Introductory Psychology
CORE 7th edition

Kalat

THOMSON
TM
WADSWORTH

Australia · Canada · Mexico · Singapore · Spain · United Kingdom · United States

THOMSON
WADSWORTH

Introductory Psychology CORE 7th edition
Kalat

Executive Editors:
Michele Baird, Maureen Staudt &
Michael Stranz

Project Development Manager:
Linda de Stefano

Marketing Coordinators:
Lindsay Annett and Sara Mercurio

**Production/Manufacturing
Supervisor:**
Donna M. Brown

Pre-Media Services Supervisor:
Dan Plofchan

Rights and Permissions Specialists:
Rights and Permissions Specialists
Kalina Hintz and Bahman Naraghi

Cover Image
Getty Images*

The Adaptable Courseware Program
consists of products and additions to
existing Thomson products that are
produced from camera-ready copy.
Peer review, class testing, and
accuracy are primarily the responsibility
of the author(s).

Introductory Psychology CORE
 7th edition
Kalat
ISBN 0-534-61604-6

International Divisions List

Asia (Including India):
Thomson Learning
(a division of Thomson Asia Pte Ltd)
5 Shenton Way #01-01
UIC Building
Singapore 068808
Tel: (65) 6410-1200
Fax: (65) 6410-1208

Australia/New Zealand:
Thomson Learning Australia
102 Dodds Street
Southbank, Victoria 3006
Australia

Latin America:
Thomson Learning
Seneca 53
Colonia Polano
11560 Mexico, D.F., Mexico
Tel (525) 281-2906
Fax (525) 281-2656

Canada:
Thomson Nelson
1120 Birchmount Road
Toronto, Ontario
Canada M1K 5G4
Tel (416) 752-9100
Fax (416) 752-8102

UK/Europe/Middle East/Africa:
Thomson Learning
High Holborn House
50-51 Bedford Row
London, WC1R 4L$
United Kingdom
Tel 44 (020) 7067-2500
Fax 44 (020) 7067-2600

Spain (Includes Portugal):
Thomson Paraninfo
Calle Magallanes 25
28015 Madrid
España
Tel 34 (0)91 446-3350
Fax 34 (0)91 445-6218

Custom Table of Contents

Preface to the Student

Welcome to introductory psychology! I hope you will enjoy reading this text as much as I enjoyed writing it. When you finish, I hope you will write your comments on the comments page, cut the page out, and mail it to the publisher, who will pass it along to me. If you are willing to receive a reply, please include a return address.

The first time I taught introductory psychology, several students complained that the book we were using was interesting to read but impossible to study. What they meant was that they had trouble finding and remembering the main points. I have tried to make this book interesting and as easy to study as possible.

Features of This Text

Modular Format

Each chapter is divided into two or more modules so that you can study a limited section at a time. Each chapter begins with a table of contents to orient you to the topics considered. At the end of each module is a summary of some important points, with page references. If a point is unfamiliar, you should reread the appropriate section. At the end of a chapter, you will find suggestions for further reading, a few Internet sites to visit, and a list of important terms.

Key Terms

When an important term first appears in the text, it is highlighted in **boldface** and defined in *italics*. All the boldface terms reappear in alphabetic order with definitions at the end of the chapter and again in the combined Subject Index and Glossary at the end of the book. You might want to find the Subject Index and Glossary right now and familiarize yourself with it. You can also consult or download a list of key terms with their definitions from this Internet site:
http://psychology.wadsworth.com/kalat_intro7e/

I sometimes meet students who think they have mastered the course because they have memorized all the definitions. You do need to understand the defined words, but don't waste time memorizing definitions word for word. It would be better to try to use each word in a sentence or think of examples of each term. Better yet, when appropriate, think of evidence for or against the concept that the term represents.

Questions to Check Your Understanding and Go Further

When you read a text, you should want to find out how well you understand it. At various points in this text are Concept Checks, questions that ask you to use or apply the information you just read. Try to answer each of them and then turn to the indicated page to check your answer. If your answer is correct, you can feel encouraged. If it is incorrect, you should reread the section.

You will also find an occasional item marked A Step Further . . . Here you are asked to go beyond the text discussion and think about possible answers to a more challenging or speculative question. I hope you will spend time with these questions, perhaps talk about them with fellow students, and maybe ask your instructor for his or her opinion. (Instructors can check for my own answers in the Instructor's Resource Guide. But to these items, there is no single right answer.)

Try It Yourself Activities

The text includes many items marked Try It Yourself. Most of these can be done with little or no equipment in just a minute or two. You will understand and remember the text far better if you do try these exercises. In some cases you will understand the text *only* if you try them. I recall a couple of test questions that were answered correctly by almost all of my students who tried a particular Try It Yourself exercise and missed by almost everyone else. A word to the wise . . .

Also available are 19 Online Try It Yourself activities. These interactive exercises can be accessed through your CD-ROM or at:
http://psychology.wadsworth.com/kalat_intro7e/
The purpose of these is the same as the Try It Yourself activities in the text; the difference is that online activities can include sounds and motion. Often, the description of some research study will be easier to understand after you have experienced it yourself. You will also remember it better.

What's the Evidence Sections

Every chapter except the first includes a section titled What's the Evidence? These sections highlight research studies in more than the usual amount of detail, specifying the hypothesis (idea being tested), research methods, results, and interpretation. In some cases the discussion also mentions the limitations of the study. The purpose of these sections is to provide examples of how to evaluate evidence.

CD-ROM

Accompanying every new copy of the text is a CD-ROM. The main feature on this disc is a series of videos illustrating important points in psychology and inviting critical thinking about the meaning of various findings. The CD-ROM also includes a convenient portal to the book's Internet site.

Internet Site

The text Web site is:
http://psychology.wadsworth.com/kalat_intro7e/.
This site offers flash cards, quizzes, interactive art, an online glossary, and links to other interesting Web sites related to each chapter. It also includes a "virtual study center," in which you answer questions and then receive a personalized Self-Study Assessment and study plan. The site also includes Online Try It Yourself activities. In addition, it includes a new vMentor opportunity, in which you can ask questions and receive live tutoring from an experienced instructor during certain hours. To do so, go to your companion Web site and follow the links to the vMentor virtual classroom. All of these opportunities are highly recommended; please explore them.

Indexes and Reference List

In the front of your text note the Theme Index, which directs you to pages where general issues are discussed, such as the influences of gender and culture on behavior. A list of all the references cited in the text is at the back of the book in case you want to check something for more details. The combined Subject Index and Glossary defines key terms and indicates where in the book to find more information.

Optional Study Guide

Also available is a Study Guide to accompany this text, written by Mark Ludorf of Stephen F. Austin State University. It provides detailed chapter outlines, learning objectives, study hints, and other helpful information. The most valuable part for most students is the sample test questions, with an answer key that explains not only which answer is right but why each of the others is wrong. The Web site also offers sample questions, but not as many. The Study Guide also includes a language-building component by Eric Bohman, William Rainey Harbor College. The Study Guide is recommended for students who have not had much success with multiple-choice tests in the past,

and who are willing to spend some time in addition to reading the book and studying lecture notes. If your bookstore does not stock the Study Guide, you can ask them to order a copy. The ISBN is 0-534-62463-4.

Answers to Some Frequently Asked Questions

Do you have any useful suggestions for improving study habits? Whenever students ask me why they did badly on the last test, I ask, "When did you read the assignment?" Some answer, "Well, I didn't exactly read *all* of the assignment," or "I read it the night before the test." If you want to learn the material well, read it before the lecture, review it again after the lecture, and quickly go over it again a few days later. Then reread the textbook assignments and your lecture notes before a test. Memory researchers have clearly established that you will understand and remember something better by studying it several times spread out over days than by studying the same amount of time all at once. Also, of course, the more total time you spend studying, the better.

When you study, don't just read the text but stop and think about it. The more actively you use the material, the better you will remember it. One way to improve your studying is to read by the SPAR method: **S**urvey, **P**rocess meaningfully, **A**sk questions, **R**eview.

Survey: Know what to expect so that you can focus on the main points. When you start a chapter, first look over the outline to get a preview of the contents. When you start a new module, turn to the end and read the summary.

Process meaningfully: Read the chapter carefully, stopping to think from time to time. Tell your roommate something you learned. Think about how you might apply a concept to a real-life situation. Pause when you come to the Concept Checks and try to answer them. Do the Try It Yourself exercises. Try to monitor how well you understand the text and adjust your reading accordingly. Good readers read quickly through easy, familiar content but slowly through difficult material.

Ask questions: When you finish the chapter, try to anticipate what you might be asked later. You can use questions in the Study Guide or on the Web site or compose your own. Write out the questions and think about them, but do not answer them yet.

Review: Pause for a few hours or more. Now return to your questions and try to answer them. Check your answers against the text or the answers in the Study Guide. Reinforcing your memory a day or two after you first read the chapter will help you retain the material longer and deepen your understanding. If you study the same material several times at lengthy intervals, you increase your chance of remembering it long after the course is over.

What do those parentheses mean, as in "(Bushman & Anderson, 2001)"? Am I supposed to remember the names and dates? Psychologists generally cite references in the text in parentheses rather than in footnotes. "(Bushman & Anderson, 2001)" refers to an article written by Bushman and Anderson, published in 2001. All the references cited in the text are listed in alphabetical order (by the author's last name) in the References section at the back of the book.

You will also notice a few citations that include two dates separated by a slash, such as "(Wundt, 1862/1961)." This means that Wundt's document was originally published in 1862 and was republished in 1961.

No, you should not memorize the parenthetical source citations. They are provided so you can look up the source of a statement and check for further information. The names that *are* worth remembering, such as B. F. Skinner, Jean Piaget, and Sigmund Freud, are emphasized in the discussion itself.

Can you help me read and understand graphs? The graphs in this book are easy to follow. Just take a minute or so to study them carefully. You will encounter four kinds: pie graphs, bar graphs, line graphs, and scatter plots. Let's look at each kind.

Pie graphs show how a whole is divided into parts. Figure 1 shows that more than one third of all psychologists take a starting job with a college or some other educational institution. Another one third work in hospitals, clinics, and businesses. The total circle represents 100% of all psychologists.

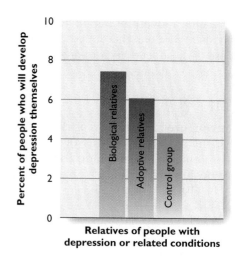

FIGURE 2

Bar graphs show how often events fall into one category or another. Figure 2 shows the percentage of relatives of people with depression or related disorders who develop depression as well.

Line graphs show how one variable is related to another variable. In Figure 3 you see that to memorize a list of 7 or fewer nonsense syllables, one reading was usually enough. To memorize a longer list took more repetitions.

Scatter plots are similar to line graphs, with this difference: A line graph shows averages, whereas a scatter plot shows individual data points. By looking at a scatter plot (Figure 4), we can see how much variation occurs among individuals.

To prepare a scatter plot, we make two observations about each individual. In Figure 4 each student is represented by one point. If you take that point and

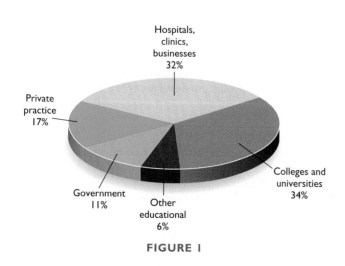

FIGURE I

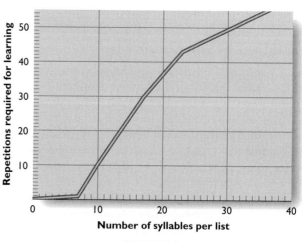

FIGURE 3

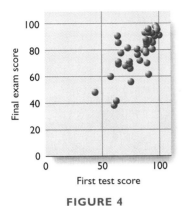

FIGURE 4

scan down to the *x*-axis, you find that student's score on the first test. If you scan across the y-axis you find that student's score on the final exam. A scatter plot shows whether two variables are closely or only loosely related.

We may have to take multiple-choice tests on this material. How can I do better on those tests?

1. Read each choice carefully. Do not choose the first answer that looks correct; first make sure that the other answers are wrong. If two answers seem reasonable, decide which of the two is better.

2. If you don't know the correct answer, make an educated guess. Eliminate answers that are clearly wrong. An answer that includes absolute words such as *always* or *never* is probably wrong; don't choose it unless you have a good reason to support it. Also eliminate any answer that includes unfamiliar terms. If you have never heard of something, it is probably not the right answer.

3. After you finish a test, go back and check your answers and rethink them. You have probably heard the advice, "Don't change your answers; stick with your first impulse." No matter how often you have heard that advice, it is wrong. J. J. Johnston (1975) tested it by looking through the answer sheets of a number of classes that had taken a multiple-choice test. He found that of all the students who changed one or more answers, 71 students improved their scores by doing so and only 31 lowered their scores. Similar results have been reported in a number of other studies. Your reconsidered answer might be better than the first for a variety of reasons. Sometimes when you read the questions that appear later in a test, one of them may remind you of something that helps you correct an earlier answer. Sometimes you reread a question and realize that you misunderstood it the first time.

Why, then, do so many students (and professors) believe that it is a mistake to change an answer? Think of what happens when you get a test paper back. When you look it over, which items do you examine most carefully? The ones you got wrong, of course. You may notice three items that you originally answered correctly and then changed. You overlook the five other items you changed from wrong to right.

Last Words Before We Start . . .

Most of all, I hope you enjoy the text. I have tried to include the liveliest examples I can find. The goal is not just to teach you some facts but to teach you a love of learning so that you will continue to read more and educate yourself about psychology long after your course is over.

James Kalat

What is Psychology?

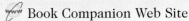

If you are like most students, you start off assuming that just about everything you read in your textbooks and everything your professors tell you must be true.

But what if it isn't? Suppose that a group of impostors has replaced the faculty of your college. They pretend to know what they are talking about and they all vouch for one another's competence, but in fact they are all unqualified. They have managed to find textbooks that support their own prejudices, but the information in the textbooks is all wrong too. If that happened, how would you know?

As long as we are entertaining such skeptical thoughts, why limit ourselves to colleges? When you read advice columns in the newspaper, read books about how to invest money, or listen to political commentators, how do you know who has the right answers?

The answer is that *no one* has the right answers all of the time. Professors, textbook authors, advice columnists, politicians, and others have strong reasons for some beliefs and weak reasons for others, and sometimes they think they have strong reasons but discover to their embarrassment that they were wrong. I don't mean to imply that you should disregard everything you read or hear. But you should expect people to tell you the reasons for their conclusions and then draw your own conclusions. At least if you make a mistake, it will be your own and not someone else's.

You have just encountered the theme of this book: Evaluate the evidence. You have heard and you will continue to hear all sorts of claims concerning psychology. Some are valid, some are wrong, many are partly valid under certain conditions, and some are too vague to be either right or wrong. When you finish this book, you will be in a better position to examine evidence and to judge for yourself which claims to take seriously.

▌ *Who has the correct answers? None of us do, at least not always. Even when people we trust seem very confident of their opinions, we should ask for their evidence or reasoning.*

What is psychology?

What philosophical questions motivate psychologists?

What do various kinds of psychologists do?

Should you consider majoring in psychology?

The term *psychology* derives from the Greek roots *psyche,* meaning "soul" or "mind," and *logos,* meaning "word"; thus, psychology is literally the study of the mind or soul. In the late 1800s and early 1900s, psychology was defined as the scientific study of the mind. Around 1920 psychologists became disenchanted with the idea of studying the mind. First, mind is private and not easily available to scientific study. Second, talking about "the mind" seemed to imply that mind is a "thing" as opposed to a series of processes. At any rate, through the middle 1900s, psychologists defined their field simply as the study of behavior.

However, people care about what they see, hear, and think, not just about what they do. When you look at this optical illusion and say that the horizontal part of the top line looks longer than that of the bottom line (although really they are the same), we want to know why it *looks* longer to you, not just why you *said* it looks longer. So for a compromise, let's define **psychology** as *the systematic study of behavior and experience.* The word *experience* lets us discuss your perceptions without implying a mind that exists independently of your body.

The kind of psychologist familiar to most people is a clinical psychologist—that is, a psychologist who tries to help worried, depressed, or otherwise troubled people. The last two chapters of this book will deal with abnormal behavior and its treatment, but that field is only part of psychology. Psychology also includes research on sensation and perception, learning and memory, hunger and thirst, sleep, attention, child development, and more. You might expect that a course in psychology will teach you to "analyze" people, to understand hidden aspects of their personality, perhaps even to use psychology to control them. It will not. You will learn to understand some aspects of

behavior, but you will gain no dazzling powers. Ideally, you will learn to be more skeptical of those who claim to analyze people's hidden personality from small samples of their behavior.

Psychology and Common Sense

Almost everyone tries to understand why people act the way they do, and every culture has developed a "folk psychology" to try to explain people's feelings and actions. Much of folk psychology is at least good enough to be useful, and common sense is usually more accurate about psychology than it is about, say, physics. But your common sense is not the same as someone else's, especially someone from a different culture, and when we carefully evaluate our common-sense ideas, we find that some are correct, some are partly correct, and others are wrong. Psychological researchers collect systematic data to try to improve upon common sense. People also have many beliefs that are not quite common sense, but are based on statements they have heard and accepted without questioning. Let's try a few questions about psychology. Choose an answer for each item:

1. Typically, we use only 10% of our brains.
   true   uncertain   false
2. Alcoholism is a disease.
   true   uncertain   false
3. A drink of alcohol kills about 5,000 brain cells.
   true   uncertain   false
4. People will not do anything under hypnosis that they would refuse to do otherwise.
   true   uncertain   false
5. People often dream they are flying, but they never dream they hit the ground. If you did dream you hit the ground, you would die.
   true   uncertain   false
6. If you want to change people's behavior, first you have to change their attitudes.
   true   uncertain   false
7. A polygraph test can reveal whether or not a person is telling the truth.
   true   uncertain   false
8. Acts of violence are more common on nights of a full moon.
   true   uncertain   false

9. After finishing a test, you should:
   a. go back, rethink your answers, and consider changing some of them.
   b. stick with your first impulse.
10. Infants can recognize their own mother's voice on the day of birth.
    true   uncertain   false

Finished? Okay, now here are the answers that the research supports:

1. **Typically, we use only 10% of our brains.** *False.* I have heard this statement many times, and you probably have too. Does it mean that you could lose 90% of your brain and still do what you do now? If so, it's false. Does it mean that only 10% of your brain cells are active at any time? If so, again it's false.

   Granted, each of us could probably do much more with our brains than we are doing now, but that doesn't mean we use only part of our brains. I'm a poor athlete, but that's not because I use only 10% of my muscles. I use them all, just not very skillfully. Chapter 3 discusses brain functioning in detail.

2. **Alcoholism is a disease.** Here the best answer is *uncertain.* It depends on what you mean by "disease." Alcoholism resembles medical diseases in some ways but not others, and medical treatment for alcoholism is not consistently effective. We consider this issue further in Chapter 15.

3. **A drink of alcohol kills about 5,000 brain cells.** Again, the best answer is *uncertain.* The next time you hear someone say that an alcoholic drink kills some number of brain cells, ask, "Who counted?" We do know that people who drink enormous amounts of alcohol over many years lose brain cells, but part of their brain damage is due to poor diet. We shall consider brain functioning in Chapter 3, alcohol abuse in Chapter 16.

4. **People will not do anything under hypnosis that they would refuse to do otherwise.** Again, the best answer is *uncertain.* Hypnotized people will sometimes do some odd, even dangerous acts, but so do people who are not hypnotized, especially if they know they are in an experiment. That is, it's hard to find anything that we are sure people would "refuse to do otherwise"! Chapter 5 elaborates on this point.

5. **People often dream they are flying, but they never dream they hit the ground. If you did dream you hit the ground, you would die.** If this were true, how would anyone know? At best this statement is *uncertain,* but some people say they have dreamt they hit the ground (and they sur-

vived), so let's call this one *false.* Chapter 5 considers the research on dreaming.

6. **If you want to change people's behavior, first you have to change their attitudes.** *False.* As we'll see in Chapter 14, sometimes it's pretty easy to change people's behavior, and then they change their attitudes to match their behavior.

7. **A polygraph test can reveal whether or not a person is telling the truth.** *It depends.* ("It depends" is frequently a good answer in psychology.) Here it depends on how much accuracy you expect from the test. If you have to decide whether someone is lying, a polygraph is more accurate than flipping a coin, but it makes many mistakes. Chapter 12 goes into more detail.

8. **Acts of violence are more common on nights of a full moon.** *False.* Although many people believe this statement, research studies have consistently failed to support it. This is an "illusory correlation," as discussed in Chapter 2.

9. **After finishing a test, you should: (a) go back, rethink your answers, and consider changing some of them or (b) stick with your first impulse.** *Go back and consider changing your answers.* If you missed this one, you should go back and read the Preface to the Student.

10. **Infants can recognize their own mother's voice on the day of birth.** *True.* After all those false or uncertain statements, I thought I should give you one that's true. It probably doesn't sound like it would be true, and you might wonder how anyone could know. If you can't contain your curiosity, look ahead to Chapter 10.

Note that sometimes the best answer was "uncertain" or "it depends." If uncertainty makes you uncomfortable and you insist on statements that are definitely right or wrong, I suggest you consider a career in mathematics, not psychology. In psychology most answers are tentative.

Also note the range of questions we just considered, from brain mechanisms to the treatment of alcoholism. You can consider this little quiz a preview of the breadth of psychology. Psychologists want to understand why we think and act the way we do—and that task is a big one.

Major Philosophical Issues in Psychology

Many psychological concerns date back to the philosophers of ancient Greece. Although psychology has moved away from philosophy in its methods, it continues to be motivated by some of the same questions. Three of the most profound are free will versus determinism, the mind–brain problem, and the nature–nurture issue.

Free Will Versus Determinism

One of the key points of the scientific approach is seeking the *immediate* causes of an event (what led to what) instead of the *final* causes (the purpose of the event in an overall plan). That is, scientists act on the basis of **determinism**, *the assumption that everything that happens has a cause, or determinant, in the observable world.*

Is the same true for human behavior? We are, after all, part of the physical world, and our brains are made of chemicals. According to the *determinist* assumption of human behavior, everything we do has causes. This view seems to conflict with the impression all of us have that "*I make the decisions about my actions. Sometimes when I am making a decision, like what to eat for lunch or which sweater to buy, I am in doubt right up to the last second. The decision could have gone either way. I wasn't controlled by anything, and no one could have predicted what I would do.*" *The belief that behavior is caused by a person's independent decisions* is known as free will.

Some psychologists argue that free will is an illusion (Wegner, 2002): What you call a decision is really more a prediction than a cause of your behavior. When you have the conscious experience of "deciding" to move a finger, the behavior is already starting to happen. What you feel as your "will" or "intention" is the result of many forces within you, of which you are unaware; it is not the cause of anything.

❚ Behavior is guided by external forces, such as waves, and by forces within the individual. According to the determinist view, even those internal forces follow physical laws.

© Rick Doyle/CORBIS

Other psychologists and philosophers reply that yes, of course, in a sense you *do* make decisions. A person walking down a mountainside is not like a rock bouncing down the same path. When you order soup and salad for lunch, the decision was a product of forces within you. The kind of person you are also determines what career you will choose, how hard you will work at it, how kind you will be to others, and so forth. However, your behavior is still a product of cause and effect. The "you" that makes all these decisions is itself a product of your heredity and all the events of your life until now. (You did not create yourself.) In this sense, yes, you have a will, and you might even call it "free" will depending on what you mean by "free" (Dennett,

2003). If you mean uncaused or random, some of the events of subatomic particles are apparently random, but at the scale of visible events, the random subatomic events cancel out. Furthermore, you probably wouldn't want to have a random will. You would prefer for it to be "determined" by the kind of person you are.

The test of determinism is ultimately empirical: If everything we do has a cause, our behavior should be predictable. In some cases it definitely is. For example, if you hear a sudden, unexpected, extremely loud noise, I can predict that, unless you are deaf, in a coma, or paralyzed, you will tense your muscles. I can even be more precise and predict you will tense your neck muscles within a quarter of a second.

In other cases psychologists' predictions are more like those of a meteorologist. A meteorologist who wants to predict tomorrow's weather for some city will want to know the location and terrain of that city, today's weather, and so forth. Even with all that information, the meteorologist will predict something such as, "High temperature around 30, low temperature around 20, with a 10% chance of precipitation." The lack of precision and occasional errors do not mean that the weather is "free" but only that it is subject to so many influences that no one can predict it exactly.

Similarly, a psychologist trying to predict your behavior for the next few days will want to know as much as possible about your past behavior, that of your friends and family, your current health, your genetics, where you live, and a great deal more. Even with all that information, the psychologist cannot predict perfectly.

Determinists are unembarrassed; after all, human behavior is subject to a great many influences, including many that are difficult to measure. Still, the more knowledge we gain, the better predictions we can make. Anyone who rejects determinism must insist that predictions of behavior could *never* become accurate, even with *complete* information about the person and the situation. To that idea a determinist replies that the only way to find out is to try.

Let's note an important point here: The assumption that behaviors follow cause and effect seems to work, and anyone planning to do research on behavior is almost forced to start with this assumption. Still, to be honest, it is an assumption, not a certainty.

CRITICAL THINKING:
A STEP FURTHER
Determinism

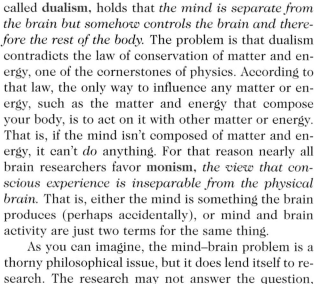

What kind of evidence, if any, would support the concept of free will? To support the concept of free will, one would need to demonstrate that no conceivable theory could make correct predictions about some aspect of behavior. Should a psychologist who believes in free will conduct the same kind of research that determinists conduct, a different kind, or no research at all?

The Mind–Brain Problem

Everything we experience or do depends on the physics and chemistry of the nervous system. Then what, if anything, is the mind? The *philosophical question of how experience is related to the brain* is the **mind–brain problem** (or mind–body problem). In a universe composed of matter and energy, why is there such a thing as a conscious mind? One view, called **dualism,** holds that *the mind is separate from the brain but somehow controls the brain and therefore the rest of the body.* The problem is that dualism contradicts the law of conservation of matter and energy, one of the cornerstones of physics. According to that law, the only way to influence any matter or energy, such as the matter and energy that compose your body, is to act on it with other matter or energy. That is, if the mind isn't composed of matter and energy, it can't *do* anything. For that reason nearly all brain researchers favor **monism,** *the view that conscious experience is inseparable from the physical brain.* That is, either the mind is something the brain produces (perhaps accidentally), or mind and brain activity are just two terms for the same thing.

As you can imagine, the mind–brain problem is a thorny philosophical issue, but it does lend itself to research. The research may not answer the question, but it can at least nibble away at it, determining what

FIGURE 1.1 PET scans show the brain activity of normal people engaged in different activities. Left column: Brain activity with no special stimulation, while passively watching something or listening to something. Center column: Brain activity while listening to music, language, or both. Right column: Brain activity during performance of a cognitive task, an auditory memory task, and the task of moving the fingers of the right hand. Red indicates the highest activity, followed by yellow, green, and blue. Arrows indicate the most active areas. *(Courtesy of Michael E. Phelps and John C. Mazziotta, University of California, Los Angeles, School of Medicine)*

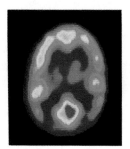

Resting state

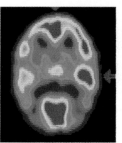

Music

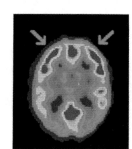

Cognitive

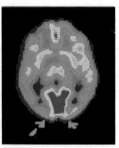

Visual

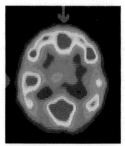

Language

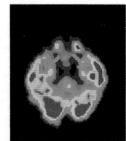

Memory

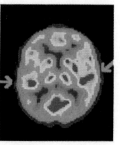

Auditory

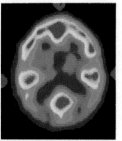

Language and music

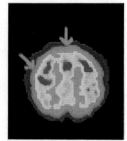

Motor

aspects of brain activity are necessary for consciousness (Crick & Koch, 2003). For example, participants in one study watched as words were flashed on a screen for a mere 29 milliseconds each. Sometimes they could identify a word consciously and say it; other times they reported only a blur or nothing at all. Brain scans demonstrated that all the flashed words activated the same brain areas but activated them more strongly on occasions when people could identify the words consciously (Dehaene et al., 2001). That is, consciousness has something to do with the total amount of brain stimulation.

The photos in Figure 1.1 show brain activity while a person is engaged in nine different tasks, as measured by a technique called positron-emission tomography (PET). Red indicates the highest degree of brain activity, followed by yellow, green, and blue. As you can see, the various tasks increase activity in different brain areas, although all areas show some activity at all times (Phelps & Mazziotta, 1985). Data such as these show a close relationship between brain activity and psychological events. You might well ask: Did the brain activity cause the thoughts, or did the thoughts cause the brain activity? Most brain researchers reply that neither brain activity nor mental activity "causes" the other; rather, brain activity and mental activity are the same thing (see Dennett, 1991).

Even if we accept this position, we are still far from understanding the mind–brain relationship. Is mental activity associated with all brain activity or just certain types? Why does conscious experience exist at all? Could a brain get along without it? Research studies are not about to resolve these questions and put philosophers out of business. But research results do constrain the philosophical answers that we can seriously consider. The hope of learning more about the mind–brain relationship is one of the ultimate goals for many psychologists, especially those whose work we shall study in Chapters 3 and 4.

CRITICAL THINKING:
A STEP FURTHER
Mind and Brain

One way to think about the mind–brain relationship is to ask whether something other than a brain—a computer, for example—could have a mind. How would we know? What if we built a computer that could perform all the intellectual functions that humans perform? Could we then decide that the computer is conscious, as human beings are?

The Nature–Nurture Issue

Why do most little boys spend more time than little girls do with toy guns and trucks and less time with dolls? Are such behavioral differences mostly the result of genetic differences between boys and girls, or are they mostly the result of differences in how society treats boys and girls?

Alcohol abuse is a big problem in some cultures and a rare one in others. Are these differences entirely a matter of social custom, or do genes influence alcohol use also?

Certain psychological disorders are more common in large cities than in small towns and in the

❚ Why do different children develop different interests? They may have had different hereditary tendencies, but they have also experienced different environmental influences. Separating the roles of nature and nurture can be difficult.

countryside. Does life in crowded cities somehow cause psychological disorders? Or do people develop such disorders because of a genetic predisposition and then move to big cities in search of jobs, housing, and welfare services?

Each of these questions is related to the **nature–nurture issue**: *How do differences in behavior relate to differences in heredity and environment?* The nature–nurture issue shows up from time to time in practically all fields of psychology, and it seldom has a simple answer.

CRITICAL THINKING:
A STEP FURTHER
Nature and Nurture

Suppose researchers found that alcohol abuse is uncommon in Turkey because of Turkey's strict legal sanctions against alcohol use. Should we then assume that the differences in alcohol use among people in other countries is also due to nongenetic causes?

CONCEPT CHECK ☑

1. In what way does all scientific research presuppose determinism?
2. What is one major objection to dualism? (Check your answers on page 16.)

What Psychologists Do

We have considered some major philosophical issues related to the entire field of psychology. However, psychologists usually deal with smaller, more answerable questions.

Psychology is an academic discipline that includes many branches and specialties, ranging from the helping professions to research on brain functions. The educational requirements for becoming a psychologist vary from one country to another (Newstead & Makinen, 1997). In the United States and Canada, a psychologist starts with a bachelor's degree (usually requiring 4 years of college) and then probably a PhD degree (at least another 4 or 5 years, often more). Some people practice psychology with a master's degree (intermediate between a bachelor's and a doctorate), and a growing number have a PsyD (doctor of psychology) degree, which generally requires less research experience than a PhD but a similar period of training. Any psychologist specializes in a particular branch of psychology, such as experimental, developmental, clinical, or industrial.

Psychologists work in many occupational settings, as shown in Figure 1.2. The most common settings are

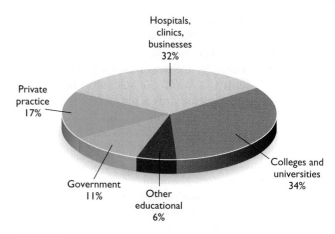

FIGURE 1.2 More than one third of psychologists work in academic institutions; the remainder find positions in a variety of settings. *(Based on data of Chamberlin, 2000)*

colleges and universities, private practice, hospitals and mental health clinics, and government agencies.

Psychologists in Teaching and Research

Many psychologists, especially those who are not clinical psychologists, have positions in colleges and universities where they teach and do research that will ideally lead to a greater understanding of behavior and experience and perhaps have useful applications. A small percentage of psychologists work in full-time research institutions. Here we preview a few major categories of psychological research.

Biological Psychology

A **biopsychologist** (or **behavioral neuroscientist**) *tries to explain behavior in terms of biological factors, such as electrical and chemical activities in the nervous system, the effects of drugs and hormones, genetics, and evolutionary pressures.* For example, the evidence suggests that certain genes influence the probability that someone will develop schizophrenia, depression, or alcoholism. However, the behavioral outcome depends on experiences as well as genetics.

Biopsychologists also study the effects of brain damage. Brain damage can result from such things as a sharp blow to the head, a ruptured blood vessel in the brain, an interruption of oxygen supply, prolonged malnutrition, or exposure to toxic chemicals. The effects of brain damage on behavior depend on the location and extent of the damage, as well as the age and overall health of the person.

Another research interest is the effects of drugs. For example, drugs such as amphetamine and cocaine usually increase activity levels, whereas heroin or morphine decrease them. Biopsychologists try to explain those effects. They have traced most drug effects to the chemical communication between one neuron and another at junctions called *synapses.*

So, according to biopsychologists, people differ from one another because they have different genes, different brain anatomies, and different hormonal patterns. Some have suffered brain damage. Others are under the influence of drugs or of nutritional deficiencies that affect the brain. Anything that affects the body, especially the brain, will also affect behavior. Chapter 3 provides much more information about biological psychology.

Evolutionary Psychology

An evolutionary psychologist *tries to explain behavior in terms of the evolutionary history of the species, including reasons evolution might have favored a tendency to act in particular ways.* It offers explanations such as, "The animal behaves this way because previous members of the species that behaved this way managed to survive and reproduce, whereas those that behaved another way were less successful." With nonhuman species we are accustomed to the idea that evolution has molded both behavior and appearance in ways that promote survival and reproduction. For example, the reptile in Figure 1.3 has evolved an appearance that blends in with its environment but also has evolved behaviors that get it into the position shown. In addition it has evolved a tendency to remain motionless for long periods; the lack of motion is critical to its camouflage.

Evolutionary psychologists apply the same kind of explanations to any behavior that is widespread within a species. In some cases the explanations are just as convincing for humans as for any other species. For example, humans have reflexes and built-in behavior tendencies (e.g., sleeping and yawning) that serve adaptive functions, even if we do not fully understand those functions. Presumably, we evolved these mechanisms because they aid us in survival and reproduction. However, although some evolutionary explanations of behavior are persuasive, others are uncertain or doubtful (de Waal, 2002). For one example of a controversial proposal,

FIGURE 1.3 This species of gecko (a kind of lizard) blends in so well with its environment that a potential predator could easily miss it. However, behavior is an important part of the camouflage. The gecko remains motionless in this position for long times; any quick movement will destroy the illusion that it is part of the plant.

Michael & Patricia Fogden/Minden Pictures

men tend to show more sexual jealousy than women do when a partner is suspected of being unfaithful. The strength of that tendency varies from one culture to another, but no culture is known in which women are more jealous than men. Evolutionary psychologists have argued that a woman always knows her baby is her own, but a man does not know his wife's baby is his, unless he is the only man who had sex with her (Buss, 2000). Therefore, throughout human evolutionary history, men were more likely to pass on their genes if they prevented their wives from having sex with other men; women gained less from being similarly jealous.

Not everyone finds this explanation convincing. Granted, evolution molds the brain as much as any other organ, and therefore also behavior. The question is whether evolution has micromanaged our behavior. Do we have (or need?) a specific mechanism in the brain that tells men to guard their girlfriends and wives jealously? Even when a general trend in behavior occurs in cultures throughout the world, it remains possible that people learned similar behaviors. For example, people throughout the world clean their food before eating it, but we do not assume they have a gene for food-cleaning. We shall return to evolutionary issues in several later chapters, especially Chapter 14.

Learning and Motivation

The research field of **learning and motivation** studies *how behavior depends on the outcomes of past behaviors and on current motivations.* How often we engage in any particular behavior depends on the results of that behavior in the past. For example, you undoubtedly have a friend whose interests differ from yours. One of you likes dancing, and the other likes painting, or one likes to play the guitar, and the other is politically active. The one who likes dancing may have received praise for dancing or may experience some good bodily sensations while dancing. The one who enjoys painting may once have tripped while dancing and therefore sought something else to do. Our current behavior depends on our past experiences.

Researchers in this field (most of whom call themselves *behaviorists*) study how the consequences of an action modify future behavior. For example, what are the effects of a payoff (money, praise, etc.) if it is infrequent and inconsistent? If someone were expecting a large payoff and instead got a smaller one, what would be the effect? What are the effects of punishment? Notice the theoretical orientation: The behaviorist studies what the person *does* as a result of the consequences of past actions, not what the person *thinks*. Because of this emphasis on actions instead of thoughts, behaviorists can conduct many of their studies on nonhuman animals. We shall consider this approach more thoroughly in Chapter 6.

Cognitive Psychology

Cognition refers to *thinking and acquiring knowledge.* A **cognitive psychologist** *studies those processes.* (The root *cogn-* also shows up in the word *recognize,* which literally means "to know again.") As a rule cognitive psychologists do not simply ask people to describe their thought processes. (If people thoroughly understood their own thoughts, there would be less need for psychologists!) Cognitive psychologists conduct experiments to infer what people know, how they came to know it, and how they use their knowledge to solve new problems. Some cognitive psychologists develop computer models of how people think.

One typical question for a cognitive psychologist is: What do experts know or do that sets them apart from other people? Much of the answer is simply that the expert knows more facts. Consider a subject on which you are an expert: how to find your way around your college campus. A fellow student asks you, "How do I get from here to the biology building?" To answer, you draw on the knowledge you share with the other student: "It's between the library and the math building." That communication works because you and the other student share a good deal of knowledge about the campus.

Now consider how you communicate with a visitor to the campus. You say, "Go over toward the library . . . " "Wait, where's the library?" "Well, go out this door, make a right, go to the next street . . . " Someone with little or no previous knowledge needs much more detailed instructions (Isaacs & Clark, 1987). Cognitive psychology is the focus of Chapters 7 and 8.

Developmental Psychology

Developmental psychologists *study the behavioral capacities typical of different ages and how behavior changes with age,* "from womb to tomb." In a typical study, developmental psychologists examine a particular behavior across a certain age span, such as language from age 2 to 4 or memory from age 60 to 80.

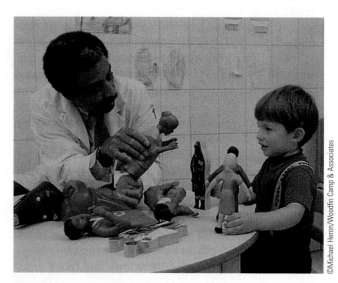

❚ Developmental psychologists study the behavioral differences among people of different ages.

The first question is: What do people do at one age that they do *not* do at another age? The second question is: Why? Was the change due to a biological process, to changes in experience, or to a complex combination of both? Developmental psychologists frequently deal with the nature–nurture issue. Because everything we do develops, developmental psychology is central to psychology and overlaps all other subdisciplines. Chapter 10 deals with developmental psychology.

Social Psychology

Social psychologists *study how an individual influences other people and is influenced by them.* When we are with other people, we tend to take our cues from them about what we should do. Suppose you arrive at a party and notice that the other guests are walking around, talking, and helping themselves to snacks. You do the same. When you go to a religious service or an art museum, you again notice how other people are acting and conform your behavior to theirs. Certainly, if you had grown up in a different country, you would have developed vastly different customs. Even within a given culture, though, individuals acquire different behaviors because of the people around them. If you had made friends with a different set of people in high school, how would you be different today?

According to social psychologists, people are also greatly influenced by other people's expectations. For example, parents often intentionally or unintentionally convey expectations that boys will be more competitive and girls will be more cooperative or that teenagers will be immature and 25-year-olds will be responsible. At least to some extent, people's behavior tends to live up to—or down to—the expectations of others. In Chapter 14 we deal with social psychology in more detail.

CONCEPT CHECK ☑

3. **a.** Of the kinds of psychological research just described—biological psychology, learning and motivation, cognitive psychology, developmental psychology, and social psychology—which field concentrates most on children?
   b. Which is most concerned with how people behave in groups?
   c. Which concentrates most on thought and knowledge?
   d. Which is most interested in the effects of brain damage?
   e. Which is most concerned with studying the effect of a reward on future behavior? (Check your answers on page 16).

Service Providers to Individuals

When most people hear the term *psychologist,* they first think of *clinical psychologists,* who constitute one type of mental health professionals. Clinical psychologists deal with problems ranging from depression, anxiety, and substance abuse to marriage conflicts, difficulties making decisions, or even the mere feeling that "I should be getting more out of life." Some clinical psychologists are college professors and researchers, but most are full-time practitioners.

It is important to distinguish among several types of mental health professionals. The term *therapist* itself has no precise meaning, and in many places even untrained, unlicensed people can hang out a shingle and call themselves therapists. Some of the main kinds of service providers for people with psychological troubles are clinical psychologists, psychiatrists, social workers, and counseling psychologists.

Clinical Psychology

Clinical psychologists *have an advanced degree in psychology, with a specialty in understanding and helping people with psychological problems.* Most have a PhD, which requires research training and the completion of a substantial research dissertation, or a PsyD, which places less emphasis on research. Also, as part of their training, clinical psychologists undergo at least a year of supervised clinical work called an *internship.*

Clinical psychologists can base their work on any of various theoretical viewpoints, or they can use a pragmatic, trial-and-error approach. They try, in one way or another, to understand why a person is having difficulties and then help that person overcome the difficulties.

Psychiatry

Psychiatry is a *branch of medicine that deals with emotional disturbances.* To become a psychiatrist, someone first earns an MD degree and then takes an additional 4 years of residency training in psychiatry. Psychiatrists and clinical psychologists provide similar services for most clients: They listen, ask questions, and try to help. Psychiatrists, however, are medical doctors and can therefore prescribe drugs, such as tranquilizers and antidepressants, whereas in most places psychologists cannot. Some states now permit psychologists with additional specialized training to prescribe drugs.

Does psychiatrists' ability to prescribe drugs give them an advantage over psychologists in places where psychologists cannot prescribe them? Sometimes but not always. Some psychiatrists habitually treat anxiety and depression with drugs, whereas psychologists treat problems by changing the person's way of living. Drugs can be useful, but relying on them too extensively can be a hazard.

Some Other Mental Health Professionals

Several other kinds of professionals also provide help and counsel. **Psychoanalysts** are *therapy providers who rely heavily on the theories and methods pioneered by the early 20th-century Viennese physician Sigmund Freud and later modified by others.* Freud and his followers attempted to infer the hidden, unconscious, symbolic meaning behind people's words and actions, and in various ways psychoanalysts today continue that effort.

There is some question about who may rightly call themselves psychoanalysts. Some people apply the term to anyone who attempts to uncover unconscious thoughts and feelings, perhaps even including followers of Carl Jung or others who broke away from Freud's views in significant ways. Others apply the term only to graduates of a 6- to 8-year program at an institute of psychoanalysis. These institutes admit only people who are already either psychiatrists or clinical psychologists. Thus, people completing psychoanalytic training will be at least in their late 30s.

A **clinical social worker** is *similar to a clinical psychologist but with different training.* In most cases a clinical social worker has a master's degree in social work with a specialization in psychological problems. A master's degree takes less education than a doctorate and requires much less research experience. In many cases health maintenance organizations (HMOs) steer most of their clients toward clinical social workers instead of psychologists or psychiatrists because the social workers, with less formal education, charge less per hour. Some psychiatric nurses (nurses with additional training in psychiatry) provide similar services.

Counseling psychologists *help people with educational, vocational, marriage, health-related, and other decisions.* A counseling psychologist has a doctorate degree (PhD, PsyD, or EdD) with supervised experience in counseling. The activities of a counseling psychologist overlap those of a clinical psychologist, but the emphasis is different. Whereas a clinical psychologist deals mostly with anxiety, depression, and other emotional distress, a counseling psychologist deals mostly with important life decisions and family or career readjustments, which, admittedly, can cause anxiety or depression! Counseling psychologists work in educational institutions, mental health centers, rehabilitation agencies, businesses, and private practice.

You may also have heard of **forensic psychologists,** *those who provide advice and consultation to police, lawyers, courts, or other parts of the criminal justice system.* Forensic psychologists are, in nearly all cases, trained as clinical or counseling psychologists with additional training in legal issues. They help with such decisions as whether a defendant is mentally competent to stand trial and whether someone eligible for parole is dangerous (Otto & Heilbrun, 2002). Several popular films have depicted forensic psychologists helping police investigators develop a "psychological profile" of a serial killer. That may sound like an exciting, glamorous profession, but bear in mind that very few psychologists engage in such activities (and the accuracy of their profiles is uncertain). We shall consider psychological profiling in Chapter 13.

Table 1.1 compares various types of mental health professionals.

CONCEPT CHECK ☑

4. Can psychoanalysts prescribe drugs? (Check your answer on page 16.)

Service Providers to Organizations

Psychologists also work in business, industry, and school systems in some capacities that might be unfamiliar to you, doing things you might not think of as psychology. The job prospects in these fields have been good, however, and you might find these fields interesting.

Industrial/Organizational Psychology

The psychological study of people at work is known as **industrial/organizational (I/O) psychology.** It deals with issues you might not think of as psychology, such as matching the right person with the right job, training people for jobs, developing work teams, determining salaries and bonuses, planning an organizational

TABLE 1.1 Several Types of Mental Health Professionals

Type of Therapist	Education
Clinical psychologist	PhD with clinical emphasis or PsyD plus internship. Ordinarily, 5+ years after undergraduate degree.
Psychiatrist	MD plus psychiatric residency. Total of 8 years after undergraduate degree.
Psychoanalyst	Psychiatry or clinical psychology plus 6–8 years in a psychoanalytic institute. Many others who rely on Freud's methods also call themselves psychoanalysts.
Psychiatric nurse	From 2-year (AA) degree to master's degree plus supervised experience.
Clinical social worker	Master's degree plus 2 years of supervised experience. Total of at least 4 years after undergraduate degree.
Counseling psychologist	PhD, PsyD, or EdD plus supervised experience in counseling.
Forensic psychologist	Doctorate, ordinarily in clinical psychology or counseling psychology, plus additional training in legal issues.

structure, and organizing the workplace so that workers will be both productive and satisfied. I/O psychologists study the behavior of both the individual and the organization, including the impact of economic conditions and governmental regulations. We shall consider work motivation in Chapter 11.

Here's an example of a concern for industrial/organizational psychologists (Campion & Thayer, 1989): A company that manufactures complex electronic equipment needed to publish reference and repair manuals for its products. The engineers who designed the devices did not want to spend their time writing the manuals, and none of them were skilled writers anyway. So the company hired a technical writer to prepare the manuals. After a year she received an unsatisfactory performance rating because the manuals she wrote contained too many technical errors. She countered that, when she asked various engineers in the company to check her manuals or to explain technical details to her, they were always too busy. She found her job complicated and frustrating; her office was badly lit, noisy, and overheated; and her chair was uncomfortable. Whenever she mentioned any of these problems, however, she was told that she "complained too much."

In a situation such as this, an industrial/organizational psychologist can help the company evaluate the problem and develop possible solutions. Maybe the company hired the wrong person for this job. If so, they should fire her and hire some expert on electrical engineering who is also an outstanding writer and *likes* a badly lit, noisy, overheated, uncomfortable office. However, if the company cannot find or afford such a person, then it needs to improve the working conditions and provide the current employee with more training or more help with the technical aspects of the job.

In other words, when a company criticizes its workers, I/O psychologists try to discover whether the problem is poor workers or a difficult job. Depending on the answer, they then try to improve the hiring decisions or improve the working conditions.

CRITICAL THINKING:
A STEP FURTHER
I/O Psychology

I/O psychologists usually consult with business and industry, but suppose they were called on to help a university where certain professors had complained that "the students are too lazy and stupid to understand the lectures." How might the I/O psychologists react?

Ergonomics

Many years ago my son Sam, then about 16 years old, turned to me as he rushed out the door and asked me to turn off his stereo. I went to the stereo in his room and tried to find an on–off switch or a power switch. No such luck. I looked in vain for the manual. Finally, in desperation I had to unplug the stereo.

Learning to operate our increasingly complex machinery is one of the perennial struggles of modern life. Sometimes the consequences can be serious. Imagine an airplane pilot who intends to lower the landing gear and instead raises the wing flaps. Or a worker in a nuclear power plant who fails to notice a warning signal. In one field of psychology, an **ergonomist**, or human factors specialist, *attempts to facilitate the operation of machinery so that ordinary people can use it efficiently and safely.* The term *ergonomics* is derived from Greek roots meaning "laws of work." Ergonomics was first used in military settings, where complex technologies sometimes required soldiers to spot nearly invisible targets, understand speech through deafening noise, track objects in three dimensions while using two hands, and make life-or-death decisions in a split second. The military turned to psychologists to determine what skills their personnel could master and to redesign the tasks to fit those skills.

Ergonomists soon applied their experience not only to business and industry but also to everyday devices. As Donald Norman (1988) pointed out, many intelligent and educated people find themselves un-

Ergonomists help redesign machines to make them easier and safer to use. An ergonomist uses principles of both engineering and psychology.

able to use all the features on a camera or a microwave oven; some even have trouble setting the time on a digital watch.

At various universities the ergonomics program is part of the psychology department, engineering, or both. Regardless of who administers the program, ergonomics necessarily combines features of psychology, engineering, and computer science. It is a growing field with many jobs available.

School Psychology

Many if not most children have academic problems at one time or another. Some children have trouble sitting still or paying attention. Others get into trouble for misbehavior. Others have specialized problems with reading, spelling, arithmetic, or other academic skills. Other children master their schoolwork very quickly and become bored. They too need special attention.

School psychologists are *specialists in the psychological condition of students,* usually in kindergarten through the 12th grade. Broadly speaking, school psychologists identify the educational needs of children, devise a plan to meet those needs, and then either implement the plan themselves or advise teachers how to implement it.

School psychology can be taught in a psychology department, a branch of an education department, or a department of educational psychology. In some countries it is possible to practice school psychology with only a bachelor's degree. In the United States the minimum is usually a master's degree, but job opportunities are much greater for people with a doctorate degree, and a doctorate may become necessary in the future. Job opportunities in school psychology have been strong and continue to grow. Most school psychologists

TABLE 1.2 Some Major Specializations in Psychology

Specialization	General Interest	Example of Interest or Research Topic
Biopsychologist	Relationship between brain and behavior	What body signals indicate hunger and satiety?
Clinical psychologist	Emotional difficulties	How can people be helped to overcome severe anxiety?
Cognitive psychologist	Memory, thinking	Do people have several kinds of memory?
Community psychologist	Organizations and social structures	Would improved job opportunities decrease psychological distress?
Counseling psychologist	Helping people make important decisions	Should this person consider changing careers?
Developmental psychologist	Changes in behavior over age	At what age can a child first distinguish between appearance and reality?
Educational psychologist	Improvement of learning in school	What is the best way to test a student's knowledge?
Environmental psychologist	How noise, heat, crowding, etc. affect behavior	What building design can maximize the productivity of the people who use it?
Ergonomist	Communication between person and machine	How can an airplane cockpit be redesigned to increase safety?
Evolutionary psychologist	Evolutionary history of behavior	Why do men generally show more sexual jealousy than women?
Industrial/organizational psychologist	People at work	Should jobs be made simple and foolproof or interesting and challenging?
Learning and motivation specialist	Learning in humans and other species	What are the effects of reinforcement and punishment?
Personality psychologist	Personality differences	Why are certain people shy and others gregarious?
Psychometrician	Measuring intelligence, personality, interests	How fair are current IQ tests? Can we devise better tests?
School psychologist	Problems that affect schoolchildren	How should the school handle a child who regularly disrupts the classroom?
Social psychologist	Group behavior, social influences	What methods of persuasion are most effective for changing attitudes?

work for a school system; others work for mental health clinics, guidance centers, and other institutions.

Table 1.2 summarizes some of the major fields of psychology, including several that have not been discussed.

Should You Major in Psychology?

Can you get a job if you major in psychology? Psychology is one of the most popular majors in the United States, Canada, and Europe. So if psychology majors cannot get jobs, a huge number of people are going to be in trouble!

The bad news is that very few jobs specifically advertise for college graduates with a bachelor's degree in psychology. The good news is that an enormous variety of jobs are available for graduates with a bachelor's degree, not specifying any major. Therefore, if you earn a degree in psychology, you will compete with history majors, English majors, astronomy majors, phys ed majors, and everyone else for jobs in government, business, and industry. According to one survey, only 20 to 25% of people who graduated with a degree in psychology took a job closely related to psychology, such as personnel work or social services (Borden & Rajecki, 2000). Still, many other jobs were good ones, even if they were not exactly in psychology.

Even if you get a job that seems remote from psychology, your psychology courses will have taught you much about how to evaluate evidence, organize and write papers, handle statistics, listen carefully to what people say, understand and respect cultural differences, and so forth. You will, of course, also gain useful background in your other courses. Regardless of your major, you should develop your skills in communication, mathematics, and computers. (If you don't have those skills, you will work for someone who does!)

Psychology also provides a good background for people entering professional schools. Many students major in psychology and then apply to medical school, law school, divinity school, or other programs. Find out what coursework is expected for the professional program of your choice and then compare the coursework required for a psychology major. You will probably find that the psychology major is compatible with your professional preparation.

If you want a career as a psychologist, you should aspire to an advanced degree, preferably a doctorate. A doctorate will qualify you to apply for positions as a college professor or, depending on your area of specialization, jobs in hospitals, clinics, private practice, school systems, or research. An increasing percentage of doctorate-level psychologists now work in business, industry, and the military doing research related to practical problems. If you are a first- or second-year college student now, it is hard to predict what the job market will be by the time you finish an advanced degree. If you are just looking for a safe, secure way to make a living, psychology offers no guarantees. A career in psychology is for those whose excitement about the field draws them irresistibly to it.

For more information about majoring in psychology, prospects for graduate school, and a great variety of jobs for psychology graduates, visit either of these Internet sites:

www.drlynnfriedman.com/

www.apa.org/students/

The types of people majoring in psychology have become more diverse over the years. Today, women receive about two thirds of the psychology PhDs in North America and most of those in Europe also (Newstead & Makinen, 1997; Sanderson & Dugoni, 1999). In some subfields such as developmental psychology, women receive as much as 80% of the new PhD degrees. Women are about as likely as men to assume leadership in the major psychological organizations and editorship of the major journals.

Minorities constitute a growing percentage of psychologists, although the total number is still small. Figure 1.4 shows the distribution for PhD degrees in psychology granted in 1996 in the United States

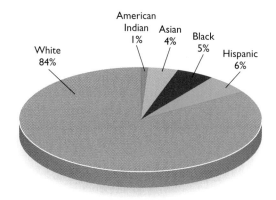

FIGURE 1.4 New psychology PhDs by race/ethnicity.

(Sanderson & Dugoni, 1999). Universities have been actively seeking more applications from minorities who are interested in graduate studies.

IN CLOSING

Types of Psychologists

An experimental psychology researcher, a clinical psychologist, an ergonomist, and an industrial/organizational psychologist are all psychologists, even though their daily activities have little in common. What does unite psychologists is a dedication to progress through research.

I have oversimplified this discussion of the various psychological approaches in several ways. First, biological psychology, cognitive psychology, social psychology, and the other fields all have their own specialized interests and questions, but they also constitute different ways of approaching many of the same questions. Furthermore, the various approaches overlap significantly. Nearly all psychologists combine insights and information gained from a variety of approaches. To understand why one person differs from another, psychologists combine information about biology, learning experiences, social influences, and much more.

As we proceed through this book, we shall consider one type of behavior at a time and, generally, one approach at a time. That is simply a necessity; we cannot talk intelligently about many topics at once. But bear in mind that all these processes do ultimately fit together; what you do at any given moment depends on a great many influences acting together.

Summary

The page number after an item indicates where the topic is first discussed.

- *What is psychology?* Psychology is the systematic study of behavior and experience. Psychologists deal with both theoretical and practical questions. (page 3)

- *Determinism/free will.* Determinism is the view that everything that occurs, including human behavior, has a physical cause. That view is difficult to reconcile with the conviction that humans have free will—that we deliberately, consciously decide what to do. (page 5)
- *Mind–brain.* The mind–brain problem is the question of how conscious experience is related to the activity of the brain. (page 6)
- *Nature–nurture.* Behavior depends on both nature (heredity) and nurture (environment). Psychologists try to determine the influence of these two factors on differences in behavior. The relative contributions of nature and nurture vary from one behavior to another. (page 7)
- *Research fields in psychology.* Psychology as an academic field has many subfields, including biological psychology, learning and motivation, cognitive psychology, developmental psychology, and social psychology. (page 8)
- *Psychology and psychiatry.* Clinical psychologists have either a PhD, PsyD, or master's degree; psychiatrists are medical doctors. Both clinical psychologists and psychiatrists treat people with emotional problems, but only psychiatrists can prescribe drugs and other medical treatments. Counseling psychologists help people deal with difficult decisions; they sometimes but less often also deal with psychological disorders. (page 11)
- *Service providers to organizations.* Nonclinical fields of application include industrial/organizational psychology, ergonomics, and school psychology. (page 12)
- *Job prospects.* People with a bachelor's degree in psychology enter a wide variety of careers or continue their education in professional schools. Those with a doctorate in psychology have additional possibilities depending on their area of specialization. In psychology, as in any other field, job prospects can change between the start and finish of one's education. (page 14)

Answers to Concept Checks

1. Any attempt to make discoveries about nature presupposes that we live in a universe of cause and effect. (page 8)
2. Dualism conflicts with the principle of the conservation of matter and energy. A nonmaterial mind could not influence anything in the universe. (page 8)
3. **a.** Developmental psychology. **b.** Social psychology. **c.** Cognitive psychology. **d.** Biological psychology. **e.** Learning and motivation. (page 11)
4. Most psychoanalysts can prescribe drugs because most are psychiatrists, and psychiatrists are medical doctors. However, psychoanalysts who are psychologists are not medical doctors and therefore cannot prescribe drugs. (page 12)

Psychology Then and Now

How did psychology get started?

What were the interests of psychologists in the early days?

How has psychology changed over the years?

Imagine yourself as a young scholar in about 1880. Enthusiastic about the new scientific approach in psychology, you have decided to become a psychologist yourself. Like other early psychologists, you have a background in either biology or philosophy. You are determined to apply the scientific methods of biology to the problems of philosophy.

So far, so good. But what questions will you address? A good research question is both interesting and answerable. (If it can't be both, it should at least be one or the other!) In 1880 how would you choose a research topic? You cannot get research ideas from a psychological journal because the first issue won't be published until next year. (And incidentally, it will be all in German.) You cannot follow in the tradition of previous researchers because there haven't *been* any previous researchers. Thus, you are on your own.

Furthermore, in the late 1800s and early 1900s, psychologists were not yet sure which questions were answerable. Sometimes they are still unsure: Should we try to study the nature of consciousness, or should we concentrate entirely on observable behavior? Many of the changes that have occurred during the history of psychology have been changes in investigators' decisions about which questions are answerable.

In the next several pages, we shall explore some of these changes in psychological research questions, including projects that dominated psychology for a while and then faded from interest. We shall discuss additional historical developments in later chapters, especially those that stood the test of time and continue to be highly influential today. Figure 1.5 outlines some major historical events inside and outside psychology. For additional information about the history of psychology, visit either of these Internet sites:

www.cwu.edu/warren/today.html

www.uakron.edu/ahap

The Early Era

At least since Aristotle (384–322 B.C.), philosophers and fiction writers have debated why people act the way they do, why they have the experiences they do,

and why one person is different from another. Without discounting the importance of these great thinkers, several 19th-century scholars wondered whether a scientific approach would be fruitful. They were impressed by the great strides made in physics, chemistry, and biology; they believed that similar progress could be made in psychology if evidence were collected and evaluated scientifically.

Wilhelm Wundt and the First Psychological Laboratory

The origin of psychology as we now know it is generally dated to 1879, when medical doctor and sensory researcher Wilhelm Wundt (pronounced "voont") set up the first psychology laboratory in Leipzig, Germany. Wundt and others had conducted psychological experiments before, but this was the first time anyone had established a laboratory exclusively for psychological research.

Wundt's broad interests ranged from the physiology of the sense organs to cultural differences in behavior, with emphases on motivation, voluntary control, and cognitive processes (Zehr, 2000). One of Wundt's fundamental questions was: What are the components of experience, or mind? He proposed that experience is composed of elements and compounds, like those of chemistry. Psychology's elements were, he maintained, sensations and feelings (Wundt, 1896/1902).[1] So at any particular moment, you might experience the taste of a fine meal, the sound of good music, and a certain degree of pleasure. These would merge into a single experience (a compound), but that experience would still include the separate elements. Furthermore, Wundt maintained, your experience is partly under your voluntary control; you can shift your attention from one element to another and get a different experience.

Wundt's question about the components of experience was a philosophical one, but Wundt, unlike the philosophers, tried to test his opinions by collecting data. He presented various kinds of lights, textures, and sounds and asked subjects to report the intensity

---

[1] A reference containing a slash between the years, such as this one, refers to a book originally published in the first year (1896) and reprinted in the second year (1902). All references are listed at the end of the book.

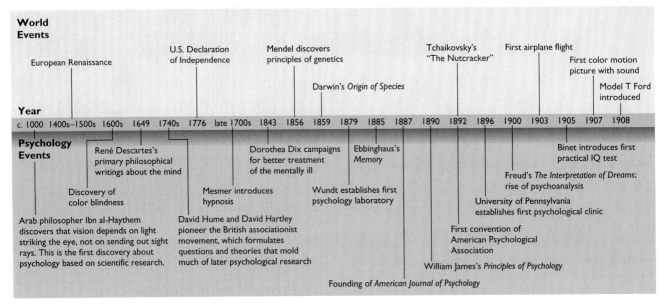

World Events

European Renaissance — U.S. Declaration of Independence — Mendel discovers principles of genetics — Darwin's *Origin of Species* — Tchaikovsky's "The Nutcracker" — First airplane flight — First color motion picture with sound — Model T Ford introduced

Year

c. 1000 | 1400s–1500s | 1600s | 1649 | 1740s | 1776 | late 1700s | 1843 | 1856 | 1859 | 1879 | 1885 | 1887 | 1890 | 1892 | 1896 | 1900 | 1903 | 1905 | 1907 | 1908

Psychology Events

Arab philosopher Ibn al-Haythem discovers that vision depends on light striking the eye, not on sending out sight rays. This is the first discovery about psychology based on scientific research.

Discovery of color blindness

René Descartes's primary philosophical writings about the mind

David Hume and David Hartley pioneer the British associationist movement, which formulates questions and theories that mold much of later psychological research

Mesmer introduces hypnosis

Dorothea Dix campaigns for better treatment of the mentally ill

Wundt establishes first psychology laboratory

Ebbinghaus's *Memory*

Founding of *American Journal of Psychology*

William James's *Principles of Psychology*

First convention of American Psychological Association

University of Pennsylvania establishes first psychological clinic

Freud's *The Interpretation of Dreams*; rise of psychoanalysis

Binet introduces first practical IQ test

FIGURE 1.5 Dates of some important events in psychology and elsewhere. *(Based partly on Dewsbury, 2000a)*

and quality of their sensations. That is, he asked them to **introspect**—*to look within themselves.* He measured the changes in people's experiences as he changed the stimuli.

Wundt also demonstrated that it was possible to conduct meaningful psychological experiments. For example, in one of his earliest studies, he set up a pendulum that struck metal balls and made a sound at two points on its swing (points b and d in Figure 1.6). People would watch the pendulum and indicate where it appeared to be when they heard the sound. Often,

the pendulum appeared to be slightly in front of or behind the ball when people heard the strike. The apparent position of the pendulum at the time of the sound differed from its actual position by an average of $\frac{1}{8}$ of a second (Wundt, 1862/1961). Apparently, the time we think we see or hear something is not the same as when the event occurred. Wundt's interpretation was that a person needs about $\frac{1}{8}$ of a second to shift attention from one stimulus to another. (The same idea has been rediscovered in other contexts, as we shall see in Chapter 8.)

© The Walt Disney Company

FIGURE 1.6 (Left) In one of Wilhelm Wundt's earliest experiments, the pendulum struck the metal balls (b and d), making a sound each time. To an observer, however, the ball appeared to be somewhere else at the time of the sound, generally the distance that it would travel in about $\frac{1}{8}$ of a second. Wundt inferred that a person needs about $\frac{1}{8}$ of a second to shift attention from one stimulus to another. (Right) The Walt Disney studios rediscovered Wundt's observation decades later: The character's mouth movements seem to be in synchrony with the sounds if the movements precede the sounds by $\frac{1}{8}$ to $\frac{1}{6}$ of a second.

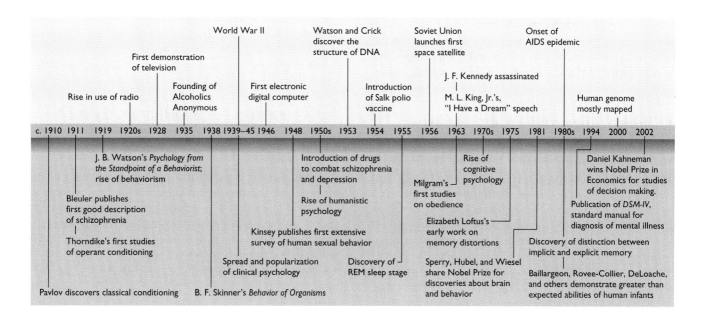

Wundt and his students were prolific investigators; the brief treatment here does not do him justice. He wrote more than 50,000 pages about his research, but his most lasting impact came from setting the precedent of studying psychological questions by collecting scientific data.

Edward Titchener and Structuralism

At first most of the world's psychologists received their education from Wilhelm Wundt himself. One of Wundt's students, Edward Titchener, came to the United States in 1892 as a psychology professor at Cornell University. Like Wundt, Titchener believed that the main question of psychology was the nature of mental experiences.

Titchener (1910) typically presented a stimulus and asked his subject to analyze it into its separate features—for example, to look at a lemon and describe its yellowness, its brightness, its shape, and so forth. He called his approach **structuralism,** *an attempt to describe the structures that compose the mind,* particularly sensations, feelings, and images. Later researchers were more interested in what those elements *do* (their functions).

If you asked psychologists today whether they thought Titchener correctly described the structures of the mind, you would probably get blank looks or shoulder shrugs. After Titchener died in 1927, psychologists virtually abandoned his research methods and even his questions. Why? Remember that a good scientific question is both interesting and answerable. Regardless of whether Titchener's questions about the elements of the mind were interesting, they appeared to be unanswerable.

For example, imagine you are the psychologist: I look at a lemon and tell you my experience of its brightness is totally separate from my experience of its yel-

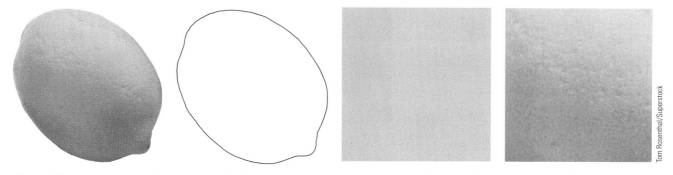

▌ Edward Titchener asked subjects to describe their sensations. For example, they might describe their sensation of shape, their sensation of color, and their sensation of texture while looking at a lemon. Titchener had no way to check the accuracy of these reports, however, so later psychologists abandoned his methods.

Tom Rosenthal/Superstock

lowness. How do you know whether I am lying, telling you what I think you want me to say, or even deceiving myself? Psychologists' frustration with Titchener's approach eventually turned many of them against studying the mind and toward studying observable behaviors.

William James and Functionalism

Almost simultaneously with the work of Wundt and Titchener, Harvard University's William James articulated some of the major issues of psychology and won eventual recognition as the founder of American psychology. James's book *The Principles of Psychology* (1890) defined the questions that dominated psychology for years afterward and even to a large extent today.

James had little patience with any search for the elements of the mind. He focused on the actions that the mind *performs* rather than what the mind *is*. That is, instead of trying to isolate the elements of consciousness, he preferred *to learn how people produce useful behaviors*. For this reason we call his approach **functionalism**. He suggested the following examples of good psychological questions (James, 1890):

- How can people strengthen good habits?
- Can someone attend to more than one item at a time?
- How do people recognize that they have seen something before?
- How does an intention lead to action?

James proposed possible answers but did little research of his own. His main contribution was to inspire later researchers to address the questions that he posed.

Studying Sensation

One of early psychologists' main research topics was the relationship between physical stimuli and psychological sensations. To a large extent, the study of

sensation *was* psychology. The first English-language textbook of the "new" scientifically based psychology devoted almost half of its pages to a discussion of the senses and the related topic of attention (Scripture, 1907). By the 1930s standard psychology textbooks devoted less than 20% of their pages to these topics (Woodworth, 1934), and today, it is down to about 5 to 10%. Why were early psychologists so interested in sensation?

One reason was philosophical: They wanted to understand mental experience, and experience consists of sensations. The other reason was strategic: A scientific psychology had to begin with answerable questions, and questions about sensation are more answerable than those about, say, personality.

Early psychologists discovered that what we see, hear, and otherwise sense is not the same as what is actually there. For example, the *perceived* intensity of a stimulus is not directly proportional to the *actual* physical intensity of the stimulus: A light that is twice as intense as another one does not look twice as bright. Figure 1.7 shows the relationship between the intensity of light and its perceived brightness. *The mathematical description of the relationship between the physical properties of a stimulus and its perceived properties* is called the **psychophysical function** because it relates psychology to physics. Such research demonstrated that, at least in the study of sensation, scientific methods can provide nonobvious answers to psychological questions.

CONCEPT CHECK ☑

5. What topic was the main focus of research for the earliest psychologists, and why?
6. What was the difference between structuralists and functionalists? (Check your answers on page 25.)

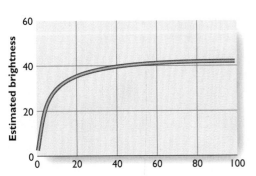

FIGURE 1.7 This graph of a psychophysical event shows the perceived intensity of light versus its physical intensity. When a light becomes twice as intense physically, it does not seem twice as bright. *(Adapted from Stevens, 1961)*

Darwin and the Study of Animal Intelligence

Charles Darwin's theory of evolution by natural selection (Darwin, 1859, 1871) had an enormous impact on psychology as well as biology. Darwin argued that humans and other species share a remote common ancestor. This idea implied that each species has specializations adapted to its own way of life, but also that all vertebrate species have many basic features in common. It further implied that nonhuman animals should exhibit varying degrees of human characteristics, including intelligence.

Based on this last implication, early **comparative psychologists**, *specialists who compare different animal species,* did something that seemed more reasonable at first than it did later: They set out to measure animal intelligence. They apparently imagined that they could rank-order animals from the smartest to the dullest. Toward that goal they set various species to such tasks as the delayed-response problem and the detour problem. In the *delayed-response problem,* an animal was given a signal indicating where it could find food. Then the signal was removed, and the animal was restrained for a while (Figure 1.8) to see how long it could remember

FIGURE 1.9 Another task popular among early comparative psychologists was the detour problem. An animal needed to first go away from the food in order to move toward it.

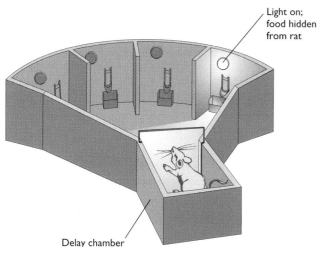

FIGURE 1.8 Early comparative psychologists assessed animal intelligence with the delayed-response problem. A stimulus was presented and a delay ensued; then the animal was expected to respond to the remembered stimulus. Variations on this delayed-response task are still used today.

the signal. In the *detour problem,* an animal was separated from food by a barrier (Figure 1.9) to see whether it would take a detour away from the food in order to get to it.

However, measuring animal intelligence turned out to be more difficult than it sounded. Too often a species seemed dull-witted on one task but brilliant on another. For example, zebras are generally slow to learn to approach one pattern instead of another for food, unless the patterns happen to be narrow stripes versus wide stripes, in which case they suddenly excel (Giebel, 1958) (see Figure 1.10). Rats seem unable to find food hidden under the object that looks different from the others, but they easily learn to choose the object that *smells* different from the others (Langworthy & Jennings, 1972).

Eventually, psychologists realized that the relative intelligence of nonhuman animals was a difficult

FIGURE 1.10 Zebras learn rapidly when they have to compare stripe patterns (Giebel, 1958). How "smart" a species is perceived to be depends in part on what ability or skill is being tested.

and probably meaningless question. The study of animal learning can illuminate general principles of learning and perhaps shed light on evolutionary questions (Papini, 2002), but because each species has somewhat different strengths, no one measurement applies to all.

Psychologists today do study animal learning and intelligence, but the emphasis has changed. The question is no longer simply which animals are the smartest, but "What can we learn from animal studies about the mechanisms of intelligent behavior?" and "How did each species evolve the behavioral tendencies it shows?"

Measuring Human Intelligence

While some psychologists studied animal intelligence, others pursued human intelligence. Francis Galton, a cousin of Charles Darwin, was among the first to try to measure intelligence and to ask whether intellectual variations were based on heredity. Galton was fascinated with trying to measure almost everything (Hergenhahn, 1992). For example, he invented the weather map, measured degrees of boredom during lectures, suggested the use of fingerprints to identify individuals, and—in the name of science—attempted to measure the beauty of women in different countries.

In an effort to determine the role of heredity in human achievement, Galton (1869/1978) examined whether the sons of famous and accomplished men tended to become eminent themselves. (Women in 19th-century England had little opportunity for fame.) Galton found that the sons of judges, writers, politicians, and other noted men had a high probability of similar accomplishment themselves. He attributed this edge to heredity. (I'll leave this one for you to judge: Did he have adequate evidence for his conclusion? If the sons of famous men become famous themselves, is heredity the only explanation?)

Galton also tried to measure intelligence using simple sensory and motor tasks, but his measurements were unsatisfactory. In 1905 a French researcher, Alfred Binet, devised the first useful intelligence test, which we shall discuss further in Chapter 9. At this point just note that the idea of testing intelligence became popular in the United States and other Western countries. Psychologists, inspired by the popularity of intelligence tests, later developed tests of personality, interests, and other psychological characteristics. Note that measuring human intelligence faces some of the same problems as animal intelligence: People have a great many intelligent abilities, and it is possible to be more adept at one than another. However, a great deal of research has been done to try to make tests of intelligence fair and accurate.

The Rise of Behaviorism

Earlier in this chapter, I casually defined psychology as "the systematic study of behavior and experience." For a substantial period of psychology's history, most experimental psychologists would have objected to the words "and experience." Some psychologists still object today, though less strenuously. From about 1920 to 1960 or 1970, most researchers described psychology as the study of behavior, period. These researchers had little to say about minds, experiences, or anything of the sort. (According to one quip, psychologists had "lost their minds.") What did psychologists have against mind or experience?

Recall the failure of Titchener's effort to analyze experience into its components. Most psychologists concluded that questions about the mind were unanswerable. Instead, they addressed questions about observable behaviors: What do people and other animals do and under what circumstances? How do changes in the environment alter what they do? What is learning and how does it occur? These questions were clearly meaningful and answerable, although the answers might be complex.

John B. Watson

Many regard John B. Watson as the founder of **behaviorism**, *a field of psychology that concentrates on observable, measurable behaviors and not on mental processes.* Watson was not the first behaviorist—it is uncertain who was the first—but he systematized the approach, popularized it, and stated its goals and assumptions (Watson, 1919, 1925). Here are two quotes from Watson:

> Psychology as the behaviorist views it is a purely objective experimental branch of natural science. Its theoretical goal is the prediction and control of behavior. (1913, p. 158)

> The goal of psychological study is the ascertaining of such data and laws that, given the stimulus, psychology can predict what the response will be; or, on the other hand, given the response, it can specify the nature of the effective stimulus. (1919, p. 10)

Studies of Learning

Inspired by Watson, many researchers set out to study animal behavior, especially animal learning. One advantage of studying nonhuman animals is that the researcher can control the animals' diet, waking–sleeping schedule, and so forth far more completely than with humans. The other supposed advantage was that nonhuman learning might be simpler to understand. Many psychologists optimistically expected to discover simple, basic laws of behavior, more or less the same from one species to another and from one situation to another. Just as physicists could study gravity by dropping any object in any location, many psychologists in the mid-1900s thought they could learn all about behavior by studying rats in mazes. One highly influential psychologist, Clark Hull, wrote, "One of the most persistently baffling problems which confronts modern psychologists is the finding of an adequate explanation of the phenomena of maze learning" (1932, p. 25). Another wrote, "I believe that everything important in psychology (except perhaps . . . such matters as involve society and words) can be investigated in essence through the continued experimental and theoretical analysis of the determiners of rat behavior at a choice-point in a maze" (Tolman, 1938, p. 34).

As research progressed, however, psychologists found that even the behavior of a rat in a maze was more complicated than they had expected, and such research declined in popularity. Just as psychologists of the 1920s abandoned Titchener's structuralist approach to the mind, later psychologists abandoned the hope that studying rats in mazes would uncover universal principles of behavior. Other approaches based on animal research have, however, remained influential. In Chapter 6 we shall consider the important ideas of B. F. Skinner.

The behaviorist emphasis continues to be highly influential, however, as we shall see especially in Chapter 6 (learning) and also in Chapters 15 and 16 (abnormal behavior and therapy). Many successful forms of therapy focus on describing problematic behaviors and then changing them through learning.

From Freud to Modern Clinical Psychology

In the early 1900s, clinical psychology was a small field devoted largely to visual, auditory, movement, and memory disorders (Routh, 2000). The treatment of psychological disorders (or mental illness) was mostly the province of psychiatry, a branch of medicine. The Austrian psychiatrist Sigmund Freud revolutionized and popularized psychotherapy with his methods of analyzing patients' dreams and memories. He tried to trace current behavior to early childhood experiences, including children's sexual fantasies. We shall examine Freud's theories in much more detail in Chapter 13. Here let me foreshadow that discussion by saying that Freud's influence has decreased sharply over the years. Freud was a very persuasive speaker and writer, but the evidence he proposed for his theories was extremely weak. In fact he changed his theory several times and often cited the same observations to support a new theory that he previously had cited as evidence to support the old theory! In other

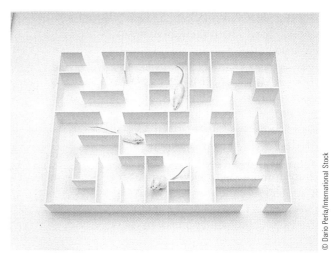

■ Early behaviorists studied rats in mazes, hoping to find general laws of behavior. As they discovered that this apparently simple behavior was very complicated, their interest declined and they turned to other topics.

© Dario Perla/International Stock

words his theories did not follow from his observations; he reinterpreted the observations to fit the theories. Nevertheless, Freud's influence was enormous, and by the mid-1900s, most psychiatrists in the United States and Europe were following his methods, at least in part.

During World War II more people wanted help, especially soldiers traumatized by war experiences. Because psychiatrists could not keep up with the need, psychologists began providing therapy. Clinical psychology became a much more popular field and much more similar to psychiatry, except without the license to prescribe drugs. Research began to compare the effectiveness of different methods, and new methods have taken the place of Freud's procedures, as we shall see in Chapters 15 and 16.

More Recent Trends in Psychology

The rest of this book will focus on the current era in psychology, with occasional flashbacks on the history of particular topics. Psychology today is an extremely diverse field, ranging from the study of simple visual processes to interventions intended to change whole communities. Recall that some of the earliest psychological researchers wanted to study the conscious mind, but the introspective methods of Titchener led nowhere. Since the mid-1960s, cognitive psychology (the study of thought and knowledge) has risen in prominence as psychologists found that they could indeed collect meaningful data about thought and knowledge (Robins,

Gosling, & Craik, 1999). Instead of asking people about their thoughts, today's cognitive psychologists carefully measure the accuracy and speed of responses under various circumstances to draw inferences about the underlying processes. They also use brain scans to determine what happens in the brain while someone is performing some task. Cognitive psychologists study human information processing in much the same way they would the information processing of a computer.

New fields of application have also arisen. For example, health psychologists study how people's health is influenced by their behaviors, such as smoking, drinking, sexual activities, exercise, diet, and reactions to stress. They also try to help people change their behaviors to promote better health. Sports psychologists apply psychological principles to helping athletes set goals, train, concentrate their efforts during a contest, and so forth.

Psychologists today have also broadened their scope to include more of human diversity. In its early days, around 1900, psychology was more open to women than most other academic disciplines, but even so, the opportunities for women were limited (Milar, 2000). Mary Calkins (Figure 1.11), an early memory researcher, was described as the best graduate student the Harvard psychology department had had to that point, but she was denied a PhD because Harvard insisted on its tradition of granting degrees to men only (Scarborough & Furomoto, 1987). She did, however, serve as president of the American Psychological Association, as did Margaret Washburn, another important woman in the early days of psychology.

Early psychological researchers tended not only to be men but also to focus their research attention on the limited population of people around them. For certain purposes it is reasonable to conduct research on "just anybody"—college students, for example. In fact many of the general principles of vision, hearing, and nervous system functioning are so widespread that we can learn about them by studying laboratory animals. However, many principles of cognition, motivation, and social behavior differ from one culture to another, and the results from a study in the United States may not apply in China, for example (Nisbett, Peng, Choi, & Norenzayan, 2001). Psychologists have become more aware of cultural influences, and cross-cultural research has become more prominent than in the past.

What will psychology be like in the future? We don't know, of course, but we assume it will reflect the changing needs of humanity. A few likely trends are foreseeable. Advances in medicine have enabled

FIGURE 1.11 Mary Calkins, one of the first prominent women in U.S. psychology.

We can learn much about what is or is not a stable feature of human nature by comparing people of different cultures.

people to live longer, while advances in technology have enabled them to build where there used to be forests and wetlands, heat and cool their homes, travel by car or plane to distant locations, and buy and discard enormous numbers of products. In short, we are quickly destroying our environment, using up natural resources, and polluting our air and water. Sooner or later it will become necessary either to decrease the population or to decrease the average person's use of resources (Howard, 2000). Convincing people to change their behavior is partly a political matter, but likely it will also be partly a task for psychologists.

IN CLOSING

Psychology Through the Years

Throughout the early years of psychology, many psychologists went down blind alleys, devoting enormous efforts to projects that produced disappointing results. Not all the efforts of early psychologists were fruitless by any means; in later chapters you will encounter some classic studies that have withstood the test of time. Still, if psychologists of the past spent countless years on fashionable projects, only to decide later that their efforts were misguided, how do we know that many psychologists aren't on the wrong track right now?

We don't, of course. In later chapters you will read about careful, cautious psychological research that has amassed what seems in many cases to be strong evidence, but you are welcome to entertain doubts. Maybe some psychologists' questions are not as simple as they seem; perhaps some of their answers are not very solid; perhaps you can think of a better way to approach certain topics. Psychologists have better data and firmer conclusions than they used to, but still they admit they do not have all the answers.

But that is not a reason for despair. Much like a rat in a maze, researchers make progress by trial and error. They pose a question, try a particular research method, and discover what happens. Sometimes the results support fascinating and important conclusions; other times they lead to rejections of old conclusions and therefore a search for replacements. In either case the experience leads ultimately to better questions and better answers. ▮

Summary

- *Choice of research questions.* During the history of psychology, researchers have several times changed their opinions about what constitutes an interesting, important, answerable question. (page 17)
- *First experiments.* In 1879 Wilhelm Wundt established the first laboratory devoted to psychological research. He demonstrated the possibility of psychological experimentation. (page 17)

- *Limits of self-observation.* One of Wundt's students, Edward Titchener, attempted to analyze the elements of mental experience, relying on people's own observations. Other psychologists became discouraged with this approach. (page 19)
- *The founding of American psychology.* William James, generally considered the founder of American psychology, focused attention on how the mind guides useful behavior rather than on the contents of the mind. By doing so James paved the way for the rise of behaviorism. (page 20)
- *Early sensory research.* In the late 1800s and early 1900s, many researchers concentrated on studies of the senses, partly because they were more likely to find definite answers on this topic than on other topics. (page 20)
- *Darwin's influence.* Charles Darwin's theory of evolution by natural selection influenced psychology in many ways; it prompted some prominent early psychologists to compare the intelligence of different species. That question turned out to be more complicated than anyone had expected. (page 21)
- *Intelligence testing.* The measurement of human intelligence was one concern of early psychologists that has persisted through the years. (page 22)
- *The era of behaviorist dominance.* As psychologists became discouraged with their attempts to analyze the mind, they turned to behaviorism. For many years psychological researchers concentrated on behavior, especially animal learning, to the virtual exclusion of mental experience. (page 22)
- *Maze learning.* Clark Hull exerted great influence for a number of years. Eventually, his approach became less popular because rats in mazes did not seem to generate simple or general answers to major questions. (page 22)
- *Psychological research today.* Today, psychologists study a wide variety of topics. Still, we cannot be certain that we are not currently going down some blind alleys, just as many psychologists did before us. (page 23)

Answers to Concept Checks

5. Early psychological research focused mainly on sensation, because sensation is central to experience and because the early researchers believed that sensation questions were answerable. (page 20)
6. Structuralists wanted to understand the components of the mind. They based their research mainly on introspection. Functionalists wanted to explore what the mind could *do,* and they focused mainly on behavior. (page 20)

CHAPTER ENDING

Key Terms and Activities

Key Terms

You can check the page listed for a complete description of a term. You can also check the glossary/index at the end of the text for a definition of a given term, or you can download a list of all the terms and their definitions for any chapter at this Web site:

http://psychology.wadsworth.com/kalat_intro7e/

behaviorism: a field of psychology that concentrates on observable, measurable behaviors and not on mental processes (page 22)

biopsychologist (or behavioral neuroscientist): a specialist who tries to explain behavior in terms of biological factors, such as electrical and chemical activities in the nervous system, the effects of drugs and hormones, genetics, and evolutionary pressures (page 8)

clinical psychologist: someone with an advanced degree in psychology, with a specialty in understanding and helping people with psychological problems (page 11)

clinical social worker: a person with a degree in social work instead of psychology, who helps people with psychological problems in ways similar to those of a clinical psychologist (page 11)

cognition: thinking and acquiring knowledge (page 10)

cognitive psychologist: a specialist who studies thought processes and the acquisition of knowledge (page 10)

comparative psychologist: a specialist who compares different animal species (page 21)

counseling psychologist: someone trained to help people with educational, vocational, marriage, health-related, and other decisions (page 12)

determinism: the assumption that all behavior has a cause, or *determinant,* in the observable world (page 5)

developmental psychologist: a specialist who studies the behavioral capacities of different ages and how behavior changes with age (page 10)

dualism: the view that the mind is separate from the brain (page 6)

ergonomist (or human factors specialist): a psychologist with engineering skills who works to facilitate the operation of machinery so that the average person can use it as efficiently and as safely as possible (page 13)

evolutionary psychologist: one who tries to explain behavior in terms of the evolutionary history of the species, including reasons evolution might have favored a tendency to act in particular ways (page 9)

forensic psychologist: one who provides advice and consultation to police, lawyers, courts, or other parts of the criminal justice system (page 12)

free will: the doctrine that behavior is caused by a person's independent decisions, not by external determinants (page 5)

functionalism: an attempt to understand how mental processes produce useful behaviors (page 20)

industrial/organizational (I/O) psychology: the psychological study of people at work (page 12)

introspection: looking within oneself (page 18)

learning and motivation: the study of how behavior depends on the outcomes of past behaviors and on current motivations (page 9)

mind–brain problem: the philosophical question of how the conscious mind is related to the physical nervous system, including the brain (page 6)

monism: the view that consciousness is inseparable from the physical brain (page 6)

nature–nurture issue: the question of the relative roles played by heredity (nature) and environment (nurture) in determining differences in behavior (page 8)

psychiatry: a branch of medicine that deals with emotional disturbances (page 11)

psychoanalyst: a psychotherapist who relies heavily on the theories of Sigmund Freud (page 11)

psychology: the systematic study of behavior and experience (page 3)

psychophysical function: the mathematical description of the relationship between the physical properties of a stimulus and its perceived properties (page 20)

school psychologist: a specialist in the psychological condition of students (page 13)

social psychologist: a specialist who studies how an individual influences others and is influenced by other people (page 10)

structuralism: an attempt to describe the structures that compose the mind (page 19)

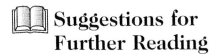

Suggestions for Further Reading

Sechenov, I. (1965). *Reflexes of the brain.* Cambridge, MA: MIT Press. (Original work published 1863). One of the first attempts to deal with behavior scientifically and still one of the clearest statements of the argument for determinism in human behavior.

Book Companion Web Site

Need help studying? Go to

http://psychology.wadsworth.com/kalat_intro7e/

for a virtual study center. You'll find a personalized Self-Study Assessment that will provide you with a study plan based on your answers to a pretest. Also study using flashcards, quizzes, interactive art, and an online glossary.

Check out interactive **Try It Yourself** exercises on the companion site! These exercises will help you put what you've learned into action.

Your companion site also has direct links to the following Web sites. These links are checked often for changes, dead links, and new additions.

Careers in Psychology

www.drlynnfriedman.com/

Clinical psychologist Lynn Friedman offers advice on majoring in psychology, going to graduate school, and starting a career.

Nontraditional Careers in Psychology

www.apa.org/students

Advice and information for students from the American Psychological Association.

Today in the History of Psychology

www.cwu.edu/~warren/today.html

Warren Street, at Central Washington University, offers a sample of events in the history of psychology for every day

of the year. Pick a date, any date (as they say), from the History of Psychology Calendar and see what happened on that date. The APA sponsors this site, which is based on Street's book, *A Chronology of Noteworthy Events in American Psychology.*

More About the History of Psychology

www.uakron.edu/ahap

The University of Akron has assembled a museum of old psychology laboratory equipment and other mementos from psychology's past.

What Else Would You Like to Know?

www.psywww.com

www.psychology.org

Both of these sites provide annotated links to a vast array of information about psychology.

Try It Yourself CD-ROM
with Critical Thinking Video Exercises

Use your CD to access **videos** related to activities designed to help you think critically about the important topics discussed. You'll also find an easy portal link to the book companion site where you can access your personalized **Self-Study Assessments** and interactive Try It Yourself exercises.

PsychNow! 2.0

PsychNow! is a fun interactive CD designed to help you with the difficult concepts in psychology. Check out the Accessing Psychology section for the following topics that relate to this chapter:

Study Skills: learning styles video, study habit lesson, and printable schedule.

Psychology and its History: quizzes, historical facts, timeline.

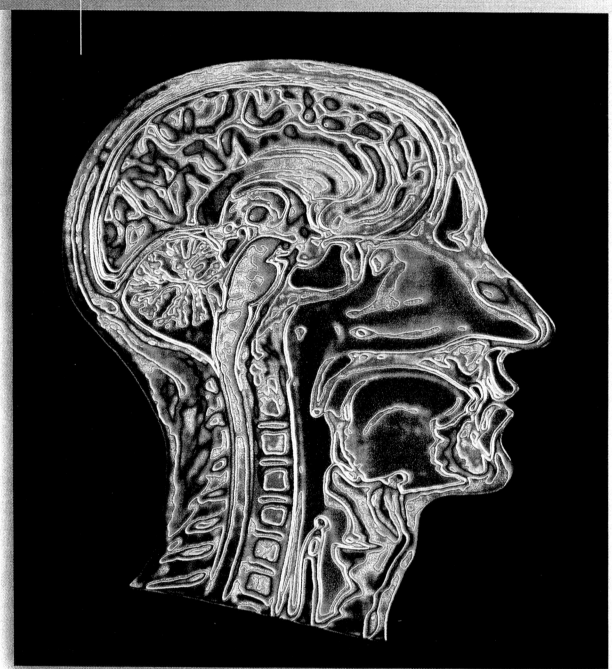

Biological Psychology

It is easy to look at a human brain, which weighs only 1.2 to 1.4 kg (2.5 to 3 lb), and marvel at its abilities. A bee's brain is microscopically small, but even a bee has amazingly complex behaviors. It locates flowers, finds food in the flowers, evades predators, finds its way back to the hive, and then does a dance that tells other bees where it found the food. When necessary, it also takes care of the queen bee, protects the hive against intruders, and so forth. Not bad for a microscopic brain.

Understanding brain processes is a daunting challenge. Researchers necessarily proceed piecemeal, first answering the easiest questions. We now know a great deal about how nerves work and how brains record sensory experiences. What we understand least is why and how brain activity produces conscious experience. (Philosopher David Chalmers calls this "the hard problem.")

■ A bee has amazingly complex behavior, but we have no way to get inside the bee's experience to know what (if anything) it feels like to be a bee.

Will we someday understand nerves well enough to "read minds" or understand the origins of consciousness? Maybe, maybe not, but the fascination of the mind–brain question motivates many researchers to tireless efforts.

Biological explanations will play a key role in many chapters and are hardly limited to this one. One major biological influence is genetics, and research on genetics plays an increasingly central role in psychology. We shall consider genetics more systematically in Chapter 10 (Development). In this chapter we focus on the cells of the nervous system and the overall structure of the nervous system.

Neurons and Behavior

Can we explain our experiences and our behavior in terms of the actions of single cells in the nervous system?

One highly productive strategy in science is *reductionism*—the attempt to explain complex phenomena by reducing them to combinations of simpler components. Biologists explain breathing, blood circulation, and metabolism in terms of chemical reactions and physical forces. Chemists explain chemical reactions in terms of the properties of the elements and their atoms. Physicists explain the properties of the atom in terms of a few fundamental forces.

How well does reductionism apply to psychology? Can we explain human behavior and experience in terms of chemical and electrical events in the brain? The only way to find out is to try. Here we explore efforts to explain behavior based on single cells of the nervous system.

Nervous System Cells

You experience your "self" as a single entity that senses, thinks, and remembers. And yet neuroscientists have found that the nervous system responsible for your experiences consists of an enormous number of separate cells. The brain processes information in **neurons** (NOO-rons), or *nerve cells*. Figure 3.1 shows estimates of the numbers of neurons in various parts of the human nervous system (R. W. Williams & Herrup, 1988). The nervous system also contains another kind of cells called **glia** (GLEE-uh), *which support the neurons in many ways such as by insulating them and removing waste products.* The glia are about one tenth the size of neurons but about 10 times more numerous.

How do so many separate neurons and glia combine forces to produce the single stream of experiences that is you? The secret is communication. Each neuron receives information and transmits it to other cells by conducting electrochemical impulses. Sensory neurons carry information from the sense organs to the central nervous system, where neurons process the information, compare it to past information, and exchange information with other neurons, and ultimately, motor neurons send commands to the muscles and glands.

To understand our nervous system, we must first understand the properties of both the individual neurons and the connections among them. Neurons have

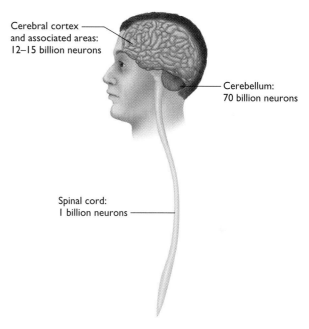

FIGURE 3.1 Estimated distribution of the neurons in the adult human central nervous system. No one has attempted an exact count, and the number varies substantially from one person to another. *(Based on data of R. W. Williams & Herrup, 1988).*

a variety of shapes depending on whether they receive information from a few sources or many and whether they send impulses over a short or a long distance (Figure 3.2).

A neuron consists of three parts: a cell body, dendrites, and an axon (Figure 3.3). The **cell body** *contains the nucleus of the cell.* The **dendrites** (from a Greek word meaning "tree") are *widely branching structures that receive transmissions from other neurons.* The **axon** is a *single, long, thin, straight fiber with branches near its tip.* Some vertebrate axons are covered with *myelin,* an insulating sheath that speeds up the transmission of impulses along an axon. As a rule an axon transmits information to other cells, and the dendrites or cell body of each cell receives that information. That information can be either excitatory or inhibitory; that is, it can increase or decrease the probability that the next cell will send a message of its own. Inhibitory messages are important for many purposes. For example, during a period of painful stimulation, your brain has mechanisms to inhibit further sensation of pain.

FIGURE 3.2 Neurons, which vary enormously in shape, consist of a cell body and branched attachments called axons (coded blue for easy identification) and dendrites. The neurons in (a) and (b) receive input from many sources, the neuron in (c) from only a few sources, and the neuron in (d) from an intermediate number of sources. The sensory neurons (e) carry messages from sensory receptors to the brain or spinal cord. Inset: Electron micrograph showing cell bodies in brown and axons and dendrites in green. The color was added artificially; electron micrographs are made with electron beams, not light, and therefore, they show no color.

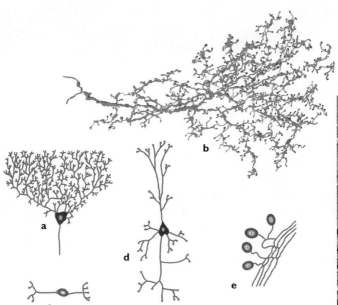
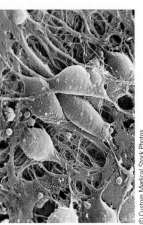

© Custom Medical Stock Photos

CONCEPT CHECK

1. Which part of a neuron receives input from other neurons? Which part sends messages to other cells? (Check your answers on page 77.)

The Action Potential

Axons are specialized to convey information over distances ranging to a meter or more. Imagine what would happen if they relied on electrical conduction: Electricity is extremely fast, but with a poor conductor such as any part of an animal body, electrical impulses weaken noticeably as they travel. The farther from your brain some information started, the less you would feel it. Short people would feel a pinch on their toes more intensely than tall people would . . . if indeed either felt their toes at all.

Instead, axons convey information by a special combination of electrical and chemical processes called an **action potential,** *an excitation that travels along an axon at a constant strength, no matter how far it must travel.* An action potential is a yes/no or on/off message, like a standard light switch. (Most switches don't let you make the light dimmer or brighter. It's either on or off.) This principle is known as the *all-or-none law.*

The advantage of an action potential over simple electrical conduction is that action potentials from distant places like your toes reach your brain at full strength. The disadvantage is that action potentials are slower than electrical conduction. Your knowledge of what is happening to your toes is at least a twentieth of a second out of date. A twentieth of a second is seldom worth worrying about, but your information

about different body parts is out of date by different delays. Consequently, if you are touched on two or more body parts at almost the same time, your brain cannot accurately gauge which touch came first.

Here is a quick description of how the action potential works:

1. When the axon is not stimulated, its membrane has a **resting potential,** *an electrical polarization across the membrane (or covering) of an axon, with a negative charge inside the axon.* A typical value is –70 millivolts on the inside relative to the outside. The resting potential depends largely on negatively charged proteins inside the axon. In addition a mechanism called the sodium-potassium pump pushes sodium ions out of the axon while pulling potassium ions in. In Figure 3.4 the sodium ions are marked Na^+, and the potassium ions are marked K^+, their chemical symbols. Both have a charge of +1 unit. The result of the sodium-potassium pump is that sodium ions are more concentrated outside the axon and potassium ions are more concentrated inside.

2. An action potential starts in either of two ways: First, many axons produce spontaneous activity. Second, input from other axons can excite a neuron's membrane. In either case, when the action potential starts, sodium gates open and allow sodium ions to enter (Figure 3.5). As the sodium ions enter the axon, they drive the inside of the cell to a slightly positive charge. Whenever that charge is great enough to reach the *threshold* of the axon, it opens narrow channels that permit still more sodium ions to enter, bringing with them their positive charges. This influx of positively charged sodium ions is the action potential.

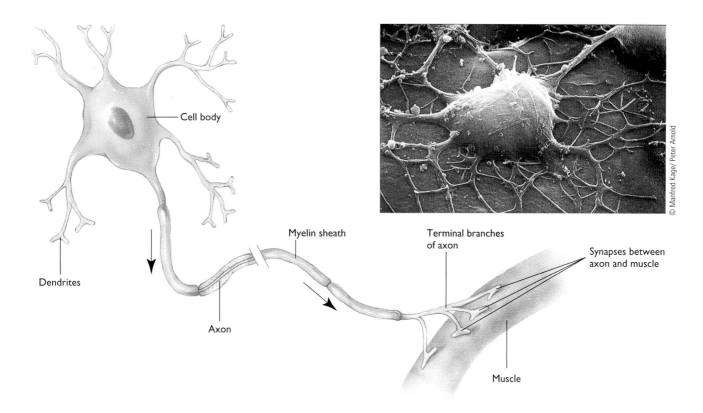

© Manfred Kage/ Peter Arnold

FIGURE 3.3 The generalized structure of a motor neuron shows the dendrites, the branching structures that receive transmissions from other neurons, and the axon, a single, long, thin, straight fiber with branches near its tip. Inset: A photomicrograph of a neuron.

3. After the sodium gates have been open for barely an instant, they snap shut. Then potassium gates open to allow potassium ions to leave the axon. The potassium ions each carry a positive charge, so their exit drives the inside of the axon back to its original resting potential (Figure 3.6b).

4. Eventually, the sodium-potassium pump removes the invading sodium ions and recaptures the escaping potassium ions.

You will recall that the axon does not conduct like an electrical wire. The action potential travels down the axon like a wave of energy, and the stimulation at each point excites the next point along the axon. You could imagine it like a fire burning along a string: The fire at each point ignites the next point, which in turn ignites the

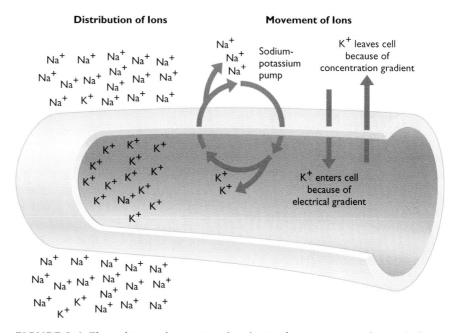

FIGURE 3.4 The sodium and potassium distribution for a resting membrane. Sodium ions (Na^+) are concentrated outside the neuron; potassium ions (K^+) are concentrated inside. Because of negatively charged proteins inside the neuron, the inside of the cell is negatively charged relative to the outside. Protein and chloride ions (not shown) bear negative charges inside the cell. At rest very few sodium ions cross the membrane except by the sodium-potassium pump. Potassium tends to flow into the cell because it is attracted by the negative charge inside the cell. It tends to flow out because it is more concentrated inside than outside.

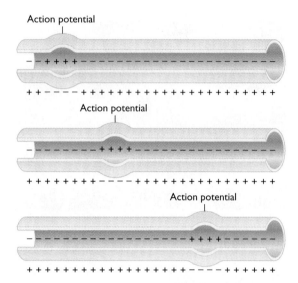

FIGURE 3.5 Ion movements conduct an action potential along an axon. At each point along the membrane, sodium ions enter the axon and alter the distribution of positive and negative charges. As each point along the membrane returns to its original state, the action potential flows to the next point.

next point. That is, after sodium ions enter some point along an axon, some of them diffuse to the neighboring portion of the axon and thereby excite that part of the membrane enough to open its own sodium gates. The action potential spreads to this next area and so on down the axon, as shown in Figure 3.6. In this manner the action potential re-

mains equally strong all the way to the end of the axon.

All of this information is clearly important to investigators of the nervous system, but why should a psychology student care? First, it explains why sensations on points on your fingers and toes do not fade away by the time they reach your brain. Second, an understanding of action potentials is one step toward understanding the communication between one neuron and the next. Third, certain drugs operate by blocking action potentials. For example, anesthetic drugs (e.g., Novocain) silence neurons by clogging the sodium gates. When your dentist drills a tooth, the receptors in your tooth send out the message "Pain! Pain! Pain!" But that message does not get through to the brain because a shot of Novocain has blocked the sodium gates and thereby halted the sensory messages.

CONCEPT CHECK ☑

2. If a mouse and a giraffe both get pinched on the toes at the same time, which will respond faster? Why?
3. Fill in these blanks: When the axon membrane is at rest, the inside has a _____ charge relative to the outside. When the membrane reaches its threshold, _____ ions enter from outside to inside, bringing with them a _____ charge. That flow of ions constitutes the _____ _____ of the axon. (Check your answers on page 77.)

Synapses

Communication between one neuron and the next is not like transmission along an axon. At a **synapse** (SIN-aps), *the specialized junction between one neuron and another* (Figure 3.7), *a neuron releases a chemical that either excites or inhibits the next neuron.* That is, the chemical can make the next neuron either more or less likely to produce an action potential. At other kinds of synapses, a neuron releases a chemical that excites a muscle or gland. The events at synapses are central to everything that your nervous system does because synapses determine which cells will be active at any moment.

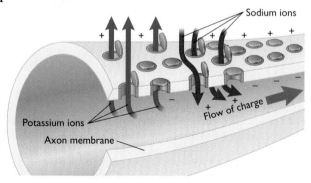

FIGURE 3.6 (a) During an action potential, sodium gates in the neuron membrane open, and sodium ions enter the axon, bringing a positive charge with them. (b) After an action potential occurs at one point along the axon, the sodium gates close at that point and open at the next point along the axon. When the sodium gates close, potassium gates open, and potassium ions flow out of the axon, carrying a positive charge with them. (*Modified from Starr & Taggart, 1992*)

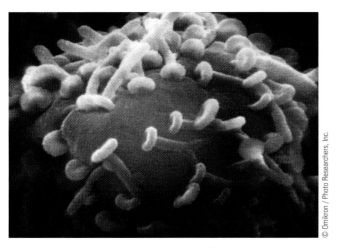

© Omikron / Photo Researchers, Inc.

FIGURE 3.7 The tips of axons swell to form terminal boutons, which form synapses onto the surface of another cell, as shown in this electron micrograph.

charged or negatively charged ions to enter. The postsynaptic neuron produces an action potential of its own if the total excitation at any moment outweighs the total inhibition coming from a variety of synapses. The process resembles making a decision: When you are trying to decide whether to do something, you weigh all the pluses and minuses and act if the pluses are stronger.

Inhibition is not the absence of excitation; it is like stepping on the brakes. For example, when a pinch on your foot causes you to raise it, thus contracting one set of muscles, inhibitory synapses in your spinal cord block activity in the muscles that would move your leg in the opposite direction. Those inhibitory synapses prevent messages from trying to raise your leg and extend it at the same time.

After a neurotransmitter excites or inhibits a receptor, it separates from the receptor, terminating the

A typical axon has several branches, each ending with a little bulge called a *presynaptic ending,* or **terminal bouton** (or **button**), as shown in Figure 3.8. When an action potential reaches the terminal bouton, it releases molecules of a **neurotransmitter,** *a chemical that has been stored in the neuron and that can activate receptors of other neurons* (Figure 3.8). Several dozen chemicals are used as neurotransmitters in various brain areas, although any given neuron releases only one or a few of them. The neurotransmitter molecules diffuse across a narrow gap to the **postsynaptic neuron,** *the neuron on the receiving end of the synapse.* There the neurotransmitter molecules attach to receptors on the neuron's dendrites or cell body (or for special purposes on the tip of its axon). The neural communication process is summarized in Figure 3.9.

Depending on the neurotransmitter and the type of receptor, the attachment can either excite or inhibit the postsynaptic neuron. That is, it enables either positively

FIGURE 3.8 The synapse is the junction of the presynaptic (message-sending) cell and the postsynaptic (message-receiving) cell. At the end of the presynaptic axon is the terminal bouton, which contains many molecules of the neurotransmitter. The thick, dark area at the bottom of the cell is the synapse.

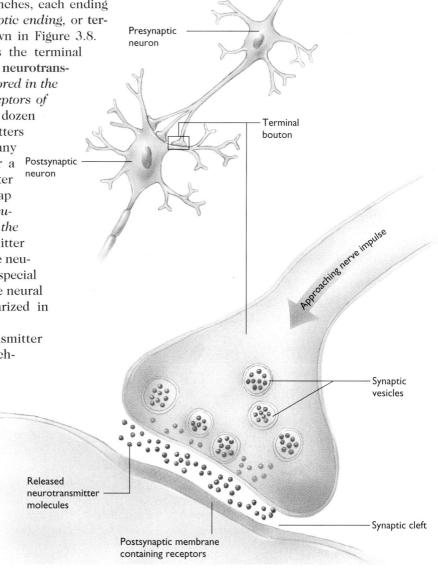

Presynaptic neuron

Terminal bouton

Postsynaptic neuron

Approaching nerve impulse

Synaptic vesicles

Synaptic cleft

Released neurotransmitter molecules

Postsynaptic membrane containing receptors

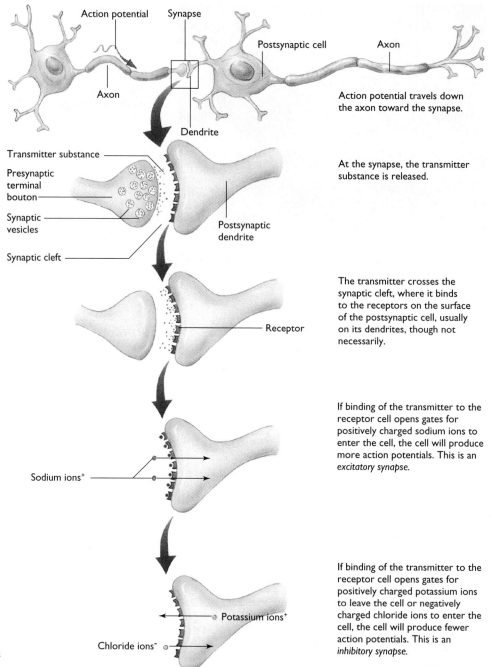

FIGURE 3.9 The complex process of neural communication takes only 1–2 milliseconds.

message. From that point on, the fate of the receptor molecule varies. It could become reabsorbed by the axon that released it (through a process called *reuptake*); it could diffuse away, get metabolized, and eventually show up in the blood or urine; or it could bounce around for a moment, return to the postsynaptic receptor, and reexcite it. Many antidepressant drugs act by blocking reuptake and therefore prolonging the effects of one transmitter or another.

Different neurotransmitters are associated with different functions, although it is misleading to as-

sign a specific behavior (e.g., sleep or pleasure) to a specific transmitter. Any complex behavior depends on many transmitter systems, and each transmitter contributes to many aspects of behavior. Still, an alteration of a particular kind of synapse will affect some behaviors more than others. For that reason it is possible to develop drugs that decrease depression, anxiety, appetite, and so forth by increasing or decreasing activity of a certain type of synapse. However, because each transmitter has several behavioral functions, drugs intended for one purpose almost always have other results, referred to as "side effects."

CONCEPT CHECK ✓

4. What is the difference between the presynaptic neuron and the postsynaptic neuron?
5. GABA is a neurotransmitter that inhibits postsynaptic neurons. If a drug were injected to prevent GABA from attaching to its receptors, what would happen to the postsynaptic neuron? (Check your answers on page 77.)

CRITICAL THINKING: *WHAT'S THE EVIDENCE?*
Neurons Communicate Chemically

You have just learned that neurons communicate by releasing chemicals at synapses. Perhaps you are perfectly content to take my word for it and go on with something else. Still, it is advisable to pause and contemplate the evidence responsible for an important conclusion.

Today, neuroscientists have a wealth of evidence that neurons release chemicals at synapses. They can radioactively trace where chemicals go and what happens when they get there; they also can inject purified chemicals at a synapse and use extremely fine electrodes to measure the response of the postsynaptic neuron. But scientists of the 1920s had no fancy equipment, yet they still managed to establish that neurons communicate with chemicals.

Otto Loewi conducted a simple, clever experiment, as he later described in his autobiography (Loewi, 1960).

Hypothesis If a neuron releases chemicals, an investigator should be able to collect some of those chemicals, transfer them from one animal to another, and thereby get the second animal to do what the first animal had been doing. Loewi had no method of collecting chemicals released within the brain itself, so he worked with axons communicating with the heart muscle. (The communication between a neuron and a muscle is similar to that between neurons.)

Method Loewi began by electrically stimulating some axons connected to a frog's heart. These particular axons slowed down the heart rate. As he continued to stimulate those axons, he collected some of the fluid on and around that heart and transferred it to the heart of a second frog.

Results When Loewi transferred the fluid from the first frog's heart, the second frog's heart rate also slowed (Figure 3.10).

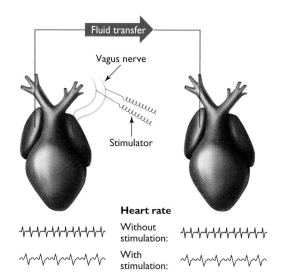

FIGURE 3.10 Otto Loewi demonstrated that axons release chemicals that can affect other cells. Using a frog, he electrically stimulated a set of axons known to decrease the heart rate. Then he collected some fluid from around the heart and transferred it to the surface of another frog's heart. When that heart slowed its beat, Loewi concluded that the axons in the first heart must have released a chemical that slows the heart rate.

Interpretation Evidently, the stimulated axons had released a chemical that slows heart rate. At least in this case, neurons send messages by releasing chemicals.

Loewi eventually won a Nobel Prize in physiology for this and related experiments. Even outstanding experiments have limitations, however. In this case the main limitation was the uncertainty about whether axons release chemicals at most synapses, all, or only a few. Answering *that* question required technologies not available until several decades later. (The answer is that *most* communication by neurons depends on chemicals; a few synapses use electrical communication.)

Neurotransmitters and Behavior

The use of drugs that affect neurotransmitters has already revolutionized psychiatry, and investigating the role of these neurotransmitters has produced major theoretical implications for psychology. The brain has dozens of neurotransmitters, and each activates many kinds of receptors. For example, serotonin activates at least 15 kinds, probably more (Roth, Lopez, & Kroeze, 2000). Each receptor type controls somewhat different aspects of behavior. For example, serotonin type 3 receptors are responsible for nausea, and this fact makes it possible to develop drugs that block nausea without major effects on other aspects of behavior (Perez, 1995).

Any drug that increases or decreases the activity of a particular type of receptor produces specific ef-

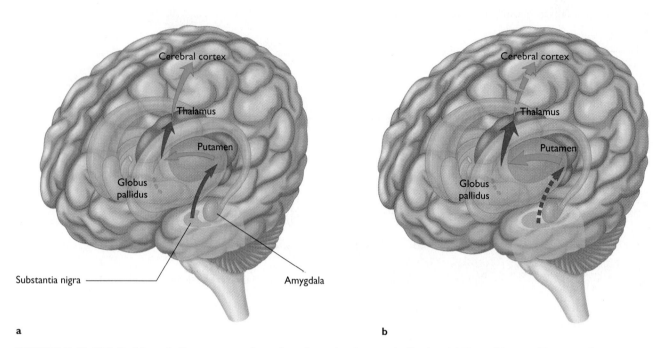

a   b

FIGURE 3.11 With Parkinson's disease, axons from the substantia nigra gradually die. (a) Normal brain. (b) Brain of person with Parkinson's disease. Green = excitatory path; red = inhibitory.

fects on behavior. One hypothesis, therefore, is that any unusual behavior is due to an excess or deficiency of some kind of synaptic activity. One example is **Parkinson's disease,** *a condition that affects about 1% of people over the age of 50. The main symptoms are difficulty in initiating voluntary movement, slowness of movement, tremors, rigidity, and depressed mood.* All of these symptoms can be traced to a gradual decay of a pathway of axons that release *the neurotransmitter* **dopamine** (DOPE-uh-meen) (Figure 3.11). One common treatment is the drug L-dopa, which enters the brain, where neurons convert it into dopamine. The effectiveness of this treatment for most people with mild cases of Parkinson's disease supports our beliefs about the link between the transmitter and the disease.

An example that shows more of the difficulty of interpreting results is **attention deficit disorder (ADD),** *a condition marked by impulsive behavior and short attention span.* ADD is usually treated with amphetamine or methylphenidate (Ritalin), and researchers know how these drugs work: Both prevent presynaptic neurons from reabsorbing (and thus recycling) the neurotransmit-

ters dopamine and serotonin after releasing them (Volkow et al., 1998). Amphetamine also increases the release of dopamine (Giros, Jaber, Jones, Wightman, & Caron, 1996). So both drugs prolong the activity of dopamine and serotonin at their synaptic receptors. It might seem, therefore, that the underlying problem in ADD is either a deficiency of those transmitters or an abnormality of their receptors. However, most people with ADD have normal dopamine release and receptors, and many people with abnormal dopamine receptors do not have ADD (Faraone & Biederman,

Former boxing champion Muhammad Ali developed symptoms of Parkinson's disease.

1998; Swanson et al., 2000). Perhaps understanding the drugs that relieve the problem doesn't tell us what caused the problem. One study found that methylphenidate improves attention even for normal healthy children, who presumably have normal dopamine activity (Zahn, Rapoport, & Thompson, 1980).

As we shall see in Chapter 16, drugs that alleviate depression and schizophrenia also act on dopamine and serotonin synapses, but again the relationship between the neurotransmitters and the behavior is complex. We still have much to learn about the relationship between the elements of the nervous system and their behavioral outcomes.

CONCEPT CHECK ☑

6. People suffering from certain disorders are given haloperidol, a drug that blocks activity at dopamine synapses. How would haloperidol affect someone with Parkinson's disease? (Check your answer on this page.)

IN CLOSING

Neurons and Behavior

Here is an imperfect analogy for the nervous system: At U.S. high school or college football games, one section of the stands is sometimes set aside for fans holding large cards. When their leader calls out a signal, such as "16," each of them holds up the appropriate card. If you were one of the fans, your card 16 might be all red, providing no clue about what the overall message might be. But the pattern provided by a few hundred fans might spell "Go, State." The message of neurons is a little like that because the activity or inactivity of any cell or synapse is part of a large overall pattern. The analogy is imperfect because the card message tells something to viewers on the other side of the field, whereas nothing reads the message of the neurons, except for the neurons themselves. However, the analogy works in some regards: Each neuron conveys a message that means nothing by itself but becomes part of an important message in context. Also, a mistake by one cardholder or one neuron is not too costly, and the overall message still gets through. Only a systematic mistake by a whole group of individuals (neurons) could garble the message.

Summary

- *Neuron structure.* A neuron, or nerve cell, consists of a cell body, dendrites, and an axon. The axon conveys information to other neurons. (page 69)
- *The action potential.* Information is conveyed along an axon by an action potential, which is regenerated without loss of strength at each point along the axon. (page 70)
- *Mechanism of the action potential.* An action potential depends on the entry of sodium into the axon. Anything that blocks this flow will block the action potential. (page 70)
- *How neurons communicate.* A neuron communicates with another neuron by releasing a chemical called a neurotransmitter at a specialized junction called a synapse. A neurotransmitter can either excite or inhibit the next neuron. (page 72)
- *Neurotransmitters and behavioral disorders.* An excess or a deficit of a particular neurotransmitter can lead to abnormal behavior, such as that exhibited by people with Parkinson's disease. However, understanding what happens at some kind of synapse is far removed from understanding the entire behavior pattern. (page 75)

Answers to Concept Checks

1. Dendrites receive input from other neurons. Axons send messages. (page 70)
2. The mouse will react faster because the action potentials have a shorter distance to travel in the mouse's nervous system than in the giraffe's. (page 72)
3. negative . . . sodium . . . positive . . . action potential (page 72)
4. The presynaptic neuron releases a neurotransmitter that travels to the postsynaptic neuron, where it activates an excitatory or inhibitory receptor. (page 75)
5. Under the influence of a drug that prevents GABA from attaching to its receptors, the postsynaptic neuron will receive less inhibition than usual. If we presume that the neuron continues to receive a certain amount of excitation, it will then produce action potentials more frequently than usual. (page 75)
6. Haloperidol would increase the severity of Parkinson's disease. In fact large doses of haloperidol can induce symptoms of Parkinson's disease in anyone. (page 77)

The Nervous System and Behavior

If you lose part of your brain, do you also lose part of your mind?

Why should psychologists care about the brain and the effects of brain damage? The reasons are both practical and theoretical. A practical reason is to distinguish between people who act strangely because of bad experiences and people who have brain disorders. There's no point in talking to someone about deep-seated psychological conflicts if the real problem is a brain tumor.

A theoretical reason is that studying the brain helps explain the organization of behavior. In some manner behavior must be made up of component parts, but what are they? Is behavior composed of ideas? Sensations? Movements? Personality characteristics? And how do the various components combine to produce the overall pattern? One way to answer such questions is to take behavior apart, one piece at a time, and brain damage does exactly that.

A related reason is that studying the brain sheds light on the mind–brain relationship discussed in Chapter 1. According to brain researchers, the mind *is* brain activity. But what exactly does that statement mean? And if it is so, why is it so? And how does brain activity produce experience? We cannot answer these questions, but studies of the brain at least help us come closer to an understanding.

The Major Divisions of the Nervous System

Psychologists and biologists distinguish between the central nervous system and the peripheral nervous system.

The **central nervous system** consists of *the brain and the spinal cord.* The central nervous system communicates with the rest of the body by the **peripheral nervous system,** which is composed of *bundles of axons between the spinal cord and the rest of the body.* The *peripheral nerves that communicate with the skin and muscles* are collectively called the **somatic nervous system.** Those that control the heart, stomach, and other organs are called the *autonomic nervous system.* Figure 3.12 summarizes these major divisions of the nervous system.

Early in its embryological development, the central nervous system of vertebrates, including humans, is a tube with three lumps, as shown in Figure 3.13. These lumps develop into the *forebrain,* the *midbrain,* and the *hindbrain;* the rest of the tube develops into the spinal cord (Figure 3.14). The forebrain, which contains the cerebral cortex and other struc-

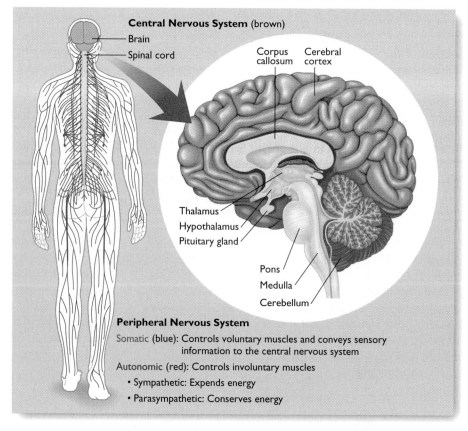

FIGURE 3.12 The nervous system has two major divisions: the central nervous system and the peripheral nervous system. Each of these has major subdivisions, as shown.

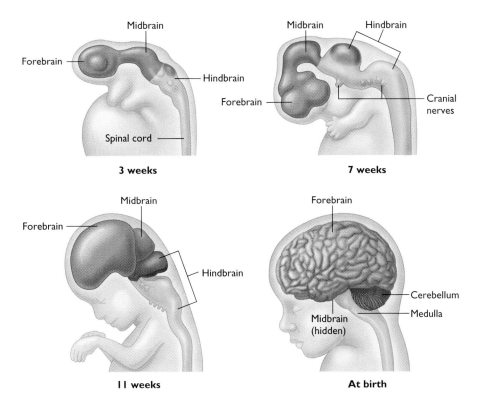

FIGURE 3.13 The human brain begins development as three lumps. By birth the forebrain has grown much larger than either the midbrain or the hindbrain, although all three structures perform essential functions.

tures, is by far the dominant portion of the brain in mammals, especially in humans.

The Forebrain

The forebrain consists of two **hemispheres,** *the left and right halves* (Figure 3.15). Each hemisphere is responsible for sensation and motor control on the opposite side of the body. Why does each hemisphere control the opposite side instead of its own side? People have speculated, but no one knows. We shall consider the differences between the left and right hemisphere in more detail later in this chapter.

The *outer covering of the forebrain,* known as the **cerebral cortex,** is especially prominent in humans. You have probably heard people talk about "having a lot of gray matter." Gray matter is composed of cell bodies and dendrites, which are grayer than the axons, and the cerebral cortex is by far your biggest area of gray matter. The interior of the forebrain beneath the cerebral cortex consists of axons, many of them covered with *myelin,* a white insulation. You can see areas of gray matter and white matter in Fig-

ure 3.16. If you would like to compare the brain anatomy of humans and many other mammalian species, see this Web site:

www.brainmuseum.org/sections/ index.html

For the sake of convenience, we describe the cortex in terms of four *lobes:* occipital, parietal, temporal, and frontal, as shown in Figure 3.17. The **occipital lobe,** *at the rear of the head, is specialized for vision.* People with damage in this area have *cortical blindness:* They have no conscious vision, no object recognition, and no visual imagery (not even in dreams), although they still have visual reflexes, such as eye blinks, that do not depend on the cerebral cortex. They also tend to set their wake–sleep cycles so they wake up in the day and get sleepy at night, again because this aspect of behavior depends on subcortical brain areas, not the cerebral cortex.

The **parietal lobe,** *just anterior (forward) from the occipital lobe, is specialized for the body senses, including touch, pain, temperature, awareness of the location of body parts, and perception of location of the body in space.* The **primary somatosensory** (body-sensory) **cortex,** *a strip in the anterior portion of the parietal lobe, has neurons*

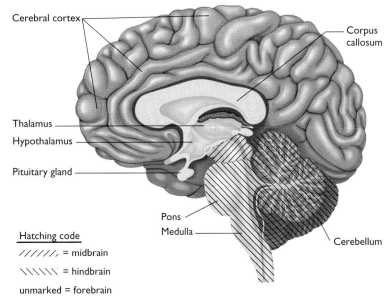

Hatching code
/ / / / / / = midbrain
\ \ \ \ \ \ = hindbrain
unmarked = forebrain

FIGURE 3.14 The major divisions of the human central nervous system, as seen from the midline.

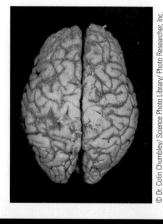

© Dr. Colin Chumbley/ Science Photo Library/ Photo Researcher, Inc.

a

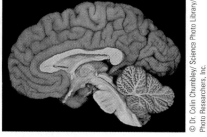

© Dr. Colin Chumbley/ Science Photo Library/ Photo Researchers, Inc.

b

FIGURE 3.15 The human cerebral cortex: (a) left and right hemispheres; (b) inside view of a complete hemisphere. The folds greatly extend the brain's surface area.

sensitive to touch in different body areas, as shown in Figure 3.18. Note that in Figure 3.18a larger areas are devoted to touch in the more sensitive parts of the body, such as the lips and hands, than to less sensitive areas, such as the abdomen and the back. Damage to any part of the somatosensory cortex will impair sensation from the corresponding part of the body. Extensive damage here also interferes with spatial attention. After parietal damage,

people see something but cannot decipher where it is relative to their body; consequently, they have trouble reaching toward it, walking around it, or shifting attention from one object to another. Because they cannot locate objects in space, they often confuse two objects. While looking at a yellow lemon and a red tomato, they might report seeing a yellow tomato and no lemon at all (Robertson, 2003). Most intact people can hardly imagine what the world must look like after parietal damage.

The **temporal lobe** of each hemisphere, *located toward the left and right sides of the head, is the main processing area for hearing and some of the complex aspects of vision.* People with damage to small areas of the temporal lobe show striking and specialized deficits, such as an inability to recognize faces and other complex patterns (Tarr & Gauthier, 2000); difficulty perceiving visual motion (Zihl, von Cramon, & Mai, 1983); or difficulty recognizing melodies and other complex sounds. One area in the temporal lobe of the left hemisphere is important for language comprehension. Damage in this area produces *Wernicke's aphasia,* characterized by trouble remembering the names of objects and understanding speech, although these people do a little better if someone speaks slowly. Their own speech, largely lacking nouns and verbs, is hard to understand, and they resort to made-up expressions, as do normal people if they are pressured to talk faster than they can think of the correct words (Dick et al., 2001).

Other parts of the temporal lobe are critical for certain aspects of emotion. The *amygdala* (Figure 3.19), a structure within the temporal lobe, responds strongly to emotional situations and to facial expressions that convey emotion. People with damage to the amygdala are slow to process emotional information (Baxter & Murray, 2002). Apparently, their problem is not that they cannot feel fear, for example, but that they are not sure when to feel fear. If you were driving down a steep, winding mountain road and suddenly discovered that your brakes weren't working, how frightened would you be? On a scale from 0 to 9, almost everyone rates this situation as 9, but someone with amygdala damage rates it about 6 (Adolphs, Russell, & Tranel, 1999).

FIGURE 3.16 (a) This cross section of a human brain shows gray matter (mostly cell bodies and dendrites) and white matter (axons). The whiteness comes from myelin, a fatty sheath that surrounds many axons. (b) The H-shaped structure in the center of the spinal cord is gray matter, composed largely of cell bodies. The surrounding white matter consists of axons. (*Source: Manfred Kage/Peter Arnold, Inc.*)

a

Courtesy of Dr. Dana Copeland

b

© Manfred Kage/ Peter Arnold

In later chapters we shall return to examine some of the structures that you see in Figure 3.19. The hippocampus is a key topic in Chapter 7 (Memory), and the hypothalamus and amygdala are important for emotional and motivated behaviors (Chapters 11 and 12).

The **frontal lobe**, *at the anterior (forward) pole of the brain,* includes the **primary motor cortex**, *a structure that is important for the planned control of fine movements,* such as moving one finger at a time. As with the primary somatosensory cortex, each area of the primary motor cortex controls a different part of the body, and larger areas are devoted to precise movements of the tongue and fingers than to, say, the shoulder and elbow muscles. The *anterior sections of the frontal lobe,*

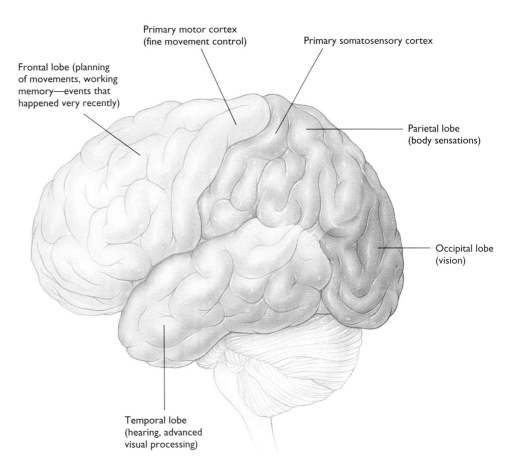

FIGURE 3.17 The four lobes of the human cerebral cortex, with indications of some of their major functions.

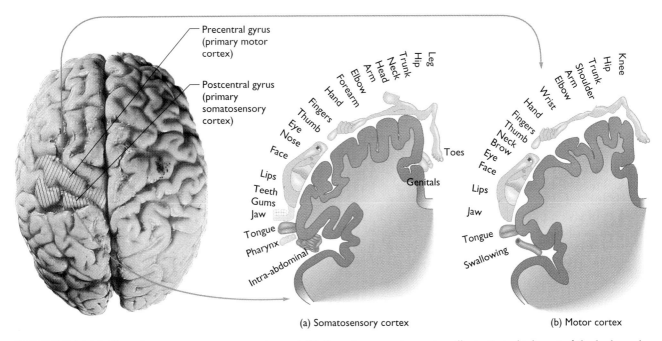

FIGURE 3.18 (a) The primary somatosensory cortex and (b) the primary motor cortex, illustrating which part of the body each brain area controls. Larger areas of the cortex are devoted to body parts that need to be controlled with great precision, such as the face and hands. *(Parts a and b adapted from* The Cerebral Cortex of Man *by W. Penfield and T. Rasmussen, Macmillan Library Reference. Reprinted by permission of Gale, a division of Thomson Learning.)*

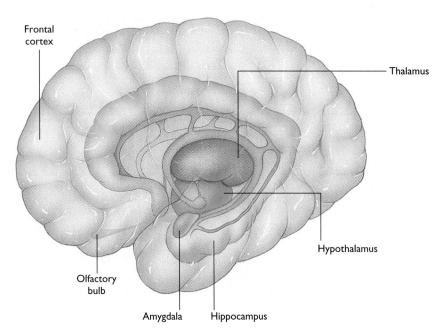

FIGURE 3.19 A view of the forebrain, showing internal structures as though the cerebral cortex were transparent.

called the **prefrontal cortex**, contribute to the organization and planning of movements and to certain aspects of memory. Indeed, planning a movement depends on memory. Recall, for example, the delayed-response task (Chapter 1): The individual must remember a signal during a delay and then make the appropriate movement. Certain areas in the left frontal lobe are essential for producing language.

CONCEPT CHECK ☑

7. The following five people are known to have suffered damage to the cerebral cortex. From their behavioral symptoms, state the probable location of each one's damage:
   a. impaired touch sensations and spatial localization
   b. impaired hearing and some changes in emotional experience
   c. inability to make fine movements with the right hand
   d. loss of vision in the left visual field
   e. poor performance on a delayed-response task, indicating difficulty remembering what has just happened. (Check your answers on page 91.)

How the Cerebral Cortex Communicates with the Body

The only sensory information that goes directly to the cerebral cortex is olfaction (the sense of smell). Touch, pain, and other skin senses enter the spinal cord, which

sends information that eventually reaches the **thalamus**, *a forebrain area that relays information to the cerebral cortex* (Figure 3.19). Vision, hearing, and taste information also goes through several synapses before reaching the thalamus and then the cerebral cortex.

The cerebral cortex does not directly control the muscles. It sends information to the **pons** and **medulla**, *which control the muscles of the head* (e.g., for chewing, swallowing, and breathing), and the **spinal cord**, *which controls the muscles from the neck down* (Figures 3.14 and 3.20). The spinal cord also controls many reflexes that do not require the forebrain. A **reflex** is a *rapid, automatic response to a stimulus*, such as unconscious adjustments of your legs while you are walking or quickly jerking your hand away from something hot.

The medulla, pons, and midbrain also contain the *reticular formation* and several other systems that send messages throughout the forebrain to regulate its arousal (Young & Pigott, 1999). A malfunction in these systems, depending on its nature and location, can render someone either persistently sleepy or persistently aroused.

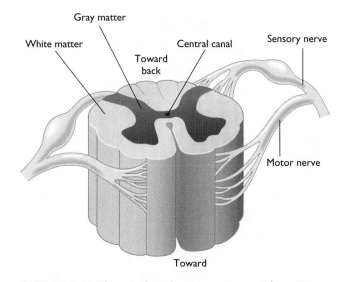

FIGURE 3.20 The spinal cord receives sensory information from all parts of the body except the head. Motor nerves in the spinal cord send messages to control the muscles and glands.

The **cerebellum** (Latin for "little brain"), *another part of the hindbrain,* is important for any behavior that requires aim or timing, such as tapping out a rhythm, judging which of two visual stimuli is moving faster, and judging whether the delay between one pair of sounds is shorter or longer than the delay between another pair (Ivry & Diener, 1991; Keele & Ivry, 1990). It is also essential to learned responses that require precise timing (Krupa, Thompson, & Thompson, 1993).

CONCEPT CHECK ☑

8. People who have become intoxicated on alcohol have slow, slurred speech and cannot walk a straight line. From these observations which part of the brain would you think the alcohol has most greatly impaired? (Check your answer on page 91.)

The Autonomic Nervous System and Endocrine System

The **autonomic nervous system,** closely associated with the spinal cord, *controls the internal organs such as the heart.* The term *autonomic* means involuntary, or automatic, in the sense that we have little voluntary control of it. We are generally unaware of its activity, although it does receive information from, and sends information to, the brain and the spinal cord.

The autonomic nervous system has two parts: (a) The *sympathetic nervous system,* controlled by a chain of neurons lying just outside the spinal cord, increases heart rate and breathing rate and readies the body for vigorous fight-or-flight activities. (b) The *parasympathetic nervous system,* controlled by neurons at the very top and very bottom levels of the spinal cord, decreases heart rate, increases digestive activities, and in general promotes activities of the body that take place during rest (Figure 3.21). We shall return to this topic in more detail in the discussion of emotions (Chapter 12).

The autonomic nervous system has some control over the **endocrine system,** *a set of glands that produce hormones and release them into the blood.* Hormones controlled by the hypothalamus and pituitary gland also regulate the endocrine system. Figure 3.22 shows some of the major endocrine glands. **Hormones** are *chemicals released by glands and conveyed via the blood to alter activity in various organs.* Hormones' effects resemble those of neurotransmitters. The difference is that a neurotransmitter is released immediately adjacent to a synapse, whereas a hormone flows with the blood. Some hormonal effects are brief, such as

Sympathetic system	Parasympathetic system
Uses much energy	**Conserves energy**
• Pupils open	• Pupils constrict
• Saliva decreases	• Saliva flows
• Pulse quickens	• Pulse slows
• Sweat increases	• Stomach churns
• Stomach less active	
• Epinephrine (adrenaline) secreted	

FIGURE 3.21 The sympathetic nervous system prepares the body for brief bouts of vigorous activity; the parasympathetic nervous system promotes digestion and other nonemergency functions. Although both systems are active at all times, the balance can shift from a predominance of one to a predominance of the other.

changes in blood pressure, but others can last months, such as preparation for migration or hibernation.

CONCEPT CHECK ☑

9. Just after a meal, the pancreas produces increased amounts of the hormone insulin, which increases the conversion of the digested food into fats in many cells throughout the body. How is a hormone more effective for this purpose than a neurotransmitter would be? (Check your answer on page 91.)

Measuring Brain Activity

Up to this point, you have been reading about the functions of various brain areas, as well as those of endocrine organs and so forth. But how did we learn about these functions? For many years nearly all the conclusions came from studies of medical patients, especially brain-damaged patients, but their brain damage could not be examined until after death. Researchers can now supplement such evidence with modern techniques that examine brain anatomy and activity in living people.

An **electroencephalograph** (EEG) *uses electrodes on the scalp to record rapid changes in brain electrical activity* (Figure 3.23). A similar method is a **magnetoencephalograph** (MEG), *which records magnetic changes.* Both of these methods provide data on a millisecond-by-millisecond basis, so they can measure people's reactions to lights and sounds, as well as how reactions depend on instructions, previous experience, and so forth. However, because EEG and MEG record from the surface of the scalp, they provide little detail about the location of the brain activity.

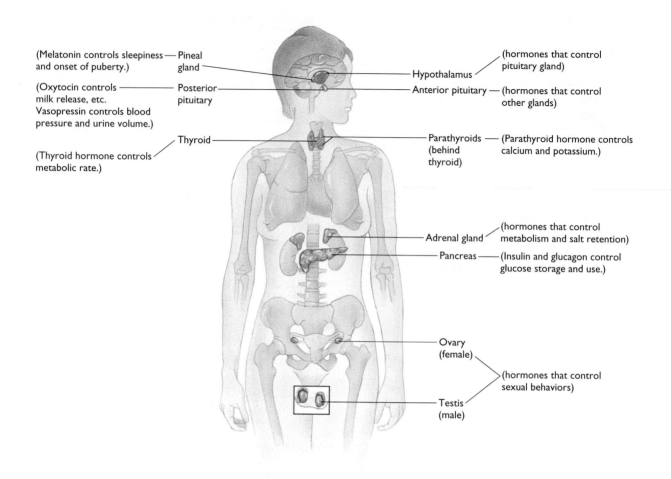

(Melatonin controls sleepiness — Pineal gland and onset of puberty.)

(Oxytocin controls — Posterior milk release, etc. pituitary Vasopressin controls blood pressure and urine volume.)

(Thyroid hormone controls — Thyroid metabolic rate.)

Hypothalamus — (hormones that control pituitary gland)

Anterior pituitary — (hormones that control other glands)

Parathyroids (behind thyroid) — (Parathyroid hormone controls calcium and potassium.)

Adrenal gland — (hormones that control metabolism and salt retention)

Pancreas — (Insulin and glucagon control glucose storage and use.)

Ovary (female) — (hormones that control sexual behaviors)

Testis (male)

FIGURE 3.22 Glands in the endocrine system produce hormones and release them into the bloodstream. This figure shows only some of the endocrine glands and some of their most abundant hormones.

Another method offers much better anatomical localization, with information on a minute-by-minute basis: **Positron-emission tomography (PET)** *records radioactivity of various brain areas emitted from injected chemicals* (Phelps & Mazziotta, 1985). First someone receives an injection of a radioactively labeled compound such as glucose. Glucose, a simple sugar that is the brain's main fuel (almost its only fuel), is absorbed mainly in the most active brain areas. Therefore, radioactivity comes primarily from those areas. Detectors around the head record the amount of radioactivity coming from each brain area and send that information to a computer, which generates an image such as the one in Figure 3.24. Red indicates areas of greatest activity, followed by yellow, green, and blue. Unfortunately, PET scans are expensive and require exposing the brain to radioactivity, a risky procedure, especially with repeated use.

Another technique, **functional magnetic resonance imaging (fMRI),** *uses magnetic detectors outside the head to compare the amounts of hemoglobin with and without oxygen in different brain areas* (J.

D. Cohen, Noll, & Schneider, 1993). (Adding or removing oxygen changes the response of hemoglobin to a magnetic field.) Highly active brain areas use much oxygen and therefore decrease the oxygen bound to hemoglobin in the blood. The fMRI technique thus indicates which brain areas are currently the most active, as in Figure 3.25. For more detail about brain scan techniques, see this Web site:

http://www.musc.edu/psychiatry/fnrd/primer_index.htm

Brain scans are a potentially powerful research tool, but interpreting the results requires careful research. For example, suppose we want to determine which brain areas are important for recent memory. We record activity while someone is engaged in a memory task and compare that activity to times when the person is doing . . . what? Doing nothing? That comparison wouldn't work; the memory task presumably includes sensory stimuli, motor responses, attention, and other processes besides memory. Researchers must design a comparison task that requires

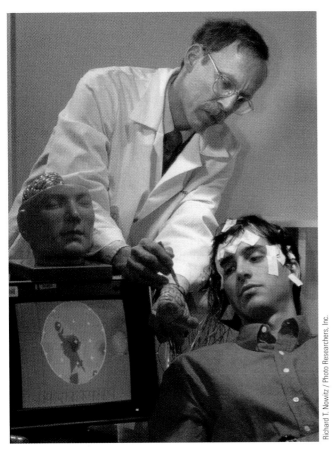

Richard T. Nowitz / Photo Researchers, Inc.

FIGURE 3.23 An EEG records momentary changes in electrical potential from the scalp, revealing an average of the activity of brain cells beneath each electrode.

attention to the same sensory stimuli, the same hand movements, and so forth as the memory task.

CRITICAL THINKING:
A STEP FURTHER
Testing Psychological Processes

Suppose you want to determine which brain areas are active during recent memory. Try to design some task that requires memory and a comparison task that is similar in every other way except for the memory requirement.

Effects of Experience on Brain Structure

Several illustrations in this text have been labeled "the" human nervous system. We do not need to specify whose nervous system because the gross structure is about the same from one person to another anywhere in the world. The detailed anatomy does vary,

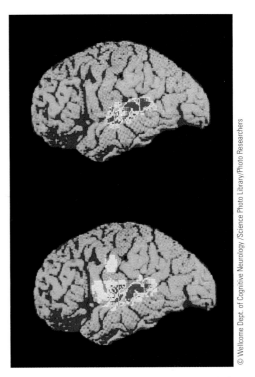

© Wellcome Dept. of Cognitive Neurology /Science Photo Library/Photo Researchers

FIGURE 3.24 A PET scan of the human brain. Red shows areas of most-increased activity during some task, yellow shows areas of next most-increased activity.

however. For example, brain volume tends to shrink in old age (Sowell et al., 2003), and it declines sharply with Alzheimer's disease and other medical conditions. The brain also shows small beneficial changes as a result of experience. Both axons and dendrites almost constantly withdraw old branches and grow new ones, producing a periodic turnover of synapses. Dendritic changes and synaptic renewal are particularly common in young animals (and presumably humans also) and become progressively less vigorous with advancing age (Grutzendler, Kasthuri, & Gan, 2002).

Can you improve your brain functioning by "exercising" your brain, as you can with your muscles? People have long assumed so. In former times students were taught ancient Latin and Greek on the assumption that they would acquire mental discipline that would make them more accomplished in whatever other tasks they undertook. Today, a similar argument is sometimes offered for why students should study Shakespeare or calculus. But is it true? There is such a thing as learning to study, but otherwise, it is difficult to demonstrate that studying one topic carries over to unrelated topics (Barnett & Ceci, 2002). For example, practicing chess would make you better at chess but not at anything else.

When we look at brain anatomy, the result is that practicing a particular skill expands the dendritic spread and probably the cell bodies of the brain areas

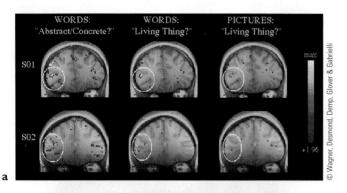

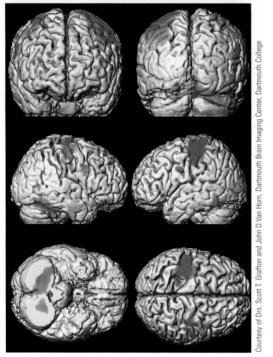

FIGURE 3.25 (a) This brain scan was made with functional magnetic resonance imaging (fMRI). Participants looked at words or pictures and judged whether each item was abstract or concrete, living or nonliving. Yellow shows the areas most activated by this judgment; red shows areas less strongly activated. *(From Wagner, Desmond, Demb, Glover, & Gabrieli, 1997. Photo courtesy of Anthony D. Wagner)* (b) A male volunteer, using his dominant right hand, was either rotating a small cylinder or resting in alternating 30-second intervals during a 5-minute fMRI scan, yielding six perspectives in which motor areas of the left brain are highlighted.

relevant to that skill. For example, professional musicians have a larger than average auditory cortex (Schneider et al., 2002) and expansions of several other brain areas important for timing and other musical processes (Gaser & Schlaug, 2003). The brain area representing the fingers expands in people who spend much time reading Braille (Pascual-Leone, Wasserman, Sadato, & Hallett, 1995). The longer someone has been a London taxi driver, the larger the posterior hippocampus, a brain area important for spatial memory (Maguire et al., 2000).

The hypothesis that using your brain in general expands your brain in general is harder to demonstrate. Rats that live in large cages with other rats do show brain enlargement relative to those in small individual cages (Greenough, 1975), but much or all of that effect can be attributed to increased physical activity, which increases blood flow to the head (van Praag, Kempermann, & Gage, 2000). Physical activity also benefits human brain size, especially in old age (Colcombe et al., 2003). Brain autopsies have shown that people with more education or greater mental activity in their daily lives tend to have greater branching in their dendrites (Jacobs, Schall, & Scheibel, 1993). However, we cannot draw a cause-and-effect conclusion. It is possible that education and mental activity promote brain growth but also possible that people who started with more dendritic branching succeeded well in their education and were drawn to more intellectual activities. In short, no evidence available so far indicates unambiguously that "exercising" your brain expands it anatomically.

For many decades researchers believed that all neurons formed before birth or early after it, so that beyond early infancy one could only lose neurons and never gain new ones. However, later researchers found that in a few brain areas, it is possible for *undifferentiated cells called* **stem cells** to develop into additional neurons (Gage, 2000; Graziadei & deHan, 1973; Song, Stevens, & Gage, 2002). Development of new neurons is well established in rats and songbirds, although not yet clear in humans, as the studies in humans may not have distinguished adequately between new neurons and new glia cells (Eriksson et al., 1998; Rakic, 2002). At most, however, new neurons form slowly, sporadically, and only in certain brain areas. It is not a routine matter like growing new skin cells or blood cells.

CONCEPT CHECK ☑

10. Under some conditions the axons and dendrites of a neuron increase their branching. Will the number of synapses change? (Check your answer on page 91.)

The "Binding Problem"

As researchers answered certain questions about brain function, a new one arose: One part of your brain is responsible for hearing, another for touch, several other areas for various aspects of vision, and so forth, and those areas have few if any direct connections with one another. So how do you get the experience of being a single "self"? If you shake a baby's toy rattle, how do you know that the object you see is also what you hear and feel? *The question of how separate brain areas combine forces to produce a unified perception of a single object* is the **binding problem** (Treisman, 1999). The binding problem is at the heart of the profound and difficult mind–brain problem mentioned in Chapter 1.

A naive explanation would be that all the various parts of the brain funnel their information to a "little person in the head" who puts it all together. Although no one takes that concept seriously, the underlying idea is hard to abandon, and brain researchers have sometimes imagined a "master area" of the brain that would serve the same purpose. Research on the cerebral cortex, however, has found no master area or central processor. Few neurons receive a combination of visual and auditory information or visual and touch information.

In fact the mystery deepens: Even in vision, different brain areas specialize in different aspects of the stimulus, such as shape, color, and movement. When you see a brown rabbit hopping, one brain area is most sensitive to the shape, another most sensitive to the movement, and another most sensitive to the brownness. The division of labor is not complete, but it is enough to make researchers wonder how we combine the different aspects, or "bind" them into a single object (Gegenfurtner, 2003).

The answer is not fully known, but part of the answer lies with the parietal cortex, important for spatial perception. Go back to shaking a toy rattle: If you can identify the location of your hand, the location of the rattle you see, and the location of the sound source, you probably can link the sensations together. If, like someone with parietal cortex damage, you cannot locate anything in space, you probably won't bind sensations into a single experience (Robertson, 2003). We also know that binding occurs only for precisely simultaneous events. Have you ever watched a film or television show in which the soundtrack is noticeably ahead of or behind the picture? If so, you knew that the sound wasn't coming from the performers on screen. You get the same experience watching a poorly dubbed foreign-language film. However, when you watch a ventriloquist, the motion of the dummy's mouth simultaneous with the sound causes you to perceive the sound as coming from the dummy.

We also know that binding takes time. If you see a brief flash on the screen showing a red circle and a green square, you might see red, green, circle, and square but not be sure which color went with which shape. The more complex the stimulus, the longer it takes to bind its elements into a whole (Holcombe & Cavanagh, 2001). People with parietal lobe damage have trouble binding a stimulus even with prolonged exposure (Treisman, 1999; Wheeler & Treisman, 2002).

©Bettmann/CORBIS

▎ We hear the sound as coming from the dummy's mouth only if sound and movements are synchronized. In general, binding depends on simultaneity of two kinds of stimuli.

The Corpus Callosum and the Split-Brain Phenomenon

What would happen if the two hemispheres of your brain could not communicate with each other? Such a situation occurs after damage to the **corpus callosum,** *a set of axons connecting the cerebral cortex of the left and right hemispheres* (Figure 3.26). Corpus callosum damage prevents someone from comparing sights seen on the left to those on the right and from comparing something felt with the left hand to something in the right. In some ways the person now has two half-brains side by side, and maybe even two spheres of consciousness.

Occasionally, brain surgeons cut the corpus callosum in an effort to relieve **epilepsy,** *a condition in which neurons somewhere in the brain emit abnormal rhythmic, spontaneous impulses.* Depending on where the abnormal impulses start and spread, epilepsy can produce varied effects. Most people with epilepsy respond well to antiepileptic drugs and live normal lives. A few, however, continue to have frequent major seizures. When all else fails, surgeons sometimes recommend cutting the corpus callosum. The original idea was that epileptic seizures would be limited to one hemisphere and therefore less incapacitating.

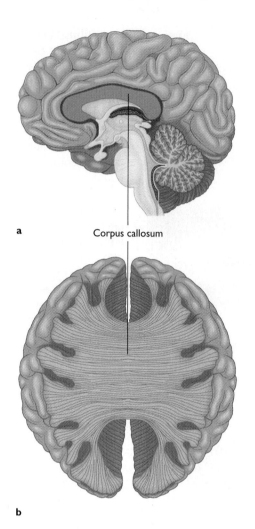

a

Corpus callosum

b

FIGURE 3.26 The corpus callosum is a large set of axons that convey information between the two hemispheres of the cerebral cortex. (a) A midline view showing the location of the corpus callosum. (b) A horizontal section showing how each axon of the corpus callosum links one spot in the left hemisphere to a corresponding spot in the right hemisphere.

The operation was more successful than expected. Not only are the seizures limited to one side of the body, but they also become less frequent. A possible explanation is that the operation interrupts the feedback loop between the two hemispheres that allows an epileptic seizure to echo back and forth. However, although these split-brain patients resume a normal life, they have some interesting behavioral effects. First, we need to consider some anatomy.

Connections Between the Eyes and the Brain

Note: This section presents a concept that is contrary to most people's expectations, and the left-right–right-left connections can be confusing. So please read carefully!

Because each hemisphere of the brain controls the muscles on the opposite side of the body, each half of the brain needs to see the opposite side of the

world. This does *not* mean that your left hemisphere sees with the right eye or that your right hemisphere sees with the left eye.

Convince yourself: Close one eye, then open it, and close the other. Note that you see almost the same view with both eyes. You see each half of the world with part of your left eye and part of your right eye.

Online Try It Yourself

Figure 3.27, which shows the human visual system, warrants careful study. Light from each half of the world strikes receptors on the opposite side of *each* retina. (The retina is the lining in the back of each eye. The retina is lined with receptors.) Information from the left half of each retina travels via the *optic nerves* to the left hemisphere of the cerebral cortex; information from the right half of each retina travels via the optic nerves to the right hemisphere.

Here is one way to remember this material: *Light from each side of the world strikes the opposite side of the retina. The brain is connected to the eyes so that each hemisphere sees the opposite side of the world.* If you remember those two statements, you should be able to deduce that each hemisphere is connected to the half of each retina *on the same side*, as shown in Figure 3.27. You might also draw the diagram for yourself.

What about the very center of the retina? The cells in a thin strip down the center of each retina send axons to both sides of the brain.

Effects of Severing the Corpus Callosum

For almost all right-handed people and about 60% of left-handed people, parts of the left hemisphere control speech. For most other left-handers, both hemispheres control speech. Complete right-hemisphere control of speech is rare. The right hemisphere is critical for understanding the emotional aspects of speech, however, as we shall see later.

Assuming you have left-hemisphere control of speech, can you talk about something you feel with the left hand or see in the left visual field? Yes, easily, if your brain is intact: The information enters your right hemisphere but then passes quickly across the corpus callosum to your left hemisphere.

The result is different if the corpus callosum is severed. A split-brain patient (someone whose corpus callosum has been cut) feels something with the left hand but cannot describe it because the information goes to the right (nonspeech) hemisphere (Nebes, 1974; Sperry, 1967). If asked to point to it, the person points correctly only with the left hand. In fact, while correctly pointing with the left hand, the person might say, "I have no idea what it was. I didn't feel anything." Evidently, the right hemisphere can understand the in-

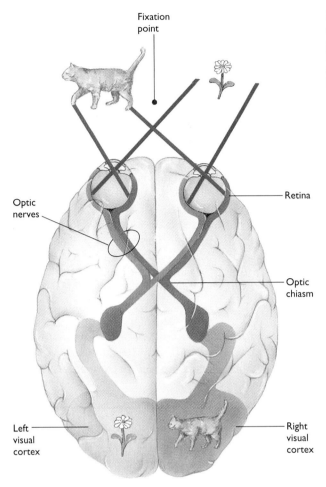

Fixation point

Retina

Optic nerves

Optic chiasm

Left visual cortex

Right visual cortex

FIGURE 3.27 In the human visual system (viewed here from above), light from either half of the world crosses through the pupils to strike the opposite side of each retina. Axons from the left half of each retina travel to the left hemisphere of the brain; axons from the right half of each retina travel to the right hemisphere of the brain.

structions and answer with the hand it controls, but it cannot talk.

Now consider what happens when a split-brain patient sees something (Figure 3.28). Ordinarily, the person moves the eyes and sees the same thing in both hemispheres. In the laboratory, however, researchers can flash information faster than the eyes can move. The person in Figure 3.28 focuses the eyes on a point in the middle of the screen. The investigator flashes a word such as *hatband* on the screen for a split second, too briefly for an eye movement, and asks for the word. The reply is, "band," which is what the left hemisphere saw. (Information from the right side, you will recall, goes to the left side of each retina and from there to the left hemisphere.) To the question of what *kind* of band it might be, the reply is, "I don't know. Jazz band? Rubber band?" However, the left hand points to a hat (which the right hemisphere saw).

Split-brain people get along reasonably well with common behaviors such as walking or even tying shoes because well-practiced behaviors don't need much input from the cerebral cortex anyway. The problem comes with unfamiliar behaviors. Two split-brain people were asked "pretend you're threading a needle" and "pretend you're attaching a fishhook to a line." The two behaviors require almost the same movements. The person who had frequently threaded a needle before the operation had no trouble threading an imaginary needle but couldn't show how to attach a fishhook. Another who had previously attached many fishhooks but never used a sewing needle had the opposite results (Franz, Waldie, & Smith, 2000).

In special circumstances the two hemispheres cooperate in clever ways. One split-brain person was looking at pictures flashed on a screen, as in Figure 3.28a. He could seldom name the objects flashed in the left visual field, but after some delay, he could name simple shapes. Here is how he did it: After seeing the object in the left visual field (with the right hemisphere), he let his eyes move around the room. (Both hemispheres control the eye muscles.) When the right hemisphere

a

b

c

FIGURE 3.28 (a) When the word hatband is flashed on a screen, a split-brain patient reports only what the left hemisphere saw, *band* and (b) writes *band* with the right hand. However, (c) the left hand (controlled by the right hemisphere) points to a hat, which is what the right hemisphere saw.

saw something with the same shape as the object it had just seen, it would stop moving the eyes. The left hemisphere just waited for the eyes to stop moving and then called out the shape of the object it saw.

CONCEPT CHECK ☑

11. Light from the left side of the world strikes the _____ side of each retina, which sends information to the _____ side of the brain.
12. After damage to the corpus callosum, a person can describe some of what he or she sees, but not all. Where must the person see something to describe it in words? That is, which half of each retina? Which visual field? (Check your answers on page 91.)

The Right and Left Hemispheres

How does the right hemisphere differ from the left? The right hemisphere does not speak, but it understands language, especially with short words and simple grammar. It is especially important for understanding the emotional content of speech; people with right-hemisphere damage often can't tell when a speaker is being sarcastic, and they frequently don't understand jokes (Beeman & Chiarello, 1998). The right hemisphere is also better than the left for recognizing and understanding facial expressions (Stone, Nisenson, Eliassen, & Gazzaniga, 1996) and for tasks that are hard to put into words, such as drawing pictures or arranging puzzle pieces.

Let me describe an interesting study. It will seem that I am changing the subject, but later you will see that I am not. People watched a videotape that showed each of 10 people speaking twice. In one speech they described themselves honestly, and in the other case they told nothing but lies. Do you think you could tell when someone was telling the truth? The average for MIT undergraduates was 47% correct, slightly *less* than they should have done by random guessing. Other groups did about equally badly, except for one group that managed to get 60% correct. (That's not great, but it's better than anyone else did.) Guess who could tell lies from truth. They were people with left-hemisphere brain damage! They could understand almost nothing of what people were saying, so they relied on gestures and facial expressions—which the right hemisphere understands quite well (Etcoff, Ekman, Magee, & Frank, 2000).

Split-brain surgery is rare. We study such patients not because you are likely to meet one but because they teach us something about brain organization: Although we cannot fully explain our experience of a unified consciousness, we see that it depends on communication across brain areas. If communication be-

tween the two hemispheres is lost, then each hemisphere becomes partly independent of the other.

Before closing this section, I want to caution you about a common misunderstanding. The left hemisphere is specialized for language and the right hemisphere for emotional perception and complex visuospatial tasks. Some writers have gone beyond this generalization to claim that the left hemisphere is logical and the right hemisphere is creative, so logical people are left brained and creative people are right brained. Some have even suggested that we could all become more creative if we could find a way to exercise the right hemisphere.

In fact, although certain tasks activate one hemisphere more than the other, complex tasks require both. What's the evidence that some people are left brained or that others are right brained? We have *no* evidence, except in the rare cases of people who have had damage to one hemisphere or the other. Nevertheless, the hypothesis is popular. Some people excuse themselves for thinking illogically by saying, "I'm a right-brained person," with the implication that *because* they are illogical, *therefore* they are creative!

IN CLOSING

Brain and Self

One of the persistent issues of brain science has been whether the brain operates as a whole or as a collection of independent parts. This in turn has implications for psychology. Are you a single thinking, behaving individual or a collection of pieces?

The correct answer is probably somewhere in between. After localized brain damage, a person will lose one kind of behavior (e.g., face recognition) more than others, but in no case does someone lose one function completely without any loss of other functions. No brain area is so specialized that it contributes to just one behavior. Similarly, no behavioral skill is totally independent of the others.

Summary

- *Central and peripheral nervous systems.* The central nervous system consists of the brain and the spinal cord. The peripheral nervous system consists of nerves that communicate between the central nervous system and the rest of the body. (page 78)
- *The cerebral cortex.* The four lobes of the cerebral cortex and their primary functions are: occipital lobe, vision; temporal lobe, hearing and some aspects of vision; parietal lobe, body sensations; frontal lobe, preparation for movement. Damage in the cerebral cortex can produce specialized deficits depending on the location of damage. (page 79)

- *Communication between the cerebral cortex and the rest of the body.* Information from the cerebral cortex passes to the medulla and then on into the spinal cord. The medulla and spinal cord have axons that receive sensory input from the periphery and other axons that send output to the muscles and glands. (page 82)
- *Autonomic nervous system and endocrine system.* The autonomic nervous system controls the body's organs, preparing them for emergency activities or for vegetative activities. The endocrine system consists of organs that release hormones into the blood. (page 83)
- *Imaging brain activity.* Modern technology enables researchers to develop images showing the structure and activity of various brain areas in living, waking people. (page 83)
- *Experience and brain structure.* The anatomy of the nervous system is constantly in flux in small ways. Extensive practice of a behavior can modify brain structure, especially if the practice begins early in life. (page 85)
- *The binding problem.* Brain researchers cannot yet explain how we develop a unified experience of an object even though our registers of hearing, touch, vision, and so forth occur in different brain areas that do not connect directly to one another. Even different aspects of vision depend on different brain areas. (page 86)
- *Corpus callosum.* The corpus callosum is a set of axons through which the left and right hemispheres of the cortex communicate. If the corpus callosum is damaged, information that reaches one hemisphere cannot be shared with the other. (page 87)
- *Connections from eyes to brain.* In humans information from the *left* visual field strikes the *right* half of both retinas, from which it is sent to the *right* hemisphere of the brain. Information from the *right* visual field strikes the *left* half of both retinas, from which it is sent to the *left* hemisphere. (page 88)
- *Split-brain patients.* The left hemisphere is specialized for language in most people, so split-brain people can describe information only if it enters the left hemisphere. Because of the lack of direct communication between the left and right hemispheres in split-brain patients, such people show signs of having separate fields of awareness. (page 88)

Answers to Concept Checks

7. **a.** parietal lobe; **b.** temporal lobe; **c.** primary motor cortex of the left frontal lobe; **d.** right occipital lobe; **e.** prefrontal cortex. (page 82)
8. Alcohol impairs the cerebellum faster and more visibly than most other brain areas. Many of the common symptoms of alcohol intoxication are due to suppressed activity in the cerebellum. (page 83)
9. Hormones have prolonged effects in widespread areas of the body, whereas a neurotransmitter affects cells close to its point of release. (page 83)
10. Increased branching of axons and dendrites makes it possible for them to form more synapses. (page 86)
11. right . . . right. (page 90)
12. To describe something, a person must see it with the left half of the retina of either eye. The left half of the retina sees the right visual field. (page 90).

Key Terms and Activites

Key Terms

action potential: an excitation that travels along an axon at a constant strength, no matter how far it must travel (page 70)

attention deficit disorder (ADD): a condition marked by impulsive behavior and short attention span (page 76)

autonomic nervous system: a system of neurons that controls the internal organs such as the heart (page 83)

axon: a single, long, thin, straight fiber that transmits information from a neuron to other neurons or to muscle cells (page 69)

binding problem: the question of how separate brain areas combine forces to produce a unified perception of a single object (page 87)

cell body: the part of the neuron that contains the nucleus of the cell (page 69)

central nervous system: the brain and the spinal cord (page 78)

cerebellum: (Latin for "little brain") a hindbrain structure that is active in the control of movement, especially for complex, rapid motor skills and behaviors that require precise timing (page 83)

cerebral cortex: the outer surface of the forebrain (page 79)

corpus callosum: a large set of axons connecting the left and right hemispheres of the cerebral cortex and thus enabling the two hemispheres to communicate with each other (page 87)

dendrite: one of the widely branching structures of a neuron that receive transmissions from other neurons (page 69)

dopamine: a neurotransmitter that promotes activity levels and facilitates movement (page 76)

electroencephalograph (EEG): a device that uses electrodes on the scalp to record rapid changes in brain electrical activity (page 83)

endocrine system: a set of glands that produce hormones and release them into the bloodstream (page 83)

epilepsy: a condition characterized by abnormal rhythmic activity of brain neurons (page 87)

frontal lobe: a portion of each cerebral hemisphere at the anterior pole, with sections that control movement and certain aspects of memory (page 81)

functional magnetic resonance imaging (fMRI): a technique that uses magnetic detectors outside the head to measure the amounts of hemoglobin, with and without oxygen, in different parts of the brain and thereby provides an indication of current activity levels in various brain areas (page 84)

glia: a cell of the nervous system that insulates neurons, removes waste materials (e.g., dead cells), and performs other supportive functions (page 69)

hemisphere: the left or right half of the brain; each hemisphere is responsible for sensation and motor control on the opposite side of the body (page 79)

hormone: a chemical released by glands and conveyed by the blood to other parts of the body, where it alters activity (page 83)

magnetoencephalograph (MEG): a device that records rapid magnetic changes during brain activity (page 83)

medulla: a structure that is located in the hindbrain and is an elaboration of the spinal cord; controls many muscles in the head and several life-preserving functions, such as breathing (page 82)

neuron: a cell of the nervous system that receives information and transmits it to other cells by conducting electrochemical impulses (page 69)

neurotransmitter: a chemical that is stored in the terminal of an axon and that, when released, activates receptors of other neurons (page 73)

occipital lobe: the rear portion of each cerebral hemisphere, critical for vision (page 79)

parietal lobe: a portion of each cerebral hemisphere; the main receiving area for the sense of touch and for the awareness of one's own body and perception of location of the body in space (page 79)

Parkinson's disease: a condition that affects about 1% of people over the age of 50; the main symptoms are difficulty in initiating voluntary movement, slowness of movement, tremors, rigidity, and depressed mood (page 76)

peripheral nervous system: the bundles of axons that convey messages between the spinal cord and the rest of the body (page 78)

pons: a structure adjacent to the medulla that receives sensory input from the head and controls many muscles in the head (page 82)

positron-emission tomography (PET): a technique that provides a high-resolution image of brain activity by recording radioactivity emitted from injected chemicals (page 84)

postsynaptic neuron: a neuron on the receiving end of a synapse (page 73)

prefrontal cortex: an area in the anterior portion of the frontal lobes, critical for planning movements and for certain aspects of memory (page 82)

primary motor cortex: a strip in the posterior (rear) part of the frontal cortex that controls fine movements, such as hand and finger movements (page 81)

primary somatosensory cortex: a strip in the anterior (forward) part of the parietal lobe that receives most touch sensations and other information about the body (page 79)

reflex: a rapid, automatic response to a stimulus (page 82)

resting potential: electrical polarization that ordinarily occurs across the membrane of an axon that is not undergoing an action potential (page 70)

somatic nervous system: peripheral nerves that communicate with the skin and muscles (page 78)

spinal cord: that part of the central nervous system that communicates with sensory neurons and motor neurons below the level of the head (page 82)

stem cells: undifferentiated cells (page 86)

synapse: the specialized junction between one neuron and another; at this point one neuron releases a neurotransmitter, which either excites or inhibits the next neuron (page 72)

temporal lobe: a portion of each cerebral hemisphere; the main processing area for hearing, complex aspects of vision, and certain aspects of emotional behavior (page 80)

terminal bouton (or button): a bulge at the end of an axon from which the axon releases a chemical called a neurotransmitter (page 73)

thalamus: a forebrain area that relays information to the cerebral cortex (page 82)

Suggestions for Further Reading

Kalat, J. W. (2004). *Biological psychology* (8th ed.). Belmont, CA: Wadsworth. Chapters 1 through 4 deal with the material discussed in this chapter in more detail.

Klawans, H. L. (1996). *Why Michael couldn't hit.* New York: Freeman. Informative and entertaining account of how the rise and fall of various sports heroes relates to what we know about the brain.

Book Companion Web Site

Need help studying? Go to

http://psychology.wadsworth.com/kalat_intro7e/

for a virtual study center. You'll find a personalized Self-Study Assessment that will provide you with a study plan based on your answers to a pretest. Also study using flashcards, quizzes, interactive art, and an online glossary.

Check out interactive **Try It Yourself** exercises on the companion site! For example, the Illustration of Binding and Hemisphere Control exercises tie to what you've learned in this chapter.

Your companion site also has direct links to the following Web sites. These links are checked often for changes, dead links, and new additions.

The Whole Brain Atlas

www.med.harvard.edu/AANLIB/home.html

Stunning photographs of both normal and abnormal brains.

Brain Scans

www.biophysics.mcw.edu

Click various links to see images and movies of the three-dimensional structure of the brain.

Brain Images

http://www.musc.edu/psychiatry/fnrd/primer_index.htm

Extensive detail about PET scans and other ways of forming images of living human brains.

Brain Anatomy of Various Species

www.brainmuseum.org/sections/index.html

Compare the brains of humans, chimpanzees, dolphins, weasels, hyenas, polar bears, and a great many other mammals.

Try It Yourself CD-ROM
with Critical Thinking Video Exercises

Use your CD to access **videos** related to activities designed to help you think critically about the important topics discussed. For example, the video about neural networks ties to what you've learned in this chapter. You'll also find an easy portal link to the book companion site where you can access your personalized **Self-Study Assessments** and interactive **Try It Yourself** exercises.

PsychNow! 2.0

PsychNow! is a fun interactive CD designed to help you with the difficult concepts in psychology. Check out the Accessing Psychology section for the following topics that relate to this chapter:

Neurons and Synaptic Transmission: neuron concentration game, parts of the neuron, 3-D virtual brain animation, and quiz.

Brain and Behavior: explore potassium depletion, cerebral cortex and subcortex lesson, and a brain and behavior review. *ExperimentNOW! Research Experiments:* Neurocognition—Brain Asymmetry

Sensation and Perception

When my son Sam was 8 years old, he asked me, "If we went to some other planet, would we see different colors?" He did not mean a new mixture of familiar colors. He meant colors that were as different from familiar colors as yellow is from red or blue. I told him that would be impossible, and I tried to explain why.

No matter where we go in outer space, no matter what unfamiliar objects or atmospheres we might encounter, we could never experience a color or a sound or any other sensation that would be fundamentally different from what we experience on Earth. Different combinations, perhaps. But fundamentally different sensory experiences, no.

No matter how exotic some other planet might be, it could not have colors we do not have here. The reason is that our eyes can see only certain wavelengths of light, and color is the experience our brains create from those wavelengths.

Three years later, Sam told me he wondered whether people who look at the same thing are all having the same experience: When different people look at something and call it "green," how can we know whether they are all seeing the same "green"? I agreed that there is no way of knowing for sure.

Why am I certain that colors on a different planet would look the same as they do here on Earth and yet uncertain whether colors look the same to different people here? The answer may be obvious to you. If not, I hope it will be after you have read this chapter.

Sensation is the *conversion of energy from the environment into a pattern of response by the nervous system.* It is the registration of information. **Perception** is *the interpretation of that information.* For example, light rays striking your eyes give rise to sensation. When you conclude from that sensation, "I see my roommate," you are expressing your perception. (In practice the distinction between sensation and perception is often difficult to make.)

Vision

How do our eyes convert light energy into something that we can experience?

How do we perceive colors?

We are constantly surrounded by **stimuli**—*energies that affect what we do.* Our eyes, ears, and other sensory organs are packed with **receptors**—*specialized cells that convert environmental energies into signals for the nervous system.* We see, hear, and so forth because stimuli activate receptors, which in turn send messages to the brain, which eventually uses this information to guide our behavior.

You have probably already learned this account in a high school or even elementary school science class. But did you believe it? Evidently, not everyone does. One survey posed the questions, "When we look at someone or something, does anything such as rays, waves, or energy go out of our eyes? Into our eyes?" Among first graders (about age 6), 49% answered (incorrectly) that energy went out of the eyes, and 54% answered that energy came into the eyes. (It was possible to say *yes* to both.) Among college students, 33% said that energy went out of the eyes; 88% said that energy came in (Winer & Cottrell, 1996).

Follow-up studies revealed that the students did not simply misunderstand the question. They really believed that their eyes sent out rays and that those rays were essential to vision. Even after reading a textbook chapter that explained vision, they did no better. After a psychologist patiently explained that the eyes do *not* send out sight rays, most answered correctly, but when asked again a few months later, almost half had gone back to believing their eyes sent out sight rays (Winer, Cottrell, Gregg, Fournier, & Bica, 2002). (It is hard to imagine a more discouraging comment on the ineffectiveness of education.)

Many people have additional misconceptions about vision. We are often led astray because we imagine that what we see is a copy of the outside world, but it is not. For example, color is not a property of objects; it is something your brain creates in response to light of different wavelengths. Brightness is not the same as the intensity of the light. (Light that is twice as intense does not appear twice as bright.) Our experiences *translate* the stimuli of the outside world into very different representations.

The Detection of Light

What we call *light* is just one part of the electromagnetic spectrum. As Figure 4.1 shows, the **electromagnetic spectrum** is *the continuum of all the frequencies of radiated energy*—from gamma rays and x-rays with very short wavelengths, through ultraviolet, visible light, and infrared to radio and TV transmissions with very long wavelengths.

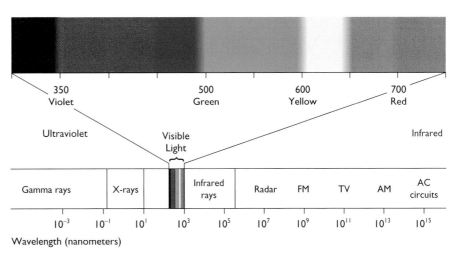

FIGURE 4.1 Visible light, what human eyes can see, is only a small part of the entire electromagnetic spectrum. While experimenting with prisms, Isaac Newton discovered that white light is a mixture of all colors, and color is a property of light. A carrot looks orange because it reflects orange light and absorbs all the other colors.

What makes "visible light" visible? The answer is our receptors, which are equipped to respond to wavelengths from 400 to 700 nanometers (nm). With different receptors we might see a different range of wavelengths. Some species—bees, for example—respond to wavelengths shorter than 350 nm, which are invisible to humans.

The Structure of the Eye

When we see an object, light reflected from that object passes through the **pupil**, *an adjustable opening in the eye through which light enters.* The **iris** is *the colored structure on the surface of the eye, surrounding the pupil.* It is the structure we describe when we say someone has brown, green, or blue eyes. When the light is dim, muscles widen the pupil to let in more light. When the light is bright, muscles narrow the pupil.

After light passes through the pupil, it travels through the *vitreous humor* (a clear jellylike substance) and strikes the retina at the back of the eyeball. The **retina** is *a layer of visual receptors covering the back surface of the eyeball* (Figure 4.2). As light passes through the eye, the cornea and the lens focus the light on the retina as shown. The **cornea**, *a rigid transparent structure on the outer surface of the eyeball,* always focuses light in the same way. The **lens** is a *flexible structure that can vary in thickness,* enabling the eye to **accommodate**, that is, *to adjust its focus for objects at different distances.* When we look at a distant object, for example, our eye muscles relax and let the lens become thinner and flatter, as shown in Figure 4.3a. When we look at a close object, our eye muscles tighten and make the lens thicker and rounder (Figure 4.3b).

The **fovea** (FOE-vee-uh), *the central area of the human retina,* is adapted for highly detailed vision (Figure 4.2). Of all retinal areas, the fovea has the greatest density of receptors; also, more of the cerebral cortex is devoted to analyzing input from the fovea than input from other areas. If you want to see something in detail, such as letters of the alphabet, you focus it on the fovea.

Hawks, owls, and other predatory birds have a greater density of receptors on the top of the retina (for looking down) than on the bottom of the retina

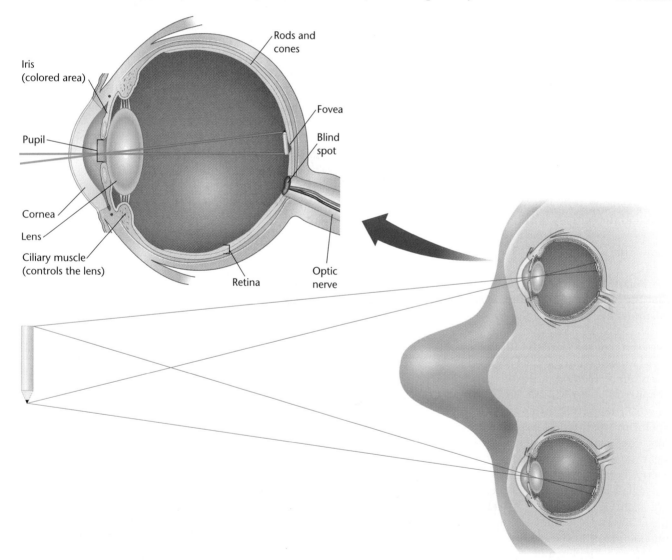

Iris (colored area)

Pupil

Cornea

Lens

Ciliary muscle (controls the lens)

Retina

Rods and cones

Fovea

Blind spot

Optic nerve

FIGURE 4.2 The lens gets its name from Latin for *lentil,* referring to its shape—an appropriate choice, as this cross section of the eye shows. The names of other parts of the eye also refer to their appearance.

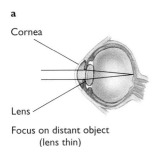

a

Cornea

Lens

Focus on distant object
(lens thin)

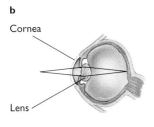

b

Cornea

Lens

Focus on close object
(lens thick)

FIGURE 4.3 The flexible, transparent lens changes shape so that objects (a) far and (b) near can come into focus. The lens bends entering light rays so that they fall on the retina. In old age the lens becomes rigid, and people find it harder to focus on nearby objects.

(for looking up). When these birds are flying, this arrangement enables them to see the ground beneath them in detail. When they are on the ground, however, they have trouble seeing above themselves (Figure 4.4).

FIGURE 4.4 The consequence of having receptors mostly on the top of the retina: Birds of prey, such as these owlets, can see down much more clearly than they can see up. In flight that arrangement is helpful. On the ground they have to turn their heads almost upside down to see above them.

Some Common Disorders of Vision

As people grow older, they gradually develop **presbyopia,** *decreased flexibility of the lens and therefore inability to focus on nearby objects.* (The Greek root *presby* means "old." This root also shows up in the word *presbyterian,* which means "governed by the elders.") Many people's eyes are not quite spherical. A person whose eyeballs are elongated, as shown in Figure 4.5a, can focus well on nearby objects but has difficulty focusing on distant objects. Such a person is said to be *nearsighted,* or to have **myopia** (mi-O-pee-ah). About half of all 20-year-olds are nearsighted and must wear glasses or contact lenses to see well at a distance. An older person with both myopia and presbyopia needs bifocal glasses to help with both near focus and distant focus. A person whose eyeballs are flattened, as shown in Figure 4.5b, has **hyperopia,** or *farsightedness.* Such a person can focus well on distant objects but has difficulty focusing on close objects.

Two other common visual disorders are glaucoma and cataracts. **Glaucoma** is a *condition characterized by increased pressure within the eyeball;* the result can be damage to the optic nerve and therefore a progressive loss of peripheral vision ("tunnel vision"). A **cataract** is a *disorder in which the lens becomes cloudy.* People with severe cataracts can have the lens surgically removed and replaced with a contact lens. Because the normal lens filters out more blue and ultraviolet light than other light, people with artificial lenses sometimes report seeing blue more clearly and distinctly than they ever had before (Davenport & Foley, 1979). They do, however, suffer increased risk of damage to the retina from ultraviolet light.

CONCEPT CHECK ☑

1. Suppose you have normal vision and you try on a pair of glasses made for a person with myopia. How will the glasses affect your vision? (Check your answer on page 110.)

The Visual Receptors

The visual receptors of the eye, specialized neurons in the retina at the back of the eyeball, are so sensitive to light that they are capable of responding to a single photon, the smallest possible quantity of light. There are two types of visual receptors: cones and rods, which differ in appearance, as Figure 4.6 shows, and in function. The **cones** are *receptors adapted for color vision, daytime vision, and detailed vision.* The **rods** are *receptors adapted for vision in dim light.*

About 5 to 10% of all the visual receptors in the human retina are cones. Most birds have at least that high a proportion of cones and correspondingly have good color vision. Species that are active mostly at

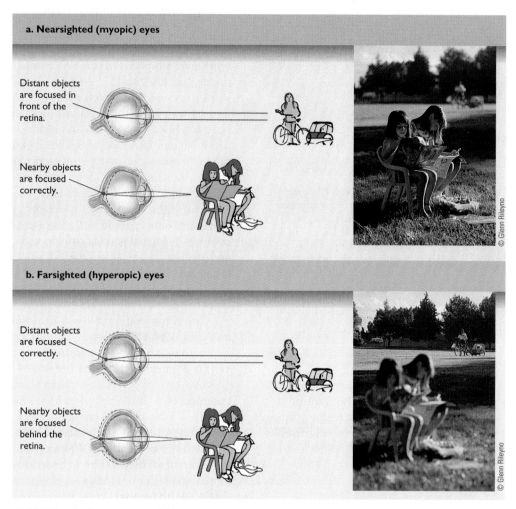

a. Nearsighted (myopic) eyes

Distant objects are focused in front of the retina.

Nearby objects are focused correctly.

b. Farsighted (hyperopic) eyes

Distant objects are focused correctly.

Nearby objects are focused behind the retina.

© Glenn Rileyno

FIGURE 4.5 The structure of (a) nearsighted and (b) farsighted eyes distorts vision. Because the nearsighted eye is elongated, light from a distant object focuses in front of the retina. Because the farsighted eye is flattened, light from a nearby object focuses behind the retina. (The dashed line shows the position of the normal retina in each case.)

night—rats and mice, for example—have mostly rods and thus good perception in faint light.

The proportion of cones is highest toward the center of the retina. The fovea consists solely of cones (Figure 4.2). Away from the fovea, the proportion of cones drops sharply. For that reason you are color-blind in the far periphery of your eye.

Try this experiment: Hold several pens or pencils of different colors behind your back. (Any objects will work as long as they have about the same size and shape and approximately the same brightness.) Pick one at random without looking at it. Hold it behind your head and bring it very

Try It Yourself

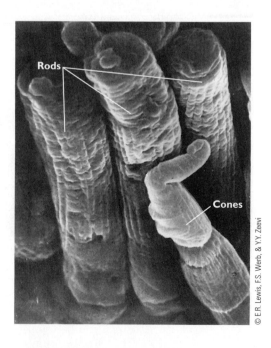

Rods

Cones

© E.R. Lewis, F.S. Werb, & Y.Y. Zeevi

FIGURE 4.6 Rods and cones seen through a scanning electron micrograph. The rods, which number over 120 million in humans, provide vision in dim light. The 6 million cones in the retina can distinguish gradations of color in bright light; they enable us to see that roses are red, magenta, ruby, carmine, cherry, vermilion, scarlet, and crimson—not to mention pink, yellow, orange, and white.

slowly into your field of vision. When you just barely begin to see it, you will probably not be able to tell what color it is. (If glaucoma or another medical problem has impaired your peripheral vision, you will have to bring the object closer to your fovea before you can see it at all, and then you will see its color at once.) Go to http://psychology.wadsworth.com/kalat_intro7e. Navigate to the student Web site, then to the Online Try it Yourself section, and click on Blindness in Visual Periphery.

Online Try It Yourself

The rods are more effective than the cones for detecting dim light for two reasons: First, a rod is slightly more responsive to faint stimulation than a cone is. Second, the rods pool their resources. Only a few cones converge their messages onto the next cell, called a *bipolar cell,* whereas many rods converge their messages. In the far periphery of the retina, more than 100 rods send messages to a bipolar cell (see Figure 4.7). Table 4.1 summarizes some of the key differences between rods and cones.

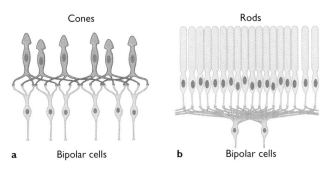

FIGURE 4.7 Because so many rods converge their input into the next layer of the visual system, known as bipolar cells, even a small amount of light falling on the rods stimulates the bipolar cells. Thus, the periphery of the retina, with many rods, readily detects faint light. However, because bipolars in the periphery get input from so many receptors, they have only imprecise information about the location and shape of objects.

CONCEPT CHECK ✓

2. Why is it easier to see a faint star in the sky if you look slightly to the side of the star instead of straight at it? (Check your answer on page 110.)

Dark Adaptation

Suppose you go into a basement at night trying to find your flashlight. The only light bulb in the basement is burned out. A little moonlight comes through the basement windows, but not much. At first you can hardly see anything. A minute or two later, you are beginning to see well enough to find your way around, and eventually, you can see well enough to find the flashlight. This *gradual improvement in the ability to see in dim light* is called **dark adaptation.**

The mechanism behind dark adaptation is this: Exposure to light causes a chemical change in certain molecules called *retinaldehydes,* thereby stimulating the visual receptors. (Retinaldehydes are derived from vitamin A.) Under normal (moderate) light, the receptors *regenerate* (rebuild) the molecules about as fast as the light alters them, and the person maintains about a constant level of visual sensitivity. In darkness or very dim light, however, the receptors can regenerate their molecules without interruption, so the person gradually becomes better able to detect faint lights.

The cones and rods adapt to the dark at different rates. During the day our vision ordinarily relies overwhelmingly on cones. When we enter a dark place, our cones regenerate their retinaldehydes faster than the rods do, but by the time the rods finish their regeneration, they are far more sensitive to faint light than the cones are. At that point we are seeing mostly with rods.

Here is how a psychologist demonstrates this process of dark adaptation (E. B. Goldstein, 1989): You are taken into a room that is completely dark except for one tiny flashing light. You have a knob that

TABLE 4.1   Differences Between Rods and Cones

	Rods	Cones
Shape	Nearly cylindrical	Tapered at one end
Prevalence in human retina	90–95%	5–10%
Abundant in	All vertebrate species	Species active during the day (birds, monkeys, apes, humans)
Area of the retina	Toward the periphery	Toward the fovea
Important for color vision?	No	Yes
Important for detail?	No	Yes
Important in dim light?	Yes	No
Number of types	Just one	Three types

controls the intensity of the light; you are told to make the light so dim that you can barely see it. Over the course of 3 or 4 minutes, you will gradually decrease the intensity of the light, as shown in Figure 4.8a. Note that a decrease in the intensity of the light indicates an increase in the sensitivity of your eyes. If you stare straight at the point of light, your results will demonstrate the adaptation of your cones to the dim light. (You have been focusing the light on your fovea, which has no rods.)

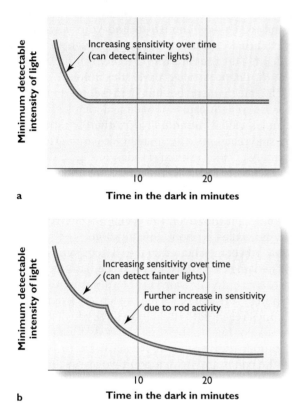

FIGURE 4.8 These graphs show dark adaptation to (a) a light you stare at directly, using only cones, and (b) a light in your peripheral vision, which you see with both cones and rods. *(Based on E. B. Goldstein, 1989)*

Now the psychologist repeats the study with one change in procedure: You are told to stare at a very faint light while another light flashes somewhat to the side of the fovea, where it stimulates both rods and cones. You turn a control knob until the flashing light in the periphery is just barely visible. (Figure 4.8b shows the results.) During the first 7 to 10 minutes, the results are the same as before. But then your rods become more sensitive than your cones, and you begin to see even fainter lights. Your rods continue to adapt to the dark over the next 20 minutes or so.

To demonstrate dark adaptation for yourself without any apparatus, try this: At night turn on one light in your room. Close one eye and cover it tightly with your hand for at least 1 minute, preferably longer. Your covered eye will adapt to the dark while your open eye remains adapted to the light. Next turn off your light and open both eyes. You will see better with your dark-adapted eye than with the light-adapted eye. (This instruction assumes you still have some faint light coming through the window. In a *completely* dark room, of course, you will see nothing with either eye.)

CONCEPT CHECK ☑

3. You may have heard people say that cats can see in total darkness. Is that possible?
4. After you have thoroughly adapted to extremely dim light, will you see more objects in your fovea or in the periphery of your eye? (Check your answers on pages 110, 111.)

The Visual Pathway

If you or I were designing an eye, we would probably run the axons of the cones and rods straight to the brain. Nature chose a different method. The visual receptors send their impulses *away from* the brain, toward the center of the eye, where they make synaptic contacts with other neurons called bipolar cells. The bipolar cells in turn make contact with still other neurons, the **ganglion cells**, which are *neurons that receive their input from the bipolar cells*. The *axons from the ganglion cells join to form* the **optic nerve**, *which turns around and exits the eye*, as Figures 4.2 and 4.9 show. Half of each optic nerve crosses to the opposite side of the brain at the optic chiasm (KI-az-m). Axons from the optic nerve then separate and go to several locations in the brain. In humans most go to the thalamus, which then sends information to the primary visual cortex in the occipital lobe. People vary in the number of axons they have in the optic nerve; some have up to three times as many as others. Those with the thickest optic nerves can see fainter or briefer lights and can detect smaller amounts of movement (Andrews, Halpern, & Purves, 1997; Halpern, Andrews, & Purves, 1999).

The *retinal area where the optic nerve exits* is called the **blind spot**. There is no room for receptors here because the exiting axons take up all the space. Ordinarily, you are unaware of your blind spot.

To illustrate, cover your left eye and stare at the center of Figure 4.10; then slowly move the page forward and backward. When your eye is about 25 to 30 cm

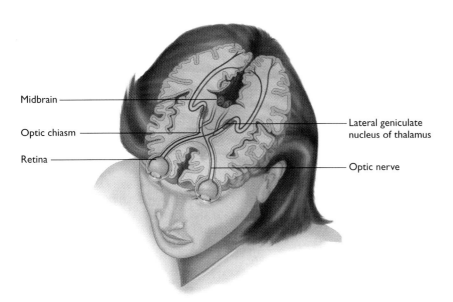

Midbrain

Optic chiasm

Retina

Lateral geniculate
nucleus of thalamus

Optic nerve

FIGURE 4.9 Axons from cells in the retina depart the eye at the blind spot and form the optic nerve. In humans about half the axons in the optic nerve cross to the opposite side of the brain at the optic chiasm. Some optic nerve axons carry information to the midbrain; others carry it to the thalamus, which relays information to the cerebral cortex.

some large blood vessels, and many receptors in the retina fall in the shadow of these blood vessels. We do not notice them, however, as our brain fills in the gaps with what "must" be there (Adams & Horton, 2002).

Information from the left and right eyes remains separate until it reaches the visual cortex. Each cell in the visual cortex receives input from one part of the left retina and a corresponding part of the right retina—that is, two retinal areas that ordinarily focus on the same point in space. Under normal conditions the input coming from the left retina is almost the same as that coming from the right retina, and the two effects summate. However, examine Figure 4.11 to see what happens if the retinal images conflict.

(10 to 12 inches) away from the page, the lion disappears because it falls into your blind spot. In its place you perceive a continuation of the circle. Go to http://psychology.wadsworth.com/kalat_intro7e. Navigate to the student Web site, then to the Online Try it Yourself section, and click on Filling in the Blind Spot.

Online Try It Yourself

In fact we have little "blind spots" throughout the retina. The retina has

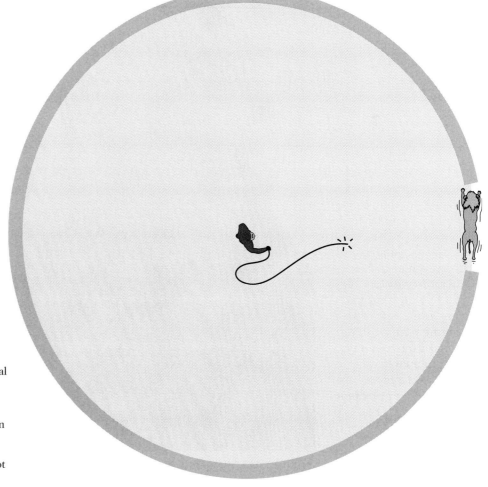

FIGURE 4.10 Close your left eye and focus your right eye on the animal trainer. Move the page toward your eyes and away from them, until you find the point where the lion on the right disappears. At that point the lion is focused on the blind spot of your retina, where you have no receptors. What you see there is not a blank spot but a continuation of the circle.

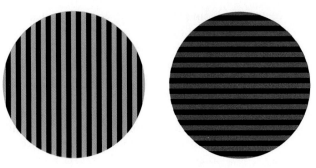

FIGURE 4.11 To produce binocular rivalry, move your eyes toward the page until the two circles seem to merge. You will alternate between seeing red lines and green lines.

Look at the two circles in Figure 4.11 and bring the page so close to your eyes that your nose touches or almost touches the page. At this point the two circles seem to merge. Some of the neurons in your visual cortex respond to vertical lines. When you merge the two circles, those cells are stimulated by the green and black vertical stripes and inhibited by the red and black horizontal stripes. For a short while, the stimulation dominates, but then for a while, the inhibition dominates. Meanwhile, inhibition and stimulation are also alternating for cells that respond to horizontal lines. The net effect is that you see green lines, then red lines, then green lines again, and so forth. With effort you can voluntarily direct attention toward the red lines or the green lines, but you cannot maintain control for long; soon the other pattern emerges again (Blake & Logothetis, 2002). The *alternation between seeing the pattern in the left retina and the pattern in the right retina* is known as **binocular rivalry.**

We become aware of visual information only after it reaches the cerebral cortex. Someone who has intact eyes but a damaged visual cortex is blind and even loses visual imagery. However,

someone with damaged eyes and an intact brain can at least imagine visual scenes. One laboratory has developed a way to bypass damaged eyes and send visual information directly to the brain. As shown in Figure 4.12, a camera attached to a blind person's sunglasses sends messages to a computer, which then sends messages to electrodes that stimulate appropriate spots in the person's visual cortex (Dobelle, 2000). After hours of practice, such people can see well enough to find their way around, to identify simple shapes, and to count how many fingers someone holds up. The goal is a more elaborate array of electrodes that might be more useful than a guide dog without being much more expensive.

Color Vision

As Figure 4.1 shows, different colors of light correspond to different wavelengths of electromagnetic energy. (White light consists of an equal mixture of all the visible wavelengths.) How does the visual system convert these wavelengths into our perception of color? The process begins with three kinds of cones, which respond to different wavelengths of light. Later cells in the visual path code this wavelength information in terms of pairs of opposites—roughly, red versus green, yellow versus blue, and white versus black. Finally, cells in the cerebral cortex compare the input from various parts of the visual field to synthesize a color experience for each object. We shall examine these three stages in turn.

The Trichromatic Theory

Thomas Young was an English physician of the 1700s who, among other accomplishments, helped to decode the Rosetta stone (making it possible to understand Egyptian hieroglyphics), introduced the modern concept of energy, revived and popularized the wave theory of light, showed how to calculate annuities

FIGURE 4.12 William Dobelle has developed an apparatus that takes an image from a camera attached to a blind person's sunglasses, transforms it by a computer, and sends a message to electrodes in the visual cortex. By this means someone with damaged eyes regains some vision.

for insurance, and offered the first theory about how people perceive color (Martindale, 2001). His theory, elaborated and modified by Hermann von Helmholtz in the 1800s, came to be known as the **trichromatic theory** or the **Young-Helmholtz theory**. It is called *trichromatic* because it claims that our receptors respond to three primary colors. In modern terms we say that *color vision depends on the relative rate of response by three types of cones.* Each type of cone is most sensitive to a particular range of light wavelengths (Figure 4.13). One type is most sensitive to short wavelengths (which we generally see as blue), another to medium wavelengths (seen as green), and another to long wavelengths (red). Each wavelength prompts varying levels of activity in the three types of cones. So, for example, green light excites mostly the medium-wavelength cones, red light excites mostly the long-wavelength cones, and yellow light excites the medium-wavelength and long-wavelength cones about equally. Every wavelength of light produces its own distinct ratio of responses by the three kinds of cones. White light excites all three kinds of cones equally.

Young and Helmholtz proposed their theory long before experiments confirmed the existence of these three types of cones (Wald, 1968). They relied entirely on a behavioral observation: Observers can take three different colors of light and then, by mixing them in various proportions, match all other colors of light. (Note that mixing light of different colors is not the same as mixing paints of different colors. Mixing yellow and blue *paints* produces green; mixing yellow and blue *lights* produces white.)

The short-wavelength cones, which respond most strongly to blue, are less numerous than the other two types of cones, especially in the fovea. Consequently, a tiny blue point may look black. For the retina to detect blueness, the blue must extend over a moderately large area.

Figure 4.14 illustrates this effect. Count the red spots and then the blue spots. Then stand farther away and count the spots again. You will probably see as many red spots as before but fewer blue spots.

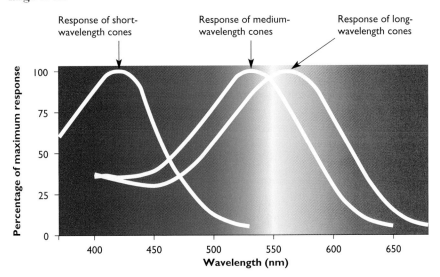

FIGURE 4.14 Blue spots look black unless they cover a sizable area. Count the red dots; then count the blue dots. Try again while standing farther away from the page.

CONCEPT CHECK ☑

5. According to the trichromatic theory, how does our nervous system tell the difference between bright yellow-green and dim yellow-green light? (Check your answer on page 111.)

The Opponent-Process Theory

Young and Helmholtz were right about how many cones we have, but our perception of color has some complicated features that the trichromatic theory cannot easily handle. For example, four colors, not three, *seem* primary or basic to most people: red, green, yellow, and blue. Yellow simply does not seem like a mixture of reddish and greenish experiences, nor is green a yellowish blue. More important, if you stare for a minute or so at something red and look away, you see a green afterimage. If you stare at something green, yellow, or blue, you see a red, blue, or yellow afterimage. The trichromatic theory provides no easy explanation for these afterimages.

Therefore, a 19th-century scientist, Ewald Hering, proposed the **opponent-process theory** of color vision: *We perceive color not in terms of independent colors but in terms of a system of paired opposites—red versus green, yellow versus blue, and white versus black.* This idea is best explained with an example.

FIGURE 4.13 Sensitivity of three types of cones to different wavelengths of light. *(Based on data of Bowmaker & Dartnall, 1980)*

Stare at one of Daffy's pupils near the center of the Figure 4.15 for a minute or so under a bright light without moving your eyes or your head. Then look at a plain white or gray background. *Do this now.*

Try It Yourself

FIGURE 4.15 Use this image to see the negative afterimages of opposite colors, which rebound after sufficient stimulation. Stare at one of Daffy's pupils for a minute or more; then focus on a white background.

© USPS 1998

1999

AP/Wide World Photos

When you looked away, you saw the cartoon in its normal coloration. After staring at something blue, you get a yellow afterimage. Similarly, after staring at yellow, you see blue; after red, you see green; after green, you see red; after white, black; and after black, white. These *experiences of one color after the removal of another* are called **negative afterimages.**

Presumably, the explanation depends on cells somewhere in the nervous system that maintain a spontaneous rate of activity when unstimulated, increase their activity in the presence of, say, green, and decrease it in the presence of red. After prolonged green stimulation fatigues them, they become less active than usual—in other words responding as if in the presence of red. Similarly, other cells would be excited by red and inhibited by green, excited by yellow and inhibited by blue, and so forth. Patterns of this type have been found in many neurons at various locations in the visual parts of the nervous system (DeValois & Jacobs, 1968; Engel, 1999).

CONCEPT CHECK ☑

6. Which theory most easily explains negative color afterimages?
7. The negative afterimage that you created by staring at Figure 4.15 may seem to move against the background. Why doesn't it stay in one place? (Check your answers on page 111.)

The Retinex Theory

The opponent-process theory accounts for many phenomena of color vision but overlooks an important one. Suppose you look at a large white screen illuminated entirely with green light in an otherwise dark room. How would you know whether this is a white screen illuminated with green light or a green screen illuminated with white light? Or a blue screen illuminated with yellow light? (The possibilities go on and on.) The answer is, you wouldn't know. But now someone wearing a brown shirt and blue jeans stands in front of the screen. Suddenly, you see the shirt as brown, the jeans as blue, and the screen as white, even though all the objects are reflecting more green light than anything else. The point is that we do not ordinarily perceive the color of an object in isolation. We perceive color by comparing the light an object reflects to the light that other objects in the scene reflect. As a result we can perceive blue jeans as blue and bananas as yellow regardless of the type of light. This *tendency of an object to appear nearly the same color under a variety of lighting conditions* is called **color constancy** (see Figure 4.16).

In response to such observations, Edwin Land (the inventor of the Polaroid Land camera) proposed the **retinex theory**. According to this theory, *we perceive color through the cerebral cortex's comparison of various retinal patterns*. (*Retinex* is a combination of the words *retina* and *cortex*.) The cerebral cortex compares the patterns of light coming from different areas of the retina and synthesizes a color perception for each area (Land, Hubel, Livingstone, Perry, & Burns, 1983; Land & McCann, 1971).

As Figure 4.16 emphasizes, it is wrong to call short-wavelength light "blue" or long-wavelength light "red" as the text implied a few pages ago. In Figure 4.16 a gray pattern looks blue in one context and yellow in another (Lotto & Purves, 2002; Purves & Lotto, 2003). The "color" is a construction by our brain, not a property of the light itself, and which color our brain constructs depends on multiple circumstances.

In the 1800s the trichromatic theory and the opponent-process theory were considered rival theories, but vision researchers today consider both of them, as well as the retinex theory, correct statements that address different aspects of vision. The trichromatic theory is certainly correct in stating

FIGURE 4.16 (a) When the block is under yellow light (left) or blue light (right), you can still recognize individual squares as blue, yellow, white, red, and so forth. However, the actual light reaching your eyes is different in the two cases. Parts b and c show the effects of removing more and more of the background: The squares that appear blue in the left half of part a are actually grayish; so are the squares that appear yellow in the right half. (*Why We See What We Do,* by D. Purves and R. B. Lotto, *figure 6.10, p. 134. Copyright 2003 Sinauer Associates, Inc. Reprinted by permission.*)

that human color vision starts with three kinds of cones. The opponent-process theory explains how the bipolar cells and later cells organize color information. The retinex theory adds the final touch, noting that the cerebral cortex compares color information from various parts of the visual field.

CRITICAL THINKING:
A STEP FURTHER
Color Afterimages

If you stare for a minute at a small green object on a white background and then look away, you will see a red afterimage. But if you stare at a green wall nearby so that you see nothing but green in all directions, then when you look away, you do not see a red afterimage. Why not?

Color Vision Deficiency

For a long time, people apparently assumed that anyone with normal vision could see and recognize colors (Fletcher & Voke, 1985). Then during the 1600s, the phenomenon of color vision deficiency (or colorblindness) was unambiguously recognized. Here was the first clue that color vision is a function of our eyes and brains and not just of the light itself.

The older term color-*blindness* is misleading because very few people are totally unable to distinguish one color from another. However, about 8% of men and less than 1% of women have difficulty distinguishing red from green and distinguishing either one from yellow (Bowmaker, 1998). The ultimate cause is a recessive gene on the X chromosome. Because men have only one X chromosome, they need just one gene to become red-green color deficient. Women need two such genes to develop the condition because they have two X chromosomes. The result is either a lack of long-wavelength or medium-wavelength cones or a decreased responsiveness of one of those cone types (Fletcher & Voke, 1985). A much smaller number of people have trouble distinguishing yellow from blue, caused by a lack of short-wavelength cones.

Figure 4.17 gives a crude but usually satisfactory test for red-green color vision deficiency. What do you see in each part of the figure? (To interpret your answers, refer to answer A on page 111.)

How does the world look to people who are colorblind? They describe the world with all the usual color words: Roses are red, violets are blue, bananas are yellow, grass is green. But their answers do not mean that they perceive colors the same as other people do. Can they tell us what a "red" rose actually looks like? In most cases no. Certain rare individuals, however, are red-green colorblind in one eye but have normal vision in the other eye. Because they know what the

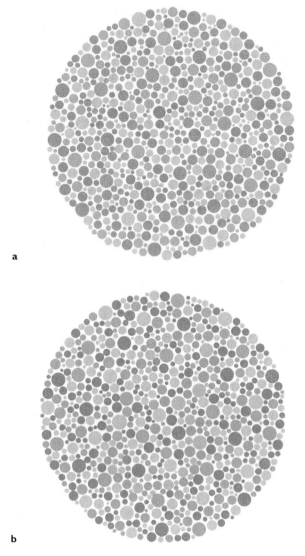

a

b

FIGURE 4.17 These items provide an informal test for red-green color vision deficiency, an inherited condition that mostly affects men. What do you see? Compare your answers to answer A on page 111. *(Reproduced from Ishihara's Test for Color Blindness. Kanehara & Co., Ltd., Tokyo, Japan. A test for color blindness cannot be conducted with this material. For accurate testing, the original plate should be used. Reprinted with permission.)*

color words really mean (from experience with their normal eye), they can tell us what their colorblind eye sees. They say that objects that look red or green to the normal eye look yellow or yellow-gray to the colorblind eye (Marriott, 1976).

If you have normal color vision, Figure 4.18 will show you what it is like to be red-green colorblind. First, cover part b, a typical item from a colorblindness test, and stare at part a, a red field, under a bright light for about a minute. (The brighter the light and the longer you stare, the greater the effect will be.) Then look at part b. Staring at the red field has fatigued your red cones, so you will now have only a weak sensation of red. As the red cones recover, you will see part b normally.

Now stare at part c, a green field, for about a minute and look at part b again. Because you have fatigued your green cones, the figure in b will stand out even more strongly than usual. In fact, certain people with red-green colorblindness may be able to see the number in b only after staring at c. (Refer to answer B on page 111.)

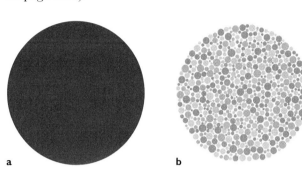 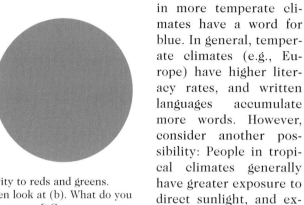

a   b   c

FIGURE 4.18 Adaptation to these stimuli temporarily alters sensitivity to reds and greens. First, stare at pattern (a) under bright light for about a minute and then look at (b). What do you see? Next stare at (c) for a minute and look at (b) again. Now what do you see? Compare your answer to answer B on page 111. (*Reproduced from Ishihara's Test for Color Blindness. Kanehara & Co., Ltd., Tokyo, Japan. A test for color blindness cannot be conducted with this material. For accurate testing, the original plate should be used. Reprinted with permission.*)

Color Vision, Color Words, and Culture

Some languages have more color words than others. For example, English has many words for shades of red, including carnation, crimson, maroon, ruby, and scarlet. Some languages do not even have a word for blue. They either use the same word for blue as for green (think of it as something like "grue") or a single word that means either blue or dark. Can we find any explanation behind this cultural difference? That is, *why* do some cultures have a separate word for blue whereas others do not?

One interesting speculation is based on the pattern shown in Figure 4.19. Many cultures in the tropics lack a separate word for blue, whereas those in more temperate climates have a word for blue. In general, temperate climates (e.g., Europe) have higher literacy rates, and written languages accumulate more words. However, consider another possibility: People in tropical climates generally have greater exposure to direct sunlight, and exposure to the sun accelerates aging of the lens of the eye. The more time someone spends in bright sunlight, the yellower the lens gets and therefore the harder it is to see short-wavelength (blue) light. As the lens ages, what used to appear as blue becomes greenish or dark. The suggestion is that physiological changes in the eye make it difficult for many tropical people to see blue, and consequently, they do not use a word for blue (Lindsey & Brown,

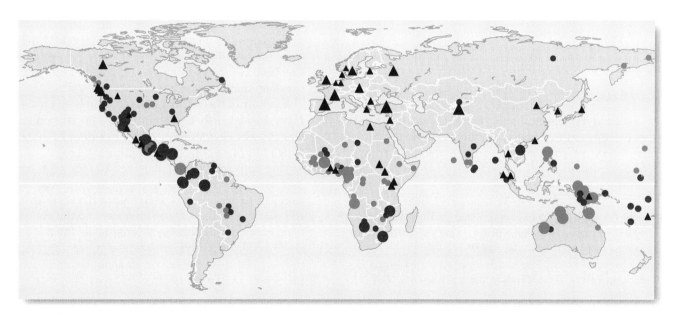

FIGURE 4.19 Each symbol represents one culture. Those with a blue triangle have a separate word for "blue"; those with a red circle have a word meaning "green or blue." Those with a green circle refer to blue objects using the same word as "dark." Note that the cultures lacking a separate word for "blue" are concentrated mostly in or near the tropics. (*Lindsey, D. T., and Brown, A. M., "Color naming and the phototoxic effects of sunlight on the eye," Psychological Science, 13, 506-512. Figure 2, p. 508. Reprinted with permission.*)

2002). (As I said, this explanation is speculative. Can you imagine a good way to test it?)

In the introduction to this chapter, I suggested that we would see no new colors on another planet and that we cannot be certain that different people on Earth really have the same color experiences. Now try to explain the reasons behind those statements.

IN CLOSING

How We See

Before there were any people or other color-sighted animals, was there any color on Earth? *No.* There was light, to be sure, and different objects reflected different wavelengths of light, but color exists only in brains, not in the objects themselves. Our vision is not just a copy of the outside world; it is a construction that enables us to interact with the world to our benefit.

To many readers vision and our other senses seem more complicated than some of the later topics in this book, such as motivation or emotion. It seems that way because researchers have learned so much more about the senses. The more we learn about any topic, the more sophisticated questions we can ask. (If we understand something poorly, neither the questions nor the answers can be very complicated.) The complexity of what we now know about vision is a tribute to many generations of researchers.

Summary

- *Common misconceptions.* The eyes do not send out "sight rays," nor does the brain build little copies of the stimuli it senses. It converts or translates sensory stimuli into an arbitrary code that represents the information. (page 97)
- *Focus.* The cornea and lens focus the light that enters through the pupil of the eye. If the eye is not spherical or if the lens is not flexible, corrective lenses may be needed. (page 98)
- *Cones and rods.* The retina contains two kinds of receptors: cones and rods. Cones are specialized for detailed vision and color perception. Rods detect dim light. (page 99)
- *Blind spot.* The blind spot is the area of the retina through which the optic nerve exits; this area has no visual receptors and is therefore blind. (page 102)
- *Binocular rivalry.* Under normal circumstances the two retinas receive similar information patterns and provide the brain with information for three-dimensional perception. If the two retinas receive incompatible patterns, we experience a competition in which one pattern or the other dominates at any given moment. (page 104)
- *Color vision.* Color vision depends on three types of cones, each most sensitive to a particular range of light wavelengths. The cones transmit messages so that the bipolar and ganglion cells in the visual system are excited by light of one color and inhibited by light of the opposite color. Then the cerebral cortex compares the responses from different parts of the retina to determine the color of light coming from each area of the visual field. (page 104)
- *Color vision deficiency.* Complete colorblindness is rare. Certain people have difficulty distinguishing reds from greens; in rare cases some have difficulty distinguishing yellows from blues. (page 108)

Answers to Concept Checks

1. If your vision is normal, then wearing glasses intended for a myopic person will make your vision blurry. Such glasses alter the light as though they were bringing the object closer to the viewer. Unless the glasses are very strong, you may not notice much difference when you are looking at distant objects because you can adjust the lens of your eyes to compensate for what the glasses do. However, nearby objects will appear blurry in spite of the best compensations that the lenses of your eyes can make. (page 99)
2. The center of the retina consists entirely of cones. If you look slightly to the side, the light falls on an area of the retina that consists partly of rods, which are more sensitive to faint light. (page 101)
3. As do people, cats can adapt well to dim light. No animal, however, can see in complete darkness. Vision is the detection of light that strikes the eye. (Similarly, the x-ray vision attributed to the comic book character Superman is impossible. Even if he could send out x-rays, he would not see anything unless those x-rays bounced off an object and back into his eyes.) (page 102)

4. You will see more objects in the periphery of your eye. The fovea contains only cones, which cannot become as sensitive as the rods do in the periphery. (page 102)

5. Although bright yellow-green and dim yellow-green light would evoke the same ratio of activity by the three cone types, the total amount of activity would be greater for the bright yellow-green light. (page 105)

6. The opponent-process theory most easily explains negative color afterimages because it assumes that we perceive colors in terms of paired opposites, red vs. green and yellow vs. blue (as well as white vs. black). (page 106)

7. The afterimage is on your eye, not on the background. When you try to focus on a different part of the afterimage, you move your eyes and the afterimage moves with them. (page 106)

Answers to Other Questions in the Module

A. In Figure 4.17a a person with normal color vision sees the numeral 74; in Figure 4.17b the numeral 8.

B. In Figure 4.18b you should see the numeral 29. After you have stared at the red circle in part a, the 29 in part b may look less distinct than usual, as though you were red-green colorblind. After staring at the green circle, the 29 may be even more distinct than usual. If you do not see either of these effects at once, try again, but this time stare at part a or c a little longer and continue staring at part b a little longer. The effect does not appear immediately, only after a few seconds.

How do hearing, the vestibular sense, skin senses, pain, taste, and smell work?

Consider these common expressions:

- I *see* what you mean.
- I *feel* your pain.
- I am deeply *touched* by everyone's support and concern.
- The Senate will *hold* hearings on the budget proposal.
- She is a person of fine *taste*.
- He was *dizzy* with success.
- The policies of this company *stink*.
- That *sounds* like a good job offer.

Each sentence expresses an idea in terms of sensation, though we know that these terms are not meant to be taken literally. If you compliment people on their "fine taste," you are not referring to their tongues.

The broad metaphorical use of terms of sensation is not accidental. Our thinking and brain activity deal mostly, if not entirely, with sensory stimuli. Perhaps you doubt that assertion: "What about abstract concepts?" you might object. "Sometimes I think about numbers, time, love, justice, and all sorts of other nonsensory concepts." Yes, but how did you learn those concepts? Didn't you learn numbers by counting objects you could see or touch? Didn't you learn about time by observing changes in sensory stimuli? Didn't you learn about love and justice from specific events that you saw, heard, and felt? Could you explain any abstract concept without referring to something you detect through your senses?

We have already considered how we detect light. Now let's discuss how we detect sounds, head tilt, skin stimulation, and chemicals.

Hearing

What we familiarly call the "ear" is a fleshy structure technically known as the *pinna*. It serves to funnel sounds to the inner ear, where the receptors lie. The mammalian ear converts sound waves into mechanical displacements that a row of receptor cells can detect. **Sound waves** are *vibrations of the air or of another medium*. They vary in both frequency and amplitude (Figure 4.20). The frequency of a sound wave is the number of *cycles (vibrations) that it goes through per second*, designated **hertz (Hz)**. **Pitch** is a *perception closely related to frequency*. We perceive a high-frequency sound wave as high pitched and a low-frequency sound as low pitched.

Loudness is a *perception that depends on the amplitude of sound waves*—that is, their intensity. Other things being equal, the greater the amplitude of a sound, the louder it sounds. Because pitch and loudness are psychological experiences, however, they are influenced by factors other than the physical frequency and amplitude of sound waves. For example, tones of different frequencies may not sound equally loud, even though they have the same physical amplitude.

The ear, a complicated organ, converts relatively weak sound waves into more intense waves of pressure in the *fluid-filled canals of the snail-shaped organ* called the **cochlea** (KOCK-lee-uh), *which contains the receptors for hearing* (Figure 4.21). When

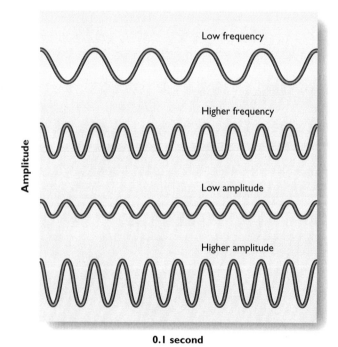

0.1 second

FIGURE 4.20 The period (time) between the peaks of a sound wave determines the frequency of the sound; we experience frequencies as different pitches. The vertical range, or amplitude, of a wave determines the sound's intensity and loudness.

sound waves strike the eardrum, they cause it to vibrate. The eardrum is connected to three tiny bones: the hammer, the anvil, and the stirrup (also known by their Latin names: malleus, incus, and stapes). As the weak vibrations of the large eardrum travel through these bones, they are transformed into stronger vibrations of the much smaller stirrup. The stirrup in turn transmits the vibrations to the fluid-filled cochlea, where the vibrations displace hair cells along the basilar membrane in the cochlea. These hair cells, which act much like touch receptors on the skin, are connected to neurons whose axons form the auditory nerve. The auditory nerve transmits impulses to the brain areas responsible for hearing.

Our knowledge of the mechanisms of hearing enables us to understand and explain hearing loss. One kind of hearing loss is conduction deafness, which *results when the bones connected to the eardrum fail to transmit sound waves properly to the cochlea.* Surgery can sometimes correct conduction deafness by removing whatever is obstructing the bones' movement. Someone with conduction deafness can still hear his or her own voice because it is conducted through the skull bones to the cochlea, bypassing the eardrum altogether. The other type of hearing loss is nerve deafness, which *results from damage to the cochlea, the hair cells, or the auditory nerve.* Nerve deafness can result from heredity, disease, or prolonged exposure to loud noises. Surgery cannot correct nerve deafness. Hearing aids can compensate for hearing loss in most people with either type of deafness (Moore, 1989). Hearing aids merely increase the intensity of the sound, however, so they are of little help in cases of severe nerve deafness.

Many people have hearing impairments for only certain frequencies. For example, people with damage to certain parts of the cochlea have trouble hearing high frequencies or medium-range frequencies. Modern hearing aids can be adjusted to intensify only the frequencies that a given person has trouble hearing.

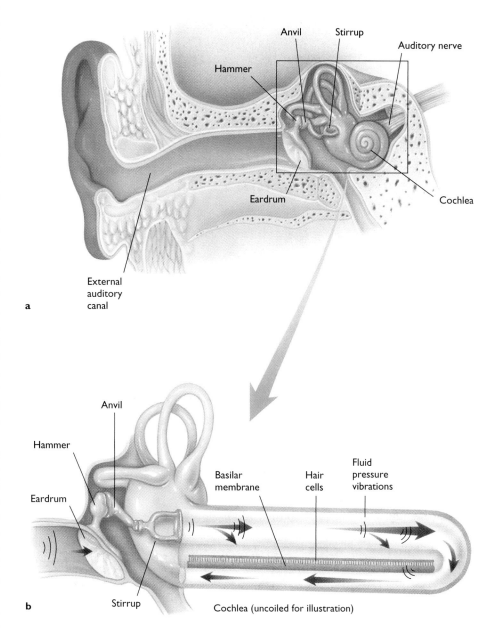

FIGURE 4.21 When sound waves strike the eardrum (a), they cause it to vibrate. The eardrum is connected to three tiny bones—the hammer, anvil, and stirrup—that convert the sound wave into a series of strong vibrations in the fluid-filled cochlea (b). These vibrations displace the hair cells along the basilar membrane in the cochlea, which is aptly named after the Greek word for snail. Here the dimensions of the cochlea have been changed to make the general principles clear.

▌ Hearing is the sensing of vibrations. Evelyn Glennie, profoundly deaf since childhood, has become a famous percussionist. Although she cannot hear her music, she detects the vibrations through her stocking feet.

Pitch Perception

Adult humans can hear sound waves from about 15–20 hertz to about 15,000–20,000 Hz (cycles per second). The low frequencies are perceived as low pitch; the high frequencies are perceived as high pitch, but frequency is not the same as pitch. (For example, doubling the frequency doesn't make the pitch seem twice as high; it makes it one octave higher.) The upper limit of hearing declines with age and also after exposure to loud noises. Thus, children hear higher frequencies than adults do.

We hear pitch by different mechanisms at different frequencies. At low frequencies (up to about 100 Hz), *a sound wave through the fluid of the cochlea vibrates all the hair cells, which produce action potentials in synchrony with the sound waves.* This is the **frequency principle.** For example, a sound with a frequency of 50 Hz makes each hair cell send the brain 50 impulses per second.

Beyond about 100 Hz, hair cells cannot keep pace. (A neuron never fires more than about 1,000 action potentials per second, and it cannot maintain that rate for long.) Even so, each sound wave excites at least a few hair cells, and *"volleys" of them (groups) respond to each vibration by producing an action potential* (Rose, Brugge, Anderson, & Hind, 1967). This is known as the **volley principle.** Thus, a tone at 1000 Hz might send 1,000 impulses to the brain per second, even though no single neuron was firing that rapidly. Volleys can keep up with most speech and music sounds up to about 4000 Hz. (The highest note on a piano is 4224 Hz.)

At still higher frequencies, we must rely on a different mechanism. At each point along the cochlea, the hair cells are tuned resonators that vibrate only for sound waves of a particular frequency. That is, *the highest frequency sounds vibrate hair cells near the stirrup end and lower frequency sounds (down to about 100–200 Hz) vibrate hair cells at points farther along the membrane* (Warren, 1999). This is the **place principle.** Note that tones less than about 100 Hz excite all the hair cells equally, and we hear them by the frequency principle. We identify tones from 100 to 4000 Hz by a combination of the volley principle and the place principle. Beyond 4000 Hz we identify tones only by the place principle. Figure 4.22 summarizes the three principles of pitch perception.

CONCEPT CHECK ☑

8. Suppose a mouse emits a soft high-frequency squeak in a room full of people. Which kinds of people are least likely to hear the squeak?
9. When hair cells at one point along the basilar membrane produce 50 impulses per second, we hear a tone at 5000 Hz. What do we hear when the same hair cells produce 100 impulses per second? (Check your answers on page 124.)

You have heard of people who can listen to a note and identify its pitch by name: "Oh, that's a C-sharp." That ability, called absolute pitch or perfect pitch, is found mostly in people with extensive musical training beginning in childhood (Takeuchi & Hulse, 1993).

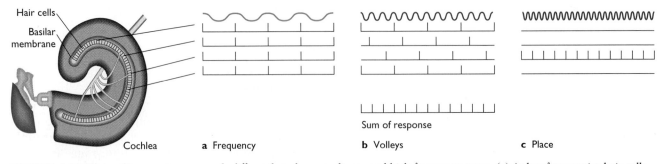

FIGURE 4.22 The auditory system responds differently to low-, medium-, and high-frequency tones. (a) At low frequencies hair cells at many points along the basilar membrane produce impulses in synchrony with the sound waves. (b) At medium frequencies different cells produce impulses in synchrony with different sound waves, but a volley (group) still produces one or more impulses for each wave. (c) At high frequencies only one point along the basilar membrane vibrates; hair cells at other locations remain still.

If you are amazed at absolute pitch, your own ability to recognize (though not name) a specific pitch might surprise you. In one study 48 college students with no special talent or training listened to 5-second segments from television theme songs, played either in their normal key or one-half or one note higher or lower. The students usually could choose which version was correct *if* they had repeatedly watched the program but not if they were unfamiliar with the program (Schellenberg & Trehub, 2003). That is, they remembered the familiar pitches.

You probably also have heard of people who are "tone-deaf." Anyone who was *completely* tone-deaf would be unable even to understand speech, as slight pitch changes differentiate one speech sound from another. However, for unknown reasons, some people are greatly impaired at detecting pitch changes. The result is that any melody sounds the same as any other, and music is no more pleasant than random noise (Peretz et al., 2002).

Localization of Sounds

What you hear is a stimulus in your ear, but you experience the sound as "out there," and you can generally estimate its approximate place of origin. What cues do you use?

The auditory system determines the direction of a source of sound by comparing the messages coming from the two ears. If a sound is coming from a source directly in front, the messages will arrive at the two ears simultaneously with equal loudness. If it comes from the left, however, it will arrive at the left ear slightly before the right ear, and it will be louder in the left ear (Figure 4.23). The timing is important for localizing low-frequency sounds; intensity is the cue for localizing high-frequency sounds.

The auditory system can also detect the approximate distance of a sound source. If a sound grows louder, you interpret it as coming closer. If two sounds differ in pitch, you assume the one with more high-frequency tones is closer. (Low-frequency tones carry better over distance, so if you can hear a high-frequency tone, its source is probably close.) However, loudness and frequency tell

you only the *relative* distances of sound sources, not the *absolute* distance. The only cue for absolute distance is the amount of reverberation (Mershon & King, 1975). In a closed room, you first hear the sound waves coming directly from the source and a little later the waves that reflected off the walls, floor, ceiling, or other objects. If you hear many reflected sounds (echoes), you judge the source of the sound to be far away. In a noisy room, the echoes are hard to hear, so people have trouble localizing sound sources; because they hear few echoes, all sounds seem nearby (McMurtry & Mershon, 1985).

CONCEPT CHECK ✓

10. Why is it difficult to tell whether a sound is coming from directly in front of or directly behind you?
11. If someone who needs hearing aids in both ears wears one in only the left ear, what will be the effect on sound localization?
12. Suppose you are listening to a monaural (nonstereo) radio. Can the station play sounds that you will localize as coming from different directions, such as left, center, and right? Can it play sounds that you will localize as coming from different distances? Why or why not? (Check your answers on page 124.)

FIGURE 4.23   The ear located closest to the sound will receive the sound waves first. That cue is important for localizing low-frequency sounds.

The Vestibular Sense

In the inner ear on each side of the head, adjacent to the structures responsible for hearing, is a structure called the *vestibule*. The **vestibular sense** that it controls *tells us the direction of tilt and amount of acceleration of the head and the position of the head with respect to gravity.* It plays a key role in posture and balance and is responsible for the sensations we experience when we are riding on a roller coaster or sitting in an airplane during takeoff. Intensive vestibular sensations are responsible for the phenomenon of motion sickness.

The vestibular sense also enables us to keep our eyes fixated on a target when our head is moving. When you walk down the street, you can keep your eyes fixated on a distant street sign, even though your head is bobbing up and down. The vestibular sense detects each head movement and controls the movement of your eyes to compensate for it.

To illustrate, try to read this page while you are jiggling the book up and down and from side to side, keeping your head steady. Then hold the book steady and move your head up and down and from side to side. You probably will find it much easier to read when you are moving your head than when you are jiggling the book. The reason is that your vestibular sense keeps your eyes fixated on the print during head movements. People who have suffered injury to

tilts, the particles excite different sets of hair cells. The otolith organs report the direction of gravity and therefore which way is up.

If the otoliths provide unreliable information, we can use vision instead. For astronauts in the zero-gravity environment of outer space, the otoliths cannot distinguish up from down; indeed, the up–down dimension is almost meaningless. Instead, they learn to rely entirely on visual signals, such as distance and direction to the walls of the ship (Lackner, 1993).

The Cutaneous Senses

What we commonly think of as the sense of touch consists of several partly independent senses: pressure on the skin, warmth, cold, pain, vibration, movement across the skin, and stretch of the skin. These sensations depend on several kinds of receptors, as Figure 4.25 shows (Iggo & Andres, 1982). A pinprick on the skin feels different from a light touch, and both feel different from a burn, because each excites different receptors. Collectively, these sensations are known as the **cutaneous senses,** meaning the *skin senses.* Although they are most prominent in the skin, we also have them in our internal organs, enabling us to feel internal pain, pressure, and temperature. Therefore, the cutaneous senses are sometimes known as the *somatosensory system,* meaning *body-sensory system.*

One way of studying the cutaneous senses is to examine people who have suffered impairments. After certain kinds of nervous-system damage, people sometimes lose one kind of touch sensation while keeping others. One patient lost the connections of light touch to the primary somatosensory part of his cerebral cortex. He could still feel pain and temperature but had very little sensation from soft touch. For example, if someone stroked a brush across his skin, he reported a "pleasant" sensation, but he could not describe the sensation further and could not tell which direction the brush went (Olausson et al., 2002).

Have you ever wondered about the sensation of itch? Is it a kind of touch or pain or what? The receptors have not been identified, but we know they are stimulated by histamine, a chemical released by injured tissues. When a mosquito bites you or when you are recovering from a wound, released histamines cause an itching sensation. It is definitely unlike pain; in fact it is inhibited by pain (Andrew & Craig, 2001).

© Julie Lemberger/CORBIS

▍ The vestibular sense plays a key role in posture and balance as it reports the position of the head.

their vestibular sense report that their vision is blurry while they are walking. To read street signs, they must come to a stop.

The vestibular system is composed of three semicircular canals, oriented in three separate directions, and two otolith organs (Figure 4.24b). The *semicircular canals* are lined with hair cells and filled with a jellylike substance. When the body accelerates in any direction, the jellylike substance in the corresponding semicircular canal pushes against the hair cells, which send messages to the brain. The two *otolith organs* shown in Figure 4.24b also contain hair cells (Figure 4.24c), which lie next to the *otoliths* (calcium carbonate particles). Depending on which way the head

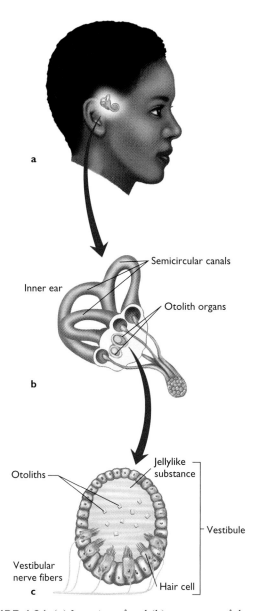

FIGURE 4.24 (a) Location of and (b) structures of the vestibule. (c) Moving your head or body displaces hair cells that report the tilt of your head and the direction and acceleration of movement.

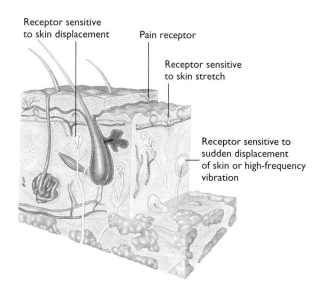

FIGURE 4.25 Cutaneous sensation is the product of many kinds of receptors, each sensitive to a particular kind of information.

When you scratch an itchy spot, your scratching has to produce some pain to relieve the itch. For example, if a dentist anesthetizes one side of your mouth prior to dental surgery, as the anesthesia wears off, the itch receptors sometimes recover before the pain and touch receptors. At that point you can scratch the itchy spot, but you don't feel the scratch and it does not relieve the itch.

Tickle is another kind of cutaneous sensation. Have you ever wondered why you can't tickle yourself? Actually, you can, a little, but it's not the same as when someone else tickles you. The reason is that when you are about to touch yourself, certain parts of your brain build up an anticipation response that is quite similar to the result of the actual stimulation (Carlsson, Petrovic, Skare, Petersson, & Ingvar, 2000). That is, when you try to tickle yourself, the sensation comes as no surprise.

Pain

Pain is a cutaneous sensation of obvious importance in medicine and a topic of interest to psychologists as well because of its relation to depression and anxiety. The experience of pain is a complicated mixture of sensation (the information about tissue damage) and emotion (the unpleasant reaction). The sensory and emotional qualities are governed by different brain areas (Craig, Bushnell, Zhang, & Blomqvist, 1994; Fernandez & Turk, 1992). The brain area responsive to the emotional aspect of pain—the *anterior cingulate cortex*—also responds to the emotional "pain" of feeling rejected by other people (Eisenberger, Lieberman, & Williams, 2003). Telling people to expect pain or distracting them from the pain changes the emotional response, including the activity in the anterior cingulate cortex, but does not change the sensation itself (Ploghaus et al., 1999).

The Gate Theory of Pain

You visit a physician because of severe pain, but as soon as the physician tells you the problem is nothing to worry about, the pain starts to subside. Have you ever had such an experience? Pain can increase or decrease greatly because of expectations.

Recall the term *placebo* from Chapter 2: A placebo is a drug or other procedure that has no important effects other than those that result from people's expectations; researchers ordinarily give placebos to control groups. Placebos have little effect on most medical conditions, but they sometimes relieve pain, or at least the emotional distress of pain, quite impressively (Hróbjartsson. & Gøtzsche, 2001). Even the effects of the drug itself depend partly on expectations. When people have a catheter in their arm and receive painkilling medicine without knowing it, the drug is less effective than when people know they are receiving it (Amanzio, Pollo, Maggi, & Benedetti, 2001).

In one experiment college students had a smelly brownish liquid rubbed onto one finger. It was in fact just a placebo, but they were told that it was a painkiller. Then they were given a painful pinch stimulus to that finger and a finger of the other hand. They consistently reported less pain on the finger with the placebo (Montgomery & Kirsch, 1996). How placebos work is far from clear, but these results eliminate mere relaxation, which would presumably affect both hands equally.

Because of observations such as these, Ronald Melzack and P. D. Wall (1965) proposed the gate theory of pain, the idea that *pain messages must pass through a gate, presumably in the spinal cord, that can block the messages.* For example, if you injure yourself, rubbing the surrounding skin sends inhibitory messages to the spinal cord, closing the pain gates. Pleasant or distracting events also send inhibitory messages. The gate can also enhance the pain messages; for example, inflamed skin (e.g., after sunburn) increases sensitivity of the spinal cord neurons so that almost any stimulation becomes painful (Malmberg, Chen, Tonegawa, & Basbaum, 1997). In short, the activities of the rest of the nervous system can facilitate or inhibit the transmission of pain messages (Figure 4.26).

Mechanisms of Decreasing Pain

Some people are completely insensitive to pain. Before you start to envy them, consider: They often burn themselves by picking up hot objects, scald their tongues on hot coffee, cut themselves without realizing it, and bite their tongues hard, possibly even biting off the tip. They sit in a single position for hours without growing uncomfortable, thereby damaging their bones and tendons (Comings & Amromin, 1974).

Although it would be a mistake to rid ourselves of pain altogether, we would like to limit it. One way is to provide distraction. For example, postsurgery patients in a room with a pleasant view complain less about pain, take less painkilling medicine, and recover faster than do patients in a windowless room or a room with a poor view (Ulrich, 1984).

Several other methods depend on medications. *Pain stimuli cause the nervous system to release a neurotransmitter,* called **substance P,** for intense pains and another transmitter, glutamate, for all pains including mild ones. Mice that lack substance P receptors react to all painful stimuli as if they were mild (DeFelipe et al., 1998). Another set of neurons release **endorphins,** *neurotransmitters that inhibit the release of substance P and thereby weaken pain sensations* (Pert & Snyder, 1973) (see Figure 4.27). The term *endorphin* is a combination of the terms *endogenous* (self-produced) and *morphine.* The drug morphine, which stimulates endorphin synapses, has

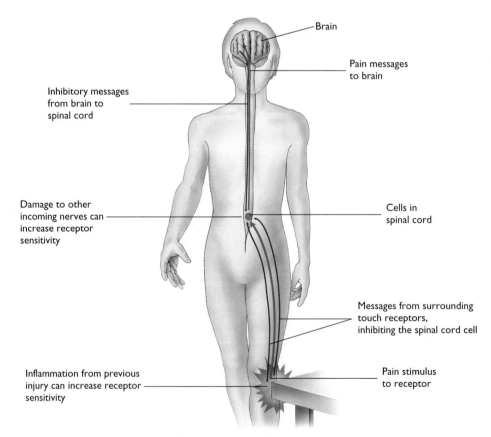

FIGURE 4.26 Pain messages from the skin are relayed from spinal cord cells to the brain. According to the gate theory of pain, those spinal cord cells serve as a gate that can block or enhance the signal. The proposed neural circuitry is simplified in this diagram. Green lines indicate axons with excitatory inputs; red lines indicate axons with inhibitory inputs.

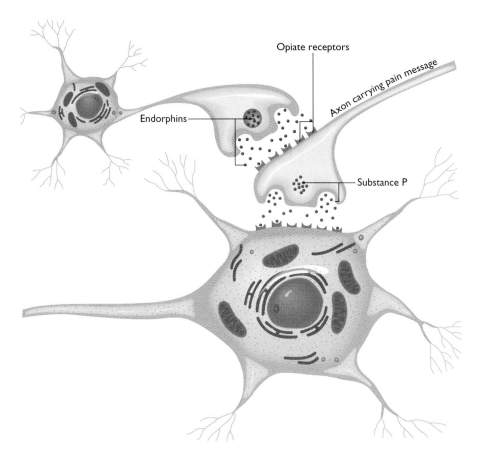

Opiate receptors

Endorphins

Axon carrying pain message

Substance P

FIGURE 4.27 Substance P is the neurotransmitter most responsible for pain sensations. Endorphins are neurotransmitters that block the release of substance P, thereby decreasing pain sensations. Opiates decrease pain by imitating the effects of endorphins.

long been known for its ability to inhibit dull, lingering pains. Endorphins are also released by pleasant experiences, such as sexual activity or thrilling music (A. Goldstein, 1980). (That effect may help to explain why a pleasant view helps to ease postsurgical pain.) In short, endorphins are a powerful method of closing pain gates.

Paradoxically, another method of decreasing pain begins by inducing it. The *chemical* capsaicin *stimulates receptors that respond to painful heat* (Caterina, Rosen, Tominaga, Brake, & Julius, 1999) and thereby *causes the release of substance P.* Capsaicin is the chemical that makes jalapeños and similar peppers taste hot. Injecting capsaicin or rubbing it on the skin produces a temporary burning sensation (Yarsh, Farb, Leeman, & Jessell, 1979). However, after that burning sensation subsides, the skin becomes less sensitive to pain than usual. Several skin creams intended for the relief of aching muscles contain capsaicin. One reason capsaicin decreases pain is that it releases substance P faster than the neurons can resynthesize it. However, that explanation cannot be complete because rapid repetition of capsaicin (which should deplete substance P even more) increases the pain instead of decreasing it (B. G. Green, 1996).

CONCEPT CHECK ☑

13. Naloxone, a drug used as an antidote for an overdose of morphine, is known to block the endorphin synapses. How could we use naloxone to determine whether a pleasant stimulus releases endorphins?
14. Psychologist Linda Bartoshuk recommends candies containing moderate amounts of jalapeño peppers as a treatment for people with pain in the mouth. Why? (Check your answers on page 124.)

Phantom Limbs

A particularly fascinating phenomenon is the **phantom limb,** *a continuing sensation of an amputated body part.* For example, someone might report occasional feelings of touch, tingling, or pain from an amputated hand, arm, leg, foot, or any other amputated part. The phantom sensation might last only days or weeks after the amputation, but it sometimes lasts years or even a lifetime (Ramachandran & Hirstein, 1998).

Physicians and psychologists have long wondered about the cause of phantom sensations. Some believed

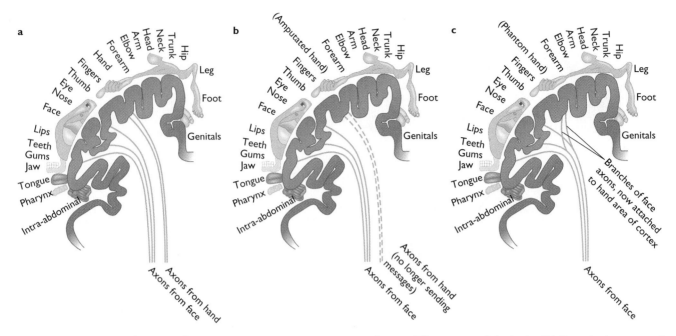

FIGURE 4.28 (a) Each area in the somatosensory cortex gets its input from a different part of the body. (b) If one body part, such as the hand, is amputated, its part of the cortex no longer gets its normal input. (c) However, the axons from a neighboring area, such as the face, can branch out to excite the vacated area or strengthen existing synapses. Now any stimulation of the face will excite both the face area and the hand area. But when it stimulates the hand area, it feels like the hand, not the face.

it was an emotional reaction, and others believed it began with irritation of nerves at the stump where the amputation occurred. Research in the 1990s established that the problem lies within the brain.

In the last chapter, Figure 3.18 shows how each part of the somatosensory cortex gets its input from a different body area. Figure 4.28a repeats part of that illustration. Part b shows what happens immediately after an amputation of the hand: The hand area of the cortex becomes inactive because the axons from the hand are inactive. (You might think of the neurons in the face area of the cortex as "widows" that have lost their old partners and are signaling their eagerness for new partners.) As time passes, axons from the face, which ordinarily excite only the face area of the cortex, form (or strengthen) branches to the hand area of the cortex, which is adjacent to the face area. So any stimulation of the face continues to excite the face area but now also excites the hand area. When it stimulates the hand area, it produces a hand experience—in other words a phantom limb (Flor et al., 1995; Ramachandran & Blakeslee, 1998).

One way is known to relieve phantom sensations: Individuals with amputations who learn to use an artificial limb gradually lose their phantoms (Lotze et al., 1999). Evidently, the hand and arm areas of their

cortex start experiencing the artificial limb (!), and this sensation displaces the abnormal sensation coming from the face.

CONCEPT CHECK

15. A phantom hand sensation is greater at some times than others. When should it be strongest? (Check your answer on page 124.)

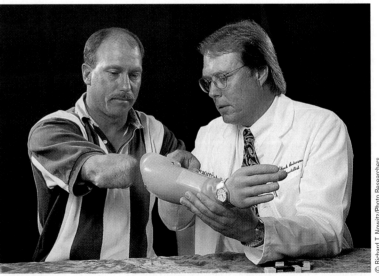

▌ After a person with an amputation gains experience using an artificial limb, phantom limb sensations fade or disappear altogether.

The Chemical Senses

Many textbooks on sensation ignore taste and smell or mention them only briefly. If rats or raccoons wrote sensation textbooks, however, they would probably devote as much coverage to taste and smell as they would to hearing and mention vision only briefly. Many invertebrates have no vision or hearing at all, surviving with only chemical senses and touch.

Taste

Vision and hearing enable humans to find food and water, avoid danger, keep our balance, and find suitable mates. The sense of **taste,** which *detects chemicals on the tongue,* serves just one function: It governs our eating and drinking.

The *taste receptors are* in the **taste buds,** *located in the folds on the surface of the tongue,* almost exclusively along the outside edge of the tongue in adults (Figure 4.29). (Children's taste buds are more widely scattered.)

Try this demonstration (based on Bartoshuk, 1991): Soak something small (a cotton swab will do) in sugar water, salt water, or vinegar. Then touch it to the center of your tongue, not too far back. You will feel it but taste nothing. Then slowly move the soaked substance toward the side or front of your tongue. Suddenly, you taste it.

If you go in the other direction (first touching the side of the tongue and then moving toward the center), you will continue to taste the substance even when it reaches the center of your tongue. The explanation is not that you suddenly grew new taste buds.

Rather, your taste buds tell you nothing about location. Once you have stimulated any taste buds, you will continue tasting the substance, but the taste receptors do not tell you *where* you are tasting the substance. If you now stimulate *touch* receptors elsewhere on your tongue, your brain interprets the taste perception as coming from the spot you are touching, even though the taste sensation is in fact coming from somewhere else.

Different Types of Taste Receptors

Researchers now have a reasonably clear understanding of how taste receptors work (Lindemann, 1996). Traditionally, Western cultures have talked about four primary tastes: sweet, sour, salty, and bitter. However, the taste of monosodium glutamate (MSG), common in many Asian cuisines, cannot be fully described in terms of those four primaries (Kurihara & Kashiwayanagi, 1998; Schiffman & Erickson, 1971), and researchers have found a taste receptor specific to MSG (Chaudhari, Landin, & Roper, 2000). So it may be better to talk about five primary tastes. English has never had a word for the taste of MSG (similar to the taste of unsalted chicken soup), so researchers have adopted the Japanese word *umami.*

Bitter taste is hard to explain because such diverse chemicals taste bitter. About the only thing they have in common is that most bitter substances are poisonous or at least harmful in large amounts. How could such diverse chemicals all excite the same receptor? The answer is that they don't. We have a large number of different bitter receptors—about 40 to 80—each sensitive to different types of chemicals (Adler et al., 2000; Matsunami, Montmayeur, & Buck, 2000). Any chemical that excites any of these receptors produces the same

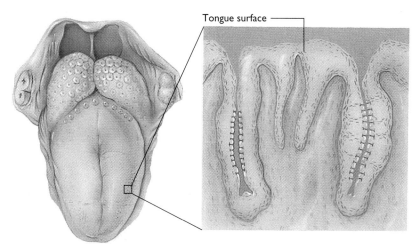
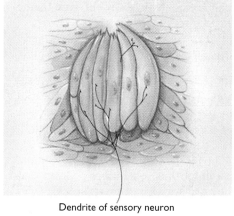

FIGURE 4.29 (a) Taste buds, which react to chemicals dissolved in saliva, are located along the edge of the tongue in adult humans but are more widely distributed in children. (b) A cross section through part of the surface of the tongue showing taste buds. (c) A cross section of one taste bud. Each taste bud has about 50 receptor cells within it.

bitter sensation. One consequence is that a wide variety of harmful chemicals taste bitter. Another consequence is that we do not always detect low concentrations of bitter chemicals; with so many different kinds of bitter receptors, we do not have many of any one kind.

Individual Differences

Researchers in the 1930s discovered that the chemical phenothiocarbamide (PTC) tasted bitter to some people but was tasteless to others. Later researchers traced the difference to a single gene (Kim et al., 2003). Most people who are insensitive to PTC, called *nontasters,* have less than average sensitivity to other tastes as well. Another group of people, called *supertasters,* have more than the usual number of taste buds, again for genetic reasons, and detect most tastes extremely strongly. Most supertasters dislike black coffee, black breads, hot peppers, sour fruits such as grapefruit, and strong-tasting vegetables such as radishes and Brussels sprouts (Bartoshuk, Duffy, Lucchina, Prutkin, & Fast, 1998; Drewnowski, Henderson, Short, & Barratt-Fornell, 1998). They also tend to be content with smaller portions of food, and most of them are relatively thin. In short, genes can affect food intake by altering taste receptors.

Taste sensitivity also depends on other factors (Yamauchi, Endo, & Yoshimura, 2002): It declines with age, especially after age 70. Cigarette smokers have decreased sensitivity, especially for bitter tastes. After about age 20, women have greater taste sensitivity than men, apparently as a result of estrogens (female-typical hormones). Women's taste sensitivity fluctuates over the monthly cycle and reaches a peak early in pregnancy (Prutkin et al., 2000).

Smell

The *sense of smell* is known as **olfaction.** The olfactory receptors, located on the mucous membrane in the rear air passages of the nose (Figure 4.30), detect the presence of certain airborne molecules. Chemically, these receptors are much like synaptic receptors, but they are stimulated by chemicals from the environment instead of chemicals released by other neurons. The axons of the olfactory receptors form the olfactory tract, which extends to the olfactory bulbs at the base of the brain.

How many kinds of olfactory receptors do we have? Until 1991 researchers had virtually no idea. In principle researchers could determine the number of receptor types with behavioral data. With color vision, for example, the researchers of the 1800s established that people can mix three colors of light in various amounts to match any other color. Therefore, even before the technology existed to examine the cones in the retina, researchers had reason to believe that the retina had three kinds of cones. Regarding olfaction, however, no one reported such behavioral results. Can people match all possible odors by mixing appropriate amounts of three, four, seven, or ten, or however many primary odors?

Perhaps it is just as well that no one spent a lifetime trying to find out. Linda Buck and Richard Axel (1991) used modern biochemical technology to demonstrate that the human nose has at least 100 types of olfactory receptors, and later research put the number at several hundred, whereas rats and mice

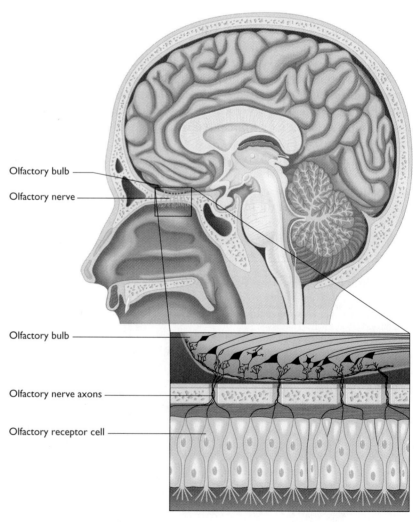

Olfactory bulb
Olfactory nerve
Olfactory bulb
Olfactory nerve axons
Olfactory receptor cell

FIGURE 4.30 The olfactory receptor cells lining the nasal cavity send information to the olfactory bulb in the brain. There are at least 100 types of receptors with specialized responses to airborne chemicals.

have about 1,000 (Zhang & Firestein, 2002). Each olfactory receptor can detect only a small group of closely related chemicals (Araneda, Kini, & Firestein, 2000). Such extreme specificity is rare in the body; the only other example is the immune system.

Much remains to be learned about olfaction. Of course it depends on stimulation of the receptors in the nose, but the brain processes the information further (Figure 4.31). For example, you will find it easier to distinguish one smell from another if both are familiar to you than if either is new (Stevenson & Boakes, 2003).

Olfaction is particularly important for food selection. Neurons in the prefrontal cortex receive both taste and olfactory information, producing the combined sensation that we call *flavor*. These cells also receive input that indicates hunger, and they respond vigorously to the flavor of a food only when the individual is hungry (Rolls, 1997).

Olfaction also serves social functions, especially in nonhuman mammals that identify one another by means of **pheromones**, which are *chemicals they release into the environment*. Nearly all nonhuman mammals rely on pheromones for sexual communication. For example, a female dog in her fertile and sexually responsive time of year emits pheromones that attract every male dog in the neighborhood that is free to move. Pheromones act primarily on the vomeronasal organ, a set of receptors near, but separate from, the standard olfactory receptors (Monti-Bloch, Jennings-White, Dolberg, & Berliner,

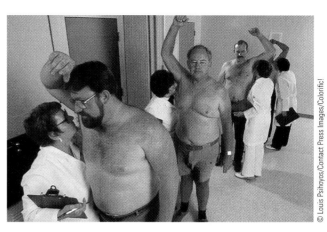

Professional deodorant tester: That's a career option you probably never considered. U.S. industries spend millions of dollars to eliminate the kinds of personal odors that are essential to other mammalian species.

1994). Each of those receptors responds to one and only one chemical, and they respond to it even at extremely low concentrations (Leinders-Zufall et al., 2000).

Humans prefer *not* to recognize one another by smell. The deodorant and perfume industries exist for the sole purpose of removing and covering up human odors. But perhaps we respond to pheromones anyway, unconsciously. For example, young women who are in frequent contact, such as roommates in a college dormitory, tend to synchronize their menstrual cycles, probably as a result of pheromones they secrete (McClintock, 1971).

One study examined women in Bedouin Arab families. The advantages of studying that culture are that the mother and sisters within a family have extensive daily contact, unmarried women have almost no contact with men, and very few women use oral contraceptives. Thus, pheromones have a maximum opportunity to show their effects. The results showed that the women in most families were at least partly synchronized; they might not begin to menstruate on exactly the same day, but they were close (Weller & Weller, 1997).

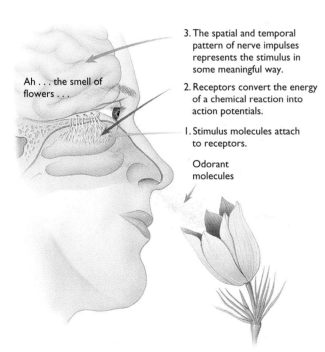

3. The spatial and temporal pattern of nerve impulses represents the stimulus in some meaningful way.

2. Receptors convert the energy of a chemical reaction into action potentials.

1. Stimulus molecules attach to receptors.

Ah . . . the smell of flowers . . .

Odorant molecules

FIGURE 4.31 Olfaction, like any other sensory system, converts physical energy into a complex pattern of brain activity.

IN CLOSING

Sensory Systems

The world as experienced by a bat (which can hear frequencies of 100,000 Hz) or a dog (which can discriminate odors that you and I would never notice) or a mouse (which depends on its whiskers when exploring the world) is in many ways a different world from the one that people experience. The function of our senses is not to tell us about everything in the world, but to alert us to the information we are most likely to use, given our way of life.

Summary

- *Pitch.* At low frequencies of sound, we identify pitch by the frequency of vibrations of hair cells. At intermediate frequencies, we identify pitch by volleys of responses from many neurons. At high frequencies, we identify pitch by the location where the hair cells vibrate. (page 114)

- *Localizing sounds.* We localize the source of a sound by detecting differences in the time and loudness of the sounds our two ears receive. We localize the distance of a sound source mostly by the amount of reverberation, or echoes, following the main sound. (page 115)

- *Vestibular system.* The vestibular system tells us about the movement of the head and its position with respect to gravity. It enables us to keep our eyes fixated on an object while the rest of our body is in motion. (page 115)

- *Cutaneous receptors.* We experience many types of sensation on the skin, each dependent on different receptors. Itch is a sensation based on tissue irritation, inhibited by pain. Tickle depends on the unpredictability of the stimulus. (page 116)

- *Pain.* The experience of pain can be greatly inhibited or enhanced by other simultaneous experiences, including touch to surrounding skin or the person's expectations. Pain depends largely on stimulation of neurons that are sensitive to the neurotransmitter substance P, which can be inhibited by endorphins. (page 117)

- *Phantom limbs.* After an amputation the corresponding portion of the somatosensory cortex stops receiving its normal input. Soon axons from neighboring cortical areas form branches that start exciting the silenced areas of cortex. When they receive the new input, they react the old way, producing a phantom sensation. (page 119)

- *Taste receptors.* Even before researchers identified the taste receptors, they knew that there must be at least four kinds because certain procedures affect one taste quality (e.g., sweetness) without affecting the others. An adult human has taste receptors only along the edges of the tongue. (page 121)

- *Olfactory receptors.* The olfactory system—the sense of smell—depends on at least 100 types of receptors, each with its own special sensitivity. Olfaction is important for many behaviors, including food selection and (especially in nonhuman mammals) identification of potential mates. (page 122)

Answers to Concept Checks

8. Obviously, the people farthest from the mouse are least likely to hear it. In addition older people would be less likely than young people are to hear the squeak because the ability to hear high frequencies declines in old age. Another group unlikely to hear the squeak are those who have had repeated exposure to loud noises. For this reason you should avoid attending loud rock concerts and listening to recorded music played at a loud volume. You could damage your hearing in the long run, even if you do not realize it now. (page 114)

9. We still hear a tone at 5000 Hz, but it is louder than before. For high-frequency tones the pitch we hear depends on which hair cells are most active, not how many impulses per second they fire. (page 114)

10. We localize sounds by comparing the input into the left ear with the input into the right ear. If a sound comes from straight ahead or from directly behind us (or from straight above or below), the input into the left ear will be identical with the input into the right ear. (page 115)

11. Sounds will be louder in the left ear than in the right, and therefore, they may seem to be coming from the left side even when they aren't. (However, a sound from the right will still strike the right ear before the left, so time of arrival at the two ears will compete against the relative loudness.) (page 115)

12. Various sounds from the radio cannot seem to come from different directions because your localization of the direction of a sound depends on a comparison between the responses of the two ears. However, the radio can play sounds that seem to come from different distances because distance localization does not depend on a difference between the ears. It depends on the amount of reverberation, loudness, and high-frequency tones, all of which can be varied with a single speaker. Consequently, the radio can easily give an impression of people walking toward you or away from you, but not of people walking left to right or right to left. (page 115)

13. First determine how much the pleasant stimulus decreases the experience of pain for several people. Then give half of them naloxone and half of them a placebo. Again measure how much the pleasant stimulus decreases the pain. If the pleasant stimulus decreases pain by releasing endorphins, then naloxone should impair its painkilling effects. (page 119)

14. The capsaicin in the jalapeño peppers will release substance P faster than it can be resynthesized, thus decreasing the later sensitivity to pain in the mouth. (page 119)

15. The phantom hand sensation should be strongest when something is rubbing against the face. (page 120)

The Interpretation of Sensory Information

What is the relationship between the real world and the way we perceive it?

Why are we sometimes wrong about what we think we see?

No doubt you have heard the expression "a picture is worth a thousand words." If so, what is one one-thousandth of a picture worth? One word? Perhaps not even that.

Printed photographs, such as the one on page 123, are composed of a great many dots. Ordinarily, you will be aware of only the overall patterns and objects, but if you magnify a photo, as in Figure 4.32, you can see the individual dots. Although one dot by itself tells us almost nothing, the pattern of dots as a whole constitutes a meaningful picture.

Actually, our vision is like this all the time. Your retina includes about 126 million rods and cones, each of which sees one dot of the visual field. What you perceive is not dots, however, but lines, curves, and complex objects. In a variety of ways, your nervous system starts with an array of details and extracts the meaningful information.

Perception of Minimal Stimuli

Some of the very earliest psychological researchers asked, "What is the weakest sound, the weakest light, the weakest touch, and so forth that a person can de-

tect?" They assumed that this question would be easy to answer and therefore a good starting point for further research. As is often the case, however, a question that appeared simple became more complicated.

Sensory Thresholds and Signal Detection

Imagine a typical experiment to determine the threshold of hearing—that is, the minimum intensity that one can hear: Participants are presented with tones of varying intensity in random order, and sometimes no tone occurs at all. Each time, the participants are asked to say whether they heard anything. Figure 4.33 presents typical results. Notice that no sharp line separates sounds that people hear from sounds they do not. Researchers therefore define an **absolute sensory threshold** as the *intensity at which a given individual can detect a stimulus 50% of the time*. Note, however, that people sometimes report stimuli below the threshold or fail to report stimuli above it. Note also that people sometimes report hearing a tone when none was present. We should not be surprised. Throughout the study they have been listening to faint tones and saying "yes" when they heard almost nothing. The difference between nothing and almost nothing is pretty slim.

FIGURE 4.32 Although this photograph is composed entirely of dots, we see objects and patterns. The principles at work in our perception of this photograph are at work in all our perceptions.

© Louis Psihoyos/Contact Press Images/Colorific!

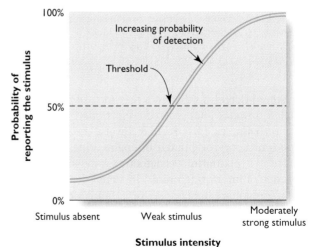

FIGURE 4.33 Typical results of an experiment to measure an absolute sensory threshold. There is no sharp boundary between stimuli that you can perceive and stimuli that you cannot perceive.

Your threshold can change drastically from one time to another. For example, if you have been outdoors on a bright, sunny day and you now walk into a darkened movie theater, you will have trouble seeing the seats at first. After a few minutes, your threshold drops (i.e., your sensitivity increases) and you can see better. Your threshold would drop still further in a completely darkened room.

When people try to detect weak stimuli, they can be correct in two ways: reporting the presence of a stimulus (a "hit") and reporting its absence (a "correct rejection"). They can also be wrong in two ways: failing to detect a stimulus when present (a "miss") and reporting a stimulus when none was present (a "false alarm"). Figure 4.34 outlines these possibilities.

FIGURE 4.34 People can make two kinds of correct judgments (green backgrounds) and two kinds of errors (red backgrounds). Someone who too readily reports the stimulus present would get many hits but also many false alarms.

Signal-detection theory is the *study of people's tendencies to make hits, correct rejections, misses, and false alarms* (D. M. Green & Swets, 1966). (Signal-detection theory originated in engineering, where it is applied to such matters as detecting radio signals in the presence of interfering noise.) In signal-detection studies, we compare responses for stimulus-present and stimulus-absent trials. For example, suppose that someone reports a stimulus present on 80% of the trials when it is actually present. That statistic is meaningless unless we also know how often the person said it was present when it was not. For example, the person might have reported a stimulus present on 80% of trials when it was absent. In that case we would conclude that

the person can't tell the difference between stimulus-present and stimulus-absent.

In a signal-detection experiment, people's responses depend on their willingness to risk a miss or a false alarm. (When in doubt, you have to risk one or the other.) Suppose you are the participant and I tell you that you will receive a 10-cent reward whenever you correctly report that a light is present, but you will be fined 1 cent if you say "yes" when it is absent. When you are not sure, you will probably guess "yes," and the results will resemble those in Figure 4.35a. Then I change the rules: You will receive a 1-cent reward for correctly reporting the presence of a light, but you will suffer a 10-cent penalty and an electrical shock if you report a light when none was present. Now you will say "yes" only when you are certain, and the results will look like those in Figure 4.35b. In short, people's answers depend on the instructions they receive and the strategies they use, not just what their senses tell them.

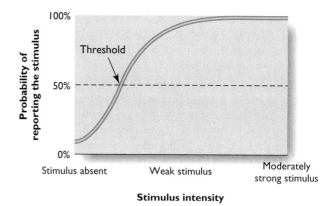

Instructions: You will receive a 10-cent reward for correctly reporting that a light is present. You will be penalized 1 cent for reporting that a light is present when it is not.

a

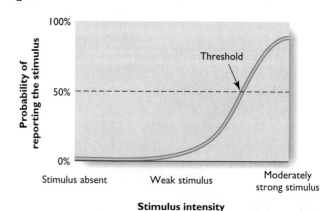

Instructions: You will receive a 1-cent reward for correctly reporting that a light is present. You will be penalized 10 cents *and* subjected to an electric shock for reporting that a light is present when it is not.

b

FIGURE 4.35 Results of experiments to measure a sensory threshold using two different sets of instructions.

People become cautious about false alarms for other reasons too. In one experiment participants were asked to read words that were flashed on a screen for a split second. They performed reasonably well with ordinary words such as *river* or *peach.* For emotionally loaded words such as *penis* or *bitch,* however, they generally said they were not sure what they saw. Several explanations are possible (e.g., G. S. Blum & Barbour, 1979); one is that participants hesitate to blurt out an emotionally charged word unless they are certain they are right.

The signal-detection approach is useful in many settings remote from a psychologist's laboratory. For example, the legal system is also a signal-detection situation. When we examine the evidence and try to decide whether someone is guilty or innocent, we can be right in two ways and wrong in two ways:

	Defendant is actually guilty	Defendant is actually innocent
Jury votes "guilty"	Hit	False alarm
Jury votes "not guilty"	Miss	Correct rejection

Most people agree it is more important to avoid false alarms (finding an innocent person guilty). Therefore, we insist on convincing evidence before convicting someone of a crime.

CONCEPT CHECK ☑

16. Suppose we find that nearly all alcoholics and drug abusers have a particular pattern of brain waves. Can we now use that pattern as a way to identify people with an alcohol or drug problem? (Check your answer on page 145.)

Subliminal Perception

You have probably heard of **subliminal perception,** the idea that *a stimulus can influence our behavior even when it is presented so faintly or briefly or along with such strong distracters that we do not perceive it consciously.* (*Limen* is Latin for "threshold"; thus, subliminal means "below the threshold.") Generally, the operational definition of "not perceived consciously" is that the person reports not seeing it. Is subliminal perception powerful, meaningless, or something in between?

What Subliminal Perception Cannot Do

Many years ago claims were made that subliminal messages could control people's buying habits. For example, an unscrupulous theater owner might insert a single frame, "EAT POPCORN," in the middle of a film. Customers who were not consciously aware of the message could not resist it, so they would flock to the concession stand to buy popcorn. Despite many tests of this claim, no one found any evidence to support it (Bornstein, 1989).

Another claim is that certain rock-'n'-roll recordings contain "satanic" messages that were recorded backward and superimposed on the songs. Some people allege that listeners unconsciously perceive these messages and then follow the evil advice. The issue for psychologists is not whether any rock band ever inserted such a message. (There are a lot of rock bands, after all.) The issue is whether a backward message has any influence. If people hear a backward message, can they understand it? Even if they don't, does it influence their behavior? Researchers have recorded various messages (nothing satanic) and asked people to listen to them backward. So far, no one listening to a backward message has been able to discern what it would sound like forward, and listening to it has not influenced behavior in any detectable way (Vokey & Read, 1985). In other words even if certain music does contain messages recorded backward, we have no evidence that the messages matter. (To hear some examples of backward speech, although not necessarily a scientific interpretation of them, visit this Web site: **www.reversespeech.com/.**)

A third unsupported claim: "Subliminal audiotapes" can help you improve your memory, quit smoking, lose weight, raise your self-esteem, and so forth. In one study psychologists asked more than 200 volunteers to listen to a popular brand of audiotape. But they intentionally mislabeled some of the tapes. That is, some tapes with self-esteem messages were labeled "memory tapes," and some tapes with memory messages were labeled "self-esteem tapes." After 1 month of listening, most who *thought* they were listening to self-esteem tapes said they had greatly improved their self-esteem; those who *thought* they were listening to memory tapes said their memory had greatly improved. What they actually heard made no difference. In other words the memory improvement was a result of people's expectations, not the tapes themselves (Greenwald, Spangenberg, Pratkanis, & Eskanazi, 1991).

What Subliminal Perception Can Do

Subliminal messages do produce effects, although they are in most cases brief, subtle, and hard to measure. For example, people in one study viewed a happy, neutral, or angry face flashed on a screen for less than one thirtieth of a second, followed immediately by a neutral face. Under these conditions no one reports seeing a happy or angry face, and even if asked to guess, people do no better than chance. However, when they see a happy face, they slightly and briefly move their facial muscles in the direction of a smile; after seeing an angry face, they tense their muscles slightly and briefly in the direction of a frown (Dimberg, Thunberg, & Elmehed, 2000).

In another study students watched a screen where they saw a word flash for one third of a second, followed by a 133-millisecond response window in which they were supposed to press one computer key if they saw a "pleasant" word (e.g., HAPPY or WARM) and a different key if they saw an "unpleasant" word (e.g., SCUM or KILL). They do see the word, but because they are forced to respond so quickly, they find the task difficult and make many mistakes. The additional element of this procedure is that prior to the flashed word, another word was also flashed *very* briefly, under conditions that made it impossible for anyone to identify it consciously. That is, it was subliminal. The full procedure is outlined as follows:

1 Blank screen	**2** Masking stimulus such as KQHYTPDQFPBYL for 150 milliseconds
3 Subliminal stimulus such as FRIEND for 50 ms	**4** Another interfering stimulus for 17 ms
5 Target stimulus such as HAPPY for 333 ms	**6** Response window for 133 ms

Although none of the participants could identify any of the subliminal words (step 3), or even noticed them at all, they responded more accurately to the target stimulus (step 5) if both the subliminal and target stimuli were pleasant, or both were unpleasant, than if one was pleasant and the other unpleasant. In other words a pleasant subliminal word (step 3) primed them to respond better to a pleasant target word (step 5), and an unpleasant subliminal word primed them to respond to an unpleasant target word (Abrams, Klinger, & Greenwald, 2002). Other research has indicated that unpleasant subliminal words have a slightly stronger effect than pleasant ones (Dijksterhuis & Aarts, 2003).

The fact that subliminal perception affects behavior at all is theoretically interesting. It shows that we are not consciously aware of all the information we process or all the events that influence us (Greenwald & Draine, 1997). However, notice that what has been demonstrated is a small, brief facilitation of one response or another, and researchers

have to average results over many participants and many trials to demonstrate any effect at all. The evidence does not indicate any powerful or long-lasting subliminal influences.

Perception and the Recognition of Patterns

How do you know what you're looking at? Take what seems like a very simple example: When you look at something, how does your brain decide how bright it is? We might guess that the answer would be simply that the more intense the light, the brighter the appearance.

However, perceived brightness depends on comparison to the surrounding objects. **Brightness contrast** *is the increase or decrease in an object's apparent brightness because of the effects of objects around it*. Consider Figure 4.36. Compare the pink bars in the middle left section to those in the middle right. The ones on the right probably look darker, but in fact they are the same. Then examine Figure 4.37.

Compare the little square in the center of the upper face of the cube to the one in the center of the front face. The one on the top face looks brown, whereas the one on the front face looks yellow or orange. Amazingly, they are physically the same (Lotto & Purves, 1999). Don't believe it? Cover everything on the page except those two squares and then compare them. Go to http://psychology.wadsworth.com/ kalat_intro7e. Navigate to the student Web site, then to the Online Try it Yourself section, and click on Brightness Contrast.

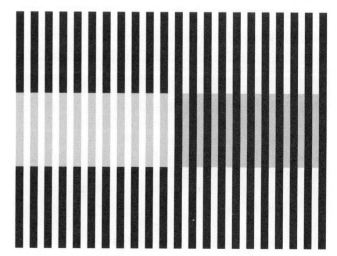

FIGURE 4.36 Because pink bars appear to lie above the dark bars on the left and below them on the right, we see a contrast between pink and dark red on the left, pink and white on the right. Therefore, we see the pink bars on the right as darker, even though they are actually the same shade as the others.

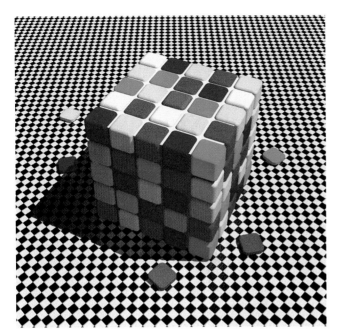 

FIGURE 4.37 The little squares in the center of the top and front faces of the left cube look very different, but they are physically identical. The cube on the right has those same squares, but the context has been removed. Try covering everything on the left cube except the two central squares, or fold the page so you can match the squares of the right cube with those of the left. *(From Lotto & Purves, 1999)*

If two spots on the page reflect light the same way, why don't we see them the same? Apparently, when the brain sees something, it uses its past experience to calculate how that pattern of light probably was generated (Lotto & Purves, 1999). In Figure 4.37 the context clearly indicates that the top face is in bright light, whereas the front face is in a shadow. The square you see in the top face is seen as a dark object, brown in color. The square you see in the front face is rather bright considering that it's in a shadow, and therefore, it looks yellow or orange. Your brain calculates what the object probably *is,* not just what light strikes your retina.

Similarly, in Figure 4.36 we see what appears to be a partly clear white bar covering the center of the left half of the grid, and the pink bars look very light. The corresponding section to the right also has pink bars, but these appear to be under the red bars and on top of a white background; here the pink looks much darker. As you will have guessed by now, the pink bars on the left are the same brightness and color as those on the right.

CONCEPT CHECK ✓

17. Of the three theories of color vision discussed earlier in this chapter (trichromatic, opponent-process, and retinex), which one best accounts for your perception of Figure 4.37? (Check your answer on page 145.)

If just perceiving brightness is that complicated, imagine how hard it is to explain something like face recognition. People are amazingly good at recognizing faces, though inept at explaining how they do it. When you someday attend your 25th high school reunion, you will probably recognize many people despite major changes in their appearance.

Can you match the high school photos in Figure 4.38 with the photos of the same people as they looked 25 years later? Probably not, but other people who had attended that high school succeeded with a respectable 49% accuracy (Bruck, Cavanagh, & Ceci, 1991). Go to http://psychology. wadsworth.com/kalat_intro7e. Navigate to the student Web site, then to the Online Try it Yourself section, and click on Matching High School Photos.

We recognize faces by whole patterns, and certain areas in the temporal lobe of the brain appear to be specialized for facial recognition (Farah, 1992; Kanwisher, 2000). Changing even one feature can sometimes make a face hard to recognize. Perhaps you have had the experience of seeing people who have just changed their hair style and for a moment you cannot recognize them. Can you identify the person in Figure 4.39?

The Feature-Detector Approach

Even explaining how we recognize a simple letter of the alphabet is difficult enough. According to one explanation, we begin recognition by breaking a com-

High-school photos

a   b   c   d   e

25 years later

1   2   3   4   5

6   7   8   9   10

M. Bruck, P. Cavanagh & S.J. Ceci "Fortysomething: Recognizing Faces at One's 25th Reunion." in *Memory & Cognition*, 19:221–228, 1991. Reprinted by permission of M. Bruck.

FIGURE 4.38 High school photos and the same people 25 years later. Can you match the photos in the two sets? (Check your answers by going online for a drag and drop version of this figure or check answer C on page 145.)

plex stimulus into its component parts. For example, when we look at a letter of the alphabet, *specialized neurons in the visual cortex,* called **feature detectors,** *respond to the presence of certain simple features, such as lines and angles.* That is, one neuron might become active only when you are looking at a horizontal line in a particular location. That feature detector would be detecting the feature "horizontal line." Other neurons might detect horizontal lines in other locations, vertical lines, and so forth.

CRITICAL THINKING:
WHAT'S THE EVIDENCE?
Feature Detectors

What evidence do we have for the existence of feature detectors in the brain? We have two kinds of evidence: one from laboratory animals and one from humans.

EXPERIMENT I

Hypothesis Neurons in the visual cortex of cats and monkeys will respond specifically when light strikes the retina in a particular pattern.

Method Two pioneers in the study of the visual cortex, David Hubel and Torsten Wiesel (1981 Nobel Prize winners in physiology and medicine), inserted thin electrodes into cells of the occipital cortex of cats and monkeys and then recorded the activity of those

© San Francisco Exploratorium

FIGURE 4.39 Who is this? We recognize people partly by hair as well as facial features. If you're not sure who it is, check answer D, page 145.

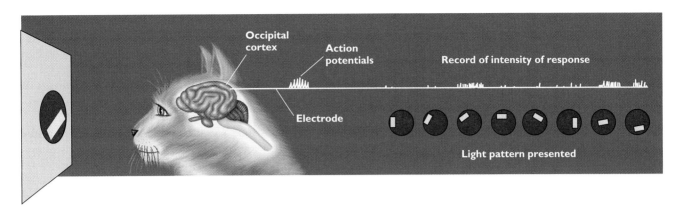

FIGURE 4.40 Hubel and Wiesel implanted electrodes to record the activity of neurons in the occipital cortex of a cat. Then they compared the responses evoked by various patterns of light and darkness on the retina. In most cases a neuron responded vigorously when a portion of the retina saw a bar of light oriented at a particular angle. When the angle of the bar changed, that cell became silent but another cell responded.

cells when various light patterns struck the animals' retinas. At first they used mere points of light; later they tried lines (Figure 4.40).

Results   They found that each cell responds best in the presence of a particular stimulus (Hubel & Wiesel, 1968). Some cells become active only when a vertical bar of light strikes a given portion of the retina. Others become active only when a horizontal bar strikes the retina. In other words such cells appear to act as feature detectors. In later experiments Hubel and Wiesel and other investigators found cells that respond to other kinds of features, such as movement in a particular direction.

Interpretation   Hubel and Wiesel reported feature-detector neurons in both cats and monkeys. If the organization of the occipital cortex is similar in species as distantly related as cats and monkeys, it is likely (though not certain) to be similar in humans.

A second line of evidence is based on the following reasoning: If the human cortex does contain feature-detector cells, one type of cell should become fatigued after we stare for a time at the features that excite it. When we look away, we should see an aftereffect created by the inactivity of that type of cell. (Recall the negative afterimage in color vision, as shown by Figure 4.15.) Try the Online Try It Yourself activity. Go to http://psychology.wadsworth.com/kalat_intro7e. Navigate to the student Web site, then to the Online Try It Yourself section, and click on Motion Aftereffect.

One example of this phenomenon is the **waterfall illusion:** *If you stare at a waterfall for a minute or more and then turn your eyes to some nearby cliffs, the cliffs will appear to flow upward.* By staring at the waterfall, you fatigue the neurons that respond to downward motion. When you look away, those neurons become inactive, but

others that respond to upward motion continue their normal activity. Even though the motionless cliffs stimulate those neurons only weakly, the stimulation is enough to produce an illusion of upward motion. For another example here is a demonstration that you can perform yourself.

EXPERIMENT 2

Hypothesis   After you stare at one set of vertical lines, you will fatigue the feature detectors that respond to lines of a particular width. If you then look at lines slightly wider or narrower than the original ones, they will appear to be even wider or narrower than they really are.

Method   Cover the right half of Figure 4.41 and stare at the little rectangle in the middle of the left half for at least 1 minute. (Staring even longer will increase the effect.) Do not stare at just one point; move your focus around within the rectangle. Then look at the square in the center of the right part of the figure and compare the spacing between the lines of the top and bottom gratings (Blakemore & Sutton, 1969). Try the Online Try it Yourself activity. Go to http://psychology.wadsworth.com/kalat_intro7e. Navigate to the student Web site, then to the Online Try it Yourself section, and click on Afterimage.

Results   What did you perceive in the right half of the figure? People generally report that the top lines look narrower and the bottom lines look wider, even though they are the same.

Interpretation   Staring at the left part of the figure fatigues neurons sensitive to wide lines in the top part of the figure and neurons sensitive to narrow lines in the bottom part. Then, when you look at lines of medium width, the fatigued cells become inactive.

FIGURE 4.41 Use this display to fatigue your feature detectors and create an afterimage. Follow the directions in Experiment 2. *(From Blakemore & Sutton, 1969)*

Therefore, your perception is dominated by cells sensitive to narrower lines in the top part and to wider lines in the bottom part.

To summarize, we have two types of evidence for the existence of visual feature detectors: (a) The brains of other species contain cells with the properties of feature detectors, and (b) after staring at certain patterns, we see aftereffects that can be explained as fatigue of feature-detector cells in the brain.

The research just described was only the start of an enormous amount of activity by laboratories throughout the world; later results have led to revised views of what the earlier results mean. For example, even though certain neurons respond better to a single vertical line

than to points or lines of other orientations, the vertical line may not be the best stimulus for exciting those neurons. Most respond even more strongly to a sine-wave grating of lines:

Thus, the feature that such cells detect is probably more complex than just a line. Furthermore, because

each cell responds to stimuli as different as a line and a group of lines, obviously no one cell provides an unambiguous message about what someone is seeing at any moment.

One important point about scientific advances: A single line of evidence—even excellent, Nobel Prize-winning evidence—seldom provides the final answer to any question. We should always look for multiple ways to test a hypothesis; even if several kinds of evidence support a conclusion, a great many unanswered questions can still remain.

CONCEPT CHECK ☑

18. What is a feature detector, and what evidence supports the idea of feature detectors? (Check your answer on page 145.)

Do Feature Detectors Explain Perception?

The neurons I have just described are active during the early stages of visual processing. Do we simply add up the responses of a great many feature detectors so that the sum of enough feature detectors constitutes your perception of, say, your psychology professor's face?

No, feature detectors cannot provide a complete explanation even for how we perceive letters, much less faces. For example, we perceive the words in Figure 4.42a as CAT and HAT, even though the A in CAT is identical to the H in HAT, and therefore, both of them stimulate the same feature detectors. Likewise, the character in the center of Figure 4.42b can be read as either the letter B or the number 13. The early stages of visual perception use feature detectors, but the perception of a complex pattern requires more.

a   b

FIGURE 4.42 We perceive elements differently depending on their context. In (a) the A in CAT is the same as the H in HAT, but we perceive them differently. In (b) the central character can appear to be a B or the number 13 depending on whether we read horizontally or vertically. *(Part b from Inversions, by S. Kim. W. H. Freeman and Company. Copyright © 1989 by Scott Kim.)*

© Courtesy of McDonnell Douglass

FIGURE 4.43 According to Gestalt psychology, the whole is different from the sum of its parts. Here we perceive an assembly of several hundred people as an airplane.

Gestalt Psychology

Figure 4.43, which we see as the overall shape of an airplane, is a photo of several hundred people. The plane is the overall pattern, not the sum of the parts. Recall also Figure 4.32 from earlier in this chapter: The photograph is composed of dots, but we perceive a face, not just dots.

Such observations derive from **Gestalt psychology**, a field that focuses on our ability to perceive overall patterns. *Gestalt* (geh-SHTALT) is a German word translated as "overall pattern or configuration." The founders of Gestalt psychology rejected the idea that a perception can be broken down into its component parts. A melody broken up into individual notes is no longer a melody. Their slogan was, "The whole is different from the sum of its parts." According to Gestalt psychologists, visual perception is an active creation, not just the adding up of lines, dots, or other pieces. We considered an example of this principle in Figure 4.42. Here are some further examples.

In Figure 4.44 you may see animals or you may see meaningless black and white patches. You might see only patches for a while, and then one or both animals suddenly emerge. (If you give up, check answer E on page 145.) To perceive the animals, you must separate **figure and ground**—that is, you must distinguish the *object from the background*. Ordinarily, you make that distinction almost instantly; you become aware of the process only when it is difficult (as it is here).

Figure 4.45 contains five **reversible figures**, *stimuli that can be perceived in more than one way.* In effect we test hypotheses: "Is this the front of the object or is that the front? Is the object facing left or right? Is this section the foreground or the background?" In Figure 4.45 part a is called the *Necker cube,* after the psychologist who first called

a

b

FIGURE 4.44 Do you see an animal in each picture? If not, check answer E on page 145. *(Part b from Dallenbach, 1951)*

attention to it. Which is the front face of the cube? If you look long enough, you will see it two ways. You can see part b either as a vase or as two profiles.

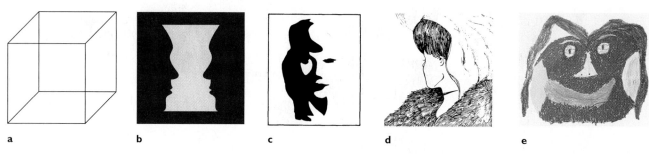

FIGURE 4.45 Reversible figures: (a) The Necker cube. Which is the front face? (b) Faces or a vase. (c) A sax player or a woman's face ("Sara Nader"). (d) An old woman or a young woman. (e) A face or what? (*Part c from Shepard, 1990; part d from Boring, 1930*)

In part c, with a little imagination, you might see a woman's face or a man blowing a horn. (If you need help, check answer F on page 145.) Part d shows both an old woman and a young woman. Almost everyone sees one or the other immediately, but many people lock into one perception so tightly that they cannot see the other one. Part e was drawn by an 8-year-old girl who intended it as the picture of a face. Can you find another possibility? (If you have trouble with parts d or e, check answers G and H on page 145.) Overall, the point of the reversible figures is that we perceive by imposing order on an array, not just by adding up lines and points.

CONCEPT CHECK ☑

19. In what way does the phenomenon of reversible figures conflict with the idea that feature detectors explain vision? (Check your answer on page 145.)

The Gestalt psychologists described several principles of how we organize perceptions into meaningful wholes, as illustrated in Figure 4.46. **Proximity** is the *tendency to perceive objects that are close together as belonging to a group.* The objects in part a form two groups because of their proximity. The *tendency to perceive objects that resemble each other as forming a group* is called **similarity.** The objects in part b group into Xs and Os because of similarity. When lines are interrupted, as in part c, we may perceive **continuation,** *a filling in of the gaps.* You probably perceive this illustration as a rectangle covering the center of one very elongated hot dog.

When a familiar figure is interrupted, as in part d, we perceive a **closure** of the figure; that is, *we imagine the rest of the figure.* The figure we imagine completes what we already see in a way that is simple, symmetrical, or consistent with our past experience (Shimaya, 1997). For example, you probably see the following as an orange rectangle overlapping

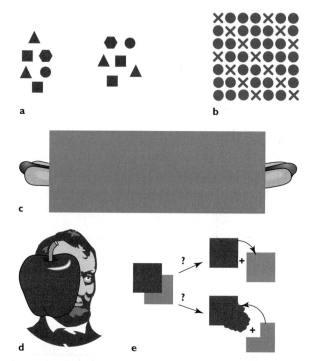

FIGURE 4.46 Gestalt principles of (a) proximity, (b) similarity, (c) continuation, (d) closure, and (e) good figure.

a blue diamond, although you don't really know what, if anything, is behind the rectangle:

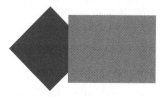

Of course, the principle of closure is similar to that of continuation. With a complicated pattern, however, closure takes into account more than a continuation of the lines. For example, in Figure 4.46c you fill in the gaps to perceive one long hot dog. With some additional context, you would probably perceive the same pattern as two shorter hot dogs:

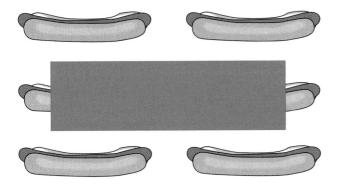

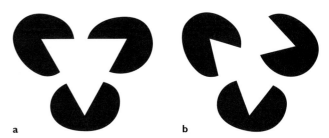

FIGURE 4.47 In (a) we see a triangle overlapping three irregular ovals. We see it because triangles are "good figures" and symmetrical. If we tilt the ovals, as in (b), they appear as irregular objects, not as objects with something on top of them. *(From "Contour Completion and Relative Depth: Petter's Rule and Support Ratio," by M. Singh, D. D. Hoffman and M. K. Albert, Psychological Science, 1999, 10, 423-428. Copyright © 1999 Blackwell Publishers Ltd. Reprinted by permission.)*

Yet another Gestalt principle is **common fate:** *We perceive objects as being part of the same group if they change or move in similar ways at the same time.* Suppose you see an array of miscellaneous objects differing in shape, size, and color. If some of them move in the same direction and speed, we see them as a related group. Also if some of them grow brighter or darker together, again we see them as related (Sekuler & Bennett, 2001).

In everyday life the principle of common fate is a useful tool. Imagine you see a snake's head sticking out of one hole in the ground and a tail sticking out of another. When the head starts moving forward, if the tail also moves down into the ground, you perceive it as all one snake. If the head moves and the tail doesn't, you see that you have two snakes to deal with.

Finally, when possible, we tend to perceive a **good figure**—*a simple, familiar, symmetrical figure.* Many important, familiar objects in the world are geometrically simple or close to it: The sun and moon are round, tree trunks meet the ground at almost a right angle, faces and animals are nearly symmetrical, and so forth. When we look at a complex pattern, we tend to focus on regular patterns. If we can see something as a circle, square, or straight line, we do. In Figure 4.46e the part on the left could represent a red square overlapping a green one or a green backward L overlapping a red object of irregular shape. We are powerfully drawn to the first interpretation because it includes "good," regular, symmetrical objects.

In Figure 4.47a we perceive a white triangle overlapping three ovals (Singh, Hoffman, & Albert, 1999). That perception is so convincing that you may have to look carefully to persuade yourself that there is no line establishing a border for the triangle. However, if we tilt the black objects slightly, as in Figure 4.47b, the illusion of something lying on top of them disappears. We "see" the overlapping object only if it is a symmetrical, good figure.

Similarities Between Vision and Hearing

The perceptual organization principles of Gestalt psychology apply to hearing as well as to vision. There are reversible figures in sound, just as there are in vision. For instance, you can hear a clock going "tick, tock, tick, tock" or "tock, tick, tock, tick." You can hear your windshield wipers going "dunga, dunga" or "gadung, gadung."

The Gestalt principles of continuation and closure work best when we see something that has interrupted something else. For example, consider Figure 4.48. In parts c and d, the context suggest objects partly blocking our view of a three-dimensional cube. In parts

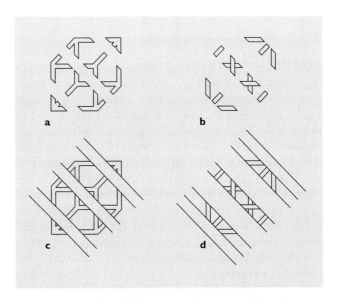

FIGURE 4.48 (a) and (b) appear to be arrays of flat objects. Introducing a context of overlapping lines causes a cube to emerge in (c) and (d). *(From Organization in Vision: Essays on Gestalt Perception, by Gaetano Kanizsa, pp. 7-9. Copyright © 1979 by Gaetano Kanizsa. Reproduced with permission of Greenwood Publishing Group, Westport, CT.)*

a and b, we are much less likely to see a cube, as nothing suggests an object occluding our view. Similarly, in Figure 4.49a we see a series of meaningless patches. In Figure 4.49b the addition of some black glop helps us see these patches as the word *psychology* (Bregman, 1981). We get continuation or closure

FIGURE 4.49 Why is the word "psychology" easier to read in (b) than in (a)? *(After Bregman, 1981)*

mainly when we see that something has blocked the presumed object in the background.

The same is true in hearing. If a speech or song is broken up by periods of silence, we do not fill in the gaps and we find the utterance hard to understand. However, if the same gaps are filled by noise, we "hear" what probably occurred during those gaps; in other words we apply continuation and closure (C. T. Miller, Dibble, & Hauser, 2001; Warren, 1970).

Feature Detectors and Gestalt Psychology

The Gestalt approach to perception does not conflict with the feature-detector approach as much as it might seem. The feature-detector approach describes the first stages of perception—how the brain takes individual points of light and connects them into lines and then into more complex features. According to the feature-detector approach, the brain says, "I see these points here, here, and here, so there must be a line. I see a line here and another line connecting with it here, so there must be a letter L." The Gestalt approach describes how we combine visual input with our knowledge and expectations. According to the Gestalt interpretation, the brain says, "I see what looks like a circle, so the missing piece must be part of a circle too."

Which view is correct? Both, of course. Our perception must assemble the individual points of light or bits of sound, but once it forms a tentative interpretation of the pattern, it uses that interpretation to organize or reorganize the information.

Perception of Movement and Depth

As an automobile drives away from us, its image on the retina grows smaller, yet we perceive it as moving, not as shrinking. That perception illustrates **visual constancy**—our *tendency to perceive objects as keeping their shape, size, and color, even though what actually strikes our retina changes from time to time.* Figure 4.50 shows examples of two visual constancies: shape constancy and size constancy. Constancies depend on our familiarity with objects and on our ability to estimate distances and angles of view. For example, we know that a door is still rectangular even when we view it from an odd angle. But to recognize that an object keeps its shape and size, we have to perceive movement or changes in distance. How do we do so?

Perception of Movement

Moving objects capture our attention, and for a good reason. A moving object could be a person or animal, something people have made (e.g., a car), something thrown, or something that has fallen. In any case it is more likely to require our immediate attention than something stationary.

The detection of motion raises some interesting issues, including how we distinguish between our own movement and the movement of objects. Try this simple demonstration: Hold an object in front of your eyes and then move it to the right. Now hold the object in front of your eyes and move your eyes to the

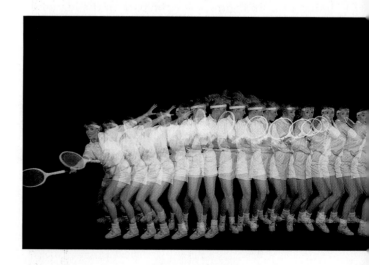

a

b

FIGURE 4.50 (a) Shape constancy: We perceive all three doors as rectangles. (b) Size constancy: We perceive all three hands as equal in size.

left. The image of the object moves across your retina in the same way when you move the object or move your eyes. Yet you perceive the object as moving in one case but not in the other. Why?

The object looks stationary when you move your eyes for two reasons. One is that the vestibular system informs the visual areas of the brain about your head movements. When your brain knows that your eyes have moved to the left, it interprets a change in what you see as being a result of that movement. One man

with a rare kind of brain damage could not connect his eye movements with his perceptions. Whenever he moved his head or eyes, the world appeared to be moving, and frequently, he became dizzy and nauseated (Haarmeier, Thier, Repnow, & Petersen, 1997).

The second reason that the object does not appear to move is that we perceive motion when an object moves *relative to the background* (Gibson, 1968). For example, when you walk forward, stationary objects in your environment move across your retina. If something fails to move across your retina, you perceive it as moving in the same direction as you are.

What do we perceive when an object is stationary and the background is moving? That seldom happens, but when it does, we may *incorrectly perceive the object as moving against a stationary background,* a phenomenon called **induced movement.** For example, when you watch clouds moving slowly across the moon, you might perceive the clouds as stationary and the moon as moving. Induced movement is a form of *apparent movement,* as opposed to *real movement.*

You have already read about the waterfall illusion (page 131), another example of apparent movement. Yet another is **stroboscopic movement,** an *illusion of movement created by a rapid succession of stationary images.* When a scene is flashed on a screen and is followed a split second later by a second scene slightly different from the first, you perceive the objects as having moved smoothly from their location in the first scene to their location in the second scene (Figure 4.51). Motion pictures are actually a series of still photos flashed on the screen.

We also experience an *illusion of movement created when two or more stationary lights separated by a short distance blink on and off at regular intervals.* Your brain creates the sense of motion in what is called the **phi effect.** You may have noticed signs in front of restaurants or motels that use this effect. As the lights blink on and off, an arrow seems to move and invite you in.

Our ability to detect visual movement played an interesting role in the history of astronomy. In 1930 Clyde Tombaugh was searching the skies for a possible undiscovered

FIGURE 4.51 A movie consists of a series of still photographs flickering at 86,400 per hour. You perceive moving objects, however, not a series of stills. Here you see a series of stills spread out in space instead of time.

planet beyond Neptune. He photographed each region of the sky twice, several days apart. A planet, unlike a star, moves from one photo to the next. However, how would he find one dot that moved among all the countless unmoving dots in the sky? He put each pair of photos on a machine that would flip back and forth between one photo and the other. When he came to the correct pair of photos, the machine flipped back and forth between them, and he immediately noticed the one moving dot (Tombaugh, 1980). We now know that little dot as the planet Pluto (Figure 4.52).

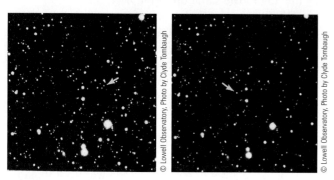

FIGURE 4.52 Clyde Tombaugh photographed each area of the sky twice, several days apart. Then he used a machine to flip back and forth between the two photos of each pair. When he came to one part of the sky, he immediately noticed one dot that moved between the two photos. That dot was the planet Pluto.

Perception of Depth

Although we live in a world of three dimensions, our retinas are in effect two-dimensional surfaces. **Depth perception,** our *perception of distance,* enables us to experience the world in three dimensions. This perception depends on several factors.

One factor is **retinal disparity**—*the difference in the apparent position of an object as seen by the left and right retinas.* Try this: Hold one finger at arm's length. Focus on it with one eye and then with the other. Note that the apparent position of your finger shifts with respect to the background. Now hold your finger closer to your face and repeat the experiment. Notice that the apparent position of your finger shifts even more. The discrepancy between the slightly different views the two eyes see becomes greater as the object comes closer. We use the amount of discrepancy to gauge distance. If you watch a three-dimensional movie while wearing special glasses, the principle is that the lenses enable your two eyes to see different views of the same scene.

A second cue for depth perception is the **convergence** of the eyes—that is, the *degree to which they turn in to focus on a close object* (Figure 4.53). When you focus on a distant object, your eyes are looking in

FIGURE 4.53 Convergence of the eyes as a cue to distance. The more this viewer must converge her eyes toward each other to focus on an object, the closer the object must be.

almost parallel directions. When you focus on something close, your eyes turn in, and you sense the tension of your eye muscles. The more the muscles pull, the closer the object must be.

Retinal disparity and convergence are called **binocular cues** because they *depend on the action of both eyes.* **Monocular cues** enable a person to *judge depth and distance with just one eye* or when both eyes see the same image, as when you look at a picture, such as Figure 4.54. The ability to use these monocular cues to interpret an illustration depends on our experience, including specifically experiences

FIGURE 4.54 We judge depth and distance in a photograph using monocular cues (those that would work even with just one eye): (a) Closer objects occupy more space on the retina (or in the photograph) than do distant objects of the same type. (b) Nearer objects show more detail. (c) Closer objects overlap certain distant objects. (d) Objects in the foreground look sharper than objects do on the horizon.

FIGURE 4.55 Which animal is the hunter attacking? Most readers of this text, using monocular cues to distance, will reply that the hunter is attacking the antelope. However, many African people unfamiliar with drawings thought he was attacking a baby elephant because the hunter is physically closer to the elephant in the drawing. *(From Hudson, 1960)*

with photographs and drawings. For example, in Figure 4.55, does it appear to you that the hunter is aiming his spear at the antelope? When this drawing was shown to African people who had seldom seen drawings, many said the hunter was aiming at a baby elephant (Hudson, 1960). Clearly, people have to learn how to judge depth in drawings.

Let's consider some of the monocular cues we use to perceive depth:

Object size: Other things being equal, a nearby object produces a larger image than a distant one. However, this cue is useful only for objects of known sizes. For example, the jogger in Figure 4.54 produces a larger image than do any of the houses, which we know are actually larger. So we see the jogger as closer. However, the mountains in the background differ in actual as well as apparent size, so we cannot assume the ones that look bigger are closer.

Linear perspective: As parallel lines stretch out toward the horizon, they come closer and closer together. Examine the road in Figure 4.54. At the bottom of the photo (close to the viewer), the edges of the road are far apart; at greater distances they come together.

Detail: We see nearby objects, such as the jogger, in more detail than objects in the distance.

Interposition: A nearby object interrupts our view of a more distant object. For example, the closest telephone pole (on the right) interrupts our view of the closest tree, so we see that the telephone pole is closer than the tree.

Texture gradient: Notice the distance between one telephone pole and the next. At greater distances the poles come closer and closer together. The "packed together" appearance of objects gives us another cue to their approximate distance.

Shadows: Shadows help us gauge sizes as well as relative locations of objects.

Accommodation: The lens of the eye *accommodates*—that is, it changes shape—to focus on nearby objects, and your brain detects that change and thereby infers the distance to an object. Accommodation could help tell you how far away the photograph itself is, although it provides no information about the relative distances of objects in the photograph.

Motion parallax: Another monocular cue helps us perceive depth while we are moving, although it does not help with a photograph. When we are walking or riding in a car, close objects seem to pass by swiftly, while distant objects seem to pass by very slowly. *The faster an object passes by, the closer it must be.* This is the principle of **motion parallax.** Television and film crews use this principle. If the camera moves very slowly, you see closer objects move more than distant ones and get a good sense of depth.

© Steve McCurry/Magnum Photos

▌ If you were a passenger on this train, the ground beside the tracks would appear to pass by more quickly than the more distant elements in the landscape. In this photo's version of motion parallax, the ground is blurred and more distant objects are crisp.

20. Which monocular cues to depth are available in Figure 4.55?
21. With three-dimensional photography, cameras take two views of the same scene from different locations through lenses with different color filters or with different polarized-light filters. The two views are then superimposed. The viewer looks at the composite view through special glasses so that one eye sees the view taken with one camera and the other eye sees the view taken with the other camera. Which depth cue is at work here? (Check your answers on page 145.)

Optical Illusions

Many people claim to have seen ghosts, flying saucers, the Loch Ness monster, Bigfoot, or people floating in the air. Maybe they are lying, maybe they did see something extraordinary, or maybe they saw something ordinary but misinterpreted it. An **optical illusion** is a *misinterpretation of a visual stimulus*. Figure 4.56 shows a few examples. Also see the Online Try It Yourself called Muller-Lyer Illusion. For more, visit: www.exploratorium.edu/exhibits

Psychologists would like to develop a single explanation for all optical illusions. (Remember the principle of parsimony from Chapter 2.) They can explain many, though not all, optical illusions from the relationship between size perception and depth perception.

The Relationship Between Depth Perception and Size Perception

If you can estimate the size of an object, you can deduce its distance. If you can estimate its distance, you can deduce its size. Figure 4.57 shows that a given image on the retina may represent either a small, close object or a large, distant object.

Watch what happens when you take a single image and change its apparent distance: Stare at Figure 4.15 again to form a negative afterimage. First examine the afterimage while you are looking at the wall across the room. Then look at the afterimage against a sheet of paper. Suddenly, the image becomes smaller. As you move the paper backward and forward, you can make the apparent size change.

In the real world, we usually have many cues for judging the size and distance of objects. However, when you have fewer cues, you can become confused (Figure 4.58). I once saw an airplane overhead and was unsure whether it was a small, remote-controlled toy airplane or a distant, full-size airplane. Airplanes come in many sizes, and the sky has few cues to distance.

A similar issue arises in reported sightings of UFOs. When people see an unfamiliar object in the

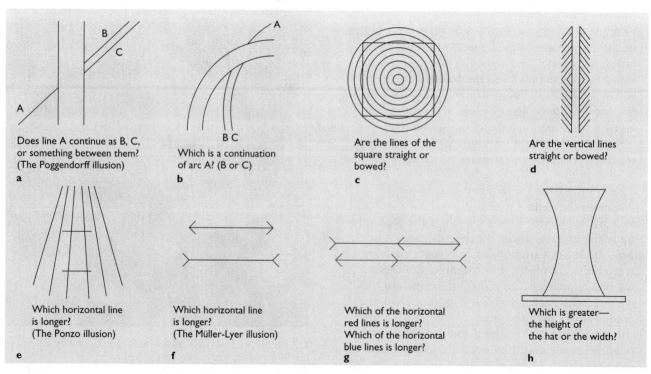

FIGURE 4.56 These geometric figures illustrate optical illusions. Answers (which you are invited to check with ruler and compass): (a) B, (b) B, (c) straight, (d) straight, (e) equal, (f) equal, (g) equal, (h) equal.

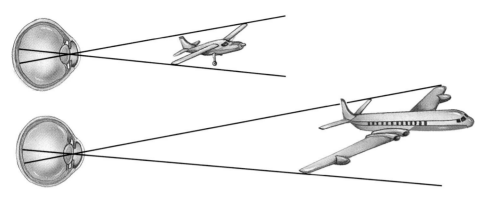

FIGURE 4.57 The trade-off between size and distance: A given image on the retina can indicate either a small, close object or a large, distant object.

sky, they can easily misjudge its distance. If they overestimate its distance, they also will overestimate its size and speed.

What does all this have to do with optical illusions? Whenever we misjudge distance, we misjudge size as well. For example, Figure 4.59a shows people in the Ames room (named for its designer, Adelbert Ames). The room is designed to look like a normal rectangular room, though its true dimensions are as shown in Figure 4.59b.

FIGURE 4.58 Because fish come in many sizes, we can estimate the size of a fish only if we know how far away it is or if we can compare its size to other nearby objects. See what happens when you cover the man and then cover the hand.

The right corner is much closer than the left corner. The two young women are actually the same height. If we eliminated all the background cues, we would correctly perceive the women as being the same size but at different distances. However, the apparently rectangular room provides such powerful (though misleading) cues to distance that the women appear to differ greatly in height.

Even a two-dimensional drawing on a flat surface can offer cues that lead to erroneous depth perception. People who have had much experience with photos and drawings tend to interpret two-dimensional drawings as if they were three-dimensional. Figure 4.60 shows a bewildering two-prong/three-prong device and a round staircase that seems to run uphill all the way clockwise or downhill all the way counterclockwise. Both drawings puzzle us because we try to interpret them as three-dimensional objects.

In Figure 4.61 linear perspective suggests that the right of the picture is farther away than the left. We therefore see the cylinder on the right as being the farthest away. If it is the farthest away and still produces the same size image on the retina as the other two, then it would have to be the largest. In short, by perceiving two-dimensional representations as if they were three-dimensional, we misjudge distance and consequently misjudge size. When we are somehow misled by the cues that ordinarily ensure constancy in size and shape, we experience an optical illusion (Day, 1972).

We can experience an *auditory illusion* by a similar principle: If we misestimate the distance to a sound source, we misestimate the intensity of the sound. That is, if you hear a sound that you think is coming from a distant source, you hear it as loud. (It would have to be for you to hear it so well from a distance.) If you hear the same sound but think it is coming from a source near you, it sounds softer (Kitigawa & Ichihara, 2002; Mershon, Desaulniers, Kiefer, Amerson, & Mills, 1981).

Further Evidence Linking Illusions to Depth Perception

The illusions occur because your brain does its best to judge distances and depths and then constructs an image of what the objects it sees *really are* (as opposed to what pattern of light strikes the retina). Let's belabor this point with two more examples.

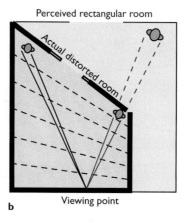
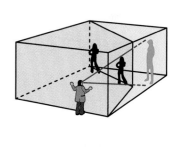

a

b

© The Exploratorium/ S. Schwartzenberg

FIGURE 4.59 The Ames room is a study in deceptive perception, designed to be viewed through a peephole with one eye. **(a)** Both of these people are actually the same height. We are so accustomed to rooms with right angles that we can't imagine how this apparently ordinary room creates this optical illusion. **(b)** This diagram shows the positions of the people in the Ames room and demonstrates how the illusion of distance is created. *(Part b from J. R. Wilson et al., 1964)*

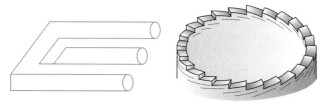

FIGURE 4.60 These two-dimensional drawings puzzle us because we try to interpret them as three-dimensional objects.

The first, shown in Figure 4.62, is the tabletop illusion (Shepard, 1990). Here, almost unbelievably, the vertical dimension of the blue table equals the horizontal dimension of the yellow table, and the horizontal dimension of the blue table equals the vertical dimension of the yellow table. (Take measurements at the center of each table. The shapes

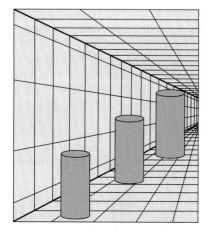

FIGURE 4.61 Many optical illusions depend on misjudging distances. The jar on the right seems larger because the context makes it appear farther away.

of the two tables are not exactly the same.) The blue table appears long and thin compared to the yellow one because we interpret it in depth. In effect your brain constructs what each table would have to really *be* in order to look this way (Purves & Lotto, 2003).

Now consider the Poggendorff illusion, first shown in Figure 4.56a, with a modified version in Figure 4.63. A diagonal line interrupted by something else appears to be not quite straight, not quite continuous. Branka Spehar and Barbara Gillam (2002) have suggested an explanation: When we see a diagonal line, we ordinarily interpret it as a line receding into the distance, such as a path moving away from us toward the horizon. In Figure 4.63a the object that interrupts a diagonal line is consistent with that interpretation and even encourages it. In that case the illusion weakens or disappears; we see each line on the right as a continuation of the correct line on the left. However, in part b the bar provides a context that conflicts with the idea of a receding line, and we have more trouble processing the information.

The Moon Illusion

To most people, the *moon close to the horizon appears about 30% larger than it appears when it is higher in the sky.* This **moon illusion** is so convincing that some people have tried to explain it by referring to the bending of light rays by the atmosphere or another physical phenomenon. The explanation, however, must depend on the observer, not the light rays. If you measure the moon image with navigational or photographic equipment, you will find that it is the same size at the horizon as it is higher in the sky. For example, Figure 4.64 shows

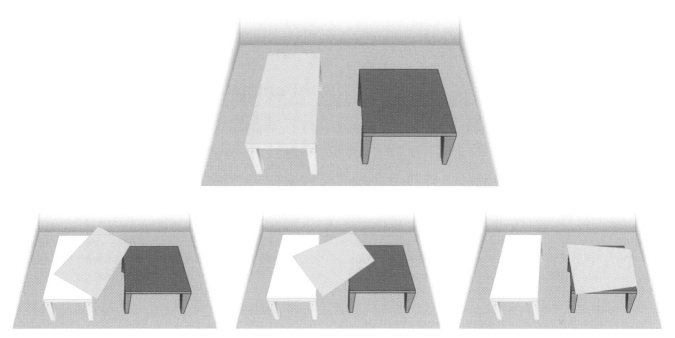

FIGURE 4.62 The tabletop illusion. The blue table is as wide as the yellow table is long, and as long as the yellow table is wide, if you measure in the middle of each table. The parts below show rotation of the blue table to overlap the yellow one.

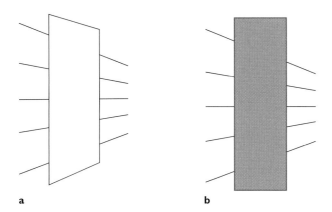

a   b

FIGURE 4.63 Variations of the Poggendorff illusion. If the interrupting bar encourages the perception of a line receding into the distance, we see the lines as continuous and straight. However, if the bar suggests the line has not receded, the lines appear distorted. *(From Spehar & Gillam, 2002)*

the moon at two positions in the sky; you can measure the two images to demonstrate that they are really the same size. (The atmosphere's bending of light rays makes the moon look orange near the horizon, but it does not increase the size of the image.) However, photographs do not capture the full strength of the moon illusion as we see it in real life. In Figure 4.64 (or any similar pair of photos), the moon looks almost the same at each position; in the actual night sky, though, the moon looks enormous at the horizon.

One explanation is that the vast terrain between the viewer and the horizon provides a basis for size comparison. When you see the moon at the horizon, you can compare it to other objects you see at the horizon, which look tiny. By contrast the moon looks

FIGURE 4.64 Ordinarily, the moon looks much larger at the horizon than it does overhead. In photographs this illusion disappears almost completely, but the photographs do serve to demonstrate that the physical image of the moon is the same in both cases. The moon illusion requires a psychological explanation, not a physical one.

© Mark Antman/The Image Works

large. When you see the moon high in the sky, however, it is surrounded only by the vast, featureless sky, so in contrast it appears smaller (Baird, 1982; Restle, 1970).

A second explanation is that the terrain between the viewer and the horizon gives an impression of great distance. When the moon is high in the sky, we have no basis to judge distance, and perhaps we unconsciously see the overhead moon as closer than when it is at the horizon. If we see the "horizon moon" as more distant, we will perceive it as larger (Kaufman & Rock, 1989; Rock & Kaufman, 1962). This explanation is appealing because it relates the moon illusion to our misperceptions of distance, a factor already accepted as important for many other illusions.

Many psychologists are not satisfied with this explanation, however, primarily because they are not convinced that the horizon moon looks farther away than the overhead moon. If we ask people which looks farther away, many say they are not sure. If we insist on an answer, most say the horizon moon looks *closer,* contradicting the theory. Some psychologists reply that the situation is complicated: We unconsciously perceive the horizon as farther away; consequently, we perceive the horizon moon as very large; then, because of the perceived large size of the horizon moon, we secondarily and consciously say it looks closer, although we continue to unconsciously perceive it as farther (Rock & Kaufman, 1962).

One major message arises from work on optical illusions and indeed from all the research on visual perception: What we perceive is not the same as what is "out there." Our visual system does an amazing job of providing us with useful information about the world around us, but under unusual circumstances we can be very wrong about what we think we see.

IN CLOSING

Making Sense Out of Sensory Information

You have probably heard the expression, "Seeing is believing." The saying is true in many ways, including that what you believe influences what you see. Perception is not just a matter of adding up all the events striking the retina; we look for what we expect to see, we impose order on haphazard patterns, we see three dimensions in two-dimensional drawings, and we see optical illusions. The brain does not simply compute what light is striking the retina, but what objects probably exist "out there" and what they are doing.

Summary

- *Perception of minimal stimuli.* There is no sharp dividing line between sensory stimuli that can be perceived and sensory stimuli that cannot be perceived. (page 125)
- *Signal detection.* To determine how accurately someone can detect a signal or how accurately a test diagnoses a condition, we need to consider not only the ratio of hits to misses when the stimulus is present but also the ratio of false alarms to correct rejections when the stimulus is absent. (page 126)
- *Subliminal perception.* Under some circumstances a weak stimulus that we do not consciously identify can influence our behavior, at least weakly or briefly. However, the evidence does not support claims of powerful effects. (page 127)
- *Face recognition.* People are amazingly good at recognizing faces. (page 129)
- *Detection of simple visual features.* In the first stages of the process of perception, feature-detector cells identify lines, points, and simple movement. Visual afterimages can be interpreted in terms of fatiguing certain feature detectors. (page 129)
- *Perception of organized wholes.* According to Gestalt psychologists, we perceive an organized whole by identifying similarities and continuous patterns across a large area of the visual field. (page 133)
- *Visual constancies.* We ordinarily perceive the shape, size, and color of objects as constant, even though the pattern of light striking the retina varies from time to time. (page 136)
- *Motion perception.* We perceive an object as moving if it moves relative to its background. We can generally distinguish between an object that is actually moving and a similar pattern of retinal stimulation that results from our own movement. (page 136)
- *Depth perception.* To perceive depth, we use the retinal discrepancy between the views that our two eyes see. We also learn to use other cues that are just as effective with one eye as with two. (page 138)
- *Optical illusions.* Many, but not all, optical illusions result from interpreting a two-dimensional display as three-dimensional or from other faulty estimates of depth. (page 140)
- *The size-distance relationship.* Our estimate of an object's size depends on our estimate of its distance

from us. If we overestimate its distance, we will also overestimate its size. (page 140)

Answers to Concept Checks

16. We have been told the hit rate, but we cannot evaluate it unless we also know the false alarm rate. That is, how many people without any alcohol or drug problem have this same pattern of brain waves? If that percentage is large, the test is useless. The smaller that percentage is, the better. (page 127)

17. The retinex theory is the only one that accounts for your perception of Figure 4.37. According to the retinex theory, your cortex compares your input in various parts of the retina to synthesize a perception of each part based on the whole context. (page 129)

18. A feature detector is a neuron in the visual system of the brain that responds mostly in the presence of a particular feature, such as a straight horizontal line. One kind of evidence is that recordings from neurons in laboratory animals indicate increased response of different cells to different visual stimuli. Another line of evidence is that people who have stared at one kind of stimulus become temporarily less sensitive to that kind of stimulus, as if the feature detectors for that stimulus have become fatigued. (page 132)

19. Feature detectors cannot fully explain how we see a reversible figure in two or more ways. If vision were simply a matter of stimulating various line detectors and adding up their responses, then a given display would always produce the same perceptual experience. (page 134)

20. Object size and linear perspective are cues that the elephant must be far away. (page 140).

21. Retinal disparity. (page 140)

Answers to Other Questions in the Module

C. a. **7.** b. **1.** c. **5.** d. **9.** e. **4.**

D.

E.

F.

G.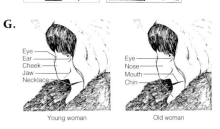

H.

I. Line d is the same length as the one on the right. (Check it with a ruler.)

Key Terms and Activities

Key Terms

absolute sensory threshold: the intensity at which a given individual can detect a sensory stimulus 50% of the time; a low threshold indicates the ability to detect faint stimuli (page 125)

accommodation of the lens: an adjustment of the thickness of the lens to focus on objects at different distances (page 98)

binocular cues: visual cues that depend on the action of both eyes (page 138)

binocular rivalry: the alteration between seeing the pattern in the left retina and the pattern in the right retina (page 104)

blind spot: the area where the optic nerve exits the retina (page 102)

brightness contrast: an increase or decrease in an object's apparent brightness because of the effects of objects around it (page 128)

capsaicin: a chemical that stimulates the release of substance P (page 119)

cataract: a disorder in which the lens of the eye becomes cloudy (page 99)

closure: in Gestalt psychology the tendency to imagine the rest of an incomplete, familiar figure (page 134)

cochlea: the snail-shaped, fluid-filled structure that contains the receptors for hearing (page 112)

color constancy: the tendency of an object to appear nearly the same color under a variety of lighting conditions (page 107)

common fate: the tendency to perceive objects as being part of the same group if they change or move in similar ways at the same time (page 135)

conduction deafness: a hearing loss that results when the bones connected to the eardrum fail to transmit sound waves properly to the cochlea (page 113)

cone: the type of visual receptor that is adapted for color vision, daytime vision, and detailed vision (page 99)

continuation: in Gestalt psychology the tendency to fill in the gaps in an interrupted line (page 134)

convergence: the degree to which the eyes turn in to focus on a close object (page 138)

cornea: a rigid, transparent structure on the surface of the eyeball (page 98)

cutaneous senses: the skin senses, including pressure on the skin, warmth, cold, pain, vibration, movement across the skin, and stretch of the skin (page 116)

dark adaptation: a gradual improvement in the ability to see in dim light (page 101)

depth perception: the perception of distance, which enables us to experience the world in three dimensions (page 138)

electromagnetic spectrum: the continuum of all the frequencies of radiated energy (page 97)

endorphin: any of the neurotransmitters that decrease the perception of pain (page 118)

feature detector: a neuron in the visual system of the brain that responds to the presence of a certain simple feature, such as a horizontal line (page 130)

figure and ground: an object and its background (page 133)

fovea: the central part of the retina that has a greater density of receptors, especially cones, than any other part of the retina (page 98)

frequency principle: the identification of pitch by the frequency of action potentials in neurons along the basilar membrane of the cochlea, synchronized with the frequency of sound waves (page 114)

ganglion cells: neurons in the eye that receive input from bipolar cells, which in turn receive their input from the visual receptors (page 102)

gate theory: the proposal that pain messages must pass through a gate, probably in the spinal cord, that can block these messages (page 118)

Gestalt psychology: an approach to psychology that seeks to explain how we perceive overall patterns (page 133)

glaucoma: a condition characterized by increased pressure within the eyeball, resulting in damage to the optic nerve and therefore a loss of vision (page 99)

good figure: in Gestalt psychology the tendency to perceive simple, symmetrical figures (page 135)

hertz (Hz): a unit of frequency representing one cycle (vibration) per second (page 112)

hyperopia: farsightedness; the inability to focus on nearby objects (page 99)

induced movement: a perception that an object is moving and the background is stationary when in fact the object is stationary and the background is moving (page 137)

iris: the colored structure on the surface of the eye, surrounding the pupil (page 98)

lens: a flexible structure that can vary its thickness to enable the eye to focus on objects at different distances (page 98)

loudness: a perception that depends on the amplitude of a sound wave (page 112)

monocular cues: visual cues that are just as effective with one eye as with both (page 138)

moon illusion: the apparent difference between the size of the moon at the horizon and its size when viewed higher in the sky (page 142)

motion parallax: the apparently swift motion of objects close to a moving observer and the apparently slow motion of objects farther away (page 139)

myopia: nearsightedness; the inability to focus on distant objects (page 99)

negative afterimage: a color that a person sees after staring at its opposite color for a while (page 106)

nerve deafness: a hearing loss that results from damage to the cochlea, the hair cells, or the auditory nerve (page 113)

olfaction: the sense of smell; the detection of chemicals in contact with the membranes inside the nose (page 122)

opponent-process theory: the theory that we perceive color in terms of a system of paired opposites: red versus green, yellow versus blue, and white versus black (page 105)

optic nerve: a set of axons that extend from the ganglion cells of the eye to the thalamus and several other areas of the brain (page 102)

optical illusion: a misinterpretation of a visual stimulus as being larger or smaller, or straighter or more curved, than it really is (page 140)

perception: the interpretation of sensory information (page 96)

phantom limb: a continuing sensation of an amputated body part (page 119)

pheromone: an odorous chemical, released by an animal, that changes how other members of the species respond to that animal socially (page 123)

phi effect: the illusion of movement created when two or more stationary lights separated by a short distance flash on and off at regular intervals (page 137)

pitch: a perception closely related to the frequency of sound waves (page 112)

place principle: the identification of pitch by determining which auditory neurons, coming from which part of the basilar membrane, are most active (page 114)

presbyopia: a decreased flexibility of the lens and therefore the inability to focus on nearby objects (page 99)

proximity: in Gestalt psychology the tendency to perceive objects that are close together as belonging to a group (page 134)

pupil: the adjustable opening in the eye through which light enters (page 98)

receptor: a specialized cell that converts environmental energies into signals for the nervous system (page 97)

retina: a layer of visual receptors covering the back surface of the eyeball (page 98)

retinal disparity: the difference in the apparent position of an object as seen by the left and right retinas (page 138)

retinex theory: the theory that color perception results from the cerebral cortex's comparison of various retinal patterns (page 107)

reversible figure: a stimulus that you can perceive in more than one way (page 133)

rod: the type of visual receptor that is adapted for vision in dim light (page 99)

sensation: the conversion of energy from the environment into a pattern of response by the nervous system (page 96)

signal-detection theory: the study of people's tendencies to make hits, correct rejections, misses, and false alarms (page 126)

similarity: in Gestalt psychology the tendency to perceive objects that resemble each other as belonging to a group (page 134)

sound waves: vibrations of the air or of another medium (page 112)

stimulus: energy in the environment that affects what we do (page 97)

stroboscopic movement: an illusion of movement created by a rapid succession of stationary images (page 137)

subliminal perception: the ability of a stimulus to influence our behavior even when it is presented so faintly or briefly or along with such strong distracters that we do not perceive it consciously (page 127)

substance P: a neurotransmitter responsible for much of the transmission of pain information in the nervous system (page 118)

taste: the sensory system that responds to chemicals on the tongue (page 121)

taste bud: the site of the taste receptors, located in one of the folds on the surface of the tongue (page 121)

trichromatic theory (or Young-Helmholtz theory): the theory that color vision depends on the relative rate of response of three types of cones (page 105)

vestibular sense: a specialized sense that detects the direction of tilt and amount of acceleration of the head and the position of the head with respect to gravity (page 115)

visual constancy: the tendency to perceive objects as unchanging in shape, size, and color, despite variations in what actually reaches the retina (page 136)

volley principle: the identification of pitch by groups of hair cells responding to each vibration by producing an action potential (page 114)

waterfall illusion: a phenomenon in which prolonged staring at a waterfall and then looking at nearby cliffs causes those cliffs to appear to flow upward (page 131)

Suggestions for Further Reading

Purves, D., & Lotto, R. B. (2003). *Why we see what we do.* Sunderland, MA: Sinauer Associates. Insightful and creative account of human perception.

Ramachandran, V. S., & Blakeslee, S. (1998). *Phantoms in the brain.* New York: Morrow. Fascinating explanation of phantom limbs and related phenomena.

Warren, R. M. (1999). *Auditory perception: A new analysis and synthesis.* Cambridge, England: Cambridge University Press. Superb treatment of hearing, with a CD-ROM disk that includes demonstrations of auditory phenomena.

 ## Book Companion Web Site

Need help studying? Go to

http://psychology.wadsworth.com/kalat_intro7e/

for a virtual study center. You'll find a personalized Self-Study Assessment that will provide you with a study plan based on your answers to a pretest. Also study using flashcards, quizzes, interactive art, and an online glossary.

Check out interactive **Try It Yourself** exercises on the companion site! For example, the Motion Aftereffect, Brightness Contrast, Blind Spot, and Matching High School Photos exercises are pulled directly from sections in this chapter.

Online Try It Yourself

Your companion site also has direct links to the following Web sites. These links are checked often for changes, dead links, and new additions.

More Illusions

www.exploratorium.edu/exhibits

Here are wonderful illusions, both visual and auditory. Enjoy.

Seeing, Hearing, and Smelling

www.hhmi.org/senses/

Elaborate psychological and medical information, courtesy of the Howard Hughes Medical Institute.

Smells and Flavors

http://www.leffingwell.com/

Rich source of information about olfaction, ranging from the chemistry of perfumes to the olfactory receptors and how our brains handle olfaction.

Reverse Speech Home Page

www.reversespeech.com/

You've heard that particular recordings contain hidden messages that can be heard only if the material is played backward. One person had the time and patience to research such claims. You will need the RealAudio plug-in, available for free at

www.realaudio.com/products/player/index.html.

Can you provide a better explanation for the reversed messages?

Try It Yourself CD-ROM
with Critical Thinking Video Exercises

Use your CD to access **videos** related to activities designed to help you think critically about the important topics discussed. For example, the video about visual impairment relates to what you've learned in this chapter. You'll also find an easy portal link to the book companion site where you can access your personalized **Self-Study Assessments** and interactive **Try It Yourself** exercises.

PsychNow! 2.0

PsychNow! is a fun interactive CD designed to help you with the difficult concepts in psychology. Check out the Accessing Psychology section for the following topics that relate to this chapter:

Vision and Hearing: roller coaster video, lesson about the path from stimulus to brain, and a transduction path quiz.

Chemical and Somesthetic Senses: muscular directionality exercise, kinesthesia, balance, smell, taste, and touch lesson as well as a chemical and somesthetic sense video.

Perception: interactive 3-D "Magic Eye" image, vision cues lesson, interactive Escher drawing to show perception.

InteractNOW! Online Collaborative Lab: Perception and Motion Aftereffects

ExperimentNOW! Research Experiments: Perception—Apparent motion, attention blink, signal detection, visual search, and the Stroop effect

Learning

Learning is a change in behavior, or the potential for future behavior, as a result of experience.[1] Suppose we set up a simple experiment on animal learning. We put a monkey midway between a green wall and a red wall. If it approaches the green wall, it receives a few raisins; if it approaches the red wall, it gets nothing. After a few trials, the monkey consistently approaches the green wall. After it has made the correct choice, say, 12 times in a row, we are satisfied that the monkey has learned something.

Now imagine the same experiment with an alligator. We use the same procedure, but the alligator strains our patience, sitting motionless for hours at a time. When it finally does move, it is as likely to approach one wall as the other. Eventually, *we* learn something: not to go into the alligator-training business! But we see little evidence that the alligator has learned anything.

Should we conclude that alligators are slow learners? Not necessarily. Maybe they are not hungry. Maybe they can't see the difference between red and green. Maybe they learn but also forget quickly, so they cannot put together a long streak of consecutive correct approaches. Maybe they learn poorly in this situation but well in some other.

Similar problems arise when we evaluate human learning. If little Joey is having academic troubles, should we consider him a "slow learner"? Not necessarily. Like the alligator, perhaps he is not motivated, or he may have visual or hearing problems. Maybe he is distracted by his emotional troubles at home. (That's a possibility we probably wouldn't consider with the alligator.)

Psychologists have devoted an enormous amount of research to learning. One key finding is how important it is to consider all the influences that might interfere with learned performance. Psychologists have developed and polished many of their research skills by conducting experiments on learning.

■ Understanding how an animal learns or why it fails to learn requires careful testing of all the factors that can influence behavior.

This chapter is about the procedures that produce changes in behavior—why you lick your lips at the sight of tasty food, why you turn away from a food that once made you sick, why you get nervous if a police car starts to follow you, and why you shudder at the sight of a ferocious person charging toward you with a chain saw. This chapter is also about why you persevere longer at some tasks than others. In Chapter 7 we proceed to the topic of memory. Obviously, any change in behavior implies some sort of memory, and any memory implies previous learning. Still, the study of learning is based on a different research tradition from that of memory.

[1] A better definition of learning would limit the term to just certain kinds of experience. For example, spending an hour on a sunny beach without sunglasses will weaken your sensitivity to faint light and therefore change certain aspects of your behavior temporarily, but we would not call that change learning. However, a "better" definition of learning would be neither brief nor simple.

Behaviorism

How and why did the behaviorist viewpoint arise?

What is its enduring message?

A monitor lizard eats smaller lizards. When it sees one of the small lizards, instead of chasing it at once, the monitor heads for the nearest pile of rocks, which is the only place the smaller lizard might be able to escape. The small lizard, now with no place to go, is easy prey (Sweet & Pianka, 2003). Should we describe this as intelligent, insightful behavior by the monitor lizard? Or does it reflect simple trial-and-error learning, where the monitor has simply learned to obtain food by going first to the rocks?

A case like this can ultimately be decided by extensive research—if anyone cares to spend the necessary effort—but psychologists differ in their initial inclinations as to what is a likely explanation. The study of learning, especially animal learning, has been dominated by **behaviorists**, *psychologists who insist that psychologists should study only observable, measurable behaviors, not mental processes.* Their inclination has been overwhelmingly to assume the simplest possible explanation for behavior and to resist interpretation in terms of understanding or insight. At least, they insist, we should exhaust attempts at simple explanations before we adopt more complex ones. You will recognize this idea as the principle of parsimony from Chapter 2.

The term *behaviorist* applies to theorists and researchers with quite a range of views (O'Donohue & Kitchener, 1999). Two major categories are *methodological behaviorists* and *radical behaviorists.* **Methodological behaviorists** *study only the events that they can measure and observe*—in other words the environment and the individual's actions—*but they sometimes use those observations to make inferences about internal events* (Day & Moore, 1995). For example, depriving an animal of food, presenting it with very appealing food, or making it exercise will increase the probability that the animal will eat food, work for food, and so forth. From such observations a psychologist can infer an **intervening variable**, *something that we cannot directly observe but that links a variety of procedures to a variety of possible responses.* In this case the intervening variable is *hunger:*

Similarly, one could use other kinds of observations to infer different intervening variables, such as

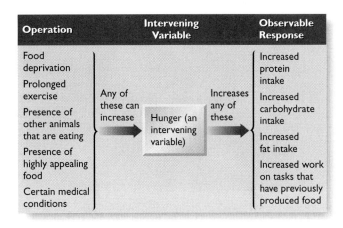

thirst, sex drive, anger, fear, and so forth. Note that any of these intervening variables is inferred from behavior, never observed directly. The important point is that a methodological behaviorist will use such terms only after anchoring them firmly to observable procedures and responses—that is, after giving them a clear operational definition (as discussed in Chapter 2). Many psychological researchers are methodological behaviorists, even if they do not use that term.

CRITICAL THINKING: A STEP FURTHER
Intervening Variables

Choose an intervening variable, such as fear or anger, and describe what measurements you could use to infer it. In the process do you in fact establish an operational definition?

Radical behaviorists do not deny that private events such as hunger or fear exist, and they agree it is possible to study the circumstances that cause people to *say,* "I am hungry," "I am frightened," and so forth. The distinguishing feature of radical behaviorists is that they *deny that hunger, fear, or any other internal, private event causes behavior* (Moore, 1995). For example, they would say if food deprivation leads to hunger and hunger leads to eating, why not just say that food deprivation leads to eating? What do we gain by introducing the word *hunger?* According to radical behaviorists, any internal state is

▌ Behaviorists agree that all psychological investigations should be based on behavioral observations. A methodological behaviorist might use observations of, say, facial expressions to make inferences about such processes as "sadness." A radical behaviorist, however, would study the facial expressions themselves, but not as a means of inferring something else.

protest movement against structuralism. Behaviorists insisted that it is useless to ask people to report their own private experiences. For example, if someone says, "My idea of roundness is stronger than my idea of color," we have no way to check the accuracy of the report. We are not even certain what it means. If psychology is to be a scientific enterprise, behaviorists insisted, it must deal with only observable, measurable events—that is, behavior and its relation to the environment.

To avoid any mention of the mind, thoughts, or knowledge, some behaviorists went to the opposite extreme. One of the forerunners of behaviorism, Jacques Loeb (1918/1973), argued that much of animal behavior, and perhaps human behavior as well, could be described in terms of simple responses to simple stimuli—for example, approaching light, turning away from strong smells, clinging to hard surfaces, walking toward or away from moisture, and so forth (see Figure 6.1). Complex behavior, he surmised, is just the result of adding together many changes of speed and direction elicited by various stimuli. Loeb's view of behavior was an example of **stimulus–response psychology,** *the attempt to explain behavior in terms of how each stimulus triggers a response.*

caused by an event in the environment (or by the individual's genetics), and therefore, the ultimate cause of any behavior lies in the observable events that led up to the behavior, not the internal states.

According to this point of view, discussions of mental events are just sloppy language. For example, as B. F. Skinner (1990) argued, when you say, "I *intend* to . . . ," what you really mean is "I am about to . . . " or "In situations like this, I usually . . . " or "This behavior is in the preliminary stages of happening . . . ." That is, any statement about mental experiences can be converted into a description of behavior.

CONCEPT CHECK ☑

1. How does a radical behaviorist differ from a methodological behaviorist? (Check your answer on page 194.)

The Rise of Behaviorism

Behaviorism should be understood within the historical context in which it arose. During the early 1900s, one highly influential group within psychology, the *structuralists* (see Chapter 1), studied people's thoughts, ideas, and sensations by asking people to describe them. The early behaviorists began as a

FIGURE 6.1 Jacques Loeb, an early student of animal behavior, argued that much or all of invertebrate behavior could be described as responses to simple stimuli, such as approaching light, turning away from light, or moving opposite to the direction of gravity.

Although the term *stimulus–response psychology* was appropriate for Loeb, it is a misleading description of today's behaviorists. Behaviorists believe that behavior is a product of not only the current stimuli but also the individual's history of stimuli and responses and their outcomes, plus the internal state of the organism, such as wakefulness or sleepiness (Staddon, 1999).

If behaviorists are to deal successfully with complex behaviors, they must be able to explain changes in behavior. The behaviorist movement became the heir to a tradition of animal learning research that had begun for other reasons. Charles Darwin's theory of evolution by natural selection inspired many early psychologists to study animal learning and intelligence (Dewsbury, 2000b). At first they were interested in comparing the intelligence of various species. By about 1930, however, most had lost interest in that topic because it seemed unanswerable. (A species that seems more intelligent on one task can be less intelligent on another.) Nevertheless, the behaviorists carried forth the tradition of experiments on animal learning, although they asked different questions.

If nonhumans learn in more or less the same way as humans do, behaviorists reasoned, then it should be possible to discover the basic laws of learning by studying the behavior of a convenient laboratory animal, such as a pigeon or a rat. This enterprise was ambitious and optimistic; its goal was no less than to determine the basic laws of behavior, analogous to the laws of physics. Most of the rest of this chapter will deal with behaviorists' research about learning.

The Assumptions of Behaviorism

Behaviorists make several assumptions, including determinism, the ineffectiveness of mental explanations, and the power of the environment to select behaviors (Moore, 1995). Let's consider each of these points.

Determinism

Behaviorists assume that we live in a universe of cause and effect; in other words they accept the idea of *determinism* as described in Chapter 1. Given that our behavior is part of the universe, it too must have causes that can be understood through scientific methods. That is, behavior follows laws, and if we determine those laws and learn enough about an individual, we should be able to predict that individual's behavior. (Of course, it is impractical to predict behavior completely, just as it is with the weather.)

Here is one simple example of a behavioral law: An individual deprived of food will increase the rate of any behavior that leads to food. Behaviorists seek more and more detailed laws of behavior, and they test their understanding by trying to predict or control behavior.

▌ Behaviorists emphasize the role of experience in determining our actions—both our current experience and our past experiences in similar situations.

The Ineffectiveness of Mental Explanations

In everyday life we commonly refer to our motivations, emotions, and mental state. However, behaviorists insist that such statements explain nothing:

Q. Why did she yell at that man?
A. She yelled because she was angry.
Q. How do you know she was angry?
A. We know she was angry because she was yelling.

Here the reference to mental states lured us into circular reasoning. Behaviorists, especially radical behaviorists, avoid mental terms as much as possible. B. F. Skinner, the most famous and influential behaviorist, resisted using even apparently harmless words such as *hide* because they imply an intention (L. D. Smith, 1995). Skinner preferred simply to describe what the individuals *did* instead of inferring what they were *trying* to do.

The same insistence on description is central to the British and American legal systems: A witness is asked, "What did you see and hear?" An acceptable answer would be, "The defendant was sweating and trembling, and his voice was wavering." A witness should not say, "The defendant was nervous and worried," because that statement requires an inference that the witness is not entitled to make. (Of course, the jury might draw an inference.)

The Power of the Environment to Mold Behavior

Behaviors produce outcomes. Eating your carrots has one kind of outcome; insulting your roommate has another. The outcome determines how often the behavior will occur in the future. In effect our environment selects successful behaviors, much as evolution selects successful animals.

Behaviorists have sometimes been accused of believing that the environment controls practically all aspects of behavior. The most extreme statement of environmental determinism came from John B. Watson, one of the founders of behaviorism, who said, "Give me a dozen healthy infants, well-formed, and my own specified world to bring them up in and I'll guarantee to take any one at random and train him to become any type of specialist I might select—doctor, lawyer, artist, merchant-chief, and yes, even beggar-man thief—regardless of his talents, penchants, tendencies, abilities, vocations, and race of his ancestors. I am going beyond my facts and I admit it, but so have the advocates of the contrary" (1925, p. 82).

Today, few psychologists would claim that variations in behavior depend entirely on the environment (or that they depend entirely on heredity, for that matter). Although behaviorists do not deny the importance of heredity, they do not generally emphasize it. Their research focuses on how the environment selects one behavior over another, and their explanations of individual differences concentrate on how different people's behaviors emerge from different learning histories.

CONCEPT CHECK ☑

2. Why do behaviorists reject explanations in terms of thoughts? (Check your answer on this page.)

IN CLOSING

Behaviorism as a Theoretical Orientation

Many students quickly dismiss behaviorism because, at least at first glance, it seems so ridiculous: "What do you *mean,* my thoughts and beliefs and emotions don't cause my behavior?!" The behaviorists' reply is, "Exactly right. Your thoughts and other internal states do not cause your behavior because events in your present and past environment caused those thoughts.

The events that caused the thoughts are therefore the real causes of your behavior, and psychologists should spend their time trying to understand the influence of the events, not trying to analyze your thoughts." Don't be too quick to agree or disagree. Just contemplate this: If you believe that your thoughts or other internal states cause behaviors *independently* of your previous experiences, what evidence could you provide to support your claim?

Summary

- *Range of positions among behaviorists.* Behaviorists insist that psychologists should study behaviors and their relation to observable features of the environment. Methodological behaviorists use these observations to draw inferences about internal states. Radical behaviorists insist that internal states are of little scientific use and that they do not control behavior. The causes of the internal states themselves, as well as of the behaviors, lie in the environment. (page 191)
- *The origins of behaviorism.* Behaviorism began in part as a protest against structuralists, who asked people to describe their own mental processes. Behaviorists insisted that the structuralist approach was futile and that psychologists should study observable behaviors. (page 192)
- *Behaviorists' interest in learning.* Before the rise of the behaviorist movement, other psychologists had studied animal intelligence. Behaviorists adapted some of the methods used in previous studies but changed the questions, concentrating on the basic mechanisms of learning. (page 193)
- *Behaviorists' assumptions.* Behaviorists assume that all behaviors have causes (determinism), that mental explanations are unhelpful, and that the environment acts to select effective behaviors and suppress ineffective ones. (page 193)

Answers to Concept Checks

1. All behaviorists insist that conclusions must be based on measurements or observations of behavior. However, a methodological behaviorist will sometimes use behavioral observations to make inferences about motivations or other internal states. A radical behaviorist avoids discussion of internal events as much as possible and insists that internal events are never the cause of behavior. (page 192)
2. We cannot directly observe or measure thoughts or other internal events. We infer them from observed behaviors, and therefore, it is circular to use them as an explanation of behavior. (page 194)

Classical Conditioning

When we learn a relationship between two stimuli, what happens?

Do we start responding to one stimulus as if it were the other?

Or do we learn how to use information from one stimulus to predict something about the other?

You are sitting in your room when your roommate flicks a switch on the stereo. Your experience has been that the stereo is set to a deafening level. You flinch not because of the soft flicking sound of the switch itself but because of the loud noise it predicts.

Many aspects of our behavior consist of learned responses to signals. However, even apparently simple responses to simple stimuli no longer seem as simple as they once did. Psychologists' efforts to discover what takes place during learning have led them to conduct thousands of experiments on both humans and nonhumans.

For certain kinds of learning, such as birdsong learning, the results depend heavily on which species is being studied, but for many other kinds of learning, the similarities among species are more impressive than the differences. Even insects learn in ways that are surprisingly similar to our own (Giurfa, Zhang, Jennett, Menzel, & Srinivasan, 2001). In some ways it is easier to study nonhumans because a researcher can better control what and when they eat and many other variables likely to influence performance.

Pavlov and Classical Conditioning

Aristotle explained falling objects by saying that objects sought the ground, which was their natural resting place. Later explanations of falling objects, first by Newton and then by Einstein, eliminated the "seeking" and explained falling objects in purely mathematical terms.

The behaviorists tried to do the same for learning. If a cat claws at the refrigerator and meows, you might say that it "expects" food or "knows" food is in the refrigerator, but behaviorists would not. Instead, they sought simple mechanical explanations.

Therefore, the mood of the time was ready for the simple theories of Ivan P. Pavlov, a Russian physiologist who had won a Nobel Prize in physiology in 1904 for his research on digestion. As Pavlov continued his research, one day he noticed that a dog would salivate or secrete stomach juices as soon as it saw the lab worker who customarily fed the dogs. Because this secretion undoubtedly depended on the dog's previous experiences, Pavlov called it a "psychological" secretion. Pavlov enlisted the help of other specialists, who then discovered that "teasing" a dog with the sight of food produced salivation that was as predictable and automatic as any reflex. Pavlov adopted the term *conditional reflex,* implying that he only *conditionally* (or tentatively) accepted it as a reflex (Todes, 1997). However, the term has usually been translated into English as *conditioned reflex,* and that term is now well established in the literature.

▌ Ivan P. Pavlov (with the white beard) with students and a dog. Pavlov focused on limited aspects of the dog's behavior—primarily salivation—and devised some apparently simple principles to describe that behavior.

Pavlov's Procedures

Pavlov guessed that animals are born with certain *automatic connections*—we call them **unconditioned reflexes**—*between a stimulus such as food and a response such as secreting digestive juices.* He conjectured that animals acquire new reflexes by transferring a response from one stimulus to another. For example, if a neutral stimulus (e.g., a buzzer) always preceded food, an animal might begin to respond to the buzzer as it responds to food. Thus, the buzzer would also elicit digestive secretions.

The *process by which an organism learns a new association between two paired stimuli—a neutral stimulus and one that already evokes a reflexive response*—has come to be known as **classical conditioning**, or **Pavlovian conditioning**. (It is called classical because it has been known and studied for a long time.)

Pavlov used an experimental setup like the one in Figure 6.2 (Goodwin, 1991). First, he selected dogs with a moderate degree of arousal. (Highly excitable dogs would not hold still long enough, and highly inhibited dogs would fall asleep.) Then he attached a tube to one of the salivary ducts in the dog's mouth to measure salivation. He could have measured stomach secretions, but it was easier to measure salivation.

Pavlov found that, whenever he gave a dog food, saliva flowed in the dog's mouth. The food → salivation connection was automatic, requiring no training. Pavlov called the food the unconditioned stimulus, and he called the salivation the unconditioned response. The **unconditioned stimulus (UCS)** is *an event that consistently, automatically elicits an un-*

conditioned response, and the **unconditioned response (UCR)** is *an action that the unconditioned stimulus automatically elicits.*

Next Pavlov introduced a new stimulus, such as a metronome. Upon hearing the metronome, the dog lifted its ears and looked around but did not salivate, so the metronome was a neutral stimulus with regard to salivation. Then Pavlov sounded the metronome a couple of seconds before giving food to the dog. After a few pairings of the metronome with food, the dog began to salivate as soon as it heard the metronome (Pavlov, 1927/1960).

We call the metronome the **conditioned stimulus (CS)** because the dog's *response to it depended on the preceding conditions*—that is, the pairing of the CS with the UCS. The salivation that followed the sounding of the metronome was the **conditioned response (CR)**. The conditioned response is simply *whatever response the conditioned stimulus begins to elicit as a result of the conditioning (training) procedure.* At the start of the conditioning procedure, the conditioned stimulus does *not* elicit a conditioned response. After conditioning, it does.

In Pavlov's experiment the conditioned response (salivation) closely resembled the unconditioned response (also salivation). However, in some cases it is quite different. For example, the unconditioned response to an electric shock includes shrieking and jumping or at least flinching. The conditioned response to a stimulus paired with shock (i.e., a warning signal for shock) is a tensing of the muscles and lack of activity (e.g., Pezze, Bast, & Feldon, 2003).

To summarize, the *unconditioned stimulus (UCS)*, such as food, automatically elicits the *unconditioned response (UCR)*, such as salivating. A neutral stimulus, such as a sound, that is paired with the UCS becomes a *conditioned stimulus (CS)*. At first this neutral stimulus elicits either no response or some irrelevant response, such as just looking around. After some number of pairings of the CS with the UCS, the conditioned stimulus elicits the *conditioned response (CR)*, which usually resembles the UCR. The key difference between the CR and UCR is that the CS (conditioned stimulus) elicits the CR (conditioned response) and the UCS (unconditioned stimulus) elicits the UCR (unconditioned response). Figure 6.3 diagrams these relationships.

All else being equal, conditioning occurs more rapidly if the conditioned stimulus is unfamiliar. For example, if you heard a tone many times (followed by nothing) and then started hearing the tone followed by a puff of air to your left eye, you would be slow to show signs of conditioning. Similarly, imagine two people who are bitten by a snake. One has never been close to a snake before; the other has spent years tending snakes at the zoo. You can guess which one will develop a fear of snakes.

FIGURE 6.2 Pavlov used dogs for his experiments on classical conditioning and salivation. The experimenter can ring a buzzer (CS), present food (UCS), and measure the responses (CR and UCR). Pavlov himself collected saliva with a simple measuring pouch attached to the dog's cheek; his later colleagues used a more complex device.

At first,

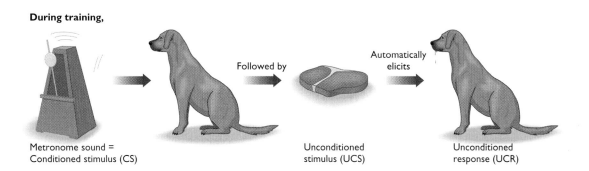

Metronome sound =
Neutral stimulus

No response.

FIGURE 6.3 With classical conditioning a conditioned stimulus is followed by an unconditioned stimulus. At first the conditioned stimulus elicits no response, and the unconditioned stimulus elicits the unconditioned response. After sufficient pairings the conditioned stimulus begins to elicit the conditioned response, which can resemble the unconditioned response.

During training,

Metronome sound =
Conditioned stimulus (CS)

Followed by

Unconditioned
stimulus (UCS)

Automatically
elicits

Unconditioned
response (UCR)

After some number of repetitions,

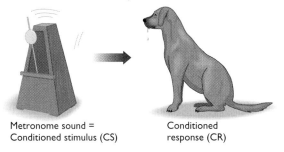

Metronome sound =
Conditioned stimulus (CS)

Conditioned
response (CR)

More Examples of Classical Conditioning

Here are some other examples of classical conditioning:

- You hear a tone and then you get a puff of air to your eyes. After a few repetitions, hearing the tone makes you blink your eyes.

Unconditioned stimulus = air puff → Unconditioned response = eye blink

Conditioned stimulus = tone → Conditioned response = eye blink

- Your alarm clock makes a faint clicking sound a couple of seconds before the alarm goes off. At first the click by itself does not awaken you, but the alarm does. After a week or so, however, you awaken as soon as you hear the click.

Unconditioned stimulus = alarm → Unconditioned response = awakening

Conditioned stimulus = click → Conditioned response = awakening

- You hear the sound of a dentist's drill shortly before the unpleasant experience of the drill on your teeth. From then on the sound of a dentist's drill arouses anxiety.

Unconditioned stimulus = drilling → Unconditioned response = tension

Conditioned stimulus = sound of the drill → Conditioned response = tension

- A nursing mother responds to her baby's cries by putting the baby to her breast, stimulating the flow of milk. After a few days of repetitions, the sound of the baby's cry is enough to start the milk flowing.

Unconditioned stimulus = baby sucking → Unconditioned response = milk flow

Conditioned stimulus = baby's cry → Conditioned response = milk flow

Note the usefulness of classical conditioning in each of these cases: It prepares an individual for likely events. In some cases, however, the effects can be unwelcome.

For example, many cancer patients who have had repeated chemotherapy treatments become nauseated when they approach or even imagine the building where they received treatment (Dadds, Bovbjerg, Redd, & Cutmore, 1997).

Form an image of a lemon, a nice fresh juicy one. You cut it into slices and then suck on a slice. And then another slice. Imagine that sour taste. As you imagine the lemon, do you notice yourself salivating? If so, your imagination produced enough resemblance to the actual sight and taste of a lemon to serve as a conditioned stimulus.

Try It Yourself

CONCEPT CHECK ✓

3. At the start of training, the CS elicits ___ and the UCS elicits ___. After many repetitions of the CS followed by the UCS, the CS elicits ___ and the UCS elicits ___.
4. In this example identify the CS, UCS, CR, and UCR: Every time an army drill sergeant calls out "Ready, aim, fire," the artillery shoots, making a painfully loud sound that causes you to flinch. After a few repetitions, you tense your muscles after the word "fire," before the shot itself. (Check your answers on page 204.)

The Phenomena of Classical Conditioning

We start by discussing mostly laboratory studies but later come to an application of classical conditioning to some human experiences. The *process that establishes or strengthens a conditioned response* is known as **acquisition**. Figure 6.4 shows how the strength of a conditioned response increases after pairings of the conditioned and unconditioned stimuli. Acquisition is not the end of the story, however, because any response that can be learned can also be unlearned.

Once Pavlov had demonstrated how classical conditioning occurs, curious psychologists wondered what would happen after various changes in the procedures. Their investigations have extended our knowledge of classical conditioning. Here are a few of the main phenomena.

Extinction

Suppose I sound a buzzer and then blow a puff of air into your eyes. After a few repetitions, you will start to close your eyes as soon as you hear the buzzer (Figure 6.5). Now I sound the buzzer repeatedly without the puff of air. What do you do?

You will blink your eyes the first time and perhaps the second and third times, but before long you will stop. This decrease of the conditioned response is called **extinction** (see Figure 6.4). *To extinguish a classically conditioned response, repeatedly present the conditioned stimulus (CS) without the unconditioned stimulus (UCS).* That is, acquisition of a response (CR) occurs if the CS predicts the UCS; extinction occurs if the CS no longer predicts the UCS.

Extinction is not the same as forgetting. Both weaken a learned response, but they arise in different ways. Forgetting occurs when we have no opportunity to practice a certain behavior over a period of time. Extinction occurs as the result of a specific experience—the presentation of the conditioned stimulus without the unconditioned stimulus.

Extinction does not erase the original connection between the CS and the UCS. You might think of acquisition as learning to do a response and extinction as learning to inhibit it. For example, suppose you have gone through original learning in which a tone regularly preceded a puff of air to your eyes. You learned to blink your eyes at the tone. Then you went through an extinction process in which you heard the tone many times but received no air puffs. You extinguished, so the tone no longer elicited a blink. Now, without warning, you get another puff of air to your eyes. As a result, the next time you hear the tone, you will blink your eyes. Extinction inhibited your response to the CS (here, the tone), but a sudden puff of air weakens that inhibition (Bouton, 1994).

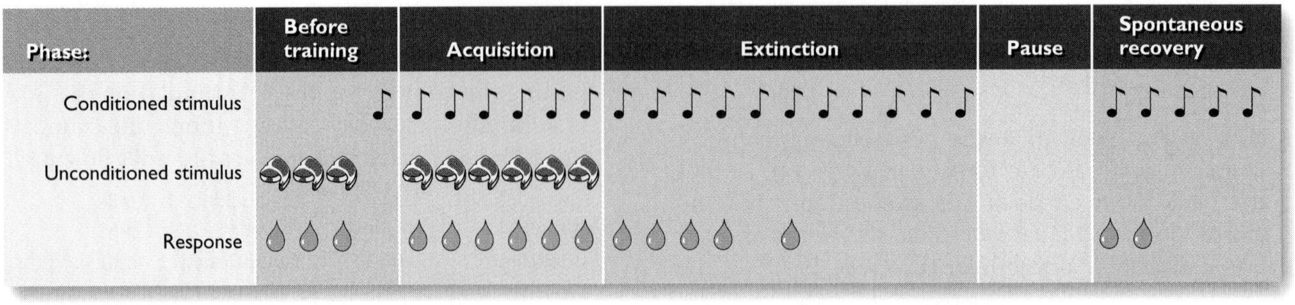

FIGURE 6.4 If the conditioned stimulus regularly precedes the unconditioned stimulus, acquisition occurs. If the conditioned stimulus is presented by itself, extinction occurs. A pause after extinction yields a brief spontaneous recovery.

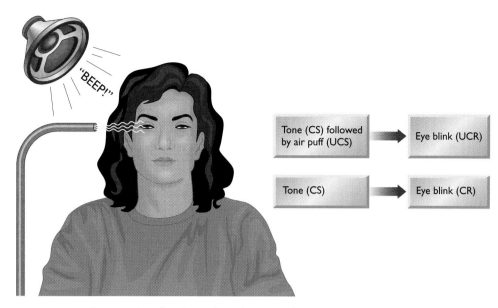

FIGURE 6.5 The procedure for classical conditioning of the eye-blink response.

Spontaneous Recovery

Suppose you are in a classical conditioning experiment. At first you repeatedly hear a buzzer sound (CS) that is always followed by a puff of air to your eyes (UCS). Then the buzzer stops predicting an air puff, and after a few trials, your response to the buzzer extinguishes. Now suppose you sit there for a long time with nothing happening and then suddenly you hear another buzzer sound. What do you suppose you will do? Chances are that you will blink your eyes at least slightly. **Spontaneous recovery** is *this temporary return of an extinguished response after a delay* (see Figure 6.4). Spontaneous recovery requires no additional CS–UCS pairings.

Why does spontaneous recovery take place? Think of it this way: At first the buzzer predicted a puff of air to your eyes, and then it didn't. You behaved in accordance with the more recent experiences. Hours later neither experience is much more recent than the other, and the effects of the original acquisition are almost as strong as those of extinction.

CONCEPT CHECK ☑

5. In Pavlov's experiment on conditioned salivation in response to a buzzer, what procedure could you use to produce extinction? What procedure could you use to produce spontaneous recovery? (Check your answers on page 204.)

Stimulus Generalization

Suppose your alarm clock makes a faint clicking sound (CS) a few seconds before the alarm (UCS), and you have learned to awaken as soon as you hear the click. What if you now buy a new alarm clock? It makes a different clicking sound before the alarm goes off. Will the click awaken you?

It probably will. The closer the sound of the new click is to the original one, the more likely you are to respond by awakening (Figure 6.6). **Stimulus generalization** is the *extension of a conditioned response from the training stimulus to similar stimuli.*

This definition may sound pretty straightforward, but in fact psychologists find it difficult to specify exactly what "similar" means (Pearce, 1994). For example, if you hear a clicking sound somewhere other than in your bedroom or at a time other than your usual awakening time, it may be ineffective. So your response at any moment depends on how similar the total configuration of stimuli is to the set on which you were trained, and that similarity is hard to measure.

Discrimination

Suppose your alarm clock makes one kind of click when the alarm is about to ring but occasionally makes a different kind of click at other times. Eventually, you will learn to **discriminate** between these two clicks: You will *respond differently to the two stimuli*

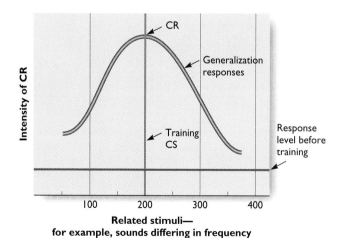

FIGURE 6.6 Stimulus generalization is the process of extending a learned response to new stimuli that resemble the one used in training. As a rule a stimulus similar to the training stimulus elicits a strong response; a less similar stimulus elicits a weaker response.

because they predicted different outcomes. You will awaken when you hear one click but not when you hear the other. Similarly, you learn that one bell signals that it is time for class to start, and a different bell signals a fire.

CRITICAL THINKING:
A STEP FURTHER
Discrimination

We can easily determine how well human subjects discriminate between two stimuli. We can simply ask, "Which note has the higher pitch?" or "Which light is brighter?" How could we determine how well a nonhuman can discriminate between two stimuli?

CRITICAL THINKING:
WHAT'S THE EVIDENCE
Emotional Conditioning Without Awareness

In many situations conditioning occurs fastest when people are aware of the connection between the CS and UCS (Knuttinen, Power, Preston, & Disterhoft, 2001). (With laboratory animals, it is hard to ask!) However, several studies indicate that emotional responses sometimes become conditioned without awareness. If so, the implications are far-reaching. We shall examine one study in detail. In some ways this discussion will seem out of place: The whole idea of

discussing attitudes, emotions, and so forth is contrary to the customs of radical behaviorism. Nevertheless, we see here how other psychologists have taken the idea of classical conditioning and applied it more broadly.

Hypothesis   People will form favorable attitudes toward items paired with something they like and unfavorable attitudes toward items paired with something they dislike, even if they are not aware of the connection (Olson & Fazio, 2001).

Method   Forty-five female college students viewed a series of slides. Most included a Pokemon image, as shown in Figure 6.7, although a few were blank. Most of those with a Pokemon also included another picture or a word. Each student's task was to look for a particular "target" Pokemon and press a computer key whenever she saw it, ignoring all the other pictures and words. One of the "other" nontarget Pokemon images was always paired with something likable, such as a picture of tasty food or the word "excellent." Another nontarget Pokemon image was always paired with something negative, such as a picture of a cockroach or the word "terrible." Still other Pokemon images were paired with neutral or varying words and pictures. After viewing all the slides repeatedly, each student was asked to look at all the Pokemon images (by themselves) and rate how pleasant or unpleasant they were. They were also asked whether they remembered what other items had paired with each Pokemon.

FIGURE 6.7 One Pokemon was the target, and the participant was to press a key whenever she saw it. Among the others, which she was to ignore, one was always paired with a pleasant word or image, another was always paired with something unpleasant, and still others were not consistently paired with anything either pleasant or unpleasant.

Results On the average the women gave a higher pleasantness rating to the Pokemon that had been associated with favorable words and pictures and lower ratings to the one associated with unfavorable words and pictures. However, they did not remember what words or pictures had been associated with each Pokemon. (They hadn't been told to pay attention to those pairings, and they didn't.)

Interpretation The attitudes that people express ("I like it" or "I don't like it") presumably reflect emotional responses. These results show classical conditioning of attitudes or emotional responses based on pairings of words and images, even though people did not notice them enough to report explicit memories.

Drug Tolerance as an Example of Classical Conditioning

Classical conditioning sometimes occurs in surprising ways. One example is **drug tolerance:** *Users of certain drugs experience progressively weaker effects after taking the drugs repeatedly.* Consequently, the users crave ever larger amounts of the drug.

Drug tolerance depends partly on classical conditioning. Consider: When drug users inject themselves with morphine or heroin, the drug injection procedure is an elaborate stimulus that includes the time and place as well as the needle injection itself. This total stimulus reliably predicts a second stimulus, the drug's entry into the brain, which triggers a variety of body defenses against its effects—for example, changes in hormone secretions, heart rate, and breathing rate.

First stimulus → Second stimulus → Automatic response
(Injection   (Drug enters   (Body's defenses)
procedure)   brain)

Whenever one stimulus predicts a second stimulus that produces an automatic response, the conditions are present for classical conditioning. The first stimulus becomes the CS, the second becomes the UCS, and its response is the UCR. So we can relabel as follows:

Conditioned → Unconditioned → Unconditioned
stimulus   stimulus   response
(Injection   (Drug enters   (Body's defenses)
procedure)   brain)

If conditioning occurs here, what would be the consequences? Suppose the CS (drug injection) produces a CR that resembles the UCR (the body's defenses against the drug). The result is that as soon as the person starts injecting the drug, before it even en-

ters the body, the body is already mobilizing its defenses against the drug. Therefore, the drug will have less effect. In other words the body develops tolerance. Shepard Siegel (1977, 1983) has confirmed that classical conditioning occurs during drug injections. That is, after many drug injections, the injection procedure by itself evokes the body's anti-drug defenses:

Conditioned stimulus → Conditioned response
(Injection procedure)   (Body's defenses)

One prediction was as follows: If the injection procedure serves as a conditioned stimulus, then the body's defense reactions should be strongest if the drug is administered in the usual way, in the usual location, with as many familiar stimuli as possible. (The whole experience constitutes the conditioned stimulus.)

The evidence strongly supports this prediction for a variety of drugs (Marin, Perez, Duero, & Ramirez, 1999; Siegel, 1983). For example, a rat that is repeatedly injected with alcohol develops a tolerance, improving its balance while intoxicated. But if it is now tested in the presence of loud sounds and strobe lights, its balance suffers. Conversely, if it had practiced its balance while intoxicated in the presence of loud sounds and strobe lights, its balance suffers if it is tested *without* those stimuli (Larson & Siegel, 1998). In short, the tolerance depends on learning.

Why do some people die of a drug overdose that is no larger than the dose they normally tolerate? They probably took the fatal overdose in an unfamiliar setting. For example, someone who is accustomed to taking a drug at home in the evening could suffer a fatal reaction from taking it at a friend's house in the morning. Because the new setting did not serve as a CS, it failed to trigger the usual drug tolerance.

CONCEPT CHECK ☑

6. When an individual develops tolerance to the effects of a drug injection, what are the conditioned stimulus, the unconditioned stimulus, the conditioned response, and the unconditioned response?

7. Within the classical-conditioning interpretation of drug tolerance, what procedure should extinguish tolerance? (Check your answers on page 204.)

Explanations of Classical Conditioning

What is classical conditioning, really? As is often the case, the process appeared at first to be fairly simple, but later investigation found it to be a more complex and indeed more interesting phenomenon.

Pavlov noted that conditioning depended on the timing between CS and UCS, as shown here:

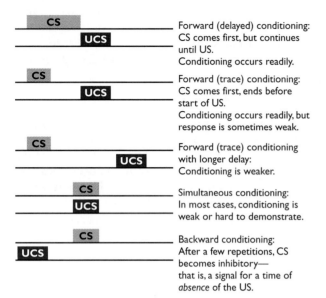

CS ████
UCS ████
Forward (delayed) conditioning: CS comes first, but continues until US.
Conditioning occurs readily.

CS ████
UCS ████
Forward (trace) conditioning: CS comes first, ends before start of US.
Conditioning occurs readily, but response is sometimes weak.

CS ████
UCS ████
Forward (trace) conditioning with longer delay:
Conditioning is weaker.

CS ████
UCS ████
Simultaneous conditioning: In most cases, conditioning is weak or hard to demonstrate.

CS ████
UCS ████
Backward conditioning: After a few repetitions, CS becomes inhibitory— that is, a signal for a time of *absence* of the US.

In these displays read time left to right. Pavlov surmised that presenting the CS and UCS at nearly the same time caused the growth of a connection in the brain so that the animal treated the CS as if it were the UCS. Figure 6.8a illustrates the connections before the start of training: The UCS excites a UCS center in the brain, which immediately stimulates the UCR center. Figure 6.8b illustrates connections that develop during conditioning: Pairing the CS and UCS causes the development of a connection between their brain representations. After this connection develops, the CS excites the CS center, which excites the UCS center, which excites the UCR center and produces a response.

Later studies contradicted that idea. For example, a shock (UCS) causes rats to jump and shriek, but a conditioned stimulus paired with shock makes rats freeze in position. They react to the conditioned stimulus as a danger signal, not as if it were itself a shock. Also, in delay conditioning (Figure 6.8), where a delay separates the end of the CS from the start of the UCS, the animal does not make a conditioned response immediately after the conditioned stimulus, but instead waits until almost the end of the usual delay between CS and UCS. Again, it is not treating the CS as if it were the UCS; it is using it as a predictor, a way to prepare for the UCS (Gallistel & Gibbon, 2000).

It is true, as Pavlov suggested, that the longer the delay between the CS and the UCS, the weaker the conditioning, all other things being equal. However, just having the CS and UCS close together in time is

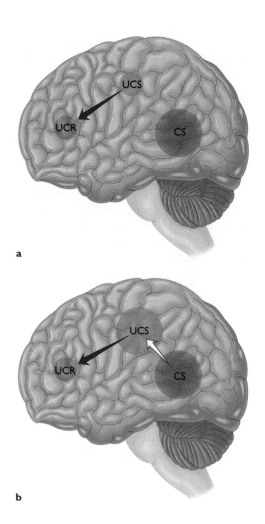

a

b

FIGURE 6.8 Pavlov believed that conditioning depended on presenting the CS and UCS at nearly the same time: (a) At the start of conditioning, activity in the UCS center automatically causes activation of the UCR center. At this time activity of the CS center does not affect the UCS center. (b) After sufficient pairings of the CS and UCS, their simultaneous activity causes the growth of a connection between the CS and UCS centers. Afterward, activity in the CS center will flow to the UCS center and therefore excite the UCR center.

not enough. What is essential is for them to occur more often together than they occur apart. That is, there must be some contingency or predictability between them. Consider this experiment: For rats in both Group 1 and Group 2, every presentation of a CS is followed shortly thereafter by a UCS, as shown in Figure 6.9. However, for Group 2, the UCS also appears at many other times, without the CS. In other words, for this group, the UCS is going to happen every few seconds anyway, and it isn't much more likely with the CS than without it. Group 1 learns a strong response to the CS; Group 2 does not (Rescorla, 1968, 1988).

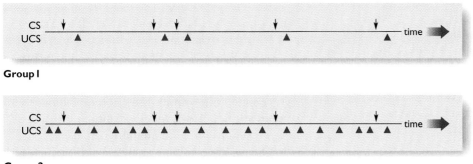

Group I

Group 2

FIGURE 6.9 In Rescorla's experiment the CS was always followed by the UCS in both groups, but Group 2 received the UCS frequently at other times also. Group 1 developed a strong conditioned response to the CS; Group 2 did not.

 CONCEPT CHECK ☑

8. If classical conditioning depended *entirely* on presenting the CS and UCS at nearly the same time, what result should the experimenters have obtained in this experiment? (Check your answer on page 205.)

Also consider this experiment: One group of rats receives a light (CS) followed by shock (UCS) until they respond consistently to the light. (The response is to freeze in place.) Then they get a series of trials with both a light and a tone, again followed by shock. Do they learn a response to the tone? No. The tone always precedes the shock, but the light already predicted the shock, and the tone adds nothing new. The same pattern occurs with the reverse order: First rats learn a response to the tone and then they get light–tone combinations before the shock. They continue responding to the tone, but not to the light, again because the new stimulus predicted nothing that wasn't already predicted (Kamin, 1969) (see Figure 6.10). These results demonstrate the **blocking effect:** *The previously established association to one stimulus blocks the formation of an association to the added stimulus.* Again, it appears that conditioning depends on more than presenting two stimuli together in time; learning occurs only when one stimulus predicts another.

Group I

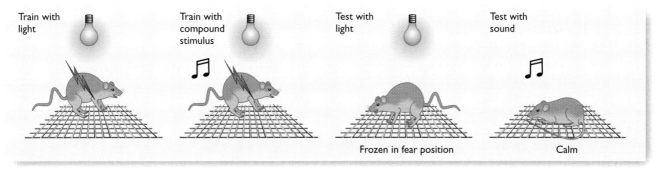

Group 2

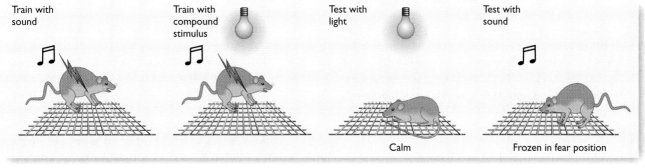

FIGURE 6.10 Each rat first learned to associate either light or sound with shock. Then it received a compound of both light and sound followed by shock. Each rat continued to show a strong response to the old stimulus (which already predicted shock) but little to the new one.

9. Suppose you have already learned to flinch when you hear the sound of a dentist's drill. Now your dentist turns on some soothing background music at the same time as the drill. The background music is paired with the pain just as much as the drill sound is. Will you learn to flinch at the sound of that background music? (Check your answer on page 205.)

IN CLOSING

Classical Conditioning Is More Than Drooling Dogs

People sometimes use the term "Pavlovian" to mean simple, mechanical, robotlike behavior. But Pavlovian or classical conditioning is not a mark of stupidity: It is a way of responding to relationships among events, a way of preparing us for what is likely to happen. Classical conditioning requires processing a fair amount of information.

Classical conditioning is important for some aspects of our behavior but less important for others. It alters our motivational or emotional reactions to stimuli, including responses related to fear, preparations for eating, preparations for a drug injection, and so forth. But it does not control walking toward or away from various stimuli. That is, classical conditioning might tell us to be afraid, but it does not tell us how to avoid the frightening item. It might tell us to salivate in preparation for eating, but it does not tell us how to find food. Other types of learning can answer these other questions, as we shall see in the next module.

Summary

- *Classical conditioning.* Ivan Pavlov discovered classical conditioning, the process by which an organism learns a new association between two stimuli that have been paired with each other—a neutral stimulus (the conditioned stimulus) and one that initially evokes a reflexive response (the unconditioned stimulus). The organism displays this association by responding in a new way (the conditioned response) to the conditioned stimulus. (page 195)
- *Extinction.* After classical conditioning has established a conditioned response to a stimulus, the response can be extinguished by repeatedly presenting that stimulus by itself. (page 198)

- *Spontaneous recovery.* If the conditioned stimulus is not presented at all for some time after extinction and is then presented again, the conditioned response may return to some degree. That return is called spontaneous recovery. (page 199)
- *Stimulus generalization.* An individual who learns to respond to one stimulus will respond similarly to similar stimuli. However, it is difficult to specify how we should measure similarity. (page 199)
- *Discrimination.* If one stimulus is followed by an unconditioned stimulus and another similar stimulus is not, the individual will come to discriminate between these two stimuli. (page 199)
- *Emotional conditioning without awareness.* In many situations conditioning is strongest if the learner is aware of the CS–UCS connection. However, some subtle emotional responses can be conditioned even if the learner is not aware of the connection or even not aware of the CS at all. (page 200)
- *Drug tolerance.* Drug tolerance is partly a form of classical conditioning in which the drug administration procedure comes to evoke defensive responses by the body. (page 201)
- *Basis for classical conditioning.* Pavlov believed that conditioning occurred because presenting two stimuli close to each other in time caused the growth of a connection between their representations in the brain. Later research showed that animals do not treat the conditioned stimulus as if it were the unconditioned stimulus. Also, being close in time is not enough; learning requires that the first stimulus predict the second stimulus. (page 201)

Answers to Concept Checks

3. No response (or at least nothing of interest) . . . the UCR . . . the CR . . . still the UCR. (page 198)
4. The conditioned stimulus is the sound "Ready, aim, fire." The unconditioned stimulus is the artillery shot. The unconditioned response is flinching; the conditioned response is tensing. (page 198)
5. To bring about extinction, present the buzzer repeatedly without presenting any food. To bring about spontaneous recovery, first bring about extinction; then wait hours or days and present the buzzer again. (page 199)
6. The conditioned stimulus is the injection procedure. The unconditioned stimulus is the entry of the drug into the brain. Both the conditioned response and the unconditioned response are the body's defenses against the drug. (page 201)
7. To extinguish tolerance, present the injection procedure (conditioned stimulus) without injecting the drug (unconditioned stimulus). Instead,

inject just water or salt water. Siegel (1977) demonstrated that repeated injections of salt water do reduce tolerance to morphine in rats. (page 201)

8. If classical conditioning depended entirely on presenting the CS and UCS at nearly the same time, the rats in both groups would have responded equally to the conditioned stimulus, regardless of how often they received the unconditioned stimulus at other times. (page 203)

9. No, you will not learn to flinch at the sound of the background music. Because the drill sound already predicted the pain, the new stimulus is uninformative and will not be strongly associated with the pain. (page 204)

How do the consequences of our behaviors affect future behaviors?

Sometimes a simple idea, or at least one that sounds simple, can be amazingly powerful. In this module we consider the simple but powerful idea that behaviors become more likely or less likely because of their consequences. In other words we either repeat a behavior or cease it depending on the outcome.

Thorndike and Operant Conditioning

Shortly before Pavlov's research, Edward L. Thorndike (1911/1970), a Harvard graduate student, began training some cats in a basement. Saying that earlier experiments had dealt only with animal intelligence, never with animal stupidity, he devised a simple behavioristic explanation of learning. Thorndike put cats into puzzle boxes (Figure 6.11) from which they could escape by pressing a lever, pulling a string, or tilting a pole. Sometimes he placed food outside the box. (Usually, though, cats worked just to escape from the box.) The cats learned to make whatever response opened the box, especially if the box opened immediately.

The learning was strictly trial and error. When a cat had to tilt a pole to escape from the box, it would first paw or gnaw at the door, scratch the walls, or

FIGURE 6.11 Each of Thorndike's puzzle boxes had a device that could open it. Here tilting the pole will open the door. *(Based on Thorndike, 1911/1970)*

pace back and forth. Eventually, it would bump against the pole by accident and the door would open. The next time, the cat would go through the same repertoire of behaviors but might bump against the pole a little sooner. Over many trials the time it took the cat to escape grew shorter in a gradual and irregular fashion. Figure 6.12 shows a learning curve to represent this behavior. A **learning curve** is *a graph of the changes in behavior that occur over the course of learning.*

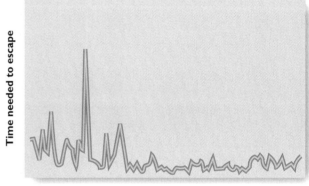

Trial number

FIGURE 6.12 As the data from one of Thorndike's experiments show, the time that a cat needs to escape from a puzzle box decreases gradually, but in an irregular manner. Thorndike concluded that the cat did not at any point "suddenly get the idea." Instead, reinforcement gradually increased the probability of the successful behavior.

Had the cat "figured out" how to escape? Had it come to "understand" the connection between bumping against the pole and opening the door? No, said Thorndike. If the cat had gained a new insight at some point, its speed of escaping would have increased suddenly at that time. Instead, the cat's performance improved slowly and inconsistently, suggesting no point of insight or understanding.

Thorndike concluded that learning occurs only when certain behaviors are strengthened at the expense of others. An animal enters a given situation with a certain repertoire of responses such as pawing the door, scratching the walls, pacing, and so forth (labeled R_1, R_2, R_3, . . . in Figure 6.13). First, the animal engages in its most probable response for this situation (R_1). If nothing special happens, it proceeds to other responses, eventually reaching a response that opens the door—for example, bumping against the pole (R_7 in this example). The opening of the door serves as a reinforcement.

A **reinforcement** is *an event that increases the future probability of the most recent response*. Thorndike said that it "stamps in," or strengthens, the response. The next time the cat is in the puzzle box, it has a slightly higher probability of bumping the lever; after each succeeding reinforcement, the probability goes up another notch until it becomes the most probable response and the cat escapes quickly (Figure 6.13c).

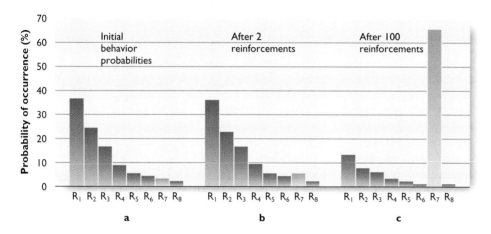

FIGURE 6.13 According to Thorndike, a cat starts with a large set of potential behaviors in a given situation. When one of these, such as bumping against a pole, leads to reinforcement, the future probability of that behavior increases. We do not need to assume that the cat understands what it is doing or why.

Thorndike summarized his views in the **law of effect** (Thorndike, 1911/1970, p. 244): *"Of several responses made to the same situation, those which are accompanied or closely followed by satisfaction to the animal will, other things being equal, be more firmly connected with the situation, so that, when it recurs, they will be more likely to recur."* In other words the animal becomes more likely to repeat the responses that led to favorable consequences even if it does not understand why. In fact it doesn't need to "understand" anything at all. A fairly simple machine could produce responses at random and then repeat the ones that led to reinforcement.

Thorndike revolutionized the study of animal learning, substituting experimentation for the collection of anecdotes. He also demonstrated the possibility of simple explanations for apparently complex behaviors (Dewsbury, 1998). On the negative side, he set the example of studying animals in contrived laboratory situations unrelated to their normal way of life (Galef, 1998).

The kind of learning that Thorndike studied is known as **operant conditioning** (because the subject

operates on the environment to produce an outcome), or **instrumental conditioning** (because the subject's behavior is *instrumental* in producing the outcome). Operant or instrumental conditioning is *the process of changing behavior by following a response with reinforcement*. The defining difference between operant conditioning and classical conditioning is the procedure: *In operant conditioning the subject's behavior determines an outcome and is affected by the outcome. In classical conditioning the subject's behavior has no effect on the outcome (the presentation of either the CS or the UCS).* For example, in classical conditioning the experimenter (or the world) presents two stimuli at particular times, regardless of what the individual does or doesn't do. In operant conditioning the individual has to make some response before the reinforcement can occur.

In general the two kinds of conditioning also differ in the behaviors they affect. Classical conditioning applies primarily to **visceral** responses (i.e., *responses of the internal organs*), such as salivation and digestion, whereas operant conditioning applies primarily to **skeletal** responses (i.e., *movements of leg muscles, arm muscles, etc.*). However, this distinction sometimes breaks down. For example, if a tone is consistently followed by an electric shock (a classical-conditioning procedure), the tone will make the animal freeze in position (a skeletal response) as well as increase its heart rate (a visceral response).

CONCEPT CHECK ☑

10. When I ring a bell, an animal sits up on its hind legs and drools; then I give it some food. Is the animal's behavior an example of classical conditioning or operant conditioning? So far, you do not have enough information to answer the question. What else would you need to know before you could answer? (Check your answer on page 219.)

Reinforcement and Punishment

What constitutes reinforcement? From a practical standpoint, a **reinforcer** is *an event that follows a response and increases the later probability or fre-*

Items that serve as reinforcers for one person might not for another. Lucy Pearson (left) has collected over 110,000 hubcaps. Jim Hambrick (right) collects Superman items.

quency of that response. However, from a theoretical standpoint, we would like to have some way of predicting what would be a reinforcer and what would not. We might guess that reinforcers are biologically useful to the individual, but in fact many are not. For example, saccharin, a sweet but biologically useless chemical, can be a reinforcer. For many people alcohol and tobacco are stronger reinforcers than vitamin-rich vegetables. So biological usefulness doesn't define reinforcement.

In his law of effect, Thorndike described reinforcers as events that brought "satisfaction to the animal." That definition won't work, either. We do not know what brings "satisfaction," and more important, we see that people will work very hard for a paycheck, a decent grade in a course, or other outcomes that don't produce clear evidence of pleasure (Berridge & Robinson, 1995).

David Premack (1965) proposed a simple rule, now known as the **Premack principle:** *The opportunity to engage in frequent behavior* (e.g., eating) *will be a reinforcer for any less frequent behavior* (e.g., lever pressing). A great strength of this idea is that it recognizes that what is a reinforcer for one individual may not be for another and what works at one time may not work at another. For example, if you ordinarily spend more time reading than watching television, someone could increase your television watching by reinforcing you with books. For someone else it might be possible to reinforce reading by opportunities to watch television.

The limitation of the Premack principle is that we are sometimes reinforced by opportunities for uncommon behaviors. For example, if we watched how often people did various acts, we might not guess that someone who almost never had sex would be strongly reinforced by an opportunity for sex. Also, how much time do you spend clipping your toenails during an average week? Almost none? Still, if you are badly overdue for

clipping them, an opportunity to do so would be reinforcing. So the key is not how often you do something, but whether you have recently been doing it less often than you would like. According to the **disequilibrium principle** of reinforcement, *each of us has a normal, or "equilibrium," state. When at equilibrium, we divide our time among activities in a preferred way, and if we are removed from that state, a return to it will be reinforcing* (Farmer-Dougan, 1998; Timberlake & Farmer-Dougan, 1991). For example, suppose that if you had no one telling you what to do, you would spend 30% of your day sleeping, 10% eating, 12% exercising, 11% reading, 9% talking with friends, 3% grooming, 3% playing the piano, and so forth. If you have been forced to spend less than this amount of time on one of those activities, then the opportunity to engage in that activity will be reinforcing to you.

CONCEPT CHECK ☑

11. Suppose you want to reinforce a child for doing chores around the house, and you don't know what would be a good reinforcer. According to the disequilibrium principle, how should you proceed? (Check your answer on page 219.)

Primary and Secondary Reinforcers

Psychologists distinguish between **primary reinforcers** (or *unconditioned reinforcers), which are reinforcing because of their own properties,* and **secondary reinforcers** (or *conditioned reinforcers), which became reinforcing because of previous experiences.* Food and water are primary reinforcers. Coins and bills (secondary reinforcers) become reinforcing because they can be exchanged for food or other primary reinforcers. A student learns that good grades will win the approval of parents and teachers;

▌ Many conditioned reinforcers are surprisingly powerful. Consider, for example, how hard some children will work for a little gold star that the teacher pastes on an assignment.

an employee learns that increased sales will win the approval of an employer. In this case secondary just means learned; do not by any means assume that secondary reinforcers are weak. We spend most of our time working for secondary reinforcers.

Punishment

In contrast to a *reinforcer*, which increases the probability of a response, a **punishment** is *an event that decreases the probability of a response*. A reinforcer can be either the presentation of something (like food) or the removal of something (like pain). A punishment can be either the presentation of something (like pain) or the removal of something (like food).

In some cases punishment or the threat of punishment is ineffective. You already know that from human behavior; if the threat of punishment were always effective, we wouldn't have to worry about crime. B. F. Skinner (1938) also showed punishment to be ineffective in a famous laboratory study. He first trained food-deprived rats to press a bar to get food and then stopped reinforcing their bar presses. For the first 10 minutes, some rats not only failed to get food but had the bar slap their paws every time they pressed it. The punished rats temporarily suppressed their bar-pressing, but in the long run, they made as many presses as did the unpunished rats. Skinner concluded that punishment temporarily suppressed behavior but produced no long-term effects.

That conclusion, however, is an overstatement (Staddon, 1993). A better conclusion would have been that punishment does not greatly weaken a response when no other response is available. Skinner's food-deprived rats had no other way to seek food. Similarly, if someone punished you for breathing, you would continue breathing, but not because you were a slow learner.

Is physical punishment of children, such as spanking, a good or bad idea? Most American parents spank their children at times, whereas spanking is uncommon or even illegal in many other countries. Many psychologists recommend against it, although the research findings are marred by several difficulties. Researchers almost always have to rely on parents' self-reports, which no doubt misstate the amount of spanking. Also, many studies do not distinguish adequately between mild spanking and physical abuse.

A review of the literature found that physical punishment had one clear benefit, which was immediate compliance. That is, if you want your child to stop doing something at once, a quick spank or slap on the hand will work (Gershoff, 2002). Punishment produces compliance especially if it is quick and predictable. If you *might* get punished a long time from now, the effects are weak and variable. The threat of punishment for crime is often ineffective because the punishment is uncertain and long delayed.

On the negative side, however, children who are spanked tend to be more aggressive than other children, more prone to antisocial and criminal behavior in both adolescence and later adulthood, and less healthy mentally. On the average they have a worse relationship with their parents, and they are more likely than others later to become abusive toward their own children or spouse (Gershoff, 2002).

Now, can we draw the conclusion that physical punishment leads to all these undesirable consequences? I hope you see immediately that we cannot. A quick summary of the results is that parents who spank their children are more likely than others to have ill-behaved children. Sure, it is possible that spanking *caused* children to become violent and poorly adjusted, but it is also possible that being violent and poorly adjusted led to the spankings (Baumrind, Larzelere, & Cowan, 2002).

Psychologists are virtually unanimous in recommending against severe punishment or any physical punishment before age 18 months or after the onset of puberty (Baumrind et al., 2002). On the issue of mild physical punishment for children between 18 months and puberty, the research data are not conclusive. (You might contemplate the difficulty of obtaining conclusive results, given the ethical impossibility of randomly assigning children to spanking or nonspanking groups.)

12. The U.S. government imposes strict punishments for selling illegal drugs. Based on what you have just read, why are those punishments ineffective for many people? (Check your answer on page 219.)

Categories of Reinforcement and Punishment

As mentioned, a reinforcement can be either the onset of something like food or the removal of something like pain. Of course, what works as a reinforcer for one person at one time may not for another person or at another time. A punishment also can be either the onset or offset of something. Psychologists use different terms to distinguish these possibilities, as shown in Table 6.1.

Note that the upper left and lower right of the table both show reinforcement; either gaining food or preventing pain will *increase* the behavior. The items in the upper right and lower left are both punishment; preventing food or gaining pain will *decrease* the behavior. Food and pain are, of course, just examples; many other events serve as reinforcers or punishers. Let's go through these terms and procedures, beginning in the upper left of the table and proceeding clockwise.

Positive reinforcement is the *presentation of an event* (e.g., food or money) *that strengthens or increases the likelihood of a behavior.*

Punishment occurs when a response is followed by an event such as pain; the frequency of the response then decreases. For example, you put your hand on a hot stove and burn yourself, and you learn to stop doing that. Punishment is also called **passive**

avoidance learning because *the individual learns to avoid an outcome by being passive* (e.g., by *not* putting your hand on the stove).

Try not to be confused by the term negative reinforcement. Remember that **negative reinforcement** is *a kind of reinforcement (not a punishment), and therefore it increases the frequency of a behavior. It is "negative" in the sense that the reinforcement is the absence of something.* For example, you learn to apply sunscreen to avoid skin cancer, and you learn to brush your teeth to avoid tooth decay. With negative reinforcement the behavior increases and the outcome deceases. Negative reinforcement is also known as **avoidance learning** *if the response prevents the outcome altogether* or **escape learning** *if it makes some outcome stop after it has already begun.* Most people find the terms "escape learning" and "avoidance learning" less confusing than "negative reinforcement" (see Kimble, 1993), but you should understand all of these terms.

If reinforcement by avoiding something bad is negative reinforcement, then *punishment by avoiding something good* is **negative punishment**. If your parents punished you by taking away your allowance, your television privileges, or your travel privileges ("grounding you"), they were using negative punishment. Another example is a teacher punishing a child by a "time out" session away from classmates. Although this practice is common, the term negative punishment is not widely used. The practice is usually known simply as punishment or as **omission training** *because the omission of the response leads to restoration of the usual privileges.*

Classifying some procedure in one of these four categories is sometimes tricky. If you are told you

TABLE 6.1 Four Categories of Operant Conditioning

	Event Such as Food	Event Such as Pain
Behavior leads to the event	**Positive Reinforcement** *Result*: Increase in the behavior, reinforced by presentation of food. *Example*: "If you clean your room, I'll get you a pizza tonight."	**Punishment = Passive Avoidance Learning** *Result*: Decrease in the behavior, and therefore a decrease in pain. *Example*: "If you insult me, I'll slap you." 
Behavior avoids the event	**Negative Punishment = Omission Training** *Result*: Decrease in the behavior, and therefore food continues to be available. *Example*: "If you hit your little brother again, you'll get no dessert."	**Negative Reinforcement = Escape or Avoidance Learning** *Result*: Increase in the behavior, and therefore a decrease in pain. *Example*: "If you go into the office over there, the doctor will remove the thorn from your leg."

can be suspended from school for academic dishonesty, you can think of it as being honest in order to stay in school (positive reinforcement), being honest in order to avoid suspension (negative reinforcement or avoidance learning), decreasing dishonesty in order to avoid suspension (punishment or passive avoidance), or decreasing dishonesty in order to stay in school (negative punishment or omission training). Sorry about that. Just attend to how something is worded: Are we talking about increasing or decreasing some behavior, and increasing or decreasing some outcome? Practice with the concept check that follows.

CONCEPT CHECK ✓

13. Identify each of the following examples using the terms in Table 6.1:
    a. Your employer gives you bonus pay for working overtime.
    b. You learn to stop playing your accordion at 5 A.M. because your roommate threatens to kill you if you do it again.
    c. You turn off a dripping faucet, ending the "drip drip drip" sound.
    d. You learn to drink less beer than you once did because you have felt sick after drinking too much.
    e. Your swimming coach says you cannot go to the next swim meet (which you are looking forward to) if you break a training rule.
    f. If you get a speeding ticket, you will temporarily lose the privilege of driving the family car.
    g. You learn to come inside when a storm is brewing to avoid getting wet. (Check your answers on page 219.)

CRITICAL THINKING:
A STEP FURTHER
Using Reinforcement

Your local school board proposes to improve class attendance by lowering the grades of any student who misses a certain number of classes. Might the board achieve the same goal more effectively by using positive reinforcement?

Additional Phenomena of Operant Conditioning

Recall the concepts of extinction, generalization, and discrimination in classical conditioning. The same concepts apply to operant conditioning, although the procedures are a little different.

Extinction

No doubt you are familiar with the saying, "If at first you don't succeed, try, try again." Better advice is, "Try again, but differently!" After all, you may be doing something wrong.

In operant conditioning **extinction** *occurs if responses stop producing reinforcements.* For example, you were once in the habit of asking your roommate to join you for supper. The last five times you asked, your roommate said no, so you stop asking. In classical conditioning extinction is achieved by presenting the CS without the UCS; in operant conditioning, the procedure is response without reinforcement. Table 6.2 compares classical and operant conditioning.

TABLE 6.2 Classical Conditioning and Operant Conditioning

	Classical Conditioning	Operant Conditioning
Terminology	CS, UCS, CR, UCR	Response, reinforcement
Behavior	Does not control UCS	Controls reinforcement
Paired during acquisition	Two stimuli (CS and UCS)	Response and reinforcement (in the presence of certain stimuli)
Responses	Mostly visceral (internal organs)	Mostly skeletal muscles
Extinction procedure	CS without UCS	Response without reinforcement

Generalization, Discrimination, and Discriminative Stimuli

Someone who receives reinforcement for a response in the presence of one stimulus will probably make the same response in the presence of a similar stimulus. *The more similar a new stimulus is to the original reinforced stimulus, the more likely the same response.* This phenomenon is known as **stimulus generalization.** For example, you might reach for the turn signal in a rented car in the same place you would find it in your own car.

If reinforcement occurs for responding to one stimulus and not another, the result is a **discrimination** between them and *a response to one stimulus and not the other.* For example, you walk toward a parked car that you think is yours, but then you realize it is not. After several such experiences, you learn to identify your own car from a distance.

A stimulus that indicates which response is appropriate or inappropriate is called a **discriminative**

stimulus. A great deal of our behavior is governed by discriminative stimuli. For example, you learn ordinarily to be quiet in class but to talk when the professor encourages discussion. You learn to drive fast on some streets and slow on others. Throughout your day one stimulus after another signals which behaviors will yield reinforcement, punishment, or neither. *The ability of a stimulus to encourage some responses and discourage others* is known as **stimulus control.**

Why Are Certain Responses Learned More Easily Than Others?

Thorndike's cats learned to push and pull various devices in their efforts to escape from his puzzle boxes. But when Thorndike tried to teach them to scratch or lick themselves to receive the same reinforcement, they learned very slowly and performed inconsistently. Why?

One possible reason is **belongingness,** the *concept that certain stimuli "belong" together or that a given response is more readily associated with certain outcomes than with others.* For example, it is easier for cats to associate a puzzle box opening with the response of pushing a door than the response of scratching the neck. Belongingness is an idea that Thorndike himself suggested, although psychologists neglected it for decades. Eventually, psychologists revived the concept, also sometimes known as "preparedness" (Seligman, 1970). For example, dogs can readily learn that a sound coming from one location means "raise your left leg" and a sound coming from another location means "raise your right leg," but they are slow to learn that a ticking metronome means raise the left leg and a buzzer means raise the right leg (Dobrzecka, Szwejkowska, & Konorski, 1966) (see Figure 6.14). Similarly, people learn more easily to turn a wheel clockwise to move something to the right and counterclockwise to move it to the left (as when turning the steering wheel of a car). Ergonomists do much research to find which procedures are easiest for people to learn so that machines can be designed to match people's tendencies.

However, belongingness may not be the whole explanation for why Thorndike's cats were slow to associate scratching themselves with escaping from a box: Perhaps a cat scratches itself only when it itches (Charlton, 1983). Suppose someone said you could win a large prize if you finished first in a rapid saliva-swallowing contest. (Why not? People compete at everything else.) You quickly swallow once, twice, maybe three times, but each successive swallow gets harder and harder. (Go ahead and try it.) Some behaviors are just harder to produce without their normal stimulus (such as a mouth full of saliva or an itchy spot on the skin).

B. F. Skinner and the Shaping of Responses

The most influential radical behaviorist, B. F. Skinner (1904–1990), demonstrated many uses of operant conditioning. Skinner was an ardent practitioner of parsimony (Chapter 2), always seeking simple explanations in terms of reinforcement histories rather than more complex mental processes.

Dog easily learns to raise the leg closer to the sound source.

Dog does not easily learn to raise one leg when it hears a metronome and a different leg when it hears a buzzer.

FIGURE 6.14 According to the principle of belongingness, some items are easy to associate with each other because they "belong" together; others do not. For example, dogs easily learn to use the direction of a sound as a signal for which leg to raise, but they have trouble using the type of sound as a signal for which leg to raise.

One problem confronting any student of behavior is how to define a response. For example, imagine watching a group of children and trying to count "aggressive behaviors." What is an aggressive act and what isn't? Psychologists studying intelligence, emotion, or personality spend much of their time trying to find the best method of measurement. Even simple food-getting or shock-escaping responses are hard to define and measure.

Skinner simplified the question by simplifying the situation (Zuriff, 1995): He set up a box, called an *operant-conditioning chamber* (or *Skinner box,* a term that Skinner himself never used), in which a rat presses a lever or a pigeon pecks an illuminated disk, or "key," to receive food (Figure 6.15). He then operationally defined the response as anything that the animal did to depress the lever or key. So if the rat pressed the lever with its snout instead of its paw, the response still counted; if the pigeon batted the key with its wing instead of pecking it with its beak, it still counted. The behavior was defined by its outcome, not by muscle movements.

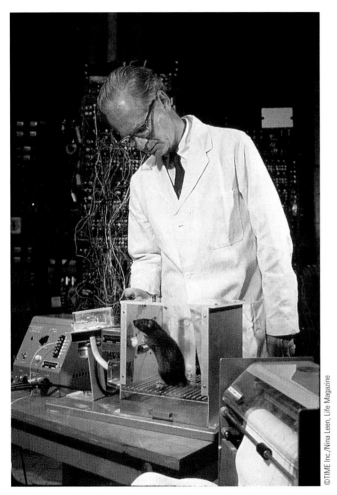

FIGURE 6.15 B. F. Skinner examines one of his laboratory animals in an operant-conditioning chamber. When the light above the bar is on, pressing the bar is reinforced. A food pellet rolls out of the storage device (left) and down the tube into the cage.

Does that definition make sense? Skinner's reply was that it did because it led to consistent results in his research. Skinner's procedures became standard in many laboratories. When deciding how to define a term (e.g., *response*), the best definition is the one that produces the clearest results.

Shaping Behavior

Suppose you want to train a rat to press a lever. If you put the rat in a box and wait, the rat might never press it. To avoid interminable waits, Skinner introduced a powerful technique, called **shaping,** for *establishing a new response by reinforcing successive approximations to it.*

To *shape* a rat to press a lever, you might begin by reinforcing the rat for standing up, a common behavior in rats. After a few reinforcements, the rat stands up more frequently. Now you change the rules, giving food only when the rat stands up while facing the lever. Soon it spends more time standing up and facing the lever. (It extinguishes its behavior of standing and facing in any other direction because those responses are not reinforced.)

Next you provide reinforcement only when the rat stands facing the correct direction while in the half of the cage nearest the lever. You gradually move the boundary, and the rat moves closer to the lever. Then the rat must touch the lever and, finally, apply weight to it. Through a series of short, easy steps, you might shape the rat to press a lever in a matter of minutes.

Shaping works with humans too, of course. All of education is based on the idea of shaping: First, your parents or teachers praise you for counting your fingers; later, you must add and subtract to earn their congratulations; step by step, your tasks get more complex, until you are doing calculus.

Chaining Behavior

To produce complex sequences of behavior, psychologists use a procedure called **chaining.** Assume that you want to train an animal, perhaps a guide dog or a show horse, to go through a sequence of actions in a particular order. You could *chain* the behaviors, *reinforcing each one with the opportunity to engage in the next one.* First, the animal learns the final behavior for a reinforcement; then it learns the next to last behavior, which is reinforced by the opportunity to perform the final behavior. And so on.

For example, a rat might first be placed on the top platform as shown in Figure 6.16f, where it eats food. Then it is put on the intermediate platform with a ladder in place leading to the top platform. The rat learns to climb the ladder. After it has done so repeatedly, it is placed again on the intermediate platform, but this time the ladder is not present. It must learn to pull a string to raise the ladder so that it can climb to the top platform. Then the rat is placed on the bottom platform (Figure 6.16a). It now has to learn to climb the ladder to the intermediate platform, pull a string to raise the ladder, and then climb the ladder again. We could, of course, extend the chain still further. Each behavior is reinforced with the opportunity for the next behavior, except for the final behavior, which is reinforced with food.

People learn to make chains of responses too. First, you learned to eat with a fork and spoon. Later, you learned to put your own food on the plate before eating. Eventually, you learned to plan a menu, go to the store, buy the ingredients, cook the meal, put it on the plate, and then eat it. Each behavior is reinforced by the opportunity to engage in the next behavior.

To show how effective shaping and chaining can be, Skinner performed this demonstration: First, he trained a rat to go to the center of a cage. Then he trained it to do so only when he was playing a certain piece of music. Next he trained it to wait for the music, go to the center of the cage, and sit up on its hind legs. Step by step, he eventually trained the rat to wait for the music (which happened to be the "Star-Spangled Banner"), move to the center of the cage, sit up on its hind legs, put its claws on a string next to a pole, pull the string to hoist the U.S. flag, and then salute it. Only then did the rat get its reinforcement. Needless to say, a display of patriotism is not part of a rat's usual repertoire of behavior.

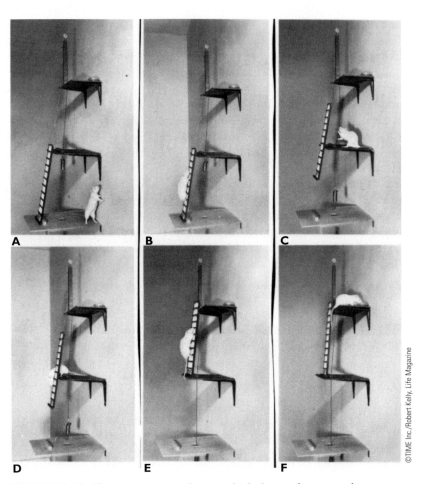

FIGURE 6.16 Chaining is a procedure in which the reinforcement for one behavior is the opportunity to engage in the next behavior. To reach food on the top platform, this rat must climb a ladder (a, b) and pull a string to raise the ladder (c, d) so that it can climb up again (e, f). The final behavior is reinforced by food.

Schedules of Reinforcement

The simplest procedure in operant conditioning is to provide reinforcement every time the correct response occurs. **Continuous reinforcement** refers to *reinforcement for every correct response.* As you know, not every response in the real world leads to reinforcement.

Reinforcement for some responses and not for others is known as **intermittent reinforcement.** We behave differently when we learn that only some of our responses will be reinforced. Psychologists have investigated the effects of many **schedules of reinforcement,** which are *rules or procedures for the delivery of reinforcement.* Four schedules for delivery of intermittent reinforcement are fixed ratio, fixed interval, variable ratio, and variable interval (see

TABLE 6.3 Some Schedules of Reinforcement

Type	Description
Continuous	Reinforcement for every response of the correct type
Fixed ratio	Reinforcement following completion of a specific number of responses
Variable ratio	Reinforcement for an unpredictable number of responses that varies around a mean value
Fixed interval	Reinforcement for the first response that follows a given delay since the previous reinforcement
Variable interval	Reinforcement for the first response that follows an unpredictable delay (varying around a mean value) since the previous reinforcement

Table 6.3). A ratio schedule provides reinforcements depending on the number of responses. An interval schedule provides reinforcements depending on the timing of responses.

Fixed-Ratio Schedule

A fixed-ratio schedule *provides a reinforcement only after a certain (fixed) number of correct responses have been made*—after every sixth response, for example. We see similar behavior among pieceworkers in a factory whose pay depends on how many pieces they turn out or among fruit pickers who get paid by the bushel.

The response rate for a fixed-ratio schedule tends to be rapid and steady. Researchers sometimes graph the results with a *cumulative record,* in which each response is noted by a movement upward that is added to the previous level. That is, the line is flat when the animal does not respond; it moves up with each response. For a fixed-ratio schedule, a typical result would look like this:

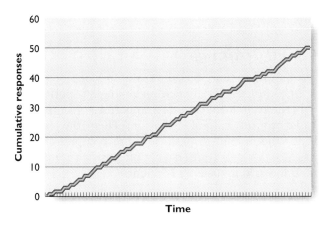

However, if the schedule requires a large number of responses for reinforcement, there may be a temporary interruption after each reinforced response. For example, if you have just completed 10 calculus problems, you may pause briefly before starting your French assignment; after completing 100 problems, you would pause even longer.

Variable-Ratio Schedule

A **variable-ratio schedule** is similar to a fixed-ratio schedule except that *reinforcement is provided after a variable number of correct responses.* For example, reinforcement may come after an average of six responses but may come after just one or two and sometimes after twenty or more. Variable-ratio schedules generate steady response rates.

Variable-ratio schedules, or reasonable approximations of them, occur whenever each response has about an equal probability of success. For example,

when you apply for a job, you might or might not get it. The more times you apply, the better your chances, but you cannot predict how many applications you need to submit before receiving a job offer.

Fixed-Interval Schedule

A fixed-interval schedule *provides reinforcement for the first response made after a specific time interval.* For instance, an animal might get food for only the first response it makes after each 15-second interval. Then it would have to wait another 15 seconds before another response would be effective. Animals (including humans) on such a schedule usually learn to pause after each reinforcement and begin to respond again only as the end of the time interval approaches. The cumulative record would look like this:

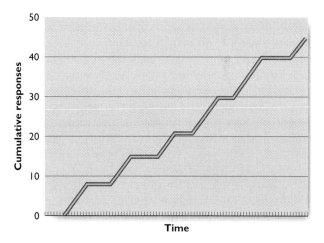

Checking your mailbox is an example of behavior on a fixed-interval schedule. If your mail is delivered at about 3 P.M., you will get no reinforcement for checking your mailbox at 2 P.M. If you are eagerly awaiting an important package, you might begin to check around 2:30 and continue checking every few minutes until it arrives.

Variable-Interval Schedule

In a **variable-interval schedule**, *reinforcement is available after a variable amount of time has elapsed.* For example, reinforcement may come for the first response after 2 minutes, then for the first response after the next 7 seconds, then after 3 minutes 20 seconds, and so forth. There is no way to know how much time will pass before the next response is reinforced. Consequently, responses on a variable-interval schedule occur at a slow but steady rate. Checking your e-mail is an example: A new message could appear at any time, so you check occasionally but not constantly.

Stargazing is also reinforced on a variable-interval schedule. The reinforcement for stargazing—finding a comet, for example—appears at irregular, unpredictable intervals. Consequently, both professional and amateur astronomers scan the skies regularly.

Extinction of Responses Reinforced on Different Schedules

Suppose you and a friend go to a gambling casino and bet on the roulette wheel, choosing bets with an almost 50% chance of winning, such as "red." Amazingly, your first 8 bets are all winners. Your friend wins 8 times out of the first 16 tries. Then both of you go into a prolonged losing streak. Presuming that the two of you have the same amount of money available and no unusual personality quirks, which of you is likely to continue betting longer?

Your friend is, even though you had a more favorable early experience. Extinction of responses is slower after a schedule of intermittent reinforcement (either a ratio schedule or an interval schedule) than after continuous reinforcement (reinforcement for every response). One explanation is that the lack of reinforcement is nothing new for someone who has been responding for intermittent reinforcement. Someone who has had continuous reinforcement can immediately notice the change.

CONCEPT CHECK ☑

14. Identify which schedule of reinforcement applies to each of the following examples:
    a. You attend every new movie that appears at your local theater, although you enjoy about one fourth of them.

    b. You phone your best friend and hear a busy signal. You don't know how soon your friend will hang up, so you try again every few minutes.
    c. You tune your television set to an all-news cable channel, and you look up from your studies to check the sports scores every 30 minutes.
15. Stargazing in the hope of finding a comet was cited as an example of a variable-interval schedule. Why is it *not* an example of a variable ratio?
16. A novice gambler and a longtime gambler both lose 20 bets in a row. Which one is more likely to continue betting? Why? (Check your answers on page 219.)

Applications of Operant Conditioning

Although operant conditioning arose from purely theoretical concerns, it has a long history of applications. Here are four examples.

Animal Training

Most animal acts are based on training methods similar to Skinner's. To induce an animal to perform a trick, the trainer first trains it to perform a simple act similar to its natural behavior. Then the trainer shapes the animal to perform more complex behaviors. Most animal trainers rely on positive reinforcement and seldom use punishment.

▌ Monkeys can be trained to help the disabled. (a) Monkeys are proving useful for indoor tasks for people with limited mobility. (b) This monkey is being trained to retrieve objects identified with a laser beam. Such training relies on shaping—building a complex response by reinforcing sequential approximations to it.

Sometimes what an animal learns is not exactly what the trainer intended (Rumbaugh & Washburn, 2003). Once some psychologists tried to teach a chimpanzee to urinate in a pan instead of on the floor. They gave her some chocolate candy every time she used the pan. Quickly, she learned to urinate just a few drops at a time, holding out her hand for candy each time. When at last she could urinate no more, she *spat* into the pan and again held out her hand for candy!

Persuasion

How could you persuade someone to do something that he or she did not want to do? To use an extreme example, how could you convince a prisoner of war to cooperate with the enemy?

The best way is to start by reinforcing a slight degree of cooperation and then working up to the goal little by little. This principle has been applied by people who had probably never heard of B. F. Skinner, positive reinforcement, or shaping. During the Korean War, the Chinese Communists forwarded some of the letters written home by prisoners of war but intercepted others. (The prisoners could tell from the replies which letters had been forwarded.)

The prisoners began to suspect that they would have better luck getting their letters through if they said something mildly favorable about their captors. So from time to time, they would include a brief remark that the Communists were not really so bad, that certain aspects of the Chinese system seemed to work pretty well, or that they hoped the war would end soon.

After a while the Chinese devised essay contests, offering a little extra food or other privileges to the soldier who wrote the best essay (in the captors' opinion). Most of the winning essays contained a statement or two that complimented the Communists on minor matters or admitted that "the United States is not perfect." Gradually, more and more soldiers started to include such statements. Then the Chinese might ask, "You said the United States is not perfect. We wonder whether you could tell us some of the ways in which it is not perfect, so that we can better understand your system." Then they would ask the soldier to read aloud the lists of what was wrong with the United States. Gradually, without torture and with only modest reinforcements, the Chinese induced prisoners to make public statements denouncing the United States, make false confessions, inform on fellow prisoners, and even reveal military secrets (Cialdini, 1993).

The point is clear: Whether we want to get rats to salute the flag or soldiers to denounce it, the most effective training technique is to start with easy behaviors, reinforce those behaviors, and then gradually shape more complex behaviors.

Applied Behavior Analysis/ Behavior Modification

In one way or another, people are almost constantly trying to influence other people's behavior. Psychologists have developed influence procedures based on operant conditioning.

In **applied behavior analysis**, also known as **behavior modification**, *a psychologist first determines the reinforcers that sustain an unwanted behavior and then tries to alter that behavior by reducing the reinforcers for the unwanted behavior and providing suitable reinforcers for more acceptable behaviors.* For example, one mentally retarded man had a habit of "inappropriate" speech, including lewd sexual comments. Psychologists found that telling him not to say such things actually increased their frequency; getting people's attention was reinforcing. So they switched to ignoring his inappropriate comments and responding attentively to all acceptable comments. The result was increased appropriate and decreased inappropriate comments (Dixon, Benedict, & Larson, 2001).

Another example: Many children get injured on playgrounds, often by using equipment improperly, such as going down the slide head first. The reinforcement for such risky behavior is simply the thrill of it. To stop such behavior, a safety officer talked to elementary school classes about playground safety and offered rewards to the whole class if everyone shifted to safer playground behaviors. College students observed the children in the playground and reported instances of risky behavior. The reinforcements here were almost trivial, such as a blue ribbon for every student or a colorful poster for the door. Nevertheless, the result was decreased head-first sliding and other risky behaviors, and the improved safety continued for weeks afterward (Heck, Collins, & Peterson, 2001).

CONCEPT CHECK ☑

17. Of the procedures characterized in Table 6.1, which one applies to giving more attention to someone's appropriate speech? Which one applies to decreasing attention to inappropriate speech? (Check your answers on page 219.)

Breaking Bad Habits

Some people learn to conquer their own bad habits by means of reinforcements. Nathan Azrin and Robert Nunn (1973) recommend this three-step method:

1. Become more aware of your bad habit. Interrupt the behavior and isolate it from the chain of normal activities. Then you might imagine an association between the behavior and something re-

pulsive. For example, to break a nail-biting habit, imagine your fingernails covered with sewage.

2. If no one else will reinforce you for making progress, provide your own reinforcements. For example, buy yourself a special treat after you have abandoned your bad habit for a certain period of time.

3. Do something incompatible with the offending habit. For example, if you have a nervous habit of hunching up your shoulders, practice depressing your shoulders.

Figure 6.17 shows an example of a college student setting up a list of reinforcements and punishments to support her goal of decreasing her smoking. If she successfully limits her smoking, she will treat herself to a movie. If she breaks the vow, she must clean the room by herself on the weekend. If you decide to try this approach, set clear goals, choose realistic reinforcers, and keep track of your successes and failures. Telling your roommate or someone else about the plan, as in this example, makes the plan work better. (It's harder for you to give up on it.)

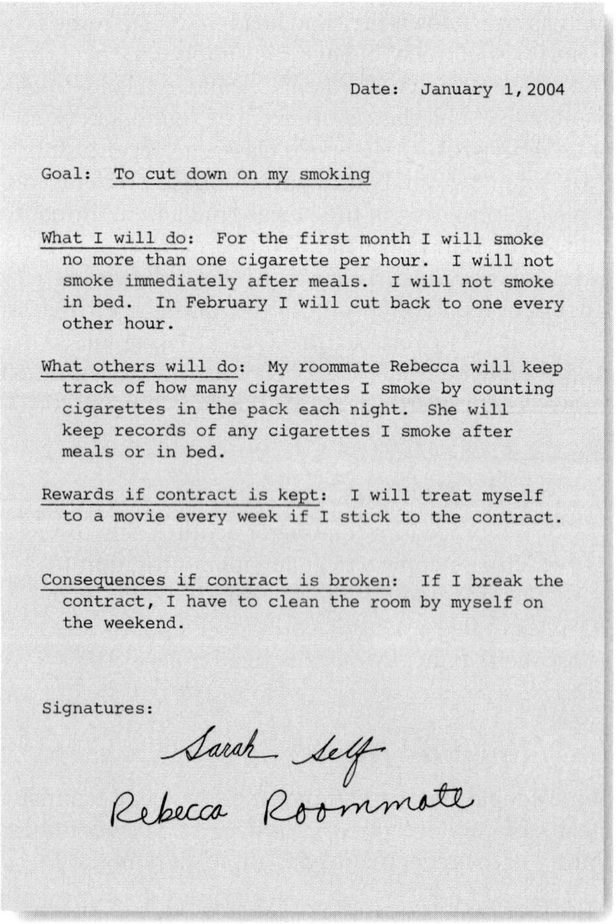

```
                                Date:  January 1, 2004

Goal:   To cut down on my smoking

What I will do:  For the first month I will smoke
  no more than one cigarette per hour.  I will not
  smoke immediately after meals.  I will not smoke
  in bed.  In February I will cut back to one every
  other hour.

What others will do:  My roommate Rebecca will keep
  track of how many cigarettes I smoke by counting
  cigarettes in the pack each night.  She will
  keep records of any cigarettes I smoke after
  meals or in bed.

Rewards if contract is kept:  I will treat myself
  to a movie every week if I stick to the contract.

Consequences if contract is broken:  If I break the
  contract, I have to clean the room by myself on
  the weekend.

Signatures:
              Sarah Self
              Rebecca Roommate
```

FIGURE 6.17 Sometimes people try to change their own behavior by setting up a system of reinforcements and punishments.

IN CLOSING

Operant Conditioning and Human Behavior

Suppose one of your instructors announced that everyone in the class would receive the same grade at the end of the course, regardless of performance on tests and papers. Would you study hard in that course? Probably not. Or suppose your employer said that all raises and promotions would be made at random, with no regard to how well you do your job. Would you work as hard as possible? Not likely. Our behavior depends on its consequences, just like that of a rat, pigeon, or any other animal. That is the main point of operant conditioning.

Summary

- *Reinforcement.* Edward Thorndike introduced the concept of reinforcement. A reinforcement increases the probability that the preceding response will be repeated. (page 207)
- *Operant conditioning.* Operant conditioning is the process of controlling the rate of a behavior through its consequences. (page 207)
- *The nature of reinforcement.* The opportunity to engage in a more probable behavior will reinforce a less probable behavior. Something that an individual can exchange for a reinforcer becomes a reinforcer itself. (page 207)
- *Reinforcement and punishment.* Behaviors can be reinforced (strengthened) by presenting favorable events or by omitting unfavorable events. Behaviors can be punished (suppressed) by presenting unfavorable events or by omitting favorable events. (page 210)
- *Extinction.* In operant conditioning a response becomes extinguished if it is no longer followed by reinforcement. (page 211)
- *Shaping.* Shaping is a technique for training subjects to perform difficult acts by reinforcing them for successive approximations to the desired behavior. (page 213)
- *Schedules of reinforcement.* The frequency and timing of a response depend on the schedule of reinforcement. In a ratio schedule of reinforcement, an individual is given reinforcement after a fixed or variable number of responses. In an interval schedule of reinforcement, an individual is given reinforcement after a fixed or variable period of time. (page 214)
- *Applications.* People have applied operant conditioning to animal training, persuasion, applied behavior analysis, and the breaking of bad habits. (page 216)

Answers to Concept Checks

10. You would need to know whether the bell was always followed by food (classical conditioning) or whether food was presented only if the animal sat up on its hind legs (operant conditioning). (page 207)

11. Begin by determining how this person spends his or her time—for example, exercising, reading, watching television, visiting with friends. Then determine something that he or she has recently not had much opportunity to do. Activities for which one has only limited opportunities become good reinforcers. (page 208)

12. To be effective, punishments must be quick and predictable. Punishments for drug dealing are neither. Furthermore, punishment most effectively suppresses a response when the individual has alternative responses that can gain reinforcements. Many people who gain enormous profits by selling drugs have no alternative way to gain similar profits. (page 210)

13. **a.** positive reinforcement; **b.** punishment or passive avoidance; **c.** escape learning or negative reinforcement; **d.** punishment or passive avoidance; **e.** omission training or negative punishment; **f.** omission training or negative punishment; **g.** avoidance learning or negative reinforcement. (page 211)

14. **a.** variable ratio. (You will be reinforced for about one fourth of your entries to the theater but on an irregular basis.) **b.** variable interval. (Calling will become effective after some interval of time, but the length of that time is unpredictable.) **c.** fixed interval. (page 216)

15. In a variable-ratio schedule, the number of responses matters, but the timing does not. If you have already checked the stars tonight and found no comets, checking three more times tonight will probably be fruitless. Checking at a later date gives you a better chance. (page 216)

16. The longtime gambler will continue longer because he or she has a history of being reinforced for gambling on a variable-ratio schedule, which retards extinction. (For the same reason, an alcoholic who has had both good experiences and bad experiences while drunk is likely to keep on drinking even after several bad experiences.) (page 216)

17. Increasing attention for appropriate speech is positive reinforcement. Decreasing attention for inappropriate speech is omission training or negative punishment. (If you called it "lack of positive reinforcement," you would not be wrong, and calling it simply "punishment" is acceptable for most purposes.) (page 217)

Other Kinds of Learning

What kinds of learning do not fit neatly into the categories of classical or operant conditioning?

How do we learn from the successes and failures of others without trying every response ourselves?

Operant and classical conditioning both depend on an association between a first event (response or CS) and a second event (reinforcement or UCS). The main difference is that in operant conditioning the first event is something the individual does, whereas in classical conditioning the first event is a stimulus in the outside world. It might seem that all possible examples of learning would fall into either of these two categories; several, however, are difficult to classify or require special treatment.

Conditioned Taste Aversions

If you eat something with an unfamiliar flavor and then feel ill, you will quickly learn to avoid that flavor. The same process works in rats and every other species researchers have tested. Most psychologists describe this process as classical conditioning, with the taste as CS and illness as US. In fact, however, because it occurs after just one trial, its classification is ambiguous: Do you (or a rat) associate the *taste* with illness or do you associate your *response* (eating or drinking that substance) with illness? If the illness depends on your response, then we should call it operant conditioning. In any case this type of learning has several special features.

An *association between eating something and getting sick* is conditioned taste aversion, first documented by John Garcia and his colleagues (Garcia, Ervin, & Koelling, 1966). One of its special features is the fact that it occurs reliably after a single pairing of food with illness, even with a long delay between them. For example, a rat is drinking a saccharin solution, which it has never tasted before. Saccharin tastes sweet, and in moderate amounts it is neither healthful nor harmful. After the rat has drunk for a few minutes, the experimenter removes the bottle, waits minutes or even hours, and then injects a small amount of poison, making the rat moderately ill. The experimenter then waits long enough for the rat to recover and offers it a choice between the saccharin solution and unflavored water. The rat will strongly prefer the unflavored water (Garcia et al., 1966). In contrast, rats that have not been poisoned, or that have been poisoned after drinking something else, strongly prefer the saccharin solution. In most other cases of either classical or operant conditioning, learning is greatest with a 1- or 2-second delay between the events to be associated and hard to demonstrate at all with delays over 20 seconds (Kimble, 1961).

An animal that learns a conditioned taste aversion to a particular food treats that food as if it tasted bad (Figure 6.18) (Garcia, 1990). Some ranchers in the western United States have used this type of learning to deter coyotes from eating sheep. They offer the coyotes sheep meat containing enough lithium salts to produce nausea but not enough to be dangerous. Afterward, the coyotes become less likely to attack sheep, although they continue to hunt rabbits and other prey. One study reported that this method reduced coyotes' sheep kills to about half of what had occurred the previous year (Gustavson, Kelly, Sweeney, & Garcia, 1976). This technique has the potential of protecting sheep without killing the coyotes, which are a threatened species.

©Stuart Ellins

FIGURE 6.18 This coyote previously fell ill after eating sheep meat containing a mild dose of lithium salts. Now it reacts toward both live and dead sheep as it would toward bad-tasting food.

Conditioned taste aversions are probably responsible for some of our choices of food and beverage. Mice that have trouble metabolizing alcohol get sick after drinking it and learn to avoid it or anything else they tasted prior to consuming it (Broadbent, Muccino, & Cunningham, 2002). Similarly, people who have trouble metabolizing alcohol also get sick after they drink it and learn to avoid it (Tu & Israel, 1995). Many women who get nauseated during pregnancy learn aversion to the foods they have been eating (Crystal, Bowen, & Bernstein, 1999), and many cancer patients learn aversions to foods they ate just prior to chemotherapy or radiation therapy (Bernstein, 1991).

Conditioned taste aversions are special in another regard as well: Recall that an animal can associate a food with feeling ill hours later. No doubt the animal had many other experiences between the food and the illness. Nevertheless, animals are predisposed to associate illness mostly with what they eat. In one classic experiment (Garcia & Koelling, 1966), rats were allowed to drink saccharin-flavored water from tubes that were set up so that, whenever the rats licked the water, they turned on a bright light and a loud noise. Some of the rats were exposed to x-rays (which can induce nausea) while they drank. Others were given electric shocks to their feet 2 seconds after they started drinking. After the training was complete, each rat was tested separately with a tube of saccharin-flavored water and a tube of unflavored water that produced lights and noises. (Figure 6.19 illustrates the experiment.)

The rats that received x-rays avoided the flavored water. The rats that received shocks avoided the tube that produced lights and noises. Evidently, rats (and other species) have a built-in predisposition to associate illness mostly with what they eat or drink. They associate skin pain mostly with what they see or hear. (This tendency is an example of preparedness, mentioned earlier in this chapter.) Such predispositions are presumably beneficial because foods are more

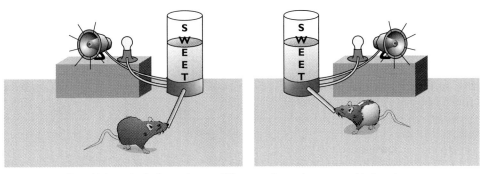

Rats drink saccharin-flavored water. Whenever they make contact with the tube, they turn on a bright light and a noisy buzzer.

Then

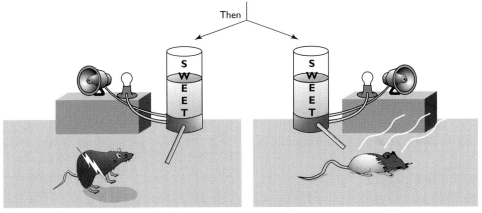

Some rats get electric shock.

Some rats are nauseated by x-rays.

Next day: Rats are given a choice between a tube of saccharin-flavored water and a tube of unflavored water hooked up to the light and the buzzer.

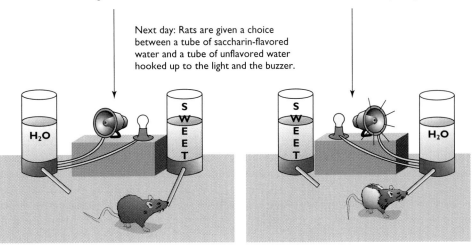

Rats that had been shocked avoid the tube with the lights and noises.

Rats that had been nauseated by x-rays avoid the saccharin-flavored water.

FIGURE 6.19 An experiment by Garcia and Koelling (1966): Rats "blame" an illness on what they ate; they blame pain on what they saw or heard or where they were.

likely to cause internal events, and lights and sounds are more likely to signal external events.

One problem remains with all of this: I have described associations between food and "illness," but some drugs that make the animal very ill produce only weak learned aversions, and some procedures such as x-rays that hardly make the animal ill at all (and produce only slight nausea in humans) produce powerful aversions to recently eaten foods. Rats will work for an opportunity to get into a running wheel, and they prefer to be in a distinctive cage associated with a running wheel instead of other cages. Nevertheless, running evidently produces some mild stomach distress (probably analogous to riding a roller coaster), and rats learn to avoid the taste of anything they drank just before getting into the running wheel (Lett, Grant, Koh, & Smith, 2001). The fact that running in a wheel can simultaneously increase preference for the cage while decreasing preference for a food indicates that conditioned taste aversion is a special kind of learning. It also indicates that a single event can be reinforcing for one response and punishing for another!

▌ A male white-crowned sparrow learns his song in the first months of life but does not begin to sing it until the next year.

©Joe McDonald/CORBIS

CONCEPT CHECK

18. Which kind of learning takes place despite a long delay between the events to be associated?
19. What evidence indicates that conditioned taste aversion is different compared to other kinds of learning? (Check your answers on page 226.)

Birdsong Learning

Birdsongs brighten the day for people who hear them, but they are earnest business for the birds themselves. For most species only males sing, and they sing only in spring, the mating season. As a rule a song indicates, "Here I am. I am a male of species ___. If you're a female of my species, please come closer. If you're a male of my species and you can hear me, you're too close. If I find you, I'll attack."

(Among the delights of birdsongs are the exceptions to the rule. Mockingbirds copy all the songs they hear and defend their territory against intruders of all species—sometimes even squirrels, cats, people, and automobiles. Carolina wrens sing male-and-female

duets throughout the year. Woodpeckers don't sing, but rely on the rhythm and loudness of their pecks to signal others. That woodpecker banging on the metal siding of your house in spring is *trying* to make a racket to impress the females. But on to more relevant matters.)

If you were to rear an infant songbird in isolation from others of its species, would it develop a normal song on its own? Maybe or maybe not depending on its species. Some species have to learn their song. For example, in several sparrow species, a male develops a normal song only if he hears the song of his own species. He *learns most readily during a* **sensitive period** *early in his first year of life.* The young bird learns better from a live tutor, such as his father, than from a tape-recorded song in a laboratory (Baptista & Petrinovich, 1984; Marler & Peters, 1987, 1988). It will not learn at all from the song of another species. Evidently, a fledgling sparrow is equipped with mechanisms to produce approximately the right song and ways of identifying which songs to imitate (Marler, 1997).

Birdsong learning resembles human language learning in that both take place in a social context, both occur most easily in early life, both start with babbling and gradually improve, and both deteriorate gradually if the individual becomes deaf later (Brainard & Doupe, 2000). Song learning differs, however, from standard examples of classical and operant conditioning. During the sensitive period, the infant bird only listens. We cannot call the song he hears an unconditioned stimulus because it elicits no apparent response. At no time in this sensitive period does the bird receive any apparent reinforcement.

Nevertheless, he learns a representation of how his song should sound, even though we cannot classify the learning as either classical or operant. The following spring, when the bird starts to sing, we see a trial-and-error process with a strange form of operant conditioning. At first his song is a disorganized mixture of sounds, somewhat like a babbling human infant. As time passes he eliminates some sounds and rearranges others until he matches the songs he heard the previous summer (Marler & Peters, 1981, 1982). But there is no external reinforcer; the only reinforcer is somehow "knowing" that he has sung correctly.

The point is that the principles of learning vary from one situation to another. If a situation poses special problems (e.g., food selection, song learning in birds, probably language learning in humans), we can expect to find that species have evolved their own special ways of learning (Rozin & Kalat, 1971).

CONCEPT CHECK ☑

20. What aspects of birdsong learning set it apart from classical and operant conditioning? (Check your answer on page 226.)

Social Learning

According to the **social-learning approach** (Bandura, 1977, 1986), *we learn about many behaviors before we try them the first time. Much learning, especially in humans, results from observing the behaviors of others and from imagining the consequences of our own behavior.* For example, if you want to learn how to swim, paint pictures, or drive a car, you *could* try to learn strictly by trial and error, but you would probably start by watching someone who is already skilled. When you do try the task yourself, your attempt will be subject to reinforcement and punishment; therefore, it falls into the realm of operant conditioning. However, because you will be facilitated by your observations of others, we treat social learning as a special case.

"Social-learning theory" is not a *theory* in the sense described in Chapter 2. The social-learning approach is more a field of emphasis, with a focus on observation, imitation, setting goals, and self-reinforcement.

▌ A Japanese toilet is a hole in the ground with no seat. Western visitors usually have to ask how to use it. (You squat.)

▌ According to the social-learning approach, we learn many behaviors by observing what others do, imitating behaviors that are reinforced, and avoiding behaviors that are punished.

Modeling and Imitation

If you visit another country with customs unlike your own, you may find yourself bewildered about things you used to take for granted. Ordering food in a restaurant is not done the way you did it back home; paying for the meal is done differently too. A hand gesture such as ⟨hand image⟩ is considered friendly in some countries but rude and vulgar in others. Many visitors to Japan are confused by the toilets. With effort you learn foreign customs either because someone explains them to you or because you watch and copy. We say that you *model* your behavior after others or *imitate* others. On a smaller scale, you also model or imitate the customs of a religious organization, a fraternity or sorority, a new place of employment, or any other group you join.

Albert Bandura, Dorothea Ross, and Sheila Ross (1963) studied the role of imitation for learning aggressive behavior. They asked two groups of children to watch films in which an adult or a cartoon character violently attacked an inflated "Bobo" doll. Another group watched a film in which the adult or character did not attack the doll. They then left the children in a room with a Bobo doll. Only the children who had watched films with attacks on the doll attacked the doll themselves, using many of the same movements they had just seen (Figure 6.20). The clear implication is

FIGURE 6.20 A child will mimic an adult's behavior even when neither one is reinforced for the behavior. This girl attacks a doll after seeing a film of a woman hitting it. People who witness violent behavior, including violence at home, may be more prone than others to turn to violent behavior themselves.

that children copy the aggressive behavior they have seen in others.

CONCEPT CHECK ☑

21. Many people complain that they cannot find much difference between the two major political parties in the United States because so many American politicians campaign using similar styles and take similar stands on the issues. Explain this observation in terms of social learning. (Check your answer on page 226.)

Vicarious Reinforcement and Punishment

Six months ago, your best friend quit a job with Consolidated Generic Products to open a restaurant. Now you are considering quitting your job and opening your own restaurant. How do you decide what to do?

You would probably start by asking how successful your friend has been. You imitate behavior that apparently has been reinforcing to someone else. In other words you learn by **vicarious reinforcement or vicarious punishment**—that is, by *substituting someone else's experience for your own.*

Whenever a new business venture succeeds, other companies copy it. For example, the first few successful Internet companies were followed by a horde of imitators. When a sports team wins consistently, other teams

copy its style of play. When a television program wins high ratings, other producers are sure to present look-alikes the following year. Advertisers depend heavily on vicarious reinforcement; they show you happy, successful people using their product, with the implication that if you use their product, you too will be happy and successful. The people promoting state lotteries show the ecstatic winners—never the losers!—suggesting that if you try the lottery, you too can win a fortune.

> **CRITICAL THINKING:**
> *A STEP FURTHER*
> *Vicarious Learning*

Might vicarious learning lead to monotony of behavior and excessive conformity? How can we learn vicariously without becoming just like everyone else?

Although we can think of many examples of vicarious reinforcement, vicarious punishment seems less effective. If someone gets caught cheating, either in a classroom or in business, or if someone goes to prison for a crime, do other people quit those behaviors? Not necessarily. We are often reminded of the health risks associated with cigarette smoking, overweight, risky sex, lack of exercise, or failure to wear seat belts, but many people ignore the dangers. Even the death penalty, an extreme example of vicarious punishment, does not demonstrably lower the murder rate.

Why is vicarious punishment often so ineffective? One explanation is

■ States that sponsor lotteries provide publicity and an exciting atmosphere for each big payoff. They hope that this publicity will provide vicarious reinforcement to encourage other people to buy lottery tickets.

that we are influenced by vicarious reinforcement or punishment to someone we consider to be like ourselves. Most of us think of ourselves as successful people and therefore unlike the "loser" who is being punished.

Self-Efficacy in Social Learning

We primarily imitate people we regard as successful. So, when you watch an Olympic diver win a gold medal for a superb display of physical control, do you then go out and try to imitate those dives? Probably not. People imitate someone else's behavior only if they have a sense of **self-efficacy**—*the perception that they themselves could perform the task successfully.* You observe your past successes and failures, compare yourself to the successful person, and estimate your chance of success.

We see this effect in children's life aspirations. Nearly anyone would like a high-paying, high-prestige profession, but many think they could never rise to that level, so they don't try (Bandura, Barbaranelli, Caprara, & Pastorelli, 2001). One reason for trying to get more women and minorities into high-visibility leadership jobs in business, education, and government is to provide role models—that is, to show young people that the gates are not closed, and strong effort can be rewarded.

❚ We tend to imitate the actions of successful people, but only if we feel self-efficacy, a belief that we could perform the task well.

Sometimes people know that they cannot do much themselves but gain confidence in what they can do with a group effort (Bandura, 2000). Even groups differ in their feeling of efficacy or nonefficacy; a group with confidence in its abilities accomplishes much more than a group with doubts.

❚ We acquire a sense of self-efficacy mainly through our own successes but also partly by watching and identifying with role models.

Self-Reinforcement and Self-Punishment in Social Learning

We learn by observing others who are doing what we would like to do. If our sense of self-efficacy is strong enough, we try to imitate their behavior. But actually succeeding often requires prolonged efforts. People typically set a goal for themselves and monitor their progress toward that goal. They even provide reinforcement or punishment for themselves, just as if they were training someone else. They say to themselves, "If I finish this math assignment on time, I'll treat myself to a movie and a new magazine. If I don't finish on time, I'll make myself clean the stove and the sink." (Nice threat, but people usually forgive themselves and don't impose the punishment.)

Some therapists teach clients to use self-reinforcement. One 10-year-old boy had a habit of biting his fingernails, sometimes down to the skin and even drawing blood. He learned to keep records of how much nail-biting he did in the morning, afternoon, and evening, and then he set goals for himself. If he met the goals by reducing his nail-biting, he wrote compliments such as "I'm great! I did wonderful!" The penalty for doing worse was that he would return his weekly allowance to his parents. An additional reinforcement was that his father promised that if the son made enough progress, he would let the son be the "therapist" to help the father quit smoking. Over several weeks the boy quit nail-biting altogether (Ronen & Rosenbaum, 2001).

One amusing anecdote shows how self-reinforcement and self-punishment can fail: Psychologist Ron Ash (1986) tried to teach himself to stop smoking by smoking only while he was reading *Psychological Bulletin* and other highly respected but tedious publications. He hoped to associate smoking with boredom. Two months later he was smoking as much as ever, but he was starting to *enjoy* reading *Psychological Bulletin*!

IN CLOSING

Why We Do What We Do

Almost everything you have done today was a learned behavior—from getting dressed and combing your hair this morning to reading this chapter right now. In fact you would have trouble listing much you did that was not learned. Even your bad habits were learned.

One point that I hope has emerged is that learning takes many forms. Classically conditioned salivation, operantly conditioned movements, conditioned taste aversions, and socially learned behaviors occur under diverse circumstances. The underlying mechanisms in the brain may or may not be the same, but at a descriptive level, these types of learning differ in some important ways. In short, your behavior is subject to a wide variety of learned influences.

Summary

* *Conditioned taste aversions.* Animals, including people, learn to avoid foods, especially unfamiliar ones, if they become ill afterward. This type of learning occurs reliably after a single pairing, even with a delay of hours between the food and the illness. Animals are predisposed to associate illness with what they eat or drink, not with other events. (page 220)
* *Birdsong learning.* Infant birds of some species must hear their songs during a sensitive period in the first few months of life if they are to develop a fully normal song the following spring. During the early learning, the bird makes no apparent response and receives no apparent reinforcement. (page 222)

* *Learning by observation.* We learn much by observing what other people do and what consequences they experience. (page 223)
* *Vicarious reinforcement and punishment.* We tend to imitate behaviors that have led to reinforcement for other people. We are less consistent in avoiding behaviors that have led to punishment. (page 224)
* *Self-efficacy.* Whether we decide to imitate a behavior depends on whether we believe we are capable of duplicating it and whether we believe we would be reinforced for it. (page 225)
* *Self-reinforcement and self-punishment.* Once people have decided to try to imitate a certain behavior, they set goals for themselves and may even provide their own reinforcements and punishments. (page 225)

Answers to Concept Checks

18. Conditioned taste aversions develop despite a long delay between food and illness. (page 222)
19. In addition to the fact that conditioned taste aversion occurs over long delays, animals are predisposed to associate foods and not other events with illnesses. Also, an event such as running in a wheel can be reinforcing for other responses but simultaneously decrease preference for a taste associated with it. (page 222)
20. The most distinctive feature is that birdsong learning occurs during a time when the learner makes no apparent response and receives no apparent reinforcement. Also, at least in certain sparrow species, birdsong learning occurs most readily during an early sensitive period, and the bird is capable of learning its own species' song but not the song of another species. (page 223)
21. One reason that most American politicians run similar campaigns and take similar stands is that they all tend to copy the same models—candidates who have won recent elections. Another reason is that they all pay attention to the same public opinion polls. (page 224)

Key Terms and Activities

Key Terms

acquisition: the process by which a conditioned response is established or strengthened (page 198)

applied behavior analysis (or behavior modification): a procedure for determining the reinforcers that sustain an unwanted behavior and then reducing the reinforcements for the unwanted behavior and providing suitable reinforcers for more acceptable behaviors (page 217)

avoidance learning: learning to make a response that avoids pain or some similar outcome (page 210)

behaviorist: a psychologist who insists that psychologists should study only observable, measurable behaviors, not mental processes (page 191)

belongingness: the concept that certain stimuli are readily associated with each other and that certain responses are readily associated with certain outcomes (page 212)

blocking effect: the tendency of a previously established association to one stimulus to block the formation of an association to an added stimulus (page 203)

chaining: a procedure for developing a sequence of behaviors in which the reinforcement for one response is the opportunity to engage in the next response (page 213)

classical conditioning (or Pavlovian conditioning): the process by which an organism learns a new association between two paired stimuli—a neutral stimulus and one that already evokes a reflexive response (page 196)

conditioned response (CR): whatever response the conditioned stimulus begins to elicit as a result of the conditioning procedure (page 196)

conditioned stimulus (CS): a stimulus that comes to evoke a particular response after being paired with the unconditioned stimulus (page 196)

conditioned taste aversion: the tendency to avoid eating a substance that has been followed by illness when it was eaten in the past (page 220)

continuous reinforcement: reinforcement for every correct response (page 214)

discrimination: (1) in classical conditioning making different responses to different stimuli that have been followed by different outcomes (page 199); (2) in operant conditioning learning to respond in one way to one stimulus and in a different way to another stimulus (page 211)

discriminative stimulus: a stimulus that indicates on which occasion a response will produce a certain consequence (page 211)

disequilibrium principle: the principle that an opportunity to engage in any deprived activity will be a reinforcer because it restores equilibrium (page 208)

drug tolerance: the progressively weaker effects of a drug after repeated use (page 201)

escape learning: learning to escape from an event such as shock (page 210)

extinction: (1) in classical conditioning the dying out of the conditioned response after repeated presentations of the conditioned stimulus without the unconditioned stimulus (page 198); (2) in operant conditioning the weakening of a response after a period without reinforcement (page 211)

fixed-interval schedule: a rule for delivering reinforcement for the first response that the subject makes after a specified period of time has passed (page 215)

fixed-ratio schedule: a rule for delivering reinforcement only after the subject has made a specific number of correct responses (page 215)

intermittent reinforcement: reinforcement for some responses and not for others (page 214)

intervening variable: something that we infer without directly observing it and that links a variety of procedures to a variety of possible responses (page 191)

law of effect: Thorndike's theory that a response followed by favorable consequences becomes more probable and a response followed by unfavorable consequences becomes less probable (page 207)

learning curve: a graphical representation of the changes in behavior that occur over the course of learning (page 206)

methodological behaviorist: a psychologist who studies only measurable, observable events but sometimes uses those observations to make inferences about internal events (page 191)

negative punishment: a decrease in the future probability of a response because it led to the absence of something such as food (page 210)

negative reinforcement: an increase in the future probability of a response because it led to the *absence* of something such as pain (page 210)

omission training: learning to suppress a behavior that would lead to the omission of an event such as food (page 210)

operant conditioning (or instrumental conditioning): the process of changing behavior by following a response with reinforcement (page 207)

passive avoidance learning: learning to avoid an outcome such as shock by being passive—that is, by inhibiting a response that would lead to the outcome (page 210)

positive reinforcement: strengthening a behavior through the presentation of an event such as food (page 210)

Premack principle: the principle that the opportunity to engage in a frequent behavior will reinforce a less frequent behavior (page 208)

primary reinforcer: an event that is reinforcing because of its own properties (page 208)

punishment: an event that decreases the probability that a response will be repeated (page 209)

radical behaviorist: a behaviorist who denies that internal, private events are causes of behavior (page 191)

reinforcement: an event that increases the future probability of the most recent response (page 207)

reinforcer: an event that follows a response and increases the later probability or frequency of that response (page 207)

schedule of reinforcement: a rule or procedure linking the pattern of responses to the reinforcements (page 214)

secondary reinforcer: an event that becomes reinforcing because it has previously been associated with a primary reinforcer (page 208)

self-efficacy: the perception of one's own ability to perform a task successfully (page 225)

sensitive period: a time early in life during which some kind of learning occurs most readily (page 222)

shaping: a technique for establishing a new response by reinforcing successive approximations (page 213)

skeletal responses: movements of the muscles that move the limbs, trunk, and head (page 207)

social-learning approach: the view that people learn by observing and imitating the behavior of others and by imagining the consequences of their own behavior (page 223)

spontaneous recovery: the temporary return of an extinguished response after a delay (page 199)

stimulus control: the ability of a stimulus to encourage some responses and discourage others (page 212)

stimulus generalization: (1) in classical conditioning the extension of a conditioned response from the training stimulus to similar stimuli (page 199); (2) in operant conditioning the tendency to make a similar response to a stimulus that resembles one that has already been associated with reinforcement (page 211)

stimulus–response psychology: a field that attempts to explain behavior in terms of how each stimulus triggers a response (page 192)

unconditioned reflex: an automatic connection between a stimulus and a response (page 196)

unconditioned response (UCR): an automatic response to an unconditioned stimulus (page 196)

unconditioned stimulus (UCS): a stimulus that automatically elicits an unconditioned response (page 196)

variable-interval schedule: a rule for delivering reinforcement after varying amounts of time (page 215)

variable-ratio schedule: a rule for delivering reinforcement after varying numbers of correct responses (page 215)

vicarious reinforcement (or vicarious punishment): the observed reinforcement or punishment experienced by someone else (page 224)

visceral responses: activities of the internal organs (page 207)

Suggestions for Further Reading

Bandura, A. (1986). *Social foundations of thought and action.* Upper Saddle River, NJ: Prentice Hall. A review of social learning by its most influential investigator.

Staddon, J. (1993). *Behaviorism.* London: Duckworth. A critique of both the strengths and weaknesses of Skinner's views.

Book Companion Web Site

Need help studying? Go to

http://psychology.wadsworth.com/kalat_intro7e/

for a virtual study center. You'll find a personalized Self-Study Assessment that will provide you with a study plan based on your answers to a pretest. Also study using flashcards, quizzes, interactive art, and an online glossary.

Check out interactive **Try It Yourself** exercises on the companion site! These exercises will help you put what you've learned into action.

Your companion site also has direct links to the following Web sites. These links are checked often for changes, dead links, and new additions.

Positive Reinforcement

server.bmod.athabascau.ca/html/prtut/reinpair.htm

Lyle K. Grant of Athabasca University helps students understand what does and what does not constitute positive reinforcement. Be sure you understand the examples before you begin the practice exercise.

Dr. P's Dog Training

www.uwsp.edu/psych/dog/dog.htm

Mark Plonsky of the University of Wisconsin discusses applications of operant conditioning to obedience competition, K9 training, assistance dogs, and working dogs.

Albert Bandura

www.ship.edu/~cgboeree/bandura.html

C. George Boeree of Shippensburg University provides a short biography of Albert Bandura, a leading pioneer in the field of social learning.

 Try It Yourself CD-ROM
with Critical Thinking Video Exercises

Use your CD to access **videos** related to activities designed to help you think critically about the important topics discussed. You'll also find an easy portal link to the book companion site where you can access your personalized **Self-Study Assessments** and interactive **Try It Yourself** exercises.

PsychNow! 2.0

PsychNow! is a fun interactive CD designed to help you with the difficult concepts in psychology. Check out the Learning & Cognition section for the following topics that relate to this chapter:
Classical Conditioning: stimuli video, a stimulus and response lesson, and a CS and CR exercise.
Operant Conditioning: explore operant conditioning with explanation and take a quiz.
Observational Learning: Skinner and a rat video, TV violence video, Bandura and observational learning lesson and quiz.

Memory

Suppose I offer you—for a price—an opportunity to do absolutely anything you want for a day. You will not be limited by the usual physical constraints. You can travel in a flash from one place to another, visiting as many places as you wish, even in outer space. You can travel forward and backward through time, finding out what the future holds and witnessing the great events of the past. (You will not be able to alter history.) Anything you want to do—just name it and it is yours. Furthermore, I guarantee your safety: No matter where you choose to go or what you choose to do, you will not get hurt.

How much would you pay for this once in a lifetime opportunity? Oh, yes, I should mention, there is one catch. When the day is over, you will completely forget everything that happened. Any notes or photos will vanish. And anyone else who takes part in your special day will forget it too.

Now how much would you be willing to pay? Much less, no doubt, and perhaps nothing. Living without remembering is hardly living at all: Our memories are almost the same as our selves.

▌ With a suitable reminder, you will find that you remember some events quite distinctly, even after a long delay. Other memories, however, are lost or distorted.

Do we have different kinds of memory?

If so, what is the best way to describe those differences?

Every year people compete in the World Memory Championship in Britain. (If you would like to read about it, visit this Web site: **http://www.worldmemorychampionship.com/**). One event is speed of memorizing a shuffled deck of 52 cards. (The all-time record is 34.03 seconds.) Other events include rapidly memorizing long lists of numbers and words. Dominic O'Brien, the eight-time world champion, set an all-time record by memorizing a 316-digit number in 5 minutes. However, he admits that one time while he was practicing his card memorization, an irate friend called to complain that O'Brien had forgotten to meet him at the airport. O'Brien apologized and drove to London's Gatwick Airport, practicing card memorization along the way. When he arrived, he remembered that his friend's flight arrived at Heathrow, London's other major airport (Johnstone, 1994).

Anyone—you, me, or Dominic O'Brien—remembers some items and forgets others. Let's define memory broadly. **Memory** refers to *the process of retaining information and to the information retained*. Memory includes skills, such as how to ride a bicycle or how to eat with chopsticks. It also includes facts that never change (your birthday), facts that seldom change (your mailing address), and facts that frequently change (where you last parked your car). You remember repeated events (the changing seasons of the year), many important events (your last day of high school or first day of college), and some of the less important events. You remember many of the most interesting and important facts you were taught in school and a few of the less useful ones. (I remember learning that "Polynesians eat poi and breadfruit," although I seldom meet a Polynesian person, and I wouldn't recognize poi or breadfruit if I saw it.)

Human memory is not much like that of a computer (Bjork & VanHuele, 1992). If you hit the "store" key, your computer will store the information without pausing to consider whether it is "boring." If you try to retrieve it later, the computer will give it to you precisely. In contrast, if you try to recall an old event yourself, you remember better at some times than others, and you remember some parts correctly while losing or distorting others. You might even claim to remember events that never happened.

Ebbinghaus's Pioneering Studies of Memory

Suppose you wanted to study memory, but no one had ever done memory research before, so you couldn't copy anyone else's procedure. Where would you start? Some of the earliest psychological researchers simply asked people to describe their memories. The obvious problem was that the researchers did not know when the memories had formed, how many times they had been rehearsed, or even whether they were correct. German psychologist Hermann Ebbinghaus (1850–1909) got around these problems by an approach that was completely original at the time, although we now take it for granted: He taught new material, so that he knew exactly what someone had learned and when, and then measured memory after various delays. To be sure the material was totally new, he used lists of nonsense syllables, such as GAK or JEK. He wrote out 2,300 such syllables, assembled them randomly into

▌ Dominic O'Brien, eight-time winner of the World Memory Championship and author of several books on training your memory, admits he sometimes forgets practical information, such as promising to meet a friend at Heathrow Airport.

©Rupert Watts

233

FIGURE 7.1 Hermann Ebbinghaus pioneered the scientific study of memory by observing his own capacity for memorizing lists of nonsense syllables.

lists (Figure 7.1), and then set out to study memorization. He had no cooperative introductory psychology students to enlist for his study nor friends eager to spend many hours memorizing nonsense, so he ran all the tests on himself. Over about 6 years, he memorized thousands of lists of nonsense syllables. (He was either very dedicated to his science or uncommonly tolerant of boredom.)

Many of his findings were hardly surprising. For example, as shown in Figure 7.2, the longer a list of nonsense syllables, the more slowly he memorized it. "Of course!" you might scoff. But Ebbinghaus was not just demonstrating the obvious; he measured *how much* longer it took to memorize a longer list. You might similarly object to the law of gravity: "Of course the farther something falls, the longer it takes to hit the ground!" Nevertheless, measuring the exact acceleration of gravity was essential to progress in physics. In the same way, measuring how long it takes to learn

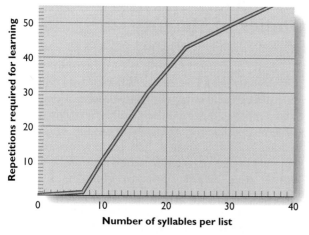

FIGURE 7.2 Ebbinghaus counted how many times he had to read a list of nonsense syllables before he could recite it once correctly. For a list of seven or fewer, one reading was usually enough. Beyond seven, the longer the list, the more repetitions he needed. *(From Ebbinghaus, 1885/1913)*

a list enables researchers to compare learning under different conditions: Do adults learn faster than children? Do we learn some kinds of lists faster than others? And so forth. Ebbinghaus's approach led to all the later research on memory, including findings that were not so obvious.

Methods of Testing Memory

Nearly everyone occasionally has a tip-of-the-tongue experience (Brown & McNeill, 1966). You are trying to think of someone's name, and all you can think of is some similar name that you know isn't right. You will probably think of the correct name later, and you are sure you would recognize it if you heard it.

In other words memory is not an all-or-none thing. You might seem to remember or seem to forget depending on how someone tests you. Let's survey the main ways of testing memory.

Free Recall

The simplest method for the tester (though not for the person tested) is to ask for **free recall**. To recall something is *to produce a response, as you do on essay tests or short-answer tests*. For instance, "Please name all the children in your third-grade class." You probably will not name many, partly because you confuse the names of the children in your third-grade class with those you knew in other grades.

Cued Recall

You will do better with **cued recall**, in which you *receive significant hints about the material*. For example, a photograph of the children in your third-grade class (Figure 7.3) or a list of their initials will

FIGURE 7.3 Can you recall the names of the students in your third-grade class? Trying to remember without any hints is *free recall*. Using a photo or a list of initials is *cued recall*.

help you remember many names. Try this: Cover the right side of Table 7.1 with a piece of paper and try to identify the authors of each book on the left. (This method is recall.) Then uncover the right side, revealing each author's initials, and try again. (This method is cued recall.)

TABLE 7.1 The Difference Between Free Recall and Cued Recall

Instructions: First try to identify the author of each book listed in the left column while covering the right column (free recall method). Then expose the right column, which gives each author's initials, and try again (cued recall).

Book	Author
Moby Dick	H. M.
Emma and *Pride and Prejudice*	J. A.
Hercule Poirot stories	A. C.
Sherlock Holmes stories	A. C. D.
I Know Why the Caged Bird Sings	M. A.
War and Peace	L. T.
This textbook	J. K.
The Canterbury Tales	G. C.
The Origin of Species	C. D.
Gone with the Wind	M. M.
Les Miserables	V. H.

(For answers, see page 244, answer A.)

Recognition

With **recognition**, a third method of testing memory, someone is *offered several choices and asked to select the correct one.* People usually recognize more items than they recall. For example, I might give you a list of 60 names and ask you to check off the correct names of children in your third-grade class. Multiple-choice tests use the recognition method.

Savings

A fourth method, the **savings method** (also known as the **relearning method**), detects weak memories *by comparing the speed of original learning to the speed of relearning.* Suppose you cannot name the children in your third-grade class and cannot even pick out their names from a list of choices. You would nevertheless learn a correct list of names faster than a list of people you had never met. That is, you save time when you relearn material that you learned in the past. The amount of time saved (time needed for original learning minus the time for relearning) is a measure of memory.

Implicit Memory

Free recall, cued recall, recognition, and savings are all tests of **explicit (or direct) memory**—*someone who states an answer regards it as a product of his or her memory.* In **implicit memory (or indirect memory)**, *an experience influences something you say or do even though you might not be aware of the influence.* If you find that definition unsatisfactory, you are not alone (Frensch & Rünger, 2003). Defining something in terms of a vague concept like "awareness" is not a good habit. Regard the current definition as tentative until we can develop a better one.

Probably the best way to explain implicit memory is by example: Suppose you are having one discussion while other people in the room are having another. You ignore the other conversation, but occasionally, words from that background conversation creep into your own. You do not even notice the influence, although an observer might.

Here is a demonstration of implicit memories. For each of the following three-letter combinations, fill in additional letters to make any English word:

CON___   DIS___
SUP___   PRO___

You could have thought of any number of words—the dictionary lists well over 100 familiar CON___ words alone. Did you happen to write any of the following: *conversation, suppose, discussion,* or *probably*? Each of these words appeared in the paragraph before this demonstration. *Reading or hearing a word temporarily* primes *that word and increases the chance that you will use it yourself,* even if you are not aware of the influence (Graf & Mandler, 1984; Schacter, 1987). However, this demonstration works better if you listen to spoken words than if you read them. To get a better sense of priming, go to http://psychology.wadsworth.com/kalat_intro7e. Navigate to the student Web site, then to the Online Try It Yourself section, and click on Implicit Memories. Table 7.2 contrasts the various memory tests.

Procedural memories, *memories of motor skills,* are also generally considered implicit memories. If you try to explain to someone how to ride a bicycle or how to use in-line skates or almost any other complex motor task, you will discover how difficult it is to put into words and how much you do without thinking about it verbally. The brain stores procedural memories differently from **declarative memories**, *memories we can readily state in words* (Schacter & Badgaiyan, 2001). People who seem to have forgotten everything—even their name—can still remember how to walk, talk, eat, use the toilet, and so forth.

TABLE 7.2 Several Ways to Test Memory

Title	Description	Example
Recall	You are asked to say what you remember.	Name the Seven Dwarfs.
Cued recall	You are given significant hints to help you remember.	Name the Seven Dwarfs. Hint: One was always smiling, one was smart, one never talked, one always seemed to have a cold . . .
Recognition	You are asked to choose the correct item from among several items.	Which of the following were among the Seven Dwarfs: Sneezy, Sleazy, Dopey, Dippy, Hippy, Happy?
Savings (relearning)	You are asked to relearn something: If it takes you less time than when you first learned that material, some memory has persisted.	Try memorizing this list: Sleepy, Sneezy, Doc, Dopey, Grumpy, Happy, Bashful. Can you memorize it faster than this list: Sleazy, Snoopy, Duke, Dippy, Gripey, Hippy, Blushy?
Implicit Memory	You are asked to generate words, without necessarily regarding them as memories	You hear the story "Snow White and the Seven Dwarfs." Later you are asked to fill in these blanks to make any words that come to mind: _ L _ _ P _ _ N _ _ Z _ _ _ C _ O _ E _ Y _ R _ _ P _ _ _ P P _ _ A _ H _ U _

CONCEPT CHECK ☑

1. For each of these examples, identify the method of measuring memory.
   a. Although you thought you had completely forgotten your high school French, you do better in your college French course than your roommate, who never had French in high school.
   b. You don't have a telephone directory and are trying to remember the phone number of the local pizza parlor.
   c. You hear a song on the radio without paying much attention to it. Later, you find yourself humming a melody, but you don't know what it is or where you heard it.
   d. You forget where you parked your car, so you scan the parking lot hoping to pick yours out among all the others.
   e. Your friend asks, "What's the name of our chemistry lab instructor? I think it's Julie or Judy something."
2. Is remembering how to tie your shoes a procedural memory or a declarative memory? Is remembering the color of your shoes a procedural or a declarative memory? (Check your answers on page 244.)

Application: Suspect Lineups as Recognition Memory

Suppose you witness a crime, and now the police would like you to identify the guilty person. They ask you to look at a few suspects in a lineup or to examine a book of photos. Your task is a clear example of recognition memory; you are trying to identify the correct item among a group of distracters.

The task raises a problem, which is familiar to you from your own experience. When you take a multiple-choice test—another clear example of recognition memory—you pick the best available choice. Sometimes you are not sure that any of the choices are quite right, but you can eliminate some as obviously wrong, and you settle on what seems the best of the others. Now imagine you do the same with a book of photos. You look through the choices, eliminate some, and pick the one that looks most like the perpetrator of the crime. You tell the police you think suspect 42 is the guilty person. "Think?" the police ask. "Your testimony won't be worth much in court unless you're sure." You look again. You would like to cooperate, and after all you're *pretty* sure. Finally, you say yes, you're sure. The police say, "Good, that's the person we thought did it," and with that confirmation you now become confident. You testify in court, and the suspect is convicted. But is justice done? Since the advent of DNA testing, investigators have identified many innocent people who were convicted by the testimony of a confident witness.

Memory researchers have proposed ways to improve suspect lineups, and most U.S. police investigators now follow these recommendations. One is to avoid hinting which person the police actually suspect and to avoid any sign of agreeing with a tentative choice (Wells, Olson, & Charman, 2003; Zaragoza, Payment, Ackil, Drivdahl, & Beck, 2001). Another is to record the witness's confidence *immediately* at the time of initial identification, before the witness has heard of any other evidence against that suspect

(Wells, Olson, & Charman, 2002). Also, the lineup should be done sequentially—that is, one suspect at a time (Wells et al., 2000). For each suspect the witness says "yes" or "no." As soon as the witness says yes, the procedure is finished; after all, there is no point in looking at additional suspects if the witness has already decided. Most important, the witness should have no opportunity to go back and reexamine photos after rejecting them. The witness's decision should be certain, not just the best of the available choices.

CRITICAL THINKING:
A STEP FURTHER
Lineups and Multiple-Choice Testing

What would happen if classroom multiple-choice tests were done with sequential answers? That is, after each question you would have to say yes or no to each answer before reading the next answer.

The Information-Processing View of Memory

Over the years psychologists have repeatedly tried to explain the mechanisms of behavior by analogy to the technologies of their time. In the early 1900s, psychologists suggested that learning and thinking worked like a telephone switchboard, unplugging old connections and making new ones. Later, they compared behavior mechanisms to a computer. A computer has three kinds of memory. First, if you type letters faster than they can appear on the screen, the computer will store a few letters in a temporary buffer until it can display them. (Older computers showed this effect more often than today's faster models.) Second, the material you have written without saving it is in random access memory (RAM). RAM is vulnerable, as you learned if you ever had a power outage while writing something. Finally, you can save something to a disk. A hard disk or set of CDs or floppies can store vastly more information than RAM and is less vulnerable.

According to the **information-processing model** of memory, human memory resembles that of a computer: *Information enters the system, is processed, coded, and then stored* (Figure 7.4). According to a popular version of this model, information first enters a sensory store (like the computer's buffer). Some of that information is stored in short-term memory (like RAM), and some short-term memory is transferred into long-term memory (like a hard disk). Eventually, a cue from the environment causes the system to retrieve information from storage (Atkinson & Shiffrin, 1968). We shall examine each portion of this model.

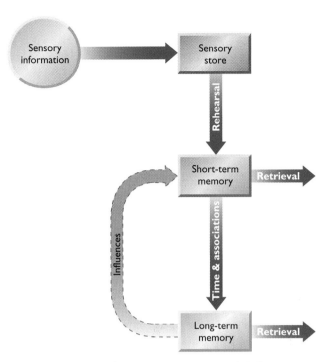

FIGURE 7.4 The information-processing model of memory resembles a computer's memory system, including temporary and permanent memory.

The Sensory Store

Close your eyes and turn your head. Then quickly blink your eyes open and shut. You will have a sudden impression that you can still "see in your mind's eye" a great deal of detail from what you just saw. However, you could not describe it all, mainly because the image fades faster than you can describe it. (It fades even faster if you look at something else instead of keeping your eyes shut.)

▌ A bolt of lightning flashes through the sky for a split second, but you can visualize it in detail for a short time afterward. That image is held momentarily in your sensory store.

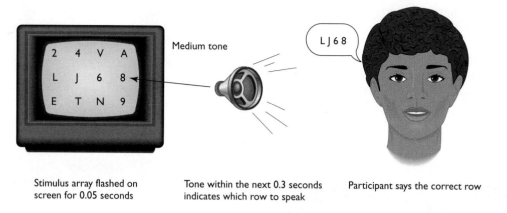

Stimulus array flashed on
screen for 0.05 seconds

Tone within the next 0.3 seconds
indicates which row to speak

Participant says the correct row

FIGURE 7.5 George Sperling (1960) flashed arrays like this on a screen for 50 milliseconds. After the display went off, a signal told the viewer which row to recite.

This *very brief storage of sensory information* is called the **sensory store**, also known as iconic memory (for visual information) and echoic memory (for auditory). George Sperling (1960) found a way to demonstrate visual sensory store. He flashed an array like the one shown in Figure 7.5 onto a screen for 50 milliseconds. When he asked viewers to report what they saw, he found that they could recall a mean of only about four items. If he had stopped his experiment at that point, he might have concluded that viewers stored only a little of the array. However, he surmised that the sensory store was probably fading while people were describing it. So he told viewers he would ask them to report only one row of the array, a different row each time.

After flashing an array on the screen, he immediately used a high, medium, or low tone to signal which row to recall. Frequently, people could name all the items in whichever row he indicated. Evidently, the whole array was briefly available to memory. When he waited for even 1 second before signaling which row to recall, though, recall was poor. That is, for the sensory store, "use it or lose it," and you had better use it fast.

You can try a version of Sperling's experiment online. Go to http://psychology. wadsworth.com/kalat_intro7e. Navigate to the student Web site, then to the Online Try It Yourself section, and click on Sperling Effect. However, this is a fragile effect (as opposed to a robust effect, which would occur under a variety of circumstances). The effect improves with practice; it also varies from one person to another and even from one computer to another depending on their speed. Give it a try, but don't be too dismayed if your results don't match the predictions.

Is the sensory store really memory, or is it perception? It is a little of both. Not everything falls neatly into our human-made categories.

CONCEPT CHECK ☑

3. Would viewers probably remember as many items if Sperling had flashed pictures of objects instead of numbers and letters? (Check your answer on page 244)

CRITICAL THINKING:
A STEP FURTHER
Sensory Storage

Sperling demonstrated the capacity of the sensory store for visual information. How could you demonstrate the capacity of the sensory store for auditory information?

Short-Term and Long-Term Memory

Of all the vast information that passes through our sensory store, most fades quickly, we deal with a little of it for temporary use, and we store even less for permanent reference. According to the traditional version of information-processing theory, we distinguish between **short-term memory**, *temporary storage of recent events*, and **long-term memory**, *a relatively permanent store*. For example, while you are playing tennis, the current score is in your short-term memory, and the rules of the game are in your long-term memory.

Psychologists distinguish two major types of long-term memory: semantic and episodic. **Semantic memory** is *memory of general principles*, and **episodic memory** is *memory for specific events in a person's life* (Tulving, 1989). For example, your memory of the rules of tennis is a semantic memory; your memory of the time you beat your roommate at tennis is an episodic memory.

Most episodic memories are more fragile than semantic memories. For example, even if you don't play tennis again for a few years, you will remember most of the rules, but you will forget most of the specific times you played tennis. Older people are especially likely to retain semantic memories but forget specific episodes (Piolino, Desgranges, Benali, & Eustache, 2002).

People also frequently remember something they have heard (a semantic memory) but forget where they heard it (an episodic memory). Therefore, they confuse reliable information with the unreliable. ("Did I hear this idea from my professor or was it on *South Park?* Did I read about brain transplants in *Scientific American* or in the *National Enquirer?*") As a result you might dismiss an idea at first because you know it came from an unreliable source, but later remember it, forget where you heard it, and start to take it seriously (Johnson, Hashtroudi, & Lindsay, 1993; Riccio, 1994). In Chapter 14 we shall again discuss this phenomenon, known as the *sleeper effect.*

Psychologists have traditionally drawn several distinctions between short- and long-term memory, including capacity, dependence on retrieval cues, and decay over time. However, on closer examination we can find exceptions at least to the latter two. Let us consider these comparisons between short- and long-term memory (see also Table 7.3).

Differences in Capacity

Long-term memory has a vast, hard-to-measure capacity. Asking how much information you could store in long-term memory is like asking how many books you could fit into a library; the answer depends on how big the books are, how you arrange them, and so forth. Short-term memory in contrast has a small, easily measured capacity. Read each of the following sequences of letters and then look away and try to repeat them from memory. Or read each aloud and ask a friend to repeat it.

Try It Yourself

E H G P H
J R O Z N Q
S R B W R C N
M P D I W F B S
Z Y B P I A F M O

Most normal adults can repeat a list of approximately seven letters, numbers, or words. Some can re-

TABLE 7.3 Comparison of Sensory Store, Short-Term Memory, and Long-Term Memory

	Sensory Store	Short-Term Memory	Long-Term Memory
Capacity	Whatever you see or hear at one moment	7 ± 2 items in healthy adults	Vast, uncountable
Duration	Fraction of a second	A period of seconds if not rehearsed	Perhaps a lifetime
Example	You see something for an instant and then recall a detail about it	You look up a telephone number, remember it long enough to dial it	You remember the house where you lived when you were 7 years old

member eight or nine; others, only five or six. George Miller (1956) referred to the short-term memory capacity as "the magical number seven, plus or minus two." When people try to repeat a longer list, however, they may fail to remember even the first seven items. It is somewhat like trying to hold objects in one hand: If you try to hold too many, you drop them all.

The limit of short-term memory depends partly on how long it takes to say a word. If you were equally fluent in English and Welsh, you would seem to have a greater short-term memory for

Short-term memory is like a handful of eggs; it can hold only a limited number of items at a time.

numbers when tested in English, just because you can say English numbers like *five* and *seven* faster than Welsh numbers like *pedwar* and *chwech* (Ellis & Hennelley, 1980). For the same reason, you would have a greater short-term memory for numbers in Chinese than in German (Lüer et al., 1998). Of

Kutbidin Atamkulov travels from one Central Asian village to another singing from memory the tale of the Kirghiz hero, Manas. The song, which lasts 3 hours, has been passed from master to student for centuries.

course, if you were more fluent in one language than the other, you would show less short-term memory in your second language.

You can also store more information in short-term memory by coding it efficiently through a process called **chunking**—*grouping items into meaningful sequences or clusters* (see Figure 7.6). For example, the sequence "ventysi" has seven letters, at the limit of most people's short-term memory capacity. However, "seventysix" has three additional letters, but can be easily remembered as "76," a two-digit number. "Seventeenseventysix" is even longer, but if you think of it as 1776, one important date in history, it now is just a single item to store.

One college student in a lengthy experiment initially could repeat about seven digits at a time, the same as average (Ericsson, Chase, & Faloon, 1980). Over a year and a half, working 3 to 5 hours per week, he gradually improved until he could repeat 80 digits, as shown in Figure 7.7, by using extraordinary strategies for chunking. He was a competitive runner, so he might store the sequence "3492 . . ." as "3 minutes, 49.2 seconds, a near world-record time for running a mile." He might store the next set of numbers as a good time for running a kilometer, a mediocre marathon time, or a date in history. With practice he started recognizing larger and larger chunks. However, when he was tested on his ability to remember a list of letters, his performance was only average because he had not developed any chunking strategies for letters.

One cautionary point before we proceed: We talk about "storing" a memory and sometimes even compare the process to holding objects in your hand or placing books on the shelf of a library. These are only loose analogies. The brain does not store a memory like an object in one place; memory representation is a diffuse set of changes in synapses spread out over a huge population of cells.

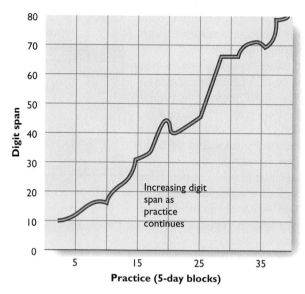

FIGURE 7.7 Most people can repeat a list of about seven numbers. One college student gradually increased his ability to repeat a list of numbers over 18 months of practice. He greatly expanded his short-term memory for digits but not for letters or words. *(Reprinted with permission from "Acquisition of a Memory Skill," by K. A. Ericsson, W. G. Chase, and S. Faloon, Science, 1980, 208, 1181-1182. Copyright © 1980 American Association for the Advancement of Science.)*

Dependence on Retrieval Cues

When you store something in long-term memory and try to find it later, you need a **retrieval cue** (*associated information that might help you regain the memory*). For example, if someone asks you what *demand characteristics* are, you might say you have no idea. Then the person says, "I think they have something to do with research methods in psychology." Still you don't remember. "Do you remember something about an experiment in which people were really in an ordinary room, but they thought they were in sensory depriva-

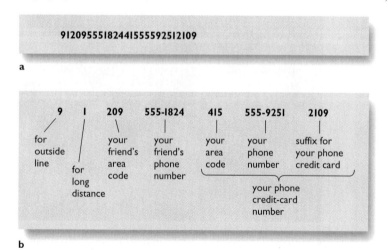

FIGURE 7.6 We overcome the limits of short-term memory through chunking. You probably could not remember the 26-digit number in (a), but by breaking it up into a series of chunks, you can remember it and dial the number correctly.

tion, so they reported hallucinations and . . . ?" Suddenly, you remember the concept.

Traditionally, psychologists have regarded retrieval cues as irrelevant to short-term memory. For example, if you fail to recall a telephone number that you heard a few seconds ago, it is presumably "gone" and no reminder will help. The results are different, though, for more meaningful materials. Suppose you hear a list of words, including "closet," and then recall as many of the words as you can. If you don't recall "closet," but someone gives you the reminder "broom . . . ," you might say, "Oh, yes, 'closet.'" So retrieval cues are helpful for some short-term memories, even if not for all (Nelson & Goodmon, 2003).

Decay of Memories Over Time

A well-learned memory can last a lifetime. Harry Bahrick (1984) found that people who had studied Spanish in school 1 or 2 years ago remembered more than those who had studied it 3 to 6 years ago, but beyond 6 years the retention appeared to be stable (Figure 7.8). If you ask your grandparents to get out an old photo scrapbook, they will recall events they had not thought about in decades. Although the photographs may have faded, it is not certain that the memories themselves fade. They gradually become harder to retrieve, but mainly because of interference from other memories.

Short-term memories do seem to fade, however. In fact neuroscientists have identified a protein that the brain makes after an experience that weakens or destroys the memory trace, presumably to avoid permanently storing unimportant information (Genoux et al., 2002). Obviously, the effects of that protein can be canceled if the information is repeated. It can also be canceled by emotional arousal, which mobilizes epi-

nephrine (adrenalin) and thereby strengthens memory formation (LaLumiere, Buen, & McGaugh, 2003).

Here is the classic behavioral demonstration of the fading of short-term memories: Lloyd Peterson and Margaret Peterson (1959) wanted to present a meaningless sequence of letters, like HOXDF, and then test people's memory after various delays. However, people who expect to be tested spend the delay rehearsing "HOXDF, HOXDF . . ." To prevent rehearsal, the experimenters gave a competing task. They simultaneously presented the letters and a number, such as 231. The instruction was to start with that number and count backward by threes, such as "231, 228, 225, 222, 219 . . ." until the end of the delay and then say the letters.

Figure 7.9 shows the results. Note that only about 10% of the participants could recall the letters after 18 seconds. In other words an unrehearsed short-term memory decays rapidly. You can demonstrate this phenomenon online. Go to http://psychology.wadsworth.com/kalat_intro7e. Navigate to the student Web site, then to the Online Try It Yourself section, and click on Decay of Short-Term Memory.

However, do not take that figure of 18 seconds too seriously. Peterson and Peterson were dealing with nonsense information, such as HOXDF. They presented a long series of trials, and the answer to each one would interfere with the others. Under other circumstances people can remember meaningful short-term memories for much longer. Certainly, you should

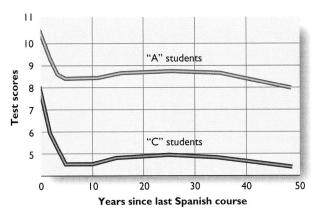

FIGURE 7.8 Spanish vocabulary as measured by a recognition test shows a rapid decline in the first few years but then long-term stability. The students who received an "A" had a better performance at the start, but both groups showed similar rates of forgetting. (*"Semantic Memory Content in Permastore: Fifty Years of Memory for Spanish Learned in School," by H. P. Bahrick,* Journal of Experiential Psychology: General, *1984, 113, 1–29. Copyright © 1984 by the American Psychological Association. Reprinted with permission of the author.*)

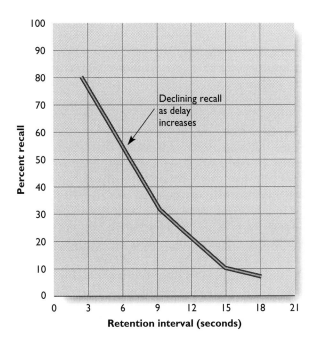

FIGURE 7.9 In a study by Peterson and Peterson (1959), people remembered a set of letters well after a short delay, but their memory faded greatly over 18 seconds if they were prevented from rehearsing during that time.

not imagine that every memory either fades within 18 seconds or so (short-term memory) or lasts a lifetime (long-term). You have many memories that you keep as long as they are current, updating them with new information as often as necessary (Altmann & Gray, 2002). For example, if you are playing basketball, you remember the score, approximately how much time is left in the game, what defense your team is using, what offense, how many fouls you have committed, and so forth. You won't (and wouldn't want to) remember all that information for the rest of your life, but you also don't need to rehearse it constantly to prevent it from fading within 18 seconds. Similarly, right now you may remember approximately how much money is in your wallet, what you plan to do next weekend, and a great deal of other information you need to store as long as it is current, until you update it with new information. So not all memories fade at the same rate.

CONCEPT CHECK ☑️

4. Is your memory of your current mailing address a semantic memory or an episodic memory? What about your memories of the day you moved to your current address?
5. How does the capacity of short-term memory compare with that of long-term memory? (Check your answers on page 244.)

Working Memory

Originally, psychologists described short-term memory as the way you store something while you are moving it into long-term storage. Eventually, problems accumulated for that idea. One problem is that *how long* information remains in short-term memory is a poor predictor of whether it will become a long-term memory. For example, you might watch a hockey game in which the score remains the same for 2 hours, but you don't remember that score permanently. In contrast, if someone tells you something important, like "Your sister just had a baby," you can form a lasting memory quickly.

Today, most researchers emphasize temporary memory storage as the information you are working with at the moment, regardless of whether you ever store it as a more permanent memory. To emphasize this different perspective, they speak of *working memory* instead of short-term memory.

Working memory is *a system for processing or working with current information.* It is almost synonymous with someone's current sphere of attention. Different psychologists have used the term in different ways, and some have broadened the term until it is al-

most synonymous with intelligence (Oberauer, Süss, Wilhelm, & Wittman, 2003).

Working memory includes at least three major components (Baddeley, 2001; Baddeley & Hitch, 1994):

- A *phonological loop,* which stores and rehearses speech information. The phonological loop, similar to the traditional view of short-term memory, enables us to repeat seven or so items immediately after hearing them. It is probably essential for anyone first learning a language (Baddeley, Gathercole, & Papagno, 1998). It is also essential for understanding a long sentence; you have to remember the words at the start of the sentence long enough to connect them to the words at the end.
- A *visuospatial sketchpad,* which stores and manipulates visual and spatial information, providing for vision what the phonological loop provides for speech (Luck & Vogel, 1997). You would use this process for recognizing pictures or for imagining what an object looks like from another angle.

  Researchers distinguish between the phonological and visuospatial stores because you can do an auditory word task and a visuospatial task at the same time without much interference but not two auditory tasks or two visuospatial tasks (Baddeley & Hitch, 1974; Hale, Myerson, Rhee, Weiss, & Abrams, 1996). People presumably have additional stores for touch, smell, and taste, but so far researchers have concentrated on the auditory and visual stores.
- A *central executive,* which governs shifts of attention. The hallmark of good working memory is the ability to shift attention as needed among different tasks. Imagine a hospital nurse who has to keep track of the needs of several patients, sometimes interrupting the treatment of one patient to take care of an emergency and then returning to complete the first patient. Also imagine yourself driving a car, watching the oncoming traffic, the cars in front of you and behind, the gauges on your dashboard, sometimes a map, and possibly a conversation with a passenger.

Psychologists are not sure precisely what they mean by "central executive" or "shifting attention," so it is not easy to find a perfect measure of it (Logan, 2003). (The same issue arises for "intelligence" in the next chapter, as well as many other terms in psychology.) Here is one simple way to measure shifting attention: Recite aloud some poem, song, or other passage that you know well. (If you can't think of a more interesting example, you can recite the alphabet.) Time how long it takes. Then measure how long it takes you to say the same thing silently. Finally, time how long it takes you to alternate—the first word aloud, the second silent, the third aloud, and so forth. Alternating takes longer because you have to keep shifting attention.

Here is another way to measure executive processes: You hear a list of words such as *maple, elm, oak, hemlock, chestnut, birch, sycamore, pine, redwood, walnut, dogwood, hickory.* After each word you are supposed to say the *previous* word. So after "maple, elm," you should say "maple." After "oak" you reply "elm." If you do well on that task, you proceed to a more difficult version: You should repeat what you heard *two* words ago. So you wait for "maple, elm, oak" and reply "maple." Then you hear "hemlock" and reply "elm." Note how you need to shift back and forth between listening to the new word and repeating something from memory.

Another example: An investigator flashes on the screen a simple arithmetic question and a word, such as

$$(2 \times 3) + 1 = 8?\ \text{SPRING}$$

As quickly as possible, you should read the arithmetic question, answer it yes or no, and then say the word. As soon as you do, you will see a new question and word; again you answer the question and say the word. After a few such items, the investigator stops and asks you to say all the words in order. To do well you have to shift your attention between doing the arithmetic and memorizing the words. This is a difficult task. Some people have trouble remembering even two words under these conditions; remembering five or six is an excellent score.

People who do well on this task (who are considered to have a "high capacity" of working memory) also do well on a variety of other tasks, including intelligence tests (Engle, Tuholski, Laughlin, & Conway, 1999; Süss, Oberauer, Wittman, Wilhelm, & Schulze, 2002). They do better than most other people at suppressing unwanted thoughts (Brewin & Beaton, 2002). They are more likely than other people to prefer a large reward later instead of a smaller reward now (Hinson, Jameson, & Whitney, 2003). They also excel at naming as many animals as possible in 10 minutes and learning several consecutive word lists without confusing one with another. Interestingly, if people have to perform an additional constantly distracting task, such as tapping a rhythm with their fingers, everyone's performance suffers, but those with the best working memory suffer the most (Kane & Engle, 2000; Rosen & Engle, 1997). They still perform better than people with less working memory but not by as much as usual. Of course, one reason is that those with poor working memory weren't doing well anyway, so they had less room to get worse. Another explanation is that people with good working memory usually do well because they direct their attention to the important aspects of the task. With a constant distracter, they lose that advantage.

CONCEPT CHECK ☑

6. Some students like to listen to music while studying. Is the music likely to help or impair their study? (What might the answer depend on?) (Check your answer on page 244.)

IN CLOSING

Varieties of Memory

Although researchers still disagree with one another on many points about memory, they do agree about what memory is *not*: Memory is not a single store into which we simply dump things and later take them out. When Ebbinghaus conducted his studies of memory in the late 1800s, he thought he was measuring the properties of memory, period. We now know that the properties of memory depend on the type of material being memorized, the individual's experience with similar materials, the method of testing, and the recency of the event. Memory is not one process, but many.

Summary

- *Ebbinghaus's approach.* Hermann Ebbinghaus pioneered the experimental study of memory by testing his own ability to memorize and retain lists of nonsense syllables. (page 233)
- *Methods of testing memory.* The free recall method reveals only relatively strong memories. Progressively weaker memories can be demonstrated by the cued recall, recognition, and savings methods. Implicit memories are changes in behavior under conditions in which the person cannot verbalize the memory or is unaware of the influence. (page 234)
- *Suspect lineups.* Suspect lineups are an example of the recognition method of testing memory. Unfortunately, witnesses sometimes choose the best available choice and then decide they are sure. Psychologists have recommended ways of improving lineups to decrease inaccurate identifications. (page 236)
- *The information-processing model.* According to the information-processing model of memory, information first enters a sensory store, then becomes a short-term memory, and finally, a long-term memory. (page 237)
- *Differences between short-term and long-term memory.* Long-term memory requires elicitation by a retrieval cue, whereas short-term memory does not. Short-term memory has a capacity of only about seven items in normal adults, although

244 CHAPTER 7 Memory

chunking can enable us to store much information in each item. Long-term memory has a very large, not easily measured capacity. Short-term memories fade over time if not rehearsed, whereas some long-term memories last a lifetime. (page 239)

- *Working memory.* As an alternative to the traditional description of short-term memory, current researchers identify working memory as a system for dealing with current information, including the ability to shift attention back and forth among several tasks as necessary. (page 242)

Answers to Concept Checks

1. **a.** savings; **b.** recall; **c.** implicit; **d.** recognition; **e.** cued recall. (page 236)
2. Remembering how to tie your shoes is a procedural memory. Remembering their appearance is a declarative memory (one you could express in words). (page 236)
3. If we assume that it would take longer to name objects than numbers or letters, people would probably name fewer. The longer it takes for people to answer, the more their sensory store fades. (page 238)
4. Your memory of your current address is a semantic memory. Your memory of the events of moving day is an episodic memory. (page 242)
5. Short-term memory has a capacity limited to only about seven items in the average adult, whereas long-term memory has a huge, difficult-to-measure capacity. (page 242)
6. If the music requires any attention at all or evokes any response, such as occasionally singing along, it will impair attention. The difference will be most noticeable for the best students. However, background music with no words and no tendency to evoke responses is probably a slight benefit if it prevents the student from noticing other sounds that might be more distracting. (page 243)

Answers to Other Questions in the Module

A. Herman Melville, Jane Austen, Agatha Christie, Arthur Conan Doyle, Maya Angelou, Leo Tolstoy, James Kalat, Geoffrey Chaucer, Charles Darwin, Margaret Mitchell, Victor Hugo. (page 235)

How can we improve our memories?

There you are, taking a geography test, unable to remember the major rivers of Africa. You remember reviewing that section in your book last night; you even remember that it was on the upper left side of the page, and there was a map to the right. You remember the cappuccino you were sipping. And the time was 9:30 P.M. You just don't remember the names of the rivers.

How can we improve our memory? The main point of this module is simple: To improve your memory, improve the way you store the material in the first place.

Meaningful Storage and Levels of Processing

If you want to memorize a definition, what would you do? Repeat it over and over? Repetition does help, other things being equal, but repetition by itself is a poor study method.

To illustrate, examine Figure 7.10, which shows a real U.S. penny and 14 fakes. If you live in the United States, you have seen pennies countless times, but can you now identify the real one? Most U.S. citizens guess wrong (Nickerson & Adams, 1979). (If you do not have a penny in your pocket, check answer B on

■ Most actors preparing for a play spend much time thinking about the meaning of what they say (a deep level of processing) and only a little time simply repeating the words.

page 251. If you are not from the United States, try drawing the front or back of a common coin in your own country.) In short, mere repetition, such as looking at a coin many times, does not guarantee a strong memory.

Suppose you read two articles of equal length from the sports pages of a newspaper. One is about a sport you follow closely, and the other is about a sport that has never interested you. Even though you spend the same amount of time reading each article, you will remember more from the article you care about. The more you already know about any topic, the easier it is to learn still more (Hambrick & Engle, 2002). The important points stand out, and you quickly associate the details to other facts you already know.

According to the **levels-of-processing principle** (Craik & Lockhart, 1972), *how easily we can retrieve a memory depends on the number and types of associations we form.* The associations establish retrieval cues. By analogy, a librarian who places a new book on the shelf also enters information into the retrieval system so that anyone who knows the title, author, or topic can find the book. The more items the librarian enters, the easier it will be for someone to find that book later. The same is true of your memory.

When you read something—this chapter, for example—you might simply read over the

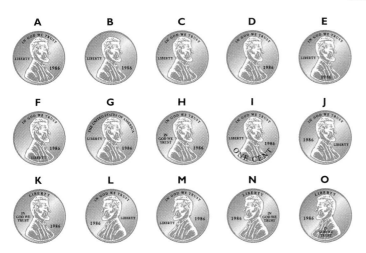

FIGURE 7.10 Can you spot the genuine penny among 14 fakes? If you're not sure (and you don't have a penny with you), check answer B on page 251. (*"Long-term Memory for a Common Object,"* by R.S. Nickerson and M.J. Adams, Cognitive Psychology, 1979, 11, 287–307. Copyright © 1979 Academic Press. Reprinted with permission.)

TABLE 7.4 Levels-of-Processing Model of Memory

Superficial processing	Simply repeat the material to be remembered: "Hawk, Oriole, Tiger, Timberwolf, Blue Jay, Bull."
Deeper processing	Think about each item. Note that two start with T and two with B.
Still deeper processing	Note that three are birds and three are mammals. Also, three are major league baseball teams and three are NBA basketball teams. Use whichever associations mean the most to you.

words, giving them little thought. We call that kind of study "shallow processing," and you will remember almost nothing at test time. Alternatively, you might stop and consider various points that you read, relate them to your own experiences, and think of your own examples of the principles. The more ways you think about the material, the "deeper" your processing is and the more easily you will remember later. Table 7.4 summarizes this model.

Imagine several groups of students who study a list of words in different ways. One group simply reads the list over and over, and a second counts the letters in each word. Both procedures yield poor recall later. A third group tries to think of a synonym for each word or tries to use each word in a sentence. These students form many associations and later recall the words better than the first two groups. Students in the fourth group ask about each word, "How does it apply to some experience in my own life?" This group does even better than the third group. For a while psychologists thought that relating words to yourself produces a special kind of strengthening, but later research found equally strong memories in students who tried to relate each word to their mothers (Symons & Johnson, 1997). The conclusion is that memory grows stronger when people elaborate and organize the material and relate it to anything they know and care about.

You can improve your level of processing in two ways (Einstein & Hunt, 1980; McDaniel, Einstein, & Lollis, 1988): First, you can think about the items on the list one by one. Second, you can look for relationships among them. You might notice, for example, that a list consists of five animals, six foods, four methods of transportation, and five wooden objects. One of the skills we gain through education is learning to organize material in this way. According to one study of the Kpelle people in West Africa, teenage children who had gone to school organized a list of words into categories and remembered the list well. Unschooled children did not sort the list into categories and did not remember it well (Scribner, 1974).

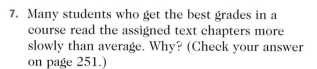

CONCEPT CHECK ☑

7. Many students who get the best grades in a course read the assigned text chapters more slowly than average. Why? (Check your answer on page 251.)

Encoding Specificity

If encoding something in a variety of ways leads to easy recall under varied circumstances, then encoding it in just one way means that only a few retrieval cues will stimulate the memory later. Those few cues, however, can be highly effective.

According to the **encoding specificity principle** (Tulving & Thomson, 1973), *the associations you form at the time of learning will be the most effective retrieval cues* (Figure 7.11). Here is an example (modified from Thieman, 1984). First, read the pairs of words (which psychologists call *paired associates*) in Table 7.5a. Then turn to Table 7.5b on page 248. For each of the words on that list, try to recall a related word on the list you just read. *Do this now.* (The answers are on page 251, answer C.)

Most people find this task difficult. Because they initially coded the word *cardinal* as a type of clergyman, for example, they do not think of it when they see the retrieval cue *bird*. If they had thought of it as a bird, then *clergyman* would not have been a good reminder.

The principle of encoding specificity extends to other aspects of experience at the time of storage. For example, if you return to a place where you haven't

FIGURE 7.11 According to the principle of encoding specificity, the way we code a word during original learning determines which cues will remind us of that word later. For example, when you hear the word *queen,* you may think of that word in any of several ways. If you think of *queen bee,* then the cue *playing card* will not remind you of it later. If you think of the *queen of England,* then *chess piece* will not be a good reminder.

TABLE 7.5a

Clergyman—Cardinal	Geometry—Plane
Trinket—Charm	Tennis—Racket
Type of wine—Port	Music—Rock
U.S. politician—Bush	Magic—Spell
Inch—Foot	Envelope—Seal
Computer—Apple	Graduation—Degree

been in years, you may remember events that happened there. In one study college students who were fluent in both English and Russian were given a list of words such as *summer, birthday,* and *doctor,* some in English and some in Russian. For each word they were asked to describe any related event they remembered. In response to Russian words, they recalled mostly events that happened when they were speaking Russian. In response to English words, they recalled mostly events when they were speaking English (Marian & Neisser, 2000).

More examples: If you experience something while you are sad, you will remember it better when you are sad again (Eich & Macaulay, 2000). If you learn something while frightened, you will remember it better when you are frightened again, and if you learn while calm, you will remember better when calm (Lang, Craske, Brown, & Ghaneian, 2001). Strong drugs can induce this effect also. **State-dependent memory** is *the tendency to remember something better if your body is in the same condition during recall as it was during the original learning.* State-dependent memory, however, is a small effect that is often difficult to demonstrate (Eich, 1995).

The encoding specificity principle has a couple of clear implications. First, if you want to remember something at a particular time and place, make your study conditions similar to the conditions when you will try to remember. On the other hand, if you want to remember the material for life, under a wide variety of conditions, then you should vary your study habits.

CONCEPT CHECK ☑

8. Suppose someone cannot remember what happened at a party last night. What steps might help improve the memory? (Check your answer on page 251.)

The Timing of Study Sessions

If you need to take a test on some topic, should you study a little at a time or wait until shortly before the test? Even if you sometimes do wait until just before

the test, you probably know how risky this strategy is. On the day before the test, some unforeseen event might arise that prevents you from studying at all. Also, if the material is complicated, you might not be able to understand it all in one reading.

But let's change the question in a way that makes the answer less obvious: Suppose you don't wait until the day before the test, but you nevertheless study the material all at once on a day when you have plenty of time and no distractions. Will your result be better, worse, or about the same as if spread out your study over days or weeks?

The answer is that studying all at once is worse, for a variety of reasons. One is that if you study all at once, you are not sure when you have studied "enough." Most students overestimate how well they understand something, and below-average students are especially likely to overestimate (Dunning, Johnson, Ehrlinger, & Kruger, 2003). If you overestimate your understanding, you stop studying too soon. However, if you spread out your study over days, then when you return after an absence, you notice how much you have forgotten, and therefore study it again.

Imagine yourself in the following study: A three-letter combination appears on a computer screen. It might be a word like BUG or a meaningless combination like FXH. You are instructed to study it for as long as you want—absolutely no rush—until you are sure you will be able to recall it later. There will be 27 such three-letter combinations. Take your time with each one. Don't proceed until you are sure you have

▌ People need to monitor their understanding of a text to decide whether to continue studying or whether they already understand it well enough. Most readers have trouble making that judgment correctly.

TABLE 7.5b

Instructions: For each of these words, write one of the second of the paired terms from the list in Table 7.5a.

Animal—	Stone—
Part of body—	Personality—
Transportation—	Write—
Temperature—	Bird—
Crime—	Harbor—
Shrubbery—	Fruit—

learned it well, and then press the key to move on to the next item. At the end, theoretically, you should get them all correct. However, when this study was actually conducted, the average student recalled only 49% of them (Nelson & Leonesio, 1988). Two conclusions follow: (a) It is hard to judge how well you have learned something if you haven't waited long enough to see whether you will forget (Maki & Serra, 1992; Weaver & Kelemen, 1997). (b) Studying something once is seldom effective, even if you study it very hard that one time.

A second reason for spreading out your study is that if you study under a variety of conditions, you will establish a wide variety of retrieval cues and therefore remember under a variety of conditions. Psychologist Harry Bahrick and members of his family studied foreign language vocabulary, varying the frequency of study. Some had a study session every 2 weeks; others studied the same number of hours but spread out over longer times, such as once every 8 weeks. The result: More frequent study led to faster learning, but less frequent study led to better long-term retention, as measured years later (Bahrick, Bahrick, Bahrick, & Bahrick, 1993).

Results of many other studies confirm the same general principle: If you want to remember something under a variety of conditions, practice it under a variety of conditions (Schmidt & Bjork, 1992). Varying the conditions may actually slow down the original learning and make the task seem more difficult, but in the long run it helps. In one experiment a group of 8-year-old children practiced throwing a small beanbag at a target on the floor 3 feet away. Another group practiced with a target sometimes 2 feet away and sometimes 4 feet away, but never 3 feet away. Then both groups were tested with the target 3 feet away. The children who had been practicing with the 3-foot target missed it by a mean of 8.3 inches. The children who had been practicing with 2-foot and 4-foot targets actually did better, missing by a mean of only 5.4 inches, even though they were aiming at the 3-foot target for the first time (Kerr & Booth, 1978). In another experiment young adults

practiced a technique for mentally squaring two-digit numbers—for example, $23 \times 23 = 529$. Those who practiced with just a small range of numbers learned the technique quickly but also forgot it quickly; those who practiced with a wider range of numbers learned more slowly but remembered better at a later time and applied the technique better to a new set of problems (Sanders, Gonzalez, Murphy, Pesta, & Bucur, 2002).

The SPAR Method

One systematic way to organize your study is the SPAR method:

Survey. Get an overview of what the passage is about. Scan through it; look at the boldface headings; try to understand the organization and goals of the passage.

Process *meaningfully.* Read the material carefully. Think about how you could use the ideas or how they relate to other things you have read. Evaluate the strengths and weaknesses of the argument. The more actively you think about what you read, the better you will remember the material.

Ask *questions.* If the text provides questions, like the Concept Checks in this text, try to answer them. Then pretend you are the instructor; write the questions you would ask on a test and answer them yourself. In the process you will discover which sections of the passage you need to reread.

Review. Wait a day or so and then retest your knowledge. Spreading out your study over time increases your ability to remember it over the long term.

CONCEPT CHECK ☑

9. If you want to do well on the final exam in this course, what should you do now—review this chapter or review the first three chapters in the book?
10. How does the advice to spread out your study over a long time instead of doing it all at one sitting fit or contrast with the encoding specificity principle? (Check your answers on page 251.)

Emotional Arousal and Memory Storage

People usually remember emotionally arousing events. Chances are you vividly remember your first day of college, your first kiss, the time your team won the big game, and times you were extremely frightened.

The effects of arousal on memory have been known for centuries. In England in the early 1600s, when people sold land, they did not yet have the custom of recording the sale on paper. (Paper was expensive and few people could read anyway.) Instead, local residents would gather around while someone announced the sale and instructed everyone to remember it. Of all those present, whose memory of the sale was most important? The children because they would live the longest. And of all those present, who were least interested? Right, again, it's the children. To increase the chances that the children would remember, the adults would kick them while telling them about the business deal. The same idea persisted in the custom, still common in the early 1900s, of slapping schoolchildren's hands with a stick to make them pay attention.

However, although emotional arousal enhances memory, what you remember may not be what you want to remember. Furthermore, your "flashbulb" memories of where you were, what you were doing, and so forth when you heard some shocking news may be emotionally intense but not necessarily accurate. In one study Israeli students were interviewed 2 weeks after the assassination of Israel's Prime Minister, Itzhak Rabin, and again 11 months later. About 36% of the emotionally intense memories they reported at the later time differed from what they had reported earlier (Nachson & Zelig, 2003). In another study U.S. students reported their memories of where they were, what they were doing, and so forth at the time of hearing about the terrorist attacks on September 11, 2001. They reported their memories on the day after the attacks and then again weeks or months later. Over time the students continued to report high vividness of the memories and high confidence in them, but the accuracy of their memory reports gradually declined, just as do any other memories (Talarico & Rubin, 2003).

Advertisers try to get you to remember their product by making their ads exciting or (for television ads) by airing them on exciting programs. However, excitement from one event doesn't always carry over to memory for another. For example, an ad featuring attractive people in skimpy bathing suits may get you excited, but you may or may not remember the product. If it is an ad for swimsuits, sunscreen, or something else related to beaches, then yes. However, a sexually exciting ad won't help you remember an ad for kitchen appliances or farm equipment. Similarly, watching a violent television program is emotionally arousing, but it actually decreases memory of the products advertised, which are generally unrelated to violence (Bushman & Phillips, 2001). The best advice for advertisers is to get the viewer or listener excited about the product itself or to advertise on an exciting program related to the product. Similarly, the advice for a student is that if you want to remember something, get excited about the content itself. Find some way to see it as interesting.

Why are emotionally arousing events generally so memorable? The physiological explanation is that emotional arousal increases the release of the hormones cortisol and epinephrine (adrenaline) from the adrenal gland. Some of the cortisol reaches the brain, and the epinephrine stimulates peripheral nerves that extend into the brain. The net effect is increased excitation of the *amygdala* and other brain areas that enhance memory storage (Cahill & McGaugh, 1998; Williams, Men, Clayton, & Gold, 1998).

CONCEPT CHECK ☑

11. Most people with posttraumatic stress disorder have lower than normal levels of cortisol. What would you predict about their memory? (Check your answer on page 251)

▌ Do you remember the first time you saw a comet? Most people recall emotionally arousing events, sometimes in great detail, although not always accurately.

Mnemonic Devices

If you needed to memorize something lengthy and not especially exciting—for example, a list of all the bones in the body—how would you do it? One effective strategy is to attach systematic retrieval cues to each term so that you can remind yourself of the terms when you need them.

A mnemonic device is *any memory aid that relies on encoding each item in a special way.* The word *mnemonic* (nee- MAHN-ik) comes from a Greek root meaning "memory." (The same root appears in the word *amnesia,* "lack of memory.") Some mnemonic devices are simple, such as "Every Good Boy Does Fine" to remember the notes EGBDF on the treble clef in music. If you have to remember the functions of various brain areas, you might try links like those shown in Figure 7.12 (Carney & Levin, 1998).

A parachute lets you coast down slowly, like the parasympathetic nervous system.

If the symphony excites you, it arouses your sympathetic nervous system.

FIGURE 7.12 A simple mnemonic device is to think of a short story or image that will remind you of what you need to remember. Here you might think of images to help remember functions of different brain areas.

Suppose you had to memorize a list of Nobel Peace Prize winners (Figure 7.13). You might try making up a little story: "Dun (Dunant) passed (Passy) the Duke (Ducommun) of Gob (Gobat) some cream (Cremer). That made him internally ILL (Institute of In-

Nobel Peace Prize Winners

1901	H. Dunant and F. Passy
1902	E. Ducommun and A. Gobat
1903	Sir W. R. Cremer
1904	Institute of International Law
1905	Baroness von Suttner
1906	T. Roosevelt
1907	E. T. Moneta and L. Renault
1908	K. P. Arnoldson and F. Bajer
1909	A. M. F. Beernaert and Baron d'Estournelles de Constant

1990	M. Gorbachev
1991	A. S. Suu Kyi
1992	Rigoberta Menchú
1993	Nelson Mandela and Frederik W. de Klerk
1994	Yasir Arafat, Yitzhak Rabin, and Shimon Peres
1995	Joseph Rotblat and Pugwash Conferences on Science and World Affairs
1996	Carlos Felipe Ximenes Belo and José Ramos-Horta
1997	Jody Williams and International Committee to Ban Landmines
1998	John Hume and David Trimble
1999	Doctors Without Borders
2000	Kim Dae Jung
2001	Kofi Annan
2002	Jimmy Carter, Jr.
2003	Shirin Ebadi

FIGURE 7.13 A list of Nobel Peace Prize winners: Mnemonic devices can be useful when people try to memorize long lists like this one.

ternational Law). He suited (von Suttner) up with some roses (Roosevelt) and spent some money (Moneta) on a Renault (Renault) . . ." You'd still have to study the names, but your story might help.

Another mnemonic device is the **method of loci** (method of places). *First, you memorize a series of places, and then you use a vivid image to associate each of these locations with something you want to remember.* For example, you might start by memorizing every location along the route from your dormitory room to, say, your psychology classroom. Then you link the locations, in order, to the names.

Suppose the first three locations you pass are the desk in your room, the door to your room, and the corridor. To link the first Nobel Peace Prize winners, Dunant and Passy, to your desk, you might imagine a Monopoly game board on your desk with a big sign "DO NOT (Dunant) PASS (Passy) GO." Then you link the second pair of names to the second location, your door: A DUKE student (as in Ducommun) is standing at the door, giving confusing signals. He says "DO COME IN (Ducommun)" and "GO BACK (Gobat)." Then you link the corridor to Cremer, perhaps by imagining someone has spilled CREAM (Cremer) all over the floor (Figure 7.14). You continue in this manner until you have linked every name to a location. Now, if you can remember all those locations in order and if you have good visual images for each one, you will be able to recite the list of Nobel Peace Prize winners.

How useful are elaborate mnemonic devices? Few people find mnemonics useful for everyday tasks such as remembering where you parked your car, but mnemonics can be helpful in their proper place. For is most effective if it is similar to the links we formed at the time of storage. (page 246)

- *Timing of study.* If you study all at one time, you cannot be sure how much you have learned and how much you will forget. It is best to spread out the study, and the more you spread it out, the longer you are likely to remember it. (page 247)
- *Emotional arousal.* Emotionally exciting events tend to be remembered vividly if not always accurately. (page 248)
- *Mnemonics.* Specialized techniques for establishing systematic retrieval cues can help people remember ordered lists of names or terms. (page 249)

Answers to Concept Checks

7. Students who read slowly and frequently pause to think about the meaning of the material are engaging in deep processing and are likely to remember the material well, probably better than those who read through the material quickly. (page 246)
8. Sometimes someone who claims not to remember simply does not want to talk about it. However, presuming the person really wants to remember, it would help to return to the place of the party, with the same people present, perhaps even at the same time of day. If he or she used alcohol or other drugs, take them again. The more similar the conditions of original learning and later recall, the better the probability of remembering. (page 247)
9. To prepare well for the final exam, you should review all the material at irregular intervals. Thus, you might profit by skimming over Chapters 2 and 3 right now. Of course, if you have a test on Chapter 7 in a day or two, your goal is different and your strategy should be different. (page 248)
10. If you study all at one sitting, the memory will be encoded specifically to what you are thinking about at that time. If you study at several times, the memory will attach to a greater variety of retrieval cues instead of being specific to just one set. (page 248)
11. Because of the lower cortisol levels, they should have trouble storing memories and therefore report frequent memory lapses. (page 249)

Answers to Other Questions in the Module

B. The correct coin is A. (page 245)
C. Animal—Seal; Part of body—Foot; Transportation—Plane; Temperature—Degree; Crime—Racket; Shrubbery—Bush; Stone—Rock; Personality—Charm; Write—Spell; Bird—Cardinal; Harbor—Port; Fruit—Apple. (page 248)

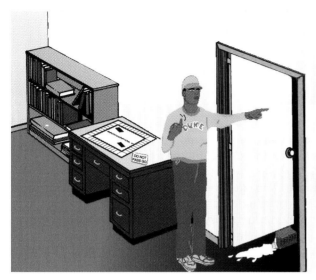

FIGURE 7.14 The method of loci is one of the oldest mnemonic devices. First, learn a list of places, such as "my desk, the door of my room, the corridor, . . ." Then link each of these places to the items on a list of words or names, such as a list of the names of Nobel Peace Prize winners.

example, you might find mnemonics useful for remembering people's names (e.g., you might remember someone named Harry Moore by picturing him as "more hairy" than everyone else).

IN CLOSING

Improving Your Memory

You have probably heard of people taking gingko biloba or other herbs or drugs to try to improve their memory. These chemicals do produce small but measurable memory benefits for patients with impaired blood flow to the brain (Gold, Cahill, & Wenk, 2002; McDaniel, Maier, & Einstein, 2002). However, no one has demonstrated any benefits for healthy people. Some people do remember better than others, even when they have studied equally, and someday—who knows—perhaps researchers will find "the secret" to improving overall memory. Until then, by far the best strategy is to think carefully about anything you want to remember, study it under a variety of conditions, and review frequently.

Summary

- *Levels-of-processing principle.* According to the levels-of-processing principle, a memory becomes stronger (and easier to recall) if we think about the meaning of the material and relate it to other material. (page 245)
- *Encoding specificity.* When we form a memory, we store it with links to the way we thought about it at that time. When we try to recall the memory, a cue

Why is memory retrieval sometimes difficult?

Why do we sometimes report confident but inaccurate memories?

Imagine that you have written a term paper on your computer, and when you click the icon to retrieve it, the computer gives you this error message: "I know it's around here somewhere, but I just can't find it. Try asking me again in a few hours." Or suppose it displays, not the correct term paper, but another one that you wrote the previous semester. Or odder yet, it prints out an elaborate, complicated term paper that you never wrote!

A computer doesn't make those errors (unless it has a virus or some other strange problem). Human memory does, however. This module is titled "Retrieval of Memories," but in fact much of the discussion focuses on failures and errors of retrieval.

Retrieval and Interference

A moment ago I said a computer would not make the mistake of displaying the wrong material. That is true for its internal memory, but when a computer searches for something on the Internet, it will often display the wrong material. When you look for a particular Web site, your search engine may display hundreds of others that resemble it.

Human memory also makes mistakes by confusing the sought material with similar information. If you want to recall a particular memory, then the more often you have learned something similar, the harder it will be to recall the correct information. The first experimental demonstration of this principle was accidental. Remember Hermann Ebbinghaus, who pioneered experimental research on memory. Ebbinghaus measured how long he could remember various lists of 13 nonsense syllables each. The results appear as the blue line on Figure 7.15. On the average he forgot more than half of each list within the first hour (Ebbinghaus, 1885/1913). What a discouraging graph! If people typically forget that fast, then education would seem pointless. However, later replications of this procedure with college students produced the red line of Figure 7.15. Note that most students remembered nearly 90% of the list 24 hours later (Koppenaal, 1963).

Why do you suppose most college students remember a list so much better than Ebbinghaus did? You may be tempted to say that college students are

■ Ebbinghaus could learn new lists of nonsense syllables, but he forgot them quickly because of interference from all the previous lists he had learned. People who memorize many similar lists start to confuse them with one another.

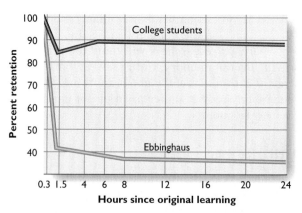

FIGURE 7.15 Blue line: Recall of lists of syllables by Ebbinghaus (1885/1913) after delays of various lengths. Red line: Recall of lists by college students after delays of various lengths. Ebbinghaus learned as fast as other people but forgot faster. *(Based on Koppenaal, 1963).*

very intelligent. Well, yes, but Ebbinghaus was no dummy either. Or you might suggest that college students "have had so much practice at memorizing nonsense." (Sorry if you think so.) But the explanation is the opposite: Ebbinghaus had memorized *too much* nonsense—thousands of lists of syllables. If you memorize large amounts of similar material, your memory becomes like a cluttered room: The clutter doesn't prevent you from bringing in still more clutter, but it makes it harder to find the item you want. Ebbinghaus forgot new lists quickly because of interference from older lists.

If you learn several sets of related materials, the old interferes with the new and the new interferes with the old. The *old materials increase forgetting of the new materials* through **proactive interference** (acting forward in time); the *new materials increase forgetting of the old materials* through **retroactive interference** (acting backward in time). Figure 7.16 shows the distinction between these two kinds of interference.

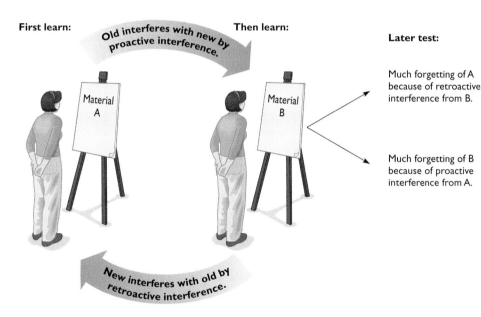

FIGURE 7.16 When someone learns two similar sets of materials, each interferes with retrieval of the other.

Interference is a major cause of forgetting. You may forget where you parked your car because of proactive interference from all the previous times you parked in the same lot. You may forget last week's French vocabulary list because of retroactive interference from this week's list.

CONCEPT CHECK ☑

12. Professor Tryhard learns the names of his students every semester. After several years he learns them as quickly as ever but forgets them

faster. Does he forget because of retroactive interference or proactive interference?

13. Remember the concept of spontaneous recovery from Chapter 6, page 199? Can you explain it in terms of proactive interference? (Hint: Original learning comes first and extinction comes second. What would happen if the first interfered with the second?) (Check your answers on page 262.)

Distinctiveness

Let's consider an application of this idea of interference. Read the following list and then recall, in any order, as many items as you can:

Brussels, Oslo, Bangkok, Calcutta, Kyoto, chocolate, Buenos Aires, Tripoli, Johannesburg, Istanbul

Later test:

Much forgetting of A because of retroactive interference from B.

Much forgetting of B because of proactive interference from A.

In this list of world cities, the word *chocolate* stands out as different, and you are therefore likely to remember it. If one of the cities had been printed in large purple letters, you would probably remember that one too. When many items are similar and one is different, the similar items interfere with one another, and the distinctive item is easier to retrieve.

Similarly, we tend to remember unusual people and those with unusual names. If you meet several men of ordinary appearance and similar names, like John Stevens, Steve Johnson, and Joe Stevenson, you will have trouble learning their names. You will more quickly remember a 7-foot-tall, redheaded man named Stinky Rockefeller.

Let's reconsider a classic study from the first module of this chapter: Peterson and Peterson demonstrated decay of short-term memories over 18 seconds. For example, if you read the letters BKLRE and then count backward by 3s from 228, you probably will forget the letters within 18 seconds. That result is correct if we take the average over many trials, but it is *not* true on the first trial. On the first trial, you have no interference from previous letter sequences, and you probably will remember for well beyond the usual time (Keppel & Underwood, 1962). Evidently, short-term memories

Bob Williams was one of 40 aging former paratroopers who reenacted his parachute jump on the 50th anniversary of D-day. We forget most events from 50 years ago but remember the distinctive ones.

fade fast only because of proactive interference from similar materials.

Serial Order and Retrieval

In addition to the most distinctive items on a list (e.g., *chocolate* among a list of world cities), we are also particularly likely to remember the items at the beginning and end of a list. This tendency, known as the **serial-order effect**, includes two aspects: *The primacy effect is the tendency to remember well the first items, partly because of the lack of proactive interference. The recency effect is the tendency to remember the final items, partly because of the lack of retroactive interference.*

The primacy and recency effects are consistent and robust and occur for many reasons. If you try to list all the people you have ever dated, all the long-distance trips you have ever taken, or all the teachers you have ever had, you will almost certainly include the most recent ones and probably the earliest ones too.

CONCEPT CHECK ☑

14. If you memorize a list of words, which ones are you most likely to remember well? How does interference explain your answer? (Check your answers on page 262.)

Reconstructing Past Events

If you try to retrieve a memory of some experience, you will start with the details that you remember clearly and **reconstruct** the rest to fill in the gaps: *During an original experience, we construct a memory. When we try to retrieve that memory, we reconstruct an account based partly on surviving memories and partly on our expectations of what must have happened.* For example, you might recall studying in the library three nights ago. With a little effort, you might remember where you sat, what you were reading, who sat next to you, and where you went for a snack afterward. If you aren't quite sure, you fill in the gaps with what usually happens during an evening at the library. Within weeks you gradually will forget that evening, and if you try to remember it, you will rely more and more on "what must have happened" with a consequent decline in accuracy of details (Schmolck, Buffalo, & Squire, 2000). However, if you happen to fall in love with the person who sat next to you that evening, the events will become a lifetime memory. Still, when you try to recall it, you will have to reconstruct the details. You might remember where you went for a snack and some of what the two of you said, but if you wanted to recall the book you were reading, you would have to reason it out: "Let's see, that semester I was taking a chemistry course that took a lot of study, so maybe I was reading a chemistry book. No, wait, I remember. When we went out to eat, we talked about politics. So maybe I was reading my political science text."

Reconstruction and Inference in List Memory

Try this demonstration: Read the words in list A once; then turn away from the list, pause for a few seconds, and write as many of the words as you can remember. Repeat the same procedure for lists B and C. *Please do this now, before reading the following paragraph.*

List A	List B	List C
bed	candy	fade
rest	sour	fame
weep	sugar	face
tired	dessert	fake
dream	salty	date
wake	taste	hate
snooze	flavor	late
keep	bitter	mate
doze	cookies	rate
steep	fruits	
snore	chocolate	
nap	yummy	

After you have written out your lists, check how many of the words you got right. If you omitted many, you are normal. The point of this demonstration is not how many you got right, but whether you included *sleep* on the first list, *sweet* on the second, or *fate* on the third. Many people include one or more of these (which are not on the lists), and some do so with great confidence (Deese, 1959; Roediger & McDermott, 1995). Apparently, while learning the individual words, people also learn the gist of what they are all about, and when they are trying to retrieve the list later, they reconstruct a memory of a word that the list implied (Seamon et al., 2002). This powerful effect occurs under a wide variety of conditions, even if people are warned about it before they hear the list (Roediger & McDermott, 2000). Evidently, we reconstruct what "must have" been on the list.

In list B *sweet* is related to the other words in meaning; in list C *fate* resembles the others in sound. In list A *sleep* is related to most of the words in meaning, but the list also includes three words that rhyme with sleep (*weep, keep,* and *steep*). This combined influence is even more effective, producing false recall in a higher percentage of people. With a still longer list that includes an equal number of similar-meaning and similar-sounding words, up to 65% of people report the implied but absent word (Watson, Balota, & Roediger, 2003).

If you did not include *sleep, sweet,* or *fate,* try the Online Try It Yourself activity. Go to http://psychology.wadsworth.com/kalat_intro7e. Navigate to the student Web site, then to the Online Try It Yourself section, and click on False Memory. Hearing a list (as you can with the online demonstration) produces a bigger effect than reading a list.

The effect occurs mostly when people have neither a strong nor a very weak memory, but something intermediate. If a list is short or if you have a chance to learn it well, you are unlikely to infer an extra word not on the list. On the other hand, if you had such a defective memory that you could not remember any of the words on the list, you could not use them to infer another word on the list, and again you would not show a false memory (Schacter, Verfaellie, Anes, & Racine, 1998). As people grow old, their ability to remember the correct words on the list becomes less reliable, and they compensate for their loss of detailed memory by relying on gist, therefore becoming more likely to report words implied but not actually on a list (Lövdén, 2003).

CONCEPT CHECK ☑

15. If you studied a list such as "candy, sour, sugar, dessert, salty, taste . . ." thoroughly instead of hearing it just once, would you be more likely or less likely to include "sweet," which isn't on the list? Why? (Check your answers on page 262.)

Reconstructing Stories

Suppose you listen to a story about a teenager's day, including a mixture of normal events (watching television) and oddities (clutching a teddy bear and parking a bicycle in the kitchen). Which would you remember better—the normal events or the oddities? You might expect to remember the unusual and distinctive events, and you would be right—*if* you are tested while your memory is still strong. However, if you start forgetting the story, you probably will reconstruct a more typical day for the teenager, recalling the normal events, omitting the unlikely ones, and adding other likely events that the story omitted, such as "the teenager went to school in the morning." In short, the less certain your memory is, the more you rely on your expectations (Heit, 1993; Maki, 1990). If you retell something several times over a period of time—either a story you heard or an event from your own experience—the retellings gradually become more coherent and make more sense (Ackil, Van Abbema, & Bauer, 2003; Bartlett, 1932). They make more sense because you rely more on the gist, keeping the details that fit the overall theme and omitting or distorting those that do not.

In a study that highlights the role of expectations, U.S. and Mexican adults tried to recall three stories. Some were given U.S. versions of the stories; others were given Mexican versions. (For example, in the "going on a date" story, the Mexican version had the man's sister go along as a chaperone.) On the average U.S. participants remembered the U.S. versions better, whereas the Mexicans remembered the Mexican versions better (R. J. Harris, Schoen, & Hensley, 1992).

CONCEPT CHECK ☑

16. When you read an account of history, it often seems that one event led to another in a logical order, whereas in everyday life events often seem illogical, unconnected, and unpredictable. Why? (Check your answer on page 262.)

Hindsight Bias

Let's try another demonstration. First read the following paragraph and then answer the question that follows:

> For some years after the arrival of Hastings as governor general of India, the consolidation of British power involved serious war. The first of these wars took place on the northern frontier of Bengal where the British were faced by the plundering raids of the Gurkas of Nepal. Attempts had been made to stop the raids by an exchange of lands, but the Gurkas would not give up their claims to country under British control, and Hastings decided to deal with them once and for all. The campaign began in November, 1814. It was not glorious. The Gurkas were only some 12,000 strong; but they were brave fighters, fighting in territory well-suited to their raiding tactics. The older British commanders were used to war in the plains where the enemy ran away from a resolute attack. In the mountains of Nepal it was not easy even to find the enemy. The troops and transport animals suffered from the extremes of heat and cold, and the officers learned caution only after sharp reverses. Major-General Sir D. Octerlony was the one commander to escape from these minor defeats. (Woodward, 1938, pp. 383–384)

Question

In light of the information in this passage, what was the probability of each of the four possible outcomes listed below? (The probabilities should total 100%.)

a. a British victory   ___%
b. a Gurka victory   ___%
c. military stalemate with no peace settlement   ___%
d. military stalemate with a peace settlement   ___%

Note that each of these possible outcomes seems possible, given what you have read. Now that you have made your estimates of the probabilities, I can tell you what really happened: The two sides reached a military stalemate without any settlement. The British had the advantages of superior numbers and superior equipment, but the Gurkas knew the territory and refused to give up, so battles continued indecisively for years. Now that you know the outcome, would you like to revise your estimates of the probabilities? Perhaps if you reread the paragraph, you will decide that you had overestimated the probabilities of some outcomes and underestimated others.

Subjects in one experiment read the preceding passage about the British and the Gurkas. Some were told which outcome "actually occurred" (although some were misinformed); all were then asked to estimate the probabilities of the four possible outcomes. Each group listed a high estimated probability for the "actual" outcome they had been given (Fischhoff, 1975). That is, once they knew what "really" happened (or incorrectly *thought* they knew), they reinterpreted the information with extra emphasis on the facts that fit the eventual (supposed) outcome (Figure 7.17). Their behavior illustrates **hindsight bias**, *the tendency to mold our recollection of the past to fit how events later turned out.* Something happens and we then say, "I *knew* that was going to happen!" (Oh, incidentally, I lied about the outcome of the British–Gurkas war. Actually, the British won. Would you like to reevaluate your estimates *again*?)

In another study, three weeks before the impeachment trial of U.S. President Clinton in 1999, college students were asked to predict the outcome. On the average they estimated the probability of a conviction at 50.5%. A week and a half after Clinton was not convicted, they were asked, "What would you have said 4 1/2 weeks ago was the chance [of a conviction]?" On the average, they reported a 42.8% estimate (Bryant & Guilbault, 2002).

Hindsight bias is not altogether irrational. When you are making a prediction, you receive a huge array of information, some of it unimportant or even wrong. When you get the final outcome, you quite reasonably conclude that the information that had pointed in the correct direction was the best. You want to focus on that information so you can pay more attention to it in the future (Hoffrage, Hertwig, & Gigerenzer, 2000). In the process you may accidentally convince yourself that you were already strongly influenced by that information.

CRITICAL THINKING:
A STEP FURTHER
Hindsight Bias

Can you interpret people's beliefs that they had a "psychic hunch" in terms of hindsight bias?

The "Recovered Memory" Versus "False Memory" Controversy

Occasionally, someone tells a therapist about vague unpleasant feelings, and the therapist replies, "Symptoms like yours are usually found among people who were abused, especially sexually abused, in childhood. Do you think you were?" In some cases the client says

a Subjects told outcome was a British victory

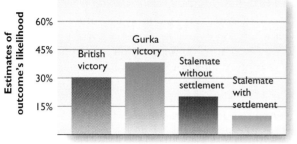

b Subjects told outcome was a Gurka victory

c Subjects told outcome was a stalemate without settlement

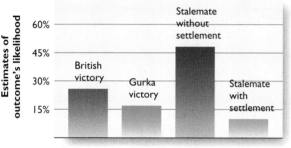

d Subjects told outcome was a stalemate with settlement

FIGURE 7.17 People who thought the British had won said that under the circumstances the British had a very high probability of victory. Those who thought the Gurkas had won said that was the most likely outcome under the circumstances and so forth. *(Based on data of Fischhoff, 1975)*

"no," but the therapist persists: "The fact that you can't remember doesn't mean that it didn't happen. It may have been so painful that you repressed it." The therapist may then recommend hypnosis, repeated attempts to remember, or other techniques. Several ses-

sions later the client may say, "It's starting to come back to me. . . . I think I do remember. . . . " Most therapists would not use such aggressive techniques to try to recover old memories, but some do. *Reports of long-lost memories, prompted by clinical techniques, are known as* **recovered memories.**

Sexual abuse in childhood does occur, and no one knows how often. Some abused children do develop long-lasting psychological scars. But when people claim to recover long-forgotten memories, has the therapist uncovered the truth, distorted the truth, or convinced the client to believe something that never happened? Since the early 1990s, this issue has been one of the most heated debates in psychology. When a commission of respected therapists and researchers met to consider the evidence, they found that they disagreed on many points and had to issue competing reports (Alpert, Brown, & Courtois, 1998; Ornstein, Ceci, & Loftus, 1998).

Some reports are bizarre. In one case two sisters accused their father of raping them many times, both vaginally and anally; bringing his friends over on Friday nights to rape them; and forcing them to participate in satanic rituals that included cannibalism and the slaughter of babies (L. Wright, 1994). The sisters had not remembered any of these events until repeated sessions with a therapist. In another case a group of 3- and 4-year-old children, after repeated urgings from a therapist, accused their Sunday school teacher of sexually abusing them with a curling iron, forcing them to drink blood and urine, hanging them upside down from a chandelier, dunking them in toilets, and killing an elephant and a giraffe during Sunday school class (M. Gardner, 1994). There was no physical evidence to support the claims, such as scarred tissues or giraffe bones.

Even when recovered-memory claims are much less bizarre, their accuracy is uncertain. If a 30-year-old woman claims that her father sexually abused her when she was 8, that she had not told anyone about it at the time, and in fact had forgotten it until now, how could anyone check her accuracy? One might consult old school records for any mention of physical and emotional scars, but even the best of such records are incomplete.

Some related questions are, however, testable: When people have abusive experiences, are they likely to forget them for years? And is it possible to persuade someone to "remember" an event that never actually happened just by suggesting it?

Memory for Traumatic Events

Sigmund Freud, whom we shall consider more fully in Chapter 13, introduced the term **repression** as *the process of moving an unbearably unacceptable memory or impulse from the conscious mind to the unconscious mind.* Although many therapists continue to use the concept of repression, the research on memory has found no clear, unambiguous support for the idea (Holmes, 1990). Experiments that were designed to demonstrate repression have produced small effects that one could explain without the concept of repression. Many clinicians now prefer the term **dissociation,** referring to *memory that is stored but cannot be retrieved* (Alpert et al., 1998). However, most of the doubts about the term *repression* also apply to the similar concept of *dissociation.*

Do people forget traumatic events? It depends. (Almost always a good answer in psychology.) Partly it depends on what we mean by "forget." Someone with a painful memory might avoid thinking or talking about it and might say "I don't remember" to avoid talking about it (Pope, Hudson, Bodkin, & Oliva, 1998).

In general, however, people seldom forget traumatic events. One study examined 16 children who had witnessed the murder of one of their parents. All had recurring nightmares and haunting thoughts of the experience; none had forgotten (Malmquist, 1986). Other studies have examined prisoners of war who had been severely mistreated (Merckelbach, Dekkers, Wessel, & Roefs, 2003), children who had been kidnapped or forced to participate in pornographic movies (Terr, 1988), and others who had additional horrible experiences. People almost always remembered the events, or they forgot only about as much as one might expect for very old events. Evidently, if repression of traumatic experiences occurs at all, it does so only under rare and undefined circumstances.

Memory for a traumatic experience depends on someone's age at the time of the event, its severity, and the reaction of other family members. In one study investigators interviewed 129 young adult women who had been brought to a hospital emergency ward because of sexual assault at ages 1 to 12 years. Most reported remembering the sexual assault, although 38% did not (L. M. Williams, 1994). Generally, those who were at least 7 years old at the time of the attack remembered better than those who were younger. In a similar study, researchers interviewed 168 young adults who had been victims of criminally prosecuted child sexual abuse. Of these, 142 reported the sexual abuse during a telephone conversation, and 12 more reported it in a follow-up mailing or face-to-face interview, leaving only 14 (8%) who did not report it at all (Goodman et al., 2003). Recall was more likely among those who were older at the time of the offense, those who had more severe or repeated abuse, and those who received more family support and encouragement. Better memory by those who were older is unsurprising; people almost always remember later events better than those of early childhood. Better recall for more severe and repeated abuse is important: It is what we would expect based on memory research—

greater recall of stronger, repeated, more important events. The result, however, is contrary to what one would predict based on the idea of repression: Theoretically, people should repress the more severely distressing experiences. In short, the results suggest that early traumatic memories are similar to other memories and are not likely to be lost.

Areas of Agreement and Disagreement

Psychologists agree that some people have had abusive childhood experiences that they later cannot remember. However, these cases are not common, except among those who were very young at the time of the abuse. Even when someone does forget a horrible experience, the question is why. Many clinicians believe that repression or dissociation is a possible explanation; if so, then attempts to recover the memory are at least a theoretical possibility (Alpert et al., 1998). (Whether recovering them would be *beneficial* is, however, not at all certain.) The alternative view, favored by most memory researchers, is that traumatic memories are like other memories: If we don't think about something for a long time, we find them harder to retrieve, and if we try to reconstruct them later, the result will be an uncertain mixture of truth and distortion.

CONCEPT CHECK   ☑

17. Based on material earlier in this chapter, why should we expect traumatic events to be remembered better than most other events? (Check your answer on page 262.)

CRITICAL THINKING:
WHAT'S THE EVIDENCE?
Suggestions and False Memories

Critics of attempts to help people recover lost memories have suggested that a therapist who repeatedly encourages a client to recall lost memories can unintentionally implant a **false memory** (or false report), *a report that someone believes to be a memory but that does not correspond to real events* (Lindsay & Read, 1994; Loftus, 1993). We shall examine three representative experiments.

EXPERIMENT I
Hypothesis   If people are asked questions that suggest or presuppose a certain fact, many people will later report remembering that "fact," even if it never happened.

Method   Elizabeth Loftus (1975) asked two groups of students to watch a videotape of an automobile accident. Then she asked one group but not the other, "Did you see the children getting on the school bus?" In fact the videotape did not show a school bus. A week later she asked both groups 20 new questions about the accident, including this one: "Did you see a school bus in the film?"

Results   Of the first group (those who were asked about seeing children get on a school bus), 26% reported that they had seen a school bus; of the second group, only 6% said they had seen a school bus.

Interpretation   The question "Did you see the children getting on the school bus?" implies that there *was* a school bus. Some of the students who heard that question reconstructed events by combining what they actually saw, what they believed must have happened, and what the researcher suggested afterward.

EXPERIMENT 2
The first experiment demonstrated that a suggestion can distort memories of something that people watched. But could a suggestion implant a memory of an experience that never really occurred?

Hypothesis   If people are told about a childhood event by a trusted person, they will come to remember it as something they experienced, even if in fact they did not.

Method   The participants, aged 18 to 53, were told that the study concerned their memories of childhood. Each participant was given four paragraphs, and each paragraph described a different event. Three of the events had actually happened. (The experimenters had contacted parents to get descriptions of childhood events.) A fourth event was a plausible story about getting lost, which had not happened. An example for one Vietnamese woman: "You, your Mom, Tien, and Tuan, all went to the Bremerton Kmart. You must have been 5 years old at the time. Your Mom gave each of you some money to get a blueberry ICEE. You ran ahead to get into the line first, and somehow lost your way in the store. Tien found you crying to an elderly Chinese woman. You three then went together to get an ICEE." After reading the four paragraphs, each participant was asked to write whatever additional details he or she could remember of the event. Participants were asked to try again 1 week later and then again after another week (Loftus, Feldman, & Dashiell, 1995).

Results   Of 24 participants, 6 reported remembering the suggested (false) event. Participants generally described the false memories in fewer words than the correct memories, but some did provide a fair amount of additional detail. The woman in the foregoing example said, "I vaguely remember walking around Kmart crying and looking for Tien and Tuan. I thought I was lost forever. I went to the shoe department, because we always spent a lot of time there. I went to the handkerchief place because we were there last. I circled all over the store it seemed 10 times. I just remember walking around crying. I do not remember the Chinese woman, or the ICEE (but it would be raspberry ICEE if I was getting an ICEE) part. I don't even remember being found."

Interpretation   A simple suggestion can provoke some people to recall a personal experience in moderate detail, even though the event never happened. Granted, the suggestion influenced fewer than half of the people tested, and most of them reported only vague memories. Still, the researchers achieved this effect after only a single brief suggestion. In a similar study, 13 of 47 participants reported detailed false memories of getting lost or getting attacked by an animal or another child, and 18 more participants reported partial recollection (Porter, Birt, Yuille, & Lehman, 2000).

One objection is that perhaps this "false" memory was not entirely false. Maybe this young woman *was* lost at some point—if not in a Kmart at age 5, then somewhere else at some other age. Some later studies tried to establish memories of virtually impossible events. In one study college students read fake advertisements for Disneyland that depicted people meeting and shaking hands with Bugs Bunny (a Warner Brothers character who would *never* appear at Disneyland). About 30% of those who read this ad later reported that they too had met Bugs Bunny at Disneyland. Some reported touching his ears or tail (Loftus, 2003). In another study British students who were asked to imagine certain experiences later reported that they actually remembered those experiences, including "having a nurse remove a skin sample from my little finger"—a procedure that never occurs in Britain (Mazzoni & Memon, 2003). In short, suggestions can lead people to report memories of events that we can be confident never happened.

EXPERIMENT 3
Some therapists recommend that their clients examine photographs from their childhood to help evoke old memories. They are certainly right that old photographs do bring back memories. The question, however, is whether looking at old photographs might also increase the report of false memories.

Hypothesis   A false suggestion about a childhood event will evoke memory reports more readily if people have examined photographs from when they were that age.

Method   The researchers contacted the parents of 45 college students and asked each to provide a report of some event that happened while these students were in third or fourth grade and another that happened in fifth or sixth grade. Both were supposed to be events that the student might or might not remember, not an event that the family had repeatedly discussed. The researchers also asked the parents to confirm that the following "false memory" event—the one they planned to suggest—had *not* happened: In the first grade, the child took a "Slime" toy to school, and then she and another child slid it into the teacher's desk and received a mild punishment. Finally, the researchers asked the parents for copies of class photographs from first grade, third or fourth, and fifth or sixth.

After all these preparations, they brought in the students and briefly described for each student the two correct events (provided by the parents) and the one false event. For each they asked the students to provide whatever additional information they remembered. Half of them (randomly selected) were shown their class photographs and half were not. At the end of the session, they were asked to think about the first-grade event for the next week and try to remember more about it. Those in the photograph group took the photo with them. A week later the students returned and again reported whatever they thought they remembered (Lindsay, Hagen, Read, Wade, & Garry, 2003).

Results Most students reported clear memories of the two real events. For the false event of first grade, Figure 7.18 shows the percentage of students who reported some memory of the event in the first and second sessions. Memories increased from the first to the second session, and students who saw the pho-

tographs reported more memories than those who did not see photographs. By the second session, almost two thirds of the students who saw a class photograph reported some memory of the false event.

At the end of the study, the researchers explained that the first-grade event did not really happen. Many of the students expressed surprise, such as "No way! I remember it! That is so weird!" (Lindsay et al., 2004, page 153).

Interpretation Examining an old photograph evokes old memories, but it also increases suggestibility about false memories. Looking at the photo helps the person remember, "Oh, yes, that's what my first grade teacher looked like. And that was my closest friend back then . . ." If the person tries to remember acting with a friend to pull a prank on the teacher, the visual image becomes more vivid and therefore more convincing. At any rate the message is that combining a suggestion about a possible memory with a photograph from that time is risky; it may strengthen false memories as well as real ones.

The question still remains, however, about clinicians' reports of recovering lost memories of early trauma. Many clinicians object that the kinds of false memories implanted in research settings (being lost in a mall, first-grade mischief, etc.) are different from emotionally intense memories of sexual abuse. To this criticism researchers reply that, ethically, they could not try to implant painful memories of traumatic abuse just to demonstrate the possibility.

If someone reports remembering some event after many years of not remembering it, we may never know whether the event actually happened. No one recommends disbelieving all such reports (Pope, 1996). The recommendation is to withhold judgment about the accuracy of a "recovered" memory unless someone has independent evidence to support it. Furthermore, the more suggestions someone was given prior to the recall, the more skeptical we should be.

CONCEPT CHECK ☑

18. In what way is hindsight bias similar to an implanted "false memory"? (Check your answer on page 262.)

Children as Eyewitnesses

Finally, should we trust the reports of young children who are witnesses or victims of a crime? On the one hand, if we routinely disregard their testimony, anyone who abuses children can be sure of avoiding prosecution. On the other hand, we know that young chil-

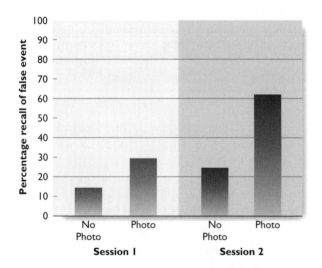

FIGURE 7.18 More students who saw a first-grade class photograph reported remembering the suggested (false) event. The percentage of recall increased from the first session to the second, a week later, especially among those who saw the photograph. (*"Recall of False Event," by D.S. Lindsay, L. Hagen, J.D. Read, K.A. Wada, and M. Garry. True Photographs and False Memories.* Psychological Science. *Copyright 2004 Blackwell Publishing. Reprinted with permission.*)

dren sometimes confuse fantasy with reality or say what they think someone wants them to say.

Research here can be tricky. No ethical researcher would abuse children or tell children they had been abused. A better approach is to ask children to recall a medical or dental examination, where a stranger probed various parts of a child's body. How well can the child report what happened?

In such studies researchers found that children as young as 3 years old report accurately under proper conditions. Children 3 to 5 years old volunteer very little when asked, "Tell me what happened." However, they do answer correctly to specific questions such as, "Did the doctor shine a light in your eyes?" We might worry that the children were responding to suggestions or agreeing to whatever someone asked them. However, they consistently respond "no" to questions about acts that did not happen, such as, "Did the doctor cut your hair?" Children's accuracy is reasonably good even 6 weeks after the physical exam (Baker-Ward, Gordon, Ornstein, Larus, & Clubb, 1993). However, after persistent questioning and prodding, young children do start reporting elaborate false memories (Ceci, 1995).

Several factors influence the accuracy of children's reports:

- **The delay between event and questioning.** If 4- to 6-year-old children are asked about a likely event that did *not* occur in the most recent physical exam, they correctly deny it if they are asked within 6 weeks but report it if asked later. Evidently, they start to confuse the most recent exam with the usual exam (Ornstein et al., 1998).
- **Suggestive questions.** To an invitation such as, "Tell me what happened," a young child's answer is usually short but accurate. To a suggestive question such as, "Did he touch you under your clothing?" the probability of a false report increases (Lamb & Fauchier, 2001).
- **The understandability of the questions.** Three-year-olds who understand a question will usually answer correctly. When they don't understand, instead of saying they don't understand, they usually answer "yes" (Imhoff & Baker-Ward, 1999).

  Sometimes a questioner thinks a child understands, but the child does not. Once my son and his family were on a trip, and the parents told my granddaughter, then 3 years old, that they would stop at a barbecue restaurant for dinner. She was so excited that she could hardly wait. She spent most of the trip asking, "Now how long till barbecue?" As they finally approached the restaurant, she asked, "Will other children be there too, with their Barbies?"
- **Repetition of the question.** A 3-year-old who is asked the same question twice within a single ses-

sion is likely to answer differently the second time (Poole & White, 1993). Evidently, the child assumes that the first answer must have been wrong. However, asking the question every few days helps the child remember, and that persistence is important if a child has to testify in court at a later date (Poole & White, 1995).
- **Use of doll props.** We might imagine that children's reports are limited by their small vocabulary. Some psychologists try to help them by providing anatomically detailed dolls and asking them to act out what happened. The idea sounds reasonable, but when researchers ask children to act out a doctor's exam (where we know what actually happened), they act out many events that did not happen (Greenhoot, Ornstein, Gordon, & Baker-Ward, 1999). If a child acts out a sexual contact, we cannot assume that the child was sexually molested. In fact, if you point to a child's elbow and then ask the child to find the doll's elbow, many young children cannot. Interpreting a child's doll play is a very uncertain matter (Ceci, 1995; Koocher et al., 1995).

The general recommendations for children's eyewitness testimony are simple: If a child is asked simple questions, without suggestions or pressure and reasonably soon after the event, even children as young as 3 can be believable (Ceci & Bruck, 1993). However, a young child can be highly influenced by suggestions.

CRITICAL THINKING: A STEP FURTHER
Unlikely Memory Reports

Some people claim to have been abducted by aliens from another planet. Apparently, most of these people are neither mentally ill nor deliberately lying (Banaji & Kihlstrom, 1996). Presuming that they were not actually abducted by aliens, how might we explain their reports?

IN CLOSING
Memory Distortions

Memory distortions are sometimes a serious problem, but they are the by-product of a useful process. That process is our ability to focus on the essential gist. When we are reasoning and making decisions, we need to focus on trends and general principles, and depending on the question, we may or may not need the details (Brainerd & Reyna, 2002). The older some experience is, the less likely we are to need its details. If we do need the details, we can usually reason them out well enough for most purposes. So memory distortions are not evidence of something going wrong. They are a necessary consequence of the way our memory normally works. The following dialogue captures well our tendency to forget details:

He: We met at nine.
She: We met at eight.
He: I was on time.
She: No, you were late.
He: Ah, yes! I remember it well. We dined with friends.
She: We dined alone.
He: A tenor sang.
She: A baritone.
He: Ah, yes! I remember it well. That dazzling April moon!
She: There was none that night. And the month was June.
He: That's right! That's right!
She: It warms my heart to know that you remember still the way you do.
He: Ah, yes! I remember it well.
　—"I Remember It Well" from the musical *Gigi* by Alan Jay Lerner and Frederick Loewe

Summary

- *Interference.* When someone learns several similar sets of material, the earlier ones interfere with retrieval of later ones by proactive interference. The later ones interfere with earlier ones by retroactive interference. (page 252)
- *Distinctiveness and serial order.* It is easiest to remember items that are least blocked by interference, such as the first and last items on a list and any unusual items. (page 253)
- *Reconstruction.* When remembering stories or events from their own lives, people recall some of the facts and fill in the gaps based on logical inferences of what must have happened. They rely particularly heavily on inferences when their memory of the details is weak. (page 254)
- *Reconstructions from a word list.* If people read or hear a list of related words and try to recall them, they are likely to include closely related words that were not on the list. They have remembered the gist and reconstructed what else must have been on the list. (page 254)
- *Story memory.* Someone who tries to retell a story after memory of the details has faded will rely on the gist and therefore leave out some details that seemed irrelevant and add or change other facts to fit the logic of the story. (page 255)

- *Hindsight bias.* People often revise their memories of what they previously expected, saying that how events turned out was what they had expected all along. (page 256)
- *The "recovered memory" vs. "false memory" debate.* Some therapists have used hypnosis or suggestive lines of questioning to try to help people remember painful experiences. Suggestions can induce people to distort memories or report events that did not happen. It is difficult to distinguish accurate memories from distorted or false ones. (page 256)
- *Children as eyewitnesses.* Even children 3 to 5 years old can correctly report events if they are asked simple questions without pressure soon after the event. However, suggestive questions can lead them astray. (page 260)

Answers to Concept Checks

12. It is due to proactive interference—interference from memories learned earlier. Much of the difficulty of retrieving long-term memories is due to proactive interference. (page 253)
13. First, someone learns the response; the second learning is the extinction of the response. If the first learning proactively interferes with the later extinction, spontaneous recovery will result. (page 253)
14. It will be easiest to remember the first, last, and most unusual items on the list. The first is spared from proactive interference; the last is spared from retroactive interference; and an unusual item is not greatly weakened by either kind of interference. However, low interference is not the only explanation for the serial order effect. (page 254)
15. You would be less likely to add a word not on the list. We rely on inferences mostly when the actual memory is weak. (page 255)
16. Long after the fact, a historian puts together a coherent story based on the gist of events, emphasizing details that fit the pattern and omitting others. In your everyday life, you are aware of all the facts, including those that do not fit any pattern. (page 256)
17. Emotionally arousing memories are usually more memorable than other events. Any emotionally arousing event stimulates cortisol release and in other ways activates the amygdala, a brain area that helps store memories. (page 258; see also page 249)
18. In a case of hindsight bias, something that you learn later operates like a suggestion, so that when you try to remember what you previously thought, you are influenced by that suggestion and change your reported memory to fit it. (page 260)

Amnesia

| Why do some people have severe memory problems?

Imagine you defied the advice given to computer owners and passed your computer through a powerful magnetic field. Chances are you would erase all the memory, but suppose you found that you had erased only the text files and not the graphics files. Or suppose the old memories were intact but you could no longer store new ones. From the damage you would gain hints about how your computer's memory works.

The same is true of human memory. Various kinds of brain damage impair one kind of memory and not another, enabling us to draw inferences about how memory is organized.

Normal forgetting depends largely on interference from similar memories. It also depends on the absence of appropriate retrieval cues. For example, if you learn something in a particular place, time, and state of mind, you may forget it in another. In addition to these normal mechanisms of forgetting, some people have more serious problems.

Amnesia After Damage to the Hippocampus

Amnesia is a *loss of memory*. Even in the most severe cases, people don't forget everything they ever learned. For example, they don't forget how to walk, talk, or eat.

(If they did, we would call it *dementia,* not amnesia.) Amnesia can result from many kinds of brain damage, including damage to the hippocampus.

In 1953 a man with the initials H. M. was suffering from many small daily epileptic seizures and about one major seizure per week. He did not respond to any antiepileptic drugs, so in desperation, surgeons removed most of his **hippocampus,** *a large forebrain structure in the interior of the temporal lobe* (Figure 7.19), where they believed his epileptic seizures were originating. They also removed some surrounding brain areas. At the time researchers knew very little about the hippocampus and did not know what to expect. Had they known the behavioral outcome, H. M. almost certainly would have preferred to continue having epileptic seizures instead of undergoing this operation.

The surgery did greatly decrease the frequency and severity of H. M.'s seizures. His personality remained the same, but he became more passive (Eichenbaum, 2002). His IQ score increased slightly, presumably because of the decreased epileptic interference. However, he suffered severe memory problems (Corkin, 1984; Milner, 1959). H. M. suffered a massive **anterograde** (ANT-eh-ro-grade) **amnesia,** *inability to store new long-term memories.* For years after the operation, he cited the year as 1953 and his own age as 27. Later, he took wild guesses (Corkin, 1984). He would read the same issue of a

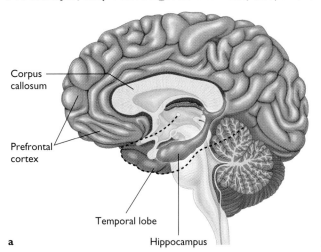

a

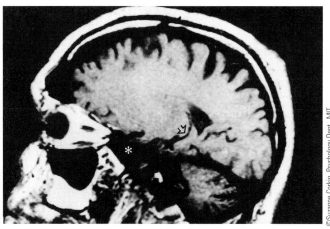

b

FIGURE 7.19 (a) The hippocampus is a large subcortical structure of the brain. (b) After damage to the hippocampus and related structures, patient H. M. had great difficulty storing new long-term memories. The photo shows a scan of the brain of H. M. formed by magnetic resonance imaging. The asterisk indicates the area from which the hippocampus is missing. The arrow indicates a portion of the hippocampus that is preserved. *(Photo courtesy of Suzanne Corkin and David Amaral)*

263

magazine repeatedly without recognizing it. He could not even remember where he had lived. He also suffered a moderate **retrograde amnesia,** *loss of memory for events that occurred shortly before the brain damage* (see Figure 7.20). That is, he had some trouble recalling events that had happened within the last 1 to 3 years before the operation. Any loss of consciousness, such as after a concussion or excessive alcohol intake, can produce retrograde amnesia, although seldom as extensive as 1 to 3 years (Riccio, Millin, & Gisquet-Verrier, 2003).

FIGURE 7.20 Brain damage induces retrograde amnesia (loss of old memories) and anterograde amnesia (difficulty storing new memories).

H. M. could form normal short-term memories, such as repeating a short list of words or numbers, and he could retain them as long as he kept rehearsing them. However, a brief distraction would eliminate the memory. For example, he might tell the same person the same story several times within a few minutes, each time forgetting that he had told it before (Eichenbaum, 2002).

Like Rip van Winkle (the story character who slept for 20 years and awakened to a vastly changed world), H. M. became more and more out of date with each passing year (Gabrieli, Cohen, & Corkin, 1988; M. L. Smith, 1988). He did not recognize the names or faces of people who became famous after the mid-1950s. He could not name the president of the United States even when Ronald Reagan was president, although he remembered Reagan as an actor. He did not understand the meaning of words and phrases that entered the English language after his surgery. For example, he treated *Jacuzzi* and *granola* as nonwords (Corkin, 2002). He guessed that *soul food* means "forgiveness" and that a *closet queen* might be "a moth" (Gabrieli et al., 1988). Seldom-used words like *squander* gradually slipped out of his vocabulary (James & McKay, 2001).

In spite of H. M.'s massive memory difficulties, he could still acquire and retain new skills. Recall the distinction between procedural memory (skills) and declarative memory (facts). H. M. learned to read material written in mirror fashion (N. J. Cohen & Squire, 1980), such as shown at top right. However, he could not remember having learned this skill or any of the

others he acquired, and always expressed surprise at his success.

He cuold read sentences written backwards, like this.

The results for H. M. led researchers to study both people and laboratory animals with similar damage. The following points have emerged:

- The hippocampus is important for storing most long-term memories.
- Although H. M. and others with damage to the hippocampus can still retrieve old memories, an intact hippocampus is ordinarily active during retrieval (Maguire & Frith, 2003).
- Other things being equal, the more difficult a memory task, the more it depends on the hippocampus (Reed & Squire, 1999).
- The hippocampus is less important for implicit than explicit memory (Ryan, Althoff, Whitlow, & Cohen, 2000), perhaps because tests of implicit memory can detect weaker memories.
- The hippocampus is important for remembering details. One man with hippocampal damage could sketch the general layout of his home neighborhood but could not identify photos of houses and other landmarks within the neighborhood (Rosenbaum et al., 2000).

CONCEPT CHECK ☑

19. Which kinds of memory are most impaired in H. M.? Which kinds are least impaired? (Check your answers on page 268.)

Amnesia After Damage to the Prefrontal Cortex

Amnesia can also arise after damage to the prefrontal cortex (see Figure 7.19). Because the prefrontal cortex receives extensive input from the hippocampus, the symptoms of prefrontal cortex damage overlap those of hippocampal damage. However, some special deficits also arise.

Prefrontal cortex damage can be the result of a stroke, trauma to the head, or **Korsakoff's syndrome,** *a condition caused by a prolonged deficiency of vitamin B_1 (thiamine), usually as a result of chronic alcoholism.* This deficiency leads to widespread loss or shrinkage of neurons, especially in the prefrontal cortex and areas connected to it. Patients suffer apathy, confusion, and severe amnesia, both retrograde and anterograde (Squire, Haist, & Shimamura, 1989). If given a long list of words to remember, they forget those at the beginning of the list before they reach the end and soon forget those at the end also (Stuss et al., 1994).

Patients with prefrontal cortex damage answer many questions with **confabulations,** which are *attempts to fill in the gaps in their memory.* Most confabulations include out-of-date information, indicating a failure to suppress inappropriate memories (Schnider, 2003). For example, a hospitalized dentist might insist that patients are waiting for his or her attention, or an aged woman might insist that she had to go home to feed her baby. Confabulations are not exactly attempts to hide their inability to answer a question, as they almost never confabulate on a question such as "Where is Premola?" or "Who is Princess Lolita?" (Schnider, 2003). That is, if they never knew the answer, they freely admit not knowing. The following interview is a typical example (Moscovitch, 1989, pp. 135–136). Note the mixture of correct information, confabulations that were correct at some time in the past, and imaginative attempts to explain the discrepancies between one answer and another:

Psychologist: How old are you?
Patient: I'm 40, 42, pardon me, 62.
Psychologist: Are you married or single?
Patient: Married.
Psychologist: How long have you been married?
Patient: About 4 months.
Psychologist: What's your wife's name?
Patient: Martha.
Psychologist: How many children do you have?
Patient: Four. (He laughs.) Not bad for 4 months.
Psychologist: How old are your children?
Patient: The eldest is 32; his name is Bob. And the youngest is 22; his name is Joe.
Psychologist: How did you get these children in 4 months?
Patient: They're adopted.
Psychologist: Who adopted them?
Patient: Martha and I.
Psychologist: Immediately after you got married you wanted to adopt these older children?
Patient: Before we were married we adopted one of them, two of them. The eldest girl Brenda and Bob, and Joe and Dina since we were married.
Psychologist: Does it all sound a little strange to you, what you are saying?
Patient: I think it is a little strange.
Psychologist: I think when I looked at your record it said that you've been married for over 30 years. Does that sound more reasonable to you if I told you that?
Patient: No.
Psychologist: Do you really believe that you have been married for 4 months?
Patient: Yes.

Patients with prefrontal cortex damage confidently defend their confabulations and often maintain the same confabulation from one time to the next. Actually, the same is true of normal people when they learn something poorly. In one study college students listened to complicated 2-minute descriptions of topics they knew little about and then answered detailed questions. Once a week for the next 4 weeks, the process repeated; they heard the complicated description and answered the same questions. Generally, they repeated the same incorrect guesses from one week to the next (Fritz, Morris, Bjork, Gelman, & Wickens, 2000).

Why do people with prefrontal damage confabulate so much more than the rest of us? According to Morris Moscovitch (1992), the prefrontal cortex is necessary for *working with memory,* the strategies we use to reconstruct memories that we cannot immediately recall. For example, if you are asked what is the farthest north that you have ever traveled or how many salads you ate last week, your answer requires reasoning. People with prefrontal cortex damage have difficulty making reasonable inferences.

Blue Planet Software, Inc. Tetris © Elorg 1987–2002

❚ People who spend many hours playing the game Tetris report seeing images of Tetris blocks, especially as they are falling asleep. So do people with severe amnesia, even though they don't remember playing the game.

Despite their impoverished memory in other regards, people with brain damage are nearly normal on most tests of implicit memory. For example, after hearing a list of words, a patient may not be able to say any of the words on the list and may not even remember that there was a list. However, when given a set of three-letter stems such as CON— and TRA—, the patient completes them to make words that were on the list (Hamann & Squire, 1997).

Another example: After patients repeatedly practiced playing the video game Tetris, they said they did not remember playing the game before, although they did improve from one session to the next. When they closed their eyes to go to sleep at night, they said they saw little images of blocks but did not know what they were (Stickgold, Malia, Maguire, Roddenberry, & O'Connor, 2000).

One important conclusion emerges from all the studies of brain damage and amnesia: We have several different types of memory. It is possible to impair one type, such as explicit and declarative, without equally damaging another type, such as implicit and procedural.

CONCEPT CHECK ☑

20. Although confabulation is a kind of false memory, how does it differ from the suggested false memories discussed in the previous module? (Check your answer on page 268.)

Memory Impairments in Alzheimer's Disease

A more common cause of memory loss is **Alzheimer's** (AHLTZ-hime-ers) **disease,** *a condition occurring mostly in old age, characterized by increasingly severe memory loss, confusion, depression, disordered thinking, and impaired attention.* Several genes have been found that lead to an onset of Alzheimer's disease before age 60 (Goate et al., 1991; Murrell, Farlow, Ghetti, & Benson, 1991; Schellenberg et al., 1992; Sherrington et al., 1995). However, more than 99% of the people with Alzheimer's disease have a later onset, and most cases of the late-onset form are not linked with any identified gene. Moreover, the effects of these genes are not inevitable. The genes linked to Alzheimer's disease in the United States are also found among the Yoruba people of Nigeria (Hendrie, 2001), but the Yoruba almost never get Alzheimer's disease. Which aspect of their culture shields them from Alzheimer's is uncertain, although diet is a likely candidate.

Alzheimer's disease is marked by a gradual accumulation of harmful proteins in the brain and deterioration of brain cells, leading to a loss of arousal and attention. The memory problem is broad, including both anterograde and retrograde amnesia. Alzheimer's patients have deficits in semantic memory as well as episodic memory (Beauregard, Chertkow, Gold, & Bergman, 2001). As a rule they can learn new skills and other implicit memories much better than new explicit memories. For example, they can be taught to use a mobile phone (Lekeu, Wojtasik, Van der Linden, & Salmon, 2002). However, even their implicit memory is deficient in some cases (McGeorge, Taylor, Della Sala, & Shanks, 2002). Like Korsakoff's patients, they often confabulate (Nedjam, Dalla Barba, & Pillon, 2000). This mixture of memory problems should not be surprising, given the overall decrease of arousal and attention. Weak arousal and impaired attention cause problems for almost any aspect of memory.

CONCEPT CHECK ☑

21. What evidence indicates that Alzheimer's disease is not strongly dependent on genetic influences? (Check your answer on page 268.)

Infant Amnesia

Can you recall events from when you were 8 years old? How about age 6? Age 4? Most people report a cutoff somewhere around age 5. The exact age varies, but before the cutoff age, one has few if any memories. The *near absence of early declarative memories* is known as **infant amnesia,** or **childhood amnesia.** (People retain procedural memories from early childhood, such as memory of how to walk, but of course they practiced those skills from then on.) Although psychologists have proposed many theories of infant amnesia, none are fully persuasive (Howe & Courage, 1997).

In what may have been the earliest proposal on this issue, Sigmund Freud suggested that children go through emotionally difficult experiences at ages 4 to 5 that are so disturbing that a child represses everything experienced at that time or before. However, neither Freud nor anyone else has ever offered any evidence to support this idea.

A more modern proposal is that the hippocampus, known to be important for memory, is slow to mature, so memories from the first few years are not well stored (Moscovitch, 1985). A weakness of that suggestion is that young children do form long-term memories. A typical 4-year-old can accurately describe experiences from ages 2 and 3, such as birthday parties, holiday celebrations, and visits to grandparents (Bauer, 1996). Even 2-year-olds remember events that happened months ago, although we have to test them in nonverbal ways to demonstrate the memories (Bauer, 2002; Liston & Kagan, 2002). In short, young children establish long-term memories, but those memories last only months or years, not a lifetime as later memories do.

Another proposal is that a permanent memory of an experience requires a "sense of self" that develops between ages 3 and 4 (Howe & Courage, 1993). A difficulty with this idea is that rats, pigeons, and other nonhuman species develop long-lasting memories. If we want to avoid saying that rats have a "sense of self" and 3-year-old children do not, we could argue that rats' memories aren't the same as the kind of memory we are discussing for adult humans. However, at best, this idea is not yet convincing.

Another possibility is that after we come to rely on language, we lose access to memories encoded earlier, nonverbally. That idea will not explain why a 4-year-old can describe what happened at age 3, whereas a 7-year-old cannot. Still, some interesting research supports the onset of language as one factor in infant amnesia: Psychologists let some 3-year-olds play with a "magic shrinking machine." A child could place a large toy into a slot, crank a handle, and then see a smaller version of the same toy come out, as if the machine had shrunk the toy. When the children returned 6 months or a year later, they clearly remembered the machine and how to work it. However, when they were asked to describe how the machine worked or to name the toys that it shrank, the children described their experience using only the words they had known at the time they originally played with the machine (Simcock & Hayne, 2002). For example, a child who knew the word "teddy bear" at age 3 would use it later, but a child who did not know the term at age 3 would not (even after learning it in the meantime).

One more possibility is that infant amnesia relates to encoding specificity (page 246). If we learn something in one time, place, physiological condition, or state of mind, we remember it more easily under the same or similar conditions. Maybe we forget our early years just because we don't have enough of the right retrieval cues to find those infant memories.

At this point none of these hypotheses is well established. Infant amnesia probably has several explanations, not just one.

CONCEPT CHECK ☑

22. What evidence indicates that infant amnesia is not due to a failure to establish long-term memories? (Check your answer on page 268.)

The Complexities of Amnesia

Some degree of memory loss is normal and even healthy (Schacter, 1999). If you remembered everything that ever happened to you, and none of those memories faded for even a moment, you would be overwhelmed with more and more information, most of it useless.

However, people with amnesia forget useful information, sometimes even information about themselves. We still have much to learn about amnesia. In this module the emphasis has been on brain damage (or brain maturation, in the case of infants), but the situation is often more complex. Almost every patient with severe amnesia has some degree of brain damage, but in some cases the person has relatively mild brain damage and additional problems in handling emotions and life events (M. D. Kopelman, 2000). Emotional problems by themselves seldom if ever cause prolonged amnesia, but they do compound and magnify organic problems. Important psychological phenomena seldom have a single, simple explanation.

Summary

- *Amnesia after damage to the hippocampus.* H. M. and other patients with damage to the hippocampus have great difficulty storing new long-term declarative memories, although they form normal short-term, procedural, and implicit memories. (page 263)
- *Damage to the frontal lobes.* Patients with damage to the frontal lobes fail to suppress old, irrelevant information and therefore give confident wrong answers, known as confabulations. (page 264)
- *Alzheimer's disease.* Patients with Alzheimer's disease, a condition that occurs mostly after age 60 to 65, have a variety of memory problems, although implicit and procedural memory are more intact than explicit, declarative memory. Their problems stem largely from impairments of arousal and attention. (page 266)
- *Lessons from amnesia.* Studies of people with brain damage demonstrate the value of distinguishing among different types of memory, such as declarative and procedural or explicit and implicit. (page 266)
- *Infant amnesia.* Most people remember little from early childhood, even though preschoolers have clear recollections of experiences that happened months or even years ago. No one explanation is fully convincing. However, research shows that as children develop language, they do not apply their newly learned words to old memories. (page 266)

Answers to Concept Checks

19. H. M. is greatly impaired at forming new declarative memories. His short-term memory is intact, as is his memory for events long before the operation and his ability to form new procedural memories. (page 264)

20. Most confabulated statements were true at one time, though not now. Also, people with brain damage seldom confabulate answers to questions they never could have answered in the past. That is, they seldom make up totally new information. (page 266)

21. Identified genes have been linked to early-onset Alzheimer's disease but not to many people with the more common late-onset type. Also, even the genes that do lead to Alzheimer's disease fail to do so in some cultures, indicating that environmental influences alter the effects of the genes. (page 266)

22. Young children remember events that happened months or even years ago. However, a few years later, they lose those memories. (page 267)

CHAPTER ENDING

Key Terms and Activities

Key Terms

Alzheimer's disease: a condition occurring mostly in old age, characterized by increasingly severe memory loss, confusion, depression, and disordered thinking (page 266)

amnesia: the severe loss or deterioration of memory (page 263)

anterograde amnesia: the inability to store new long-term memories (page 263)

chunking: the process of grouping digits or letters into meaningful sequences (page 240)

confabulations: attempts made by amnesic patients to fill in the gaps in their memory, mostly with out-of-date information (page 265)

cued recall: a method of testing memory by asking someone to remember a certain item after being given a hint (page 234)

declarative memory: the recall of factual information (page 235)

dissociation: a condition in which memory is stored but cannot be retrieved (page 258)

encoding specificity principle: the tendency for the associations formed at the time of learning to be more effective retrieval cues than other associations (page 246)

episodic memory: a memory for specific events in a person's life (page 238)

explicit memory (or direct memory): a memory that a person can state, generally recognizing that it is the correct answer (page 235)

false memory: a report that someone believes to be a memory but that does not actually correspond to real events (page 258)

free recall: a method of testing memory by asking someone to produce a certain item (e.g., a word) without substantial hints, as on an essay or short-answer test (page 234)

hindsight bias: the tendency to mold our recollection of the past to fit how events later turned out (page 256)

hippocampus: a forebrain structure in the interior of the temporal lobe that is important for storing certain kinds of memory (page 263)

implicit memory (or indirect memory): a memory that influences behavior without requiring conscious recognition that one is using a memory (page 235)

infant amnesia (or childhood amnesia): a relative lack of declarative memories from early in life (page 266)

information-processing model: the view that information is processed, coded, and stored in various ways in human memory as it is in a computer (page 237)

Korsakoff's syndrome: a condition caused by a prolonged deficiency of vitamin B_1, which results in both retrograde amnesia and anterograde amnesia (page 264)

levels-of-processing principle: the concept that the number and types of associations established during learning determine the ease of later retrieval of a memory (page 245)

long-term memory: a relatively permanent store of information (page 238)

memory: the process of retaining information or the information retained (page 233)

method of loci: a mnemonic device that calls for linking the items on a list with a memorized list of places (page 250)

mnemonic device: any memory aid that is based on encoding each item in a special way (page 249)

priming: the temporarily increased probability of using a word as a result of recently reading or hearing it (page 235)

proactive interference: the hindrance that an older memory produces on a newer one (page 253)

procedural memory: the retention of learned skills (page 235)

recognition: a method of testing memory by asking someone to choose the correct item from a set of alternatives (page 235)

reconstruction: putting together an account of past events, based partly on memories and partly on expectations of what must have happened (page 254)

recovered memory: a report of a long-lost memory, prompted by clinical techniques (page 257)

repression: according to Freudian theory, the process of moving a memory, motivation, or emotion from the conscious mind to the unconscious mind (page 257)

retrieval cue: information associated with remembered material, which can be useful for helping to recall that material (page 240)

retroactive interference: the impairment that a newer memory produces on an older one (page 253)

retrograde amnesia: the loss of memory for events that occurred before the brain damage (page 264)

savings method (or relearning method): a method of testing memory by measuring how much faster someone can relearn something than learn something for the first time (page 235)

semantic memory: memory of general principles (page 238)

sensory store: a very brief storage of sensory information (page 238)

serial-order effect: the tendency to remember the items near the beginning and end of a list better than those in the middle (page 254)

short-term memory: a temporary storage of a limited amount of information (page 238)

SPAR method: a systematic way to monitor and improve understanding of a text by surveying, processing meaningfully, asking questions, and reviewing (page 248)

state-dependent memory: the tendency to remember something better if your body is in the same condition during recall as it was during the original learning (page 247)

working memory: a system that processes and works with current information, including three components—a central executive, a phonological loop, and a visuospatial sketchpad (page 242)

📖 Suggestion for Further Reading

Schacter, D. L. (1996). *Searching for memory*. New York: Basic Books. Discusses current theories and research in an accessible manner.

 ## Book Companion Web Site

Need help studying? Go to

http://psychology.wadsworth.com/kalat_intro7e/

for a virtual study center. You'll find a personalized Self-Study Assessment that will provide you with a study plan based on your answers to a pretest. Also study using flashcards, quizzes, interactive art, and an online glossary.

Check out interactive **Try It Yourself** exercises on the companion site! For example, the Sperling Effect, Decay of Short-Term Memory, and False and Implicit Memories exercises tie to what you've learned in this chapter.

Your companion site also has direct links to the following Web sites. These links are checked often for changes, dead links, and new additions.

The Magic Number Seven, Plus or Minus Two

www.well.com/user/smalin/miller.html

This is George Miller's classic article about the limits of short-term memory, complete with graphs and references, as it originally appeared in the *Psychological Review* in 1956.

 ## Try It Yourself CD-ROM
with Critical Thinking Video Exercises

Use your CD to access **videos** related to activities designed to help you think critically about the important topics discussed. You'll also find an easy portal link to the book companion site where you can access your personalized **Self-Study Assessments** and interactive **Try It Yourself** exercises.

PsychNow! 2.0

PsychNow! is a fun interactive CD designed to help you with the difficult concepts in psychology. Check out the Learning & Cognition section for the following topics that relate to this chapter:

Memory Systems: "Lost in a Shopping Mall" video with researcher Elizabeth Loftus, memory flowchart lesson, permanent short-term memory loss video.

Forgetting: repeating musical notes in order, memory interference lesson and quiz.

InteractNOW! Online Collaborative Lab: Memory and the *ExperimentNOW! Research Experiment:* Memory—Brown-Peterson, false memory, memory span, partial report, serial position, Sternberg search

ExperimentNOW! Research Experiment: Imagery—Mental rotation

Categorization and Attention

What are concepts and attention? How can we measure them?

Cognition means *thinking, gaining knowledge, and dealing with knowledge.* Cognitive psychologists study how people think, how they acquire knowledge, what they know, how they imagine, and how they solve problems. They also deal with how people organize their thoughts into language and communicate with others.

Cognitive psychology increased in popularity after computers became popular. Although brains and computers do not work the same way, computers provide a valuable way of modeling theories of cognitive processes. A researcher may say, "Imagine that cognitive processes work as follows. . . . Now let's program a computer to go through those same steps. If we then give the computer the same information that a human has, will it draw the same conclusions and make the same errors as a human?" In short, computer modeling provides a way to test theories of cognition. Today, cognitive psychologists use a variety of methods to measure mental processes and to test theories about what we know and how we know it.

Methods of Research in Cognitive Psychology

Perhaps it seems that cognitive psychology should be simple. "If you want to find out what people think or what they know, why not ask them?" Sometimes psychologists do ask, but people can't always describe their own thought processes (Kihlstrom, Barnhardt, & Tataryn, 1992). Recall, for example, implicit memory as discussed in Chapter 7: Sometimes you see or hear something that influences your behavior without your realizing it. Similarly, we sometimes solve a problem without knowing how we did it.

Also, consider visual imagery. People often claim that they have a clear mental image of some object but then cannot correctly answer simple questions about it. To illustrate, imagine a simple cube balanced with one point (corner) on the table and the opposite point straight up. Imagine that you are holding the highest point with one finger. Now, using a finger of the opposite hand, point to all the remaining corners of the cube (not counting the one touching the table). How many corners do you touch?

You probably will say that you answered this question by "picturing" a cube in your mind as if you were actually seeing it. However, most people answer the question incorrectly, and few get it right quickly (Hinton, 1979). (Check answer A on page 284.)

In short, we cannot simply accept people's self reports about their thinking. So how *can* we measure thinking, a process that we obviously cannot observe? Physicists don't directly observe magnetic fields or electrical currents either. In each case researchers infer the unobservable processes from their effects. To illustrate, let's consider one of the classic experiments in cognitive psychology, which demonstrated a way to measure a mental process.

CRITICAL THINKING: WHAT'S THE EVIDENCE?
Mental Imagery

Roger Shepard and Jacqueline Metzler (1971) studied how humans solve visual problems. They reasoned that if people visualize mental images, then the time it takes them to rotate a mental image should be similar to the time needed to rotate a real object.

Hypothesis   When people have to rotate a mental image to answer a question, the farther they have to rotate it, the longer it will take them to answer the question.

Method   Participants examined pairs of drawings of three-dimensional objects, as in Figure 8.1, and indicated whether the two drawings represented one object and a rotated view of it or different objects. (Try to answer this question yourself before reading further. Then check answer B on page 284.)

People pulled one lever to indicate *same* and another lever to indicate *different.* When the correct answer was *same,* someone might determine that answer by rotating a mental image of the first picture until it matched the second. If so, the delay should depend on how far the image had to be rotated.

Results   Participants answered almost 97% of the items correctly. As predicted, their reaction time

273

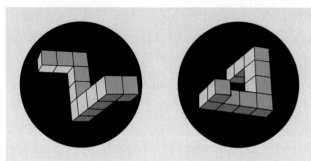

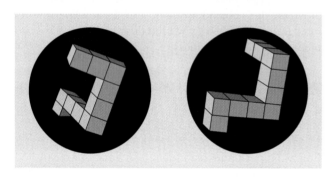

FIGURE 8.1 Examples of pairs of drawings used in an experiment by Shepard and Metzler (1971). Do the drawings for each pair represent the same object being rotated, or are they different objects? (See answer B on page 284.) (*Reprinted with permission from "Mental Rotation of Three-Dimensional Objects," by R. N. Shepard and J. N. Metzler,* Science, *1971, 171, 701-703. Copyright © 1980 American Association for the Advancement of Science.*)

when they responded *same* depended on the angular difference in orientation between the two views. For example, if the first image of a pair had to be rotated 30 degrees to match the second image, people needed a certain amount of time to pull the *same* lever. If an image had to be rotated 60 degrees to match the other, they took twice as long to pull the lever. In other words they reacted as if they were watching a model of the object rotate; the more the object needed to be rotated, the longer they took to determine the answer.

Interpretation   First, viewing a mental image is at least partly like real vision. So, in this case common sense appears to be correct. Second, it is possible for researchers to infer thought processes from someone's delay in answering a question.

Some people report that they have auditory images as well as visual images. They "hear" words or songs "in their head." What kind of evidence would we need to test this claim?

Categorization

An ancient Greek philosopher once said that you cannot step into the same river twice. He referred to the fact that the river changes, but in fact you change too from one time to the next. Nothing stays the same, and almost every concept refers to items that differ from one another. Nevertheless, to make reasonable decisions, we have to treat similar objects similarly. A major part of thinking is the formation of categories or concepts.

Ways of Describing a Category

Do we look up our concepts in a mental dictionary to determine their meaning? A few words have simple, unambiguous definitions. For example, we think of the term *bachelor* as an unmarried male. Because we would not ordinarily apply the term bachelor to a young child or to a Catholic priest, we might refine the definition to "a male who has not yet married but could." That definition pretty well explains the concept.

Many concepts are harder to define, however. Try defining *country music,* for example. Also, imagine a man who loses one hair from his head. Is he bald? Of course not. Then he loses one more hair, then another and another. Eventually, he *is* bald, so was there some point at which losing one more hair made him bald? We are forced to that absurdity if we use baldness as a yes/no category. (Similar problems arise if we try to classify everyone as depressed or not, schizophrenic or not, and alcoholic or not. Almost everything comes in degrees.)

Eleanor Rosch (1978; Rosch & Mervis, 1975) argued that many categories are best described by *familiar or typical examples* called **prototypes.** We decide whether an object belongs to a category by determining how much it resembles the prototypes of that category. For example, we define the category "vehicle" by examples: *car, bus, train, airplane, boat, truck.* Is a *blimp* also a vehicle? What about an *elevator* or *water skis*? These other items resemble the prototypes in some ways but not others, so they are marginal members of the category, which has fuzzy boundaries.

However, some categories cannot be described by prototypes (Fodor, 1998). For example, we can talk and think about "bug-eyed monsters from outer space" without ever encountering a single prototype of that category.

Conceptual Networks and Priming

Choose any concept and try to think about only it and nothing else. It's impossible. You can't really think about something without relating it to something else. When you think about some concept, for example *bird,* you link it to more specific terms, such as *sparrow,* more general terms, such as *animals,* and related terms such as *flight* and *eggs.*

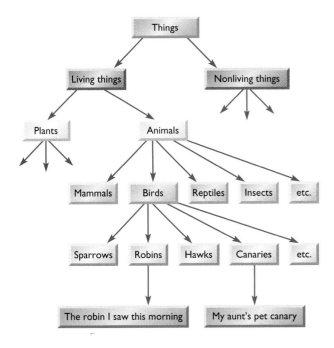

We naturally organize items into hierarchies, such as animal as a higher level category, bird as intermediate, and sparrow as a lower level category. Researchers demonstrate the reality of this kind of hierarchy by measuring the delay for people to answer various questions (A. M. Collins & Quillian, 1969, 1970). Answer the following true/false questions as quickly as possible:

- Canaries are yellow.
- Canaries sing.
- Canaries lay eggs.
- Canaries have feathers.
- Canaries have skin.

Presumably you answered "true" to all five items, but you may have answered some faster than others. Most people answer fastest on the *yellow* and *sing* items, slightly slower on the *eggs* and *feathers* items, and still slower on the *skin* item. Why? It is because yellowness and singing are distinctive char-

acteristics of canaries. You probably do not think of eggs or feathers specifically as canary features; instead you reason (quickly), "Canaries are birds, and birds lay eggs. So canaries must lay eggs." Skin is not even distinctive of birds, so you have to reason, "Canaries are birds and birds are animals. Animals have skin, so canaries must have skin." Even though this way of categorizing things delays you slightly in answering whether canaries have skin, it saves you enormous effort overall. When you learn some new fact about birds or animals in general, you don't have to learn it again separately for every individual species. Reasoning in terms of categories and subcategories simplifies our memory.

CONCEPT CHECK ☑

1. Which would people answer faster: whether politicians give speeches or whether they sometimes eat spaghetti? Why? (Check your answers on page 284.)

We also link a word or concept to other concepts related to it. Figure 8.2 shows a possible network of conceptual links that someone might have at a par-

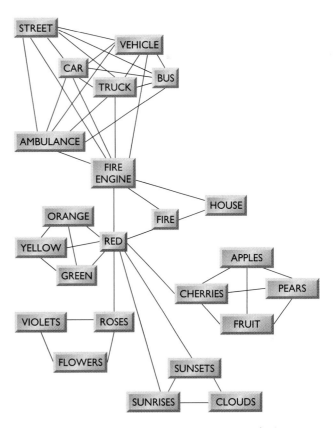

FIGURE 8.2 We link each concept to a variety of other related concepts. Any stimulus that activates one of these concepts will also partly activate (or "prime") the ones that are linked to it. *(From A. M. Collins & Loftus, 1975)*

ticular moment (A. M. Collins & Loftus, 1975). Suppose this network describes your own concepts. *Thinking about one of the concepts shown in this figure will activate, or prime, the concepts linked to it* (A. M. Collins & Loftus, 1975). This process is called **spreading activation.** For example, if you hear *flower,* you are primed to think of *rose, violet,* and various other flowers. If you also hear *red,* the combination of *flower* and *red* strongly primes you to think of *rose.* You might think of the word spontaneously, and you would recognize it more easily than usual if it were flashed briefly on a screen or spoken very softly.

Priming is important during reading. When you come to a difficult word that you barely know, you find it easier to understand if the preceding sentences were about closely related concepts (Plaut & Booth, 2000). In effect they provide hints about the meaning of the new word.

Here is an illustration that can be explained in terms of a spreading activation model. Quickly answer each of the following questions (or ask someone else):

1. How many animals of each kind did Moses take on the ark?
2. What was the famous saying uttered by Louis Armstrong when he first set foot on the moon?
3. Some people pronounce St. Louis "saint loo-iss" and some pronounce it "saint loo-ee." How would you pronounce the capital city of Kentucky?

The answers are in the footnote on this page.[1] Many people miss these questions and are then embarrassed or angry. Figure 8.3 offers an explanation in terms of spreading activation (Shafto & MacKay, 2000): The question about Louis Armstrong activates a series of sounds and concepts that are linked to one another and to other items. The sound *Armstrong* and the ideas *first astronaut on the moon* and *famous sayings* are all linked to "One small step for a man . . ."

[1]Answers: 1. None. Moses didn't have an ark; Noah did. 2. Louis Armstrong never set foot on the moon; it was Neil Armstrong. 3. The right pronunciation of Kentucky's capital is "frank-furt." (Not "loo-ee-ville"!)

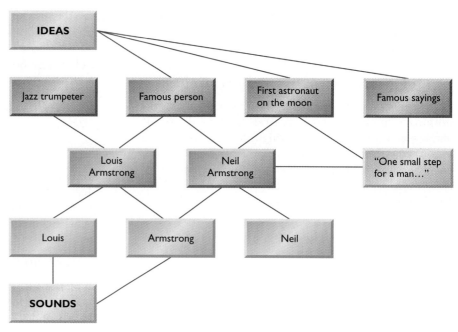

FIGURE 8.3 According to one explanation, the word *Armstrong* and the ideas *astronaut, first person on the moon,* and *famous sayings* all activate the linked saying "One small step for a man . . ." Even the word *Louis* contributes, because both Louis Armstrong and Neil Armstrong were famous people.

Even the name *Louis Armstrong* is loosely linked to *Neil Armstrong* because both are famous people. (You probably would not respond the same way to a question about "What was the famous line uttered by Jennifer Armstrong . . . ?") The combined effect of all these influences automatically triggers the answer, "One small step for a man . . ."

CONCEPT CHECK ☑

2. Suppose someone says "cardinal" and then flashes the word *bird* on a screen very briefly. Some viewers identify the word correctly, suggesting priming, and some do not. Considering both priming and the encoding specificity idea from Chapter 7, how might you explain why some people and not others identified the word *bird*? (Check your answer on page 284.)

Cross-Cultural Studies of Concepts

When you and I use the same term—river, vehicle, free will, or anything else—do we really have the same concept? Do people of different cultures and languages have the same concepts? People fluent in two languages sometimes remark that something gets lost in translation; a translated statement doesn't mean in English exactly the same as what it meant in Russian.

Let's start with one line of research that measures differences in meaning for what are regarded as equivalent words in different languages.

Hypothesis   Even though a word in one language is considered a translation of a word in another language, people will use them in different ways. For example, the English word *bottle* is considered a translation of the Spanish word *botella,* and the English word *jar* is translated as the Spanish word *frasco.* Nevertheless, they might not apply to all the same objects.

Method   Researchers showed English-, Argentinean Spanish-, and Chinese-speaking people a large array of objects, including those shown in Figure 8.4. Researchers asked them what word they would use for each. They also asked people to arrange pictures of the objects into groups of "similar" objects.

Results   U.S. English speakers used seven words for the various objects—*jar, bottle, container, can, jug, tube,* and *box.* Argentinean Spanish speakers used fifteen words for the same objects, and Chinese speakers used five. Of the sixteen objects called *bottle* in English, many were called *botella* in Spanish, but a total of six other names were given to some of them. One Chinese term applied to all the objects called *jar* in English but also applied to some of the objects considered *bottles* or *containers.*

However, when people were asked to arrange pictures of objects into groups of similar items, users of the three languages made remarkably similar categories. That is, people might put several objects into the same group, even though they gave them different names (Malt, Sloman, & Gennari, 2003; Malt, Sloman, Gennari, Shi, & Wang, 1999).

Interpretation   The simple conclusion is that words don't translate exactly. Generally, the items that English-speakers considered good examples (prototypes) of *bottle* were also considered good examples of *botella* in Spanish and so forth. However, people disagreed about how to label many marginal cases. On the other hand, differences in what people called objects had little apparent influence on which objects they considered similar. So, in this case the results suggest that people speaking different languages do not think very differently. (Obviously, we should not generalize too far based on this one example.)

Attention

You are constantly bombarded with sights, sounds, smells, and other kinds of sensation. **Attention** is *your tendency to respond to some stimuli more than others at any given time or to remember some more than others.* Attention can shift or select. That is, you attend to different items at different times.

To illustrate, recall from Chapter 4 that the fovea of your retina receives the most detail. Ordinarily, you remember mainly what was in your fovea, and that information has the biggest impact on your behavior. However, it is possible to direct your attention elsewhere. For example, you might not want someone to know that you are watching him or her, so you look off to the side, but you nevertheless concentrate on that person. You can demonstrate your ability to shift attention with the following. Fixate your eyes on the x in the center, and then without moving your eyes, read the letters in the circle around it clockwise:

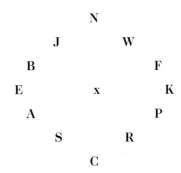

As you see, focusing your attention away from the center of your vision is difficult but possible. You can even attend to two nonadjacent spots at once—for example, the places occupied by **A** and **F** in the display above. When you increase your attention to something in your visual field, the part of your visual cortex sensitive to that area becomes more active and receives more blood flow (Müller, Malinowski, Gruber, & Hillyard, 2003). Also, if you try to pay extra attention to the color or motion of the next object to be shown on the screen, then the brain areas sensitive to color or motion become more active, even before the object appears (Driver & Frith, 2000). So attention is a process of increasing the brain's response to certain classes of stimuli. Nevertheless, explaining exactly how all this happens is a major challenge.

Preattentive and Attentive Processes

In the example just described, you deliberately shifted your attention from one letter to another. Often, however, objects grab your attention automatically when they start to move (Abrams & Christ, 2003) or because

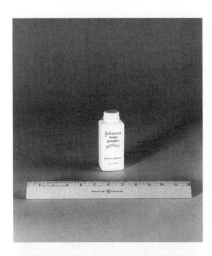

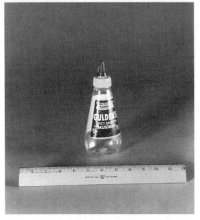

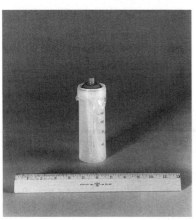

FIGURE 8.4 What word would you use for each of these objects? Would all the objects you call *bottle* translate as *botella* in Spanish? *(From Malt, Sloman, Gennari, Shi, & Wang, "Knowing vs. Naming: Similarity and the Linguistic Categorization of Artifacts,"* Journal of Memory and Language, *40, 230–262, 1999.)*

they are brightly colored or surprising in some way. I once watched an unusual costume contest. People were told to dress so distinctively that their friends or family could find them in a crowd as quickly as possible. The winner was a young man who came onto the stage naked. Although I concede that he earned the prize, there is a problem with this contest: The most distinctive clothing (or lack of it) depends on what everyone else is wearing. A naked person would be easy to spot in a shopping mall, but not quite so easy at a beach and not at all at a nudist beach. Our attention is drawn to the unusual, but what is unusual depends on the context. Ordinarily, we notice something that is flashing on and off, but if almost everything is flashing on and off, our attention is drawn to the one thing that isn't (Pashler & Harris, 2001).

To illustrate how an unusual object draws attention, look at Figure 8.5, which shows a huge flock of sandhill cranes plus one whooping crane. Find the whooping crane—the one that's different. That was easy, wasn't it? When an object differs drastically from those around it in size, shape, or color, we find it by a **preattentive process,** *meaning that it stands out immediately; we don't have to shift attention from one object to another.* Because the distinctive item jumps out preattentively, the number of sandhill cranes is irrelevant. Even if someone added or subtracted a few, you would find the whooping crane just as fast.

Contrast that task with Figure 8.6. Here the photo shows a flock of marbled godwits. Most of them are facing to your left; your task is to find the one that is facing to your right. Now you have to check each one separately, and the more birds present, the longer you will need, on the average, to find the one you are looking for. (You might find it quickly if you are lucky enough to start your search in the correct corner of the photograph.) You had to rely on an **attentive process**—*one that requires searching through the items in series* (Enns & Rensink, 1990; Treisman & Souther, 1985). (The *Where's Waldo* books are an excellent example of a task requiring an attentive process.) Studies of brain activity confirm that when we are searching through a complex display for an item that is hard to find, we are shifting attention (and the brain's responsiveness) from one area to another (Woodman & Luck, 2003).

The distinction between attentive and preattentive processes has practical applications. Imagine yourself as an ergonomist (human factors psychologist) designing machinery with several gauges. When the apparatus is running safely, the first gauge should read about 70, the second 40, the third 30, and the fourth 10, and any reading far from these normal values is dangerous. If

FIGURE 8.5 Demonstration of preattentive processes: Find the one whooping crane among the sandhill cranes. It stands out immediately. You would find the whooping crane just as fast in a much larger or much smaller flock of sandhill cranes.

FIGURE 8.6 Demonstration of attentive processes: Find the marbled godwit that is facing to the right. In this case you need an attentive process, checking the birds one at a time.

you arrange the gauges as in the top row of Figure 8.7, then people using this machine must check each gauge separately to find anything dangerous. Note how the bottom row of Figure 8.7 simplifies the process: All the gauges are arranged so that the safe range is on the right. Now someone can glance at the display and quickly (preattentively) notice anything out of position.

CONCEPT CHECK ☑

3. Suppose you are in a field full of brownish bushes and one motionless brown rabbit. Will you find the rabbit by attentive or preattentive processes? If the field has many motionless rabbits and one that is hopping, will you find the active one by attentive or preattentive processes? (Check your answers on page 284.)

The Stroop Effect

Here is another example of something that grabs our attention automatically: Read the following instructions and then examine Figure 8.8:

Notice the blocks of color at the top of the figure. Scanning from left to right, give the name of each color as fast as you can. Then notice the nonsense syllables printed in different colors in the center of the figure. Don't try to pronounce them; just say the color of each one as fast as possible. Then turn to the real words at the bottom. Don't read them; quickly state the color in which each one is printed.

Most people find it very difficult to ignore the words at the bottom of the figure. After all of your years of reading, you can hardly bring yourself to look at RED and say "green." *The tendency to read the word, instead of saying the color of ink as instructed,* is known as the **Stroop effect**, after the psychologist who discovered it.

One explanation of the Stroop effect that we can discard is the idea that words always take priority over colors. Try the following: Go back to

Figure 8.8 and notice the red, green, blue, and yellow patches at the four corners. This time, instead of saying anything, point to the correct color patch. First, try pointing to the color patch corresponding to the color of the ink; that is, when you come to RED, point to the blue patch in the lower left. Then try it again but point to the color corresponding to the meaning of the word. That is, when you come to RED, point to the red patch in the upper left. Try it now.

You probably found it easy to point to the patch that matches the color of the ink and harder to point to the color matching the word meaning (Durgin, 2000). When you are speaking, you are primed to read the words you see, but when you are pointing, you are more primed to attend to something nonverbal, such as ink color. In either case one response dominates, and it interferes with the less dominant response.

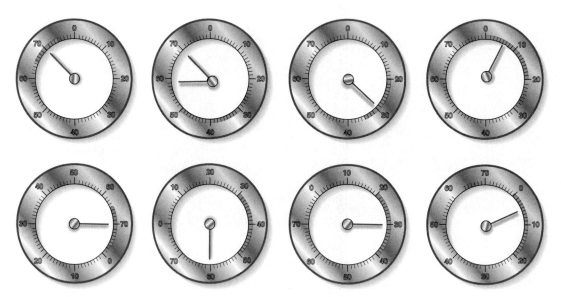

FIGURE 8.7 Each gauge represents a measurement of a different variable in a machine, such as an airplane. The top row shows one way of presenting the information. The operator must check each gauge one at a time to find out whether the reading is within the safe range for that variable. The bottom row shows the information represented in a way that is easier to read. The safe range for each variable is rotated to the same visual position. At a glance the operator can detect any reading outside the safe zone.

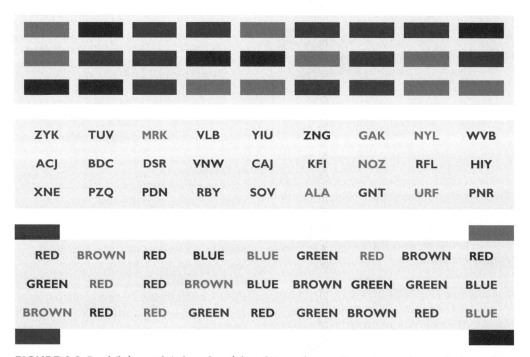

FIGURE 8.8 Read (left to right) the color of the ink in each part. Try to ignore the words themselves.

Attention Limits over Space and Time

How much can you hold in your attention at once? For example, imagine yourself in the control room of the Three Mile Island nuclear power plant, the site of a nearly disastrous accident in 1979. Figure 8.9 shows a small portion of the room as it appeared then. You notice immediately the enormous number of knobs and gauges for what is, after all, a complicated system. What you cannot see in the picture is that in certain cases the knob controlling something and the gauge measuring it were in different places.

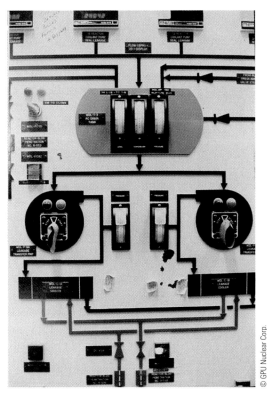

FIGURE 8.9 The Three Mile Island TMI-2 nuclear power plant had a complex and confusing control system, a small portion of which is shown here. Some of the important gauges were not easily visible, some were poorly labeled, and many alarm signals had ambiguous meanings. After the accident in 1979, the control system was redesigned and simplified.

Since then the controls have been redesigned to simplify the task. Designing good controls is a challenge for engineers and psychologists with a combination of theoretical and applied interests. One of the main issues they face is understanding the limits of human attention.

Change Blindness

If you look out your window, you see a scene with many objects. Do you see the whole scene at once? Recall the concept of *sensory store* from Chapter 7 (p. 237): If a display disappears but a signal immediately calls your attention to one part of the display, you can say what had been there. So, in a sense you did see the whole scene. However, if nothing calls your attention to a particular spot, then how much did you see and how well could you recall it? If you have scanned around the scene, briefly fixating practically everything, do you now know everything in the scene?

Most people think they do, and they believe they would notice anything that changed. However, movie directors discovered long ago that they could shoot different parts of a story segment on different days, and few viewers would notice that some of the actors had changed clothes, that some of the props had moved, or that the extra actors in the background were different people (Simons & Levin, 2003).

Psychologists have named this phenomenon **change blindness**—*the frequent failure to detect changes in parts of a scene*. If anything moves or changes its appearance suddenly in any way, it automatically draws your attention. However, if a similar change occurs slowly or during an instant you are not watching, you might not notice. Have you ever seen one of those puzzles that ask you to "find ten differences between these two pictures"? The difficulty of finding them all indicates that you don't exactly "see" everything you look at. You can experience this effect yourself. Go to http://psychology.wadsworth.com/kalat_intro7e. Navigate to the student Web site, then to the Online Try It Yourself section, and click on Change Blindness.

Online Try It Yourself

In one experiment people looked at a screen that alternated between two views of a scene, as shown in Figure 8.10. Each view appeared for 560 milliseconds (ms), followed by a blank screen for 80 ms, and then the other view for 560 ms, with the sequence repeating until the viewer detected how the two scenes differed. Generally, viewers found differences in important features of the scene faster than changes in less central details, but on the average they took almost 11 seconds to find a difference. On some pairs of pictures the average viewer needed more than 50 seconds (Rensink, O'Regan, & Clark, 1997).

CONCEPT CHECK ☑

4. Did viewers in this study detect the changes by a preattentive or an attentive mechanism? (Check your answer on page 284.)

Even without an intervening blank screen, people often fail to detect a change in the scene if the change happens while they are blinking their eyes or even while moving their eyes to focus on a different area (Henderson & Hollingworth, 2003b). They are more likely to notice a changed object if their eyes were moving toward that object than if moving away (Henderson & Hollingworth, 2003a).

Would viewers notice a change in a display even if they had already paid attention to every part of the display? In one experiment students looked at a circular array of one-digit numbers, as shown in Figure 8.11, for 2 seconds. During that time they had to attend to each digit to answer a question such as, "What is the

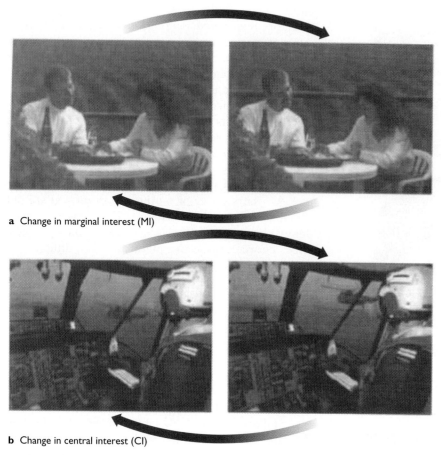

a Change in marginal interest (MI)

b Change in central interest (CI)

FIGURE 8.10 Viewers' task was to detect what was different between the two scenes, which were presented in alternation. The top scene has a change in a usually unattended detail; the lower scene has a change in a more important feature. If you can't find the changes, check answer C, page 284. *(Rensink, R.A., O'Regan, J.K., and Clark, J.J. (1997). "To see or not to see: The need for attention to perceive changes in scenes." Psychological Science, 8, 368–373. Figure 2, p. 370. Reprinted with permission of Blackwell Publishing.)*

highest digit included?" or "What is the lowest digit *not* included?" Then the display went blank for 150 milliseconds and reappeared. The viewers' task was to say whether any of the digits had changed. They detected a change only about one third of the time (Becker & Pashler, 2002).

In sound we have change deafness, analogous to change blindness. In one study students tried to re-

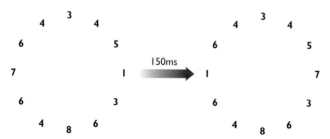

FIGURE 8.11 In the experiment by Becker and Pashler (2002), people saw a circular array of numbers for 2 seconds and then, after a 150 millisecond delay, saw the same or a changed array. People usually failed to detect the change.

peat the words they heard someone speak, as quickly as possible. After a 1-minute rest break, the procedure continued, but in some cases with a new voice speaking the words. Only about half of the students noticed the change (Vitevitch, 2003).

Overall, the apparent conclusion is that you do not maintain a detailed representation of what you have seen or heard. You hold a few details, but which details you hold vary from one time to another. (That's what we mean by attention.) You do retain the gist of the rest of the scene but not in detail (Becker & Pashler, 2002; Tatler, Gilchrist, & Rusted, 2003). Recall a similar conclusion about story memory from Chapter 7: We ordinarily remember a few details and only the gist of the rest of the story.

Shifting Attention

Paying attention to one thing detracts from attention to something else (Pashler, 1994). Can you do two things at once? Yes, you can *do* two things at once, especially if one of them is simple or highly practiced. However, you cannot *plan* two actions at once. For example, if you have to respond to one signal that tells you something to say and another signal that tells you which computer key to press, you can't make both responses as fast as you could make just one or the other (Ruthruff, Pashler, & Hazeltine, 2003; Ruthruff, Pashler, & Klaassen, 2001).

Many years ago, when automobile radios were introduced, people worried that listening to the radio would distract drivers and cause accidents. We no longer worry about radio, but we do worry about drivers using cell phones, and some states and countries have outlawed driving while holding a cell phone. Even if you don't have to hold the phone, listening with a phone on one ear tends to shift your attention toward that side of the body instead of straight ahead (Spence & Read, 2003). Also, conversations require more attention than radio, and a cell-phone conversation is more distracting than one with a passenger in the car because most passengers pause a conversation when they see that driving conditions are difficult. Research on simulated driving finds that a cell-phone conversation decreases a driver's attention to signs and increases the risk of accidents (Stayer, Drews, & Johnston, 2003).

The way you divide your attention among tasks is not fixed from birth; you can change it—perhaps unintentionally. For example, the research indicates that people who spend much time playing complex action video games learn to divide their attention widely over the video screen. That division of attention helps while playing the games, and probably in some real-life situations too, but on the other hand, it impairs the ability to concentrate on just one item. That is, habitual video game players tend to be distracted by irrelevant stimuli in their peripheral vision that most other people ignore (C. S. Green & Bavelier, 2003). Not much is known yet about this process, but it opens the way for further research: Might certain kinds of video games be either helpful or harmful to people with, say, attention deficit disorder?

The Attentional Blink

Just as we don't attend equally to every point in space, we also don't attend equally at all points in time. It takes time to shift attention from one item to another.

The demonstration of this point is called the **attentional blink:** *During a brief time after perceiving one stimulus, it is difficult to attend to something else.* Just as you don't see anything during a brief blink of the eyes, you don't attend to something during the attentional "blink." For example, suppose you watch a screen that displays a series of letters, one at a time for 90 ms each. Every series includes one letter in blue ink, and it may or may not include the letter T. Your task is to name the blue letter and say whether or not a T appeared. Here are two series and their correct answers:

D S R B J A O E C V "B, no."
Y L H F X G W K T Q "G, yes."

Most people miss the T (and say "no") if the T appears during a period about 100 to 700 ms after the blue letter. Similar results occur with many other kinds of stimuli and several variations of this procedure (Visser, Bischof, & DiLollo, 1999). It is an interesting demonstration theoretically and also a useful way of measuring how quickly various people can switch attention. For example, people with attention deficit disorder—known for their difficulty in controlling attention—have an unusually long attentional blink and often miss a target letter (T in the preceding example) even a full second after the blue letter (Hollingsworth, McAuliffe, & Knowlton, 2001). One exception: You might not notice most words if they are presented during the attentional blink, but you do notice your own name (K. L. Shapiro, Caldwell, & Sorensen, 1997).

Note that calling this phenomenon the attentional blink does not explain it. Why do we not notice a second stimulus 100 to 700 ms after the first one? "Be-

cause of the attentional blink." How do we know there is such a thing as an attentional blink? "Because we ignore a second stimulus 100 to 700 ms after the first one." Among several possible explanations that psychologists have been considering, one is that while the brain is "binding" the first stimulus into a single object, it cannot bind the second one and therefore does not fully perceive it (Raymond, 2003). Clearly, much more research is needed here.

CONCEPT CHECK ☑

5. Suppose you are playing a video game and you see two signals, about a quarter-second apart, telling you to do two things. You respond to the first one but not to the second. Why? (Check your answer on page 284.)

CRITICAL THINKING:
A STEP FURTHER
The Attentional Blink

When you read or listen to someone talk, one word or syllable follows another with very short delays. Why doesn't the attentional blink stop you from hearing or reading some of the words?

IN CLOSING

Thinking About Concepts and Attention

Behaviorists have traditionally avoided the topic of cognition because thinking and knowledge are unobservable. Although I hope this module has demonstrated that scientific research on cognition is possible and leads to new understanding, I also hope you see that the behaviorists' objections were not frivolous. Research on cognition is difficult, and each advance requires many experiments to check and recheck each conclusion and compare alternative explanations. The task is not purely theoretical; the better we can specify what we mean by "attention," for example, the better we can deal with those who have deficits in it.

Summary

* *Research methods in cognitive psychology.* Researchers cannot directly observe thinking or knowledge, but they can make inferences from observations such as people's delays in answering various questions. (page 273)

- *Mental imagery.* Mental images resemble vision in certain respects. For example, the time required to answer questions about a rotating object depends on how far the object would actually rotate between one position and another. (page 273)
- *Categorization.* People use many categories that are hard to define; we determine whether something fits the category by how closely it resembles familiar examples. Many items are marginal examples of a category, so we cannot insist on a yes/no decision. (page 274)
- *Conceptual networks.* We represent words or concepts with links to related concepts. Hearing or thinking about one concept will temporarily prime the linked concepts, and hearing several concepts can strongly prime another. (page 275)
- *Cross-cultural studies of concepts.* A word in one language may not correspond exactly to a word in another language; however, the similarities people see across objects do not depend on the words they use to name them. (page 276)
- *Attentive and preattentive processes.* We notice unusual items or items that have started to move almost at once, preattentively, regardless of potential distracters. Noticing less distinct items requires more careful attention to one possible target after another. (page 277)
- *The Stroop effect.* Sometimes it is difficult to avoid attending to certain stimuli; for example, it is difficult to state the color of the ink in which words are written while ignoring the words themselves (especially if they are color names). (page 279)
- *Attention limits.* Ordinarily, we notice only a small portion of a scene, perceiving and remembering just a vague gist of the rest. We often fail to detect changes in a scene if they occur slowly or during an eye blink or eye movement. We also frequently fail to detect a stimulus that appears 100 to 700 ms after a first stimulus that required some attention. (page 280)
- *Shifting attention.* Attending to one stimulus or activity detracts from attention to another. However, repeated practice, such as from playing video games, alters the degree to which someone divides attention across objects. (page 282)

Answers to Concept Checks

1. It would take longer to answer whether politicians sometimes eat spaghetti. Giving speeches is a distinctive feature of politicians; eating spaghetti is not. To answer the second question, you have to reason that politicians are people, and most people sometimes eat spaghetti. (page 275)

2. People who heard "cardinal" and thought of it as a bird would have spreading activation to prime the word *bird*. However, other people who thought of "cardinal" as an officer in the Catholic church would have spreading activation to prime a very different set of words, and not *bird*. (page 276)

3. Finding a motionless brown rabbit in a field full of brown objects will require attentive processes, but you could use preattentive processes to find a hopping rabbit in a field where nothing else is moving. (For this reason small animals in danger of predation stay motionless when they can.) (page 279)

4. The changes did not jump out by a preattentive mechanism. People had to use an attentive process to check each part of the scene one at a time. (page 281)

5. The second signal arrived during the attentional blink while you were still processing the first stimulus. (page 283)

Answers to Other Questions in the Module

A. The cube has six (not four) remaining corners. (page 273)

© Glenn Riley

B. The objects in pair a are the same; in b they are the same; and in c they are different. (page 274)
C. In the top scene, a horizontal bar along the wall has changed position. In the lower scene, the location of the helicopter has changed. (page 282)

Problem Solving, Expertise, and Error

How does someone become an expert?

What are some common errors of thinking?

On a college physics exam, a student was asked how to use a barometer to determine the height of a building. He answered that he would tie a long string to the barometer, go to the top of the building, and carefully lower the barometer until it reached the ground. Then he would cut the string and measure its length.

When the professor marked this answer incorrect, the student asked why. "Well," said the professor, "your method would work, but it's not the method I wanted you to use." When the student objected, the professor offered as a compromise to let him try again.

"All right," the student said. "Take the barometer to the top of the building, drop it, and measure the time it takes to hit the ground. Then, from the formula for the speed of a falling object, using the gravitational constant, calculate the height of the building."

"Hmmm," replied the professor. "That too would work. And it does make use of physical principles. But it still isn't the answer I had in mind. Can you think of another way?"

"Another way? Sure," he replied. "Place the barometer next to the building on a sunny day. Measure the height of the barometer and the length of its shadow. Also measure the length of the building's shadow. Then use the formula

height of barometer ÷ height of building = length of barometer's shadow ÷ length of building's shadow

The professor was impressed but still reluctant to give credit, so the student persisted with another method: "Measure the barometer's height. Then walk up the stairs of the building, marking it off in units of the barometer's height. At the top take the number of barometer units and multiply by the height of the barometer to get the height of the building."

The professor sighed: "Give me one more way— any other way—and I'll give you credit, even if it's not the answer I wanted."

"Really?" asked the student with a smile. "*Any* other way?"

"Yes, any other way."

"All right," said the student. "Go to the man who owns the building and say, 'Hey, buddy, if you tell me how tall this building is, I'll give you this cool barometer!'"

Whenever we face a new problem, we must devise a new solution instead of relying on a memorized or practiced solution. Sometimes people develop creative, imaginative solutions like the ones that the physics student proposed. Sometimes they offer less imaginative but reasonable solutions or something quite illogical or no solution at all. Psychologists study problem-solving behavior partly to understand the thought processes behind it and partly to look for ways to help people reason more effectively.

▮ How would you carry 98 water bottles—all at one time, with no vehicle? When faced with a new problem, sometimes people find a novel and effective solution, and sometimes they do not.

Expertise

People vary in their performance on problem-solving and decision-making tasks. In the barometer story just described, we would probably talk about the student's creativity; in other cases we might talk of expertise. Expertise is a high level of thinking and knowledge in a particular field and therefore an example of outstanding cognition.

If you want to become an expert on something, what would you have to do? Above all, you would have to learn facts . . . many, many facts. Computer programmers realized that need when they tried to develop software to answer people's questions (C. Thompson, 2001). For example, if a Web site is to advise someone on travel plans, it should be able to say, "Because you are claustrophobic, you should avoid taking the Channel Tunnel from England to France." But to do so, the program needs to be told that:

- Claustrophobic people dislike long tunnels.
- The Channel Tunnel is 31 miles long.

© David Burnett/Contact Press Images

- In this context anything more than 50 feet is considered "long."
- 31 miles is longer than 50 feet.

To get a Web site to answer various other questions, programmers had to provide the following information:

- Water is wet.
- Every person has a mother.
- You should carry a glass of water open end up.
- When people die, they stay dead.
- If you melt a statue, it is no longer a statue.

These facts are so obvious that stating them seems humorous. The point is that even the simplest decisions require a huge array of facts, and expert decisions require even more.

Practice Makes (Nearly) Perfect

Expert performance can be extremely impressive. An expert crossword puzzle solver not only completes *The New York Times* Sunday crossword—an impressive feat in itself—but tries to make it more interesting by racing against someone else. An expert bird watcher can look at a blurry photo of a bird and identify not only the species but also sometimes the subspecies and whether the bird is male or female, juvenile or adult, and in summer or winter plumage.

It is tempting to assume that experts were born with a special talent or great intelligence. Not so, say psychologists who have studied expertise. Remember the World Memory Championship from the start of Chapter 7? Winning contestants memorize a shuffled deck of cards in less than 40 seconds or a 300-digit number in 5 minutes. Psychologists tested 10 of the top memory performers and found that their mean IQ score was 111, as compared to a mean of 100 for the whole population (Maguire, Valentine, Wilding, & Kapur, 2003). A score of 111 is above average but hardly unusual. These people had developed their skills mainly by practicing the method of loci (page 250). They were no better than anyone else at remembering a series of photographs—a memory task they had not practiced because it is not part of the contest.

Similarly, in fields ranging from chess to sports to violin playing, the rule is that expertise requires about 10 years of concentrated practice (Ericsson & Charness, 1994; Ericsson, Krampe, & Tesch-Römer, 1993). The top violin players say they have practiced 3 to 4 hours every day since early childhood. A world-class tennis player spends hours working on backhand shots; a golfer works on chip shots. American writer John Irving is dyslexic and says it always took him longer than others to complete reading and writing assignments in school. By his own assessment, he is not a "talented" writer; he succeeded only because of

long, hard work and a willingness to undertake many revisions (Amabile, 2001). In short, experts are made, not born, and they are extremely impressive only in their area of specialization. In fact, the very brightest people—the top 1% of the top 1%—seldom become experts at anything because they get bored with the repetition and want to move on to something else.

Hungarian author Laszlo Polgar set out to demonstrate his conviction that almost anyone can achieve expertise with sufficient effort. He allowed his three young daughters to explore several fields; when they showed an interest in chess, he devoted enormous efforts to nurturing their chess skills. All three became outstanding chess players, and one, Judit, was the first woman and the youngest person ever to reach grand master status.

Some psychologists have argued that expertise depends *entirely* on practice, regardless of inborn predispositions. That claim is almost certainly an overstatement (H. Gardner, 1995). For obvious examples, short slow people will not become basketball stars, no matter how hard they practice, and blind people will not be-

▮ Judit Polgar confirmed her father's confidence that prolonged effort could make her an expert in her chosen field, chess. By reaching the status of grand master at age 15 years and 5 months, she beat Bobby Fisher's previous record for being the youngest.

come expert photographers. Also, in any field those who show early success are most likely to devote the necessary effort to achieve expertise. The main point, however, is that even someone born with "talent" or "potential" (whatever that means) needs years of hard work to achieve expertise on any complicated task.

Would you like to become an expert at something? In fields as competitive as chess, violin, or basketball, nearly all the great performers started young. Still, you have a choice among many other fields. (For example, if you want to be an expert psychologist, you won't have to worry about competing against people who started in childhood.) However, do not underestimate the effort required. Judit Polgar became a grand master by practicing chess about 8 hours a day from age 5 to 15, missing nearly all of the usual childhood activities. Thomas Young, a great 19th-century scientist, worked 16 hours a day, 7 days a week, including the day he died. His wife complained that she could not get pregnant because her husband almost never found time for sex (Martindale, 2001).

Expert Pattern Recognition

What exactly do experts do that other people do not? One important characteristic is that experts can look at a pattern and recognize its important features quickly.

In a typical experiment (de Groot, 1966), chess experts and beginners were shown pieces on a chessboard, as in Figure 8.12, for 5 seconds, and then asked to recall the positions of all the pieces. When the pieces were arranged as they might be in an actual game, expert players recalled 91% of the positions correctly, whereas novices recalled only 41%. When the pieces were arranged randomly, however, the expert players did no better than the novices. That is, on the average, expert chess players recognize the common chessboard patterns, but they do not have a superior overall memory. They still have to reason out the best move in a less-than-familiar situation, and even top chess players make occasional blunders when rushed for time (Chabris & Hearst, 2003), but recognizing common patterns is a huge head start.

a **b**

FIGURE 8.12 Pieces arranged on a chessboard as they might actually occur in a game (a) and in a random manner (b). Master chess players can memorize the realistic pattern much better than others can, but they are no better than average at memorizing the random pattern.

In a wide variety of other areas from bird identification to reading x-rays to judging gymnastic competitions, experts recognize key patterns that other observers overlook (Murphy & Medin, 1985; Ste-Marie, 1999). They also know the difference between relevant and irrelevant information (Proffitt, Coley, & Medin, 2000).

Here is a quick demonstration, introduced by Herbert Simon, to show what happens when you develop expertise on a simple task where you do not need 10 years of practice. First, play this game with someone: The two of you take turns choosing a number from the set 1-2-3-4-5-6-7-8-9. When one of you chooses a number, scratch it out so that the other can't choose the same number. Continue until one of you has a set of three numbers that add to 15. For example, the combination 2, 4, 9 would win because 2 + 4 + 9 = 15. After you have tried this game two or three times, turn to answer D on page 300.

Problem Solving

Problem solving can be described in terms of four phases (Polya, 1957): (a) understanding the problem, (b) generating hypotheses, (c) testing the hypotheses, and (d) checking the result (Figure 8.13). We shall discuss these four phases in detail.

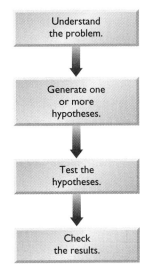

FIGURE 8.13 Four steps to solving a problem.

Understanding and Simplifying a Problem

Sometimes a problem is easy to solve once we recognize it as a problem. For years airport terminals listed incoming and outgoing flights in order of time. You can imagine the struggle to find your flight: You might remember that it was supposed to depart somewhere

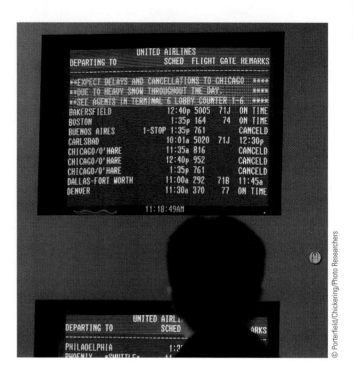

FIGURE 8.14 Switching airport terminal displays from listings by times (the old way) to listings by destinations (the new way) took little effort and had clear advantages.

between 10 and 10:30, but you didn't remember exactly when (and planes seldom leave exactly on time anyway), so you would have to sort through listings of many irrelevant flights to find the right one. Eventually, someone recognized the problem: People look for "the flight to San Jose," not "the flight at 10:27." Once the problem was recognized, the solution was obvious (Figure 8.14). (And then people wondered why they had overlooked the obvious for so long.)

When we recognize a problem but don't know how to solve it, a good strategy is to start with a simpler version. For example, here is what may appear to be a difficult, even impossible, problem: A professor hands back students' test papers at random. On the average how many students will accidentally receive their own paper?

Try It Yourself

Note that the problem does not specify how many students are in the class. If you don't see how to approach the problem, try the simplest cases: How many students will get their own paper back if there is only one student in the class? One, of course. What if there are two students? There is a 50% chance that both will get their own paper back and a 50% chance that neither will, for an average of one student getting the correct paper. What if there are three students? Each student then has one chance in three of getting his or her own paper. A one-third chance times three students means that on the average one student will get the correct paper. Already the pattern is clear: If there are n students, each student has one chance in n of getting his or her own paper back. No matter how many

students are in the class, on the average one student will get his or her own paper back.

Generating Hypotheses

After you have simplified a problem, you generate *hypotheses*—preliminary interpretations that you can evaluate or test. In some cases you can test every possible hypothesis. For example, suppose you want to connect your television set to a pair of stereo amplifiers, a VCR, and a DVD player, but you have lost the instruction manuals. You have several cables to attach, and each device has input and output channels. You could simply connect the cables by trial and error, testing every possibility until you find one that works. *A mechanical, repetitive procedure for solving a problem or testing every hypothesis* is called an **algorithm.** The rules for alphabetizing a list are one example; you check every possible item to see which one goes first, then check them all for which goes second, and so forth. You can also learn an algorithm for how to win, or at least tie, every time you play tick-tack-toe.

In many situations, however, the possible hypotheses are too numerous or vague to apply any algorithm. Consider the question, "What should I do with my life?" You could not consider every possible choice, and even if you did, you would not be sure how to evaluate them. **Heuristics** are *strategies for simplifying a problem or for guiding an investigation.* For the question about your future, you might restrict your attention to a few possible careers and then learn whatever you can about them.

▌ To find the right way to connect the lines, you could use the simple algorithm of trying every possible combination, one after the other.

To illustrate the contrast between algorithms and heuristics, consider chess. At a typical point in a game of chess, a player has about 25 legal moves, and the opponent has about 25 legal replies to each of them. To choose your best move by an algorithm, you would consider each of your possible moves, each of your opponent's possible replies, each of your next moves, and so forth, as many moves ahead as possible. Finally, you would select the move that gives you the best result, assuming that your opponent made the best possible reply at each point. Computerized chess programs do use algorithms, but human memory is more limited, so you simplify the task with heuristics: On each move you select just a few possible moves for serious consideration. You consider just a few of your opponent's likely responses, a few of your possible next moves, and so forth.

CONCEPT CHECK ☑

6. Suppose you are a traveling salesperson. You must start from your home city, visit each of several other cities, and then return home. Your task is to find the shortest route. What would be the appropriate algorithm? What would be a possible heuristic for simplifying the problem? (Check your answers on page 300.)

Testing Hypotheses and Checking the Results

If you think you have solved a problem, test whether your idea works. Many people who think they have a great idea never bother to try it out, even on a small

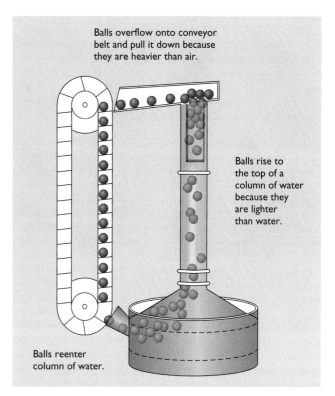

Balls overflow onto conveyor belt and pull it down because they are heavier than air.

Balls rise to the top of a column of water because they are lighter than water.

Balls reenter column of water.

FIGURE 8.15 What is wrong with this perpetual motion machine?

scale. One inventor applied for a patent on the "perpetual motion machine" shown in Figure 8.15. Rubber balls, being lighter than water, rise in a column of water and flow over the top. The balls are heavier than air, so they fall, thus moving a belt and generating energy. At the bottom they reenter the water column. Do you see why this system could never work? You would if you tried to build it. (Check answer E on page 300.)

Even if you can't physically check your idea, consider whether it is realistic. One article published in 1927 claimed that a deer botfly has a speed of 800 miles per hour (almost 1,300 kilometers per hour). Some books and Internet sources to this day list that speed as the record for the fastest species on earth. One physicist calculated that an object moving that fast would generate more than enough air pressure to squash the fly. A fly striking you at that speed would pierce you like a bullet. And the energy to move that fast would require the fly to eat 1.5 times its weight in food *per second* (May, 1999).

Generalizing Solutions to Similar Problems

You might imagine that people who had just solved one problem would quickly recognize how to solve a similar problem (see Figure 8.16). Often, they do not. For example, if you have learned to use a formula in

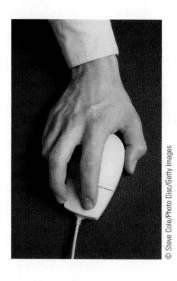

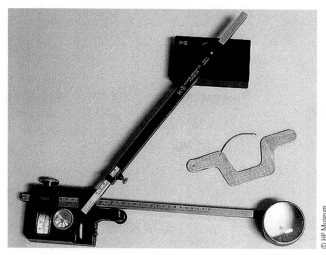

FIGURE 8.16 The computer mouse was invented by a computer scientist who was familiar with an engineering device called a planimeter that he believed could be modified for use with computers. Such insights are unusual; most people do not generalize a solution from one task to another.

mathematics, you probably won't recognize that the same formula applies to some problem in a physics class, unless someone points out the similarity (Barnett & Ceci, 2002; Gick & Holyoak, 1980). You probably would learn faster in the new situation, so the previous training was not worthless (De Corte, 2003), but still it is noteworthy how often people apply a principle in one situation but not another.

For an example of failure to transfer principle, consider Figure 8.17a, which shows a coiled garden hose. When the water spurts out, what path will it take? (Draw it.) Figure 8.17b shows a curved gun barrel. When the bullet comes out, what path will it take? (Draw it.)

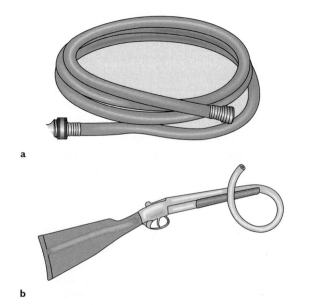

a

b

FIGURE 8.17 (a) Draw the trajectory of water as it flows out of a coiled garden hose. (b) Draw the trajectory of a bullet as it leaves a coiled gun barrel.

Almost everyone draws the water coming straight out of the garden hose, but most draw a bullet coming out of a gun in a curved path, as if the bullet remembered the curved path it had just taken (Kaiser, Jonides, & Alexander, 1986). The physics is the same in both situations: Except for the effects of gravity, both the water and the bullet will follow a straight path.

Here is another example in which people answer correctly one version of the problem but not another. Let's start with the harder version: You will be presented with a series of cards, each of which has a letter on one side and a number on the other. Your task is to test the hypothesis that "any card that has a vowel on one side has an even number on the other." The cards are shown below. Which cards do you need to turn over to test the hypothesis?

| A | | T | | 4 | | 7 |

One choice is easy (if you understand the instructions): You have to turn over the card with an A. Most people, however, turn over the card with a 4, which is unnecessary. (Either a vowel or a consonant on the back of the 4 would be okay, according to the hypothesis.) But a vowel on the back of the 7 would contradict the hypothesis, and most people do not check the 7 (Wason, 1960).

Change the task, however, and it becomes easy. Now you are told that each card represents a person. One side indicates the person's age and the other is what kind of beverage the person is drinking. You are supposed to test the hypothesis that everyone under age 21 is drinking nonalcoholic beverages. Here are the cards; which ones do you need to turn over to check the hypothesis?

| Age 18 | Age 30 | Drinking Ginger Ale | Drinking Wine |

With this version the answer is obvious: Check the 18-year-old and the person drinking wine but not the other two (Cosmides, 1989).

CRITICAL THINKING:
A STEP FURTHER
Logical Reasoning

Why was this version so much easier than the first? Some psychologists believe we are specialized to think more clearly about human social situations than about anything else. Try writing the question in some other way that pertains to realistic nonhuman events. Is your phrasing as easy as the human drinking example, as difficult as the letter–vowel example, or intermediate?

Why do we sometimes solve one problem and not another, even though they are logically similar? Part of the answer is that we sometimes apply a principle in one situation without fully understanding it or mastering it. After you have applied an approach in a few situations, you more quickly recognize its usefulness in still others (Gick & Holyoak, 1983). (This finding resembles the encoding specificity principle of memory: If you study something in just one situation, you remember it well in that one situation but probably not in others. If you study in several contexts, you remember in many.)

The other part of the answer is that, bluntly, we usually don't rely much on logical reasoning (Evans, 2002). We answer impulsively, or we look for evidence to support what we have already decided (Brownstein, 2003). In some cases people's intuitions are so strong that even solid evidence and logic fail to persuade them (Arkes, 2003; Krauss & Wang, 2003).

There is also a general point that will arise again in Chapter 10: A concept isn't something you either have or don't have. You can have it to a greater or lesser degree, find it easy or difficult to use, and use it frequently or infrequently (Siegler, 2000).

Special Features of Insight Problems

In "insight" or "aha!" problems, the correct answer occurs to you suddenly or not at all. Here is an example (M. Gardner, 1978): Figure 8.18 shows an object that was made by cutting and bending an ordinary piece of cardboard. How was it made? If you think you know, take a piece of paper and try to make it yourself. (The solution is on page 301, answer F.)

FIGURE 8.18 This object was made by cutting and folding an ordinary piece of cardboard with nothing left over. How was it done?

Sudden or Gradual Insights?

Solving insight problems differs from solving, say, algebra problems. Most people can look at an algebra problem and predict how quickly they will solve it if at all. As they work on it, they estimate how close they are to a solution. With insight problems, however—like the paper-folding problem just presented—people often think they are making no progress and then suddenly solve it (Metcalfe & Wiebe, 1987). Does the answer really come as suddenly as it seems?

If you were groping your way around in a dark room, you would have no idea how soon you were going to find the door, but nevertheless, you were making progress. You would have learned much about the room, including where the door was *not*. So maybe people are making more progress than they realize on insight problems. To test this possibility, psychologists gave students problems with the following form:

> The following three words are all associated with one other word. What is that word? color numbers oil

In this case the intended answer is paint, although you might be able to defend some other answers. As with other insight questions, participants who solved it said the answer came to them suddenly. Then the experimenters gave the students paired sets of three words each, like those shown here in Sets 1 and 2, to examine for 12 seconds. In each pair one set had a correct answer (like paint in the example just given). The other set had no correct answer. Students were asked to generate a correct answer if they could, but if not, at least to guess which set had a correct answer. Examples:

Set 1

| playing | credit | report | *or* | still | pages | music |

Set 2

| town | root | car | *or* | ticket | shop | broker |

(You can check your answers on page 301, answer G.)

The main result: Even students who did not know the correct answer usually guessed correctly which set had an answer (Bowers, Regehr, Balthazard, & Parker, 1990). Even when they said they had "no confidence" in their guesses, they were still right more often than not. In short, people often make progress on insight problems without realizing it.

The Characteristics of Creativity

Why are some people more creative than others? Creativity is not the same as expertise. An expert gymnast goes through the same motions every time, and an expert chess player may use the same strategy in game after game, but a writer, composer, or painter who kept doing the same thing again and again would not be considered creative. One hallmark of creative people is a willingness to take risks. For example, painter Claude Monet deliberately varied the style and content of his paintings instead of just producing a series of successful but similar paintings (Stokes, 2001).

Creative writers, composers, and scientists have certain features in common, such as nonconformity, risk-taking, willingness to tolerate rejection, openness to new experiences, and at least moderate intelligence (Simonton, 2000b). However, it is misleading to talk about "creative people" as if certain people are creative in everything they do. People have to know a field well before they can make creative contributions to it. That is, don't expect a creative poet to offer creative solutions to an auto-mechanics problem.

Howard Gardner (1993) studied creativity by examining the lives of seven 20th-century people who are widely regarded as creative in very different fields: Sigmund Freud (psychology), Albert Einstein (physics), Pablo Picasso (painting), Igor Stravinsky (musical composition), T. S. Eliot (poetry), Martha Graham (dance),

∎ Creative problem solving, evident in this temporary bridge made of old railroad cars, has two elements: novelty and social value.

and Mahatma Gandhi (political resistance and spirituality). Gardner found a few patterns that these people had in common, including the following:

- They worked in an atmosphere of moderate tension, sensing that the old ways of doing things were not quite right.
- They had enough background in their fields to feel confident but not so much experience that they became trapped into traditional habits.
- Early in life, each relied heavily on one or a few close friends for advice and encouragement.
- Each threw him- or herself wholeheartedly into the work, at the expense of family and friendships. Even Gandhi, a famous advocate for love and justice, had trouble developing close relationships.

∎ Howard Gardner studied the lives of seven highly creative people, including political and spiritual leader Mahatma Gandhi and dance pioneer Martha Graham, to find the features that promote creativity.

Creative careers, however, are extremely variable (Simonton, 1997). As a rule poets are recognized for their greatness early in life, generally in their 20s, whereas the greatest, most creative historians seldom do their best work before their 40s or 50s. Within any field some people start early and quit early and others bloom late. Some—such as Bach, Picasso, and Edison—produce enormous quantities of good work, whereas others produce only one or two great works.

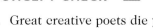

CONCEPT CHECK

7. Great creative poets die younger on the average than equally recognized historians. Why? (Hint: Imagine the distribution of ages at death for both groups.) (Check your answer on page 300.)

Reasoning by Heuristics

Heuristics, you will recall, are methods of simplifying a problem. We all have limited knowledge, limited memory, and limited time to collect information and reason out an answer. Frequently, we have to make very quick decisions with almost no time to weigh the evidence and consider alternatives. Therefore, heuristics are often an excellent guide, if not a necessity.

Furthermore, simple heuristics sometimes produce surprisingly good results. For example, people are given pairs of U.S. cities, such as San Diego and San Antonio, and pairs of German cities, such as Munich and Cologne. For each pair they are asked to pick the one with the larger population. Oddly, Americans guess more accurately with the German cities and Germans guess more accurately with American cities (Goldstein & Gigerenzer, 2002). Almost everyone relies on the heuristic, "The city I've heard of probably has more people." That heuristic works fine for a country you know a little about, but less well for your own country, where both cities are familiar. So the heuristic works best if you don't know too much!

However, heuristics can lead us astray if we use them habitually even when we have an opportunity to weigh the evidence logically. Economists generally assume that people are more or less rational. That is, they follow their own best interests as well as they can; they make decisions based on the facts; and they buy and sell products at prices that match their real values. In 2002 Daniel Kahneman won the Nobel Prize for Economics for research demonstrating that people often make illogical decisions based on heuristics, emotions, and biases.

In 2002 Princeton psychologist Daniel Kahneman (left) won the Nobel Prize for Economics. (There is no Nobel Prize in psychology.) Although others have won Nobel Prizes for research related to psychology, Kahneman was the first winner who had a PhD in psychology.

The Representativeness Heuristic and Base-Rate Information

Perhaps you have heard the saying: "If something looks like a duck, waddles like a duck, and quacks like a duck, chances are it's a duck." This saying is an example of the **representativeness heuristic**, *the tendency to assume that, if an item resembles members of a particular category, it is probably a member of that category itself.*

The assumption is usually correct, but research by Kahneman and others has shown how it leads us astray when we deal with uncommon events. For example, if you see something that looks, walks, and sounds like some rare bird, you may indeed have found a rarity, but you should check carefully to make sure it isn't some similar, more common species. In general, to decide whether something belongs in one category or another, you should consider how closely it resembles the two categories but also the **base-rate information**—that is, *how common the two categories are.*

When people apply the representativeness heuristic, they frequently overlook base-rate information. For example, consider the following question (modified from Kahneman & Tversky, 1973):

Psychologists have interviewed 30 engineers and 70 lawyers. One of them, Jack, is a 45-year-old married man with four children. He is generally conservative, cautious, and ambitious. He shows no interest in political and social issues and spends most of his free time on home carpentry, sailing, and solving mathematical puzzles. What is the probability that Jack is one of the 30 engineers in the sample of 100?

Most people estimate a rather high probability—perhaps 80 or 90%—because the description sounds more representative of engineers than lawyers. That estimate isn't really wrong, as we have no logical way to determine the true probability. The interesting point is that if some people are told the sample included 30 engineers and 70 lawyers, and others are told it included 70 engineers and 30 lawyers, both groups make about the same estimate for Jack (Kahneman & Tversky, 1973). Certainly, the base-rate information should have some influence.

Here is another example of misuse of the representativeness heuristic. Read the following description and then answer the questions following it:

> Linda was a philosophy major. She is 31, bright, outspoken, and concerned about issues of discrimination and social justice.

What would you estimate is the probability that Linda is a bank teller? What is the probability that she is a feminist bank teller? (Answer before you read on.)

The true probabilities, hard to estimate, are not the point. The interesting result is that most people estimate a higher probability that Linda is a *feminist* bank teller than the probability that she is a bank teller (A. Tversky & Kahneman, 1983). However, she could clearly not be a feminist bank teller without being a bank teller. Apparently, people regard this description as fairly typical for a feminist and thus for a feminist bank teller (or feminist anything else) but not typical for bank tellers in general (Shafir, Smith, & Osherson, 1990).

CONCEPT CHECK ☑

8. A device was built to protect airplanes by detecting explosives that people might have in their luggage. The device detects 95% of bombs and has a false alarm (saying there is a bomb when there is none) only 5% of the time. Is this device good enough to use? (Hint: Think about the base-rate probability of the presence of a bomb.) (Check your answer on page 300.)

The Availability Heuristic

When we estimate how common something is, we generally start by trying to think of examples. Try this question: In the English language, are there more words that start with *k* or more words with *k* as the third letter? Most people guess that more words start with *k*. They start by trying to think of words that start with *k*: "king, kitchen, kangaroo, key, knowledge, . . ." Those were pretty easy. Then they try to think of words with *k* as the third letter: "ask, ink, . . . uh . . ." They rely on the **availability heuristic,** *the strategy of assuming that how easily one can remember examples of some kind of event indicates how common the event itself is* (Table 8.1). Because it is easier to think of words that start with *k* than words with *k* as the third letter, people assume that more words start with *k*. In fact, however, many more words have *k* as the third letter.

Because the news media tend to emphasize the spectacular, our use of the availability heuristic leads us to overestimate some dangers and underestimate others. For example, would you guess that more people die from tornadoes or lightning? From diabetes or homicide? From stomach cancer or automobile accidents? A tornado that kills 10 people gets national publicity, whereas a bolt of lightning that kills one person may not even make the local news show. Therefore, we assume tornado deaths are more common, although in fact lightning kills more people. Similarly, diabetes and stomach cancer kill far more people than homicide or automobile accidents but get little publicity. If you guessed that homicide and automobile accidents kill more, probably you were using the availability heuristic (Ruscio, 2000).

Another example: Would you rate yourself a better than average, average, or worse than average driver? Most people rate themselves above average, although statistically it is impossible for more than half to be above

TABLE 8.1 The Representativeness Heuristic and the Availability Heuristic

	A Tendency to Assume That	Leads Us Astray When	Example of Error
Representativeness Heuristic	An item that resembles members of a category probably belongs to that category.	Something resembles members of a rare category.	Something looks like it might be a UFO, so you decide it is.
Availability Heuristic	The more easily we can think of members of a category, the more common the category is.	One category gets more publicity than another or is more memorable.	You remember more reports of airplane crashes than car crashes so you think air travel is more dangerous.

average. When people try to imagine other people's driving, it is easy to remember times when you saw someone driving extremely badly—much worse than you ever would, right?—but hard to remember anyone driving especially better than you. Similarly, almost all people say they have less than average racial prejudice. Extremely prejudiced people stand out in your memory more than people with less prejudice.

Other Common Errors in Human Cognition

Common human errors include inappropriate use of the representativeness heuristic and availability heuristic but also include many other tendencies. Although we humans pride ourselves on our intelligence and our ability to solve problems, we sometimes make embarrassing mistakes. For decades college professors have talked about the importance of **critical thinking,** *the careful evaluation of evidence for and against any conclusion.* However, even the sincerest advocates of critical thinking sometimes find that they have been repeating nonsense that they should have questioned. For example, I myself used to repeat the rumors—only I didn't know they were rumors; I thought they were facts—that "glass flows as a very slow liquid," that "when the lemming population gets very high, some of them jump off cliffs," and that "Thomas Crapper invented the flush toilet." I later learned that all these claims were false. (The story about Thomas Crapper was started by Wallace Reyburn, who wrote the book *Flushed with Pride,* a partly true, partly fictitious biography of Crapper, who manufactured toilets, but didn't invent them. Everyone might have continued to believe Reyburn's hoax if he hadn't followed it with a less plausible book, *Bust Up,* a biography of Otto Titzling, allegedly the inventor of the bra!)

Why do intelligent people sometimes come to false conclusions or accept conclusions without adequate evidence? The reasons are many; here we consider just a few.

Overconfidence

Let's start with a demonstration. Ten questions follow. Few people know any of the answers exactly, but I'm asking for only an approximation. For each question answer with a 90% confidence range; that is, give a range within which you are 90% sure the correct answer lies. For example, consider this question: In the 2000 summer Olympics in Sydney, Australia, how many silver medals did China win? You might decide that you would be surprised if they won fewer than 5 or more than 25, so you guess "5 to 25."

If so, you would be right because China won 16 silver medals. Okay, that's the idea. Now fill in your answers:

Your estimate (as a 90% confidence range)
1. How old was Martin Luther King, Jr., at the time of his death?   — to —
2. How long is the Nile River?   — to —
3. How many countries belong to OPEC?   — to —
4. How many books are in the Old Testament?   — to —
5. What is the diameter of the moon?   — to —
6. What is the weight of an empty Boeing 747?   — to —
7. In what year was Mozart born?   — to —
8. What is the gestation period of an Asian elephant? (in days)   — to —
9. How far is London from Tokyo?   — to —
10. What is the deepest known point in the ocean? (in feet or meters)   — to —

Now turn to answer H on page 301 to check your answers (Plous, 1993). How many of your ranges included the correct answer? Because you said you were 90% confident of each answer, you should be right on about nine of ten. However, most people miss more than half. That is, they were **overconfident;** *they believed their estimates were more accurate than they actually were.* These were, of course, very difficult questions. On extremely easy questions, the trend is reversed and people tend to be underconfident (Erev, Wallsten, & Budescu, 1994; Juslin, Winman, & Olsson, 2000). You can try additional items with the Online Try It Yourself exercise. Go to http://psychology.wadsworth.com/kalat_ intro7e. Navigate to the student Web site, then to the Online Try It Yourself section, and click on Overconfidence.

Philip Tetlock (1994) conducted a study of government officials and consultants, foreign policy professors, newspaper columnists, and others who make their living by analyzing and predicting world events. He asked them to predict world events over the next several years—such as what would happen in Korea, the Middle East, Eastern Europe, and Cuba—and to state their confidence in their predictions (such as 70%). Five years later he compared predictions to actual results and found very low accuracy, especially among those who were the most confident and those with a strong liberal or conservative point of view. That is, those who saw both sides of a question were more likely to be right.

Most people are overconfident of their understanding of complex physical processes. In one study college students were asked to rate how well they understood how various devices work, including a speedometer, zipper, flush toilet, cylinder lock, helicopter, quartz watch, sewing machine, and others. Then the researchers asked them in fact to explain four of the devices and answer questions about them, such as "How could someone pick a cylinder lock?" and "How does a helicopter go from hovering to forward flight?" After producing what were obviously weak answers, nearly all students lowered their ratings of understanding for these four phenomena (Rozenblit & Keil, 2002). However, curiously, some insisted that except for the four devices that the experimenters happened to choose, they really did understand all the other devices pretty well!

CONCEPT CHECK

9. When students estimate their grades for the coming semester or athletic coaches estimate their teams' success for the coming year, what mistake is likely? (Check your answer on page 300.)

Attractiveness of Valuable but Very Unlikely Outcomes

If people are faced with choices A and B, and on the average A is worth $1 and on the average B is also worth $1, then theoretically, people should like both choices equally. In reality, people don't behave that way.

Which would you rather have:

- $100,000 for sure or a 10% chance of winning $1 million?
- $10,000 or a 1% chance at $1 million?
- $1,000 or a 0.1% chance at $1 million?
- $100 or a 0.01% chance at $1 million?
- $10 or a 0.001% chance at $1 million?
- $1 or a 0.0001% chance at $1 million?

If you are like most people, you chose the $100,000 over a 10% chance at a million and $10,000 over a 1% chance. But at some point, you switched from the sure profit to the gamble. Especially if the sure profit is $10 or less, most people prefer a chance at winning a million. In fact almost half of college students said they would forego $10 to have even one chance in a million of winning a million—a gamble of very bad odds (Rachlin, Siegel, & Cross, 1994). A later study, using an Internet sample of thousands of people from 44 countries, confirmed this tendency to prefer a long-shot bet over a small but sure gain (Birnbaum, 1999), so it is not something unique to one culture.

Why do people prefer a slim chance at a fortune to a small but sure gain? First, for most people $10 is not going to raise your standard of living. A million dollars would. Second, although you understand the difference between a 10% chance and a 1% chance, it is hard to grasp the difference between a 0.001%

chance and a 0.0001% or even a 0.000001% chance. They blur together as "unlikely but not impossible," and we think, "Someone is going to win, and it might be me." In fact the unlikeliness of winning is part of the appeal: People report more pleasure from a surprising gain than from one they expected (Mellers, Schwartz, Ho, & Ritov, 1997). That is, a surprising gambling win is a bigger thrill than money you knew you were going to gain.

Confirmation Bias

Often, we make mistakes by *accepting one hypothesis and then looking for evidence to support it, instead of considering other possibilities.* This tendency is known as the **confirmation bias.** For example, examine the poorly focused photo in Figure 8.19a and guess what it depicts. Then see Figures 8.19b and 8.19c on the following pages. Many people find that seeing the extremely out-of-focus photo makes it harder to identify the items in the better focused photo. When they saw the first photo, they formed a hypothesis, probably a wrong one, which interfered with correctly perceiving the later photo (Bruner & Potter, 1964).

Peter Wason (1960) asked students to discover a certain rule he had in mind for generating sequences of numbers. One example of the numbers the rule might generate, he explained, was "2, 4, 6." He told the students that they could ask about other se-

FIGURE 8.19a People who form a hypothesis based on the first photo look at succeeding photos to find evidence that they are right. Because their first guess is generally wrong, they don't do as well as people who look at the later photos before making any preliminary guesses. Try to guess what this shows. Then examine parts b and c on pages 298 and 300.

© Susan Ashukian

quences, and he would tell them whether or not those sequences fit his rule. They should tell him as soon as they thought they knew the rule.

Most students started by asking, "8, 10, 12?" When told "yes," they proceeded with "14, 16, 18?" Each time, they were told, "Yes, that sequence fits the rule." Soon most of them guessed, "The rule is three consecutive even numbers." "No," came the reply. "That is not the rule." Many students persisted, trying "20, 22, 24?" "26, 28, 30?" "250, 252, 254?" Note that they were testing sequences that fit their rule, ignoring other possibilities. The rule Wason had in mind was, "Any three positive numbers of increasing magnitude." For instance, 1, 2, 3, would be acceptable, and so would 21, 25, 24, 601.

A special case of confirmation bias is **functional fixedness,** *the tendency to adhere to a single approach or a single way of using an item.* Here are three examples:

1. You are provided with a candle, a box of matches, some thumbtacks, and a tiny piece of string, as shown in Figure 8.20. Using no other equipment, find a way to mount the candle to the wall so that it could be lit.

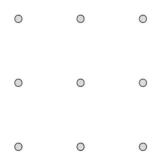

FIGURE 8.20 You are provided with a candle, a box of matches, some thumbtacks, and a tiny piece of string. What is the best way, using no other equipment, to attach the candle to a wall so that it could be lit?

2. Consider an array of nine dots:

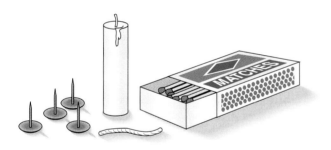

Connect all nine dots with a series of connected straight lines, such that the end of one

line is the start of the next. For example, one way would be:

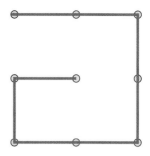

But use the fewest lines possible.

3. There are some students in a room. All but two of them are psychology majors, all but two are chemistry majors, and all but two are history majors. How many students are in the room, and what are their majors? (If your first impulse is to say "two of each," try it out: It doesn't work.) Now here's the interesting part: There are two possible solutions. After you have found one solution, discard it and find another. After you have either found solutions to these questions or given up, check answer I on page 301. (Solve these problems before reading further.)

Question 1 was difficult because most people think of the matchbox as simply a container for matches, not as a potential tool on its own. The box is "functionally fixed" for one way of using it. Question 2 was difficult because most people assume that the lines must remain within the area defined by the nine dots. On question 3 it is difficult to think of even one solution, and after thinking of it, it is hard to abandon it to think of an entirely different approach.

Framing Questions

A truly logical person would give the same answer to a question no matter how it was worded. In fact most people answer questions differently depending on how they are phrased, as you may recall from the discussion of surveys in Chapter 2.

For example, answer the following: "What's the probability that Sunday will be hotter than every other day next week?" (Please answer before you read on.)

Many people answer "50%" because it seems there are two possibilities—it will be hotter, or it won't. But now consider this rewording: "What's the probability that next week, the hottest day of the week will be Sunday?" With this wording, most people switch to the correct answer, one seventh, because they see that there are seven days with an equal chance of being the hottest (Fox & Rottenstreich, 2003).

For another example, suppose you have been appointed head of the Public Health Service, and you need to choose a plan to deal with a disease that has endangered the lives of 600 people. If you adopt plan A, you will save the lives of 200 people. If you adopt plan B, there is a 33% chance that you will save all 600 and a 67% chance that you will save no one. *Choose plan A or B before reading further.*

Now another disease breaks out; again you must choose between two plans. If you adopt plan C, 400 people will die. If you adopt plan D, there is a 33% chance that no one will die and a 67% chance that 600 will die. *Choose plan C or D now.*

Figure 8.21 shows the choices that more than 150 people made. Most chose A over B and D over C. However, note that plan A is exactly the same as C (200 live, 400 die), and plan B is exactly the same as D. Why then did so many people choose both A and D? The reason, according to Tversky and Kahneman (1981), is that most people avoid taking a risk to gain something (like saving lives) but willingly take a risk to avoid loss (like not letting people die). *The tendency to answer a question differently when it is framed (phrased) differently* is called the **framing effect.** For an additional example of the framing effect go to http://psychology.wadsworth.com/kalat_intro7e. Navigate to the student Web site, then to the Online Try It Yourself section, and click on Framing Questions.

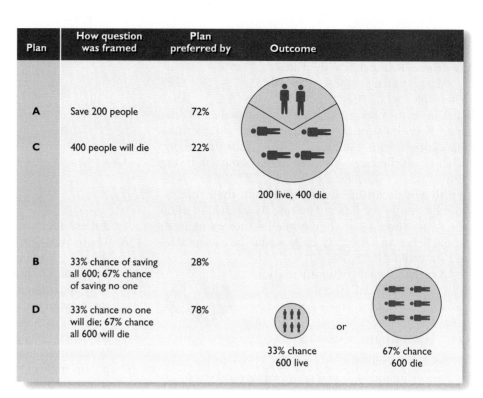

Plan	How question was framed	Plan preferred by	Outcome
A	Save 200 people	72%	
C	400 people will die	22%	200 live, 400 die
B	33% chance of saving all 600; 67% chance of saving no one	28%	
D	33% chance no one will die; 67% chance all 600 will die	78%	33% chance 600 live or 67% chance 600 die

FIGURE 8.21 Most people chose plan A over B, and D over C, although A produces the same result as C and B produces the same result as D. Amos Tversky and Daniel Kahneman (1981) proposed that most people play it safe to gain something but accept a risk to avoid a loss.

CONCEPT CHECK ☑

10. Someone says, "More than 90% of all college students like to watch late-late-night television, whereas only 20% of older adults do. Therefore, most watchers of late-late-night television are college students." What error in thinking has this person made?
11. Someone tells me that if I say "abracadabra" every morning, I will stay healthy. I say it daily and, sure enough, I stay healthy. I conclude that saying this magic word really does ensure health. What error of thinking have I made?

12. Which of the following offers by your professor would probably be more persuasive? (a) "If you do this extra project, there's a small chance I will add some points to your grade." (b) "I'm going to penalize this whole class for being inattentive today, but if you do this extra project, there's a chance I won't subtract anything from your grade." (Check your answers on page 300.)

FIGURE 8.19b

The Sunk Cost Effect

The sunk cost effect is a special case of the framing effect, but let's start with some examples:

- You have bought a $200 plane ticket to Wonderfulville and a $500 ticket to Marvelousville. Too late, you realize that they are both for the same weekend, and both are nonrefundable. You think you would prefer Wonderfulville, but you paid more for the ticket to Marvelousville. Where will you go?
- Months ago you bought an expensive ticket to a football game, but the game is today and the weather is miserably cold. You wish you hadn't bought the ticket. Do you go to the game?

Many people say they would go to Marvelousville instead of Wonderfulville because the Marvelousville ticket was more expensive and they don't want to waste the money. Many also say they will go to the football game in the bad weather, again because they don't want to waste the money. These examples illustrate the sunk cost effect, *the willingness to do something we wouldn't otherwise choose to do because of money or effort already spent* (Arkes & Ayton, 1999). This tendency arises in many situations. Someone gambles weekly on the state lottery, losing huge sums, but keeps betting because to quit without winning it back would admit that all the previous bets were a mistake. A company invests vast amounts of money in a project that now appears to be a mistake but doesn't want to cancel the project and admit it has wasted so much money. A professional sports team gives someone a huge signing bonus, and later finds the player's performance disappointing, but keeps using that player anyway to avoid wasting the money.

Curiously, young children never show the sunk cost effect. The fact that they have already wasted much time or money doesn't induce them to waste still more. No one has ever demonstrated the sunk cost effect in nonhuman animals either in spite of repeated efforts (Arkes & Ayton, 1999). Apparently, you have to be fairly intelligent to do something this stupid.

CRITICAL THINKING:
A STEP FURTHER
Framing a Question

Recall the discussion on page 297 about how the phrasing of a question influences people's answers. For example, most people will take more risks to avoid a loss than to increase a gain. Can you use this principle to explain why many gamblers on a losing streak will continue betting, sometimes increasing their bets? Is there a different way to think about the situation to decrease the temptation to continue gambling?

IN CLOSING
Successful and Unsuccessful Problem Solving

In this module we have considered thinking at its best and worst—expertise and error. Experts polish their skills through extensive practice. Of course, all of us have to make decisions about topics in which we are far from being experts, and we cannot expect perfect decisions. However, without insisting on perfection, we can at least hold ourselves to the standard of not doing anything foolish. We often make mistakes even when we have enough information, time, and skill to make a better decision. Perhaps if we become more aware of common errors, we can be more alert to avoid them.

Summary

- *Becoming an expert.* Experts are made, not born. Becoming an expert requires years of practice and effort. (page 285)
- *Expert pattern recognition.* Experts recognize and memorize familiar and meaningful patterns more rapidly than less experienced people do. (page 287)
- *Steps for solving a problem.* Problem solving can be described as a series of steps: understanding the problem, generating hypotheses, testing the hypotheses, and checking the result. (page 287)
- *Algorithms and heuristics.* People solve problems by using algorithms (repetitive means of checking every possibility) or heuristics (ways of simplifying the problem to get a reasonable solution). (page 288)
- *Generalizing.* People who have learned how to solve a problem often fail to apply that solution to a similar problem. (page 289)
- *Insight.* With insight problems people have trouble estimating how close they are to a solution. However, they may be making more progress than they realize. (page 291)
- *Creativity.* Creative people work in a field in which they have knowledge and self-confidence; no one is creative in all fields. Many highly creative people go through a period in which they rely on a small group of friends, perhaps just one, for support and encouragement. They dedicate their lives to their work, often to the exclusion of all else. (page 292)
- *Thinking by heuristics.* Heuristics simplify complex problems and help us find quick answers that are correct most of the time. However, overreliance on them or inappropriate use of them can lead to errors. (page 293)
- *Representativeness heuristic and base-rate information.* If something resembles members of some

category, we usually assume it too belongs to that category. However, that assumption is risky if the category is a rare one. (page 293)

- *Availability heuristic.* We generally assume that the more easily we can think of examples of some category, the more common that category is. However, some rare items are easy to think of because they get much publicity or because they stand out emotionally. (page 294)
- *Critical thinking.* Even people who try conscientiously to evaluate the evidence for every claim sometimes find themselves repeating a nonsensical statement that they know they should have doubted. (page 295)
- *Reasons for errors.* People tend to be overconfident about their own judgments, especially on difficult questions. They are attracted to high-payoff gambles even when the chance of winning is extremely low. They tend to look for evidence that supports their hypothesis instead of evidence that might reject it. They answer the same question differently when it is phrased differently. They sometimes take unpleasant actions to avoid admitting that previous actions were a waste of time or money. (page 295)

Answers to Concept Checks

6. An algorithm would check each possible route: For your home city (H) and three other cities (1, 2, and 3), the possible routes would be H-1-2-3-H, H-1-3-2-H, and H-2-1-3-H. (Three other routes that you could generate would be the mirror images of these three and therefore are not necessary to consider.) As the number of cities increases, the number of possible routes rises rapidly. If you had to visit 10 cities, your algorithm would have to consider almost 2 million routes. One possible heuristic would be to consider only those routes that led you from any city to one of the two cities closest to it. Another would be to consider only those routes that did not require you to cross a path already taken. (page 289)

7. Because many poets are recognized for their greatness while they are still young, it is possible to be a great poet and die young. Most historians are in their 40s or later when they do their first outstanding work; therefore, it is almost impossible to be recognized as a great historian and die young. (page 293)

8. A false-alarm rate of 5% is far too high. Imagine a plane with 100 innocent passengers, each checking two bags. Of the 200 innocent bags, this device will identify 5%—that is, 10 bags—as containing a bomb! Speer (1989) estimated that this device (which the Federal Aviation Administration actu-

ally considered using) would have 5 million false alarms for every bomb it found. (page 294)

9. Both are likely to overestimate their success. Generally, the weakest students are most likely to overestimate their success. However, the straight-A students can hardly overestimate and are therefore more likely to underestimate. (page 296)

10. Failure to consider the base rate: 20% of all older adults is a larger number than 90% of all college students. (page 298)

11. Premature commitment to one hypothesis without testing the hypothesis that one could stay healthy without the magic word. (page 298)

12. Probably (b). People are generally more willing to take a risk to avoid losing something than to gain something. (page 298)

Answers to Other Questions in the Module

D. At first you probably had no idea what strategy to use. As shown below, the game is equivalent to tick-tack-toe. If you know the correct strategy for tick-tack-toe, you now know what strategy to use for the numbers-adding-to-15 game. (page 287)

2	7	6
9	5	1
4	3	8

E. The water in the tube would leak out of the hole in the bottom. Any membrane heavy enough to keep the water in would also keep the rubber balls out. (page 289)

© Susan Ashukian

FIGURE 8.19c

F. This illustration shows how to cut and fold an ordinary piece of paper or cardboard to match the figure with nothing left over. (page 291)

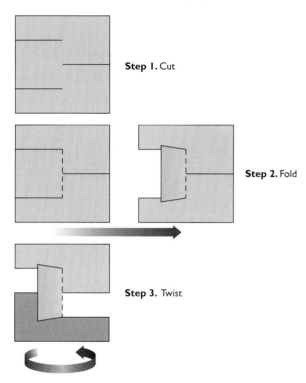

G. Set 1: The words *playing, credit,* and *report* are all associated with *card.* Set 2: The words *ticket, shop,* and *broker* are all associated with *pawn.* (page 291)

H. (1) 39 years. (2) 4,187 miles, or 6,738 kilometers. (3) 13 countries. (4) 39 books. (5) 2,160 miles, or 3,476 kilometers. (6) 390,000 pounds, or 177,000 kilograms. (7) 1756. (8) 645 days. (9) 5,959 miles, or 9,590 kilometers. (10) 36,198 feet, or 11,033 meters. (page 295)

I. (1) The best way to attach the candle to the wall is to dump the matches from the box and thumbtack the side of the box to the wall, as shown in this picture. The tiny piece of string is irrelevant.

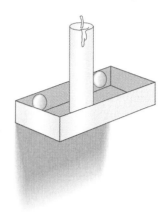

(2) The dots can be connected with four lines:

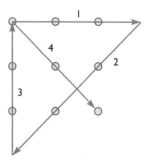

(3) One answer is three students: one psychology major, one chemistry major, and one history major. The other possibility is two students who are majoring in something else—music, for example. (If there are two music majors, all but two of them are indeed majoring in psychology etc.) (page 297)

How do we learn language?

Language is a complicated and impressive product of human cognition. It enables us to learn from the experiences of people who lived at other times and places and thereby enables education and advances in technology. Thinking and language are not synonymous, but they are certainly related closely. It sometimes seems that people speak without thinking, but presumably, their speech represented *some* kind of thinking, even if it wasn't careful thinking. Furthermore, when adult humans think about something, they usually do so in words.

Language is an extremely versatile system. Other species signal one another in various ways, but only human languages have the property of **productivity,** *the ability to express new ideas.* Every day we say and hear a few stock sentences like "Nice weather we're having," or "I can't find my keys," but we also invent new sentences that no one has ever said before. The productivity of language enables humans to communicate an ever-changing array of ideas.

You might ask, "How do you know that no one has ever said that sentence before?!" Well, of course, no one can be certain that a particular sentence is new, but we can be confident that many sentences are new (without specifying which ones) because of the vast number of possible ways to rearrange words. Imagine this exercise (but don't really try it unless you have nothing else to do with your life): Pick a sentence of more than 10 words from any book you choose. How long would you need to keep reading, in that book or any other, until you found the exact same sentence again?

In short, we do not memorize all the sentences we use. Not even infants do. Instead, we learn rules for making and understanding sentences. The famous linguist Noam Chomsky (1980) described those rules as a **transformational grammar,** *a system for converting a deep structure into a surface structure.* The deep structure is the underlying logic or meaning of a sentence. The surface structure is the sequence of words as they are actually spoken or written (Figure 8.22). According to this theory, whenever we speak, we transform the deep structure of the language into a surface structure.

Two surface structures can resemble each other without representing the same deep structure, or conversely, they can represent the same deep structure without resembling each other. For example, "John is

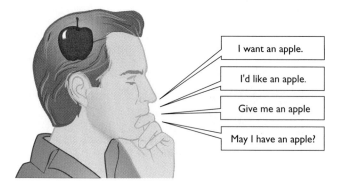

FIGURE 8.22 According to transformational grammar, we can transform a sentence with a given deep structure into any of several other sentences with different surface structures.

easy to please" has the same deep structure as "pleasing John is easy" and "it is easy to please John." These sentences all represent the same underlying idea.

In contrast consider the sentence, "Never threaten someone with a chain saw." The surface structure of that sentence maps into two quite different deep structures, as shown in Figure 8.23.

Language researcher Terrence Deacon once presented a brief talk about language to his 8-year-old's elementary school class. One child asked whether other

Deep Structure No. 1:
You are holding a chain saw. Don't threaten to use it to attack someone!

Deep Structure No. 2:
Some deranged person is holding a chain saw. Don't threaten him!

FIGURE 8.23 The sentence "Never threaten someone with a chain saw" has one surface structure but two deep structures, corresponding to different meanings.

animals have their own languages. Deacon explained that other species communicate but without the productivity of human language. The child persisted, asking whether other animals had at least a *simple* language, perhaps one with only a few words and short sentences. No, he replied, they do not have even a simple language.

Then another child asked, "Why not?" (Deacon, 1997, p. 12). Deacon paused, and then paused some more. Why not, indeed. He realized that this 8-year-old had asked a profound question. If language is so extremely useful to humans, why haven't other species evolved at least a little of it? And what makes humans so good at learning language?

Nonhuman Precursors to Language

One way to examine humans' language specialization is to ask how far another species could progress toward language with sufficient training. Beginning in the 1920s, several psychologists reared chimpanzees in their homes and tried to teach them to talk. The chimpanzees learned many human habits (Figure 8.24) but understood only a little of language.

Chimpanzees' vocal cords are poorly adapted to making voice sounds. The sounds they do make are mostly during inhaling, not exhaling. (Try to speak

a

b

c

d

e

FIGURE 8.24 Psychologists have tried to teach chimpanzees to communicate with gestures or visual symbols. (a) One of the Premacks' chimps arranges plastic chips to request food. (b) Viki in her human home, helping with the housework. After years with the Hayeses, she could make only a few sounds similar to English words. (c) Kanzi, a bonobo, presses symbols to indicate words. Among the primates bonobos have shown the most promising ability to acquire language. (d) A chimp signing *toothbrush*. (e) Roger Fouts with Alley the chimp, who is signing *lizard*.

while inhaling!) However, chimpanzees do make hand gestures in nature. R. Allen Gardner and Beatrice Gardner (1969) taught a chimpanzee named Washoe to use the sign language of the American deaf (Ameslan). Washoe eventually learned the symbols for about 100 words.

How much do these gestures resemble language? Washoe and other chimpanzees trained in this way used their symbols almost exclusively to make requests, not to describe, and rarely in new, original combinations (Pate & Rumbaugh, 1983; Terrace, Petitto, Sanders, & Bever, 1979; C. R. Thompson & Church, 1980). By contrast a human child with a vocabulary of 100 words or so starts linking them into original combinations and short sentences and frequently uses words to describe.

The results have been different, however, for another species, *Pan paniscus,* sometimes known as the pygmy chimpanzee (a misleading term because these animals are almost as large as common chimpanzees) and sometimes known as the bonobo. Bonobos' social behavior resembles that of humans in several regards: Males and females form strong attachments; females are sexually responsive throughout the month, not just during their fertile period; males contribute to infant care; and adults often share food with one another.

Several bonobos have used symbols in impressive ways. They occasionally use the symbols to name and describe objects that they are not requesting. They sometimes use the symbols to describe past events. (One with a cut on his hand explained that his mother had bit him.) Also, they frequently make original, creative requests, such as asking one person to chase another.

The most proficient bonobos seem to comprehend symbols about as well as a 2- to 2 ½-year-old child understands language (Savage-Rumbaugh et al., 1993). They have also shown considerable understanding of spoken English, following even such odd commands such as "bite your ball" and "take the vacuum cleaner outside" (Savage-Rumbaugh, 1990; Savage-Rumbaugh, Sevcik, Brakke, & Rumbaugh, 1992). They also passed the test of responding to commands issued over earphones, eliminating the possibility of unintentional "Clever Hans"-type signals, as discussed in Chapter 2 (Figure 8.25).

The explanation for this impressive success pertains partly to species differences: Apparently, bonobos have greater language capacities than common chimpanzees. Another part of the explanation pertains to the method of training: Learning by observation and imitation promotes better understanding than the formal training methods that were used in previous studies (Savage-Rumbaugh et al., 1992). People, after all, learn language by imitation. Finally, the bonobos began their language experi-

FIGURE 8.25 Kanzi, a bonobo, points to answers on a board in response to questions he hears through earphones. Experimenter Rose Sevcik sits with him but does not hear the questions, so she cannot signal the correct answer.

ence early in life. Humans learn language more easily when they are young, and the same may be true for bonobos.

CONCEPT CHECK ☑

13. Based on the studies with bonobos, can you offer advice about how to teach language to children with impaired language learning? (Check your answer on page 316.)

Human Specializations for Learning Language

Is the glass half full or half empty? Should we be impressed that bonobos understand language almost as well as a 2½-year-old child or wonder why they do not progress further? Humans are clearly specialized to learn language in a way that no other species can.

Language and General Intelligence

Did we evolve language as an accidental by-product of evolving big brains and great intelligence? The idea sounds appealing, but several observations argue strongly against it. Dolphins and whales have larger brains than humans have but do not develop language. (Yes, they communicate, but not in a flexible system resembling human language.) Some people with massive brain damage have less total brain mass than a chimpanzee but continue to speak and understand language.

Also, people in one family, all having a particular gene, develop normal intelligence except for language (Fisher, Vargha-Khadem, Watkins, Monaco, & Pembrey, 1998; Lai, Fisher, Hurst, Vargha-Khadem, & Monaco, 2001). Their pronunciation is poor and they do not fully master even simple rules, such as how to form plurals of nouns. So normal human brain size and normal intelligence do not automatically produce language.

At the opposite extreme, consider **Williams syndrome**, *a genetic condition characterized by mental retardation in most regards but skillful use of language.* Before the discovery of Williams syndrome, psychologists would have confidently said that good language was impossible without normal intelligence. One 14-year-old with Williams syndrome could write good creative stories and songs, but in other ways she performed like a 5- to 7-year-old and could not be left alone without a baby-sitter. Another child with Williams syndrome, when asked to name as many animals as he could think of, started with "ibex, whale, bull, yak, zebra, puppy, kitten, tiger, koala, dragon . . ." Another child could sing more than 1,000 songs in 22 languages (Bellugi & St. George, 2000). However, these children prefer 50 pennies to 5 dollars and, when asked to estimate the length of a bus, give answers such as "3 inches or 100 inches, maybe" (Bellugi, Lichtenberger, Jones, Lai, & St. George, 2000). Again, the conclusion is that language ability is not synonymous with overall intelligence.

Language Learning as a Specialized Capacity

Susan Carey (1978) calculated that children between the ages of 1½ and 6 learn an average of nine new words per day. But how do they infer the meanings of all those words? Suppose you are in Japan and someone points to a pillow and says "makura." You therefore conclude that *makura* is the Japanese word for *pillow.* But logically, it could have meant "soft thing," "throwable thing," or even *this particular* pillow. How did you make the correct inference that the word probably referred to the category *pillow*? More important, how did you know it meant anything at all? All you observed was that someone made a sound and pointed; you inferred the intention to communicate. That inference comes naturally to humans, but not to other species.

Noam Chomsky has argued that people learn language so easily that they must not be learning in the usual way. Children must begin with some preconceptions. The simplest and perhaps most important is the idea that words *mean* something. Children also make essential distinctions, such as between actors and actions (i.e., nouns and verbs), actors and recipients of

action, singular and plural, same and different, and so forth. They have to learn how to express those relationships in their particular language, but they do not have to learn concepts like singular and plural themselves. Chomsky and his followers therefore suggest that people are born with a **language acquisition device** or "language instinct," *a built-in mechanism for acquiring language* (Pinker, 1994).

Doubts and controversies remain, however, about exactly what is built in. Are we really born with concepts, distinctions, and a primitive grammar, or just with the ability to learn them? If we are born with a predisposition to learn language, what is the nature of that predisposition? The predisposition could be far removed from the details of language itself (Deacon, 1997; Seidenberg, 1997).

Here is one study suggesting an innate predisposition: Adult German speakers were asked to learn a little of Italian or Japanese, which were unfamiliar to them before the experiment. In all cases the experimenters used real Italian or Japanese words, but they taught some people real grammatical rules (which are unlike those of German) and other people some made-up rules unlike those of any known language. For example, one made-up rule was, "to make a sentence negative, add the negative word (*no* in Italian, *nai* in Japanese) after the third word of the sentence, whatever that word may be." Another fake rule was "to make a statement into a question, say the words in reverse order." So, *"Paolo mangia la pera"* (the Italian for "Paul eats the pear") would become *"Pera la mangia Paolo?"* ("Does Paul eat the pear?"). Those who learned either Italian or Japanese with real grammar showed increased activity in the brain areas usually associated with language. Those learning with the fake rules showed increased activity in other brain areas but not in the circuits usually important for language (Musso et al., 2003). Evidently, some grammars seem "natural" even when they are unfamiliar, whereas other grammars are recognized as "not real language."

But what conclusion do we draw? It would be a vast overstatement to say that we are literally born knowing the grammars of all possible languages. A more reasonable conclusion is that we are predisposed to learn some relationships more easily than others (Saffran, 2003). For example, making interrogatives by inverting the order of entire sentences would be difficult. Learning the rule itself would be easy, but applying it would be a difficult memory task when dealing with a long sentence.

Is it possible that infants learn all the complexities of word meanings and grammar from the apparently meager information they receive? Perhaps the information is better than we imagined. Parents throughout the world simplify the language-learning task by speaking to their infants in "parentese." I am not talking about silly "goo-goo" baby talk, but a pattern of speech that emphasizes and prolongs the vowels, making clearer than usual the difference between words such as *cat* and *cot* (Kuhl et al., 1997). Infants listen more intently to parentese than to normal speech and learn more from it. We also speak slowly, distinctly, and in simple words to someone who barely understands our language. To those who know the language well, we can speak rapidly, mumble, or speak in a noisy environment and still expect decent understanding (Calvin & Bickerton, 2000).

Several studies have found that even infants younger than 1 year old detect the regularities of the language they hear (Marcus, Vijayan, Rao, & Vishton, 1999; Saffran, 2003). For example, when adults speak they usually run all their words together without pausing between them: "Lookattheprettybaby." The infant detects which sounds go together as words by statistical relations. For example, the infant frequently hears the two-syllable combination "pre-tty" and frequently hears "ba-by" but less often hears the combination "ty-ba" and concludes that the word break comes between *pretty* and *baby.* We can infer that infants draw this conclusion because infants react to "ty-ba" as a new, attention-getting sound and don't react the same way to "pretty" or "baby" (Saffran, Aslin, & Newport, 1996). In short, infants learn the basics of language from regularities in what they hear.

Adults go through much the same process when trying to learn a foreign language (Cutler, Demuth, & McQueen, 2002). If you heard someone say, "vogubarilatusomatafikogovogurasu . . ." you would infer that the first word is either "vo," "vog," "vogu," or something longer because no word in any language is shorter than one syllable. (Whether we are born with that assumption or learn it is not known.) Because "vogu" was repeated already, but "voguba" was not, you would probably infer that "vogu" is one word of this language.

Language and the Human Brain

What aspect of the human brain enables us to learn language so easily? Studies of people with brain damage have long pointed to two brain areas as particularly important for language. People with damage in the frontal cortex, including *Broca's area* (Figure 8.26), develop **Broca's aphasia**, *a condition characterized by inarticulate speech and by difficulties with both using and understanding grammatical devices—prepositions, conjunctions, word endings, complex sentence structures, and so forth.* For example, one patient who was asked about a dental appointment slowly mumbled, "Yes . . . Monday . . . Dad and Dick . . . Wednesday nine o'clock . . . 10 o'clock . . . doctors . . . and . . . teeth" (Geschwind, 1979, p. 186). These people do not really

Wernicke's area: Brain damage leading to Wernicke's aphasia usually includes this area.

Broca's area: Brain damage leading to Broca's aphasia usually includes this area.

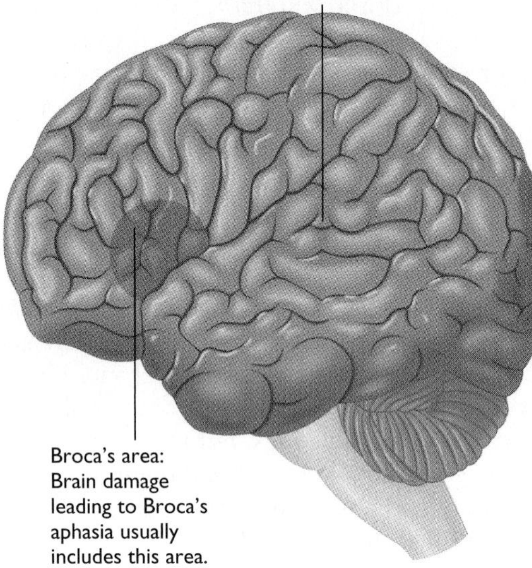

FIGURE 8.26 Brain damage that produces major deficits in language usually includes the left-hemisphere areas shown here. However, the deficits are severe only if the damage is more extensive, including these areas but extending to others as well. Many areas of the human brain contribute to language comprehension and production.

lose all grammatical understanding; they merely find it much more difficult to use and understand language, much as other people do when they are extremely distracted (Blackwell & Bates, 1995).

People with damage in the temporal cortex, including *Wernicke's area* (Figure 8.26), develop **Wernicke's aphasia,** *a condition marked by difficulty recalling the names of objects and impaired comprehension of language.* Because these people do not remember names, their speech is nonsensical even when it is grammatical. For example, one patient responded to a question about his health, "I felt worse because I can no longer keep in mind from the mind of the minds to keep me from mind and up to the ear which can be to find among ourselves" (Brown, 1977, p. 29).

However, language did not evolve simply by adding a language module to a chimpanzee brain. The brain areas important for language are critical for many other processes as well, including music (Patel, 2003) and some aspects of memory (Tyler et al., 2002). Brain damage that seriously impairs language always extends well beyond Broca's or Wernicke's area. Indeed, the nature of the language deficit varies from one person to another, and the location of the damage does accurately predict the language problems. Evidently, each person's language cortex is organized somewhat differently from everyone else's. Furthermore, PET scans or other brain recordings show widespread activation during speech (Just, Carpenter, Keller, Eddy, & Thulborn, 1996). It is hardly an exaggeration to say that the whole human brain is specialized to make language possible.

Stages of Language Development

Table 8.2 lists the average ages at which children reach various stages of language ability (Lenneberg, 1969; Moskowitz, 1978). Progression through these stages depends largely on maturation, not just extra experience (Lenneberg, 1967, 1969). Parents who expose their children to as much language as possible find that they can increase the children's vocabulary, but they hardly affect the rate of progression through language stages (Figure 8.27). At the other extreme, hearing children of deaf parents are exposed to much less spoken language, and at first they start "babbling" with rhythmic hand gestures (Petitto, Holowka, Sergio, & Ostry, 2001), but with even modest exposure to spoken language, their language development progresses on schedule.

Deaf infants babble as much as hearing infants do for about the first 6 months and then start to decline. At first, hearing infants babble only haphazard sounds, but soon they start repeating the sounds that are common in the language they have been hearing. Thus, a 1-year-old babbles a variety of sounds that resemble French, Chinese, or whatever other language the family speaks (Locke, 1994).

One of the first sounds an infant can make is *muh*, and *muh, muh-muh,* or something similar has been adopted by most of the world's languages to mean "mother." Infants also make the sounds *duh, puh,* and

FIGURE 8.27 Some overeager parents try to teach their children language at a very early age. The child may enjoy the attention, but the activity is unlikely to accelerate the child's progress in language development.

buh. In many languages the word for father is similar to *dada* or *papa. Baba* is the word for grandmother in several languages. In effect infants tell their parents what words to use for important concepts. Indeed, Deacon (1997) has argued that children do not evolve to learn language; languages evolve to be easy for children to learn.

By age 1½ most toddlers have a vocabulary of about 50 words, but they seldom link words together. Thus, a toddler will say "Daddy" and "bye-bye" but not "Bye-bye, Daddy." In context parents can usually discern considerable meaning in these single-word utterances. *Mama* might mean, "That's a picture of Mama," "Take me to Mama," "Mama went away and left me here," or "Mama, I'm hungry." At this age toddlers understand language far better than they can produce it. In a sense they "learn how to learn" the meanings of words. If they are given careful practice with the idea that names refer to the shapes of objects—for example, being taught that *box* always refers to a particular shape, regardless of the color or size—they start increasing their vocabulary faster, particularly their vocabulary of the names of objects (L. B. Smith, Jones, Landau, Gershkoff-Stowe, & Samuelson, 2002).

By age 2, children start producing "telegraphic" phrases of two or more words, including combinations such as "more page," "allgone sticky," and "allgone outside" to indicate "read some more," "my hands are now clean," and "someone has closed the door," respectively. Note the originality of such phrases; it is unlikely that the parents ever said "allgone sticky"!

By age 2½ to 3 years, most children are generating full sentences, though each child maintains a few peculiarities. For example, many young children have their own rules for forming negative sentences. A common one is to add *no* or *not* to the beginning or end of a sentence, such as, "No I want to go to bed!" One little girl formed her negatives just by saying something louder and at a higher pitch; for instance, if she shrieked, "I

TABLE 8.2
Stages of Language Development

Age	Typical Language Abilities (Much Individual Variation)
3 months	Random vocalizations.
6 months	More distinct babbling.
1 year	Babbling that resembles the typical sounds of the family's language; probably one or more words including "mama"; language comprehension much better than production.
1½ years	Can say some words (mean about 50), mostly nouns; few or no phrases.
2 years	Speaks in two-word phrases.
2½ years	Longer phrases and short sentences with some errors and unusual constructions. Can understand much more.
3 years	Vocabulary near 1,000 words; longer sentences with fewer errors.
4 years	Close to adult speech competence.

want to share my toys!" she really meant, "I do *not* want to share my toys." Presumably, she had learned this "rule" by remembering that people screamed at her when they told her not to do something. My son Sam made negatives for a while by adding the word *either* to the end of a sentence: "I want to eat lima beans either." Apparently, he had heard people say, "I don't want to do that either" and had decided that the word *either* at the end of the sentence made it an emphatic negative.

Young children act as if they were applying grammatical rules. (I say "as if" because they cannot state the rules. By the same token, baseball players chasing a high fly ball act "as if" they understood calculus.) For example, a child may learn the word *feet* at an early age and then, after learning other plurals, abandon *feet* in favor of *foots*. Later, the child begins to compromise by saying "feets," "footses," or "feetses" before eventually returning to "feet." Children at this stage say many things they have never heard anyone else say, such as "the womans goed and doed something." Clearly, they are applying rules for how to form plurals and past tenses, although they *overregularize* or *overgeneralize* the rules. My son David invented the word *shis* to mean "belonging to a female." (He had apparently generalized the rule "He–his, she–shis.") Note that all these inventions imply that children are learning rules, not just repeating word combinations.

The progression of language stages suggests that language is a developmental process that unfolds, much like growth. Do we have a "critical period" for learning language early in life? Adults can learn the vocabulary of a second language faster than children can, but children learn the pronunciation better, as well as difficult aspects of the grammar. Even those who overheard another language in childhood without paying much attention to it learn it more easily later in life (Au, Knightly, Jun, & Oh, 2002). However, researchers find no sharp age cutoff for when language becomes more difficult. That is, starting a second language is easier for 2-year-olds than 4-year-olds, but also somewhat easier for 13-year-olds than 16-year-olds (Hakuta, Bialystok, & Wiley, 2003; Harley & Wang, 1997). So the results do not support a "critical period" with a cutoff date; we have a gradual tendency toward learning quicker when younger and gradually worsen with age (as with many other kinds of learning as well).

CONCEPT CHECK ☑

14. At what age do children begin to string words into combinations that they have never heard before? Why do psychologists believe that even very young children learn some of the rules of grammar? (Check your answers on page 316.)

Children Exposed to No Language or Two Languages

Would children who were exposed to no language at all make up their own? In rare cases an infant who was accidentally separated from other people grew up in a forest without human contact until discovered years later. Such children not only fail to show a language of their own but also fail to learn much language after they are given the chance (Pinker, 1994). However, their development is so abnormal and their early life so unknown that we should hesitate to draw conclusions.

The best evidence comes from studies of children who are deaf. Children who cannot hear well enough to learn speech and who are not taught sign language invent their own sign language, which they teach to other deaf children and so far as possible to their parents. As they grow older, they make the system more complex, linking signs together into sentences with fairly consistent word order and grammatical rules—for example, "Mother, twist open the jar, blow a bubble, so I can clap it" (Goldin-Meadow, McNeill, & Singleton, 1996; Goldin-Meadow & Mylander, 1998). Observations of sign language in Nicaragua found that the language had evolved over the decades, becoming more complex and richer in information. Thus, the younger deaf people, who had learned the richer language from their early childhood, had in many ways more expressive signs than older deaf people, who had originally learned the less complex version (Senghas & Coppola, 2001).

Although each deaf child invents a different system, most systems share some interesting similarities. For example, most include some sort of marker to indicate the difference between a subject that is doing something to an object ("the mouse eats the cheese") and a subject that is doing something without an object ("the mouse is moving"). The sign languages invented by children in Taiwan resemble those of children in the United States, even though the spoken languages of those countries—Chinese and English—have very different grammars (Goldin-Meadow & Mylander, 1998).

If a deaf child starts to invent a sign language and no one responds to it, because the child meets no other deaf children and the adults fail to or refuse to learn, the child gradually abandons it and becomes totally without language. If such a child is exposed to sign language much later, such as age 12, he or she struggles to develop even weak signing skills and never catches up with those who started earlier (Harley & Wang, 1997; Mayberry, Lock, & Kazmi, 2002). This observation is our best evidence for the importance of early development in language learning: A child who doesn't learn a language while young is permanently impaired at learning one.

Some children grow up in a **bilingual** environment, *learning two languages about equally well.* Bilingualism is especially common among immigrant children, who are generally bicultural as well, learning both their parents' customs and those of their new country. The areas of brain activity during language use are the same in bilingual people as in those with only one language (Paradis, 1990; Solin, 1989). If the brain representations are so similar, how do bilingual people keep their two languages separate? The answer is that they do not, at least not completely (Francis, 1999).

Bilingualism has two disadvantages: Children take longer to master two languages than to master one (of course), and even adult bilinguals occasionally confuse words from the two languages. The primary advantage is obvious: If you learn a second language, you can communicate with more people. A second advantage is subtle: A bilingual person gains extra cognitive flexibility by learning that there are different ways of expressing the same idea. For example, children younger than 6 years old who speak only one language apparently believe that every object has only one name. If an adult gestures toward a cup and a gyroscope and says, "Please bring me the gyroscope," a child who knows the word *cup* will immediately bring the gyroscope, assuming that if one object is the cup, the other one must be the gyroscope. But the child would also fetch the gyroscope if asked to bring the *vessel,* the *chalice,* or any other synonym for *cup* that the child did not know. A bilingual child, however, is more likely to hesitate or to ask for help, understanding that an unfamiliar word could refer to the cup just as easily as the other object (Davidson, Jergovic, Imami, & Theodos, 1997).

CONCEPT CHECK ☑

15. What is the most convincing evidence that early exposure to language is necessary for language development? (Check your answer on page 316.)

Understanding Language

On a trip to Norway some years ago, I consulted my Norwegian phrase book and asked directions to the men's room: "Hvor er toalettet?" When the man answered—in Norwegian, of course—I suddenly realized the problem: It doesn't do me any good to speak the language unless I understand the answers!

Understanding a Word

We customarily describe the word *cat* as being composed of three sounds, *kuh, ah,* and *tuh.* However, the first sound in *cat* is not quite the same as the consonant sound in *kuh;* the *a* and *t* sounds are changed also. Each letter changes its sound depending on the other sounds that precede and follow it. What we hear also depends on the context and our expectations. For example, a researcher computer-modified a sound to be halfway between a normal *s* sound and a normal *sh* sound. When this intermediate sound replaced the *s* sound at the end of the word *embarrass,* people heard it as an *s* sound, but when the same sound replaced the *sh* at the end of *abolish,* people heard the same sound as *sh* (Samuel, 2001).

We also use lipreading more than we realize to understand what we hear. If lip movements do not match the sound, we sometimes "hear" something that is neither what we saw nor what we heard, but a compromise between them (McGurk & MacDonald, 1976). To experience this phenomenon go to http://psychology.wadsworth.com/kalat_intro7e. Navigate to the student Web site, then to the Online Try It Yourself section, and click on McGurk Effect.

Online Try It Yourself

In another study students listened to a tape recording of a sentence with one sound missing (Warren, 1970). The sentence was, "The state governors met with their respective legislatures convening in the capital city." However, the sound of the first *s* in the word *legislatures,* along with part of the adjacent *i* and *l,* had been replaced by a cough or a tone. The students were asked to listen to the recording and try to identify the location of the cough or tone. None of the 20 students identified the location correctly, and half thought the cough or tone interrupted one of the other words on the tape. They all claimed to have heard the *s* plainly. In fact even those who had been told that the *s* sound was missing still insisted that they had heard the sound. Apparently, the brain uses the context to fill in the missing sound.

Many English words have different meanings in different contexts. *Rose* can refer to a flower, or it can be the past tense of the verb *to rise. Dove* can refer to a bird related to pigeons, or it can be the past tense of the verb *to dive.* Consider the word *mean* in this sentence: "What did that mean old statistician mean by asking us to find the mean and mode of this distribution?" Just as we hear the word *legislatures* as a whole, not as a string of separate letters, we interpret a sequence of words as a whole, not one at a time. For example, suppose you hear a tape-recorded word that is carefully engineered to sound halfway between *dent* and *tent.* If you simply hear it and are asked to say what you heard, you might reply "dent," "tent," or "something sort of intermediate between dent and tent." But now suppose you hear that same sound in context:

1. When the *ent in the fender was well camouflaged, we sold the car.
2. When the *ent in the forest was well camouflaged, we began our hike.

Most people who hear sentence 1 report the word *dent.* Most who hear sentence 2 report *tent.* Now consider two more sentences:

3. When the *ent was noticed in the fender, we sold the car.
4. When the *ent was noticed in the forest, we stopped to rest.

For sentences 3 and 4, the context comes too late to help. People are as likely to report hearing *dent* in one sentence as in the other (Connine, Blasko, & Hall, 1991). Think for a moment what this means: In the first two sentences, the fender or forest showed up three syllables after *ent. In the second pair, the fender or forest appeared six syllables later. Evidently, when you hear an ambiguous sound, you can hold it in a temporary "undecided" state for about three syllables for the context to help you understand it. Beyond that point it is too late; you hear it one way or the other and stick with your decision, regardless of the later context.

Although a long-delayed context cannot help you hear an ambiguous word correctly, it can help you understand its meaning. Consider the following sentence from Karl Lashley (1951):

> Rapid righting with his uninjured hand saved from loss the contents of the capsized canoe.

If you hear this sentence spoken aloud, so that spelling is not a clue, you are likely at first to interpret the second word as *writing,* until you reach the final two words of the sentence. Suddenly, the phrase *capsized canoe* changes the whole scenario; now we understand that *righting* meant "pushing with a paddle." In summary only the immediate context can influence what you hear, but even a delayed context can change the word's meaning.

Understanding Sentences

Making sense of language requires knowledge about the world. For example, consider the following sentences (from Just & Carpenter, 1987):

- That store sells horse shoes.
- That store sells alligator shoes.

You interpret *horse shoes* to mean "shoes for horses to wear," but you don't interpret *alligator*

shoes as "shoes for alligators to wear." Your understanding of the sentences depended on your knowledge of the world, not just the syntax of the sentences.

Here is another example:

- I'm going to buy a pet hamster at the store, if it's open.
- I'm going to buy a pet hamster at the store, if it's healthy.

Nothing about the sentence structure told you that *it* refers to the store in the first sentence and the hamster in the second sentence. You understood because you know that stores but not hamsters can be open, whereas hamsters but not stores can be healthy.

In short, you don't base your sentence understanding just on the sentence itself. Language comprehension depends on your knowledge of the world and all the assumptions that you share with the speaker or writer of the sentence. Sometimes you even have to remember where you are because the meaning of a word differs from one place to another (Figure 8.28).

FIGURE 8.28 In England a *football coach* is a bus full of soccer fans. In the United States it's the person who directs a team of American football players.

Now consider this sentence: *While Anna dressed the baby played in the crib.* Quickly: Whom did Anna dress? And who played in the crib?
The addition of a comma would simplify the sentence, but even without it, English grammar prohibits "baby" from being both the object of *dressed* and the subject of *played.* If the baby played in the crib (as you no doubt answered), Anna must have dressed herself. Nevertheless, many people misunderstand and think Anna dressed the baby (Ferreira, Bailey, & Ferraro, 2002). Remember the example from earlier in the chapter about how many animals Moses took on the

ark? That was another example in which many people overlook the details of the sentence and construct a "good enough" interpretation of the sentence's meaning based on their knowledge and reasonable expectations. That strategy occasionally misleads us, but it proves valuable in far more cases, such as those about the alligator shoes or buying a hamster at the store.

Limits to Our Language Understanding

Some sentences that follow the rules of grammar are nevertheless nearly incomprehensible. One example is a doubly embedded sentence—a sentence within a sentence within a sentence. A singly embedded sentence is understandable, though not simple:

The dog the cat saw chased a squirrel.
The squirrel the dog chased climbed the tree.

In the first sentence, "the cat saw the dog" is embedded within "the dog chased a squirrel." In the second, "the dog chased the squirrel" is embedded within "the squirrel climbed the tree." So far, so good, but now consider a doubly embedded sentence:

The squirrel the dog the cat saw chased climbed the tree.

Doubly embedded sentences overburden our memory. In fact, if your memory is already burdened with other matters, you may have trouble understanding even a singly embedded sentence (Gordon, Hendrick, & Levine, 2002).

Double negatives are also difficult to understand. "I would not deny that . . ." means that I agree. "It is not false that . . ." means that something is true. People can understand such sentences, but with difficulty. Have you ever seen a multiple-choice test item that asks "Which of the following is not true . . ." and then one of the choices has a *not* in it? When that happens, confusion is almost certain.

Triple negatives are, of course, still worse. Consider the following sentence, which includes *four* (!) negatives (emphasis added): "If you do *not* unanimously find from your consideration of all the evidence that there are *no* mitigating factors sufficient to *preclude* the imposition of a death sentence, then you should sign the verdict requiring the court to impose a sentence *other than* death." In Illinois a judge reads those instructions to a jury in a capital punishment case to explain how to decide between a death penalty and life in prison. (Do you think many jurors will understand?)

Even single negatives are sometimes confusing. Suppose you are trying to decide whether to buy a product at the supermarket. You notice on the package, "Contains no cyanide or rat pieces!" Does that notice encourage you to buy the product? Hardly! It is as if you do not fully believe the "no." (After all, why would the manufacturer even mention the absence of something unless it might be present?) I was once on an airplane that turned around shortly after departure because one of its two engines failed. The attendant told the passengers what was happening, but until she said "Please don't panic," we didn't realize there was any reason to panic.

In one clever experiment, students watched an experimenter pour sugar into two jars. The students were then told to label one jar "sucrose, table sugar" and the other "not sodium cyanide, not poison." Then the experimenter made two cups of Kool-Aid, one from each jar of sugar, and asked the students to choose one cup to drink (Figure 8.29). Of those who expressed a preference, 35 of 44 wanted Kool-Aid made from the jar marked "sucrose," not from the one that denied cyanide and poison (Rozin, Markwith, & Ross, 1990).

FIGURE 8.29 Most students preferred Kool-Aid made with sugar labeled "sugar" instead of sugar labeled "not cyanide," even though they had placed the labels themselves. Evidently, people do not fully believe the word "not." *(Based on results of Rozin, Markwith, & Ross, 1990)*

Monitoring Understanding

Earlier, we encountered the sentence "Never threaten someone with a chain saw." Another ambiguous sentence is "The daughter of the man and the woman arrived." Who arrived—one person (the man and woman's daughter)—or two people (the man's daughter plus some other woman)? If you said something like this, you would presumably know which meaning you intended, and your listener might know too because of the context or because of your pauses, intonations, and gestures. But might you overestimate your listener's understanding?

FIGURE 8.30 Either a word or a single letter flashed on a screen and then an interfering pattern. The observers were asked, "Which was presented: *C* or *J*?" More of them identified the letter correctly when it was part of a word.

In one study people were asked to read aloud a series of ambiguous sentences, such as, "The daughter of the man and the woman arrived." In each case the speaker was told which of the two meanings was correct and was instructed to say the sentence to convey that meaning. After each sentence the speaker estimated the probability that a listener would correctly understand. On the average, speakers estimated correct understanding 72% of the time, whereas the listeners understood only 61% (Keysar & Henly, 2002). Remember from earlier in this chapter people's general tendency to be overconfident of themselves (page 295). Here we see another example.

Good writers try to avoid ambiguous or confusing sentences, and their copy editors try to catch any confusion the writer hadn't noticed. Still, some badly worded sentences make it to print. For example, a student newspaper once included this gem of a sentence: *He said Harris told him she and Brothers told French that grades had been changed.* When good readers find a sentence like that, they stop and reread it until they understand. Poorer readers tend to read everything at about a steady speed, regardless of how confusing it is.

Reading

As you will recall from earlier in this chapter, expertise achieved after 10 or so years of intensive practice enables one to recognize complex patterns at a glance. You have intensively practiced reading for more than the last 10 years, so in that regard you qualify as an expert reader. You may not think of yourself as an expert because we usually reserve the term *expert* for someone who is far more skilled than others. Nevertheless, your years of reading enable you to recognize words instantaneously, like an expert who recognizes chess patterns at a glance.

Word Recognition

Consider the following experiment: The investigator flashes one letter on a screen for less than a quarter of a second and then shows an interfering pattern and asks,

"Was the letter C or J?" Then the experimenter flashes an entire word on the screen for the same length of time and asks, "Was the first letter of the word C or J?" (Figure 8.30). Which question do you think would be easier to answer? Most people can *identify the letter more accurately when it is part of a whole word than when it is presented by itself* (Reicher, 1969; Wheeler, 1970). This is known as the **word-superiority effect.** You can experience it yourself. Go to http://psychology.wadsworth. com/kalat_intro7e. Navigate to the student Web site, then to the Online Try It Yourself section, and click on Word Superiority Effect.

In further research James Johnston and James McClelland (1974) briefly flashed words on the screen and asked students to identify one letter (whose position was marked) in each word (Figure 8.31). On some trials the experimenters told the students to focus on the center of the area where the word would appear and to try to see the whole word. On other trials they showed the students exactly where the critical letter would appear on the screen and told them to focus on that spot and ignore the rest of the screen. Most students identified the critical letter more successfully when they looked at the whole word than when they focused on just the letter itself. This benefit occurs only with a real word, like COIN, not with a nonsense combination, like CXQF (Rumelhart & McClelland, 1982).

You may have experienced the word-superiority effect yourself. To pass time on long car trips, people sometimes try to find every letter of the alphabet on the billboards. It is usually easier to spot a letter by reading complete words than by checking letter by letter.

What accounts for the word-superiority effect? According to one model (J. L. McClelland, 1988;

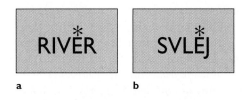

a   b

FIGURE 8.31 Students identified an indicated letter better when they focused on an entire word (a) than on a single letter in a designated spot (b).

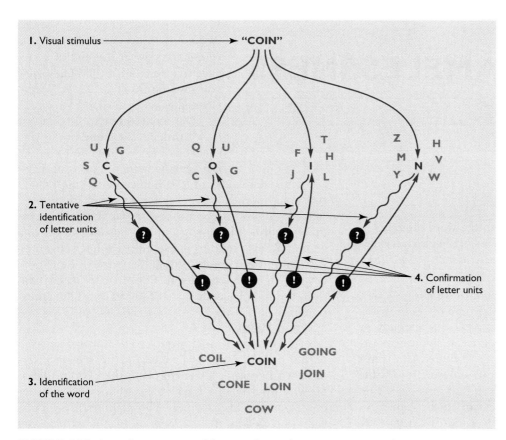

FIGURE 8.32 According to one model, a visual stimulus activates certain letter units, some more strongly than others. Those letter units then activate a word unit, which in turn strengthens the letter units that compose it. For this reason we recognize a whole word more easily than a single letter.

you tentatively perceive the word as *RED* (the only English word among those choices), the feedback strengthens the activity of the *R*, *E*, and *D* units.

Reading and Eye Movements

In an alphabetical language such as English, the printed page consists of letters that form familiar clusters that in turn form words and sentences. One kind of cluster is a **phoneme**, *a unit of sound.* A phoneme can be a single letter (such as *f*) or a combination of letters (such as *sh*). Good reading requires mastering phonics—the relationship between letters and sounds (Rayner, Foorman, Perfetti, Pesetsky, & Seidenberg, 2001). Another kind of cluster is a **morpheme**, *a unit of meaning.* For example, the noun *thrills* has two morphemes (*thrill* and

Rumelhart, McClelland, & the PDP Research Group, 1986), our perceptions and memories are represented by vast numbers of connections among "units," presumably corresponding to sets of neurons. Each unit is connected to other units (Figure 8.32). Each unit, when activated, excites some of its neighbors and inhibits others. Suppose that, at a given moment, units corresponding to the letters C, O, I, and N are moderately active. They excite a higher order unit corresponding to the word COIN. Although none of the four letter units sends a strong message by itself, the collective impact is strong (J. L. McClelland & Rumelhart, 1981). This higher level perception COIN then feeds excitation back to the individual letter-identifying units and confirms their tentative identifications.

This model helps explain our perception of Figure 8.33. Why do you see the top word in that figure as *RED* instead of *PFB*? After all, in the other words, those letters do look like *P, F,* and *B*. But in the top word, one ambiguous figure activates some *P* units and some *R* units; the next figure activates *E* and *F* units, and the third figure activates *D* and *B* units. All of those units in turn activate other more complex units corresponding to *RFB, PFB, PFD,* and *RED.* As

s). The final *s* is a unit of meaning because it indicates that the noun is plural (see Figure 8.34).

FIGURE 8.33 The combination of possible letters enables us to identify a word; word recognition in turn helps to confirm the letter identifications. Although each of the letters in the top word is ambiguous, a whole word—RED—is perceived. *("Parallel Distributed Processing: Explorations in the Microstructures of Cognition," Vol. 1: Foundations by David E. Rumethan et al., p. 8, figure 2. Series in Computational Models of Cognition and Perception. Copyright 1986 by MIT Press. Used with permission of the publisher.)*

Phonemes
(units of sound):

SHAMELESSNESS

Morphemes
(units of meaning):

FIGURE 8.34 The word *shamelessness* has nine phonemes (units of sound) and three morphemes (units of meaning).

CONCEPT CHECK ☑

16. How many phonemes are in the word *thoughtfully*? How many morphemes? (Check your answers on page 316.)

When we read, do we ordinarily read one letter, one phoneme, one morpheme, or one or more words at a time? And do we move our eyes in a steady or jerky fashion? The movements are fast, and we are ordinarily not aware of them. Psychologists have arranged devices to monitor eye movements during reading. Their first discovery was that a reader's eyes move in a jerky fashion. You can move your eyes steadily to follow a moving object, but when you are scanning a stationary object, such as a page of print, you alternate between **fixations,** *when your eyes are stationary,* and *quick eye movements called* **saccades** (sa-KAHDS) *that take your eyes from one fixation point to another.*

You read during your fixations but you are virtually blind during the saccades. To illustrate this point, try the following demonstration: Look at yourself in the mirror and focus on your left eye. Then move your focus to the right eye. Can you see your eyes moving in the mirror? (Go ahead; try it.) People generally agree that they do not see their eyes move.

"Oh, but wait," you say. "That movement in the mirror was simply too quick and too small to be seen." Wrong. Try again, but this time get someone else to look at your left eye and then shift his or her gaze to your right eye. Now you do see the other person's eye movement, so the movement itself is not too fast or too small to be seen. Go back and try your own eyes in the mirror again and observe the difference. You can see someone else's eyes moving, but you cannot see your own eyes moving in the mirror.

There are two explanations: First, certain areas in the parietal cortex monitor impending eye movements and send a message to the primary visual cortex, in effect telling the visual cortex, "The eyes are about to move, so shut down activity for a moment." Even if you are in total darkness, the visual cortex decreases its activity during saccadic eye movements (Burr,

Morrone, & Ross, 1994; Paus, Marrett, Worsley, & Evans, 1995). Second, the stationary view at the end of a saccade interferes with the blurry view you saw during the saccade (Matin, Clymer, & Matin, 1972).

The consequence is that we see during fixations and not during saccades. An average adult reading a magazine article fixates on each point for about 200 to 250 milliseconds (ms). Good readers generally have briefer fixations than poor readers do, and everyone has briefer fixations on familiar words like *girl* than on harder words like *ghoul.* We also tend to pause a little longer on words with more than one meaning, like *bark* or *lie* (Rodd, Gaskell, & Marslen-Wilson, 2002). After each fixation, the next saccade lasts 25 to 50 ms. Thus, most readers have about four fixations per second (Rayner, 1998).

(In the attentional blink experiments discussed earlier, a letter that is flashed on the screen interferes with another letter that is flashed 200 ms later. So why doesn't one fixation interfere with another one when you are reading? The main explanation is that the flashes are very brief in the attentional blink experiments. The other explanation relates to the word-superiority effect: It is easier to read whole words in a meaningful context than to identify isolated letters.)

How much can a person read during one fixation? Many people believe they see quite a bit of the page at each instant. However, research indicates that we read only about 11 characters—one or two words—at a time. To demonstrate this limitation, focus on the letter *i* marked by an arrow (↓) in the two sentences below.

↓
1. This is a sentence with no misspelled words.
↓
2. Xboc tx zjg rxunce with no mijvgab zuen.

If you permit your eyes to wander back and forth, you quickly notice that sentence 2 is mostly gibberish. But as long as you dutifully keep your eyes on the fixation point, the sentence looks all right. You can read the letter on which you fixated plus about three or four characters (including spaces) to the left and about seven to the right; the rest is a blur. Therefore, you see —*ce with no m—*, or possibly —*nce with no mi—*.

This limit of about 11 letters depends partly on the lighting; in faint light your span decreases to as little as 1 or 2 letters, and your reading ability suffers accordingly (Legge, Ahn, Klitz, & Luebker, 1997). The limit does not depend on how much fits into the fovea of your eyes. In the following display, again focus on the letter *i* in each sentence and check how many letters you can read to its left and right:

This is a sentence with no misspelled words.

This is a sentence with no misspelled words.

↓

is a sentence with no misspelled

If your reading span were limited by how many letters can fit into the fovea of your retina, you should be able to read more letters in the top sentence and fewer as the letters get larger. In fact you do at least as well, maybe even better, with a larger print sentence (up to a point).

What we can see at a glance also depends on our habits of reading. In Japanese, where each character conveys more information than English letters do, readers see fewer letters per fixation (Rayner, 1998). And in Hebrew and Farsi, which are written right to left, readers read more letters to the left of fixation and fewer to the right (Brysbaert, Vitu, & Schroyens, 1996; Faust, Kravetz, & Babkoff, 1993; Malamed & Zaidel, 1993).

Often, our 11-character window of reading includes one word plus a fragment of another. For example, suppose you have fixated on the point shown by an arrow in the following sentence:

↓

The government made serious mistakes.

Readers can see the word *serious* plus about the first three letters of *mistakes*. Three letters do not identify the word; from what the reader knows, the next word could be *misspellings, misbehavior, missiles, mishmash,* or any of a number of other *mis*-things that a government might make.

Does the preview of the next word facilitate reading? Yes. In one study college students again read passages on a computer screen while a machine monitored their eye movements. The computer correctly displayed the word the student fixated on plus the next zero, three, or four letters. So the display might look like this:

or like this:

Students who could preview the first three or four letters of the next word read significantly faster than those who could not (Inhoff, 1989). Evidently, while we are reading one word, we are previewing the next. Our preview helps guide the next eye movement and gives us a head start on identifying the next word (Inhoff, Radach, Eiter, & Juhasz, 2003).

You might wonder what speed-readers do differently from normal readers. An average adult reader has about four or five fixations per second with occasional backtracks, for an overall rate of about 200 words per minute. Speed-readers have briefer fixations with fewer backtracks. With practice people can double or triple their reading speed with normal comprehension. Some claim that they see more than 11 characters per fixation, and unfortunately, researchers haven't done enough studies to test this possibility. However, unless they increase their span enormously, reading speed has some physical limits. Each saccadic eye movement lasts 25 to 50 ms, and reading does not occur during saccades. Thus, it would be impossible to exceed 20 to 40 fixations per second, even if each fixation lasted no time at all! If we make the generous estimate that people might be able to average 2 words per fixation, the theoretical maximum would be 20 to 80 words per second, or 1,200 to 4,800 words per minute. And remember, this calculation unrealistically assumes a fixation time of zero. Yet some people claim to read 5,000 to 10,000 words per minute. In fact they are fixating on some words and guessing the rest. A combination of reading and guessing can produce very fast reading and adequate comprehension of books with predictable content, like a James Bond novel. However, the speed-reader does miss details. When speed-readers read college textbooks, they either slow their reading (Just & Carpenter, 1987) or fail the tests (Homa, 1983).

CONCEPT CHECK ☑

17. Why can we sometimes read two or three short words at a time, whereas we need a saccade or two to read the same number of longer words?
18. If a word is longer than 11 letters, will a reader need more than one fixation to read it? (Check your answers on page 316.)

IN CLOSING

Language and Humanity

At the start of this module, we considered the question, "If language is so extremely useful to humans, why haven't other species evolved at least a little of it?" None of the research directly answers this question, but we can speculate. Certain adaptations are much more useful on a large scale than on a small scale. For example, skunks survive because they are very stinky; being just slightly stinky wouldn't help much. Porcupines survive because they have long, sharp quills; having a few short quills might be slightly helpful, but not very. Similarly, a little language might be slightly helpful (like a little stink or a few short quills), but better developed language is vastly more useful. A little bit of language development is probably an unstable condition, evolutionarily speaking. Once a species such as humans had evolved a little language, those individuals with still better language abilities would have a huge selective advantage over the others.

Summary

- *Language productivity.* Human languages enable us to create new words and phrases to express new ideas. (page 302)
- *Language training in nonhumans.* Bonobos, and to a lesser extent other chimpanzees, have learned certain aspects of language. Human evolution evidently elaborated on potentials found in our apelike ancestors but developed that potential further. (page 303)
- *Language and intelligence.* It is possible to have intelligence without language or language without other aspects of intelligence. Therefore, many psychologists regard language as a specialized capacity, not just a by-product of overall intelligence. (page 304)
- *Rapid language learning in children.* Children learn language at an amazing rate, considering the unsystematic training they receive. In some way children are born with a predisposition to learn language easily. (page 305)
- *Brain organization and aphasia.* Brain damage, especially in the left hemisphere, can impair people's ability to understand or use language. However, many brain areas contribute to language in varied ways. (page 306)
- *Stages of language development.* Children advance through several stages of language development, probably reflecting maturation of brain structures necessary for language and not just the total amount of experience. From the start children's language is creative, using the rules of language to make new word combinations and sentences. (page 307)
- *Children exposed to no language or two.* If deaf children are not exposed to language, they invent a sign language of their own. However, a deaf child who has no opportunity to use sign language in childhood will be impaired on learning it or any

other language later. Children in a bilingual environment sometimes have trouble keeping the two languages separate but gain the ability to converse with many people and in certain ways show extra cognitive flexibility. (page 308)
- *Understanding language.* Much of speech is ambiguous; we understand words and sentences in context by applying the knowledge we have about the world in general. (page 309)
- *Limits to our language understanding.* Many sentences are difficult to understand, especially those with embedded clauses or more than one negative. Difficult grammar places a burden on our working memory. (page 311)
- *Reading.* When we read, we have fixation periods separated by eye movements called saccades. We read during the fixations, not the saccades. Even good readers can read only about 11 letters per fixation; people increase their speed of reading by increasing the number of fixations per second. (page 312)

Answers to Concept Checks

13. Start language learning when a child is young. Rely on imitation as much as possible, instead of providing direct reinforcements for correct responses. (page 304)
14. Children begin to string words into novel combinations as soon as they begin to speak two words at a time. We believe that they learn rules of grammar because they overgeneralize those rules, creating such words as *womans* and *goed*. (page 308)
15. Deaf children who cannot learn spoken language and who have no opportunity to communicate with signs early in life are permanently disadvantaged in learning sign language. (page 309)
16. *Thoughtfully* has seven phonemes: th-ough-t-f-u-ll-y. (A phoneme is a unit of sound, not necessarily a letter of the alphabet.) It has three morphemes: thought-ful-ly. (Each morpheme has a distinct meaning.) (page 314)
17. Two or three short words can fall within the window of about 11 letters that we can fixate at one time. If the words are longer, it may be impossible to see them all at once. (page 315)
18. Sometimes but not always. Suppose your eyes fixate on the fourth letter of *memorization*. You should be able to see the three letters to its left and the seven to its right—in other words all except the final letter. Because there is only one English word that starts *memorizatio-*, you already know the word. (page 315)

Key Terms and Activities

Key Terms

algorithm: a mechanical, repetitive procedure for solving a problem (page 288)

attention: the tendency to respond to some stimuli more than others or to remember some more than others (p. 277)

attentional blink: a brief period after perceiving a stimulus, during which it is difficult to attend to another stimulus (page 283)

attentive process: a procedure that extracts information from one part of the visual field at a time (page 278)

availability heuristic: the strategy of assuming that how easily one can remember examples of some kind of event indicates how common the event actually is (page 294)

base-rate information: data about the frequency or probability of a given item (page 293)

bilingual: able to use two languages about equally well (page 309)

Broca's aphasia: a condition characterized by inarticulate speech and by difficulties with both using and understanding grammatical devices—prepositions, conjunctions, word endings, complex sentence structures, and so forth (page 306)

change blindness: the tendency to fail to detect changes in any part of a scene to which we are not focusing our attention (page 281)

cognition: the processes of thinking, gaining knowledge, and dealing with knowledge (page 273)

confirmation bias: the tendency to accept one hypothesis and then look for evidence to support it, instead of considering other possibilities (page 296)

critical thinking: the careful evaluation of evidence for and against any conclusion (page 295)

fixation: a period when the eyes are steady (page 314)

framing effect: the tendency to answer a question differently when it is framed (phrased) differently (page 298)

functional fixedness: the tendency to adhere to a single approach to a problem or a single way of using an item (page 297)

heuristics: strategies for simplifying a problem or for guiding an investigation (page 288)

language acquisition device: a built-in mechanism for acquiring language (page 305)

morpheme: a unit of meaning (page 313)

overconfidence: the belief that one's opinions or predictions are highly correct when in fact they are not (page 295)

phoneme: a unit of sound (page 313)

preattentive process: a procedure for extracting information automatically and simultaneously across a large portion of the visual field (page 278)

productivity: the ability to express new ideas (page 302)

prototype: a familiar or typical example of a category (page 274)

representativeness heuristic: the tendency to assume that, if an item is similar to members of a particular category, it is probably a member of that category itself (page 293)

saccade: a quick jump in the focus of the eyes from one point to another (page 314)

spreading activation: the process by which the activation of one concept also activates or primes other concepts that are linked to it (page 276)

Stroop effect: the tendency to read a word, especially if it is a color name, in spite of instructions to disregard the word and state the color of the ink in which it is printed (page 279)

sunk cost effect: the willingness to do something we wouldn't otherwise choose to do because of money or effort already spent (page 299)

transformational grammar: a system for converting a deep structure of a language into a surface structure (page 302)

Wernicke's aphasia: a condition marked by difficulty recalling the names of objects and impaired comprehension of language (page 306)

Williams syndrome: a genetic condition characterized by mental retardation in most regards but skillful use of language (page 305)

word-superiority effect: identifying a letter with greater ease when it is part of a whole word than when it is presented by itself (page 312)

Suggestion for Further Reading

Pinker, S. (1999). *Words and rules: The ingredients of language.* New York: Basic Books. A discussion of language by a writer with a keen eye for excellent examples.

Book Companion Web Site

Need help studying? Go to

http://psychology.wadsworth.com/kalat_intro7e/

for a virtual study center. You'll find a personalized Self-Study Assessment that will provide you with a study plan based on your answers to a pretest. Also study using flashcards, quizzes, interactive art, and an online glossary.

Check out interactive **Try it Yourself** exercises on the companion site! For example, the Work-Superiority Effect and Overconfidence exercises relate to what you've learned in this chapter.

Your companion site also has direct links to the following Web sites. These links are checked often for changes, dead links, and new additions.

Preattentive Processes

www.csc.ncsu.edu/faculty/healey/PP/Interfere.html

A description of preattentive processes with interesting demonstrations.

Human Language

http://www.ilovelanguages.com

This site has links to many sources of information about languages.

# Try It Yourself CD-ROM
with Critical Thinking Video Exercises

Use your CD to access **videos** related to activities designed to help you think critically about the important topics discussed. You'll also find an easy portal link to the book companion site where you can access your personalized **Self-Study Assessments** and interactive **Try It Yourself** exercises.

PsychNow! 2.0

PsychNow! is a fun interactive CD designed to help you with the difficult concepts in psychology. Check out the Learning & Cognition section for the following topics that relate to this chapter:

Cognition and Language: framing pretest, interactive risk/outcome scenarios, apply solution to the pretest.

Problem Solving nd Creativity: pretests, creativity and problem solving lesson, and an animated solution to the pretest.

ExperimentNOW! Concepts: Lexical decisions and prototypes

© Joel Gordon

Human Development

Suppose you buy a robot. When you get home, you discover that it does nothing useful. It cannot even maintain its balance. It makes irritating, high-pitched noises, moves its limbs haphazardly, and leaks. The store you bought it from refuses to take it back. And for some reason you cannot turn it off. So you are stuck with this useless machine.

A few years later, your robot can walk and talk, read and write, draw pictures, and do arithmetic. It follows your directions (usually) and sometimes even finds useful things to do without being told. It often beats you at checkers and almost always at memory games.

How did all this happen? After all, you knew nothing about how to program a robot. Did your robot have some sort of built-in programming that simply took a long time to phase in? Or was it programmed to learn all these skills?

Children are a great deal like that robot. Nearly every parent wonders, "How did my children get to be the way they are?" The goal of developmental psychology is to understand everything that influences human behavior "from womb to tomb."

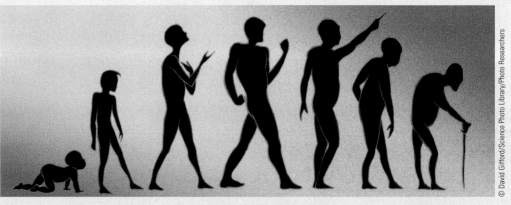

▌ As we grow older, we change in many ways—we gain in some ways and lose in others. Developmental psychologists seek to understand the changes in our behavior and the reasons behind these changes.

Getting Started: From Genetics Through Infancy

How do genes influence behavior?

How can we infer the sensation, memory, and other capacities of an infant?

Identical, or monozygotic (one egg), twins *develop from a single fertilized egg and therefore have identical genetics.* **Fraternal, or dizygotic (two eggs), twins** *develop from two eggs and share only half their genes, like brother and sister* (Figure 10.1). Many studies of nature and nurture focus on comparing the two kinds of twins, especially if the twins grew up in separate environments. When twins are put up for adoption today, adoption agencies place them both in one family, but many years ago it was common for twins to be adopted separately. One pair of identical twins who were separated at birth and reared in different western Ohio cities were reunited in adulthood (Figure 10.2). They quickly discovered that they had much in common:

Both had been named Jim by their adoptive parents. Each liked carpentry and drafting, had built a bench around a tree in his yard, and worked as a deputy sheriff. Both chewed their fingernails, gained weight at the same age, smoked the same brand of cigarettes, drove Chevrolets, and took their vacations in western Florida. Each married a woman named Linda, divorced her, and married a woman named Betty. One had a son named James Alan and the other a son named James Allen; both had a pet dog named Toy.

Undoubtedly, some of these similarities are mere coincidences. Lots of people drive Chevrolets, for example, and many people from western Ohio vacation in western Florida. It's hard to believe that they had genes causing them to marry a Linda and divorce her to marry a Betty. (If they lived in some other country, they would have had trouble finding either a Linda or a Betty. And did these women have genes that attracted them to men named Jim?)

All right, but let's consider other identical twins separated at birth. One pair of women each wore rings on seven fingers. A pair of men discovered that they used the same brands of toothpaste, shaving lotion, hair tonic, and cigarettes. When they sent each other a birthday present, their presents crossed in the mail and each discovered that he had received the same present he had sent. Another pair reported that whenever they went to the beach, they waded into the water backward and only up to their knees (Lykken, McGue, Tellegen, & Bouchard, 1992).

Researchers have examined up to 100 pairs of twins, some identical and

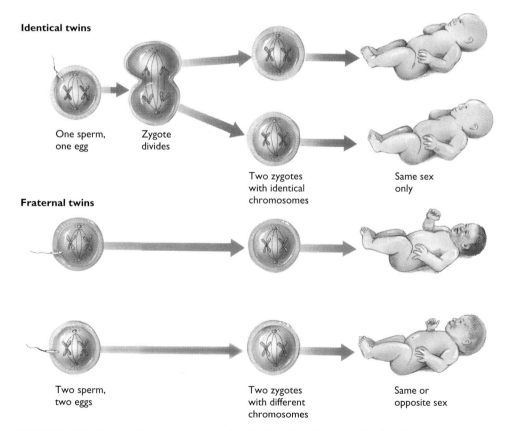

Identical twins

One sperm, one egg → Zygote divides → Two zygotes with identical chromosomes → Same sex only

Fraternal twins

Two sperm, two eggs → Two zygotes with different chromosomes → Same or opposite sex

FIGURE 10.1 Identical (monozygotic) twins develop from the same fertilized egg. Fraternal (dizygotic) twins grow from two eggs fertilized by different sperm.

353

FIGURE 10.2 Identical twins Jim Lewis and Jim Springer were separated at birth, reared in separate cities of western Ohio, and reunited in adulthood.

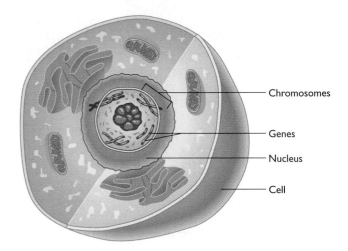

FIGURE 10.3 Genes are sections of chromosomes in the nuclei of cells. (Scale is exaggerated for illustration purposes.)

Except for your red blood cells, all of your cells contain a nucleus, which includes *strands of hereditary material* called **chromosomes** (Figure 10.3). Chromosomes provide the chemical basis of heredity. Humans have 23 pairs of chromosomes, except in egg or sperm cells, which have 23 unpaired chromosomes. At fertilization the 23 chromosomes from an egg cell combine with the 23 of a sperm to form 23 pairs for the new person (Figure 10.4).

Sections along each chromosome are known as **genes,** *which control the chemical reactions that direct development*—for example, determining proba-

others fraternal, who were reared in separate homes and then reunited as adults. The identical twins resembled each other more than did the fraternal pairs with regard to hobbies, vocational interests, consumption of coffee and fruit juices, preference for awakening early in the morning or staying up late at night, answers on personality tests, and political beliefs (DiLalla, Carey, Gottesman, & Bouchard, 1996; Hur, Bouchard, & Eckert, 1998; Hur, Bouchard, & Lykken, 1998; Lykken, Bouchard, McGue, & Tellegen, 1993; McCourt, Bouchard, Lykken, Tellegen, & Keyes, 1999). Evidently, genetic factors influence a wide range of behaviors.

But *how* do genes influence behavior? We discussed some of the issues and controversies in the last chapter with regard to intelligence. The same issues arise in almost any discussion of developmental psychology. You developed your personality, your social behavior, and all your other characteristics through a complex combination of heredity and environmental influences. But the role of heredity varies from one behavior to another. Let's first take a quick survey of genes and what they do. Then we shall explore the application of genetics to human behavior.

Genetic Principles

If you have already studied genetics in a biology class, much of this discussion will be a review. Skim what you already know and concentrate on unfamiliar material.

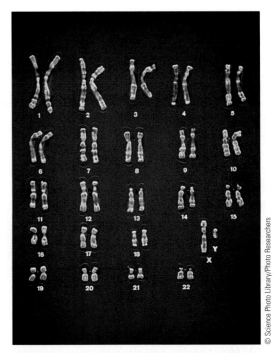

FIGURE 10.4 The nucleus of each human cell contains 46 chromosomes, 23 from the sperm and 23 from the ovum, united in pairs.

ble height or hair color. They can influence behavior by changes in the brain or sense organs or indirectly by changes in other body parts.

Genes are composed of the chemical DNA, which controls the production of other chemicals called RNA, which among other functions control the production of proteins. The proteins either become part of the body's structure or control the rates of chemical reactions in the body.

Because chromosomes come in pairs (one from the mother and one from the father), you have two of almost all genes. (The exception: Men have one X chromosome and one Y chromosome and therefore have unpaired genes on their X and Y chromosomes.) To explain the concept of genes, educators often use an example such as eye color. If you have either one or two genes for brown eyes, you will have brown eyes because the brown-eye gene is dominant. The gene for blue eyes is recessive, so you can have blue eyes only if you have two genes for blue eyes. A behavioral example is the ability to curl your tongue lengthwise (Figure 10.5). If you have this dominant gene, you can curl your tongue, and if you don't have it, you can't. (You will be seldom inconvenienced.)

FIGURE 10.5 A single gene determines whether you can curl your tongue.

© ZEFA/The Stock Market

However, examples like this are misleading. First, they imply that each gene has only one effect, whereas most genes have many. Second, they imply that a gene completely controls something so that there is nothing you could do about it. Most genes' effects vary with your age, diet, health, and other factors. Many genes increase or decrease the probability of some behavior, but the outcome depends on other influences also.

CONCEPT CHECK ☑

1. If two parents cannot curl their tongues, what can you predict about their children? (Check your answer on page 363.)

Sex-Linked and Sex-Limited Genes

One pair of chromosomes is known as **sex chromosomes** because they *determine whether an individual develops as a male or as a female.* Mammals' sex chromosomes are known as X and Y (Figure 10.6). *A female has two X chromosomes in each cell; a male has one X chromosome and one Y chromosome.* The mother contributes an X chromosome to each child, and the father contributes either an X or a Y.

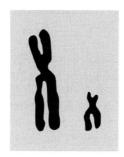

FIGURE 10.6 An electron micrograph of X and Y chromosomes shows the difference in length. *(From Ruch, 1984)*

Genes located on the X chromosome are known as X-linked or **sex-linked genes**. A sex-linked recessive gene shows its effects more often in men than in women. For example, the most common type of color vision deficiency depends on a sex-linked recessive gene. A man with that gene on his X chromosome will be colorblind because he has no other X chromosome. A woman with that gene probably has a gene for normal color vision on her other X chromosome. Conse-

a
© Gordon & Cathy Illg/Animals, Animals

b
© Tom & Pat Leeson/Photo Researchers

c
© Maslowski Wildlife Productions

▮ Albinos occur in many species, always because of a recessive gene. (a) Striped skunk. (b) American alligator. (c) Mockingbird.

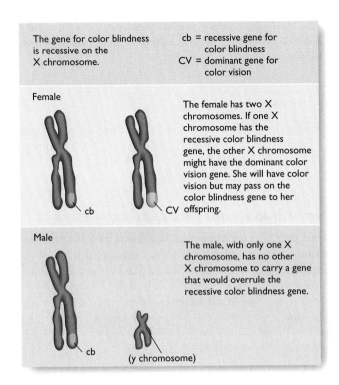

The gene for color blindness is recessive on the X chromosome.

cb = recessive gene for color blindness

CV = dominant gene for color vision

Female

The female has two X chromosomes. If one X chromosome has the recessive color blindness gene, the other X chromosome might have the dominant color vision gene. She will have color vision but may pass on the color blindness gene to her offspring.

cb   CV

Male

The male, with only one X chromosome, has no other X chromosome to carry a gene that would overrule the recessive color blindness gene.

cb   (y chromosome)

FIGURE 10.7 Why males are more likely than females to be colorblind.

quently, far more men than women have color vision deficiency (Figure 10.7).

A **sex-limited** gene *occurs equally in both sexes but exerts its effects in one but not the other* (or only slightly in the other). For example, both men and women have the genes for facial hair, but men's hormones activate those genes. Similarly, both men and women have the genes for breast development, but women's hormones activate those genes.

CONCEPT CHECK ✓

2. Suppose a father has color vision deficiency and a mother has two genes for normal color vision. What sort of color vision will their children have? (Check your answer on page 363.)

Identifying and Localizing Genes

Modern technology has enabled researchers to identify genes that increase the risk of Alzheimer's disease and other diseases. Some genes increase the risk only slightly, and others more substantially. You could (for a price) have someone examine your chromosomes and tell you which diseases you are likely to get, how likely you are to get them, and in some cases how soon you will get them (Gusella & MacDonald, 2000).

As research progresses, the possibilities for prediction will grow even stronger.

Would you want to know this information? Your answer probably depends on what you could do with it. For example, learning that you were predisposed to alcoholism might lead you to take precautions, such as not joining a fraternity or sorority with a reputation for heavy drinking. On the other hand, learning that you were likely to develop Alzheimer's disease in old age might be useless information, unless researchers found some way to prevent the disease. The following Web site documents research on the identification of human genes:

www.ornl.gov/TechResources/
Human_Genome/home.html

Estimating Heritability in Humans

You might hear someone ask whether some behavior depends on heredity or environment. That question is meaningless as it is phrased. (Take away either your heredity or your environment and there is no "you" left!) However, a change in wording makes the question meaningful: Does a given *difference* in behavior (e.g., the difference between an alcoholic and a non-alcoholic) depend more on *differences* in heredity or *differences* in environment? That is, if we want to predict who will become alcoholics, how well could we succeed if we knew their heredity, and how well if we knew their environment?

The answer to a question like this is summarized by the term **heritability,** *an estimate of the variance within a population that is due to heredity.* Heritability ranges from 1, indicating that heredity controls all the variance, to 0, indicating that it controls none of it. For example, tongue curling has a heritability of almost 1.

For an example of a condition with virtually 0 heritability, consider which language someone speaks. If you want to predict whether a child will speak English, Greek, or Bengali, you should ask which language the child's parents and community speak. Examining the child's genes will not help.

To estimate the heritability of a behavior, researchers rely on the following types of evidence (Segal, 1993):

• Do identical twins resemble each other more closely than fraternal twins do? Identical twins have the same genes; fraternal twins resemble each other genetically only as much as a brother and sister do. If fraternal twins resemble each other as much as identical twins do, then heritability is low.

If identical twins resemble each other more than fraternal twins do, a genetic influence is likely but not certain. Most identical twins share a single amniote before birth, whereas fraternal twins have separate amniotes (Figure 10.8). Therefore, identical twins have more similarities in prenatal (before-birth) influences, and what appears to be evidence for a genetic influence might also reflect similar prenatal environments (Phelps, Davis, & Schartz, 1997). Also, because of their nearly identical appearance, identical twins tend to be treated more alike after birth.

- Do twins who are adopted by separate families and reared apart resemble each other more closely than we would expect by chance? If so, again genetic similarity is a likely explanation.
- To what extent do adopted children resemble their adoptive and biological parents? Any resemblance of adopted children to their biological parents probably reflects a genetic influence, although again we should consider prenatal influences.

A low correlation with the adoptive parents can also be misleading. Recall from Chapter 2 that two variables are highly correlated if we can use measurements of one to predict the other accurately. Imagine trying to predict which adopted children will become alcoholics by examining the alcohol habits of their adoptive parents. You can't make much of a prediction because adoption agencies almost never let alcoholics adopt children. The low correlation between adopted child and adoptive parent doesn't tell us the possible effect of a severely alcoholic family (Stoolmiller, 1999).

The point is that accurately measuring heritability is difficult. Better evidence will emerge from new biochemical methods of determining which identified genes are associated with one behavior or another.

CONCEPT CHECK

3. If our society changed so that an equally good environment was provided for all children, would the heritability of behaviors increase or decrease? (Check your answer on page 363.)

How Genes Influence Behavior

Based on studies of twins and adopted children, researchers have found at least moderate heritability for almost every behavior they have examined. For example, adopted children resemble their birth parents with regard to how much time they spend watching television (Plomin, Corley, DeFries, & Fulker, 1990). Monozygotic twins reared apart resemble each other in their religious devoutness (Waller, Kojetin, Bouchard, Lykken, & Tellegen, 1990). (Their religious affiliation, however, depends on the adoptive family. There is no gene for Presbyterian.) The evidence also indicates moderate heritability for loneliness (McGuire & Clifford, 2000), neuroticism (Lake, Eaves, Maes, Heath, & Martin, 2000), and a host of other variables. How could genes affect such complicated characteristics?

Direct and Indirect Influences

Genes control maturation of brain structures, production of neurotransmitters, and production of neurotransmitter receptors. However, genes can also influence behaviors indirectly. For example, imagine a gene that makes you tall. If you live where people play basketball, you are more likely than shorter people to spend much of your time playing basketball and, therefore less time playing chess, writing poetry, and so forth.

Or imagine genes that cause you to be especially good-looking. Many people will smile at you, invite you to parties, and try to become your friend. You

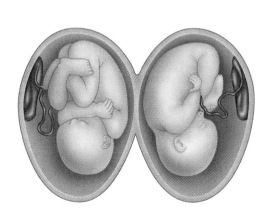 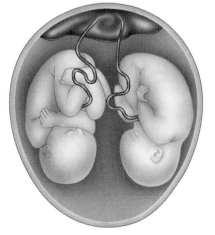

FIGURE 10.8 (a) Fraternal twins develop with separate amniotes and therefore separate blood supplies. (b) Most monozygotic (identical) twins develop with a single amniote and therefore the same blood supply, the same hormone levels, and so forth.

may develop increased self-confidence and a number of other subtle changes in personality. The genes changed your behavior by changing the way your environment treated you.

Also consider dietary choices: Almost all infants can digest *lactose,* the sugar in milk. As they grow older, most Asian children and many non-Asian children lose the ability to digest it. (They lose that ability even if they drink milk frequently. The loss depends on genes.) They can still enjoy a little milk, and more readily enjoy cheese, yogurt, and other easy-to-digest dairy products, but they get gas and cramps from consuming too much milk or ice cream (Flatz, 1987; Rozin & Pelchat, 1988). Figure 10.9 shows how the ability to digest dairy products varies from one part of the world to another. The point is that a gene can affect behavior—in this case consumption of dairy products—by altering chemical reactions outside the brain itself.

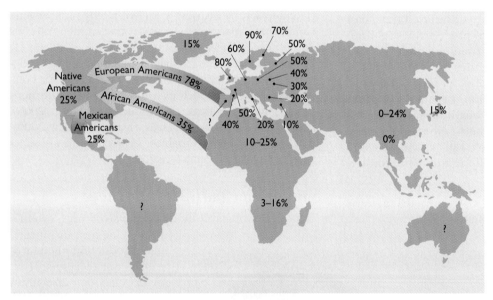

FIGURE 10.9 Adult humans vary in their ability to digest lactose, the main sugar in milk. The numbers refer to the percentage of each population's adults that can easily digest lactose. In Asian countries and other locations where most adults cannot digest lactose, cooks seldom use dairy products. *(Based on Flatz, 1987; Rozin & Pelchat, 1988)*

Phenylketonuria: Modifying Genetic Effects Through Diet

Some people assume that if something is under genetic control, we can't do anything about it. Nonsense. For example, you might have genes for straight black hair, but you could curl it, dye it blonde, or shave it off.

Here is a stronger example: **Phenylketonuria (PKU)** is *an inherited condition that, if untreated, leads to mental retardation.* About 2% of people with European or Asian ancestry, and virtually no one of African ancestry, has one copy of the recessive gene

that leads to PKU, but one copy produces no apparent harm. People who have two copies, one on each chromosome, cannot metabolize *phenylalanine,* a common constituent of proteins. On an ordinary diet, an affected child accumulates phenylalanine in the brain and becomes mentally retarded; however, following a diet low in phenylalanine protects the brain. Thus, a controlled diet prevents a disorder that is "under genetic control." One hope is that research on genetics may help us control undesirable genetic effects.

The Fetus and the Newborn

Genes control development of the body, which in turn provides for behavior. A course in psychology emphasizes behavior. However, because this chapter covers development over the life span, let's focus briefly on early physical development.

During prenatal development, everyone starts as a *fertilized egg cell,* or zygote, which develops through its first few stages until it is identified as a fetus *about 8 weeks after conception.* Even as soon as 6 weeks after conception, the brain is mature enough to produce the first few movements. By the 36th week, the brain can turn the head and eyes in response to sounds and proceeds through recognizable stages of waking, sleeping, and REM sleep (Joseph, 2000). None of this behavior requires the cerebral cortex, which matures more slowly than other brain areas.

The growing body receives nutrition from the mother. If she eats little, the baby receives little nourishment. If she takes drugs, the baby gets them too. Undernourished mothers generally give birth to small babies (Figure 10.10), and investigators have long known that newborns weighing less than about 1,750–2,000 grams (4 pounds) are at high risk of dying in infancy (Kopp, 1990). Those that survive have an increased risk of conduct problems and poor academic performance (H. G. Taylor, Klein, Minich, & Hack, 2000). These facts are beyond dispute, but their meaning is less certain.

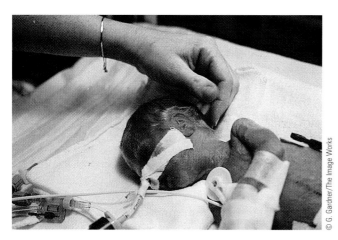

FIGURE 10.10 Low-birthweight babies are susceptible to many physical and behavioral difficulties later in life; however, we cannot be sure that low birthweight causes the problems. Many of these babies are born to mothers who are poorly nourished, who take illegal drugs, or who fail to obtain good nutrition and care.

The apparently obvious interpretation is that low birthweight leads to impaired brain development and thus to later academic and behavior problems. However, many low-birthweight babies are born with low birthweights because their mothers were poorly nourished, unhealthy, victims of family violence, possibly smoking or drinking during pregnancy, and not receiving medical care (Garcia Coll, 1990; McCormick, 1985). In short, many low-birthweight babies have other problems as well (Brooks-Gunn & Furstenberg, 1989; Zeanah, Boris, & Larrieu, 1997).

One way to study the effect of low birthweight separately from other problems is to examine pairs of twins where one twin was born much heavier than the other. In most cases the low birthweight infant develops about as well as the heavier twin (R. S. Wilson, 1987). In short, low birthweight *by itself* is not necessarily a serious problem; it correlates with developmental difficulties partly because many low-birthweight babies have other disadvantages.

A more severe risk arises if the fetus is exposed to alcohol or other substances. *If the mother drinks alcohol during pregnancy,* the infant may develop signs of **fetal alcohol syndrome,** *a condition marked by stunted growth of the head and body; malformations of the face, heart, and ears; and nervous system damage, including seizures, hyperactivity, learning disabilities, and mental retardation* (Streissguth, Sampson, & Barr, 1989). In milder cases children appear normal but have moderate deficits in language, memory, and coordination (Mattson, Riley, Grambling, Delis, & Jones, 1998). The more alcohol the mother drinks during pregnancy, the greater the risk to the fetus (see Figure 10.11).

The reason for the nervous system damage is now understood: Developing neurons require persistent excitation to survive. Without it, they activate a self-destruct program. Alcohol facilitates the main inhibitory neurotransmitter of the brain (known as GABA) and interferes with the main excitatory neurotransmitter (glutamate). It therefore decreases neurons' arousal and leads them to self-destruct (Ikonomidou et al., 2000). An implication is that pregnant women should minimize the use of tranquilizers and anesthetics because they also inhibit neuronal activity.

Women who smoke during pregnancy have an increased probability that their babies will have health problems early in life. They also run an increased risk that their children, especially sons, eventually will develop *conduct disorder,* a condition marked by discipline problems both at school and at home and potentially even criminal behavior in adulthood. Conduct disorder has been found to correlate more strongly with the mother's smoking during pregnancy than with the father's antisocial behavior, the family's

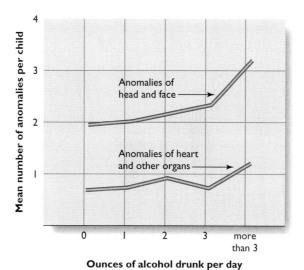

FIGURE 10.11 (a) The more alcohol a woman drinks during pregnancy, the more likely her baby is to have anomalies of the head, face, and organs. *(Based on data of Ernhart et al., 1987)* (b) A child with fetal alcohol syndrome: Note the wide separation between the eyes, a common feature of this syndrome.

economic status, lack of child supervision, or excessive punishment (Wakschlag et al., 1997). To be safe, pregnant women should avoid alcohol and tobacco and should get a physician's advice before taking any medications.

Still, it is remarkable that an occasional "high-risk" child—small at birth, perhaps exposed to alcohol or other drugs before birth, perhaps from an impoverished or turbulent family—overcomes all odds and becomes a healthy, productive, outstanding person. Resilience (the ability to overcome obstacles) is poorly understood and difficult to study (Luthar, Cicchetti, & Becker, 2000). However, the more positive influences one has in life, the easier it is to overcome negative ones. That is, most people who overcome disadvantages have some special source of strength such as a close relationship with one or more supporting people, an effective school, a strong faith, some special skill, or just a naturally easygoing disposition (Masten & Coatsworth, 1998).

CONCEPT CHECK ☑

4. Why should a pregnant woman avoid taking large amounts of tranquilizers? (Check your answer on page 363.)

Behavioral Capacities of the Newborn

Even at birth, each infant differs from others in many ways. For example, some are calm whereas others are easily aroused. The differences relate to genetics and prenatal environment. From birth onward infants begin interacting with a much wider environment and trying to make sense of it.

Studying the infant's early attempts to understand the world is both fascinating and frustrating. A newborn is like a computer that is not attached to a monitor or printer: No matter how much information it processes, it cannot tell us about it. The challenge of studying the newborn is to figure out how to attach some sort of "monitor" to find out what is going on inside.

Newborns have little control of their muscles. At first they cannot keep their head from flopping over, and their arms and legs flail about aimlessly. They gradually gain muscle control

through a combination of maturation and practice. For example, babies who are too young to support their own weight flail their arms and legs in varied and haphazard ways; as soon as they can support their weight, they quickly abandon most of their varied movement patterns and settle on the standard patterns and rhythms of human crawling (Freedland & Bertenthal, 1994).

About the only useful movements that newborns can make are eye and mouth movements, especially sucking. As the months pass, and as their control spreads from the head muscles downward, they make progressively finer movements, eventually including single finger movements.

If we want to test infants' sensory and learning abilities, we must test the responses that they can control, such as eye or head movements. If we try to train them to reach out and grab something, we will certainly underestimate their capacities.

Newborns' Vision

William James, the founder of American psychology, once said that as far as an infant can tell, the world is a "buzzing confusion," full of meaningless sights and sounds. Since James's time, psychologists have substantially increased their estimates of infants' vision.

One research method is to record the infant's eye movements. In general, infants direct their eyes toward the same kinds of objects that attract adults' attention. For example, even 2-day-old infants spend more time looking at drawings of human faces than at other patterns with similar areas of light and dark (Fantz, 1963) (see Figure 10.12).

By the age of 5 months or so, infants have had extensive visual experience but almost no experi-

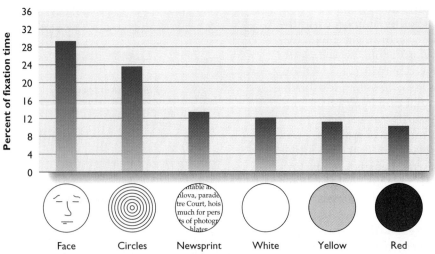

FIGURE 10.12 Infants pay more attention to faces than to other patterns. These results suggest that infants are born with certain visual preferences. *(Based on Fantz, 1963)*

ence at crawling or reaching for objects. Over the next several months, they increase their control of arm and leg movements. They learn to reach out to pick up toys, crawl around objects, avoid crawling off ledges, and in other ways coordinate what they see with what they do. Apparently, they need experience of controlling their own movements before they show a fear of heights. Infants usually take a tumble or two before they develop a fear of heights (Adolph, 2000). Those who crawl early develop a fear of heights early; those who are late to crawl are also late to develop a fear of heights (Campos, Bertenthal, & Kermoian, 1992).

Newborns' Hearing

It might seem difficult to measure newborns' responses to sounds because we cannot observe anything like eye movements. However, infants suck more vigorously when they are aroused, and certain sounds arouse them more than others do.

In one study the experimenters played a brief sound and noted how it affected an infant's sucking rate (Figure 10.13). On the first few occasions, the sound increased the sucking rate. A repeated sound produced less and less effect. We say that the infant became *habituated* to the sound. **Habituation** is *decreased response to a repeated stimulus*. When the experimenters substituted a new sound, the sucking rate increased. Evidently, the infant was aroused by the unfamiliar sound. *When a change in a stimulus produces an increase in a previously habituated response,* we say that the stimulus produced **dishabituation**.

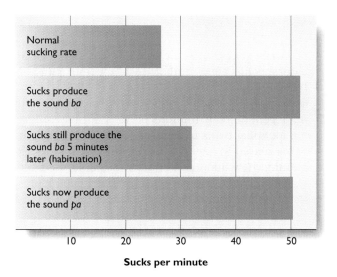

FIGURE 10.13 After repeatedly hearing a *ba* sound, the infant's sucking habituates. When a new sound, *pa*, follows, the sucking rate increases, an indication that infants hear a difference between the sounds. *(Based on results of Eimas, Siqueland, Jusczyk, & Vigorito, 1971)*

Psychologists use this technique to determine whether infants hear a difference between two sounds. For example, infants who have become habituated to the sound *ba* will increase their sucking rate when they hear the sound *pa* (Eimas, Siqueland, Jusczyk, & Vigorito, 1971). Apparently, even month-old infants can tell the difference between *ba* and *pa,* an important distinction for later language comprehension.

Similar studies have shown that infants who have habituated to hearing one language, such as Dutch, dishabituate when they hear a different language, such as Japanese. At first they show no response to a shift between Dutch and English, presumably because the sounds and rhythms are fairly similar. By age 5 months, however, they dishabituate when they hear a change from a British accent to an American accent (Jusczyk, 2002). Studies of this sort show that children can discriminate relevant language sounds long before they know what any of the words mean.

CONCEPT CHECK ☑

5. Suppose an infant habituates to the sound *ba,* and when we substitute the sound *bla,* the infant fails to increase its sucking rate. What interpretation would be likely? (Check your answer on page 363.)

Infants' Learning and Memory

Infants certainly cannot describe their memories to us. But if they respond differently to a stimulus because of previous experience with it, we can infer a memory.

Several studies have begun with the observation that infants learn to suck harder on a nipple if their sucking turns on a sound. Investigators then tried to determine whether infants work to turn on certain sounds more than others. In one study 26 babies younger than 3 days old could turn on a tape recording of their mother's voice by sucking on a nipple at certain times or at certain rates. By sucking at different times or at different rates, they could turn on a tape recording of another woman's voice. When their sucking produced their own mother's voice, they sucked more frequently (DeCasper & Fifer, 1980). They did not suck much to produce a different voice. Apparently, even very young infants recognized their own mother's voice and preferred it to an unfamiliar voice. Because they showed this preference so early—in some cases on the day of birth—developmental psychologists believe that the infants display a memory of what they heard before birth.

CONCEPT CHECK ☑

6. Suppose a newborn sucks to turn on a tape recording of its father's voice. Eventually, the baby habituates and the sucking frequency decreases. Now the experimenters substitute the recording of a different man's voice. What would you conclude if the sucking frequency increased? What if it remained the same? What if it decreased? (Check your answers on page 363.)

Using somewhat older infants, Carolyn Rovee-Collier (1997, 1999) demonstrated an ability to learn a response and remember it for days. In one series of studies, she attached a ribbon to an ankle so that an infant could activate a mobile by kicking with one leg (Figure 10.14). Two-month-old infants quickly learned this response and generally kept the mobile going nonstop for a full 45-minute session. (Earlier, I said infants cannot control their leg muscles, but they didn't need much control to keep the mobile going.) Once they have learned, they quickly remember what to do when the ribbon is reattached several days later—to the infants' evident delight. Six-month-old infants remembered the response for 2 weeks. Even after forgetting it, they could relearn it in 2 minutes and then retain it for an additional month or more (Hildreth, Sweeney, & Rovee-Collier, 2003).

In another series of studies, Rovee-Collier and her colleagues found that 9-month-olds can learn to press a lever to make a toy train go around a track. In both the mobile studies and the train studies, older infants remembered the response longer than younger ones (Hartshorn et al., 1998).

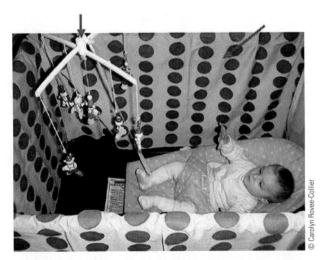

FIGURE 10.14 Two-month-old infants rapidly learn to kick to activate a mobile attached to their ankles with a ribbon. They remember how to activate the mobile when tested days later. *(From Hildreth, Sweeney, & Rovee-Collier, 2003)*

IN CLOSING

Getting Started in Life

Physicists say that the way the universe developed depended on its "initial conditions"—the array of matter and energy a fraction of a second after the start of the "big bang." The outcome of any experiment in physics or chemistry depends on the initial conditions—the type of matter, its temperature and pressure, and so forth. You had initial conditions too—your genetics and prenatal environment. Understanding those initial conditions is critical to understanding your special characteristics. However, you also have "conditions added later." At any point in your life, your behavior depends on a complex combination of your predispositions, the effects of past experiences, and all aspects of the current environment.

Research on infants' sucking, kicking, and other simple responses has enabled psychologists to infer the thoughts and perceptions of infants too young to talk. As research methods have advanced, the trend has been a steady increase in our estimation of infants' capacities. Are we now at risk of jumping from underestimates of infants' abilities to overestimates? You can see the fascination of this research topic.

Summary

- *Genes.* Genes, which are segments of chromosomes, control heredity. (page 354)
- *Sex-linked and sex-limited genes.* Genes on the X chromosome are sex linked. A sex-linked recessive gene will show its effects more frequently in males than in females. A sex-limited gene is present in both sexes, but it affects one more than the other. (page 355)
- *Locating genes.* In some cases researchers can locate specific genes linked to a specific outcome. (page 356)
- *Evidence for genetic influences.* Researchers estimate genetic contributions to behavior by comparing identical twins to fraternal twins, by comparing twins reared in separate environments, and by examining how adopted children resemble their biological and adoptive parents. However, each kind of research has limitations. (page 356)
- *How genes affect behavior.* Genes can affect behaviors indirectly, by influencing some aspect of the body that in turn influences behavior. (page 357)
- *Influence of the environment on gene expression.* It is possible to control a genetically influenced condition by changing the environment. One example is the use of a low-phenylalanine diet to prevent the mental retardation associated with phenylketonuria. (page 358)

- *Prenatal development.* Although the cerebral cortex is slow to mature, the rest of the brain begins to produce movements long before birth. Exposure to drugs such as alcohol decreases brain activity and releases neurons' self-destruct programs. (page 358)
- *Inferring infant capacities.* We easily underestimate newborns' capacities because they have so little control over their muscles. With careful testing procedures, we can demonstrate that newborns can see, hear, and remember more than we might have supposed. (page 360)
- *Infant vision and hearing.* Newborns stare at some visual patterns longer than others. Newborns habituate to a repeated sound but dishabituate to a slightly different sound, indicating that they hear a difference. (page 360)
- *Infant memory.* Newborns increase or alter their rate of sucking if a particular pattern of sucking turns on a recorded voice. They suck more vigorously to turn on a recording of their own mother's voice than some other woman's voice, indicating a memory of the sound of the mother's voice. Infants just 2 months old can learn to kick to move a mobile and remember how to do it several days later. (page 361)

Answers to Concept Checks

1. Both parents must lack the dominant gene that controls the ability to curl their tongues. Therefore, they can transmit only "noncurler" genes, and their children will be noncurlers also. (page 355)

2. The woman will pass a gene for normal color vision to all her children, so they will all have normal color vision. The man will pass a gene for deficient color vision on his X chromosome, so his daughters will be carriers for color deficiency. (page 356)

3. If all children had equally supportive environments, the heritability of behaviors would *increase.* Remember, heritability refers to how much of the difference among people is due to hereditary variation. If the environment is practically the same for all, then environmental variation cannot account for much of the variation in behavior. Whatever behavioral variation still occurs would be due mostly to hereditary variation. (Note one implication: Any estimate of heritability applies only to a given population. In another population the heritability could be much different.) (page 357)

4. Tranquilizers decrease brain stimulation, and neurons that fail to receive enough stimulation self-destruct. Tranquilizers during pregnancy therefore provide the same risk as alcohol. (page 360)

5. Evidently, the infant does not hear a difference between *ba* and *bla.* (This is a hypothetical result; the study has not been done.) (page 361)

6. If the frequency increased, we would conclude that the infant recognizes the difference between the father's voice and the other voice. If the frequency remained the same, we would conclude that the infant did not notice a difference. If it decreased, we would assume that the infant preferred the sound of the father's voice. (page 362)

| *How do children's thought processes differ from adults'?*

The artwork of young children is amazingly inventive and revealing. One toddler, 1½ years old, showed off a drawing that consisted only of dots on a sheet of paper. Puzzled adults did not understand. It is a rabbit, the child explained, while making more dots: "Look: hop, hop, hop . . . ." (Winner, 1986). When my daughter, Robin, was 6 years old, she drew a picture of a boy and a girl drawing pictures (Figure 10.15). The overall drawing has features that may not be clear; for example, both children are wearing Halloween costumes. For the little girl's drawing, Robin pasted on some wildlife photos. This array, she maintained, was what the little girl had drawn. Now look at the little boy's drawing, which is just a scribble. When I asked why the little girl's drawing was so much better than the little boy's, Robin replied, "Don't make fun of him, Daddy. He's doing the best he can."

miss the highly expressive drawings of her early childhood. The point is this: As we grow older, we gain many new abilities and skills. But we lose something too.

Studying the abilities of young children is challenging. Often, they misunderstand our questions or we misunderstand their answers. Developmental psychologists have made progress by devising increasingly careful methods of measurement.

Research Designs for Studying Development

Comparing people of different ages may sound easy, but any research method has limitations. Two major research designs are cross-sectional studies and longitudinal studies. A **cross-sectional study** *compares groups of individuals of different ages all at the same time.* For example, we could compare the drawing abilities of 6-year-olds, 8-year-olds, and 10-year-olds. The main weakness of cross-sectional studies is the difficulty of obtaining equivalent samples at different ages. For example, suppose you want to compare 20-year-olds and 60-year-olds. You might study a sample of 20-year-olds from the local college, but how will you find a comparable group of 60-year-olds?

A **longitudinal study** *follows a single group of individuals as they develop.* For example, we could study one group of children as they age from, say, 6 to 12. Table 10.1 contrasts the two kinds of studies.

FIGURE 10.15 A drawing of two children drawing pictures, courtesy of 6-year-old Robin Kalat.

© Courtesy of Robin Kalat

Sometimes, as in this case, a child's drawing can tell us a great deal about the child's worldview. As children grow older, their art changes. Robin Kalat, now an adult, draws with skill that I envy. Still, I sometimes

Longitudinal studies face practical difficulties. A longitudinal study necessarily takes years, and not everyone who participates the first time is willing and available later.

■ As we grow older, we mature in our social and emotional behaviors. However, many revert quickly to childlike behaviors in situations where such behavior is acceptable.

Furthermore, those who leave a study may differ in important ways from those who continue. Suppose a creature from outer space observes humans and discovers that about 50% of young adults are males but

that only 10 to 20% of 90-year-olds are males. The creature concludes that, as humans grow older, most males transform into females. You know why that conclusion is wrong. Males—with a few exceptions—do not change into females, but on the average they die earlier, leaving a greater percentage of older females. **Selective attrition** is *the tendency for some kinds of people to be more likely than others to drop out of a study.* Psychologists can compensate by reporting the data for only the people who stayed to the end of the study.

A longitudinal study also faces the difficulty of separating the effects of age from the effects of changes in society. For example, if people change their political views over the years, we do not know whether they changed because they grew older or because of changes in the world situation.

Despite these difficulties, certain questions logically require a longitudinal study. For example, to study the effects of divorce on children, researchers compare how each child reacts at first with how that same child reacts later. To study whether happy children are likely to become happy adults, we would follow a single group of people over time.

Sequential Designs

A sequential (or "cross-sequential") design combines the advantages of both cross-sectional and longitudinal designs. In a **sequential design**, *researchers start*

TABLE 10.1 Cross-Sectional and Longitudinal Studies

	Description	Advantages	Disadvantages	Example
Cross-sectional	Several groups of subjects of various ages studied at one time	1. Quick 2. No risk of confusing age effects with effects of changes in society	1. Risk of sampling error by getting different kinds of people at different ages 2. Risk of cohort effects	Compare memory abilities of 3-, 5-, and 7-year-olds
Longitudinal	One group of subjects studied repeatedly as the members grow older	1. No risk of sampling differences 2. Can study effects of one experience on later development 3. Can study consistency within individuals over time	1. Takes a long time 2. Some participants quit 3. Sometimes hard to separate effects of age from changes in society	Study memory abilities of 3-year-olds, and of the same children again 2 and 4 years later

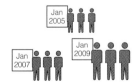

with groups of people of different ages, studied at the same time, and then study them again at one or more later times. For example, imagine we study the drawings of 6-year-olds and 8-year-olds and then examine the drawings by those same children 2 years later:

First Study	2 Years Later
Group A, age 6 years	Group A, now 8 years old
Group B, age 8 years	Group B, now 10 years old

If Group A at age 8 years resembles Group B at age 8 years, we can feel confident that the groups are comparable. We can then compare Group A at 6 years, both groups at 8 years, and Group B at 10 years.

Cohort Effects

Sometimes people differ not because of age but because of the era in which they were born. Consider: On the average who knows more about the Vietnam War, current 20-year-olds or current 60-year-olds? Who knows more about computers, 20-year-olds or 60-year-olds? Presumably, you answered *60-year-olds* to the first question and *20-year-olds* to the second. People born in a given era share life experiences with those born at the same time, and they differ in many ways from people born in other eras. Psychologists call these differences *cohort effects* (Figure 10.16). A **cohort** is *a group of people born at a particular time or a group of people who entered an organization at a particular time.*

Indeed, the era in which you grew up is one of the most important influences on your behavior. For example, people whose youth spanned the Great Depression and World War II learned to save money and to sacrifice their own pleasures for the needs of society as a whole. Even after the war was over and prosperity reigned, most remained thrifty and cautious (Rogler, 2002). In contrast the generation who lived their youth in the 1990s and early 2000s has had a great deal of leisure time to spend on television and video games (Larson, 2001). They are more extraverted than previous generations but also more depressed and prone to anxiety (Twenge, 2002).

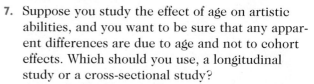

Jean Piaget's Views of Development

Attending a political rally can have a profound effect on a young adult, less effect on a preteen, and none at all on an infant. However, playing with a pile of blocks will be a more stimulating experience for a young child than for anyone older. The effect of any experience depends on a person's maturity and previous experiences. The theorist who made this point most influentially was Jean Piaget (pee-ah-ZHAY) (1896–1980).

Early in his career, Piaget administered IQ tests to French-speaking children in Switzerland. He grew bored with the tests but was fascinated by children's incorrect answers. Piaget concluded that children and adults use qualitatively different thought processes. This view contrasts with the approach of most cognitive researchers, who describe age differences as quantitative changes in memory storage, speed of pro-

FIGURE 10.16 Children of the 1920s, 1960s, and 1990s differed in their behavior because they grew up in different historical eras, with different education, nutrition, and health care. Differences based on such influences are called *cohort effects*.

© Yves de Braine/Black Star

▌ Jean Piaget (on the left) demonstrated that children with different levels of maturity react differently to the same experience.

cessing, and so forth. Piaget supported his conclusion with extensive studies of children, especially his own, relying mainly on description and not on quantitative measurements.

CRITICAL THINKING:
A STEP FURTHER
Children's Thinking

How could we know whether the difference in adult and child thought processes is qualitative or quantitative? Consider: A modern computer differs from an old one in purely quantitative ways—speed of processing and amount of memory. The basic principles of computing are the same. Yet the new computer runs programs that the old one cannot—a qualitative difference in results. Could the differences between child and adult thinking reflect just speed of processing and amount of memory?

According to Piaget a child's intellectual development is not merely an accumulation of experience or a maturational unfolding. Rather, the child constructs new mental processes as he or she interacts with the environment.

In Piaget's terminology behavior is based on schemata (the plural of *schema*). A **schema** is *an organized way of interacting with objects in the world.* For instance, infants have a grasping schema and a sucking schema. Older infants gradually add new schemata to their repertoire and adapt their old ones. The adaptation takes place through the processes of assimilation and accommodation.

Assimilation means *applying an old schema to new objects or problems.* For example, a child who observes that animals move on their own may believe that the sun and moon are alive because they seem to move on their own. (Many ancient adult humans believed the same thing.) **Accommodation** means *modifying an old schema to fit a new object or problem.* For example, a child may learn that "only living things move on their own" is a rule with exceptions and that the sun and moon are not alive.

Infants shift back and forth between assimilation and accommodation. **Equilibration** is *the establishment of harmony or balance between the two,* and according to Piaget equilibration is the key to intellectual growth. A disturbance or discrepancy occurs between the child's current understanding and some evidence to the contrary. That disturbance leads to assimilation and accommodation and then to equilibration at a higher level of functioning.

The same processes occur in adults. When you are given a new mathematical problem to solve, you try several methods until you hit upon one that works. In other words you assimilate the new problem to your old schema. However, if the new problem is different from any problem you have ever solved before, you modify (accommodate) your schema until you work out a solution. Through processes like these, said Piaget, intellectual growth occurs.

Piaget contended that children progress through four major stages of intellectual development:

1. *The sensorimotor stage* (from birth to almost 2 years)
2. *The preoperational stage* (from just before 2 to 7 years)
3. *The concrete operations stage* (from about 7 to 11 years)
4. *The formal operations stage* (from about 11 years onward)

The ages are variable, and not everyone reaches the formal operations stage. However, apparently everyone progresses through the stages in the same order. We shall encounter the same principle in other theories about stages of human development: Speed of progress through the stages varies, but order is con-

FIGURE 10.17 If someone places a bit of unscented rouge on a child's nose, a 2-year-old shows self-recognition by touching his or her own nose. A younger child ignores the red spot or points at the mirror.

stant. Let us consider children's capacities at each of Piaget's stages.

Piaget's Sensorimotor Stage

Piaget called the first stage of intellectual development the **sensorimotor stage** because *at this early age (birth to almost 2 years) behavior is mostly simple motor responses to sensory stimuli*—for example, the grasp reflex and the sucking reflex. According to Piaget infants respond only to what they see and hear right now.

Infants nevertheless notice relationships among their experiences. For example, even young infants can figure out which person in the room is talking, based on lip movements and the sound of the voice, and then look at the talking person (Lickliter & Bahrick, 2000).

As children progress through the sensorimotor stage of development, they appear to gain some concept of "self." The data are

as follows: A mother puts a spot of unscented rouge on an infant's nose and then places the infant in front of a mirror. Infants younger than 1½ years old either ignore the red spot they see on the baby in the mirror or reach out to touch the red spot. At some point after age 1½ years, infants in the same situation touch themselves on the nose, indicating that they recognize themselves in the mirror (Figure 10.17). Infants show this sign of self-recognition at varying ages; the age when they start to show self-recognition is about the same as when they begin to act embarrassed (Lewis, Sullivan, Stanger, & Weiss, 1991). That is, they show a sense of self either in both situations or in neither.

> **CRITICAL THINKING:**
> *WHAT'S THE EVIDENCE?*
> *The Infant's Thought Processes About Object Permanence*

A central point of Piaget's concept of the sensorimotor period was that infants respond only to what they see, not to what they remember. In fact he argued that infants in the first few months of life lack the concept of **object permanence**, *the idea that objects continue to exist even when we do not see or hear them.* That is, infants not only ignore what they don't see; they don't even know the objects still exist. How could Piaget know what an infant thinks? Obviously, he could only infer.

Piaget drew his inferences from observations of this type: Place a toy in front of a 6-month-old infant, who reaches out and grabs it. Later, place a toy in the same place, but before the infant has a chance to grab it, cover it with a clear glass. No problem; the infant removes the glass and takes the toy. Now repeat that procedure, but this time cover the toy with an opaque

FIGURE 10.18 (a) A 6- to 9-month-old child reaches for a visible toy, but not one that is hidden behind a barrier (b) even if the child sees someone hide the toy. According to Piaget this observation indicates that the child hasn't yet grasped the concept of object permanence.

(nonclear) glass. The infant, who watched you place the glass over the toy, makes no effort to remove the glass and obtain the toy. Or place a thin barrier between the infant and the toy. An infant who cannot see at least part of the toy does not reach for it (Piaget, 1937/1954) (see Figure 10.18). Even at 9 months, a child who has repeatedly found a toy in one location will reach there again after watching you hide it in a neighboring location.

Why not? According to Piaget the infant *does not know* that the hidden toy is there. However, one can imagine other possible explanations. A study by Renee Baillargeon (1986) suggests that infants do show signs of understanding object permanence when they are tested differently.

Hypothesis   An infant who sees an event that would be impossible (if objects are permanent) will be surprised and therefore will stare longer than will an infant that sees a similar but possible event.

Method   Infants aged 6 or 8 months watched a series of events staged by the researcher. First, the child watched the experimenter raise a screen to show nothing behind it and then watched a toy car go down a slope and emerge on the other side, as shown in the drawing below. This was called a "possible" event.

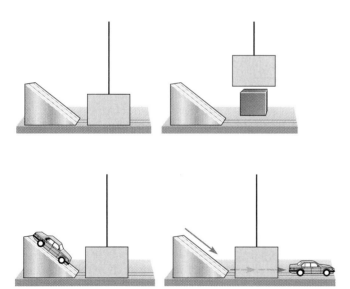

Possible event. The block appears to be behind the track, and the car passes by the block.

The researchers measured how long the child stared after the car went down the slope. They repeated the procedure until the child decreased his or her staring time for three trials in a row (showing habituation).

Then the experimenters presented two kinds of events. One kind was the possible event as just described; the other was an impossible event like this:

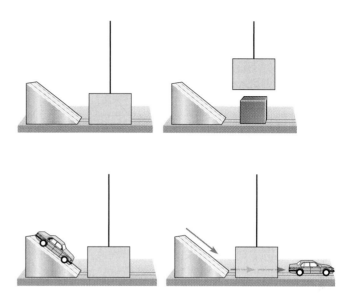

Impossible event. The raised screen shows a box on the track right where the car would pass. After the screen lowers, the car goes down the slope and emerges on the other side.

In an impossible event, the raised screen showed a box that was on the track, right where the car would pass. After the screen lowered, the car went down the slope and emerged on the other side. (The experimenters had pulled the box off the track after lowering the screen.) The experimenters measured each child's staring times after both kinds of events. They repeated both events two more times, randomizing the order of events.

Results   Figure 10.19 shows the mean looking times. Infants stared longer after seeing an impossible event than after seeing a possible event. They also stared longer during the first pair of events than after the second pair and longer after the second than the third (Baillargeon, 1986).

Interpretation   Why did the infants stare longer at the "impossible" event? The inference—and admittedly only an inference, not a certainty—is that the infants found the impossible event surprising. To be surprised, the infants had to expect that the box would continue to exist where it was hidden and that a car could not go through it. If this inference is correct, even 6-month-old infants have some understanding of the permanence of objects, as well as elementary physics. A later study with a slightly different method again measured how long infants stared at

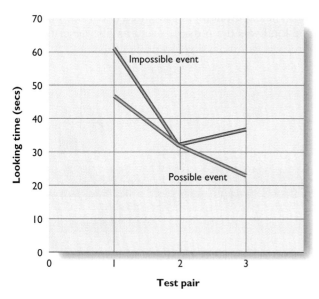

FIGURE 10.19 Mean looking times of 6- and 8-month-old infants after they had watched either possible or impossible events. *(Baillargeon, R. "Representing the existence and the location of hidden objects: Object permanence in 6- and 8-month-old infants."* Cognition, 23, 21-41. Copyright 1986. Reprinted with permission from Elsevier.)

possible and impossible events and demonstrated object permanence in infants as young as 3½ months (Baillargeon, 1987).

Still, remember that 9-month-olds failed Piaget's object permanence task of reaching out to pick up a hidden object. Do infants have the concept of object permanence or not? Perhaps there is something wrong with the question. It is possible to have a concept but use it in some situations and not others (Munakata, McClelland, Johnson, & Siegler, 1997). Even college students can pass a physics test and then fail to apply the laws of motion in a new situation or state a rule of grammar and yet make grammatical errors.

The important point is this: When dealing with infants or anyone else whose thought processes are likely to be different from our own, we should be cautious about inferring what they can or cannot do. The results may vary depending on the exact procedures.

CRITICAL THINKING:
A STEP FURTHER
Inferring "Surprise"

Suppose we play a series of musical notes and an infant stares longer toward the source of *do-re-mi-fa-so-la-ti* than *do-re-mi-fa-so-la-ti-do*. Should we infer that the infant is "surprised" by the absence of the final *do*?

Piaget's Preoperational Stage

By or before age 2, most children are learning to speak; within a few years, they will have nearly mastered their language. When a child asks for a toy, there is no longer any doubt that the child understands the concept of object permanence. Nevertheless, at this age children's understanding is not like that of adults. For example, they have difficulty understanding that a mother can be someone else's daughter. A boy with one brother will assert that his brother has no brother. Piaget refers to this period as the **preoperational stage** because *the child lacks* operations, *which are reversible mental processes.* For example, for a boy to understand that his brother has a brother, he must be able to reverse the concept of "having a brother." According to Piaget three typical aspects of preoperational thought are egocentrism, difficulty distinguishing appearance from reality, and lack of the concept of conservation.

Egocentrism: Understanding Other People's Thoughts

According to Piaget young children's thought is **egocentric.** By this term Piaget did *not* mean that children are selfish; instead, he meant that *a child sees the world as centered around himself or herself and cannot easily take another person's perspective.* If you and a preschooler sit on opposite sides of a complicated pile of blocks and you ask the child to draw or describe what the blocks would look like from your side, the child draws or describes them as they look from the child's side.

Another example: Young children hear a story about a little girl, Lucy, who wants her old pair of red shoes. Part way through the story, Lucy's brother Linus comes into the room, and she asks him to bring her red shoes. He goes and brings back her new red shoes, and she is angry because she wanted the old red shoes. Young children are often surprised that he brought the wrong shoes because *they* knew which shoes she wanted (Keysar, Barr, & Horton, 1998). In this and other studies, children up to 4, 5, or 6 years old (depending on the details) seem to assume that whatever *they* know, other people will know too (Birch & Bloom, 2003).

Unfortunately, none of us completely outgrow this tendency. In one study adults heard a story in which Jane recommends a restaurant to David. He goes there and dislikes it. Later, she asks him how he liked the restaurant, and he replies, ". . . it was marvelous, just marvelous." Adults who knew he disliked it are surprised that Jane didn't realize he was being sarcastic. Like the children, the adults were egocentric by assuming that what they knew other people would know also (Keysar et al., 1998).

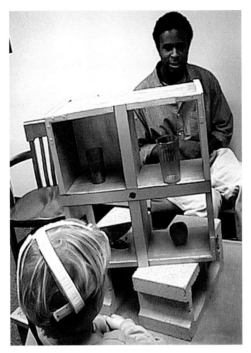 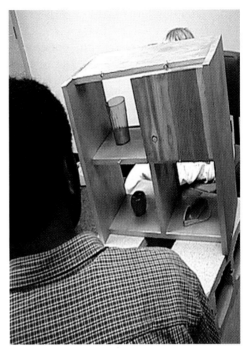

FIGURE 10.20 Sometimes a child saw that the adult could see two glasses; other times it was clear that the adult could see only one. If two glasses were visible, the child usually told the adult which glass to pick up, instead of just saying "pick up the glass." *(From Nadig, A. S., & Sedivy, J. S.,"Evidence of Perspective-Taking Constraints in Children on line Reference Resolution"* American Psychological Society, *Vol. 13, No. 4, July 2002. Photo reprinted with the permission of the author and publisher.)*

Furthermore, even young children are able to understand another person's perspective some of the time if the task is simple. In one study 5- and 6-year-old children had to tell an adult to pick up a particular glass. If a child saw that the adult could see two glasses, the child usually said to pick up the "big" or "little" glass, so the adult could get the right one. If the child saw that the adult could see only one glass, the child was more likely just to say "the glass" (Nadig & Sedivy, 2002) (see Figure 10.20).

CONCEPT CHECK ☑

10. Which of the following is the clearest example of egocentric thinking?
    a. A writer who uses someone else's words without giving credit.
    b. A politician who blames others for everything that goes wrong.
    c. A professor who gives the same complicated lecture to a freshman class that she gives to a convention of professionals. (Check your answer on page 382.)

To say that a child is egocentric is to say that he or she has trouble understanding what other people know and don't know. Psychologists say that a young child lacks, but gradually develops, **theory of mind,** which is *an understanding that other people have a mind too and that each person knows some things that other people don't know.* How can we know whether a child has this understanding? Here is one example of a research effort.

> **CRITICAL THINKING:**
> **WHAT'S THE EVIDENCE?**
> *Children's Understanding of Other People's Knowledge*

How and when do children first understand that other people have minds and knowledge? Researchers have developed some clever experiments to answer this difficult question.

Hypothesis   A child who understands that other people have minds will distinguish between someone who knows something and someone who could not.

Method   A 3- or 4-year-old child sat in front of four cups (Figure 10.21) and watched as one adult hid a candy or toy under one of the cups, although a screen prevented the child from seeing which cup. Then another adult entered the room. The "informed" adult pointed to one cup to show where he or she had just hidden the surprise; the "uninformed" adult pointed to one of the other cups. The child was then given an opportunity to look under one cup for the surprise.

This procedure was repeated 10 times for each child. The two adults alternated roles, but on each trial one or the other hid the surprise while the other was absent. That is, one was in a position to know where the surprise was hidden and the other was not.

Results   Of the 4-year-olds, 10 of 20 consistently chose the correct cup (the one indicated by the informed adult). That is, many of them showed that they understood who had the relevant knowledge and who did not. However, the 3-year-olds were just as likely to follow the lead of the uninformed adult as that of the informed adult (Povinelli & deBlois, 1992).

Interpretation   Evidently, 4-year-olds are more likely than 3-year-olds to understand other people's knowledge (or lack of it).

Other experiments, using a somewhat different procedure, have yielded similar results. For example, children in one study watched a dramatization where a girl who had a marble in her basket left the room temporarily. During her absence a second girl moved the marble from the first girl's basket to her own basket. When the first girl returned to the room, the children were asked "Where is the marble?" and "Where will the first girl look for it?" Most 4-year-olds answered that she would look in her own basket, but younger children thought she would look in the second girl's basket (Wimmer & Perner, 1983). As in the previous study, 4-year-olds inferred what various people might or might not know.

Although these are important results, we should avoid concluding that children at some point suddenly understand that other people have minds. Children sometimes act as if they understand and sometimes not depending on the situation (Yirmiya, Erel, Shaked, & Solomonica-Levi, 1998). Gaining a concept is seldom an all-or-none process.

Distinguishing Appearance from Reality

Piaget and many other psychologists have contended that children in the early preoperational stage do not distinguish clearly between appearance and reality. For example, a child who sees you put a white ball behind a blue filter will say that the ball is blue. When you ask, "Yes, I know the ball *looks* blue, but what color is it *really*?" the child replies that it really *is* blue (Flavell,

FIGURE 10.21 A child sits in front of a screen covering four cups and watches as one adult hides a surprise under one of the cups. Then that adult and another (who had not been present initially) point to one of the cups to signal where the surprise is hidden. Many 4-year-olds consistently follow the advice of the informed adult; 3-year-olds do not.

1986). Similarly, a 3-year-old who encounters a sponge that looks like a rock probably will say that it really is a rock, but a child who says it is a sponge will also insist that it *looks like* a sponge. Children have to grow a year or two older before they say that something looks like one thing but really is another.

However, other psychologists have argued that the 3-year-old's difficulty is more with language than with understanding the appearance–reality distinction. (After all, 3-year-olds do play games of make-believe, so they sometimes do distinguish appearance from reality.) In one study psychologists showed 3-year-olds a sponge that looked like a rock and let them touch it. When the investigators asked what it looked like and what it was *really*, most of the children said either "rock" both times or "sponge" both times. However, if the investigators asked, "Bring me something so I can wipe up some spilled water," the children brought the sponge. And when the investigators asked, "Bring me something so I can take a picture of a teddy bear with something that looks like a rock," they again brought the sponge. So evidently, they did understand that something could be a sponge and look like a rock, even if they didn't say so (Sapp, Lee, & Muir, 2000).

Also consider the following experiment: A psychologist shows a child a playhouse room that is a scale model of a full-size room. Then the psychologist hides a tiny toy in the small room (while the child watches) and explains that a bigger toy just like it is "in the same place" in the bigger room. (For example, if the little toy is behind the sofa in the little room, the big toy is behind the sofa in the big room.) Then the psychologist asks the child to find the big toy in the big room. Most 3-year-olds look in the correct place and find the toy immediately (DeLoache, 1989). Adult chimpanzees solve a similar problem (Kuhlmeier & Boysen, 2002). Most 2½-year-old children, however, search haphazardly (see Figure 10.22a). If the experimenter shows the child the big toy in the big room and asks the child to find the little toy "in the same place" in the little room, the results are the same: Most 3-year-olds find it, but most 2½-year-olds cannot (DeLoache, 1989).

Before we speak too confidently about what a 2½-year-old cannot do, however, consider this clever follow-up study: The psychologist hides a toy in the small room while the child watches. Then both step out of the room, and the psychologist shows the child a "machine that can make things bigger." The psychologist aims a beam from the machine at the room and takes the child out of the way. They hear some chunkata-chunkata-clunkata-clunkata sounds, and then the psychologist shows the

a A 2½-year-old is shown small room where stuffed animal is hidden.

Child is unable to find the stuffed animal in the larger room.

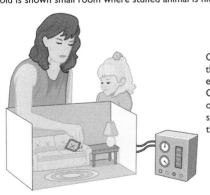

b Child is shown small room where stuffed animal is hidden.

Child is told that the machine expands the room. Child stands out of the way during some noises and then returns.

Child is able to find the stuffed animal in the "blown-up" room.

FIGURE 10.22 If an experimenter hides a small toy in a small room and asks a child to find a larger toy "in the same place" in the larger room, most 2½-year-olds search haphazardly. (a) However, the same children know where to look if the experimenter says this is the same room as before, except that a machine has expanded it (b).

full-sized "blown-up" room and asks the child to find the hidden toy. Even 2½-year-olds go immediately to the correct location (DeLoache, Miller, & Rosengren, 1997) (see Figure 10.22b). Evidently, they can use one room as a "map" of the other *if* they think of them as "the same room." (Incidentally, hardly any of the children doubted that the machine had actually expanded the room, and many continued to believe it even after the psychologist tried to explain what had really happened!) The overall conclusion is that a child can appear to have an ability or to lack it depending on how we ask the question.

Developing the Concept of Conservation

According to Piaget preoperational children lack the concept of **conservation**. They fail to *understand that objects conserve such properties as number, length, volume, area, and mass after changes in the shape or arrangement of the objects.* They cannot perform the mental operations necessary to understand such transformations. (Table 10.2 shows some typical conservation tasks.) For example, if we set up two glasses of the same size containing the same amount of water and then pour the contents of one glass into a taller, thinner glass, preoperational children will say that the second glass contains more water (Figure 10.23).

I once doubted whether children really believed what they were saying in such a situation. I thought perhaps the phrasing of the questions somehow tricks them into saying something they do not believe. If you have these same doubts, borrow someone's 6-year-old child and try it yourself with your own wording. Here's my own experience: Once when I was discussing Piaget in my introductory psychology class, I invited my son Sam, then 5½ years old, to take part in a class demonstration. I started with two glasses of water, which he agreed contained equal amounts of water. Then I poured the water from one glass into a wider glass, lowering the water level. When I

asked Sam which glass contained more water, he confidently pointed to the tall, thin one. After class he complained, "Daddy, why did you ask me such an easy question? Everyone could see that there was more water in that glass! You should have asked me something harder to show how smart I am!" The following year I brought Sam to class again for the same demonstration. He was now 6½ years old, about the age when children make the transition from preoperational thinking to the next stage. This time I poured the water from one of the tall glasses into a wider one and asked him which glass contained more water. He looked and paused. His face got red. Finally, he whispered, "Daddy, I don't know!" After class he complained, "Why did you ask me such a hard question? I'm never coming back to any of your classes again!" The question that used to be embarrassingly easy had become embarrassingly difficult.

The next year, when he was 7½, I tried again (at home). This time he answered confidently, "Both glasses have the same amount of water, of course. Why? Is this some sort of trick question?"

TABLE 10.2 Typical Tasks Used to Measure Conservation

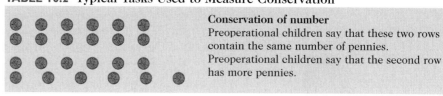

Conservation of number
Preoperational children say that these two rows contain the same number of pennies.
Preoperational children say that the second row has more pennies.

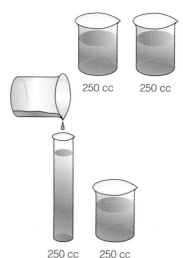

Conservation of volume

Preoperational children say that the two same-size containers have the same amount of water.

250 cc   250 cc

Preoperational children say that the taller, thinner container has more water.

250 cc   250 cc

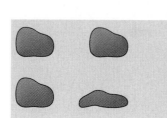

Conservation of mass
Preoperational children say that the two same-size balls of clay have the same amount of clay.
Preoperational children say that a squashed ball of clay contains a different amount of clay than the same-size round ball of clay.

FIGURE 10.23 Preoperational children, usually younger than age 7, don't understand that the volume of water remains constant despite changes in its appearance. During the transition from preoperational thinking to concrete operations, a child finds conservation tasks difficult and confusing.

Piaget's Concrete Operations Stage and Formal Operations Stage

At about the age of 7, children enter the stage of concrete operations and begin to understand the conservation of physical properties. This transition is not sudden, however. For instance, a 6-year-old child may understand that squashing a ball of clay will not change its weight but may not realize until years later that squashing the ball will not change the volume of water it displaces when it is dropped into a glass.

According to Piaget, during the **stage of concrete operations,** *children can perform mental operations on concrete objects but still have trouble with abstract or hypothetical ideas.* For example, ask this question: "How could you move a 4-mile-high mountain of whipped cream from one side of the city to the other?" Older children think of imaginative answers, but children in the concrete operations stage are likely to complain that the question is silly.

Or ask, "If you could have a third eye anywhere on your body, where would you put it?" Children in this stage generally respond immediately that they would put it right between the other two, on their foreheads. Older children suggest more imaginative ideas such as on the back of their heads, in the stomach (so they could watch food digesting), or on the tip of a finger (so they could peek around corners).

Finally, in Piaget's **stage of formal operations,** children develop *the mental processes that deal with abstract, hypothetical situations. Those processes demand logical, deductive reasoning and systematic planning.* According to Piaget children reach the stage of formal operations at about age 11. Later researchers found that many people take longer to reach this stage, and some never reach it.

Suppose we ask three children, ages 6, 10, and 14, to arrange a set of sticks in order from the longest to the shortest. The 6-year-old (preoperational) child fails to order the sticks correctly. The 10-year-old (concrete operations) eventually gets them in the right order but only after prolonged trial and error. The 14-year-old (formal operations) holds the sticks upright with their bottom ends on the table and then removes the longest one, the second longest, and so forth.

A second example: We set up five bottles of clear liquid and explain that it is possible to mix some combination of them to produce a yellow liquid. The task is to find that combination. Children in the concrete operations stage plunge right in with no plan. They try combining bottles A and B, then C and D, then perhaps A, C, and E. Soon they have forgotten which combinations they've already tried. If they do stumble onto the correct combination, it is mostly by luck.

Children in the formal operations stage approach the problem more systematically. They may first try all the two-bottle combinations: AB, AC, AD, AE, BC, and so forth. If those fail, they try three-bottle combinations: ABC, ABD, ABE, ACD, and so on. By trying every possible combination only once, they are sure to succeed.

Children do not reach the stage of formal operations any more suddenly than they reach the concrete operations stage. Reasoning logically about a particular problem requires some experience with it. A 9-year-old chess hobbyist reasons logically about chess problems and plans several moves ahead but reverts to concrete reasoning when faced with an unfamiliar problem. Table 10.3 summarizes Piaget's four stages.

TABLE 10.3 Summary of Piaget's Stages of Cognitive Development

Stage and Approximate Age	Achievements and Activities	Limitations
Sensorimotor (birth to 1½ years)	Reacts to sensory stimuli through reflexes and other responses	Little use of language; seems not to understand object permanence in the early part of this stage
Preoperational (1½ to 7 years)	Develops language; can represent objects mentally by words and other symbols; can respond to objects that are remembered but not present	Lacks operations (reversible mental processes); lacks concept of conservation; focuses on one property at a time (such as length or width), not on both at once; still has trouble distinguishing appearance from reality
Concrete operations (7 to 11 years)	Understands conservation of mass, number, and volume; can reason logically with regard to concrete objects that can be seen or touched	Has trouble reasoning about abstract concepts and hypothetical situations
Formal operations (11 years onward)	Can reason logically about abstract and hypothetical concepts; develops strategies; plans actions in advance	None beyond the occasional irrationalities of all human thought

CONCEPT CHECK ☑

11. You are given the following information about four children. Assign each of them to one of Piaget's stages of intellectual development.
    a. Child has mastered the concept of conservation; has trouble with abstract and hypothetical questions.
    b. Child performs well on tests of object permanence; has trouble with conservation.
    c. Child has schemata; does not speak in complete sentences; fails tests of object permanence.
    d. Child performs well on tests of object permanence, conservation, and hypothetical questions. (Check your answers on page 382.)

Are Piaget's Stages Distinct?

According to Piaget the four stages of intellectual development are distinct, and a transition from one stage to the next requires a major reorganization of the child's thinking, almost as a caterpillar metamorphoses into a chrysalis and then the chrysalis metamorphoses into a butterfly. In other words intellectual growth is marked by periods of revolutionary reorganization.

Later research has cast much doubt on this conclusion. If it were true, then a child in a given stage of development—say, the preoperational stage—should perform consistently at that level. In fact children's performance fluctuates as a task is made

slightly more or less difficult. For example, consider the conservation-of-number task, in which an investigator presents two rows of seven or more objects and then spreads out one row and asks which row "has more." Preoperational children reply that the spread-out row has more. However, when Rochel Gelman (1982) presented two rows of only three objects each (Figure 10.24) and then spread out one of the rows, even 3- and 4-year-old children usually answered that the rows had the same number of items. After much practice with short rows, most of the 3- and 4-year-olds also answered correctly that a spread-out row of eight items had the same number of items as a tightly packed row of eight.

FIGURE 10.24 (a) With the standard conservation-of-number task, preoperational children answer that the lower row has more items. (b) With a simplified task, the same children say that both rows have the same number of items.

Whereas Piaget believed children made distinct jumps from one stage to another, most psychologists today see development as gradual and continuous (Courage & Howe, 2002). That is, the difference between older children and younger children is not so much a matter of *having* or *lacking* an ability. Rather, younger children use their abilities only in simpler situations.

Differing Views: Piaget and Vygotsky

One implication of Piaget's findings is that children must discover certain concepts, such as the concept of conservation, mainly on their own. Teaching a concept means directing children's attention to the key aspects and then letting them discover the concept for themselves.

Another implication frequently drawn from Piaget's work is that teachers should determine a child's level of functioning and then teach material appropriate to that level. For example, teachers should not introduce abstract concepts to children who are at the concrete operations stage of development. They should wait for children to discover many concepts on their own.

In contrast Russian psychologist Lev Vygotsky (1978) argued that educators cannot wait for children to rediscover the principles of physics and mathematics. Indeed, he argued, the distinguishing characteristic of human thought is that it is based on language and symbols that enable each generation to profit from the experience of the previous ones.

However, when Vygotsky said that adults should teach children, he did not mean that adults should ignore the child's developmental level. Rather, every child has a **zone of proximal development**, which is *the distance between what a child can do alone and what the child can do with help.* Instruction should remain within that zone. For example, one should not try to teach a 4-year-old the concept of conservation of volume, and it would be a waste of time to try to teach it to an 8-year-old who understands it already. But a child around 6 years old who does not yet understand the concept might learn it

with help and guidance. Similarly, children improve their recall of a story when adults provide appropriate hints and reminders, and they can solve more complicated math problems with help than without it. Vygotsky compared this help to *scaffolding,* the temporary supports that builders use during construction: After the building is complete, the scaffolding is removed. Good advice for an educator, therefore, is to be sensitive to a child's zone of proximal development and attempt to detect how much further the child can be pushed.

CONCEPT CHECK ☑

12. What would be the opinions of Piaget and Vygotsky about the feasibility of teaching the concept of conservation? (Check your answer on page 382.)

The Development of Moral Reasoning

Just as people gradually develop their understanding of the physical world, they also gradually develop their understanding of right and wrong.

Kohlberg's Measurements of Moral Reasoning

Psychologists once regarded morality as a set of arbitrary, learned rules, such as driving on the right or left side of the road depending on the country. Lawrence Kohlberg (1969; Kohlberg & Hersh, 1977) proposed instead that moral reasoning is a process that naturally matures through a series of stages. For example, children younger than about 6 years old say that accidentally breaking something valuable is worse than intentionally breaking something of less value; older children and adults attend more to people's intentions. Although Kohlberg's stages of moral reasoning are analogous to Piaget's stages, someone might progress more rapidly through Piaget's stages than Kohlberg's, or the reverse.

Kohlberg argued that moral reasoning should not be evaluated according to someone's de-

▌ Lev Vygotsky called attention to a child's zone of proximal development: the gap between what a child can do alone and what the child can do with help. Education within that zone advances a child's reasoning abilities.

© Laura Dwight / PhotoEdit

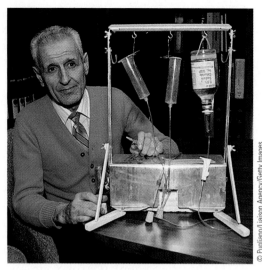

A real-life moral dilemma: Michigan physician Jack Kevorkian developed a device to help terminally ill patients kill themselves painlessly. Is it morally right or wrong to aid in someone else's suicide? According to Kohlberg the morality of an act depends on the reasoning behind it.

cisions but according to the reasons behind them. For example, do you think that designing nuclear bombs is a moral way to make a living? According to Kohlberg the answer depends on one's reasons for taking the job. Hugh Gusterson (1992) interviewed nuclear bomb designers at the Lawrence Livermore National Laboratory. When he asked them about the morality of their actions, nearly everyone said something like, "You're lucky you chose me to interview, because I, unlike all the others, think deeply about these matters." Nearly all insisted that the weapons' only function was to threaten an enemy and thereby prevent wars. If you doubt that assumption, you might disagree with the morality of the bomb designers' *actions,* but you could still respect their moral *reasoning.*

To measure the maturity of someone's moral judgments, Kohlberg devised a series of **moral dilemmas**—

problems *that pit one moral value against another.* Each dilemma is accompanied by a question such as, "What should this person do?" or "Did this person do the right thing?" Kohlberg was not concerned about the choices people make because well-meaning people disagree on the right answer. More revealing is their explanations, which are categorized into six stages, grouped into three levels (see Table 10.4). Because few people respond consistently at stage 6, many authorities combine stages 5 and 6. To emphasize: Kohlberg's stages do not represent moral or immoral decisions but only moral and less moral *reasons* for a decision.

CRITICAL THINKING:
A STEP FURTHER
Kohlberg's Stages

Suppose a military junta overthrows a democratic government and sets up a dictatorship. In which of Kohlberg's stages of moral reasoning would you classify the members of the junta? Would your answer depend on their reasons for setting up the dictatorship?

People begin at Kohlberg's first stage and then progress through the others in order, although few reach the highest stages. (The order of progression is an important point: If people were just as likely to progress in the order 3-5-4 as in the order 3-4-5, then we would have no justification for calling one stage higher than the other.) People seldom skip a stage or revert to an earlier stage after reaching a higher one. People do fluctuate from one time to another. Nevertheless, we can classify people in terms of the usual or average level of their answers. Figure 10.25 shows that most 10-year-olds' judgments are at Kohlberg's first or second stage, but 13- and 16-year-olds progress to higher levels. Kohlberg suggests that this rather swift development results from cognitive growth: 16-year-olds are capable of more mature reasoning than 10-year-olds.

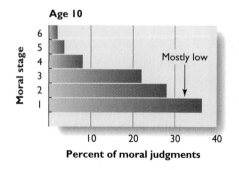 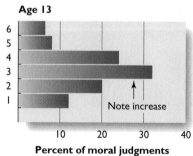 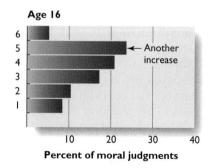

FIGURE 10.25 Most younger adolescents give answers corresponding to Kohlberg's earlier moral stages. By age 16 most of their answers are at higher levels. *(Based on Kohlberg, 1969)*

TABLE 10.4 Responses to One of Kohlberg's Moral Dilemmas by People at Six Levels of Moral Reasoning

The dilemma: Heinz's wife was near death from cancer. A druggist had recently discovered a drug that might be able to save her. The druggist was charging $2000 for the drug, which cost him $200 to make. Heinz could not afford to pay for it, and he could borrow only $1000 from friends. He offered to pay the rest later. The druggist refused to sell the drug for less than the full price paid in advance: "I discovered the drug, and I'm going to make money from it." Late that night, Heinz broke into the store to steal the drug for his wife. Did Heinz do the right thing?

Level/Stage	Typical Answer	Basis for Judging Right from Wrong	Description of Stage
The Level of Preconventional Morality 1. Punishment and obedience orientation	"No. If he steals the drug, he might go to jail." "Yes. If he can't afford the drug, he can't afford a funeral, either."	Wrong is equated with punishment. What is good is whatever is in the man's immediate self-interest.	Decisions are based on their immediate consequences. Whatever is rewarded is "good" and whatever is punished is "bad." If you break something and are punished, then what you did was bad.
2. Instrumental relativist orientation	"He can steal the drug and save his wife, and he'll be with her when he gets out of jail."	Again, what is good is whatever is in the man's own best interests, but his interests include delayed benefits.	It is good to help other people, but only because they may one day return the favor: "You scratch my back and I'll scratch yours."
The Level of Conventional Morality 3. Interpersonal concordance, or "good boy/nice girl" orientation	"People will understand if you steal the drug to save your wife, but they'll think you're cruel and a coward if you don't."	Public opinion is the main basis for judging what is good.	The "right" thing to do is whatever pleases others, especially those in authority. Be a good person so others will think you are good. Conformity to the dictates of public opinion is important.
4. "Law and order" orientation	"No, because stealing is illegal." "Yes. It is the husband's duty to save his wife even if he feels guilty afterward for stealing the drug."	Right and wrong can be determined by duty or by one's role in society.	You should respect the law—simply because it *is* the law—and work to strengthen the social order that enforces it.
The Level of Postconventional or Principled Morality 5. Social-contract legalistic orientation	"The husband has a right to the drug even if he can't pay now. If the druggist won't charge it, the government should look after it."	Laws are made for people's benefit. They should be flexible. If necessary, we may have to change certain laws or allow for exceptions to them.	The "right" thing to do is whatever people have agreed is the best thing for society. As in stage 4, you respect the law, but in addition recognize that a majority of the people can agree to change the rules. Anyone who makes a promise is obligated to keep the promise.
6. Universal ethical principle orientation	"Although it is legally wrong to steal, the husband would be morally wrong not to steal to save his wife. A life is more precious than financial gain."	Right and wrong are based on absolute values such as human life. Sometimes these values take precedence over human laws.	In special cases it may be right to violate a law that conflicts with higher ethical principles, such as justice and respect for human life. Among those who have obeyed a "higher law" are Jesus, Mahatma Gandhi, and Martin Luther King, Jr.

Source: Kohlberg, 1981.

CONCEPT CHECK ☑

13. For the moral dilemma described at the top of Table 10.4, suppose someone says that Heinz was wrong to steal the drug to save his wife's life. Which level of moral reasoning is characteristic of this judgment? (Check your answer on page 382.)

Limitations of Kohlberg's Views

Kohlberg's theory is based on several uncertain assumptions. Let us consider two major issues: (a) justice versus caring orientations to morality and (b) the relationship between moral reasoning and behavior.

Are There Other Types of Moral Reasoning?

Kohlberg assumed that most judgments of right and wrong depend on "justice." In many non-Western cultures, such as the Hindu culture of India, people seldom talk about justice, laws, or personal happiness. They talk instead of a natural sense of duty toward others (Shweder, Mahapatra, & Miller, 1987). Even in Western cultures, we don't always reason in terms of justice. Carol Gilligan (1977, 1979) pointed out that we sometimes rely on a "caring" orientation—that is, what would help or hurt other people. She proposed alternative stages of moral development, as outlined in Table 10.5, ranging from preconventional (the least mature stage) to postconventional (the most mature). Gilligan initially argued that men rely more on a justice orientation and women rely more on caring. Later research found that this gender difference is small and inconsistent (Jaffee & Hyde, 2000). Nearly everyone shows some concern with both justice and caring. However, the key point is that the two orientations can be in conflict.

For example, at one point during the Vietnam War, a group of soldiers were ordered to kill a group of unarmed civilians. One soldier, who regarded the order as immoral, refused to shoot. In terms of "justice," he acted at a high moral level, following a "higher law" that required him not to kill. However, his actions

TABLE 10.5 Carol Gilligan's Stages of Moral Development

Stage	Basis for Deciding Right from Wrong
Preconventional	What is helpful or harmful to myself?
Conventional	What is helpful or harmful to other people?
Postconventional	What is helpful or harmful to myself and others?

▌ Sometimes the two "voices" of moral reasoning—justice and caring—are in conflict with each other. From a caring standpoint, you want to help someone in distress. From a justice standpoint, you may think it wrong to encourage begging.

made no difference, as the other soldiers killed all the civilians. In terms of "caring," he would have been more moral if he had found a way to hide a few of the victims (Linn & Gilligan, 1990).

How Does Moral Reasoning Relate to Behavior?

The movie *Schindler's List* portrays a German man who risked his life to save Jewish people from the Nazi Holocaust. We all agree he did the right thing. But if you or I had been non-Jewish Germans at the time, what would we have done? I don't know. Stating the right thing to do is not the same as doing it.

Kohlberg's approach to morality has been criticized for both overestimating and underestimating people's moral behavior reasoning. I shall present both arguments and let you draw your own conclusions.

The first argument is as follows: Although many people give answers that qualify as stages 4, 5, and 6, moral *behavior* at those levels is less common, and we can understand why (Krebs, 2000). Behavior at stages 1, 2, and 3 benefits yourself: Seek rewards, avoid punishments, and cooperate with others who cooperate with you. ("You scratch my back and I'll scratch yours.") Behavior at stages 4, 5, and 6 benefits other people whom you will never meet.

On the other hand, maybe we underestimate the moral imperative. Most of us *want* to behave morally, even though we know that we often yield to temptations. Imagine the following: You and another student show up for psychological research. The researchers explain that two studies are available. One study sounds interesting and pleasant; the other is difficult and painful. You are invited to flip a coin and then announce who gets to be in the pleasant study.

■ Critics of Kohlberg's approach point out that moral reasoning is not the same as moral action. This cadet at a Russian military academy (left) could probably explain why cheating is immoral, but he cheats nevertheless.

In this situation 85 to 90% of students claim they won the toss and get to be in the pleasant experiment. Obviously, many are lying. However, suppose you were asked whether you want to flip the coin and announce the results or let the experimenter do it. Now most people say "let the experimenter do it" (Batson & Thompson, 2001). They avoid putting themselves in a situation in which they know they will be tempted to lie.

IN CLOSING

Developing Cognitive Abilities

The universe is a complicated place, and none of us fully understands it. We should not be surprised that children misunderstand a great deal. For example, when a child fails to distinguish between appearance and reality—well, it's quite natural to assume that what you see is real.

Not only do young children often misunderstand the world; we adults often misunderstand children. They cannot express themselves clearly, and infants can't even control their muscles well. When an infant appears not to understand object permanence or when a toddler seems to have trouble understanding another person's point of view or when a child says it is wrong to do something "because you'll get punished," we are tempted to assume that what we see is real—that is, the child lacks certain ideas or abilities. Maybe so, but maybe not. More extensive testing sometimes reveals greater potentials than appeared at first. Children's development is complicated, and we should be humble enough to recognize the limits of our understanding.

Summary

- *Cross-sectional and longitudinal studies.* Psychologists study development by means of cross-sectional studies, which examine people of different ages at the same time, and by means of longitudinal studies, which look at a single group of people at various times as they grow older. A sequential design combines the main advantages of both methods. (page 364)

- *Cohort effects.* Many differences between young people and old people are not due to age but to time of birth. A group of people born in a particular era is called a cohort, and one cohort can differ from another in important ways. (page 366)

- *Piaget's view of children's thinking.* According to Jean Piaget, children's thought differs from adults' thought qualitatively as well as quantitatively. He believed children grew intellectually through accommodation and assimilation. (page 366)

- *Piaget's stages of development.* Children in the sensorimotor stage respond to what they see or otherwise sense at the moment. In the preoperational stage, according to Piaget, they lack reversible operations, such as the ability to understand that a mother could be someone else's daughter. In the concrete operations stage, children can reason about concrete problems but not abstractions. Adults and older children are in the formal operations stage, in which they can plan a strategy and can deal with hypothetical or abstract questions. (page 368)

- *Egocentric thinking.* Young children sometimes have trouble understanding other people's point of view. However, the results vary depending on the procedure. (page 370)

- *Appearance and reality.* Young children sometimes seem not to distinguish between appearance and reality. However, with a simpler task or different method of testing, they do distinguish. In many cases children do not fully have or lack a concept; they show the concept under some conditions and not others. (page 372)

- *Vygotsky.* Most psychologists now doubt that children go through distinct stages. Rather, one level of performance gradually blends into the next. According to Lev Vygotsky, children must learn new abilities from adults or older children; we cannot wait for them to make the discoveries by themselves. (page 377)

- *Kohlberg's view of moral reasoning.* Lawrence Kohlberg contended that moral reasoning matures naturally through stages. According to Kohlberg moral reasoning should be evaluated on the basis of the reasons someone gives for a decision rather than the decision itself. (page 377)

- *Challenges to Kohlberg's views.* Kohlberg concentrated on "justice," ignoring a "caring" orientation that sometimes gives a conflicting view. It has been argued both that people's actions are less moral than their answers to Kohlberg's questions and that their actions are in fact more moral than their answers imply. (page 380)

Answers to Concept Checks

7. Use a longitudinal study, which studies the same people repeatedly instead of comparing one cohort with another. (page 366)
8. With a longitudinal study, you would see clothing changes over time, but you would not know whether the changes were due to age or to changes in society. A cross-sectional study would be better, but you would have problems due to cohort effects. The older generation probably has always differed in its taste from the current younger generation. (page 366)
9. Another possible explanation is that the first-year students who have the lowest grades (and therefore pull down the grade average for first-year students) do not stay in school long enough to become seniors. (page 366)
10. c is the clearest case of egocentric thought, a failure to recognize another person's point of view. (page 371)
11. **a.** concrete operations stage; **b.** preoperational stage; **c.** sensorimotor stage; **d.** formal operations stage. (page 376)
12. Piaget would recommend waiting for the child to discover the concept by himself or herself. According to Vygotsky the answer depends on the child's zone of proximal development. Some children could be taught the concept, and others are not yet ready for it. (page 377)
13. Not enough information is provided to answer this question. In Kohlberg's system any judgment can represent either a high or a low level of moral reasoning; we evaluate a person's moral reasoning by the explanation, not by the decision itself. (page 380)

Social and Emotional Development

How do we change, socially and emotionally, as we grow older?

You are a contestant on a new TV game show called *What's My Worry?* Behind the curtain is someone with an overriding concern. You are to identify that concern by questioning a psychologist who knows what it is. (You neither see nor hear the concerned person.) You must ask questions that can be answered with a single word or a short phrase. If you identify the worry correctly, you can win as much as $50,000.

Here's the catch: The more questions you ask, the smaller the prize. If you guess correctly after only one question, you win $50,000. After two questions, you win $25,000 and so on. It would therefore be poor strategy to keep asking questions until you are sure; instead, you should ask one or two questions and then make an educated guess.

What would your first question be? Mine would be: "How old is this person?" The principal worries of teenagers are different from those of most 20-year-olds, which in turn differ from those of still older people. Each age has its own characteristic concerns, opportunities, and pleasures.

Erikson's Description of Human Development

Erik Erikson divided the human life span into eight periods that he variously called ages or stages. At each stage of life, he said, people have specific tasks to master, and each generates its own social and emotional conflicts. Table 10.6 summarizes Erikson's stages, with the particular issues associated with each of them.

Erikson suggested that failure to master the task of a particular stage meant unfortunate consequences that would carry over to later stages. For example, the newborn infant deals with the issue of basic trust versus mistrust. An infant whose early environment is supportive, nurturing, and loving will form a strong attachment to the parents, and this attachment will positively influence future relationships with other people (Erikson, 1963). An infant who is mistreated will fail to form a close, trusting relationship with his or her parents and will have trouble developing close ties with anyone else later. This idea is, of course, testable, and later in this module, we shall consider some of the relevant research.

Consider also adolescence, with its issue of identity. Adolescents in Western societies have many options of how they will spend the rest of their lives. Most people consider many options before deciding, and it is possible to delay a decision or even to change one. Eventually, however, a decision becomes important. You can't work on achieving your plans until you have plans.

According to Erikson the key decision of young adulthood is intimacy or isolation—that is, sharing your life with someone else or living alone. Here is it pretty clear how a good decision can benefit the rest of your life and how a poor decision can hurt it.

If you live a full life span, you will spend about half your life in "middle adulthood," where the issue is

TABLE 10.6 Erikson's Stages of Human Development

Stages	Main Conflict	Typical Question
Infant	Basic trust versus mistrust	Is my social world predictable and supportive?
Toddler (ages 1–3)	Autonomy versus shame and doubt	Can I do things by myself or must I always rely on others?
Preschool child (ages 3–6)	Initiative versus guilt	Am I good or bad?
Preadolescent (ages 6–12)	Industry versus inferiority	Am I successful or worthless?
Adolescent (early teens)	Identity versus role confusion	Who am I?
Young adult (late teens and early 20s)	Intimacy versus isolation	Shall I share my life with another person or live alone?
Middle adult (late 20s to retirement)	Generativity versus stagnation	Will I succeed in my life, both as a parent and as a worker?
Older adult (after retirement)	Ego integrity versus despair	Have I lived a full life or have I failed?

▌Erik Erikson argued that each age group has its own special social and emotional conflicts.

generativity (producing something important, such as children or work) versus stagnation (not producing). If all goes well, you can take pride in your success. If not, then the difficulties and disappointments are almost certain to continue into old age.

Is Erikson's view of development accurate? This question is unanswerable. He provided a description, not an explanation. You might or might not find his description of development a useful way to describe life concerns, but it is not the kind of theory that one can test scientifically. However, two of his general points do seem valid: Each stage has its own special difficulties, and an unsatisfactory resolution to the problems of one stage of development will carry over as an extra difficulty in the next stage.

Now let's examine in more detail some of the major social and emotional issues that confront people at different ages. Beyond the primary conflicts that Erikson highlighted, development is marked by a succession of other significant problems.

CRITICAL THINKING:
A STEP FURTHER
Erikson's Stages

Suppose you disagreed with Erikson's analysis; for example, suppose you believe that the main concern of young adults is not "intimacy versus isolation" but "earning money versus not earning money" or "finding meaning in life versus meaninglessness." How might you determine whether your theory or Erikson's is more accurate?

Infancy and Childhood

An important aspect of human life at any age is **attachment**—*a long-term feeling of closeness toward another person*—and one of the most important events of early childhood is the formation of one's first attachments. John Bowlby (1973) developed a theoretical view that infants who develop one or more good attachments have a sense of security and safety. They can explore the world and return to their attachment figure when frightened or distressed. Those who do not develop strong early attachments will probably have trouble developing close relations later as well and need to cope with life's troubles without social support (Mikulincer, Shaver, & Pereg, 2003).

All that sounds fine in theory, but how can we measure strength of attachment to begin to test and extend the theory? Most work has used the **Strange Situation** (usually capitalized), pioneered by Mary Ainsworth (1979). In this procedure *a mother and her infant* (typically 12 or 18 months old) *come into a room with many toys. Then a stranger enters the room. The mother leaves and then returns. A few minutes later, both the stranger and the mother leave; then the stranger returns, and finally, the mother returns.* Through a one-way mirror, a psychologist observes the infant's reactions to each of these events. Observers classify infants' responses in the following categories. Of course, not all fit neatly into one category or another.

- *Securely attached.* The infant uses the mother as a base of exploration, often showing her a toy, cooing at her, or making eye contact with her. The infant shows some distress when the mother leaves but cries only briefly or not at all. When she returns, the infant goes to her with apparent delight, cuddles for a while, and then returns to the toys.
- *Anxious (or resistant).* Responses toward the mother fluctuate between happy and angry. The infant clings to the mother and cries profusely when she leaves, as if worried that she might not return. When she does return, the infant clings to her again but does not use her as a base to explore a room full of toys. A child with an anxious attachment typically shows many fears, including a strong fear of strangers.
- *Avoidant.* While the mother is present, the infant does not stay near her and does not interact much with her. The infant may or may not cry when she leaves and does not go to her when she returns.
- *Disorganized.* The infant seems not even to notice the mother or looks away while approaching her or covers his or her face or lies on the floor. The infant may alternate between approach and avoidance and shows more fear than affection.

The prevalence of the various attachment styles varies from one population to another, but these numbers are often cited as an approximation for North America: 65% secure, 10% anxious/resistant, 15% avoidant, 10% disorganized (Ainsworth, Blehar, Waters, & Wall, 1978). Of course, many children do not fit neatly into one category or another, so some who are classified as "secure" or "avoidant" are more secure or avoidant than others.

The Strange Situation also can be used to evaluate the relationship between child and father (Belsky, 1996), child and grandparent, or other relationships. As a rule the quality of one relationship correlates with the quality of others. For example, most children who have a good relationship with the mother also have a good relationship with the father, and chances are the parents are happy with each other as well (Elicker, Englund, & Sroufe, 1992; Erel & Burman, 1995). Beyond about age 18 months, the Strange Situation is no longer a useful tool, as children become much less distressed when they are left alone or with a stranger. The attachment patterns continue, though, and can be measured in other ways. For example, most infants who have a secure relationship with their parents at age 12 months continue to have a close relationship with them decades later (Waters, Merrick, Treboux, Crowell, & Albersheim, 2000). They are also likely to form close and mutually supportive relationships with friends and romantic partners, whereas those with anxious or avoidant attachments worry excessively about rejection or fail to seek others' support in times of distress (Mikulincer et al., 2003).

What influences a child's attachment pattern? That is, why do some children develop more secure attachments than others? One possibility is that children differ genetically in their tendency to fear the unfamiliar, and several studies with older children support this idea (McGuire, Clifford, Fink, Basho, & McDonnell, 2003; Schwartz, Wright, Shin, Kagan, & Rauch, 2003). However, much of the observed variance in attachment style depends on how responsive the parents are to the infants' needs, including such things as talking to the infant but also quite importantly holding and touching. Gentle touch can be very reassuring (Hertenstein, 2002). Programs that teach parents to be more responsive produce significant increases in secure attachments by the infants (Bakermans-Kranenburg, van IJzendoorn, & Juffer, 2003).

Extreme early experiences can also produce powerful effects. One study examined children adopted in Britain after living up to their first 2 years of life in Romanian orphanages where they had received little attention. Many of them did not even resemble any of the usual attachment styles. They might approach and cling to the stranger instead of the parent. Some of them approached the stranger in a friendly way at first and then withdrew, unlike typical children who avoid a stranger at first and then become more friendly (O'Connor et al., 2003).

The patterns of attachment are somewhat consistent across cultures, but not entirely. For example, in most parts of the United States, most mothers encourage their infants to be independent from an early age, and mothers who exert much physical control over their infants tend to be less sensitive to their infants, leading to an avoidant attachment style. In Puerto Rico, however, most mothers exert much physical control while nevertheless being warm and sensitive, leading to a secure attachment style (Carlson & Harwood, 2003). In Asia most mothers hold their infants much of the day and keep them in bed with the parents at night. If an Asian mother is persuaded to leave her infant with a stranger in the Strange Situation, it may be the first time the infant has been away from its mother, and it cries loud and long. By Western standards these children qualify as "anxiously attached," but the behavior means something different in its cultural context (Rothbaum, Weisz, Pott, Miyake, & Morelli, 2000).

CONCEPT CHECK ☑

14. If a child in the Strange Situation clings tightly to the mother and cries furiously when she leaves, which kind of attachment does the child have? Does the child's culture affect the answer? (Check your answers on page 390.)

Social Development in Childhood and Adolescence

The social and emotional development of children depends in part on how successfully they form friendships with other children. "Popular" children have many friends and admirers. "Rejected" children are avoided by most other children. "Controversial" children who have some social skills but an aggressive streak are liked by some but rejected by others. In most cases a child's status as popular, rejected, or controversial is consistent from year to year (Coie & Dodge, 1983).

Adolescence begins when the body reaches *puberty,* the onset of sexual maturation. Adolescence merges into adulthood, and adulthood is more a state of mind than a condition of the body. Some 12-year-

▌ Children learn social skills by interacting with brothers, sisters, and friends close to their own age.

olds act like adults, and some 30-year-olds act like adolescents.

Adolescence has sometimes been portrayed as a period of "storm and stress," characterized by moodiness, conflict with parents, and risky behaviors. To some extent those trends reflect hormonal changes and brain maturation during adolescence. Even adolescent rats and other species show risky, sensation-seeking behaviors (Spear, 2000). However, the storm and stress vary substantially among individuals, families, and cultures (Arnett, 1999). For example, in Western societies the adolescent years are typically the time when people start dating, and the romantic relationships (or lack of

them) can be a source of either great pleasure or displeasure (Furman, 2002).

In many nontechnological societies, most teenagers are married and working. In effect they move directly from childhood into adulthood. In Western culture our excellent health and nutrition have gradually lowered the average age of puberty (Okasha, McCarron, McEwen, & Smith, 2001), but our economic situation encourages people to stay in school into their 20s and to postpone marriage, family, and career (Arnett, 2000). The consequence is a long period of physical maturity without adult status. Imagine that our society decided that people should stay in college until age 30, postponing marriage, children, and career decisions until even later. Would this policy bring out the best behavior in 25- to 30-year-olds?

Identity Development

As Erik Erikson pointed out, adolescence is a time of "finding yourself," of determining "who am I?" or "who will I be?" It is when most people first construct a coherent "life story" of how they got to be the way they are and how one life event led to another (Habermas & Bluck, 2000).

In some societies most people are expected to enter the same occupation as their parents and to live in the same town. The parents may even choose their children's marriage partners. Western society offers young people choices about education, career, marriage, political and religious affiliation, where to live, and activities regarding sex, alcohol, and drugs. Remember from Chapter 8 that, even when people are

▌ (a) American teenagers are financially dependent on their parents but have the opportunity to spend much time in whatever way they choose. (b) In many nontechnological societies, teenagers are expected to do adult work and accept adult responsibilities.

given all the information they need to answer a question, they sometimes still rely on inappropriate heuristics and make illogical decisions. With regard to life's most important choices, people almost never have all the information. Having a great deal of freedom to choose a life path can be invigorating, but it can also be more than a little frightening.

An adolescent's *concern with decisions about the future and the quest for self-understanding* has been called an **identity crisis.** The term *crisis* implies more emotional turbulence than is typical. Identity development has two major elements: whether one is actively exploring the issue and whether one has made any decisions (Marcia, 1980). We can diagram the possibilities using the following grid:

	Has explored or is exploring the issues	Has not explored the issues
Decisions already made	Identity achievement	Identity foreclosure
Decisions not yet made	Identity moratorium	Identity diffusion

Those who have not yet given any serious thought to making any decisions and who in fact have no clear sense of identity are said to have **identity diffusion.** People in this stage are not actively concerned with their identity and are waiting to clarify the issues. People in **identity moratorium** are *seriously considering the issues but have not yet made any decisions.* They experiment with various possibilities and imagine themselves in different roles before deciding which one is best.

Identity foreclosure is a state of *reaching firm decisions without much thought.* For example, a young man might be told that he is expected to go into the family business with his father, or a young woman might be told that she is expected to marry and raise children. Decrees of that sort were once common in North America and Europe, and they are still common in many other societies today. Someone who accepts such decisions has little reason to explore alternative possibilities.

Finally, **identity achievement** is *the outcome of having explored various possible identities and then making one's own decisions.* Identity achievement does not come all at once. For example, you might be fully decided about your career but not about marriage or about marriage but not a career. You might also reach identity achievement and then rethink some of those decisions years later.

The "Personal Fable" of Teenagers

Answer the following items true or false:

- Other people may fail to realize their life ambitions, but I will realize mine.
- I understand love and sex in a way that my parents never did.
- Tragedy may strike other people, but probably not me.
- Almost everyone notices how I look and how I dress.

According to David Elkind (1984), teenagers are particularly likely to harbor such beliefs. Taken together, he calls them the "personal fable," the conviction that "I am special—what is true for everyone else is not true for me." Up to a point, this fable can help us to maintain a cheerful, optimistic outlook on life, but it becomes dangerous when it leads people to take foolish chances.

For example, one study found that high school girls who were having sexual intercourse without contraception estimated that they had only a small chance of becoming pregnant through unprotected sex. Girls who were either having no sex or using contraception during sex estimated a much higher probability that unprotected sex would lead to pregnancy (Arnett, 1990). Because this was a correlational study, we do not know which came first—the girls' underestimation of the risk of pregnancy or their willingness to have unprotected sex. In either case the results illustrate the attitude, "it can't happen to me."

❚ Some teenagers seriously risk their health and safety. According to David Elkind, one reason for such risky behavior is the "personal fable," the secret belief that "nothing bad can happen to me."

This attitude is hardly unique to teenagers, however. Most middle-aged adults regard themselves as more likely than other people to succeed on the job and as less likely than average to have an injury or a serious illness (Quadrel, Fischhoff, & Davis, 1993). They also overestimate their own chances of winning a lottery, especially if they get to choose their own lottery ticket (Langer, 1975). That is, few people fully outgrow the personal fable.

Adulthood and the Midlife Transition

From their 20s until retirement, the main concern of most adults is, as Erik Erikson noted: "What will I achieve and contribute to society and my family? Will I be successful?" The young adult years begin with a flurry of major decisions about marriage, career, having children, where to live, and how to live. Whether middle age is a time of satisfaction depends on the quality of those decisions.

No doubt you have heard people talk about a "midlife crisis." Few people experience enough distress to call it a crisis, but many do experience *a reassessment of personal goals,* which we call a **midlife transition.** As people realize that their lives are about half over, they reconsider their careers and other choices.

Just as the adolescent identity crisis is a bigger issue in cultures that offer many choices, the same is true for the midlife transition. If you lived in a society that offered no choices, you would not worry about the paths not taken! People in Western society, however, enter adulthood with high hopes. While you are young, you dream of all the great things you will experience and accomplish. You plan to earn an advanced degree, work at a wonderful job, excel at it, marry a wonderful person, have marvelous children, become a leader in your community, run for political office, write a great novel, compose great music, travel the world . . . You know you are not working on all of your goals right now, but you can tell yourself, "I'll do it later." But at some point as you grow older, you realize that you are running out of "later." Even if some of your dreams are still achievable, time is passing: "What am I waiting for?"

People deal with their midlife transitions in many ways. Some abandon their unrealistic goals and set new goals more consistent with the direction their lives have taken. That is, they decide to do as well as possible at what they are already doing. Others decide that they have been ignoring dreams that they are not willing to abandon. They quit their jobs and go back to school, set up a business of their own, or try something else they had always wanted to do. In one study middle-aged women who made major changes in their lives were happier and more successful than those who didn't (Stewart & Ostrove, 1998). (Of course, we don't know whether the life changes made women happy and successful or whether happy, successful women are more likely than others to make changes.)

The least satisfactory outcome is to decide, "I can't abandon my dreams, but I can't do anything about them either. I can't take the risk of changing my life, even though I am dissatisfied with it." People with that attitude become frustrated, discouraged, depressed.

The advice is clear: To increase your chances of feeling good in middle age and beyond, make good decisions now. If there is something you really care about, such that you will regret not trying it, don't wait until you have a midlife crisis. Get started on it now. Take chances. If you fail, well, at least you won't always wonder what would have happened if you had tried. Besides, in the process of trying to do what you want, you might discover a related opportunity that you would not have found otherwise. And you never know: You might succeed.

CONCEPT CHECK ☑

15. How does a midlife transition resemble an adolescent identity crisis? (Check your answer on page 390.)

Old Age

People age in different ways. Some people, especially those with Alzheimer's disease or other serious ailments, deteriorate rapidly, both intellectually and physically. However, most people over 65 continue to work at full-time or part-time jobs, volunteer work, or other activities. Many remain active and alert well into their 80s and 90s. It is difficult to remain alert without remaining active; programs that increase older people's physical exercise lead to improvements in memory and cognition as well (Colcombe & Kramer, 2003).

Your satisfaction in old age will depend largely on how you live while younger. Some older people can say, "I hope to continue living many more years, but even if I don't, I have lived my life well. I did everything that I really cared about." Others say, "There is so much that I wanted to do but never did." Feeling dignity in old age also depends on how people are treated by their families, communities, and societies. Some cultures, including the people of Korea, observe a special ceremony to celebrate a person's retirement or 70th birthday (Damron-Rodriguez, 1991). African American and Native American families traditionally honor their elders, giving them a position of status in

▌ In Tibet and many other cultures, children are taught to treat old people with respect and honor.

the family and calling on them for advice. Japanese families follow a similar tradition, at least publicly (Koyano, 1991).

Older people make some different choices than young people, but their differences are easy to understand. Suppose we ask young and old adults whether they would prefer to spend this weekend meeting interesting new people or with friends they have known for years. Young people generally opt for an exciting stranger, but older people strongly prefer longtime friends. Why? You can probably identify with the older people if we change the question slightly. You still have a choice between meeting exciting new people or visiting with longtime friends, except that you plan soon to move permanently to the other side of the world. Now whom do you want to visit? Almost certainly, you will want to use this last opportunity to visit your best friends (Carstensen & Charles, 1998).

Although an increasing percentage of people over 65 remain in the work force, most people eventually retire. Retirement decreases stress, but it also brings a sense of loss to those whose lives had centered around their work (Kim & Moen, 2001). Loss of control becomes a more serious issue still later if someone is in failing health. Consider someone who spent half a century running a business who now lives in a nursing home where staff members make all the decisions. Leaving even a few of the choices and responsi-

bilities to the residents improves their health, alertness, and memory (Rodin, 1986; Rowe & Kahn, 1987).

The Psychology of Facing Death

A man who has not found something he is willing to die for is not fit to live.
—Martin Luther King Jr. (1964)

This is perhaps the greatest lesson we learned from our patients: LIVE, so you do not have to look back and say, "God, how I have wasted my life!"
—Elisabeth Kübler Ross (1975)

The worst thing about death is the fact that when a man is dead it's impossible any longer to undo the harm you have done him, or to do the good you haven't done him. They say: live in such a way as to be always ready to die. I would say: live in such a way that anyone can die without you having anything to regret.
—Leo Tolstoy (1865/1978, p. 192)

We commonly associate death with older people, although people die at any age. Just thinking about the fact that you will eventually die evokes distress. According to **terror-management theory**, *we cope with our fear of death by avoiding thinking about death and by affirming a worldview that provides self-esteem, hope,*

▌ Pedro Zamora worked to educate people about HIV prevention and AIDS after he learned he was HIV positive. He became famous when he appeared on MTV's *Real World* and later died of AIDS-related complications.

and value in life (Pyszczynski, Greenberg, & Solomon, 2000). If someone simply reminds you that you are mortal, your probable reactions include self-assurances that you have many years to live, that your health is good, and that you will quit smoking, lose weight, or do whatever else would improve your health. You probably also will increase your ambitions temporarily, talking about the high salary you will earn and the exciting things you will do during the rest of your life (Kasser & Sheldon, 2000).

Still, even excellent health merely postpones death, so a reminder of death also redoubles people's efforts to defend a belief that life is part of something eternal. People with strong religious beliefs may have faith in a continuation of their own lives after death. Others think in terms of how their lives contribute to their families, their countries, their professions, or something else that will continue after they are gone (Pyszczynski et al., 2000). Even a casual reference to death increases people's defenses of their beliefs, whatever those beliefs are.

IN CLOSING

Social and Emotional Issues Through the Life Span

Let's close by reemphasizing a key point of Erik Erikson's theory: Each age or stage builds on the previous ones. For example, the quality of your early attachments to parents and others correlates with your ability to form close, trusting relationships later. How well you handle the identity issues of adolescence affects your adult life. Certainly, your productivity during adulthood (generativity vs. stagnation) determines how satisfied you can feel with your life when you reach old age.

We could make a similar point for Piaget's cognitive stages or Kohlberg's stages of moral reasoning, discussed in the previous module: Each of us has to master the tasks of an earlier stage before we can deal effectively with those of the next stage. Life is a continuum, and the choices you make at any age are linked with those you made before and after.

Summary

- *Erikson's view of development.* Erik Erikson described the human life span as a series of eight ages or stages, each with its own social and emotional conflicts. (page 383)
- *Infant attachment.* Infants can develop several kinds of attachment to significant people in their lives, as measured in the Strange Situation. However, the results of studies in Western society do not apply equally well in other societies. (page 384)
- *Adolescent identity crisis.* Adolescents have to deal with the question "Who am I?" Many experiment with several identities before deciding. (page 386)
- *Adults' concerns.* One of the main concerns of adults is productivity in family and career. Many adults undergo a midlife transition when they reevaluate their goals. (page 388)
- *Old age.* Dignity and independence are key concerns of old age. (page 388)
- *Facing death.* People at all ages face the anxieties associated with the inevitability of death. A reminder of death influences people to set higher goals and to defend their worldviews. (page 389)

Answers to Concept Checks

14. In the United States, this pattern would indicate an anxious or insecure attachment. In Southeast Asia, however, this behavior is normal and we should beware of applying any labels that have been established for Western children. (page 385)
15. In both cases people examine their lives, goals, and possible directions for the future. (page 388)

Temperament, Family, Gender, and Cultural Influences

What factors influence development of personality and social behavior?

If you had to describe yourself briefly, what would you say? You probably would mention your age, your family, whether you are male or female, where you live, where you work or go to school, and your main interests and activities. You might mention your political or religious affiliation and possibly your nationality or ethnic identity.

The point is this: You are a unique individual and also a member of many groups. Your group memberships mold some of your thoughts about yourself and how other people treat you. You are a complex product of both what you bring to a situation (your personality and temperament) and how a situation affects you. Let's begin with temperament.

Temperament and Lifelong Development

People differ markedly in their **temperament**—their *tendency to be either active or inactive, outgoing or reserved, and to respond vigorously or quietly to new stimuli*. Would you rather go to a party where you will meet new people or spend a quiet evening with a few old friends? Would you try a risky activity or would you watch while someone else tries it? In general, are you more impulsive or more reserved than most of the people you know?

Now consider how you just described yourself: How long have you been like that? Were you at one time a great deal more outgoing and adventurous, or shyer and more reserved, than you are now?

To test the persistence of temperament, researchers have conducted studies lasting from infancy into adulthood. Infants who frequently kick and cry are termed "difficult" or "inhibited," whereas those who seldom kick or cry are called "easy" or "uninhibited" (Thomas & Chess, 1980; Thomas, Chess, & Birch, 1968). The inhibited infants have irregular eating and sleeping habits. As children they are frequently tense and hard to comfort (Kagan, 1989). They also contract contagious diseases more often than others (Lewis, Thomas, & Worobey, 1990). (Inhibited and uninhibited children are, of course, two ends of a continuum. Many children are intermediate.)

Jerome Kagan and Nancy Snidman (1991) identified some clearly inhibited and uninhibited 4-month-old infants and then tested them again a few months later in mildly frightening situations. For example, the experimenter might uncover a rotating toy, frown, and then scream a nonsense phrase. Infants who had been inhibited at age 4 months were in general easily frightened at 9 and 14 months. When they were tested again at 7½ years, they tended to be shy, nervous, and fearful (Kagan, Reznick, & Snidman, 1988). As adults they were tested with functional magnetic resonance imaging, a procedure that measures the activity of various brain areas. As shown in Figure 10.26, when inhibited people viewed photographs of unfamiliar people, they had higher than average activity in the *amygdala,* a brain area that processes anxiety-related information (Schwartz et al., 2003).

Most people's temperaments remain fairly consistent over time. An outgoing, uninhibited child will probably continue to be outgoing and uninhibited for years, perhaps even into adulthood.

391

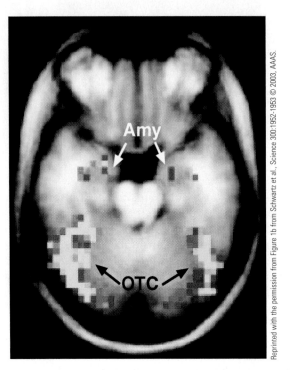

FIGURE 10.26 This horizontal section through an image of the human brain shows two areas that were more active in inhibited than uninhibited adults. Areas marked in red showed a large difference and those in yellow showed an even larger difference. "Amy" indicates the area of the amygdala (on each side of the brain). "OTC" indicates the occipital and temporal areas of the cortex.

Apparently, temperament depends at least partly on genetics. Identical twins resemble each other in temperament more than fraternal twins do (Matheny, 1989). Identical twins reared in separate and apparently rather different environments generally end up with similar temperaments (Bouchard, Lykken, McGue, Segal, & Tellegen, 1990). However, environmental factors must contribute also; otherwise, identical twins would always match each other exactly.

CONCEPT CHECK ☑

16. Were the studies of temperament over the years longitudinal or cross-sectional?
17. Why is it likely that temperament is one influence on behavior in the Strange Situation? (Check your answers on page 399.)

The Family

In early childhood our parents and other relatives are the most important people in our lives. How do those early family experiences mold our personality and social behavior?

Birth Order and Family Size

You have no doubt heard people say that first-born children are more successful in schoolwork and career accomplishments than later borns. First borns also rate themselves as more ambitious, honest, and conscientious (e.g., Paulhus, Trapnell, & Chen, 1999). On the other hand, later-born children are said to be more popular, more independent, less conforming, less neurotic, and possibly more creative.

Those generalizations are based on an enormous number of studies. However, most of those studies have used flawed research methods (Ernst & Angst, 1983; Schooler, 1972). The simplest and by far most common way to do the research is this: You ask some large number of people to tell you their birth order and something else about themselves, such as their grade point average in school. Then you measure the correlation between the measurements. Do you see any possible problem here?

The problem is that many first borns come from families with *only* one child, whereas (of course) later-born children all come from larger families. In general, highly educated and ambitious parents are more likely to have only one child and to provide that child with many advantages. Therefore, what appears to be a difference between first- and later-born children could be a difference between small and large families (Rodgers, 2001).

A better way to do the study is to compare first- versus second-born children in only families with at least two children, first- versus third-born children in only families with at least three children, and so forth. Figure 10.27 shows the results of one such study. As you can see, the average IQ is higher in small families

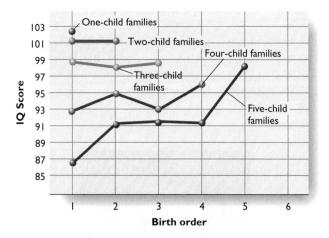

FIGURE 10.27 Children from small families tend to score higher on IQ tests than children from large families. However, within a family of a given size, birth order is not related to IQ. If we combine results for families of different sizes, first borns have a higher mean score, but only because many of them come from small families. *(Adapted from Rodgers et al., 2000)*

Reprinted with the permission from Figure 1b from Schwartz et al.. Science 300:1952-1953 © 2003, AAAS.

than in large families. However, within a family of any given size, first borns do no better than later borns on the average (Rodgers, Cleveland, van den Oord, & Rowe, 2000).

"But wait," you say. "The first born in my family does act different from the others, and most of the people I know see the same pattern in their own families." In a sense you are right: The first born takes more responsibility, identifies more with the parents, bosses the younger children around, and in many other ways, acts differently from the later-born children *while at home*. However, the way people act at home is not necessarily the way they act among friends at school (Harris, 2000).

CONCEPT CHECK ☑

18. Suppose someone found that last-born children (those with no younger brothers or sisters) do better in school than second-to-last borns. What would be one likely explanation? (Check your answer on page 400.)

Effects of Parenting Styles

If and when you have children of your own, will you be loving and kind or strict and distant? Will you give the children everything they want or make them work for rewards? Will you encourage their independence or enforce restrictions? Moreover, how much does your behavior matter?

Psychologists have done a great deal of research comparing parenting styles to the behavior and personality of the children. Much of this research is based on four parenting styles described by Diana Baumrind (1971):

Authoritative parents: These parents *set high standards and impose controls, but they are also warm and responsive to the child's communications.* They set limits but adjust them when appropriate; they encourage their children to strive toward their own goals.

Authoritarian parents: Like the authoritative parents, authoritarian parents set firm controls, but they tend to be *emotionally more distant from the child; they set rules without explaining the reasons behind them.*

Permissive parents: Permissive parents are *warm and loving but undemanding.*

Indifferent or uninvolved parents: These parents *spend little time with their children and do little more than provide them with food and shelter.*

Parenting styles are reasonably consistent within a family. For example, parents who are permissive with

one child are usually permissive with the others too (Holden & Miller, 1999). The research has found small but reasonably consistent links between parenting style and children's behavior. For example, most children of authoritative parents are self-reliant, cooperate with others, and do well in school. Children of authoritarian parents tend to be law-abiding but distrustful and not very independent. Children of permissive parents are often socially irresponsible. Children of indifferent parents tend to be impulsive and undisciplined.

However, the interpretation of the results is not as easy as it may appear. Many psychologists have drawn cause-and-effect conclusions—for example, assuming that parental indifference *leads to* impulsive, out-of-control children. However, as Judith Rich Harris (1998) pointed out, other explanations are possible. Maybe impulsive, hard-to-control children cause their parents to withdraw into indifference. Or maybe the parents and children share genes that lead to uncooperative behaviors. Similarly, the kindly behaviors of authoritative parents could encourage well-mannered behaviors in their children, but it is also possible that these children were well behaved from the start, thereby encouraging kindly, understanding behaviors in their parents.

A better approach is to study adopted children, who are genetically unrelated to the parents rearing them. If their behavior depends on the parenting style or resembles the behavior of the parents in any way, we cannot explain the relationship in terms of shared genes. The results of such studies surprise most people: Most measures of personality show nearly a zero correlation between adoptive parents and their adopted children (Heath, Neale, Kessler, Eaves, & Kendler, 1992; Loehlin, 1992; Viken, Rose, Kaprio, & Koskenvuo, 1994). For this reason Harris (1995, 1998) has argued that family life has little lasting influence on most aspects of personality (except for what people do specifically at home). Much of personality variation depends on genetic differences, and the rest of the variation, she argues, depends mostly on peer influences—that is, the other children in the neighborhood. If a researcher picks two children at random from the same classroom, they are more likely than children from different schools to resemble each other in a wide variety of behaviors (Rose et al., 2003). In short, peer influences are strong. For more information visit this Web site:

home.att.net/~xchar/tna/

As you can imagine, not everyone happily accepted Harris's conclusion. Psychologists who had spent a career studying parenting styles were not pleased to be told that their results were inconclusive. Parents were not pleased to be told that they had less influence on their children than they had thought. Harris (2000), however, chose her words carefully. She did not say that it makes no difference how you treat your children. For one thing, obviously, if you treat your children badly, they won't like you!

Also, parents control where the children live and therefore influence their choice of peers, and parents influence some aspects of life that peers usually don't care about, such as religion, exposure to music lessons, and what spices to put on food. Parents have other influences too, and indeed, Harris may have overstated her case (Vandell, 2000). What is clear, however, is that previous psychologists had overstated their case even more. Parents do have an influence on their children's psychological development but not the huge effect we used to assume.

CONCEPT CHECK ☑

19. Why is a correlation between parents' behavior and children's behavior indecisive concerning how parents influence their children? Why would a correlation between adoptive parents' behavior and that of their adopted children provide more useful information? (Check your answers on page 400.)

Parental Employment and Child Care

Many people assume that the "normal" way to rear infants is for the mother to stay with them full time because that custom was prevalent in much of North America and Europe for many years. However, child-rearing customs vary greatly from one culture to another, one era to another, and even one social class to another.

In many subsistence cultures, a mother returns to her usual tasks of gathering food and so forth shortly after giving birth, leaving her infant most of the day with other women, relatives, and older children (McGurk, Caplan, Hennessy, & Moss, 1993). For example, in the Efe culture of Africa, a mother stays with her infant only about half of the day, but the infant is seldom alone. Within the first few months, the infant establishes strong attachments to several adults and children (Tronick, Morelli, & Ivey, 1992). In wealthy families in Europe, it has long been the custom for "nannies" (paid caregivers) to take care of the children for most of the day. In short, if we consider all the people who ever lived anywhere, it is a rarity for a child to be reared exclusively by the mother.

Still, many psychologists in Europe and North America developed a theoretical belief that healthy emotional development required an infant to establish a strong attachment to a single caregiver—ordinarily, the mother. When more and more families began placing infants in day care so that both parents could return to work shortly after their infant's birth, a question arose about the psychological effect on those children.

Many studies compared children who stayed with their mothers and those who entered day care early. The studies examined attachment (as measured by the Strange Situation or in other ways), adjustment and well-being, play with other children, social relations with other adults, and intellectual development. The results were that most children develop satisfactorily, both intellectually and socially, if they receive at least adequate day care (Scarr, 1998). One longitudinal study of 2,402 low-income families examined both preschoolers and older children before and after their mothers took jobs. The preschoolers showed no behavioral changes, and the older children showed slight benefits in some aspects of adjustment (Chase-Lansdale et al., 2003). One study showed a surprising result: Children who started day care before age 1 showed more favorable attachment behaviors than those who started after age 2½ (Erel, Oberman, & Yirmiya, 2000). Perhaps those who started day care early got used to it, whereas those who started later had more trouble adjusting to the change.

Undoubtedly, the quality of day care makes a difference to children's behavior, although most studies have found big differences only for children from disadvantaged homes. Evidently, development is satisfactory when either home life or day care is good; prob-

In many cultures it has long been the custom for a mother to leave her infant for much of the day with friends, relatives, and other children.

❚ Many children today are reared by a single parent. Some are reared primarily by the father or grandparents. Some are reared by gay parents. The research says that who rears the child has little influence on long-term personality development if the caregivers are loving and dependable.

lems arise when both are bad. When children from disadvantaged homes experience good day care (with a consistent, affectionate staff and adequate facilities), they develop *better* than if they had stayed at home (McGurk et al., 1993; Scarr, Phillips, & McCartney, 1990). Children from deprived homes who experience poor day care, which is often all the parents can afford, are at a clear disadvantage.

Nontraditional Families

Western society has considered a "traditional" family to be a mother, a father, and their children. A "nontraditional" family is, therefore, anything else. Psychologists have studied the personalities of children who were reared by unmarried mothers (Weissman, Leaf, & Bruce, 1987), gay or lesbian couples (Patterson, 1994), and families where the mother works full time and the father stays home with the children (Parke, 1995). Parenting styles do differ; for example, fathers generally play with their children more, talk to them less, and tell them more facts with less praise (Leaper, Anderson, & Sanders, 1998). Single parents (usually mothers) often have trouble paying the bills, and their children have troubles resulting from poverty.

However, according to the available data, if we control for the effects of poverty, the other variables in family composition make little measurable difference. Researchers have found no consistent personality effects from being reared by one parent instead

of two or mainly by the father instead of the mother or by gay or lesbian couples instead of a heterosexual couple (Golombok et al., 2003; Silverstein & Auerbach, 1999).

At least those are the conclusions from the available data. Not many studies have examined children reared mainly by fathers or by homosexual couples, and most of those studies have a small sample size and only a modest number of behavioral observations (Redding, 2001). More extensive studies would be a good idea.

Parental Conflict and Divorce

At an earlier time in the United States, divorce was unusual and considered shameful. When Adlai Stevenson was defeated in the presidential campaign of 1952, the fact that he was divorced was considered a major explanation. By 1980, when Ronald Reagan was elected president, voters hardly noticed his divorce and remarriage.

Most children who experience the divorce of their parents show a variety of academic, social, and emotional problems compared to other children. One reason is that the children of divorced families receive less attention and suffer greater economic hardship. Also, many children in divorced families endure prolonged hostility between their parents (Amato & Keith, 1991). If the divorce takes place while the children are still too young to realize what is happening, the effects are milder (Tschann, Johnston, Kline, & Wallerstein, 1990).

Mavis Hetherington and her associates have conducted longitudinal studies of middle-class children and their families following a divorce (Hetherington, 1989). Compared to children in intact families, those in divorced families are more likely to have conflicts with their parents and other children. They pout and seek attention, especially in the first year after a divorce. The boys in particular become aggressive, both at home and at school. Generally, distress is greatest if a mother who had not worked before the divorce takes a job immediately afterward—often by economic necessity. The children then feel that they have lost both parents.

❚ Many sons of divorced parents go through a period when they act out their frustrations by starting fights.

In families where the mother remarried, the daughters were often indifferent or hostile to the stepfather and showed poorer adjustment than children of mothers who did not remarry (Hetherington, Bridges, & Insabella, 1998). Many of the girls rejected every attempt by their stepfathers to establish a positive relationship until eventually the stepfather simply gave up (Hetherington, 1989).

"Complex" or "blended" stepfamilies are composed of parents and their children from previous marriages. Such families have special opportunities and difficulties. Interestingly, the children usually get along fairly well with their new step-brothers and sisters. They may, however, show resentment toward their parents (Hetherington, Henderson, & Reiss, 1999).

Hetherington's studies concentrated on European American middle-class children, and the results differ for other cultures. Divorce is more common in African American families but as a rule more accepted and less stressful (Fine & Schwebel, 1987). Many African American families ease the burden of single parenthood by having a grandmother or other relative help with child care. As in European American families, the more upset the mother is by the divorce, the more upset the children are likely to be (R. T. Phillips & Alcebo, 1986).

Exceptions can be found to almost any generalization about the effects of divorce on children (Hetherington, Stanley-Hagan, & Anderson, 1989). Some children show emotional distress for 1 or 2 years and then gradually feel better. Others remain depressed 5 or 10 years after the divorce. A few seem to do well for years but become more distressed during adolescence. Other children are amazingly resilient throughout their parents' divorce and afterward. They keep their friends, do all right in school, and maintain good relationships with both parents. In fact even some children who are seriously maltreated or abused develop far better than one might expect (Caspi et al., 2002).

Given the emotional trauma usually associated with divorce, should parents stay together for the children's sake? Not necessarily. Children do not fare well if their parents are constantly fighting. Indeed, most children (especially boys) begin to show signs of distress years *before* their parents' divorce, perhaps in response to the parental conflict they already see (Cherlin et al., 1991).

Gender Influences

How would you be different if you had been born female instead of male or male instead of female? Males and females differ, on the average, in many regards. Generally, men fight more often than women and with less provocation. Men also swear more. Men and women generally carry books and packages in different ways, men to the side and women in front. Men are generally more likely to help a stranger change a flat tire, but women are more likely to provide long-term nurturing support (Eagly & Crowley, 1986). When giving directions, men are more likely to use directions and distances—such as "go four blocks east . . ."—whereas women are more likely to use landmarks—such as "go until you see the library . . ." (Saucier et al., 2002). The more pairs of shoes you own, the higher is the probability that you are female. The list of miscellaneous differences could go on and on.

However, many of the differences vary across circumstances. For example, many tasks that are defined as "men's work" in some cultures are "women's work" in others. A few examples are building a fire, making leather products, weaving baskets, planting crops, and milking cows (Wood & Eagly, 2002). Generally, if a culture lives in conditions that require hunting, vigorous defense of resources, or other use of physical strength, men have much greater status and power than women. When food is abundant and enemies are few, men and women have more equal status. Of course, after a culture has adopted a certain set of values, they tend to continue long after the conditions that established them (D. Cohen, 2001).

Within the United States, the percentage of women pursuing careers has greatly increased since the 1950s, as has the percentage of men devoting substantial efforts to child care (Barnett & Hyde, 2001). More women than ever before hold positions of authority in business and industry, and their leadership style differs from men's in only small ways (Eagly, Johannesen-Schmidt, & van Engen, 2003). Thus, many of the male–female differences are more flexible than we once assumed.

Cognitive Differences

Two cognitive differences between the genders are reasonably consistent. First, beginning at an early age, females tend to perform better on certain aspects of language use, especially language fluency (Maccoby & Jacklin, 1974). Second, men generally do better on spatial tasks (Collins & Kimura, 1997). Men are more likely to enter careers in mathematics, physical sciences, and engineering, even in comparison to women of similar mathematical abilities (Benbow, Lubinski, Shea, & Efekhari-Sanjani, 2000).

You might try this task and compare results with your friends: Here is a drawing of a bottle half full of water and then the same bottle tilted. Draw the water level in the tilted bottle.

Most studies—although I have never been able to see this effect with my own students—report that

most U.S. men draw the water level parallel to the ground, as shown below in the drawing on the left, whereas most women draw it partly or entirely parallel to the bottom of the bottle, as shown in the other two drawings (Vasta & Liben, 1996). (The one on the left is correct, of course.)

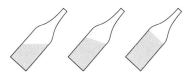

Many researchers have speculated that men evolved greater attention to spatial relationships because men in early hunter-gatherer societies had to find their way home from hunting, whereas women spent more time close to home (Silverman et al., 2000). However, we know little for sure about prehistoric human life. Also, it has been reported that male rats have better spatial learning abilities than female rats (Williams, Barnett, & Meck, 1990), so the difference is probably not specific to anything about early humans.

Differences in Social Behaviors

One idea you have encountered repeatedly is that the results of psychological research depend on details of the method. The same is true for gender differences. If you watch boys and girls at a playground, you see large, consistent differences in their play. Then you set up a laboratory test to measure those differences. You test boys and girls one at a time, and you are stunned to find almost no difference. Many of the differences between males and females emerge only in a social context

▌ One girl tested alone behaves about the same as one boy tested alone. But when boys play together, they show off to one another and to other observers (a); girls play more cooperatively (b).

(Maccoby, 1990). When boys get together with other boys or girls get together with other girls, the social influence magnifies tendencies that are hardly detectable if you examine each person individually.

Girls play competitive games too, but they are more likely than boys to play cooperatively. They take turns, present their desires as "suggestions" instead of demands, and (usually) avoid hurting each other's feelings. Boys compete with each other almost constantly, even when they are just talking: They shout orders, interrupt, threaten, boast, and insult one another.

What happens when boys and girls play together? If they are working on a task that requires cooperation, few sex differences are evident (Powlishta & Maccoby, 1990). However, in unsupervised situations the boys often dominate and intimidate the girls. In some cases the boys take control and the girls simply watch (Maccoby, 1990).

When boys grow up, they do not entirely change their ways. Deborah Tannen (1990) reports one episode at a college basketball game: At the University of Michigan at the time, the custom was for students to ignore the seat numbers on their tickets and take seats on a first-come, first-served basis. One night several men from the visiting team, Michigan State, tried to go to the seats listed on their tickets, only to find University of Michigan students, both men and women, already seated there. The Michigan State students asked the others to leave; the University of Michigan men replied rudely, and the dispute quickly escalated to insults. The women were mortified with embarrassment.

Within a few minutes, however, the Michigan State men settled into neighboring seats, and soon the two groups of men were happily discussing basketball strategies. The women didn't understand why the men had screamed insults in the first place or how they had become friends so quickly afterward.

Reasons Behind Gender Differences

It is easy to list differences between men and women but difficult to explain them. Opinions are often firmer than the evidence.

On the one hand, it is undeniable that adults treat little boys differently from little girls. In one fascinating study, researchers set up cameras and microphones to eavesdrop on 298 families who had brought a child (one child each) to a science museum. Boys and girls spent about equal time looking at each exhibit, and the parents spent about equal time telling boys or girls how to use each exhibit, but on the average they provided about three times as much scientific explanation to the boys as to the girls, regardless of how many questions the children themselves asked (Crowley, Callanen, Tenenbaum, & Allen, 2001).

On the other hand, the fact that we treat boys and girls differently does not negate the possibility that they also differ biologically. If nothing else, men are on the average taller and more muscular than women, and those differences are agreed to be biological in origin. The physical differences predispose to certain behavioral differences, and in turn those differences alter the way other people react, and other people's reactions alter further behavior. (Recall the "magnifier" effect mentioned in Chapter 9, page 338.) In short, neither biological nor cultural influences act in isolation, but only in combination with each other.

Ethnic and Cultural Influences

Membership in a minority group molds a child's development in two major ways: First, the customs of the minority group may differ from those of other groups. Second, members of a minority group are affected because other people treat them differently or expect certain behaviors from them.

Immigrants to any country undergo a period of **acculturation,** *a transition from feeling part of the culture of their original country to the culture of the country they enter.* Acculturation is gradual; people sometimes require a generation or more before they or their descendants feel fully comfortable in a new culture. Most recent immigrants to the United States have come from Latin America or Asia, and most of the children have been highly motivated to learn English and to achieve beyond the level of their parents. Delinquency, crime, and drug and alcohol abuse are less common in recent immigrants than in other U.S. residents (Fuligni, 1998).

Although most immigrant parents want their children to become successful members of their new culture, they also want them to maintain the best parts of their old cultures, such as values of hard work, cooperation, and generosity (Fuligni, 1998). The alternative to full assimilation is **biculturalism,** *the ability to alternate between membership in one culture and membership in another.* For example, people who settle in an Italian American community speak Italian and follow Italian customs in their home neighborhood but speak English and follow U.S. customs elsewhere.

The advantages of biculturalism resemble those of bilingualism: Someone who speaks two languages can communicate with more people and read a greater variety of literature than can a monolingual person. Also, bilingual people come to understand their primary language from a new perspective. Similarly, a bicultural person interacts with a great variety of other people and becomes aware of the strengths and weaknesses of each culture (Harrison, Wilson, Pine, Chan, & Buriel, 1990; LaFromboise, Coleman, & Gerton,

■ Many immigrants are bicultural, having reasonable familiarity with two sets of customs. These immigrant children attend middle school in Michigan.

1993). Many African Americans and Asian Americans identify with their ethnic groups, live in a neighborhood populated mostly by members of the same group, and rely on the help of an extended family but also join the melting pot culture at school, on the job, and in other settings.

At least to a small extent, nearly all of us learn to function in a variety of subcultures. Unless you live in a small town where everyone has the same background, religion, and customs, you have to learn to adjust what you say and do in different settings and with different groups of people. However, the transitions are more noticeable and more intense for ethnic minorities.

IN CLOSING

Understanding and Accepting Many Ways of Life

Each of us can easily fall into the trap of thinking that our own way of growing up and relating to other people is the "normal" way. In fact people differ substantially in their social development, and understanding psychology requires understanding that diversity. Developmental psychologists conduct extensive research to specify the influences behind that diversity, ranging from genetics and prenatal environment to the physical, familial, and cultural environment.

Summary

- *Temperament.* Even infants who are only a few months old differ in their characteristic way of reacting to experiences. Temperament remains fairly consistent as a person grows older. (page 391)

- *Birth order.* Most studies comparing first-born versus later-born children confound the effects of birth order with the effects of family size. If we disregard families with only one child, first borns and later borns behave about the same way when they are outside the home. (page 392)

- *Parenting styles.* Parenting style correlates with the behavior of the children. For example, caring, understanding parents tend to have well-behaved children. However, most studies do not separate the effects of social influences from genetics. Adopted children usually do not resemble their adoptive parents' personalities. Judith Rich Harris has therefore argued that personality and social behavior depend mostly on genetics and peer influences. (page 393)

- *Nontraditional child care.* Children who spend much time early in day care develop about the same as those reared at home by a parent. A child's normal personality and social development require at least one caring adult, but the number of caregivers and their gender and sexual orientation apparently matter little. (page 394)

- *Effects of divorce.* Children of divorced parents often show signs of distress, sometimes even before the divorce. The distress is generally more marked in European American families than in African American families. (page 395)

- *Gender influences.* Women tend to do better than men on certain aspects of language, whereas men tend to solve spatial problems better. Social differences between males and females are small on the average when people are tested one at a time but larger when tested in all-male or all-female groups. Individuals can differ greatly from the averages. (page 396)

- *Ethnic and cultural differences.* People also differ because of ethnic and cultural influences. Acculturation is the process of transition from one culture to another. Many people can function successfully as members of two or more cultures simultaneously. (page 398)

Answers to Concept Checks

16. Kagan and Snidman's study was longitudinal; they studied the same children at different ages. (page 392)

17. Temperament is a measure of how people react to novel stimuli, and the Strange Situation is also a test of reaction to novel stimuli. The difference is that the Strange Situation focuses specifically on social stimuli, particularly the presence or absence of the mother or some other important person in a child's life. (page 392)

18. An only child is a last born as well as a first born. A large sample of last borns will include many children from single-child families, which are often characterized by high IQ and ambitions. Second-to-last borns necessarily come from larger families. (page 393)

19. Children can resemble their parents' behavior because of either genetics or social influences. Adoptive children do not necessarily resemble their adopted parents genetically, so any similarity in behavior would reflect environmental influences. Of course, the question would remain as to whether the parents influenced the children or the children influenced the parents. (page 394)

CHAPTER ENDING

Key Terms and Activities

Key Terms

accommodation: Piaget's term for the modification of an established schema to fit a new object or problem (page 367)

acculturation: a transition from feeling part of the culture of one's original country to the culture of the country that one enters (page 398)

assimilation: Piaget's term for the application of an established schema to new objects or problems (page 367)

attachment: a long-term feeling of closeness between people, such as a child and a caregiver (page 384)

authoritarian parents: those who exert firm controls on their children, generally without explaining the reasons for the rules and without providing much warmth (page 393)

authoritative parents: those who are demanding and impose firm controls, but who are also warm and responsive to the child's communications (page 393)

biculturalism: the ability to alternate between membership in one culture and membership in another (page 398)

chromosome: a strand of hereditary material found in the nucleus of a cell (page 354)

cohort: a group of people born at a particular time (as compared to people born at different times) (page 366)

conservation: the concept that objects retain their weight, volume, and certain other properties in

spite of changes in their shape or arrangement (page 374)

cross-sectional study: a study of groups of individuals of different ages all at the same time (page 364)

dishabituation: an increase in a previously habituated response as a result of a change in the stimulus (page 361)

egocentric: the inability to take the perspective of another person; a tendency to view the world as centered around oneself (page 370)

equilibration: the establishment of harmony or balance between assimilation and accommodation (page 367)

fetal alcohol syndrome: a condition marked by stunted growth of the head and body; malformations of the face, heart, and ears; and nervous system damage, including seizures, hyperactivity, learning disabilities, and mental retardation (page 359)

fetus: an organism more developed than an embryo but not yet born (from about 8 weeks after conception until birth in humans) (page 358)

fraternal twins: twins who develop from two eggs (dizygotic) fertilized by two different sperm; they are no more closely related than are any other children born to the same parents (page 353)

gene: a segment of a chromosome that controls chemical reactions that ultimately direct the development of the organism (page 354)

habituation: a decrease in a person's response to a stimulus after it has been presented repeatedly (page 361)

heritability: an estimate of the variance within a population that is due to heredity (page 356)

identical twins: twins who develop from the same fertilized egg (monozygotic) and therefore have the same genes (page 353)

identity achievement: the outcome of having explored various possible identities and then making one's own decisions (page 387)

identity crisis: concerns with decisions about the future and the quest for self-understanding (page 387)

identity diffusion: the condition of having not yet given any serious thought to identity decisions and having no clear sense of identity (page 387)

identity foreclosure: the state of having made firm identity decisions without having thought much about them (page 387)

identity moratorium: the state of seriously considering one's identity without yet having made any decisions (page 387)

indifferent or uninvolved parents: those who pay little attention to their children beyond doing what is necessary to feed and shelter them (page 393)

longitudinal study: a study of a single group of individuals over time (page 364)

midlife transition: a time of goal reassessment (page 388)

moral dilemma: a problem that pits one moral value against another (page 378)

object permanence: the concept that objects continue to exist even when one does not see, hear, or otherwise sense them (page 368)

operation: according to Piaget a mental process that can be reversed (page 370)

permissive parents: those who are warm and loving but undemanding (page 393)

phenylketonuria (PKU): an inherited disorder in which a person lacks the chemical reactions that convert a nutrient called phenylalanine into other chemicals; unless the diet is carefully controlled, the affected person will become mentally retarded (page 358)

preoperational stage: according to Piaget the second stage of intellectual development, in which children lack operations (page 370)

schema (pl.: schemata): an organized way of interacting with objects in the world (page 367)

selective attrition: the tendency of some kinds of people to be more likely than others to drop out of a study (page 365)

sensorimotor stage: according to Piaget the first stage of intellectual development; an infant's behavior is limited to making simple motor responses to sensory stimuli (page 368)

sequential design: a procedure in which researchers start with groups of people of different ages, studied at the same time, and then study them again at one or more later times (page 365)

sex chromosomes: the pair of chromosomes that determine whether an individual will develop as a female or as a male (page 355)

sex-limited gene: a gene that affects one sex more strongly than the other, even though both sexes have the gene (page 356)

sex-linked gene: a gene located on the X chromosome (page 355)

stage of concrete operations: according to Piaget the ability to deal with the properties of concrete objects but not hypothetical or abstract questions (page 375)

stage of formal operations: according to Piaget the stage when children develop the ability to deal with abstract, hypothetical situations, which demand logical, deductive reasoning and systematic planning (page 375)

Strange Situation: a procedure in which a psychologist observes an infant's behavior in an unfamiliar room at various times as a stranger enters, leaves, and returns and the mother enters, leaves, and returns (page 384)

temperament: people's tendency to be either active or inactive, outgoing or reserved, and to respond vigorously or quietly to new stimuli (page 391)

terror-management theory: the proposal that we cope with our fear of death by avoiding thinking about death and by affirming a worldview that provides self-esteem, hope, and value in life (page 389)

theory of mind: an understanding that other people have a mind too and that each person knows some things that other people don't know (page 371)

X chromosome: a sex chromosome; females have two per cell and males have only one (page 355)

Y chromosome: a sex chromosome; males have one per cell and females have none (page 355)

zone of proximal development: the distance between what a child can do on his or her own and what the child can do with the help of adults or older children (page 377)

zygote: a fertilized egg cell (page 358)

Suggestions for Further Reading

Elkind, D. (1984). *All grown up and no place to go.* Reading, MA: Addison-Wesley. An account of the problems that teenagers and young adults face.

Tannen, D. (1990). *You just don't understand.* New York: William Morrow. A popular book that discusses the various reasons that men and women often fail to understand one another.

Book Companion Web Site

Need help studying? Go to

http://psychology.wadsworth.com/kalat_intro7e/

for a virtual study center. You'll find a personalized Self-Study Assessment that will provide you with a study plan based on your answers to a pretest. Also study using flash cards, quizzes, interactive art, and an online glossary.

Check out interactive **Try It Yourself** exercises on the companion site! For example, the Genetic Generations exercise ties to what you've learned in this chapter.

Your companion site also has direct links to the following Web sites. These links are checked often for changes, dead links, and new additions.

Human Genome Project

www.ornl.gov/TechResources/Human_Genome/home.html

This is the definitive site for understanding the Human Genome Project, from the basic science to ethical, legal, and social considerations to the latest discoveries.

The Child Psychologist

www.childpsychology.com/

Rene Thomas Folse's site focuses on "Specific Disorders and Other Reasons for Concern" about the behavior of children and on "Treatment, Resources, and Remediation." There are links to information about several specific diagnostic tests used with children.

American Academy of Child and Adolescent Psychiatry

http://www.aacap.org

Check this site for information about common psychological disorders of children and teenagers.

The Nurture Assumption

home.att.net/~xchar/tna/

Judith Rich Harris maintains this Web page about her controversial book on the importance of peers and the relative unimportance of parenting styles.

The Child Artist Grown Up

www.robinka.com

Did you like Robin Kalat's drawing at the start of Module 10.2? Check out her adult art at this site.

Try It Yourself CD-ROM
with Critical Thinking Video Exercises

Use your CD to access **videos** related to activities designed to help you think critically about the important topics discussed. For example, the video about anxiety disorders in children relates to what you've learned in this chapter. You'll also find an easy portal link to the book companion site where you can access your personalized **Self-Study Assessments** and interactive **Try It Yourself** exercises.

PsychNow! 2.0

PsychNow! is a fun interactive CD designed to help you with the difficult concepts in psychology. Check out the Human Development section for the following topics that relate to this chapter:

Infant Development: explore children's drawings over time, infant development, and then guess developmental stages.

Child Development: learn about child development stages, Piaget's stages, and his conservation tasks.

Adolescent Development: define adolescence, explore the development of identity, and take an identity self-test.

Adult Development, Aging, and Death: test existing knowledge and watch videos of adults reflecting on their lives.

InteractNOW! Online Collaborative Lab: Development and the sensorimotor stage

Personality

489

Several thousand people have the task of assembling the world's largest jigsaw puzzle, which contains more than a trillion pieces. Connie Conclusionjumper examines 20 pieces very closely, stares off into space, and announces, "When the puzzle is fully assembled, it will be a picture of the Sydney Opera House!" Prudence Plodder says, "Well, I don't know what the whole puzzle will look like, but I think I've found two little pieces that fit together."

Which of the two has made the greater contribution to completing the puzzle? We could argue either way. Clearly, the task requires an enormous number of little, unglamorous accomplishments like Prudence's. But if Connie is right, her flash of insight will be extremely valuable for assembling all the pieces. Of course, if the puzzle turns out to be a picture of a sailboat at sunset, then Connie will have misled us and wasted our time.

Some psychologists have offered grand theories about the nature of personality. Others have tried to classify personality types and understand why people act differently in specific situations. In this chapter we explore several methods of approaching personality, ranging from large-scale theories to small-scale descriptions. In the first module, we survey some of the most famous and influential theories of personality, such as that of Sigmund Freud. The second module concerns descriptions of personality. Any description is, of course, a theory, but it is a different kind of theory. The final module deals with measurements of personality.

▮ This three-dimensional jigsaw puzzle of the ocean liner *Titanic* consists of 26,000 pieces. Assembling all the pieces is an overwhelming task, but at least people know how the final product should look. Understanding personality is an even more complex puzzle, and we do not know the overall structure before we start investigating.

How can we best describe the overall structure of personality?

> Every individual is virtually an enemy of civilization. . . . Thus civilization has to be defended against the individual. . . . For the masses are lazy and unintelligent . . . and the individuals composing them support one another in giving free rein to their indiscipline.
> —Sigmund Freud (1927/1961)

> It has been my experience that persons have a basically positive direction. In my deepest contacts with individuals in therapy, even those whose troubles are most disturbing, whose behavior has been most antisocial, whose feelings seem most abnormal, I find this to be true.
> —Carl Rogers (1961)

What is human nature? The 17th-century philosopher Thomas Hobbes argued that humans are by nature selfish. Life in a state of nature, he said, is "nasty, brutish, and short." If we are to protect ourselves from one another, the government must restrain us. The 18th-century political philosopher Jean-Jacques Rousseau disagreed, maintaining that people are naturally good and that governments are the problem, not the solution. Rational people acting freely, he maintained, would advance the welfare of all.

The debate between those two viewpoints survives in modern theories of personality (Figure 13.1). Some theorists, including Sigmund Freud, have held that people are born with sexual and destructive impulses that must be held in check if civilization is to survive. Others, including Carl Rogers, believed that people will achieve good and noble goals once they have been freed from unnecessary restraints.

Which point of view is correct? Way down deep, are we good, bad, both, or neither? We cannot expect a firm scientific answer, but psychologists have developed many approaches to exploring personality.

The term *personality* comes from the Latin word *persona,* meaning "mask." In the plays of ancient Greece and Rome, actors wore masks to indicate whether they were comic or tragic characters. Unlike a mask that one can either put on or take off, however, the term *personality* implies something stable. **Personality** consists of *all the consistent ways in which the behavior of one person differs from that of others, especially in social situations.* (Differences in learning, memory, sensation, or muscle control are generally not considered personality.)

Of course, in any one aspect of your personality, you resemble many other people. For example, you might be about as cheerful as many others. Nevertheless, your particular combination of behavior tendencies and mental processes sets you apart.

In this module we concentrate largely on the theory of Sigmund Freud because it has been so influential outside psychology as well as within. However, you should evaluate it carefully before you decide how seriously to take it.

Sigmund Freud and the Psychodynamic Approach

Sigmund Freud (1856–1939), an Austrian physician, developed the first psychodynamic theory. *A* **psychodynamic theory** *relates personality to the interplay of conflicting forces within the individual, including some that the individual may not consciously recognize.* That is, we are being pushed and pulled by internal forces that we do not fully understand.

Freud's influence extends into sociology, literature, art, religion, and politics. And yet, here we are, about three fourths of the way through this text on psychology, and until now I have barely mentioned Freud. Why?

The reason is that Freud's influence within psychology has declined substantially. According to one

Hobbes	Rousseau
Government is required for protection	Humans are good
Humans are selfish	Government is a corrupting influence
Freud	**Rogers**
Natural impulses are detrimental to society	Natural impulses are noble and good

FIGURE 13.1 Sigmund Freud, like the philosopher Thomas Hobbes, stressed the more destructive aspects of human nature. Carl Rogers, like Jean-Jacques Rousseau, emphasized the more favorable aspects.

▌ Sigmund Freud interpreted dreams, slips of the tongue, and so forth to infer unconscious thoughts and motivations. Most researchers today, however, are skeptical of Freud's interpretations.

psychologist, Frederick Crews (1996, p. 63), "independent studies have begun to converge toward a verdict that was once considered a sign of extremism or even of neurosis: that there is literally nothing to be said, scientifically or therapeutically, to the advantage of the entire Freudian system or any of its constituent dogmas." Think about that: *nothing* to be said in favor of *any* of Freud's theories. Needless to say, not everyone agrees with that statement. Still, the decline of Freud's influence is striking.

▌ The fame of Sigmund Freud far exceeds that of any other psychologist. His picture has even appeared on the Austrian 50-schilling bill and bimetal millennial coin.

Freud's Search for the Unconscious

Freud would have preferred to be a professor of cultural history or anthropology; he wrote several books and articles about those topics in his later years. In Austria at the time, however, few university positions were offered to Jews. The only professions readily open to him were law, business, and medicine. Freud chose medicine, but without much commitment to healing people. His interests were almost purely theoretical.

Early in his career, Freud worked with the psychiatrist Josef Breuer, who had been treating a young woman with a fluctuating variety of physical complaints. As she talked with Breuer about her past, she remembered various traumatic, or emotionally damaging, experiences. Breuer, and later Freud also, said that remembering these experiences produced **catharsis,** *a release of pent-up emotional tension,* thereby relieving her illness. However, later scholars who reexamined the medical records found that this woman who was so famous in the history of psychoanalysis was not cured at all. She may not even have benefited from the treatment (Ellenberger, 1972).

Regardless of whether the "talking cure" had been successful, Freud began applying it to his own emotionally disturbed patients. He referred to *his method of explaining and dealing with personality, based on the interplay of conscious and unconscious forces,* as **psychoanalysis.** To this day psychoanalysts remain loyal to some version of Freud's methods and theories, although their views have of course evolved over the decades.

Psychoanalysis started out as a fairly simple theory: Each of us has an unconscious mind as well as a conscious mind (Figure 13.2). The **unconscious** is *the*

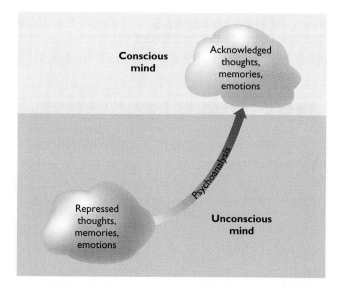

FIGURE 13.2 Freud believed that psychoanalysis could bring parts of the unconscious into the conscious mind, where the client could deal with them.

repository of memories, emotions, and thoughts, many of them illogical, that affect our behavior even though we cannot talk about them. Traumatic experiences force thoughts and emotions into the unconscious (theoretically), and the goal of psychoanalysts is to bring those memories back to consciousness. Doing so produces catharsis and enables the person to confront irrational and self-defeating impulses.

As Freud listened to his patients, however, he became convinced that the traumatic events they recalled could not account for their abnormal behavior. Some patients reacted strongly to events that others took in stride. Why? At first, in the early 1890s, Freud attributed their overreactions to sexual difficulties (Macmillan, 1997). For a while Freud claimed that increased sexual activity would cure anxiety problems, although he soon abandoned this view, and since then no one has found any reason to revive it.

People suffering from nervous exhaustion, he said, were suffering from the results of masturbation. His evidence for this idea was that all his patients who were suffering from nervous exhaustion had masturbated (!). You can see the problem: Freud boldly asserted that mentally healthy people do not masturbate. Suppose you were in his audience. Would you raise your hand and say, "Wait a minute, Dr. Freud, I think I'm mentally healthy, and I masturbate . . ."? You probably wouldn't, and neither did anyone else, so Freud concluded that he was right.

A few years later, however, Freud abandoned these hypotheses and suggested instead that the ultimate cause of psychological disorders was traumatic childhood sexual experiences, either seduction by other children or sexual abuse by adults. Freud's patients did not report any such memories, but Freud put together parts of the patients' dream reports, slips of the tongue, and so forth and claimed that they pointed to early sexual abuse.

At this point Freud's problems with evidence became serious. His ideas about inadequate sex or too much masturbation may sound ridiculous, but at least they were testable. But how was anyone to determine whether the childhood events that Freud inferred from dreams and so forth had actually happened?

A few years later, he abandoned the idea that psychological disorders resulted from childhood sexual abuse. According to Freud's own description of these events, he decided that his patients had "misled" him into believing they were sexually abused in early childhood, whereas in fact, Freud said, their claims were wishes and fantasies (Freud, 1925). Although he never fully developed his views of girls' early sexual development, he was more explicit about boys: During early childhood every boy goes through an **Oedipus complex,** *when he develops a sexual interest in his mother and competitive aggression toward his father.* (Oedipus—

EHD-ah-puhs—in the ancient Greek play by Sophocles unknowingly murdered his father and married his mother.) In short, Freud said people become psychologically disturbed not because their parents sexually molested them but because as children they wanted to have sex with their parents and couldn't.

Why did Freud switch from his idea about sexual abuse to a theory about sexual fantasies? According to one view (Masson, 1984), Freud was right the first time, and he simply lost the courage to defend his theory. According to other scholars, however, Freud never had any evidence for either theory (Esterson, 2001; Powell & Boer, 1994; Schatzman, 1992). In his earliest writings, Freud inferred his patients' sexual abuse from their symptoms and dreams despite their own denials of abuse. It was hardly fair, therefore, to complain that the patients had misled him into believing they had been abused. When he switched to saying that the patients had childhood sexual fantasies, he was again drawing inferences that his patients denied. (Freud considered his patients' protests to be signs of emotional resistance and therefore confirmation that his interpretations were correct.)

Apparently, Freud's main evidence for his interpretations was simply that he could construct a coherent story linking a patient's symptoms, dreams, and so forth to the sexual fantasies that Freud inferred (Esterson, 1993). In short, he did not distinguish between his results and his interpretations.

Consider another example of Freud's use of evidence: A patient described as "Dora" came to Freud at the insistence of her father, an acquaintance of Freud's. Since about age 8, Dora had suffered from headaches, coughing, and shortness of breath, all of which Freud interpreted as psychological in nature. She had also avoided a certain friend of her father, Mr. K, ever since she was 14, when he grabbed her and kissed her on her lips.

Freud wrote that Dora surely experienced sexual pleasure at this time because K's presumably erect penis must have rubbed up against her clitoris and excited it. Freud described Dora's disgust as "entirely and completely hysterical" (Freud, 1905/1963, p. 44). He then proceeded to try to trace Dora's behavior to her presumed love for both K and her father and her homosexual attraction to Mrs. K. As one reads Freud's elaborate discussion, one wonders what was wrong with Dora's simpler explanation—that she found the sexual advances of this middle-aged man repulsive.

Stages of Psychosexual Development in Freud's Theory of Personality

Right or wrong, Freud's theory is so well known that you should learn what his terms mean. One of his central points was that psychosexual interest and pleasure

TABLE 13.1 Freud's Stages of Psychosexual Development

Stage (approximate ages)	Sexual Interests	Effects of Fixation at This Stage
Oral stage (birth to 1 year)	Sucking, swallowing, biting	Lasting concerns with dependence and independence; pleasure from eating, drinking, and other oral activities
Anal stage (1 to 3 years)	Expelling feces, retaining feces	Orderliness or sloppiness, stinginess or wastefulness, stubbornness
Phallic stage (3 to 5 or 6 years)	Touching penis or clitoris; Oedipus complex	Difficulty feeling closeness. Males: fear of castration Females: penis envy
Latent period (5 or 6 to puberty)	Sexual interests suppressed	—
Genital stage (puberty onward)	Sexual contact with other people	—

begin in infancy. He used the term **psychosexual pleasure** broadly to include *all strong, pleasant excitement arising from body stimulation.* He maintained that how we deal with our psychosexual development influences nearly all aspects of our personality. According to Freud, just as nonhuman mammals respond sexually to sounds and smells, children respond sexually to stimulation of the mouth, anus, and other body zones that do not greatly excite human adults. Freud based his views on his patients' reconstructions of childhood; he did not systematically observe children himself.

According to Freud (1905/1925), people have a *psychosexual energy,* which he called **libido** (lih-BEE-doh), from a Latin word meaning "desire." Normally, libido is focused in an infant's mouth and "flows" to other body parts as the child grows older. Children go through five stages of psychosexual development, each with a characteristic sexual focus that leaves its mark on the adult personality. If normal sexual development is blocked or frustrated at any stage, Freud said, part of the libido becomes **fixated** at that stage; that is, it *continues to be preoccupied with the pleasure*

area associated with that stage. Table 13.1 summarizes these stages.

The Oral Stage

In the **oral stage**, from birth to about age 2—Freud was vague about the age limits—*the infant derives intense psychosexual pleasure from stimulation of the mouth, particularly while sucking at the mother's breast.* According to Freud someone fixated at this

❚ According to Freud, if normal sexual development is blocked at the oral stage, the child will seek pleasure from drinking and eating and later from kissing and smoking. Perhaps this cigarette smoker's mother weaned him too quickly—or let him nurse too long. Like most of Freud's ideas, this one is difficult to test.

stage continues to receive great pleasure from eating, drinking, and smoking and may also have lasting concerns with dependence and independence.

The Anal Stage

At about 2 years of age, children enter the **anal stage**, when *they get psychosexual pleasure from stimulation of the sensations of bowel movements.* A person fixated at this stage goes through life "holding things back"—being orderly, stingy, and stubborn—or less commonly, may go to the opposite extreme and become messy and wasteful.

The Phallic Stage

Beginning at about age 3, in the **phallic stage**, children begin to *play with their genitals* and according to Freud become sexually attracted to the opposite-sex parent. Freud claimed that boys with a phallic fixation are afraid of being castrated; girls with such a fixation develop "penis envy." These ideas have always been controversial. Some girls report fantasies about what it would be like to be a boy (Linday, 1994), but calling these fantasies "penis envy" is a stretch, and assuming that they play a major role in personality development is even more of a stretch. Similarly, few boys show clear signs of castration fears.

The Latent Period

From about age 5 or 6 until adolescence, Freud said, most children enter a **latent period** in which they *suppress their psychosexual interest.* At this time they play mostly with peers of their own sex. The latent period is evidently a product of European culture and is not apparent in all societies.

The Genital Stage

Beginning at puberty young people *take a strong sexual interest in other people.* This is known as the **genital stage**. According to Freud anyone who has fixated a great deal of libido in an earlier stage has little libido left for the genital stage. But people who have successfully negotiated the earlier stages can now derive primary satisfaction from sexual intercourse.

Evaluation of Freud's Stages

Freud's theory is vague and difficult to test (Grünbaum, 1986; Popper, 1986). When it has been tested, the results have been mostly inconclusive. For example, the characteristics of being orderly, stingy, and stubborn, which Freud described as due to anal fixation, tend to correlate with one another, suggesting that they are part of a single personality trait. However, we have no evidence that these attributes result from toilet training (Fisher & Greenberg, 1977).

Freud's Description of the Structure of Personality

Personality, Freud claimed, consists of three aspects: id, ego, and superego. (Actually, he used German words that mean *it, I,* and *over-I.* A translator used Latin equivalents instead of English words.) The **id** consists of *all our biological drives,* such as sex and hunger, that demand immediate gratification. The **ego** is *the rational, decision-making aspect of the personality.* The **superego** contains *the memory of rules and prohibitions we learned from our parents and the rest of society,* such as, "Nice little boys and girls don't do that." Sometimes the id produces sexual or other motivations that the superego considers repugnant, thus evoking feelings of guilt. However, most psychologists today find it difficult to imagine the mind in terms of three warring factions and therefore regard Freud's description as only a metaphor.

CONCEPT CHECK ☑

1. If someone has persistent problems with independence and dependence, Freud would suggest a fixation at which psychosexual stage?
2. What kind of behavior would Freud expect of someone with a strong id and a weak superego? What behavior would Freud expect of someone with an unusually strong superego? (Check your answers on page 505.)

Defense Mechanisms Against Anxiety

According to Freud *the ego defends itself against conflicts and anxieties by relegating unpleasant thoughts and impulses to the unconscious.* Among the **defense mechanisms** that the ego employs are repression, denial, rationalization, displacement, regression, projection, reaction formation, and sublimation (Figure 13.3). He saw these as normal processes that sometimes went to extremes. Descriptions of these mechanisms were largely developed and elaborated by his daughter, Anna.

Repression

The defense mechanism of **repression** is *motivated forgetting*—rejecting unacceptable thoughts, desires, and memories and banishing them to the unconscious. One example would be someone who sees a murder and later cannot remember it. Another example: Someone has an unacceptable sexual or aggressive impulse and represses it so thoroughly as to be unaware of it.

Researchers have struggled to find clear evidence of repression. As discussed in Chapter 7, most people who endure miserable experiences remember them well. Laboratory investigators have exposed participants to

FIGURE 13.3 The ego, or "rational I," has numerous ways of defending itself against anxiety, that apprehensive state named for the Latin word meaning "to strangle." We use defense mechanisms to avoid unpleasant realities. They are part of an internal battle that you fight against yourself.

various unpleasant or threatening experiences in the expectation that repression would interfere with their memories. Even in the cases where people did forget, alternative explanations were available that did not include repression (Holmes, 1990). If repression occurs at all, it occurs rarely or under very special circumstances.

Denial

The refusal to believe information that provokes anxiety ("This can't be happening") is called **denial**. Whereas repression is the motivated forgetting of certain information, denial is an assertion that the information is incorrect. For example, someone with a serious alcohol problem may insist, "I'm not an alcoholic. I can take it or leave it." A patient who is told that he or she has a fatal illness may refuse to accept the diagnosis.

Rationalization

When people *attempt to prove that their actions are rational and justifiable and thus worthy of approval,* they are using **rationalization**. For example, a student who wants to go to the movies says, "More studying won't do me any good anyway." Someone who misses a deadline to apply for a job says, "I didn't really want that job."

Displacement

By diverting a behavior or thought away from its natural target toward a less threatening target, **displacement** lets people engage in the behavior more safely or with less anxiety. For example, someone who is angry with a boss or professor might yell at a friend instead. The person is angry but feels inhibited about yelling at someone who could retaliate.

Regression

A *return to a more immature level of functioning,* **regression** is an effort to avoid the anxiety of facing one's current role in life. By adopting a childish role, a person can escape responsibility and return to an earlier, perhaps more secure, way of life. For example, after a new sibling is born, an older child may cry or pout. Adults who have just gone through a divorce or business loss may sometimes move in with their parents and depend on them.

Projection

The attribution of one's own undesirable characteristics to other people is known as **projection**. In theory, by suggesting that other people have those faults, the faults become more acceptable and less anxiety provoking. For example, someone who secretly enjoys pornography might accuse other people of enjoying it. However, the research finds that people using projection do not ordinarily decrease their anxiety or their awareness of their own faults (Holmes, 1978; Sherwood, 1981). If so, projection is not an effective defense.

Reaction Formation

To keep undesirable characteristics repressed, people may use **reaction formation** to *present themselves as the opposite of what they really are to hide the unpleasant truth either from themselves or others.* For example, a man troubled by doubts about his religious faith may try to convert others to the faith. Someone with unacceptable aggressive tendencies may join a group dedicated to preventing violence. (Not everyone who proselytizes for a faith has deep doubts about it, of course, and not everyone who tries to prevent violence is secretly a violent person. Different people have different reasons for the same actions.)

Sublimation

The transformation of sexual or aggressive energies into culturally acceptable, even admirable, behaviors is **sublimation**. According to Freud sublimation enables a person to express the impulse without admitting its existence. For example, painting and sculpture may represent a sublimation of sexual impulses. Someone may sublimate aggressive impulses by becoming a surgeon. However, if the true motives of a painter are sexual, as Freud proposed, they are well hidden indeed. Sublimation is the one proposed defense mechanism that is associated with socially constructive behavior.

CONCEPT CHECK ☑

3. Match the Freudian defense mechanisms in this list with the situations that follow: Repression, Regression, Denial, Projection, Rationalization, Reaction formation, Displacement, Sublimation.
   a. A man who is angry with his neighbor goes hunting and kills a deer.
   b. Someone with a smoking habit insists there is no convincing evidence that smoking impairs health.
   c. A woman with doubts about her religious faith tries to convert others to her religion.
   d. A man who beats his wife writes a book arguing that people have an instinctive need for aggressive behavior.
   e. A woman forgets a doctor's appointment for a test for cancer.
   f. Someone who has difficulty dealing with certain people resorts to pouting, crying, and throwing tantrums.
   g. A boss takes credit for a good idea suggested by an employee because "It's better for me to take the credit so that our department will look good and all the employees will benefit."
   h. Someone with an unacceptable impulse to shout obscenities becomes a writer of novels. (Check your answers on page 505.)

Freud's Legacy

Undeniably, Freud was a great pioneer in identifying new questions. The validity of his answers is less certain, however. He based his conclusions on inferences he drew from what his patients said and did, without testing the validity of his inferences. A growing number of psychologists today contend that Freud imposed theories onto his data instead of drawing conclusions from the data.

It is conceivable, of course, that someone might draw correct conclusions even from worthless data. If later data support a theory, the weakness of the original evidence does not matter. One reviewer of the literature (Westen, 1998) identifies the following ideas as among Freud's enduring contributions to psychology:

- Much of mental life is unconscious. We don't always know why we're doing something.
- People often have conflicting motives.
- Childhood experiences are important for the development of personality and social behavior.
- Our relationships with other people can resemble the relationships we had with other people in the past, such as our parents.

Freud's own couch is now part of our history. What is the future of the psychoanalytic couch?

- People develop through stages of psychosexual interest and relationships with the social world.

However, a critic can reply that these comments are "damning with faint praise." That is, Freud's goal was not to make generalizations such as "people often have conflicting motives" or "childhood is important"—ideas that were hardly original to Freud! Freud thought he had found a way to probe and reveal people's unconscious thoughts and motives. Furthermore, the kinds of unconscious processes that current data support are very different from Freud's concepts. For example, implicit memory (Chapter 7) and priming (Chapter 8) are unconscious in the sense that people are unaware of certain influences on their behavior. However, these processes are unconscious only because the stimulus was presented briefly, not because the person repressed offensive ideas. What Freud said about the unconscious did not lead to research on implicit memory or priming; if anything, it may have deterred and delayed research on unconscious processes. In short, how much credit we should give Freud is a matter of opinion.

Neo-Freudians

Some psychologists, known as **neo-Freudians,** *remained faithful to parts of Freud's theory while modifying other parts.* One of the most influential neo-Freudians was the German physician Karen Horney (HOR-nigh; 1885–1952), who believed that Freud exaggerated the role of the sex drive in human behavior and misunderstood women's sexual motivations. She believed, for example, that the conflict between a child and parents was a reaction to parental hostility and intimidation, not a manifestation of sexual desires. Horney emphasized the social and cultural influences on personality that give rise to anxiety. Still, she maintained many Freudian concepts such as repression and the attempt to understand people's inner conflicts. Her views were more a revision than a rejection of Freud's theories.

Other theorists, including Carl Jung and Alfred Adler, broke more sharply with Freud. Although Jung and Adler were at one point associates of Freud, each broke with Freud's theory in substantial ways and should not be classified as neo-Freudians.

Carl Jung and the Collective Unconscious

Carl G. Jung (YOONG; 1875–1961), a Swiss physician, was an early member of Freud's inner circle. Freud regarded Jung like a son, the "heir apparent" or "crown prince" of the psychoanalytic movement, until their father–son relationship deteriorated (Alexander, 1982).

Jung's own theory of personality emphasized people's search for a spiritual meaning in life and the continuity of human experience, past and present. Jung believed that every person has not only a conscious mind and a "personal unconscious" (equivalent to Freud's unconscious) but also a collective unconscious. You could think of it as a "group mind." The personal unconscious results from each person's own experience. The **collective unconscious,** present at birth, represents *the cumulative experience of preceding generations.* Because all humans share common ancestors, all have the same collective unconscious. The collective unconscious contains **archetypes,** which are *vague images that we inherited from the experiences of our ancestors.* As evidence for this view, Jung pointed out that similar images emerge in the art of cultures throughout the world (Figure 13.4) and that similar themes emerge in various religions, myths, and folklore.

Those images and themes also appear in dreams and hallucinations. So, for example, if you dream about a beetle, Jung might relate your dream to the important role that beetles have played in human mythology dating back at least to the ancient Egyptians. Given modern views of genetics, Jung's ideas are hard to defend. Having an experience does

Karen Horney, a major neo-Freudian, revised some of Freud's theories and paid greater attention to cultural influences. She was a pioneer in the development of feminine psychology.

Carl G. Jung rejected Freud's concept that dreams hide their meaning from the conscious mind: "To me dreams are a part of nature, which harbors no intention to deceive, but expresses something as best it can" (Jung, 1965).

a © Silvio Fiore/Superstock

b © Archive for Research in Archetypal Symbolism

c © Chrisine Garrigan

d © Pat Berrett

FIGURE 13.4 Carl Jung was fascinated that similar images appear in the artwork of different cultures. One recurring image is the circular mandala, a symbol of unity and wholeness. These mandalas are: (a) a Hindu painting from Bhutan; (b) a mosaic from Beth Alpha Synagogue, Israel; (c) a tie-dye tapestry created in California; and (d) a Navajo sand painting from the southwestern United States.

not change anyone's genes, and you cannot inherit a representation of your ancestors' memories. Jung's alternative to a genetic explanation was that perhaps archetypes exist on their own, independent of time, space, and brains. That idea is difficult even to understand, much less test. In short, Jung's views of the collective unconscious and archetypes are mystical (Neher, 1996).

CRITICAL THINKING:
A STEP FURTHER
Archetypes

Jung believed that the similarities in artworks throughout the world—such as the drawings he called mandalas—indicated that people inherited images or archetypes for those shapes. Can you suggest a simpler, more parsimonious explanation?

CONCEPT CHECK ☑

4. How does Jung's idea of the collective unconscious differ from Freud's idea of the unconscious? (Check your answer on page 505.)

Alfred Adler and Individual Psychology

Alfred Adler (1870–1937), an Austrian physician who, like Jung, had been one of Freud's early associates, broke with Freud because he believed Freud overemphasized the sex drive and neglected other more important influences on personality. They parted company in 1911, with Freud insisting that women experience "penis envy" and with Adler contending that women were more likely to envy men's status and power.

Adler founded a rival school of thought, which he called **individual psychology**. To Adler, this term did not mean "psychology of the individual." Rather, it meant *"indivisible psychology," a psychology of the person as a whole rather than a psychology of parts,* such as id, ego, and superego. Adler emphasized the importance of conscious, goal-directed behavior and deemphasized (but did not deny) unconscious influences.

Adler's Description of Personality

Several of Adler's early patients were acrobats who had had an arm or a leg damaged by a childhood illness or injury. As they worked to overcome their disabilities, they continued until they developed the needed strength and coordination to perform as acrobats. Perhaps, Adler surmised, people in general try to overcome their weaknesses and to transform them into strengths (Adler, 1932/1964).

As infants, Adler noted, we are small, dependent creatures who strive to overcome our inferiority. Normal experiences with failure goad people to try harder. However, persistent failures or overcritical parents and others can produce an **inferiority complex**, *an exaggerated feeling of weakness, inadequacy, and helplessness.*

▌ Alfred Adler emphasized the ways in which personality depended on people's goals, especially their way of striving for a sense of superiority.

© UPI/Bettman/CORBIS

According to Adler everyone has a natural **striving for superiority**, *a desire to seek personal excellence and fulfillment.* Each person creates a **style of life**, or *master plan for achieving a sense of superiority.* That style of life may be directed toward success in business, sports, or any other competitive activity. People can also strive for success in other ways. For example, someone who withdraws from life may gain a sense of accomplishment or superiority from being uncommonly self-sacrificing. Someone who constantly complains about illnesses or disabilities may win a measure of control over friends and family. Or someone may commit crimes to savor the attention that they bring. People also sometimes get a feeling of superiority by making excuses for their lack of achievements (and thereby imaging how great they would have been if these impediments hadn't blocked their way).

If you marry someone who is likely to thwart your ambitions, perhaps your underlying motivation is to maintain an illusion: "I could have been a great success if my spouse hadn't prevented me." Failure to study can have a similar motivation: "I could have done well on this test, but my friends talked me into going to a party the night before." Adler recognized that people are not always aware of their own style of life and the assumptions behind it and may fail to understand that the real motive behind a word or action is to manipulate others. They may engage in self-defeating behavior because they have not admitted to themselves what their goals really are.

Adler tried to determine people's real motives. For example, he would ask someone who complained of a backache, "How would your life be different if you could get rid of your backache?" Those who said they would become more active were presumably suffering from physical ailments that they were trying to overcome. Those who said they could not imagine how their life would change, or said only that they would get less sympathy from others, were presumably suffering from psychologically caused ailments or, at least, were exaggerating their discomfort.

CONCEPT CHECK ☑

5. In Adler's theory what is the relationship between striving for superiority and style of life? (Check your answer on page 505.)

Adler's View of Psychological Disorders

Any personality based on a selfish style of life is unhealthy, Adler (1928/1964) said. People's needs for one another require a **social interest**, *a sense of solidarity and identification with other people.* Note that social interest does not mean a desire to socialize; it means an interest in the welfare of society. People with a strong social interest strive for superiority and welfare of a large group of people or all of humanity. They want to cooperate with other people, not to compete. In equating mental health with a strong social interest, Adler saw mental health as a positive state, not just the absence of impairments. In Adler's view people with excessive anxieties are not suffering from an "illness." Rather, they have set immature goals, are following a faulty style of life, and show little social interest. Their response to new opportunity is "Yes, but . . ." (Adler, 1932/1964). They strive for superiority in useless ways.

For example, one of Adler's patients was a man who lived in conflict with his wife because he was constantly trying to impress and dominate her (Adler, 1927). When discussing his problems, the man revealed that he had been very slow to mature physically and had not reached puberty until he was 17 years old. Other teenagers had ignored him and had treated him like a child. He was now a physically normal adult, but he was overcompensating for those years of feeling inferior by trying to seem bigger and more important than he really was.

Adler tried to get patients to understand their own style of life and to correct the faulty assumptions on which they had based their lives. He urged them to strengthen their social interest and to strive for superiority in ways that would benefit both themselves and others.

Adler's Legacy

Adler's influence exceeds his fame, and he probably would be glad for that. His concept of the "inferiority complex" has become part of the common culture. He was the first to talk about mental health as a positive state rather than as merely the absence of impairments. Many later forms of therapy drew upon Adler's emphasis on understanding the assumptions that people make and how those assumptions influence behavior. Many psychologists also followed Adler by urging people to take responsibility for their own behavior. According to Adler the key to a healthy personality was not just freedom from disorders but "social interest," a desire for the welfare of other people.

The Learning Approach

How did you develop your personality? At least part of the answer surely depends on how you have learned to behave in certain situations. Indeed, some psychologists have argued that the whole concept of personality is overrated and that most of what we call personality is learned on a situation-by-situation basis (Mischel, 1973, 1981). For example, you might be honest about returning a lost wallet to its owner; yet you lie to your professor about why your paper is late.

So how useful is it to say that you are an honest person or even that you are "more honest than 80% of other people"? It might be more useful to describe what you do in particular situations (Mischel & Shoda, 1995). Presumably, you learned these behaviors, and different people learn different behaviors. The fact that learning is specific to a situation helps explain both variations among individuals and variations among situations for a given individual.

The Social Learning section of Chapter 6 described several ways in which we learn our personality. We learn much by imitation or by vicarious reinforcement and punishment. That is, we copy behaviors that were successful for other people and avoid behaviors that failed for others. We behave like the people that we respect and want to resemble.

Let's illustrate this idea by applying the approach to masculine and feminine personality tendencies. Part of learning how we are expected to act is developing a **gender role**, *the pattern of behavior that each person is expected to follow because of being male or*

▮ Children learn gender roles partly by imitating adults, but they probably learn more from other children.

FIGURE 13.5 Gender roles vary greatly from one culture to another and even from one time period to another within a single culture. Here a Palestinian man (a) and a Vietnamese woman (b) plow the fields. Men in Bangladesh (c) and women in Thailand (d) do the wash.

female. A gender role is the psychological aspect of being male or female, as opposed to sex, which is the biological aspect. We know that gender role is at least partly learned because certain aspects vary strikingly among cultures (Figure 13.5). For example, some cultures define cooking as "women's work" and others define it as "men's work." Men wear their hair short in some cultures and long in others.

To say that children learn their gender role does not mean that anyone teaches it intentionally. People teach mainly by example. Boys tend to imitate men, and girls tend to imitate women. In one experiment children watched adults choose between an apple and a banana. If all the men chose one fruit and all the women chose the other, the boys wanted what the men had and the girls wanted what the women had (Perry & Bussey, 1979). The choice of fruit is in itself trivial, but the study shows the potential for influence on more important behaviors. Even more powerfully, boys and girls learn their gender roles from older children. In short, the learning approach focuses on specific behaviors and attempts to relate them to specific experiences.

Humanistic Psychology

Another general perspective on personality, **humanistic psychology**, *deals with consciousness, values, and abstract beliefs, including spiritual experiences and the beliefs that people live by and die for.* According to humanistic psychologists, personality depends on what people believe and how they perceive the world. If you *believe* that a particular experience was highly meaningful, then it *was* highly meaningful. A psychologist can understand your behavior only by asking you for your own evaluations and interpretations of the events in your life. (In theology a *humanist* glorifies human potentials, generally denying or paying little attention to a Supreme Being. The term *humanistic psychologist* implies nothing about religious beliefs.)

Humanistic psychology emerged in the 1950s and 1960s as a protest against both behaviorism and psychoanalysis, the dominant viewpoints in psychology at that time (Berlyne, 1981). Behaviorists and psychoanalysts often emphasize the less noble, or at least morally neutral, aspects of people's thoughts and actions, whereas humanistic psychologists see people as essentially good and striving to achieve their best potential. Also, behaviorism and psychoanalysis, despite their many differences, are both rooted in *determinism* (the belief that every behavior has a cause) and in *reductionism* (the attempt to explain behavior in terms of its component elements).

Humanistic psychologists do not try to explain behavior in terms of its parts or hidden causes. They claim that people make deliberate, conscious decisions about what to do. For example, people might decide to devote themselves to a great cause, to sacrifice their own well-being, or to risk their lives. To the humanistic psychologist, it is fruitless to ascribe such behavior to past rewards and punishments or to unconscious thought processes.

Humanistic psychologists generally study the special qualities of a given individual, as opposed to seeking means or medians for large representative groups. Their research consists mostly of recording narratives of individuals' lives, more like a biographer than like a scientist in the usual sense. Therefore, their data are qualitative, not quantitative, and often difficult to evaluate scientifically.

Carl Rogers and the Goal of Self-Actualization

Carl Rogers, an American psychologist, studied theology before turning to psychology, and the influence of those early studies is apparent in his view of human nature. Rogers became probably the most influential humanistic psychologist.

Rogers (1980) regarded human nature as basically good. He said people have a natural drive toward **self-actualization**, *the achievement of one's full potential.* According to Rogers it is as natural for people to strive for excellence as it is for a plant to grow. The drive for self-actualization is the basic drive behind the development of personality. (Rogers's concept of self-actualization is similar to Adler's concept of striving for superiority. Adler was a forerunner of humanistic psychology.)

Children evaluate themselves and their actions beginning at an early age. They learn that what they do is sometimes good and sometimes bad. They develop a **self-concept**, *an image of what they really are,* and an **ideal self**, *an image of what they would like to be.* Rogers measured a person's self-concept and ideal self by handing the person a stack of cards containing statements such as "I am honest" and "I am suspicious of others." The person would then sort the statements into piles representing *true of me* and *not true of me* or arrange them in a continuum from *most true of me* to *least true of me.* (This method is known as a *Q-sort.*) Then Rogers would provide an identical stack of cards and ask the person to sort them into two piles: *true of my ideal self* and *not true of my ideal self.* In this manner he could determine whether someone's self-concept was similar to his or her ideal self; people who perceive a great discrepancy between the two generally feel distress. Humanistic psychologists try to help people overcome this distress either by improving their self-concept or by revising their ideal self.

To promote human welfare, Rogers maintained that people should relate to one another with **unconditional positive regard**, a relationship that Thomas Harris (1967) described as "I'm OK—You're OK." Unconditional positive regard is *the complete, unqualified acceptance of another person as he or she is,* much like the love of a parent for a child. If you feel unconditional positive regard, you might disapprove of someone's actions or intentions, but you would still accept and love that person. (This view resembles the Christian admonition to "hate the sin but love the sinner.") The alternative is *conditional positive regard,* the attitude that "I shall like you only if . . . ." People who are treated this way may feel restrained about opening themselves to new ideas or activities for fear of losing someone else's support.

Abraham Maslow and the Self-Actualized Personality

Abraham Maslow, another founder of humanistic psychology, complained that most psychologists concentrate on disordered personalities, assuming that all personality is either "normal" or worse than normal. Maslow insisted that personality can differ from normal

▌ Carl Rogers maintained that people naturally strive toward positive goals and that they do not need special urging. He recommended that people relate to one another with "unconditional positive regard."

© Bettman/CORBIS

▌ Abraham Maslow, one of the founders of humanistic psychology, introduced the concept of a "self-actualized personality," a personality associated with high productivity and enjoyment of life.

© Bettman/CORBIS

Harriet Tubman (1823–1913) © CORBIS

■ Harriet Tubman, identified by Maslow as having a self-actualized personality, was a leader of the Underground Railroad, a system for helping slaves escape from the southern states before the Civil War. Maslow defined the self-actualized personality by first identifying highly admirable people, such as Tubman, and then determining which personality features they shared.

in positive, desirable ways. He proposed that people's highest need is *self-actualization,* the fulfillment of an individual's potential. That is, of course, a difficult concept, as we have no way to know what someone's potential is or whether he or she has achieved it, but we can recognize people who seem to be coming closer than others are.

As a first step toward describing the self-actualized personality, Maslow (1962, 1971) made a list of people who in his opinion were approaching their full potential. His list included people he knew personally as well as some from history. He then sought to discover what, if anything, they had in common.

According to Maslow (1962, 1971), people with a self-actualized (or self-actualizing) personality show the following characteristics:

- An accurate perception of reality: They perceive the world as it is, not as they would like it to be. They are willing to accept uncertainty and ambiguity.
- Independence, creativity, and spontaneity: They make their own decisions, even if others disagree.
- Acceptance of themselves and others: They treat people with unconditional positive regard.

- A problem-centered outlook rather than a self-centered outlook: They think about how to solve a problem, not how to make themselves look good. They also concentrate on significant problems, such as philosophical or political issues, not just the petty issues of getting through the day.
- Enjoyment of life: They are open to positive experiences, including "peak experiences" when they feel truly fulfilled and content.
- A good sense of humor.

Critics have attacked Maslow's description on the ground that, because it is based on his own choice of examples, it may simply reflect the characteristics that he himself admired. That is, his reasoning was circular: He defined certain people as self-actualized and then inquired what they had in common to figure out what "self-actualized" means (Neher, 1991). In any case Maslow paved the way for other attempts to define a healthy personality as something more than a personality without disorder.

CONCEPT CHECK ☑

6. According to humanistic psychologists, is developing a self-actualized personality a way to achieve another person's unconditional positive regard? (Check your answer on page 505.)

IN CLOSING

In Search of Human Nature

Most psychologists would list as the three most comprehensive personality theorists Freud, Jung, and Adler, who all lived and worked in Austria in the early 1900s. Here we are, close to a century later, and most specialists in personality research neither accept any of those three theories nor attempt to replace them with something better. The whole idea of a single theory of personality seems either wrong or at best premature. These theories have been historically influential, however, and they have produced both the questions and the hypotheses that have guided much of later research.

Recall from Chapter 1 that a good research question is interesting and answerable. Fundamental questions about human nature are extraordinarily interesting, but answering them is extraordinarily difficult. Most researchers today try to answer smaller questions about specific, measurable aspects of behavior, as the next two modules will describe. If and when researchers answer a long series of simpler questions, it may make more sense to return to the big questions of "what makes people tick?"

Summary

- *Personality theories as views of human nature.* Personality consists of the stable, consistent ways in which the behavior of one person differs from that of others. Theories of personality are closely related to conceptions of human nature. Some observers believe that human beings are basically hostile and need to be restrained (Hobbes, Freud). Others believe that humans are basically good (Rousseau, Rogers). (page 491)
- *Psychodynamic theories.* Several historically influential theories have described personality as the outcome of internal forces of which people are not fully conscious. (page 491)
- *Freud.* Sigmund Freud, the founder of psychoanalysis, proposed that human behavior is greatly influenced by unconscious thoughts and motives and that much of what we do and say has hidden meanings. Critics say he twisted his evidence to fit his theories instead of deriving theories from the evidence itself. (page 492)
- *Freud's psychosexual stages.* Freud believed that many unconscious thoughts and motives are sexual in nature. He proposed that people progress through stages or periods of psychosexual development—oral, anal, phallic, latent, and genital—and that frustration at any stage fixates the libido at that stage. (page 493)
- *Defense mechanisms.* Freud and his followers argued that people defend themselves against anxiety by such mechanisms as denial, repression, projection, and reaction formation. (page 495)
- *Jung.* Carl Jung believed that all people share a "collective unconscious" that represents the entire experience of humanity. (page 498)
- *Adler.* Alfred Adler proposed that people's primary motivation is a striving for superiority. Each person adopts his or her own "style of life," or method of striving. (page 500)
- *Adler's view of a healthy personality.* According to Adler the healthiest style of life is one that emphasizes "social interest"—that is, concern for the welfare of others. (page 500)
- *The learning approach.* The behaviors that constitute personality can be learned through individual experience, or by vicarious reinforcement and punishment. Different people develop different behavior patterns ("personalities") at least partly because of different experiences. (page 501)
- *Humanistic psychology.* Humanistic psychologists emphasize conscious, deliberate decision making. (page 502)

Answers to Concept Checks

1. Freud would interpret this behavior as a fixation at the oral stage. (page 495)
2. Someone with a strong id and a weak superego could be expected to give in to a variety of sexual and other impulses that other people would inhibit. Someone with an unusually strong superego would be unusually inhibited and dominated by feelings of guilt. (page 495)
3. **a.** displacement; **b.** denial; **c.** reaction formation; **d.** projection; **e.** repression; **f.** regression; **g.** rationalization; **h.** sublimation. (page 497)
4. Jung's collective unconscious is the same for all people and is present at birth. Freud believed the unconscious developed from repressed experiences. (page 500)
5. In Adler's theory a person's style of life is a method of striving for superiority. (page 500)
6. No. People strive for self-actualization because of their own intrinsic desire for it, not for any external reward. Unconditional positive regard is like the love of a parent for a child, independent of what the other person does. (page 504)

What traits provide the best description of personality?

Why do people differ in their personalities?

With regard to human personality, which would you say?

a. Every person is different from every other.
b. Way down deep, we're all the same.
c. It depends.

I vote for "it depends." The answer depends on our purposes. By analogy, in some ways every rock is unique. If you want to know the fair market value of a rock, you cannot treat diamonds the same as granite, and if you want to predict how well a rock will conduct electricity or how easily you could break it, you need to know a good deal about the content of the rock. However, if you want to predict how fast a rock will fall if you drop it or what will happen when you throw it against a window, one kind of rock is about the same as another.

▌ Like this man playing the role of a woman in Japanese Kabuki theater, actors can present personalities that are very different from their private ones. All of us occasionally display temporary personalities that are different from our usual selves.

Similarly, people resemble one another in some ways but not others. Psychologists study personalities in two ways, called the nomothetic and the idiographic approaches. The word *nomothetic* (NAHM-uh-THEHT-ick) comes from the Greek *nomothetes,* meaning "legislator," and the **nomothetic approach** *seeks general laws about various aspects of personality,* based on studies of large groups of people. For example, we might make the nomothetic statement that people vary in a trait called *extraversion,* and the more extraverted someone is, the more likely that person will introduce himself or herself to a stranger.

In contrast the word *idiographic* is based on the root *idio-,* meaning "individual." The **idiographic approach** concentrates on *intensive studies of individuals* (Allport, 1961). For example, a psychologist might study one person in detail, trying to understand that person's goals, moods, and reactions. The conclusions would apply only to this person and anyone else who is very similar.

Personality Traits and States

Meteorologists distinguish between climate (the usual conditions) and weather (the current conditions). For example, the climate in Scotland is moister and cooler than the climate in Texas, but on a given day, the weather could be warm in Scotland and cool in Texas. Similarly, psychologists distinguish between long-lasting personality conditions and temporary fluctuations.

A consistent, long-lasting tendency in behavior, such as shyness, hostility, or talkativeness, is known as a **trait.** In contrast a **state** is *a temporary activation of a particular behavior.* For example, being afraid at a particular moment is a state; being nervous most of the time is a trait. Being quiet in a library is a state; being quiet habitually is a trait. A trait, like a climate condition, manifests itself as an average over time, though not at every moment. For example, someone who is usually quiet will have an occasional talkative moment, and someone who is usually outgoing may be shy in special circumstances.

Note that both traits and states are descriptions of behavior, not explanations. To say that someone is nervous and quiet does not explain anything; it merely tells us what we are trying to explain.

CONCEPT CHECK ☑

7. Suppose someone becomes nervous as soon as he sits down in a dentist's chair. Is this experience "trait anxiety" or "state anxiety"? (Check your answer on page 514.)

CONCEPT CHECK ☑

8. Who would be more likely to buy lottery tickets—someone with an internal or external locus of control? (Check your answer on page 514.)

The Search for Broad Personality Traits

The point of the **trait approach to personality** is the idea that *people have consistent personality characteristics that can be measured and studied.* Psychologists have described, studied, and measured a great many personality traits, such as honesty, friendliness, authoritarianism, and nervousness.

Some of the research deals with traits that are not familiar descriptions in everyday life. For example, people who *believe they are largely in control of their lives* are said to have an **internal locus of control**. Those who *believe they are controlled mostly by external forces* are said to have an **external locus of control** (Rotter, 1966). Table 13.2 lists some items from a questionnaire designed to measure locus of control. After you complete these items, check answer A on page 514. Generally, people with an internal locus of control like to choose tasks where they believe they can control the outcome, and then they persist at these tasks. At the end they take the credit or blame for the outcome.

TABLE 13.2 Sample Items from the Internal–External Scale

For each item, choose the statement you agree with more.

1. a. Without the right breaks, one cannot be an effective leader.
   b. Capable people who fail to become leaders have not taken advantage of their opportunities.
2. a. Becoming a success is a matter of hard work; luck has little or nothing to do with it.
   b. Getting a good job depends mainly on being in the right place at the right time.
3. a. As far as world affairs are concerned, most of us are the victims of forces we can neither understand nor control.
   b. By taking an active part in political and social affairs, people can control world events.
4. a. Many times I feel that I have little influence over the things that happen to me.
   b. It is impossible for me to believe that chance or luck plays an important role in my life.

Source: Rotter, 1966, pp. 11–12.

Issues in Personality Measurement

In past chapters, particularly in the discussions of intelligence and emotion, we have dealt with difficulties of measurement. Progress in any field depends on good measurement, and in personality research measurement is particularly difficult. The problem is that we care about how someone acts *in general* (the person's traits), but behavior fluctuates substantially from one moment to another. The same is true to some extent for any aspect of psychology: Your memory varies from one time to another, and so do your intelligence and even your vision and hearing. But those fluctuations are small compared to fluctuations in personality: You might be very friendly and outgoing at one time or in one situation but much less so an hour later. Theoretically, a researcher could observe your behavior nonstop for days or weeks to get an adequate sample, but by far the most common procedure is to ask you, or someone who knows you well, to report about your personality with a questionnaire.

Devising and evaluating a useful questionnaire are more difficult than you might think. Recall the discussion of reliability and validity from Chapter 9. Reliability means repeatability or consistency of scores; validity means usefulness of the scores for predicting something else. Determining the reliability of a personality questionnaire is the first step; if the reliability is low, then some of the questions may be unclear or confusing, or different questions may be measuring different aspects of personality. Validity is more difficult. When people rate their own personality, can we trust them to be accurate? For example, most Americans describe their own intelligence as well above average, whereas the British are more modest, and the Japanese are still more modest, although on actual IQ tests the British do at least as well as Americans and the Japanese usually do better (Furnham, Hosoe, & Tang, 2002). On personality questionnaires also, presumably people vary in how accurately they describe themselves.

One way to check the validity of a personality questionnaire is to compare questionnaire results to behaviors recorded in diary form. In one study 170 college students filled out questionnaires about several personality dimensions including aggressiveness and spontaneity. Then they kept daily records of such behaviors as yelling at someone (aggression) and buying something on the spur of the moment (spontaneous behavior). Both kinds of data rely on self-reports, but the daily behavior records are more detailed, closer in time to the actual events, and presumably more accurate. The questionnaire results correlated about .4 with reports of aggressive behavior, but less well with reports of spontaneous acts (Wu & Clark, 2003). That is, the questionnaire results were moderately accurate measurements.

In another study 10- to 11-year-old girls filled out a questionnaire about conscientiousness (tendency to follow the rules and keep one's promises), and a year later reported whether they had engaged in any risky sexual behaviors. Conscientiousness correlated −.42 with risky sexual behaviors; that is, those girls low in conscientiousness were the most likely to engage in risky sexual activities (Markey, Markey, & Tinsley, 2003). Again, it appears that the personality questionnaire is measuring an important aspect of behavior—not perfectly, but moderately well.

An Example of Measurement Problems: Self-Esteem

For some years a popular goal among both psychologists and the general public was to raise people's self-esteem. The belief was that low self-esteem led to self-destructive activities and violence toward others, whereas high self-esteem led to satisfaction, productivity, and a host of other good outcomes. That belief was only a hypothesis, however, and researchers needed data to test it. Psychologists developed several questionnaires to measure self-esteem and devised programs to help people raise their self-esteem. However, research results were mixed and often disappointing. On the plus side, as people increase their self-esteem, they are less likely to feel depressed (Watson, Suls, & Haig, 2002). However, raising people's self-esteem generally has little effect on aggressive behavior and in many cases leads to *decreased* performance in school or on the job (Baumeister, Campbell, Krueger, & Vohs, 2003). Evidently, if we convince people that "you're doing great," they see little need to try harder!

Part of the problem is that self-esteem means many things, and different questionnaires measure it differently. Consider some example questions on self-esteem questionnaires (Blascovich & Tomaka, 1991). Here is one set of examples:

- I feel that I have a number of good qualities.
- I am able to do things as well as most other people.
- At times I think I'm no good at all.
- I'm a failure.

An answer of "true" to the first two or "false" to the second two would count as points toward a high self-esteem score. Contrast those to the following items from a different self-esteem questionnaire, on which you are to answer from 1 (rarely or never) to 5 (usually or always):

- I feel that I am a beautiful person.
- I think that I make a good impression on others.
- I think that I have a good sense of humor.
- I feel that people really like me very much.

Would you call those items "self-esteem" or "self-evaluation"? Certainly, they highlight a different aspect of self-regard. For example, you might think you have "a number of good qualities" as in the first set of items but not describe yourself as "beautiful."

Now consider these additional true–false items:

- There are lots of things about myself I'd change if I could.
- I'm often sorry for the things I do.
- I'm not doing as well in school as I'd like.
- I wish I could change my physical appearance.

A "true" answer on any of those items would count as a point toward low self-esteem. But do the answers really indicate low self-esteem or high goals? Someone who says "true" is presumably striving for self-improvement. Someone who says "false" is satisfied with current performance, whatever that might be. In short, a self-esteem questionnaire might not be measuring what we want to measure.

Here is an additional problem: Most Americans rate themselves above average in intelligence, personality, and self-esteem. Therefore, if you rate yourself "average," you are considered to have *below-average* self-esteem! Next a survey asks what you think of minority groups or foreigners. Most Americans claim to have a "very high" opinion of minority groups and foreigners, so if you rate them "about average," you are considered to have a *below-average* opinion of them. Using these methods some studies have reported that "people with low self-esteem tend to be prejudiced," when a better statement of the data would be "people who rate themselves average rate other people average too" (Baumeister et al., 2003). As emphasized before, to evaluate anyone's conclusions, we need to examine the evidence carefully, especially the measurement methods.

CONCEPT CHECK ☑

9. If someone's questionnaire results indicate "low self-esteem," what else might the results actually mean, other than low self-esteem? (Check your answer on page 514.)

The Big Five Model of Personality

Psychologists have devised questionnaires to measure locus of control, self-esteem, aggressiveness, and hundreds of other traits. Measuring hundreds of traits is impractical; the goal should be a simple system listing no more traits than necessary. Remember the principle of parsimony from Chapter 2: If we can adequately describe personality with, say, five or ten traits, we do not need to measure more.

One way to begin is by examining our language. Many psychologists assume that any human language probably has a word for every important personality trait. Although this assumption is not a logical necessity, it seems reasonable considering how much attention people pay to other people's personalities.

Gordon Allport and H. S. Odbert (1936) plodded through an English dictionary and found almost 18,000 words that might be used to describe personality. They deleted from this list words that were merely evaluations, such as *nasty*, and terms referring to temporary states, such as *confused*. (At least we hope that being confused is temporary.) In the remaining list, they looked for clusters of synonyms, such as *affectionate, warm,* and *loving,* and kept only one of these terms. When they found opposites, such as *honest* and *dishonest,* they also kept just one of them. (*Honesty* and *dishonesty* are different extremes of one dimension, not separate traits.) After eliminating synonyms and antonyms, Raymond Cattell (1965) narrowed the original list to 35 traits.

Derivation of the Big Five Personality Traits

Although some of the 35 personality traits that Cattell identified are not exactly synonyms or antonyms of one another, many of them overlapped. To determine which traits correlate with one another, psychologists use a method called *factor analysis.* For example, if measurements of warmth, gregariousness, and assertiveness correlate strongly with one another, we can cluster them together as a single trait. But if this combined trait does not correlate highly with self-discipline, then self-discipline (and anything that correlates strongly with it) is a separate trait.

Using this approach researchers found major clusters of personality traits, which they call the **big five personality traits:** *neuroticism, extraversion, agreeableness, conscientiousness, and openness to new experience* (McCrae & Costa, 1987). The case for these five traits is that (a) each correlates with many personality dimensions for which our language has a word and (b) none of these five traits correlates highly with any of the other five, so they are not measuring the same thing.

The big five dimensions are described in the following list (Costa, McCrae, & Dye, 1991). Note that the first two, neuroticism and extraversion, are the "biggest" of the big five. Even psychologists who are skeptical of the big five model agree that neuroticism

and extraversion are powerful traits that influence much of human behavior (Block, 1995).

Neuroticism is *a tendency to experience unpleasant emotions relatively easily.* Neuroticism correlates positively with anxiety, hostility, depression, and self-consciousness. In one study college students kept a diary in which they recorded the most stressful event of the day. Students who scored high on a neuroticism questionnaire were more likely than other students to identify their most stressful event as some conflict they had with another person. They were also more likely than other students to rate the experience as highly distressing, and they were less likely than others to deal effectively with their stressful events (Gunthert, Cohen, & Armeli, 1999).

Extraversion is *a tendency to seek stimulation and to enjoy the company of other people.* The opposite of extraversion is introversion. Extraversion is associated with warmth, gregariousness, assertiveness, impulsiveness, and a need for excitement. Extraverted people tend to be risk-takers, and the unpleasant side of extraversion is an increased risk of alcohol abuse and similar problems (Martsh & Miller, 1997). The pleasant side is that extraverts tend to be happy most of the time (Francis, Brown, Lester, & Philipchalk, 1998). In one study participants reported five times a day for 2 weeks what they had been doing and how they were feeling. Generally, they reported feeling happy at the same times when they had been talkative, energetic, and adventuresome. Furthermore, when people were *instructed* to act in an extraverted way, they reported feeling happier afterward, and when instructed to act in an introverted way, they reported decreased happiness, regardless of whether they were usually extraverted or introverted (Fleeson, Malanos, & Achille, 2002). These results imply that active, outgoing behavior leads to happiness, although it is also likely that happiness leads to active, outgoing behavior.

Active, outgoing behavior   Happy feelings

Agreeableness is *a tendency to be compassionate toward others.* It implies a concern for the welfare of other people and is closely related to Adler's concept of social interest. People high in agreeableness generally trust other people and expect other people to trust them.

Conscientiousness is *a tendency to show self-discipline, to be dutiful, and to strive for achievement and competence.* People high in conscientiousness tend to show a strong work motivation (Judge & Ilies, 2002). They are likely to complete the tasks they say they will perform. If you were giving a speech or making some other kind of performance, would you prefer to have your performance rated by someone high in agreeableness or conscientiousness? As you might guess, people high in conscientiousness generally give lower, presumably more honest, ratings, whereas people high in agreeableness give higher, more generous ratings (Bernardin, Cooke, & Villanova, 2000).

Openness to experience, the big five trait that is usually the least variable and hardest to observe, is *a tendency to enjoy new intellectual experiences and new ideas.* Someone high in this trait would be likely to enjoy modern art, unusual music, thought-provoking films and plays, and so forth. People open to experience enjoy meeting different kinds of people and exploring new ideas and opinions (McCrae, 1996).

CONCEPT CHECK ☑

10. Some psychologists suggest that we should divide extraversion into two traits—which they call *ambition* and *sociability*—changing the big five

Courtesy of Morimura Yasumasa

▪ The Japanese artist Morimura Yasumasa re-creates famous paintings, substituting his own face for the original. Some people love his work; others dislike it or object to the whole idea. People high in "openness to experience" delight in new, unusual forms of art, literature, and music.

into the big six. How should psychologists determine whether to do so? (Check your answer on page 514.)

Criticisms and Problems

You may already have thought about one peculiarity of the research so far: Almost none of the research behind the big five model depended on observing people's behavior. The research was based entirely on a study of personality words in the English language and people's answers to questionnaires. Questionnaire results are moderately good predictors of real behavior, but they are far from perfect.

The research methods could overlook certain personality traits just because of quirks of the English language. For example, we identify extraversion–introversion as a big factor because it relates to so many words in the English language—sociability, warmth, friendliness, adventuresomeness, gregariousness, happiness, and so forth. Religiousness would not emerge as a major personality trait because the language has few synonyms for it. Critics of the big five approach have identified nine personality dimensions that the big five model seems to have overlooked (Paunonen & Jackson, 2000). These nine are religiousness, manipulativeness, honesty, sexiness, thriftiness, conservativeness, masculinity–femininity, snobbishness, and sense of humor. None of these correlates very strongly with any of the others or with the big five.

Other critics raise the opposite objection that five is more traits than we need. Openness to experience has a modest positive correlation with extraversion, and conscientiousness correlates negatively with neuroticism, so perhaps we could get by with just three factors: neuroticism, extraversion, and agreeableness (Eysenck, 1992).

Cross-cultural studies offer partial, but only partial, support to the big five approach. Some studies have used translations of English words or an array of personality descriptions from other languages. Others have shown pictures of people in various activities and asked, "How likely would you be to do this?" The picture approach makes it easy to test people of various cultures without first thoroughly studying their language (Paunonen, Zeidner, Engvik, Oosterveld, & Maliphant, 2000). Many studies have found results approximately consistent with the big five model (McCrae & Costa, 1997).

However, some studies did find important cross-cultural differences. For example, in many traditional cultures, almost everyone is low in what Westerners call "openness to experience" (Mastor & Cooper, 2000; Saggino, 2000; Silverthorne, 2001). A study in China identified four big traits corresponding approximately to extraversion, neuroticism, conscientiousness, and "loyalty to Chinese traditions" (Cheung et al., 1996).

Overall, how should we evaluate the five-factor description? The answer depends on our purposes. If we are interested in a theoretical understanding of personality, it is premature at best to call the five-factor description a fact of nature (as some have done). The five-factor description accounts for enough of the variability in human behavior to be useful, although for some purposes three factors may be enough and for other purposes more may be necessary. It depends on how much precision we want in describing and predicting people's behavior.

The Origins of Personality

A description of personality differences is not an explanation. What makes some people more extraverted, neurotic, agreeable, conscientious, or open to experience than other people are?

Heredity and Environment

If you want evidence that heredity can influence personality, you need look no further than the nearest pet dog. For centuries people have selectively bred dogs for the personalities they desired, ranging from the tamest and friendliest lap dogs to those that are capable of attacking ferociously.

To measure the influences of heredity and environment on human personality, researchers have relied mostly on the same kinds of data as in other areas of psychology (Bouchard & McGue, 2003). First, they compare the similarities between identical twins and fraternal twins. As Figure 13.6 shows, five studies conducted in separate locations indicated much greater similarities in extraversion between identical pairs than fraternal pairs (Loehlin, 1992). Studies in Australia and the United States found a similar pattern for neuroticism, with identical twins resembling each other much more than fraternal twins, who resembled each other no more than brothers or sisters born at different times (Lake, Eaves, Maes, Heath, & Martin, 2000).

Modern methods make it possible to search for specific genes linked to particular personality traits. Several studies have identi-

fied genes apparently linked to neuroticism or to the specific aspect of neuroticism known as *harm avoidance* or anxiety-proneness (Fullerton et al., 2003; Zohar et al., 2003). However, each of the genes identified so far makes only a small contribution, and researchers have not yet established the route by which any gene acts.

Second, researchers compare the personalities of parents, their biological children, and their adopted children. As Figure 13.7 shows, parents' extraversion levels correlate moderately with those of their biological children but hardly at all with their adopted children. Similarly, biologically related brothers or sisters growing up together resemble each other moderately in personality, and unrelated children adopted into the same family do not (Loehlin, 1992). The results shown in Figures 13.6 and 13.7 pertain to extraversion; similar studies provide a largely similar pattern for neuroticism and other personality traits (Heath, Neale, Kessler, Eaves, & Kendler, 1992; Loehlin, 1992; Viken, Rose, Kaprio, & Koskenvuo, 1994).

The low correlations between adopted children and adoptive parents imply that children learn rather little of their personalities by imitating their parents.

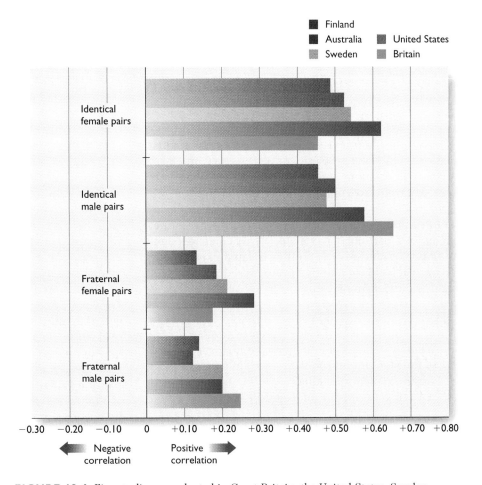

FIGURE 13.6 Five studies—conducted in Great Britain, the United States, Sweden, Australia, and Finland—found larger correlations between the extraversion levels of identical (monozygotic) twins than those of fraternal (dizygotic) twins. *(Based on data summarized by Loehlin, 1992)*

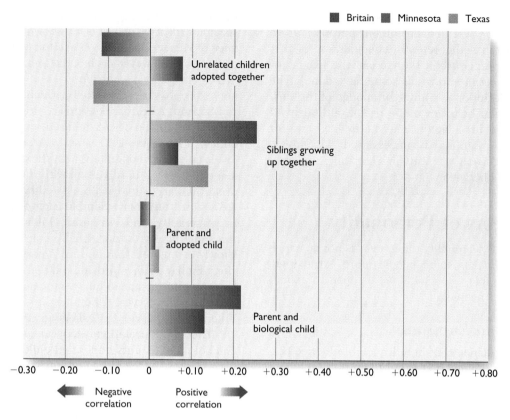

FIGURE 13.7 Studies in Britain, Minnesota, and Texas measured extraversion in members of hundreds of families. Each found moderate positive correlations between parents and their biological children and between pairs of biologically related brothers and sisters. However, all found low or even negative correlations between parents and adopted children and among adopted children living in the same family. *(Based on data summarized by Loehlin, 1992)*

(Recall from Chapter 10 that Judith Harris made this same point.) Many researchers believe that much of the variation among people's personalities relates to the **unshared environment,** *the aspects of environment that differ from one individual to another, even within a family.* Unshared environment includes the effects of a particular playmate, a particular teacher, an injury or illness, or any other isolated experience. Because of its idiosyncratic nature, unshared environment is difficult to investigate.

CONCEPT CHECK ☑

11. What evidence would indicate an important role of the *shared environment*—the influences that are the same for all children within a family? (Check your answer on page 514.)

Influences of Age and Historical Era

Do you think your personality now resembles what it was in childhood? In some aspects it probably does. In one study investigators observed the behavior of 3-year-old children and followed them longitudinally until age 26. Children who were fearful and easily upset at age 3 were more nervous and inhibited than others at age 26. Those who were impulsive and restless at age 3 tended to have been in trouble with others from then on and to feel alienated from society. On the other hand, those who were confident, friendly, and eager to explore their environment at 3 tended to be confident adults, eager to take charge of events (Caspi, Harrington, et al., 2003).

Will your personality change much in the next few years? According to the research, the older people get, the more consistent their personalities remain over time. In childhood, answers on a personality questionnaire correlate a modest .34 between two tests given 6 or 7 years apart. By college age the correlation is .54. It increases to .64 at age 30 and .74 at age 60 (Roberts & DelVecchio, 2000). Why personality becomes more fixed as we grow older is not known, but you can probably imagine a few hypotheses.

The differences that occur over age are not large, but they are fairly predictable, and many are consistent across cultures. One trend is that as people grow older, they become more conscientious. In every culture that has been studied throughout the world, middle-aged people are more likely to be highly conscientious—that is, to do what they promise they will do—than are teenagers (McCrae et al., 2000). A simple explanation is that adults are forced, whether they like it or not, to hold a job, pay the bills, repair the house, care for children, and take responsibility in other ways.

As people age, they also tend to become less extraverted, especially less sensation seeking. Again this trend is found cross-culturally (Labouvie-Vief, Diehl, Tarnowksi, & Shen, 2000). Older people also tend to be less neurotic—that is, less prone to anxieties and unpleasant mood swings—and slightly more agreeable (Cramer, 2003; McCrae et al., 2000). In the United States, young people on the average score higher on openness to new experience than older people. This trend is no surprise; we see that young people enjoy new types of music, new kinds of food, new styles of clothing, and so forth (Sapolsky, 1998), whereas older people stay with old habits. In some other cultures, however, openness to experience shows no clear trend over age (McCrae et al., 2000).

Finally, does personality change from one generation to the next? Remember the Flynn effect from Chapter 9: Over the years people's performance on IQ tests has gradually increased so that each generation does better on the tests than the previous generation. Researchers have also found generational differences in personality. For example, over the years, beginning in the 1950s, measurements of anxiety have steadily increased (Twenge, 2000). On the Child Manifest Anxiety Scale, the mean score in the 1950s was 15.1, and the mean for children in mental hospitals was 20.1. By the 1980s the mean for *all* children was 23.3! Do we really have that much more anxiety than in past generations? It is possible that people's answers do not mean exactly the same as what they used to. The more disturbing possibility is that we really do live in an age of anxiety despite our increases in health and wealth and the decreased probability of nuclear war. Compared to past generations, more children today have to live through their parents' divorce, and fewer live in a neighborhood with many friends and relatives. Might those social changes have raised the average anxiety level to what used to characterize the top 10%? The answer is uncertain, but now researchers need to worry about why people worry so much.

IN CLOSING

The Challenges of Classifying Personality

Personality descriptions refer to averages over time. We don't expect anyone to be equally extraverted at all times or equally neurotic, conscientious, agreeable, open to experience, or anything else. What you do at any moment depends largely on the situation. In a sufficiently novel situation, you may be surprised by the actions of people you know well, and even by your own behavior.

The dimensions of personality apply best in familiar situations that apply few constraints on us, allowing personality differences to emerge clearly. The first step is for researchers to describe those differences. Later, they can better address the causes of the differences—the issues of "what makes us tick" that we addressed in the first module.

Summary

- *Nomothetic and idiographic research.* Nomothetic studies examine large numbers of people briefly, whereas idiographic studies examine one or a few individuals intensively. (page 506)
- *Traits and states.* Traits are personality characteristics that persist over time; states are temporary tendencies in response to particular situations. (page 506)
- *Measurement problems.* Personality researchers rely mostly on self-reports, which are not entirely accurate. Many people misrepresent themselves, either knowingly or unintentionally. (page 507)
- *Five major traits.* Much of personality can be explained by these five traits: neuroticism, extraversion, openness to new experience, agreeableness, and conscientiousness. However, several other important dimensions may have been overlooked. (page 508)
- *Determinants of personality.* Studies of twins and adopted children indicate that heredity contributes to the observed differences in personality. Family environment evidently contributes rather little. Much of the variation in personality may be due to unshared environment, the special experiences that vary from one person to another even within a family. (page 511)
- *Changes over time.* Compared to younger people, older people tend to be higher in conscientiousness and agreeableness. They are somewhat lower in extraversion and neuroticism. Openness to experience decreases with age in the United States, but several other countries do not show this trend. (page 512)
- *Changes over historical era.* Measurements of anxiety have gradually increased over the decades so that normal people now report anxiety levels that used to characterize people in mental hospitals. (page 513)

Answers to Concept Checks

7. This nervousness is state anxiety because it is evoked by a particular situation. Trait anxiety is a tendency to become nervous in many situations. (page 507)

8. People with an external locus of control would be more likely to buy lottery tickets. Those with an internal locus of control prefer tasks where they can control the outcome. (page 507)

9. Depending on the questionnaire items, what appears to be low self-esteem might indicate high goals and therefore lack of satisfaction with one's current performance. Also, rating one's intelligence and personality as "average" could simply mean that the person tends to use the middle part of the rating scale. (page 508)

10. They should determine whether measures of ambition correlate strongly with measures of sociability. If so, then ambition and sociability can be considered two aspects of a single trait, extraversion. If not, then they are indeed separate personality traits. (page 510)

11. If the personalities of adopted children within a family correlated highly with one another, we would conclude that the similarity reflected the shared environment. The weakness of such correlations is the main evidence for the importance of the unshared environment. (page 512)

Answer to Other Question in the Module

A. Choices 1b, 2a, 3b, and 4b indicate internal locus of control; the other choices indicate external locus of control. Your answers to a longer list of such items could more accurately assess your locus of control. (page 507)

Personality Assessment

| *What inferences can we safely draw from the results of a personality test?*

A new P. T. Barnum Psychology Clinic has just opened at your local shopping mall and is offering a grand opening special on personality tests. You have always wanted to know more about yourself, so you sign up. Here is Barnum's true–false test:

Questionnaire for Universal Assessment of Zealous Youth (QUAZY)

1. I have never met a cannibal I didn't like.　T　F
2. Robbery is the only felony I have ever committed.　T　F
3. I eat "funny mushrooms" less frequently than I used to.　T　F
4. I don't care what people say about my nose-picking habit.　T　F
5. Sex with vegetables no longer disgusts me.　T　F
6. This time I am quitting glue-sniffing for good.　T　F
7. I generally lie on questions like this one.　T　F
8. I spent much of my childhood sucking on telephone cords.　T　F
9. I find it impossible to sleep if I think my bed might be clean.　T　F
10. Naked bus drivers make me nervous.　T　F
11. I spend my spare time playing strip solitaire.　T　F

You turn in your answers. A few minutes later, a computer prints out your individual personality profile:

> You have a need for other people to like and admire you, and yet you tend to be critical of yourself. While you have some personality weaknesses, you are generally able to compensate for them. You have considerable unused capacity that you have not turned to your advantage. Disciplined and self-controlled on the outside, you tend to be worrisome and insecure on the inside. At times, you have serious doubts as to whether you have made the right decision or done the right thing. You prefer a certain amount of change and variety and become dissatisfied when hemmed in by restrictions and limitations. You also pride yourself as an independent thinker and do not accept others' statements without satisfac-

tory proof. But you have found it unwise to be too frank in revealing yourself to others. At times you are extraverted, affable, and sociable, while at other times you are introverted, wary, and reserved. Some of your aspirations tend to be rather unrealistic. (Forer, 1949, p. 120)

Do you agree with this assessment? Several experiments have been conducted along these lines with psychology classes (Forer, 1949; Marks & Kammann, 1980; Ulrich, Stachnik, & Stainton, 1963). Students started by filling out a questionnaire that looked fairly reasonable, not something as preposterous as the QUAZY. Several days later, each student received a sealed envelope with his or her name on it. Inside was a "personality profile," supposedly based on the student's answers to the questionnaire. The students were asked, "How accurately does this profile describe you?" About 90% rated it as good or excellent. Some expressed amazement at its accuracy: "I didn't realize until now that psychology was an exact science." None of them realized that everyone had received exactly the same personality profile—the same one you just read.

The students accepted this personality profile partly because it vaguely describes almost everyone, much like newspaper horoscopes do, and partly because people tend to accept almost *any* statement that a psychologist makes about them (Marks & Kammann, 1980). *This tendency to accept and praise vague statements about our personality is known as the* **Barnum effect**, named after P. T. Barnum, the circus

▌ People tend to accept almost any personality assessment that someone offers them, especially if it is stated in vague, general terms that each person can interpret to fit himself or herself.

owner who specialized in fooling people out of their money.

The conclusion: Psychological testing must be done carefully. If we want to know whether a particular test measures a particular person's personality, we cannot simply ask that person's opinion. Many people will praise as "highly accurate" even the results of a worthless test. To devise a psychological test that not only *appears* to work but also actually *does* work, psychologists need to design the test carefully and determine its reliability and validity.

Standardized Personality Tests

Psychologists have devised a great variety of personality tests. A **standardized test** is *one that is administered according to exact rules that specify how to interpret the results.* One important step for standardizing a test is to determine the distribution of scores. We need to know the mean score and the range of scores for a representative sample of the population and how they differ for special populations, such as people with severe depression. Given such information, we can determine whether a particular score on a personality test is within the normal range or whether it is more typical of people with some disorder.

Most of the tests published in popular magazines have never been standardized. A magazine may herald an article: "Test Yourself: How Good Is Your Marriage?" or "Test Yourself: How Well Do You Control the Stress in Your Life?" After you take the test and compare your answers to the scoring key, the article may tell you that "if your score is greater than 80, you are doing very well . . . if it is below 20, you need to work on improving yourself!"—or some such nonsense. Unless the magazine states otherwise, you can safely assume that the author pulled the scoring norms out of thin air and never even bothered to make sure that the test items were clearly stated.

Over the years psychologists have developed an enormous variety of tests to measure both normal and abnormal personality. We shall examine a few prominent examples and explore some creative possibilities for future personality measurement.

An Objective Personality Test: The Minnesota Multiphasic Personality Inventory

Some of the most widely used personality tests are based on simple pencil-and-paper responses. We now consider in detail the MMPI, the most widely used of all personality tests (Piotrowski & Keller, 1989).

The **Minnesota Multiphasic Personality Inventory** (mercifully abbreviated **MMPI**) consists of *a series of true–false questions intended to measure certain personality dimensions and clinical conditions such as depression.* The original MMPI, developed in the 1940s and still in use, has 550 items; *the second edition,* MMPI–2, published in 1990, has 567. Typical items are "my mother never loved me" and "I think I would like the work of a pharmacist." (The items stated in this text are rewordings of the actual items.)

The MMPI was devised *empirically*—that is, based on evidence rather than theory (Hathaway & McKinley, 1940). The authors wrote hundreds of true–false questions that they thought might be useful for measuring personality. They put these questions to people who were known to be suffering from various psychological disorders and to a group of hospital visitors, who were assumed to be psychologically normal. The researchers selected those items that most of the people in a given clinical group answered differently from most of the normal people. They assumed, for example, that if you answer many questions as most people with depression do, you probably are depressed also. The MMPI had scales for reporting depression, paranoia, schizophrenia, and others. The result was a test that worked, and still works, moderately well in practice. For example, most people with scores above a certain level on the Depression scale are in fact depressed.

Some of the items on the MMPI made sense theoretically; others did not. For example, some items on the Depression scale asked about feelings of helplessness or worthlessness, which are an important part of depression. But two other items were "I attend religious services frequently" and "occasionally I tease animals." If you answered *false* to either of those items, you would get a point on the Depression scale! These items were included simply because more depressed people than others answered *false.* Why is not obvious. (Perhaps people with depression do not tease animals because they do hardly anything just for fun.)

Revisions of the Test

The MMPI was standardized in the 1940s. As time passed the meaning of certain items, or at least of certain answers, changed. For example, how would you respond to the following item?

I believe I am important.   T F

In the 1940s fewer than 10% of all people marked this item *true.* At the time the word "important" meant about the same thing as "famous," and people who called themselves important were thought to have an inflated view of themselves. Today, we stress that every person is important.

TABLE 13.3 The Ten MMPI-2 Clinical Scales

Scale	Typical Item
Hypochondria (Hs)	I have chest pains several times a week. (T)
Depression (D)	I am glad that I am alive. (F)
Hysteria (Hy)	My heart frequently pounds so hard I can hear it. (T)
Psychopathic Deviation (Pd)	I get a fair deal from most people. (F)
Masculinity–Femininity (Mf)	I like to arrange flowers. (T = female)
Paranoia (Pa)	There are evil people trying to influence my mind. (T)
Psychasthenia (Obsessive–Compulsive) (Pt)	I save nearly everything I buy, even after I have no use for it. (T)
Schizophrenia (Sc)	I see, hear, and smell things that no one else knows about. (T)
Hypomania (Ma)	When things are dull I try to get some excitement started. (T)
Social Introversion (Si)	I have the time of my life at parties. (F)

What about this item?

I like to play drop the handkerchief.   T F

Drop the handkerchief, a game similar to tag, dropped out of popularity in the 1950s. Most people born since then have never even heard of it, much less played it.

To bring the MMPI up to date, a group of psychologists rephrased some of the items, eliminated some, and added others to deal with drug abuse, suicidal thoughts, and other issues that did not concern psychologists in the 1940s (Butcher, Graham, Williams, & Ben-Porath, 1990). Then they tried out the new MMPI–2 on a large representative sample of the U.S. population. In other words they restandardized the test. (You may recall the discussion in Chapter 9 about the need to re-standardize IQ tests.) Psychologists also developed a new form, the MMPI–A, intended for use with adolescents.

The MMPI–2 has 10 clinical scales, as shown in Table 13.3. The various scales have 32 to 78 items each, scattered throughout the test rather than clustered. Most people get at least a few points on each scale; a score above a certain level indicates a probable difficulty. Figure 13.8 shows how MMPI–2 scores are plotted.

Generalizability of the MMPI

Can a single test measure personality for all kinds of people? In particular, is the MMPI (or MMPI–2 or MMPI–A) a fair measure of personality for people of different ethnic and cultural backgrounds?

This is a difficult question to answer. In general, the means and ranges on each scale are about the same for many ethnic groups, even after translation into different languages (Negy, Leal-Puente, Trainor, & Carlson, 1997). However, differences do occur. For example, Mexicans are more likely than U.S. people to say *true* to "Life is a constant strain for me." Presumably, the reason is that life really is more difficult for many people who live in Mexico. On several scales of the MMPI–2, the means for Mexicans differ from the U.S. means (Lucio, Ampudia, Durán, León, & Butcher, 2001). Consequently, the scoring standards for a personality test should differ from one country to another. Even within a country, psychologists need to be

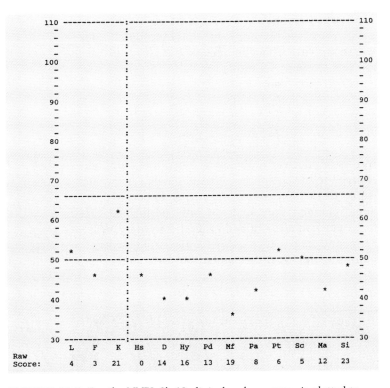

FIGURE 13.8 For the MMPI–2's 10 clinical scales, a score is plotted to profile an individual. This is the profile of a middle-aged man with no psychological problems. A person with a disorder such as hypochondria or paranoia would have scores in the range of 65 or higher on those scales. *(Minnesota Multiphasic Personality Inventory–2, © by the Regents of the University of Minnesota. Data courtesy of R. J. Huber.)*

cautious in interpreting scores for ethnic minorities (Gynther, 1989).

Detection of Deception

If you were taking the MMPI or another personality test, could you lie to make yourself look mentally healthier than you really are? Yes. Could someone catch your lies? Probably.

The designers of the MMPI and MMPI–2 included items designed to identify lying (Woychyshyn, McElheran, & Romney, 1992). For example, consider the items "I like every person I have ever met" and "occasionally I get angry at someone." If you answer *true* to the first question and *false* to the second, you are either a saint or a liar. The test authors, convinced that liars outnumber saints, would give you 1 point for each of these answers on a scale to measure lies. If you get too many points on that scale, a psychologist will distrust your answers to the other items. Strangely enough, some people lie on the test to try to make themselves look bad. The MMPI includes items to detect that kind of faking also.

A similar method detects deception on other questionnaires. For example, many employers ask job applicants about their experience with job-related skills. Suppose some employer's questionnaire asked you how much experience you have had at "determining myopic weights for periodic tables." You're not sure what that means, but you really want the job. Do you claim to have had extensive experience? If so, your claimed expertise will count *against* you because "determining myopic weights for periodic tables" is nonsense. The employer asked about it just to see whether you were exaggerating your qualifications on other items. According to the results of one study, almost half of all job applicants claimed to have experience with one or more nonexistent tasks (Anderson, Warner, & Spencer, 1984). Some claimed they had not only performed these tasks but had also trained others! The more skill an applicant claims to have on nonexistent tasks, the more the employer discounts that applicant's claims about real tasks.

CRITICAL THINKING:
A STEP FURTHER
Assessing Honesty

Could you use this strategy in other situations? Suppose a political candidate promises to increase aid to college students. You are skeptical. How could you use the candidate's statements on other issues to help you decide whether to believe this promise?

Uses of the MMPI

The MMPI is useful for personality assessment and for research on personality. It also helps clinical psychologists learn something about a client before therapy or measure a client's personality changes during therapy. The MMPI has better reliability and validity than many other personality tests (Garb, Florio, & Grove, 1998). However, to a client, the MMPI results are seldom surprising. For example, suppose you gave the following answers:

I doubt that I will ever be successful.	True
I am glad that I am alive.	False
I have thoughts about suicide.	True
I am helpless to control the important events in my life.	True

A psychologist analyzes your answer sheet and tells you that your results show indications of depression. Yes, of course. You already knew that. But even in a case like this, the results can be useful for comparing *how* depressed you are now and later.

CONCEPT CHECK ☑

12. Suppose a person thinks "True or false, black is my favorite color" would be a good item for the Depression scale of the MMPI. How would a researcher decide whether to include it?
13. Why does the MMPI include some items that ask about common flaws, such as, "Sometimes I think more about my own welfare than that of others"? (Check your answers on page 526.)

Projective Techniques

The MMPI and similar personality tests are easy to score and easy to handle statistically, but they restrict how a person can respond to a question. In hopes of learning more, psychologists ask open-ended questions that permit an unlimited range of responses.

However, to the inquiry "tell me about yourself," many people are reluctant to confide embarrassing information. Many people find it easier to discuss their problems in the abstract than in the first person. For instance, they might say, "I have a friend with this problem. Let me tell you my friend's problem and ask what my friend should do." They then describe their own problem. They are "projecting" their problem onto someone else, in Freud's sense of the word—that is, attributing it to someone else.

Rather than discouraging projection, psychologists often make use of it. They use **projective techniques**, which are *designed to encourage people to project their personality characteristics onto ambiguous* *stimuli.* This strategy helps people reveal themselves more fully than they normally would. Let's consider the best-known projective techniques: the Rorschach Inkblots and the Thematic Apperception Test.

14. Which of the following is a projective technique?
    a. A psychologist gives a child a set of puppets with instructions to act out a story about a family.
    b. A psychologist hands you a stack of cards, each containing one word, such as *tolerant,* with instructions to sort the cards into a stack of cards that apply to you and a stack of cards that do not. (Check your answers on page 526.)

The Rorschach Inkblots

The Rorschach Inkblots, *a projective technique based on people's interpretations of 10 ambiguous inkblots,* is the most famous and most widely used projective personality technique. It was created by Hermann Rorschach (ROAR-shock), a Swiss psychiatrist, who showed people inkblots and asked them to say whatever came to mind (Pichot, 1984). Rorschach was impressed that his patients' interpretations of the blots differed from his own. In a book published in 1921 (English translation 1942), he presented the 10 symmetrical inkblots that still constitute the Rorschach Inkblot Technique. (Originally, he had used a larger number, but the publisher insisted on cutting the number to 10 to reduce printing costs.) As other psychiatrists and psychologists began using these blots, they gradually developed the Rorschach into the projective technique we know today.

Administering the Rorschach

The Rorschach Inkblot Technique consists of cards similar to the one in Figure 13.9. Five are in black and white and five are in color. A psychologist administering this procedure hands you a card and asks, "What might this be?" The instructions are intentionally vague on the assumption that everything you do in an ill-defined situation reveals something significant about your personality.

Sometimes people's answers are revealing, either immediately or in response to a psychologist's probes. Here is an example (Aronow, Reznikoff, & Moreland, 1995):

Client: (looking at Card 5) Some kind of insect; it's not pretty enough to be a butterfly.
Psychologist: Any association to that?
Client: It's an ugly black butterfly, no colors.
Psychologist: What does that make you think of in your own life?
Client: You probably want me to say "myself." Well, that's probably how I thought of myself when I was younger—I never thought of myself as attractive—my sister was the attractive one. I was the ugly duckling—I did get more attractive as I got older.

Evaluation of the Rorschach

It is true that personality makes a bigger difference in an ill-defined, ambiguous situation than in one where everyone is asked to do something specific. The question is how accurately a psychologist can interpret the responses in that ambiguous situation. When I describe what I see in a picture, I sometimes see how my answer relates to a past experience or current concern. But would anyone else guess the connection?

In the 1950s and 1960s, certain psychologists made exaggerated claims, even calling the Rorschach "an x-ray of the mind." Those claims provoked vigorous criticism. The main problem was that different psychologists drew different conclusions from the same answer depending on their theoretical expectations. For example, a man with depression described one blot, "It looks like a bat that has been squashed on the pavement under the heel of a giant's boot" (Dawes, 1994, p. 149). Psychologist Robyn Dawes initially was impressed with how the Rorschach had revealed the client's sense of being overwhelmed and crushed by powers beyond his control. However, Dawes later realized that he had already known the client was depressed. If a client with a history of violence had made the same response, he would have focused on the aggressive nature of the giant's foot stomp. For a hallucinating or paranoid client, he would have made still other interpretations. Psychologists often believe the Rorschach gave them some insight, when in fact they already knew it before administering the test (Wood, Nezworski, Lilienfeld, & Garb, 2003).

James Exner (1986) developed methods for interpreting Rorschach responses that were intended to standardize the interpretations. Using Exner's system, a psychologist counts the number of times a client mentions certain kinds of themes, such as

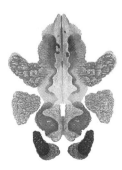

FIGURE 13.9 In the Rorschach Inkblot Technique, people study an abstract pattern and say what it looks like. The idea is that in an ambiguous situation personality will be revealed by anything that someone does and says.

aggression, how often the response refers to the whole blot or just part of it, and several other reasonably objective measurements. From comparison to standards that presumably represent normal people, a psychologist derives measures of certain kinds of mental disturbance.

However, serious problems with the Rorschach remain (Lilienfeld, Wood, & Garb, 2000; Wood et al., 2003):

• The standardization sample must have been strange because the test identifies *most* people as psychologically disturbed.
• People are asked to give as many answers as they wish on each blot, but psychologists count the *total number* of aggressive, depressive, or otherwise pathological answers. Highly intelligent or talkative people give more answers than other people do, and the more total answers you give, the more likely you are to say something that counts as "disturbed."
• Different ethnic groups have certain characteristic ways of responding that differ from the standardization group, and the test may be inappropriate for use with some groups.
• The interrater reliability of the test is only about .85. That is, different psychologists listening to the same answers do not fully agree on their counts of aggressive themes, depressive themes, and so forth. A reliability around .85 is acceptable for research purposes but is risky for making decisions about an individual.
• Many of the individual scales have doubtful validity. For example, the supposed measures of depression, anxiety, and hostility have low correlations with depressive, anxious, or hostile behavior.
• Finally and most important, the Rorschach rarely gives information that could not be obtained more easily in other ways. For example, psychologists who are given biographical and MMPI information about someone usually make the same personality judgments as psychologists who are given the same information plus the Rorschach results. In fact adding the Rorschach results sometimes makes their judgments *less* accurate.

Critics of the Rorschach stop short of calling it completely invalid. Their point is that it is not valid enough to make decisions about an individual and that it seldom provides information that a psychologist could not get more easily in other ways. For example, Rorschach results are reasonably valid for determining that someone's thinking is severely disturbed (schizophrenic), but psychologists can usually recognize a severe disturbance from a brief conversation with the person. In its defense some users of the Rorschach say they use it not for diagnosis or decisions but only as a way of starting a conversation and getting clients to

talk more freely about topics they might be reluctant to discuss (Aronow et al., 1995). Of course, if used in that way, it is no longer a personality test, and its results should not be reported. Some psychologists continue to use Rorschach results to recommend to the courts which parent should get custody of a child, which prisoners should get parole, and so forth. Using the results for those purposes should require solid evidence of validity, and that evidence is lacking (Wood et al., 2003).

CONCEPT CHECK

15. Why are highly talkative people more likely than others to have their Rorschach answers considered disturbed? (Check your answer on page 526.)

The Thematic Apperception Test

The **Thematic Apperception Test (TAT)** consists of pictures like the one shown in Figure 13.10. *The person is asked to make up a story for each picture, describing what is happening, what events led up to the scene, and what will happen in the future.* The test was devised by Christiana Morgan and Henry Murray as a means of measuring people's needs; it was revised and published by Murray (1943) and later revised by others. It includes 31 pictures in all, including some showing women, some showing men, some with both or neither, and one that is totally blank. Originally, it was intended that a psychologist would select 20 cards for use with a given client, but in actual practice most psychologists use fewer (Lilienfeld et al., 2000).

The assumption behind the TAT is that when you tell a story about a person in the drawing, you probably identify with the person and so the story is really about yourself. You might describe events and concerns in your own life, including some that you might

FIGURE 13.10 In the Thematic Apperception Test, people tell a story about what is going on in a picture such as this one. Most people include material that relates to current concerns in their lives.

be reluctant to discuss openly. For example, one young man told the following story about a picture of a man clinging to a rope:

> This man is escaping. Several months ago he was beat up and shanghaied and taken aboard ship. Since then, he has been mistreated and unhappy and has been looking for a way to escape. Now the ship is anchored near a tropical island and he is climbing down a rope to the water. He will get away successfully and swim to shore. When he gets there, he will be met by a group of beautiful native women with whom he will live the rest of his life in luxury and never tell anyone what happened. Sometimes he will feel that he should go back to his old life; but he will never do it. (Kimble & Garmezy, 1968, pp. 582–583)

This young man had entered divinity school, mainly to please his parents, but was unhappy there. He was wrestling with a secret desire to escape to a new life with greater worldly pleasures. In his story he described someone doing what he wanted to do.

Psychologists use the TAT in several ways. Many therapists use it unsystematically. They use different cards and different numbers of cards with different clients, and they interpret the results according to their "clinical judgment," without any clear rules. The results may be reasonable in some cases, but under these circumstances it is impossible to collect adequate data to estimate the reliability or validity of the test.

If you took the TAT with two psychologists, they might reach different conclusions about you. As with the Rorschach, the interrater reliability is about .85—good enough for research purposes but not for making important decisions about an individual (Cramer, 1996). When someone retakes the test a few weeks later, the test–retest reliability is generally lower, usually less than .5 (Cramer, 1996). As with the Rorschach, one criticism is that the test seldom provides information that goes beyond what we could get in other ways (Lilienfeld et al., 2000).

On the other hand, the TAT is sometimes used to measure people's need for achievement by counting all the times that they mention achievement. The test is similarly used to measure power and affiliation needs. These results are useful for many research purposes, although not necessarily for making decisions about an individual (Lilienfeld et al., 2000).

Handwriting as a Projective Technique

Based on the theory that your personality affects everything you do, some psychologists (and others) have tried analyzing people's handwriting. For example, perhaps people who dot their i's with a dash—*ı̇* —are especially energetic, or perhaps people who draw large loops above the line—as in *allow* —are highly idealistic. Carefully collected data, however, show only random relationships between handwriting and personality (Tett & Palmer, 1997).

Possible Implicit Personality Tests

The research has failed to support any of the projective tests, but the motivation behind them remains: Psychologists would like to measure personality aspects that people cannot or will not discuss openly. So the search for another kind of personality test continues.

Recall from Chapter 7 the distinction between explicit and implicit memory. If you listen to a list of words and then try to repeat them, what you recall is explicit memory. If you unknowingly use words from the list in your later conversation, your use of those words constitutes implicit memory. Implicit memory occurs even when you are not aware of remembering something.

Many researchers are trying to develop an implicit personality test—that is, one that measures some aspect of your personality without your awareness. No one knows yet whether these methods will succeed. We shall consider two examples: the Emotional Stroop Test and the Implicit Association Test.

The Emotional Stroop Test

Recall the Stroop effect from Chapter 8: People are asked to look at a display like this and read the color of the ink instead of reading the words:

| purple brown green blue yellow purple yellow red brown |

In the **Emotional Stroop Test,** *someone examines a list of words, some of which relate to a possible source of worry or concern to the person, and tries to say the color of the ink of each word.* For example, in the following display, say the color of the ink of each word as fast as possible:

| cancer venom defeat hospital rattler failure fangs blood loser slither nurses bite jobless cobra inadequate disease |

If you had a snake phobia, might you pause longer when you try to read the color of snake-related words—*venom, rattler, fangs, slither, bite, cobra?* You can collect results for yourself. Go to http://psychology. wadsworth.com/kalat_intro7e. Navigate to the student Web site, then to Online Try it Yourself, and click on Emotional Stroop Test.

Let's examine a representative study.

Online Try It Yourself

The Emotional Stroop Test is sometimes called the Personal Stroop Test because the items are individualized to concerns that some person might have. In this case the research dealt with people who had attempted suicide (Becker, Strohbach, & Rinck, 1999).

Hypothesis   It is always somewhat difficult to look at a word and say the color of ink instead of reading the word. It may be especially difficult if the word has a strong emotional meaning. In this case the hypothesis is that people who have attempted suicide will be slower than other people to read the color of words that relate to suicide.

Method   The experimenters asked 31 suicide attempters and 31 other people to look at four cards with 12 words each and say the color of ink for each word. One card had words with *positive* connotations, such as *talent* and *love*. Another card had words with *negative* connotations, such as *jail* and *stupidity*. A third card had words with *neutral* connotations, such as *ankle bone* and *square*. The final card had *suicide-related* words such as *grave, coldness,* and *darkness*. Different people looked at the cards in different orders. The experimenters timed how long each person took to say the ink colors of words on each card.

Results   Previous suicide attempters took slightly longer to read the suicide-related words. Other people took about equal times with all four cards. Here are the means for the two groups:

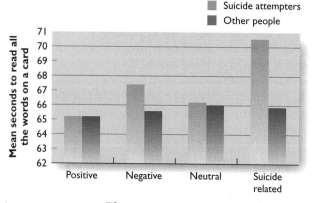

Interpretation   The previous suicide attempters apparently were distracted by the suicide-related words. The difference was not large, however. In its present form, the Emotional Stroop Test can report differences between groups, but it is not accurate enough to make decisions about any individual.

The Emotional Stroop Test has similarly shown that violent offenders have long delays on words like *anger*

and *hate* (P. Smith & Waterman, 2003), that pain sufferers respond slowly for words related to pain (Crombez, Hermans, & Adriaensen, 2000), and so forth. However, an extra delay on a word does not necessarily mean that the word reflects a fear or worry. In one study pessimistic people were slow to read the colors of unpleasant words like *germ, loser,* and *failure*, whereas optimistic people were slower with pleasant words like *joy, smile,* and *accomplish* (Segerstrom, 2001). Evidently, people were slow with words that grabbed their attention for whatever reason.

The Implicit Association Test

Recall from Chapter 9 the idea of priming: Immediately after reading or hearing a word, such as *red*, you are quicker than usual to identify a related word, such as *cherry*. The fact that you are quicker indicates that you see the two words as related. Similarly, the **Implicit Association Test** *measures whether you respond faster to a category that combines some topic with pleasant words or with unpleasant words*. The results have implications for whether you find that category pleasant or unpleasant.

To illustrate, imagine this example: You rest your left and right forefingers on a computer keyboard. When the experimenter reads a word, you are to press with your left finger if it is an unpleasant word, such as *blunder, fail,* or *shame*, and press with your right finger if it is a pleasant word, such as *joy, nice,* or *success*. Once you have mastered this procedure, we change the instructions. Now you should press the left key if you hear either an unpleasant word or a word relating to insects, and the right key if you hear either a pleasant word or one relating to flowers. Some other people have the reverse instructions: The left key means either an unpleasant word or a flower; the right key means either a pleasant word or an insect. Most people respond faster if they pair flowers with pleasant and insects with unpleasant than if they have to pair flowers with unpleasant and insects with pleasant. The conclusion is that most people like flowers and dislike insects. In this case the procedure seems more trouble than it is worth, as people could readily tell us that they like flowers more than insects. However, we can use the method to measure preferences that people did not want to admit, perhaps not even to themselves.

For example, people in one study were given the following instructions: When they saw a word in UPPERCASE letters, they should press one key if the word was pleasant (like *FRIEND*) and another key if it was unpleasant (like *UGLY*). When they saw a word in lowercase letters, they should press one key for violent words (like *kill*) and the other key for nonviolent words (like *clock*). The rule periodically changed so that sometimes pleasant was paired with violent (and unpleasant with nonviolent), and sometimes pleasant was paired with nonviolent (and unpleasant with violent). Most people responded faster when the key for pleasant words was the same as the key for nonviolent words, implying that they considered violence unpleasant. However, a group of 13 murderers responded equally fast under both conditions, implying that for them, violence was neither pleasant nor unpleasant (Gray, MacCulloch, Smith, Morris, & Snowden, 2003).

Unfortunately, the Implicit Association Test, like the Emotional Stroop Test, produces measures accurate enough for research purposes but not for classifying individuals. Research on implicit personality tests continues, though, because of the potential advantages. Mainly, it is hard for people to "fake" their results. They can try to conceal their personalities in an interview or on the MMPI, but they cannot accurately control their reaction times on the Stroop test or an association test.

CONCEPT CHECK ☑

16. On the preceding sample items of an emotional Stroop test, if you had the greatest delay in naming the ink color for *cancer, hospital, blood, nurses,* and *disease,* what would these results imply about your emotions? (Check your answer on page 526.)

Uses and Misuses of Personality Tests

Before any drug company can market a new drug in the United States, the Food and Drug Administration (FDA) requires that it be carefully tested. If the FDA

finds the drug safe and effective, it approves the drug for certain purposes but requires a warning label stating how it is to be used. After the drug is approved, however, the FDA cannot prevent a physician from prescribing it for unapproved purposes.

Personality tests are a little like prescription drugs: They should be used with caution and only for the purposes for which they have demonstrable usefulness. They are, at a minimum, helpful to psychologists as an interviewing technique to help "break the ice" and begin a good conversation. Tests can also be useful as an aid in personality assessment by a clinical psychologist. However, a test score by itself can be misleading if it is interpreted without caution. For example, suppose someone has an MMPI personality profile that resembles the profile typical for schizophrenia. Identifying schizophrenia or any other unusual condition is a signal-detection problem, as we discussed in Chapter 4—a problem of reporting a stimulus when it is present without falsely reporting it when it is absent. Suppose (realistically) that people without schizophrenia outnumber people with schizophrenia by 100 to 1. Suppose further that a particular personality profile on the MMPI–2 is characteristic of 95% of people with schizophrenia and only 5% of other people. As Figure 13.11 shows, 5% of the normal population is a *larger* group than 95% of the schizophrenic population. Thus, if we labeled as "schizophrenic" everyone with a high score, we would be wrong more often than right. (Recall the representativeness heuristic and the issue of base-rate information, discussed in Chapter 8: Someone who seems "representative" of people in a rare category does not necessarily belong to that category.) Therefore, a conscientious psychologist will look for other evidence beyond the test score before drawing

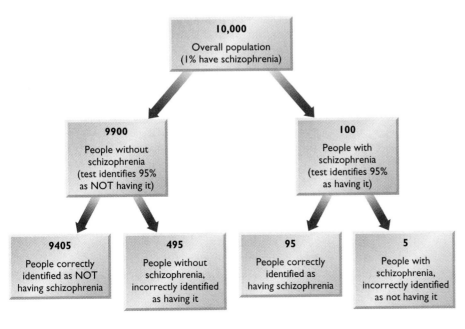

FIGURE 13.11 Assume that a certain profile occurs in 95% of people with schizophrenia and 5% of other people. If we relied entirely on this test, we would correctly identify 95 schizophrenic people, but we would also misidentify 495 normal people.

a firm conclusion. The same, of course, should be said of any test, including IQ tests.

Personality Tests in Action: Criminal Profiling

Although you might not have thought of it this way, psychological profiling of criminals is an application of personality testing. The idea is that a psychologist or experienced police investigator examines the crime scene and other information about a crime and then surmises the personality, emotions, and motivations of whoever committed the crime. Constructing such a profile presupposes that someone who commits a crime has nearly the same personality as other people who have committed similar crimes in the past.

Many movies and popular television shows have featured psychological profilers almost as superheroes. In 2003, a colleague and I informally surveyed our university's freshman psychology majors about their career plans and discovered to our amazement that about one fourth said they aspired to become forensic psychologists who would construct criminal profiles to help the police. We tried to explain that the number of freshmen at this university aspiring to be criminal profilers was probably greater than the number of people currently employed as profilers in the entire country.

How accurate are criminal profiles? Can a psychologist look at the evidence of a crime and infer the criminal's personality and background in enough detail to aid a police investigation? If so, we should be amazed, even stunned. As you have seen in this chapter, personality testing is far from an exact science, even when psychologists spend hours testing and interviewing the most cooperative people.

Even skeptics do concede the possibility of a limited degree of criminal profiling (Alison, Bennell, & Mokros, 2002; Scott, Lambie, Henwood, & Lamb, 2003). For example, most criminals live or work near the location of their crimes. Also, obviously, a rapist is more likely to be a young man than a child or an old man. Less obviously, but also less consistently, a rapist who removes all trace of his semen from the scene of the crime evidently knows something about police investigative techniques and may have been arrested for similar crimes in the past. The question is whether profilers can go beyond such general statements to infer anything about a specific individual who committed a specific crime.

A few studies have tried to collect data about the relationship between the crime and the criminal. For example, one study of sex-related murders categorized some crimes as deliberate and cruel, some as motivated more by sex than violence, others as "furious"

and possibly revenge-based, and still others as antisocial and perverse. The kinds of people who committed one kind of murder differed on the average from those who committed other kinds. However, most of the crimes the researchers examined did not fit neatly into any of these categories, and those that did fit were so few that the apparent links to personal characteristics could have been due to chance (Kocsis, Cooksey, & Irwin, 2002).

Another study examined 100 cases of stranger rape (as opposed to acquaintance rape). Researchers rated the degree of similarity among crimes and also the degree of similarity among convicted offenders. They found no consistent relationship. That is, men who had committed apparently similar crimes were no more likely than others to be similar in age, ethnic group, education, marital status, employment records, or criminal records (Mokros & Alison, 2002). If, indeed, people who commit similar crimes do not resemble one another, the prospects for criminal profiling are limited.

A few studies have directly measured the ability of profilers to infer the characteristics of people who committed specific crimes. Unfortunately, sample sizes have been small because most profilers have declined to be tested. In one study five professional profilers as well as larger numbers of police officers, psychologists, college students, and self-declared psychics were given extensive details about a murder case, including photos of the crime scene, information about the victim, and various laboratory reports. Then they were asked 30 multiple-choice questions about the probable criminal—sex, height, weight, age, marital status, religion, violent fantasies, and so forth. The results were compared to what was known about the actual murderer (who had in fact been caught, although the participants did not know about him). The number of choices per multiple-choice item varied from 2 to 9; overall, random guessing would produce 8.1 correct answers out of the 30 items. However, even an uninformed person should do better than chance, just by knowing, for example, that more crimes are committed by men than women and by guessing some common religion instead of a rare one. Of the tested groups, the profilers in fact did the best, at 13.8 correct, and the psychics did the worst, at 11.3, but the differences were small and none of the groups did well (Kocsis, Irwin, Hayes, & Nunn, 2000). Even for this modest success, we do not know that the profilers based their guesses on any information about the crime. Maybe they just have more accurate stereotypes of the "average criminal" than other people do.

A similar study compared police officers with varying levels of experience and college students with no relevant experience at all. In this case the college students outperformed the police officers, although

a   b

▌ When two snipers shot a series of people in the Washington, D.C., area, psychological profilers said to look for a White man acting alone. That description fit most previous serial killers but was wrong this time. John Allen Muhammad (a) and Lee Boyd Malvo (b) were convicted of the killings.

even the students averaged only 12.4 correct out of 30. Again, the differences among groups were small (Kocsis, Hayes, & Irwin, 2002).

We should not conclude that criminal profiling is impossible. However, as it is currently practiced, the results are certainly unimpressive. After all, 13.8 correct answers out of a possible 30, where 8.1 is random, means that profilers would give the police mostly wrong information.

Why, then, do so many police investigators insist that they find criminal profiles useful? Recall the Barnum effect mentioned in the introduction to this module: People tend to accept almost any statement about their own personality, especially vague statements that can be interpreted to fit the facts. A similar process applies here. Most actual (as opposed to television) profiles of criminals include vague or untestable statements that would apply to many people: The criminal is about the same age as the victim . . . average appearance . . . does not look out of context in the area . . . possibly unemployed . . . has a pornography collection . . . probably a very confused person . . . (Alison, Smith, & Morgan, 2003). In one study researchers gave police officers a criminal profile that an FBI profiler had prepared for the investigation of a particular murder, plus a description of the actual murderer (who had been caught), and asked the officers how well the profile fit the actual criminal. Most called it a good fit, rating it between 5 and 6 on a 1-to-7 scale. The researchers then gave a different group of police officers the same profile, plus a completely different, fictional description of the murderer, changing his age, relationship to the

victim, childhood history, and everything else. Most of this group also called the profile a good fit, again rating it between 5 and 6 (Alison et al., 2003). In short, the actual facts about the criminal made little difference to how highly the police rated the profile.

CONCEPT CHECK   ☑

17. In what way does criminal profiling illustrate the representativeness heuristic, as described in Chapter 8? (Check your answer on page 526.)

IN CLOSING

Possibilities and Limits of Personality Tests

One of most people's main topics of conversation could be described uncharitably as "gossip" or more kindly as "other people's personalities." Knowing about other people is important. You need to know whom to trust and whom to distrust.

Given this focus on personality, most of us tend to believe that personality is highly stable and governs a great deal of behavior. If so, someone should be able to look at a crime scene and discern the personality of the perpetrator. Psychologists should be able to listen to a client's answers to the Rorschach Inkblots and figure out his or her innermost secrets. So it might seem, but the research says otherwise. Personality is somewhat consistent over time and situations, but (as stated at the start of the second module) it is like climate—a trend over a long period of time but not always a good guide to what is happening at the moment.

The problem is that psychologists seldom want to watch and record anyone's behavior over months to get an accurate reading. Instead, they ask people for self-reports, using the MMPI or something similar. Such tests are useful within limits. However, we should remember those limits and avoid overconfident conclusions.

Our personalities depend on the situations at least as much as they do on consistent tendencies within us. In the next chapter, we take up the influence of social situations.

Summary

- *People's tendency to accept personality test results.* Because most people accept almost any interpretation of their personality based on a personality test, tests must be carefully scrutinized to ensure that they are measuring what they claim to measure. (page 515)
- *Standardized personality tests.* A standardized test is administered according to explicit rules, and its results are interpreted in a prescribed fashion based on the norms for the population. (page 516)
- *The MMPI.* The MMPI, a widely used personality test, consists of a series of true–false questions selected in an effort to distinguish among various personality types. The MMPI–2 is a modern version. (page 516)
- *Detection of lying.* The MMPI and certain other tests guard against lying by including items on which most people admit common faults or deny rare virtues. Denying common faults or claiming rare virtues is probably a lie. An unusual number of lying answers will invalidate the results. (page 518)
- *Projective techniques.* A projective technique, such as the Rorschach Inkblots or the Thematic Apperception Test, lets people describe their concerns indirectly while talking about the person in the picture or about other ambiguous stimuli. The results from projective techniques are difficult to interpret and have unimpressive validity for making decisions about any individual. (page 518)
- *Implicit personality tests.* The Emotional Stroop Test measures people's delays in naming the color of ink on the assumption that they will pause longer if the word has emotional meaning to them. The Implicit Association Test asks people to give one response to a particular combination of categories (e.g., social words and happy outcomes) and a different response to a different combination (e.g., nonsocial words and unhappy outcomes). So far, such tests are useful for research but not for decisions about an individual. (page 521)
- *Uses and misuses of personality tests.* Personality tests can be used as an aid for assessing personality, but their results should be interpreted cautiously and in conjunction with other evidence. (page 523)
- *Criminal profiling.* Some psychologists and police officers try to aid police investigations by constructing personality profiles of the kind of person who would probably commit a certain crime. There has been little research, but what has been conducted casts doubt on the accuracy of these profiles. (page 524)

Answers to Concept Checks

12. Researchers would determine whether people with depression were more likely than other people to answer *true*. If so, the item could be included. If people with depression answer about the same as others, the item would be discarded. (page 518)
13. Such items are intended to detect lying. If you answered *false*, you would get a point on a lying scale. (page 518)
14. **a.** The puppet activity could be a projective technique because the child is likely to project his or her own family concerns onto the puppets, using them to enact various problems. (page 519)
15. The psychologist administering the test counts the total number of answers that are considered abnormal or disturbed. The more answers someone gives, the greater the probability of saying something that seems disturbed. (On the other hand, if you give very few answers, you will be considered unimaginative and dull-witted.) (page 520)
16. The results would suggest that you are especially worried about health-related matters. (page 523)
17. The representativeness heuristic is the assumption that if something resembles category A, then it is a member of category A. In this case the idea is that if someone resembles people who have committed a particular type of crime, then he or she is a likely suspect to have committed that crime. This reasoning is risky if many people fit that description. (page 525)

Key Terms and Activities

Key Terms

agreeableness: the tendency to be compassionate toward others and not antagonistic (page 509)

anal stage: Freud's second stage of psychosexual development; here, psychosexual pleasure is focused on the anus (page 495)

archetypes: according to Jung vague images inherited from our ancestors and contained in the collective unconscious (page 498)

Barnum effect: the tendency to accept and praise vague statements about our personality (page 515)

big five personality traits: five traits that account for a great deal of human personality differences: neuroticism, extraversion, agreeableness, conscientiousness, and openness to new experience (page 509)

catharsis: the release of pent-up emotions associated with unconscious thoughts and memories (page 492)

collective unconscious: according to Jung an inborn level of the unconscious that symbolizes the collective experience of the human species (page 498)

conscientiousness: the tendency to show self-discipline, to be dutiful, and to strive for achievement and competence (page 509)

defense mechanism: a method employed by the ego to protect itself against anxiety caused by the conflict between the id's demands and the superego's constraints (page 495)

denial: the refusal to believe information that provokes anxiety (page 496)

displacement: the diversion of a thought or behavior away from its natural target toward a less threatening target (page 496)

ego: according to Freud the rational, decision-making aspect of personality (page 495)

Emotional Stroop Test: a procedure in which someone tries to say the color of ink for a number of words, some of which might pertain to a source of worry or concern (page 521)

external locus of control: the belief that external forces are largely in control of the events of one's life (page 507)

extraversion: the tendency to seek stimulation and to enjoy the company of other people (page 509)

fixation: in Freud's theory a persisting preoccupation with an immature psychosexual interest as a result of frustration at that stage of psychosexual development (page 494)

gender role: the pattern of behavior that each person is expected to follow because of being male or female (page 501)

genital stage: Freud's final stage of psychosexual development, in which sexual pleasure is focused on sexual intimacy with others (page 495)

humanistic psychology: a field that is concerned with consciousness, values, and abstract beliefs, including spiritual experiences and the beliefs that people live by and die for (page 502)

id: according to Freud the aspect of personality that consists of all our biological drives and demands for immediate gratification (page 495)

ideal self: an image of what one would like to be (page 503)

idiographic approach: an approach to the study of personality differences that concentrates on intensive studies of individuals (page 506)

Implicit Association Test: a procedure that measures how fast someone responds to a category that combines a topic with pleasant words or with unpleasant words (page 522)

individual psychology: the psychology of the person as an indivisible whole, as formulated by Adler (page 500)

inferiority complex: an exaggerated feeling of weakness, inadequacy, and helplessness (page 500)

internal locus of control: the belief that one is largely in control of the events of one's life (page 507)

latent period: according to Freud a period in which psychosexual interest is suppressed or dormant (page 495)

libido: in Freud's theory psychosexual energy (page 494)

Minnesota Multiphasic Personality Inventory (MMPI): a standardized test consisting of true–false items and intended to measure various personality dimensions and clinical conditions such as depression (page 516)

MMPI–2: the modernized edition of the MMPI (page 516)

neo-Freudians: personality theorists who have remained faithful to parts of Freud's theory while modifying other parts (page 498)

neuroticism: the tendency to experience unpleasant emotions relatively easily (page 509)

nomothetic approach: an approach to the study of individual differences that seeks general laws about how an aspect of personality affects behavior (page 506)

Oedipus complex: according to Freud a young boy's sexual interest in his mother accompanied by competitive aggression toward his father (page 493)

openness to experience: the tendency to enjoy new intellectual experiences, the arts, fantasies, and anything that exposes a person to new ideas (page 510)

oral stage: Freud's first stage of psychosexual development; here, psychosexual pleasure is focused on the mouth (page 494)

personality: all the consistent ways in which the behavior of one person differs from that of others, especially in social situations (page 491)

phallic stage: Freud's third stage of psychosexual development; here, psychosexual interest is focused on the penis or clitoris (page 495)

projection: the attribution of one's own undesirable characteristics to other people (page 497)

projective techniques: procedures designed to encourage people to project their personality characteristics onto ambiguous stimuli (page 518)

psychoanalysis: an approach to personality and psychotherapy developed by Sigmund Freud, based on identifying unconscious thoughts and emotions and bringing them to consciousness (page 492)

psychodynamic theory: a system that relates personality to the interplay of conflicting forces within the individual, including some that the individual may not consciously recognize (page 491)

psychosexual pleasure: according to Freud any strong, pleasant enjoyment arising from body stimulation (page 494)

rationalization: attempting to prove that one's actions are rational and justifiable and thus worthy of approval (page 496)

reaction formation: presenting oneself as the opposite of what one really is in an effort to reduce anxiety (page 497)

regression: the return to a more juvenile level of functioning as a means of reducing anxiety or in response to emotionally trying circumstances (page 496)

repression: according to Freudian theory, motivated forgetting, the process of moving an unacceptable memory, motivation, or emotion from the conscious mind to the unconscious mind (page 495)

Rorschach Inkblots: a projective personality technique; people are shown 10 inkblots and asked what each might be depicting (page 519)

self-actualization: the achievement of one's full potential (page 503)

self-concept: an image of what one really is (page 503)

social interest: a sense of solidarity and identification with other people (page 500)

standardized test: a test that is administered according to specified rules and its scores are interpreted in a prescribed fashion (page 516)

state: a temporary activation of a particular behavior (page 506)

striving for superiority: according to Adler a universal desire to seek personal excellence and fulfillment (page 500)

style of life: according to Adler a person's master plan for achieving a sense of superiority (page 500)

sublimation: the transformation of sexual or aggressive energies into culturally acceptable, even admirable, behaviors (page 497)

superego: according to Freud the aspect of personality that consists of memories of rules put forth by one's parents (page 495)

Thematic Apperception Test (TAT): a projective personality technique; a person is asked to tell a story about each of 20 pictures (page 520)

trait: a consistent, long-lasting tendency in behavior (page 506)

trait approach to personality: the study and measure of consistent personality characteristics (page 507)

unconditional positive regard: the complete, unqualified acceptance of another person as he or she is (page 503)

unconscious: according to Freud the repository of memories, emotions, and thoughts—often illogical thoughts—that affect our behavior even though we cannot talk about them (page 492)

unshared environment: the aspects of environment that differ from one individual to another, even within a family (page 512)

 Suggestions for Further Reading

Crews, F. C. (1998). *Unauthorized Freud.* New York: Viking Press. Devastating criticisms of Sigmund Freud's use and misuse of evidence.

Freud, S. (1924). *Introductory lectures on psychoanalysis.* New York: Boni and Liveright. Read Freud's own words and form your own opinion.

 Book Companion Web Site

Need help studying? Go to

http://psychology.wadsworth.com/kalat_intro7e/

for a virtual study center. You'll find a personalized Self-Study Assessment that will provide you with a study plan based on your answers to a pretest. Also study using flash cards, quizzes, interactive art, and an online glossary.

Check out interactive **Try It Yourself** exercises on the companion site! These exercises will help you put what you've learned into action.

Your companion site also has direct links to the following Web sites. These links are checked often for changes, dead links, and new additions.

Personality Measures and the Big Five

personality-project.org/personality.html

This site offers a wealth of information about personality traits and research, including links to many research sites.

 Try It Yourself CD-ROM
with Critical Thinking Video Exercises

Use your CD to access **videos** related to activities designed to help you think critically about the important topics discussed. You'll also find an easy portal link to the book companion site where you can access your personalized **Self-Study Assessments** and interactive **Try It Yourself** exercises.

PsychNow! 2.0

PsychNow! is a fun interactive CD designed to help you with the difficult concepts in psychology. Check out the Personality and Abnormal Psychology section for the following topics that relate to this chapter:

Theories of Personality: explore a self-image checklist, learn about personality theories, and take a test.

InteractNOW! Online Collaborative Lab: Personality and the Rorschach Inkblot Test

Social Psychology

In the *Communist Manifesto*, Karl Marx and Friedrich Engels wrote, "Mankind are more disposed to suffer, while evils are sufferable, than to right themselves by abolishing the forms to which they are accustomed. But when a long train of abuses and usurpations, pursuing invariably the same object, evinces a design to reduce them under absolute despotism, it is their right, it is their duty, to throw off such government." Fidel Castro wrote, "A little rebellion, now and then, is a good thing." Do you agree with those statements? Why or why not? Can you think of anything that would change your mind?

█ Influence depends not only on what someone says but also on what listeners think of the person who says it. Arnold Schwarzenegger, now governor of California, has advantages based on appearance and acting skills; however, some people discount his ideas because of his lack of political experience.

Oh, pardon me. . . . That first statement is not from the *Communist Manifesto*. It is from the United States' Declaration of Independence. Sorry. And that second statement is a quotation from Thomas Jefferson, not Castro. Do you agree more with these statements now that you know they came from democratic revolutionaries instead of communist revolutionaries?

What kinds of influences alter your opinions? This question is one example of the issues that interest **social psychologists**—*the psychologists who study social behavior and how individuals influence other people and are influenced by other people.* Social psychology can be described as a broad field because it includes the study of attitudes, persuasion, self-understanding, and almost all everyday behaviors of relatively normal people in their relationships with others. It can also be criticized as a narrow field because so much of its research deals with North American college students in laboratory settings (Rozin, 2001). As you will see, social psychologists have studied some very interesting phenomena, but much more remains to be learned.

Social Perception and Cognition

What factors influence our judgments of others?

How can we measure stereotypes that people do not want to admit?

How do we explain the causes of our own behavior and that of others?

People generally measure their own success by comparing themselves to others. To decide whether you are satisfied with your grades in school, your salary on the job, or even the morality of your behavior, you compare yourself to other people similar to yourself. You cheer yourself up by noting that you are doing better than some of your friends; you motivate yourself to try harder by comparing yourself to someone more successful (Suls, Martin, & Wheeler, 2002).

To make these comparisons, we need accurate information about other people. We also need that information to form expectations about how others will act, whom we can trust, and so forth. **Social perception and cognition** are *the processes we use to gather and remember information about others and to make inferences from that information.* Social perception and cognition, like any other perception and cognition, influence our observations, memory, and thinking.

First Impressions

Other things being equal, *the first information we learn about someone influences us more than later information does* (Belmore, 1987; E. E. Jones & Goethals, 1972). This tendency is known as the **primacy effect.** For example, if a professor makes a good impression on the first day of class, your favorable attitude helps you discount a lackluster performance later in the semester. A professor who seems dull at first will have a hard time impressing you later. Similarly, your professor's early impression of you can have lasting effects.

Why are first impressions so influential? If your first impression of someone is unfavorable, you may not spend enough time with that person to change your view. Also, once you have formed an impression, it alters your interpretation of later experiences. Suppose your first impression of someone is that he talks about himself too much. Later, whenever he talks about himself, you take his comments as supporting your initial impression.

Our first impressions can become **self-fulfilling prophecies,** *expectations that change one's own behavior in such a way as to increase the probability of the predicted event.* Suppose a psychologist hands you a telephone receiver and asks you to have a conversation with someone, while handing you a photo supposedly of that person. It is not actually of that person at all. Unknown to you and to the person you are talking to, the psychologist hands some people a photo of a very attractive member of the opposite sex and hands other people a much less attractive photo. Not surprisingly, you act friendlier to someone you regard as attractive. More interesting, if you think you are talking to someone attractive, that person reacts to you by becoming more cheerful and talkative. In short, your first impression changes how you act and influences the other person to live up to (or down to) your expectations (Snyder, Tanke, & Berscheid, 1977).

■ If you were a new patient of Dr. Balamurali Ambati, the world's youngest doctor (at age 17), what would your first impression probably be? An impression based only on his youthful appearance could be greatly mistaken.

©Bettmann/CORBIS

CRITICAL THINKING:
A STEP FURTHER
First Impressions

In a criminal trial, the prosecution presents its evidence first. Might that give the jury an unfavorable first impression of the defendant and increase the probability of a conviction?

CONCEPT CHECK ☑

1. Why do some professors avoid looking at students' names when they grade essay exams? Why is it more important for them to avoid looking at the names on tests given later in the semester than on the first test? (Check your answers on page 542.)

Stereotypes and Prejudices

A **stereotype** is *a generalized belief or expectation about a group of people.* It is possible to develop false stereotypes because of our tendency to remember the unusual. If we see an unusual person doing something unusual, the event is doubly memorable. For example, you might remember one left-handed redhead who cheated you and then form a false stereotype about left-handed redheads—an illusory correlation, as discussed in Chapter 2.

Stereotypes can also be based on exaggerations of correct observations. In particular, people tend to perceive and describe their political opponents as being far more extreme than they really are (Keltner & Robinson, 1996; Robinson & Keltner, 1996).

However, researchers have also come to admit that many stereotypes are correct. For example, who do you think gets into more fistfights on the average—men or women? If you answered "men," you are supporting a stereotype, but you are correct. Similarly, who do you think is more likely to be sensitive to the subtle social connotations of what people say—a liberal-arts major or an engineering major? Again, if you said "liberal-arts major," you are endorsing a stereotype, but the research supports you (Ottati & Lee, 1995).

Indeed, whenever we say that members of two cultures behave differently, we are endorsing a stereotype. In some cases members of both cultures agree on those stereotypes but express them in different words. For example, many Americans describe the Chinese as "inhibited," whereas Chinese call themselves "self-controlled." U.S. businesspeople complain that Mexicans "don't show up on time," whereas Mexicans complain that people from the United States "are always in a rush" (Lee & Duenas, 1995). People even form stereotypes about their own group, such as "we Americans are patriotic," "people in my town are very conservative," or "students at my college drink a lot of alcohol" (Prentice & Miller, 2002).

However, agreeing that some stereotype is correct on the average does not mean that it fits all individuals (Banaji & Bhaskar, 2000). For example, most 20-year-olds are more athletic than most 80-year-olds, but some 80-year-olds are in better shape than some 20-year-olds. Also, believing that a stereotype is usually correct does not mean that we have to let it influence the way we treat people. Ideally, we should strive to know people as individuals and treat them accordingly.

Aversive Racism

A **prejudice** is *an unfavorable attitude toward a group of people.* It is usually associated with **discrimination**, which is *unequal treatment of different groups,* such as minority groups, women, the physically disabled, obese people, or gays and lesbians. Decades ago many Americans admitted their prejudices and discriminated openly. Today, although some people are more prejudiced than others (Duckitt,

■ The usual stereotype of old people as inactive is largely correct on the average, but almost every stereotype has exceptions.

2001), most prejudices are subtle and not expressed openly. People may be ashamed of having such feelings, or they may not even be aware of them. In either case people *consciously express the idea that all people are equal, but nevertheless harbor negative feelings or unintentionally discriminate.* When these conflicting feelings pertain to race, psychologists use the term **aversive racism**, also known as subtle prejudice, modern racism, symbolic racism, racial ambivalence, or other similar terms (Sears & Henry, 2003). This kind of racism is called "aversive" because it is unpleasant to the person who acts this way. In a similar way, many people have **ambivalent sexism,** *an overt belief in equal treatment of the sexes joined with a lingering, often unstated belief that women should be treated differently* (Glick & Fiske, 2001).

Subtle, unstated prejudices are less harmful than the overt hostility of previous eras, but they can take their toll nevertheless. For example, if you are a victim of prejudice, you might be excluded from conversations among fellow students or workers (S. T. Fiske, 2002). People might smile at you less, offer you less help, and give you less benefit of the doubt in an uncertain situation (Crandall & Eshleman, 2003). If they see you frowning slightly, they may overestimate your hostility (Hugenberg & Bodenhausen, 2003). When you fail to get a job, promotion, or other opportunity, you may not know whether you were rejected because of something you did wrong or because of prejudices against your group (Major, Quinton, & McCoy, 2002).

Stereotypes and prejudices can also become self-fulfilling prophecies. Recall the idea of *stereotype threat* from Chapter 9 (p. 342): African American students' test performance is impaired if they are told that the test measures intelligence. In a variety of other situations and with many types of people, a general principle has emerged: People who are told "your group usually doesn't do well on this test" fail to perform as well as they could, especially if the task is difficult (Steele, Spencer, & Aronson, 2002). Perhaps they simply don't try very hard, or maybe they are distracted from the task.

Researchers have tried to measure aversive racism (unintentional, unconscious discrimination). Here is an example (Dovidio & Gaertner, 2000): Each European American college student was asked to evaluate the folder for one person applying for a job as a peer counselor. One third of the applications described strong experience and qualifications for the job, one third were marginal, and one third had weak qualifications. Of each kind of application (strong, marginal, or weak), half mentioned membership in a nearly all-White fraternity and the other half mentioned membership in the Black Student Union. So each student read what appeared to be a strong White, strong Black, marginal White, marginal Black, weak

White, or weak Black application. The following graph shows the mean results: Note that the students were slightly more generous with well-qualified or poorly qualified Black applicants than with equally qualified Whites. The big difference, however, was for the marginal applications.

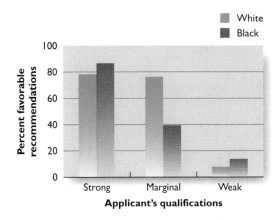

The students favorably recommended 77% of the marginal White applicants but only 40% of the marginal Black applicants (Dovidio & Gaertner, 2000). Without realizing it, the students evaluated the ambiguous qualifications more positively if they thought they applied to White applicants.

Implicit Measures of Stereotypes and Prejudice

Most people in the United States believe in fair treatment for everyone, or so we say. But if we are all as unprejudiced as we claim we are, where do all the racism, sexism, and so forth come from? Researchers have sought methods of measuring subtle prejudices that people do not want to admit, not even to themselves.

One method uses the Implicit Association Test described in Chapter 13. Recall the idea: A participant might be asked to press the left key after hearing either a pleasant word or the name of a flower and to press the right key after either an unpleasant word or the name of an insect. At another time the participant might be asked to press the left key for pleasant or insect and the right key for unpleasant or flower. The fact that "unpleasant or insect" is easier than "pleasant or insect" indicates that most people find insects unpleasant. The effect is not huge, but it has some advantages over just asking people what they like and dislike. (People often say what they think they are supposed to say instead of what they really think.)

The same strategy can be used for measuring prejudices (Greenwald, Nosek, & Banaji, 2003). Imagine yourself in the following experiment: You are seated in front of a computer screen that will sometimes show a

SET 1: Press left key if

Photo of a Black person   or   Pleasant word

PEACE

Press right key if

Photo of a White person   or   Unpleasant word

CANCER

SET 2: Press left key if

Photo of a Black person   or   Unpleasant word

BOMB

Press right key if

Photo of a White person   or   Pleasant word

JOY

© Kevin Peterson/PhotoDisc/PictureQuest (left photos); © Rubberball Productions1998/PictureQuest (right photos)

FIGURE 14.1 Procedures for an Implicit Association Test to measure prejudices.

tive sample of the population, but neither are the college students in a usual study. The Web site participants are, at least, a huge number of people varying in age, geographical region, and so forth. The results were that White participants on the average linked White-pleasant, Black-unpleasant more easily than White-unpleasant, Black-pleasant, in spite of the fact that most of them claimed to have little or no racial prejudice. The implicit prejudice was slightly stronger among political conservatives. Black participants showed an interesting pattern: Although most stated that their explicit attitude was more favorable to Blacks than to Whites, the Implicit Association Test results indicated a slight implicit attitude favoring Whites over Blacks. That is, they too linked White-pleasant, Black-unpleasant more readily than White-unpleasant, Black-pleasant, at least to a small extent. The Web site made other kinds of tests available also. For example, most participants showed an implicit attitude favoring young over old, linking young-pleasant, old-unpleasant more easily than the reverse.

photo and sometimes a word. If it is a photo of a Black person or a pleasant word (e.g., *peace, joy,* or *love*), press the left key. If it is a photo of a White person or an unpleasant word (e.g., *evil, failure,* or *death*), press the right key. After you have done it that way for a while, the rule will switch to the opposite pairing.

Figure 14.1 illustrates the procedures and Figure 14.2 summarizes the results of one study using White college students. Most of them responded faster if the responses were for *Black or unpleasant* and *White or pleasant.* They responded slower if the responses were for *Black or pleasant* and *White or unpleasant.* That is, even though most of the participants in this study claimed to have no racial stereotypes or prejudices, they evaluated White faces more favorably than Black faces (Phelps et al., 2000). A similar study reported that White students found it easier to pair pleasant words with White names, such as *Andrew* and *Brandon,* and unpleasant words with Black names, such as *Lamar* and *Jamal* (Dasgupta, McGhee, Greenwald, & Banaji, 2000).

Researchers made available a simplified version of the Implicit Association Test on a Web site, which you can try yourself:

https://implicit.harvard.edu/implicit/demo/

They have analyzed the results for more than 600,000 people who have visited this Web site over the years (Nosek, Banaji, & Greenwald, 2002). People who visit a Web site are, of course, not a representa-

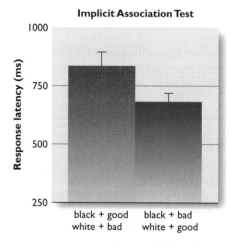

Implicit Association Test

Response latency (ms)

1000 / 750 / 500 / 250

black + good white + bad   black + bad white + good

FIGURE 14.2 On the average, White students who claimed to have no racial prejudice responded faster if they had to make one response for "Black face or unpleasant word" and a different response for "White face or pleasant word" than if the pairings were reversed—Black and pleasant, White and unpleasant. *(From "Performance on Indirect Measures of Race Evaluation Predicts Amygdala Activation" by E. A. Phelps, K. J. O'Connor, W. A. Cunningham, E. S. Funayama, J. C. Gatenby, J. C. Gore, and M. R. Banaji,* Journal of Cognitive Neuroscience, *2000, 12, 729–738. Copyright © 2000 MIT Press. Reprinted by permission.)*

All these results are important for showing that even well-meaning people can have prejudices that operate without their awareness (Greenwald & Banaji, 1995). That result is important to remember when people insist that we should evaluate college applicants or job applicants "entirely on the basis of their qualifications." The problem is that we may be influenced by stereotypes and prejudices that we do not even recognize, especially when the qualifications are hard to evaluate (Crosby, Iyer, Clayton, & Downing, 2003). Perhaps it is better to recognize that we have stereotypes and try to take them into account, instead of denying their existence.

On the other hand, it may also be that the Implicit Association Test overstates people's prejudices. In a related task, called the **bona fide pipeline**, *people alternate between looking at different kinds of faces, such as Black and White, and reading words that they need to classify as pleasant or unpleasant.* The assumption is that someone who is prejudiced against Black people will answer "unpleasant" faster after seeing a Black face than after seeing a White face. However, the results depend on the instructions. If White students just look at the faces with the expectation of trying to recognize them later, then seeing a Black or White face has little effect on how fast they say "pleasant" or "unpleasant" to the next word. If, however, they have to count the number of Black faces so that they are forced to pay attention to race, then the predicted results do occur, with faster "unpleasant" responses after seeing Black faces (Olson & Fazio, 2003). In other words the bona fide pipeline, and presumably also the Implicit Association Test, show implicit prejudice if the instructions ask people to pay attention to race. Without such urging people may react to the faces as individuals without showing clear evidence of prejudice.

CONCEPT CHECK ☑️

2. What is the advantage of the Implicit Association Test over simply asking people about their racial prejudices?
3. Under what condition are the Implicit Association Test and bona fide pipeline most likely to show evidence of implicit prejudice? (Check your answers on page 542.)

Overcoming Prejudice

After prejudices and hostility have arisen between two groups, what can anyone do to break down those barriers? Simply getting to know each other better helps sometimes, but not always. A more effective technique is to get the two groups to work toward a common goal, to think of themselves as part of a larger, combined group (Dovidio & Gaertner, 1999).

Many years ago psychologists demonstrated the power of this technique using two arbitrarily chosen groups (Sherif, 1966). At a summer camp at Robbers' Cave, Oklahoma, 11- to 12-year-old boys were divided into two groups in separate cabins. The groups competed for prizes in sports, treasure hunts, and other activities. With each competition the antagonism between the two groups grew more intense. The boys made threatening posters, shouted insults, and engaged in food fights. Each group had clearly developed prejudice and hostility toward the other.

Up to a point, the "counselors" (the experimenters) allowed the hostility to take its course, neither encouraging nor prohibiting it. Then, they tried to reverse it by stopping the competitions and setting common goals. First, they asked the two groups to work together to find and repair a leak in the water pipe that supplied the camp. Later, they had the two groups pool their treasuries to rent a movie that both groups wanted to see. Still later, they had the boys pull together to get a truck out of a rut. Gradually, hostility turned into friendship—except for a few holdouts who nursed their hatred to the bitter end! The point of this study is that competition leads to hostility; cooperation leads to friendship.

❚ People who work together for a common goal can overcome prejudices that initially divide them.

Attribution

We often try to figure out why the people we observe behave as they do. Yesterday, you won $1 million in the state lottery, and today, some classmates who previously ignored you want to be your friends. You draw inferences about their reasons. **Attribution is** *the set of thought processes we use to assign causes to our own behavior and to the behavior of others.*

Internal Versus External Causes

Fritz Heider, the founder of attribution theory, emphasized the distinction between internal and external causes of behavior (Heider, 1958). **Internal attributions** are *explanations based on someone's individual characteristics, such as attitudes, personality traits, or abilities.* **External attributions** are *explanations based on the situation, including events that presumably would influence almost anyone.* An example of an internal attribution is that your brother walked to work this morning "because he likes the exercise." An external attribution would be that he walked "because his car wouldn't start." Internal attributions are also known as *dispositional* (i.e., something about the person's disposition led to the behavior); external attributions are also known as *situational* (i.e., something about the situation led to the behavior).

You make internal attributions when someone does something that you think most people would not do. For example, if I tell you I would like to visit Hawaii, you probably draw no conclusions about me. However, if I say I would like to visit northern Norway in midwinter, you would seek an attribution to something special about my personality or interests (Krull & Anderson, 1997).

This tendency sometimes leads to misunderstandings between members of different cultures. Each person views the other's behavior as "something I would not have done" and therefore as grounds for making an attribution about the other one's personality. In fact such behavior may actually be what the other culture dictates. For example, some cultures expect people to cry loudly at funerals, whereas others expect people to be more restrained. People who are unfamiliar with other cultures may inappropriately attribute a behavior to someone's personality.

Harold Kelley (1967) proposed that we rely on three types of information when deciding whether to make an internal or an external attribution for someone's behavior:

- **Consensus information** *(how the person's behavior compares with other people's behavior).* If someone behaves the same way you believe other people would in the same situation, then you make an external attribution. If someone's behavior seems unusual, you look for an internal attribution pertaining to something about the person instead of the situation. (You can easily be wrong if you misunderstand the situation.)
- **Consistency information** *(how the person's behavior varies from one time to the next).* If someone almost always seems friendly, for example, you would make an internal attribution ("a friendly person"). If someone's friendliness varies, you look for an external attribution, such as an event that elicited a good or bad mood.
- **Distinctiveness** *(how the person's behavior varies from one situation to another).* For example, if your friend is pleasant to most people but consistently unfriendly to one particular person, you assume that person has done something to irritate your friend (an external attribution).

❚ We are sometimes surprised by people's behavior and attribute an internal cause when in fact the people are acting according to the customs of their culture. In the United States, a funeral usually calls for reserved behavior; in many other places, the opposite is true.

CONCEPT CHECK ☑

4. Classify the following as either internal or external attributions:
   a. She contributed money to charity because she is generous.
   b. She contributed money to charity because she wanted to impress her boss, who was watching.
   c. She contributed money to charity because she owed a favor to the man who was asking for contributions.
5. Juanita returns from watching *The Return of the Son of Sequel Strikes Back Again Part 2* and says it was excellent. Most other people that you know disliked the movie. Will you make an internal or external attribution for Juanita's opinion? Why? (Distinctiveness, consensus, or consistency?) (Check your answers on page 542.)

The Fundamental Attribution Error

A common error is *to make internal attributions for people's behavior even when we see evidence for an external influence on behavior.* This tendency is known as the **fundamental attribution error** (Ross, 1977). It is also known as the *correspondence bias,* meaning a tendency to assume a strong similarity between someone's current actions and his or her dispositions.

Imagine yourself in a classic study demonstrating this phenomenon. You are told that U.S. college students were randomly assigned to write essays praising or condemning Fidel Castro, the Communist leader of Cuba. You read an essay that defends Castro, criticizes the United States for its long embargo against Cuba, and compares Cuba favorably to other Latin American countries. Now what's your guess about the actual attitude of the student who wrote this essay?

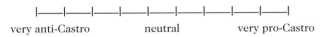

very anti-Castro   neutral   very pro-Castro

Most U.S. students in one study guessed that the author of a pro-Castro essay was at least mildly pro-Castro, even though they were informed, as you were, that the author had been told to praise Castro (E. E. Jones & Harris, 1967). In a later study, experimenters explained that one student in a creative writing class had been assigned to write a pro-Castro essay and an anti-Castro essay at different times in the course. Then the participants read the two essays and estimated the writer's true beliefs. Most thought that the writer had changed attitudes between the two essays (Allison, Mackie, Muller, &

Worth, 1993). That is, even when people are told of a powerful external reason for someone's behavior, they apparently believe the person probably had internal reasons as well (McClure, 1998).

CONCEPT CHECK ☑

6. Would people who believe they control their own destinies in life (internal locus of control) be more likely or less likely than others to make the fundamental attribution error? (Check your answer on page 542.)

Cultural Differences in Attribution and Related Matters

The fundamental attribution error is partly due to culture. In general, people of Western cultures tend to rely on internal (personality) attributions in situations where people in China, Korea, and other nearby Asian cultures tend to rely more on external (situational) attributions. For example, how would you explain the behavior of the fish designated with an arrow in this drawing? Most Americans say this fish is leading the others, whereas many Chinese say the other fish are chasing it (Hong, Morris, Chiu, & Benet-Martinez, 2000). That is, the cultures differ in whether they think the fish controls its own behavior or obeys the influence of the others.

Try It Yourself

Richard Nisbett and his colleagues have noted other cases in which Chinese and Korean people tend to focus more on the situation, and less on individual personality, than do most people in Western cultures (Nisbett, Peng, Choi, & Norenzayan, 2001). As a result they expect more change and less consistency in people's behavior from one situation to another. The Chinese and Koreans are also more likely to accept contradictions and look for compromises, instead of viewing one position as correct and another as incorrect. Here are a few examples:

- When given a description of a conflict, such as one between mother and daughter, Chinese students are more likely than Americans to see merit in both arguments, instead of siding with one or the other (Peng & Nisbett, 1999).
- Far more Chinese than English-language proverbs include apparent self-contradictions, such as "beware of your friends, not your enemies" and "too humble is half proud" (Peng & Nisbett, 1999).
- Chinese people are more likely than Americans to expect events to change and to predict that current trends—whatever they might be—will reverse themselves. For example, if life seems to have been getting better lately, most Americans predict that things will continue getting better, whereas Chinese predict that things will get worse (Ji, Nisbett, & Su, 2001).
- In one study people were told about some event and then told the final outcome. Americans often expressed surprise when Koreans said the outcome was to be expected. That is, in this study the Koreans showed a stronger hindsight bias (Chapter 7)—the tendency to say, "I knew it all along" (Choi & Nisbett, 2000).

The reported differences are interesting. Still, an important question remains: To the extent that Chinese people respond differently from Western-culture people, is that difference due to ancient traditions within the two cultures or to social, political, and economic pressures of the current time? Unfortunately, cross-cultural research is as difficult as it is important. Questionnaire studies are often misleading, as people from different cultures interpret the questions and answers differently. It is important to take cultural differences seriously but also important to avoid overstating them.

The Actor-Observer Effect

Here is another common bias related to the fundamental attribution error: *People are more likely to make internal attributions for other people's behavior and more likely to make external attributions for their own* (E. E. Jones & Nisbett, 1972). This tendency is called the **actor-observer effect.** You are an "actor" when you try to explain the causes of your own behavior and an "observer" when you try to explain someone else's behavior.

In one study investigators asked college students to rate themselves, their fathers, their best friends, and Walter Cronkite (a television news announcer at the time) on several personality traits. For each trait (e.g., "leniency"), the participants were given three choices: (a) the person possesses the trait, (b) the person possesses the opposite trait, and (c) the person's behavior "depends on the situation." Participants checked "depends on the situation"—an external at-

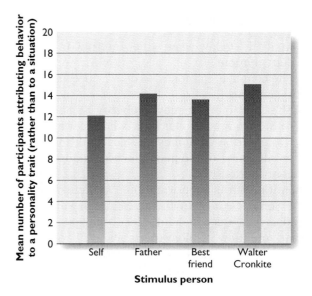

FIGURE 14.3 Participants were asked whether certain people had certain traits, the opposite traits, or whether "it depended on the situation." They were most likely to say that their own behavior depended on the situation and least likely to say "it depends" for Walter Cronkite, the person they knew the least. *(Based on data of Nisbett, Caputo, Legant, & Marecek, 1973)*

tribution—most frequently for themselves, less frequently for their fathers and friends, and least often for Walter Cronkite (Nisbett, Caputo, Legant, & Marecek, 1973). Figure 14.3 shows the results.

Why do we tend to explain our own behavior differently from that of others? First, we are aware of how our own behavior varies from one situation to another. The less well we know someone else, the less aware we are of variations from situation to situation. Second, we tend to attribute unexpected, surprising behavior to internal causes. Our own behavior seldom surprises us, so we do not attribute it to internal causes.

The third reason is perceptual. We see other people as objects in our visual field, and we tend to think that whatever we are watching is the cause of the action. The perceptual explanation for the actor-observer effect has an interesting implication: If you became an object in your own visual field, you might explain your own behavior in terms of internal traits, as you do with others. Researchers have found that if you watch a videotape of your own behavior, you do tend to explain your behavior in terms of personality factors more than situational factors (Storms, 1973).

A further application of this idea: Suppose you watch a videotape of a conversation between two people. The actual conversation is planned so that both people participate equally. However, you are randomly given one of two versions of the videotape, with the camera focused on one person or the other. You will tend to perceive the person you are watching as the one who dominated the conversation and influenced the other person. Similarly, if you watch a videotape of an interrogation between a detective and a suspect, you will judge the suspect's confession to be more voluntary if the camera is focused on the suspect and more coerced if the camera is focused on the detective (Lassiter, Geers, Munhall, Ploutz-Snyder, & Breitenbecher, 2002).

CRITICAL THINKING:
A STEP FURTHER
Attributions

Try to explain these examples of behavior:

- Why did you choose to go to the college you are attending?
- Why did your roommate choose this college?
- Why are you reading this book right now?
- Why does your roommate study so much (or so little)?

Did you attribute internal causes or external causes for these behaviors? Did you rely more on external causes to explain other people's behavior or to explain your own?

Using Attributions to Manage Perceptions of Ourselves

Even if you generally attribute your own behavior largely to external causes, you probably vary your attributions to try to present yourself in a favorable light. For example, you might credit your good grades to your intelligence and hard work (an internal attribution) but blame your bad grades on unfair tests (an external attribution). *Attributions that we adopt to maximize our credit for our success and minimize our blame for our failure* are called **self-serving biases** (D. T. Miller & Ross, 1975; van der Pligt & Eiser, 1983).

People can also protect their images with **self-handicapping strategies,** in which they *intentionally put themselves at a disadvantage to provide an excuse for a possible failure.* Suppose you fear you will do poorly on a test. You go to a party the night before and stay out late. Now you can blame your low score on your lack of sleep without admitting that you might have done poorly anyway.

In an experiment on self-handicapping strategies, Steven Berglas and Edward Jones (1978) asked some college students to work on solvable problems and asked others to work on a mixture of solvable and unsolvable problems. (The students did not know that some of the problems were impossible.) Then the experimenters told all the students that they had done well. The students who had been given solvable problems (and had solved them) felt good about their success. Those who had worked on many unsolvable problems were unsure in what way they had "done well." They certainly had no confidence that they could continue to do well.

Next the experimenters told the participants that the purpose of the experiment was to investigate the effects of drugs on problem solving and that they were now going to hand out another set of problems. The participants could choose between taking a drug that supposedly impaired problem-solving abilities and another drug that supposedly improved them. The participants who had worked on unsolvable problems the first time were more likely than the others to choose the drug that supposedly impaired performance. Because they did not expect to do well on the second set of problems anyway, they provided themselves with a convenient excuse.

CONCEPT CHECK ☑

7. Who is more likely to make the fundamental attribution error, people from Western cultures or Chinese?
8. If, instead of watching someone, you close your eyes and imagine yourself in that person's position, will you be more likely to explain the behavior with internal or external attributions? Why?
9. Why would people sometimes intentionally do something likely to harm their own performance? (Check your answers on page 542.)

IN CLOSING

How Social Perceptions Affect Behavior

We are seldom fully aware of the reasons for our own behavior, much less someone else's, but we make our best guesses. If someone you know passes by without saying hello, you might attribute that person's behavior to absent-mindedness, indifference, or outright hostility. You might attribute someone's friendly response to your own personal charm, the other person's extraverted personality, or that person's devious and manipulative personality. Whatever attributions you make are sure to influence your own social behaviors.

Summary

- *First impressions.* Other things being equal, we pay more attention to the first information we learn about someone than to later information. (page 533)

- *Stereotypes.* Stereotypes are generalized beliefs about groups of people. Even if a stereotype is true on the average, it does not apply to all individuals. (page 534)
- *Prejudice.* A prejudice is an unfavorable stereotype. Many people will not admit their prejudices, even to themselves. Through indirect measures, researchers have found ways to demonstrate subtle effects of stereotypes and prejudices even in people who deny having them. (page 534)
- *Attribution.* Attribution is the set of thought processes by which we assign internal or external causes to behavior. According to Harold Kelley, we are likely to attribute behavior to an internal cause if it is consistent over time, different from most other people's behavior, and directed toward a variety of other people or objects. (page 537)
- *Fundamental attribution error.* People frequently attribute people's behavior to internal causes, even when they see evidence of external influences. (page 539)
- *Cultural differences.* People in China and Korea are less likely than those in Western cultures to attribute behavior to consistent personality traits and more likely to attribute it to the situation. (page 539)
- *Actor-observer effect.* We are more likely to attribute internal causes to other people's behavior than to our own. (page 540)
- *Self-serving bias and self-handicapping.* People sometimes try to protect their self-esteem by attributing their successes to skill and their failures to outside influences. They can also intentionally place themselves at a disadvantage to provide an excuse for their expected failure. (page 541)

Answers to Concept Checks

1. They want to avoid being biased by their first impressions of the students. This procedure is less important with the first test because they have not yet formed strong impressions. (page 534)
2. The Implicit Association Test can reveal prejudices that people don't want to admit, perhaps even to themselves. (page 537)
3. They are most likely to show evidence of implicit prejudice if the instructions ask people to pay attention to the race of the people in the photos. (page 537)
4. **a.** internal; **b.** and **c.** external. An internal attribution relates to a stable aspect of personality or attitudes; an external attribution relates to the current situation. (page 539)
5. You probably will make an internal attribution because of *consensus.* When one person's behavior differs from others', we make an internal attribution. (page 539)
6. They would be more likely to make the fundamental attribution error because they tend to attribute behaviors to internal causes instead of situations. (page 539)
7. Westerners are more likely to make the fundamental attribution error because the Chinese tend to attribute behavior more to situational factors than do Westerners. (page 541)
8. You will be more likely to give an external attribution because you will become more like an actor and less an observer. (page 541)
9. People sometimes do something to harm their own performance to give themselves an excuse for doing poorly, especially if they thought they might do poorly anyway. (page 541)

What are some effective ways of influencing people's attitudes?

"If you want to change people's behavior, you have to change their attitudes first." Do you agree? Suppose you say "yes." Now answer two more questions: (a) What is your attitude about paying higher taxes? (b) If the government raises taxes, will you pay the higher taxes?

I assume you said that you have an unfavorable attitude about paying higher taxes, but if the taxes are raised, you will pay them. In other words, by changing the law, the government could change your behavior without changing your attitude. In fact it is often easier to change behaviors than attitudes.

So what effects do attitudes have on behavior? And what leads people to change their attitudes?

Attitudes and Their Influence

An attitude is *a like or dislike that influences our behavior toward someone or something* (Allport, 1935; Petty & Cacioppo, 1981). Your attitudes include an evaluative or emotional component (how you feel about something), a cognitive component (what you know or believe), and a behavioral component (what you are likely to do). *Persuasion* is an attempt to alter your attitudes or behavior.

One common way of measuring attitudes (and thus the effectiveness of persuasion) is through the use of attitude scales, such as Likert scales, also known as summated rating scales (Dawes & Smith, 1985). On a Likert scale (named after psychologist Rensis Likert), a person checks a point along a line ranging from 1, meaning "strongly disagree," to 7, meaning "strongly agree," for each of several statements about a topic, as illustrated in Figure 14.4.

The attitudes that people report sometimes relate closely to their behaviors but often do not. For example, many people report attitudes about cigarettes, alcohol, safe sex, wearing seat belts in a car, studying hard for tests, and so forth that do not match their behavior. Why? One reason is that people sometimes answer attitude questionnaires impulsively, especially on questions that are not important to them (van der Pligt, de Vries, Manstead, & van Harreveld, 2000). Recall that the same idea arose in Chapter 2 concerning surveys. A second reason is that people's answers to an attitude question fluctuate because of momentary influences (Lord & Lepper, 1999). For example, what is your attitude toward politicians on a scale from 1 (very unfavorable) to 7 (very favorable)? If you are thinking about the public servants you admire most, you might rate politicians favorably. At a later time, however, you might be thinking about corrupt or incompetent politicians, and you would answer differently.

A third reason, which overlaps the other two, is that people sometimes maintain mixed or contradictory attitudes (T. D. Wilson, Lindsey, & Schooler, 2000). For example, you might have long held an unfavorable attitude toward homosexuals. More recently,

Indicate your level of agreement with the items below, using the following scale:	Strongly disagree			Neutral			Strongly agree
1. Labor unions are necessary to protect the rights of workers.	1	2	3	4	5	6	7
2. Labor union leaders have too much power.	1	2	3	4	5	6	7
3. If I worked for a company with a union, I would join the union.	1	2	3	4	5	6	7
4. I would never cross a picket line of striking workers.	1	2	3	4	5	6	7
5. Striking workers hurt their company and unfairly raise prices for the consumer.	1	2	3	4	5	6	7
6. Labor unions should not be permitted to engage in political activity.	1	2	3	4	5	6	7
7. America is a better place for today's workers because of the efforts by labor unions in the past.	1	2	3	4	5	6	7

Note: Items 2, 5, and 6 are scored the opposite of 1, 3, 4, and 7.

FIGURE 14.4 Likert scales, such as this one assessing attitudes toward labor unions, are commonly used in attitude research. Participants rate their agreement or disagreement with each statement.

you have been persuaded that this attitude was unfair, and you now express a more positive attitude. You state your new explicit attitude on questionnaires, but your old attitude emerges in your nonverbal behaviors and emotional reactions.

CONCEPT CHECK ☑

10. What test or method mentioned in the first module of this chapter could demonstrate mixed or contradictory attitudes? (Check your answer on page 551.)

Central and Peripheral Routes of Attitude Change and Persuasion

Sometimes people ponder the evidence carefully and develop a thoughtfully reasoned attitude, and sometimes they form attitudes with only a superficial basis. Richard Petty and John Cacioppo (1981, 1986) proposed the following distinction: *When people take a decision seriously, they invest the necessary time and effort to evaluate the evidence and logic behind each message.* Petty and Cacioppo call this logical approach the **central route to persuasion.** In contrast, *when people listen to a message on a topic they consider unimportant, they attend to such factors as the speaker's appearance and reputation or the sheer number of arguments presented, regardless of their quality.* This superficial approach is the **peripheral route to persuasion.**

CONCEPT CHECK ☑

11. You listen to a debate about raising tuition at Santa Enigma Junior College. Later, you listen to a debate about raising tuition at your own college. In which case will you follow the central route to persuasion? (Check your answer on page 551.)

Delayed Influence

Some messages have no apparent influence at first but an important effect later. A message can have a delayed effect for many reasons; we consider two examples.

The Sleeper Effect

Suppose you reject a message because of peripheral route influences. For example, you quickly reject some idea because of your low opinion of the person who suggested it. Weeks or months later, you may forget where you heard the idea (*source amnesia*) and remember only the idea itself. At that time you evaluate it on its merits and perhaps decide it was a good idea (Hovland & Weiss, 1951; Pratkanis, Greenwald, Leippe, & Baumgardner, 1988). If you completely forget the source, you might even claim it as your own idea! Psychologists use the term **sleeper effect** to describe *delayed persuasion by an initially rejected message.*

Minority Influence

Delayed influence also occurs when a minority group, especially one that is not widely respected, proposes a worthwhile idea: The majority rejects the idea at first but reconsiders it later. By "minority group," I do not necessarily mean an ethnic minority; it could be a political minority or any other outnumbered group.

If a minority group continually repeats a single simple message and its members seem united, it has a good chance of eventually influencing the majority's decision. The minority's united, uncompromising stance forces the majority to wonder, "Why won't they conform? Maybe their idea is better than we thought." The minority's influence often increases gradually, even if the majority hesitates to admit that the minority has swayed them (Wood, Lundgren, Ouellette, Busceme, & Blackstone, 1994). A minority, by expressing its views, can also prompt the majority to generate new ideas of its own (Nemeth, 1986). That is, by demonstrating the possibility of disagreement, the minority opens the way for other people to offer new suggestions different from the original views of both the majority and the minority.

One powerful example of minority influence is that of the Socialist party of the United States, which ran candidates for elective offices from 1900 through the 1950s. The party never received more than 6% of the vote in any presidential election. No Socialist candidate was ever elected senator or governor, and only a few were elected to the House of Representatives (Shannon, 1955). Beginning in the 1930s, the party's membership and support dwindled, until eventually the party stopped nominating candidates. Was that because they had failed? No! Most of the major proposals of the party had been enacted into law (see Table 14.1). Of course, the Democrats and Republicans who voted for these changes claimed credit for the ideas. Still, the Socialist party, without winning elections, had exerted an enormous influence.

CONCEPT CHECK ☑

12. At a meeting of your student government, you suggest a new method of testing and grading students. The other members immediately reject your plan. Should you become discouraged and give up? If not, what should you do? (Check your answers on page 551.)

TABLE 14.1 Political Proposals of the U.S. Socialist Party, Around 1900

Proposal	Eventual Fate of Proposal
Women's right to vote	Established by 19th Amendment to U.S. Constitution; ratified in 1920
Old-age pensions	Included in the Social Security Act of 1935
Unemployment insurance	Included in the Social Security Act of 1935; also guaranteed by the other state and federal legislation
Health and accident insurance	Included in part in the Social Security Act of 1935 and in the Medicare Act of 1965
Increased wages, including minimum wage	First minimum-wage law passed in 1938; periodically updated since then
Reduction of working hours	Maximum 40-hour workweek (with exceptions) established by the Fair Labor Standards Act of 1938
Public ownership of electric, gas, and other utilities and of the means of transportation and communication	Utilities not owned by government but heavily regulated by federal and state government since the 1930s
Initiative, referendum, and recall (mechanisms for private citizens to push for changes in legislation and for removal of elected officials)	Adopted by most state governments

Sources: Foster, 1968; and Leuchtenburg, 1963.

Ways of Presenting Persuasive Messages

The influence of an attempt at persuasion can depend on many factors that we hardly notice. For example, a television ad may become more effective because of the pleasant music in the background. Often, we are influenced by some factor that we would insist did not affect us. Advertisers, politicians, and many others attend closely to the details of how they present their messages.

The Role of Fear

Most persuasive messages fall into one of two categories: (a) Do this to accomplish something good, and (b) do this to avoid something bad. Either approach can be effective depending on the circumstances. Figure 14.5 shows the "St. Jude" chain letter that has circulated throughout the world for decades. It has been called a "mind virus" because it inspires people to duplicate and spread the letter (Goodenough & Dawkins, 1994). Many people who receive this letter cannot resist its command to make copies and send them to others, even if they regard the message as a silly superstition. Why? The letter claims to be offering "good luck" and "love," but it follows those promises with an implied threat: Allegedly, people who have failed to follow the instructions have lost their job, lost a loved one, died, or had car problems! The threat makes people feel nervous and uneasy if they decline to follow the instructions.

Fear messages are effective in some cases, as in the St. Jude letter, but not always. Appeals for money are often accompanied by implied threats, such as "If you don't send enough money to support our cause, then our political opponents will gain power and do terrible things." According to the research, messages that appeal to fear are effective only if they can convince people that the danger is real (Leventhal, 1970). People tend to disbelieve an organization that exaggerates the threats or sends "emergency" appeals too often.

Moreover, a fear message is effective only if people believe they can easily reduce the danger. For example, most people will visit a physician for an immunization against a contagious disease or for an x-ray to test for cancer. Many people, but not all, will change their sex habits to avoid herpes or AIDS. Even fewer people consistently change their behavior to conserve natural resources or to avoid damaging the

FIGURE 14.5 If you received a copy of this chain letter, would you copy it and send it to other people, as it requests? Why or why not?

world's climate because most people doubt that their behavior will make much difference.

Fear messages sometimes backfire. To motivate action against a problem, an organization might try to describe the danger as severe. For example, an antidrug campaign might say that drug use is spreading wildly, or a conservation organization might say that pollution and destruction of the environment are out of control. The intended message is, "Take this problem seriously and act now." The unintended message that people sometimes receive is, "Drug use, pollution, etc. are normal." If the problem seems extremely widespread, people see no point in fighting it (Cialdini, 2003).

Influence of Similarity

Other things being equal, a persuasive message is more effective if the speaker conveys the message, "I resemble you." In one striking illustration of the influence of similarity, students were asked to read a very unflattering description of Grigory Rasputin, the "mad monk of Russia," and then rate Rasputin on several scales such as pleasant to unpleasant, effective to ineffective, and strong to weak. All students read the same description except for Rasputin's birth date: In some cases Rasputin's birth date had been changed to match the student's own birth date. Students who thought Rasputin had the same birth date as their own

■ Grigory Rasputin was a contemptible person whose unsavory influence on the czar of Russia led to the Communist revolution. However, people who are told Rasputin resembled them, even in trivial ways, soften their criticisms.

were more likely than others to rate him as "strong" and "effective" (Finch & Cialdini, 1989).

Influence of Group Endorsement

Imagine some preposterous idea that you reject vigorously. Now imagine that some group you respect endorses the idea. Would you suddenly think it was a good idea?

In one study psychologists used a questionnaire to identify the most politically liberal students and the most conservative ones. Then they gave each student one of two versions of what they said was a proposed law about welfare for the unemployed. One version offered extraordinarily generous benefits, including $800 per month for up to 8 years, plus full medical care, $2,000 in food stamps, subsidies for housing and day care, job training, full tuition at a community college, and more. Although this policy goes well beyond what the U.S.'s most liberal politicians have recommended, if students were told that the Republicans (the more conservative party) endorsed it, conservative students said they supported it too, while liberal students opposed it. Other students were told about a much stingier proposed law, which provided only $250 per month, with an 18-month limit, and no other benefits. Ordinarily, almost anyone would consider this policy inadequate, but if students were told that the Democrats (the more liberal party) endorsed it, liberal students supported it while conservatives did not. When students were asked the reasons for their decisions, almost none admitted that endorsement by one party or the other was a significant influence. They insisted that they decided on their own (G. L. Cohen, 2003).

CONCEPT CHECK ☑

13. A salesperson calls at your door and says that several of your neighbors (whom the salesperson names) have bought the product and recommended you as another possible customer. What techniques of persuasion is this salesperson using? (Check your answer on page 551.)

Audience Variables

Some people are more easily persuaded than others are, and someone may be more easily influenced at some times than at others. The ease of persuading someone depends on both the person and the situation.

Intelligence and Interest

Who would you guess would be persuaded more easily—more intelligent or less intelligent people? It depends. The peripheral route to persuasion is more likely to persuade less intelligent people of an illogical or poorly supported idea (Eagly & Warren, 1976). The central route to persuasion is generally more effective with highly intelligent people, who are better able to understand complicated evidence.

However, the effectiveness of the central or peripheral route also depends on people's level of interest. A clever salesperson gauges a client's interests and concentrates on personally relevant issues. For example, some customers have more patience than others for listening to a series of facts. Today, it is possible to tailor Internet ads to the individual; computers store information about you and change the emphasis of an ad depending on what kinds of information are most likely to interest and persuade you (Kreutzer & Holt, 2001).

Heightened Resistance

Psychologists long assumed that people avoided reading or listening to arguments with which they disagree. Researchers have found, however, that people do expose themselves to ideas they dislike, and they remember the arguments surprisingly well. However, they argue against them and resist any major change in their attitudes (Eagly, Kulesa, Chen, & Chaiken, 2001).

Simply informing people that they are about to hear a persuasive speech activates their resistance and weakens the effect of the talk on their attitudes (Petty & Cacioppo, 1977). This tendency is called the **forewarning effect**. Actually, the effects are somewhat complex. Suppose you have a strongly unfavorable attitude toward something—higher tuition at your college, for example. Now someone tells you that a well-informed person is going to try to persuade you in favor of higher tuition. At once, before the speech even begins, your attitudes shift slightly in that direction, toward favoring higher tuition! Exactly why is unclear; perhaps you are telling yourself, "I guess there must be some good reason for that opinion." Then when you hear the speech itself, it does have some influence, and your attitudes will shift still further toward favoring it (or at least toward neutrality), but your attitudes do not shift as much as those of someone who had not been forewarned. The warning alerts you to resist the persuasion, to criticize weak arguments, and to reject weak evidence (Wood & Quinn, 2003).

In the closely related **inoculation effect**, *people first hear a weak argument and then a stronger argument supporting the same conclusion.* After they have rejected the first argument, they are likely to reject the second one also. In one experiment people listened to speeches *against* brushing their teeth after every meal. Some of them heard just a strong argument (e.g., "Brushing your teeth too frequently wears away tooth enamel, leading to serious disease"). Others first heard a weak argument and then the strong argument 2 days later. Still others first heard an argument *for* tooth-brushing and then the strong argument against it. Only those who heard the weak antibrushing argument before the strong one resisted its influence; the other two groups found it highly persuasive (McGuire & Papageorgis, 1961). So if you want to convince people, start with your strong evidence, not with evidence that they may consider faulty.

CONCEPT CHECK ☑

14. If you want your children to preserve the beliefs and attitudes you try to teach them, should you give them only arguments that support those beliefs or should you also expose them to attacks on those beliefs? Why? (Check your answers on page 551.)

Strategies of Persuasion

People representing anything from worthless products to noble charities will sometimes ask you to give more of your time or money than you would rationally choose to spend. You should understand several of their techniques so that you can resist these appeals.

One technique is to start with a modest request, which the person accepts, and then follow it with a larger request. This procedure is called the **foot-in-the-door technique**. When Jonathan Freedman and Scott Fraser (1966) asked suburban residents in Palo Alto, California, to put a small "Drive Safely" sign in their windows, most of them agreed to do so. A couple of weeks later, other researchers asked the same residents to let them set up a large, unsightly "Drive Safely" billboard in their front yards for 10 days. They also made the request to some residents who had not been approached by the first researchers. Of those who had already agreed to display the small sign, 76% agreed to the billboard. Only 17% of the others agreed. Even agreeing to make as small a commitment as signing a petition to support a cause significantly increases the probability that people will later donate money to that cause (Schwarzwald, Bizman, & Raz, 1983).

In another approach, called the **door-in-the-face technique** (Cialdini et al., 1975), *someone follows an outrageous initial request with a more reasonable second one,* implying that if you refused the first request, you should agree to the second. For example, I once received a telephone call from a college alumni association asking me to show my loyalty by contributing $1,000. When I apologetically declined, the caller acted sympathetic (as if to say, "It's too bad you don't have a high-paying job like all our other alumni . . .") and then asked whether I could contribute $500. And if not $500, how about $200? The implication was that, if I had refused the original request, I should "compromise" by donating a smaller amount.

Robert Cialdini and his colleagues (1975) demonstrated the power of the door-in-the-face technique with a clever experiment. They asked one group of college students, chosen randomly, whether they would be willing to chaperone a group from the juvenile detention center on a trip to the zoo. Only 17% said they would. They asked other students to spend 2 hours per week for 2 years working as counselors with juvenile delinquents. Not surprisingly, all of them refused. But then the researchers asked them, "If you won't do that, would you chaperone a group from the juvenile detention center on one trip to the zoo?" Half of them said they would. Apparently, they felt that the researchers were conceding a great deal and that it was only fair to meet them halfway.

Someone using the **bait-and-switch technique** *first offers an extremely favorable deal, gets the other person to commit to the deal, and then makes additional demands*. Alternatively, the person might offer a product at a very low price to get customers to the store but then claim to be out of the product and try to sell them something else. For example, a car dealer offers you an exceptionally good price on a new car and a generous price for the trade-in of your old car. You weren't sure you wanted this make of car, but the deal is too good to resist. After you have committed yourself to buying this car, the dealer checks with the boss, who rejects the deal. Your salesperson comes back saying, "I'm so sorry. I forgot that this car has some special features that raise the value. If we sold it for the price I originally quoted, we'd lose money." So you agree to a higher price. Then the company's used car specialist looks at your old car and "corrects" the trade-in value to a lower amount. Still, you have already committed yourself, so you don't back out. Eventually, you leave with a deal that you would not have accepted at the start.

In the **that's-not-all technique**, *someone makes an offer and then improves the offer before you have a chance to reply*. The television announcer says, "Here's your chance to buy this amazing combination paper shredder and coffeemaker for only $39.95. But wait, there's more! We'll throw in a can of dog deodorant! Also this handy windshield wiper cleaner and a solar-powered flashlight and a subscription to *Modern Lobotomist*! If you call now, you can get this amazing offer, which usually costs $39.95, for only $19.95! Call this number!" People who hear the first offer and then the "improved" offer are more likely to comply than are people who hear the "improved" offer from the start (Burger, 1986).

CONCEPT CHECK ☑

15. Identify each of the following as an example of the foot-in-the-door technique, the door-in-the-face technique, or the that's-not-all technique.
    a. Your boss says, "We need to cut costs drastically. I'm afraid I'm going to have to cut your salary in half." You protest vigorously. Your boss replies, "Well, I suppose we could cut expenses some other way. Maybe I can give you just a 5% cut." "Thanks," you reply. "I can live with that."
    b. A store marks its prices "25% off" and then scratches that out and marks them "50% off!"
    c. A friend asks you to help carry some supplies over to the elementary school for an afternoon tutoring program. When you get there, the principal says that one of the tutors is late and asks whether you could take her place until she arrives. You agree and spend the rest of the afternoon tutoring. The principal then talks you into coming back every week as a tutor. (Check your answers on page 551.)

Cognitive Dissonance

Much research asks whether people's attitudes change their behavior. The theory of cognitive dissonance reverses the direction: It holds that a change in people's behavior alters their attitudes (Festinger, 1957). **Cognitive dissonance** is *a state of unpleasant tension that people experience when they hold contradictory attitudes or when their behavior is inconsistent with their attitudes, especially if they are distressed about the inconsistency.*

For example, if you pride yourself on honesty and find yourself saying something you do not believe, you feel tension. You can reduce that tension in three ways: You can change what you are saying to match your attitudes, change your attitude to match what you are saying, or find an explanation that justifies your behavior under the circumstances (Wicklund & Brehm, 1976) (see Figure 14.6). Although you might adopt any of these options, most of the existing research has focused on how cognitive dissonance changes people's attitudes.

Imagine yourself as one of the participants in this classic experiment on cognitive dissonance (Festinger & Carlsmith, 1959). The experimenters explain that they are studying motor behavior. They show you a board full of pegs. Your task is to take each peg out of the board, rotate it one fourth of a turn, and return it to the board. When you finish all the pegs, you start over from the top, rotating all the pegs again as quickly and accurately as possible for an hour. As you

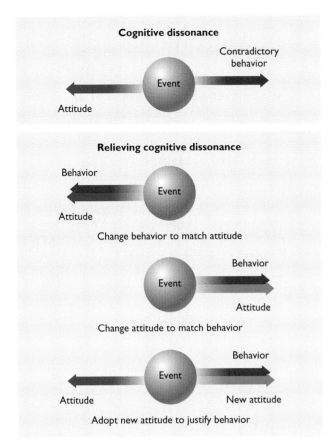

FIGURE 14.6 Cognitive dissonance is a state of tension that arises when people perceive that their attitudes do not match their behavior. They can resolve this discrepancy by changing either their attitudes or their behavior or by developing a new attitude or excuse to explain the discrepancy.

proceed an experimenter silently takes notes. You find your task tedious and boring. (In fact the researchers intentionally chose this task because it was so boring.)

At the end of the hour, the experimenter thanks you for participating and "explains" to you (falsely) that the study's purpose was to determine whether people's performances are influenced by their attitudes toward the task. You were in the neutral-attitude group, but those in the positive-attitude group are told before they start that they will enjoy this interesting experience.

In fact, the experimenter continues, right now the research assistant is supposed to give that instruction to the next participant, a young woman waiting in the next room. The experimenter excuses himself to find the research assistant and then returns distraught. The assistant is nowhere to be found, he says. He turns to you and asks, "Would you be willing to tell the next partic-

ipant that you thought this was an interesting, enjoyable experiment? If so, I will pay you." Assume that you consent, as most students in the study did. After you tell that woman in the next room that you enjoyed the study, what would you actually think of the study, assuming the experimenter paid you $1? What if he paid you $20? (This study occurred in the 1950s, before decades of inflation. In today's money that $20 would be worth more than $100.)

In this study, after participants told the woman how much fun the experiment was, they left, believing the study was over. As they walked down the hall, a representative of the psychology department greeted them and explained that the department wanted to find out what kinds of experiments were being conducted and whether they were educationally worthwhile. (The answers to these questions were the real point of the experiment.) Participants were asked how enjoyable they considered the experiment and whether they would be willing to participate in a similar experiment later.

The students who received $20 said they thought the experiment was boring and that they wanted nothing to do with another such experiment. However, contrary to what you might guess, those who received $1 said they enjoyed the experiment and would be willing to participate again (Figure 14.7).

Why? According to the theory of cognitive dissonance, those who accepted $20 to tell a lie experienced little conflict. They knew they were lying, but they also knew why: for the $20. They had no reason to change their original low opinion of the experiment. However, the students who had told a lie for only $1 felt a conflict between their true attitude and what they had said about the experiment. The small payment provided little reason for lying, so they experienced cognitive dissonance—an unpleasant tension. They did not want to feel bad about telling a lie, so the only way they could reduce their tension was to change their attitude, deciding that the experiment really had been interesting after all. ("I learned a lot of

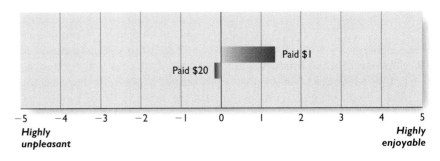

FIGURE 14.7 In a classic experiment demonstrating cognitive dissonance, participants were paid either $1 or $20 for telling another subject that they enjoyed an experiment (which was actually boring). Later, they were asked for their real opinions. Participants who were paid the smaller amount said that they enjoyed the study more than the others. *(Based on data from Festinger & Carlsmith, 1959)*

interesting things about myself, like . . . uh . . . how good I am at rotating pegs.")

The idea of cognitive dissonance attracted much attention and inspired a great deal of research (Aronson, 1997). Here are two examples:

- An experimenter left a child in a room with toys but forbade the child to play with one particular toy. If the experimenter threatened the child with severe punishment for playing with the toy, the child avoided it but still regarded it as desirable. However, if the experimenter merely said that he or she would be unhappy or disappointed if the child played with that toy, the child avoided the toy and said (even weeks later) that it was not a good toy (Aronson & Carlsmith, 1963).
- The experimenter asked college students to write an essay defending a position that the experimenter knew, from previous information, was contrary to the students' beliefs. For example, college students who favored freer access to alcohol might be asked to write essays on why the college should increase restrictions on alcohol. Those who were told they must write the essays did not change their views significantly, but those who were asked to "please" write the essay and were also reminded that they did so voluntarily generally came to agree with what they wrote (Croyle & Cooper, 1983).

The general principle is that, if you entice people to do something by means of a minimum reward or a tiny threat so that they are acting almost voluntarily, they change their attitudes to defend what they are doing and reduce cognitive dissonance. This procedure is a powerful way of changing attitudes because people are actively participating, not just quietly listening to someone.

This module began with the statement, "If you want to change people's behavior, you have to change their attitudes first." The results of cognitive dissonance experiments tell us quite the opposite: If you start by changing people's behavior, their attitudes will change too.

CONCEPT CHECK ☑

16. Suppose your parents pay you to get a good grade in a course that you consider boring. According to cognitive dissonance theory, are you more likely to develop a positive attitude toward your studies if your parents pay you $10 or $100?
17. The effort to avoid cognitive dissonance leads to consistency in behavior. Use that principle to explain the foot-in-the-door technique. (Check your answers on page 551.)

IN CLOSING

Persuasion and Manipulation

Broadly defined, attitudes influence almost everything we do. The stereotypes, prejudices, and so forth that we considered in the first module are attitudes about people or groups of people. You also have attitudes about political issues, the value of various products, and various ethical questions.

When you form an attitude about something of little consequence to you, it is understandable that you will follow the peripheral route, paying little attention to the complexities of the evidence. When you are dealing with important matters, however, such as how you will spend your time and money, you will almost certainly follow the central route, examining the facts as carefully as you can. It is important to be alert to some of the influences that might throw you off course, such as the foot-in-the-door technique, bait-and-switch, and cognitive dissonance. Advertisers, politicians, and vast numbers of others try to polish their techniques of persuasion, and not everyone has your best interest at heart.

Summary

- *Attitudes.* An attitude is a like or dislike of something or somebody that influences our behavior toward that thing or person. (page 543)
- *Two routes to persuasion.* When people consider a topic of little importance to them, they are easily persuaded by the speaker's appearance and other superficial factors. When people care about the topic, they pay more attention to logic and to the quality of the evidence. (page 544)
- *Sleeper effect.* When people reject a message because of their low regard for the person who proposed it, they sometimes forget where they heard the idea and later come to accept it. (page 544)
- *Minority influence.* Although a minority may have little influence at first, it can, through persistent repetition of its message, eventually persuade the majority to adopt its position or consider other alternatives. (page 544)
- *Influence of fear-inducing messages.* Messages that appeal to fear are effective if people perceive the danger as real and think they can do something about it. (page 545)
- *Influence of group endorsement.* People tend to accept a position endorsed by a political party or other group they favor, even if they would ordinarily doubt that position. (page 546)
- *Forewarning and inoculation effects.* If people have been warned that someone will try to persuade them of something, or if they have previously

heard a weak version of the persuasive argument, they tend to resist the argument. (page 547)

- *Strategies of persuasion.* Several procedures can influence people to do something they would not have done otherwise. These include starting with a tiny request and then increasing it, starting with an enormous request and offering to compromise, offering a generous deal and then demanding more, and offering a moderate deal and then adding inducements. (page 547)

- *Cognitive dissonance.* Cognitive dissonance is a state of unpleasant tension that arises from contradictory attitudes or from behavior that conflicts with a person's attitudes. When people's behavior does not match their attitudes, they try to eliminate the inconsistency by changing either their behavior or their attitudes. (page 548)

Answers to Concept Checks

10. Some people express one attitude openly but demonstrate another attitude on the Implicit Association Test. (page 544)
11. You will pay more attention to the evidence and logic, following the central route to persuasion, for the debate about your own college because it is worth your effort to evaluate the evidence carefully. (page 544)
12. The fact that your idea was overwhelmingly rejected does not mean that you should give up. If

you and a few allies continue to present this plan in a simple way, showing apparent agreement among yourselves, the majority may eventually endorse a similar plan—but probably without giving you credit for it. (page 544)
13. The salesperson is relying on endorsement by a group that you presumably like and trust. Also you are likely to be persuaded by people similar to yourself. (page 546)
14. You should expose them to weak attacks on their beliefs so that they will learn how to resist such attacks. (page 547)
15. a. door-in-the-face technique; b. that's-not-all technique; c. foot-in-the-door technique. (page 548)
16. You will come to like your studies more if you are paid $10 than if you are paid $100. If you are paid only $10, you won't be able to tell yourself that you are studying harder only for the money. Instead, you will tell yourself that you must be really interested.

    The theory of intrinsic and extrinsic motivation leads to the same prediction: If you study hard in the absence of any strong external reason, you will perceive that you have internal reasons for studying. (page 550)
17. Once you have agreed to a small request, you can maintain consistency (decrease dissonance) by agreeing to similar requests in the future. (page 550)

How do we choose our partners? Do men and women choose for the same reasons?

William Proxmire, a former U.S. senator, used to give Golden Fleece Awards to those who, in his opinion, most flagrantly wasted the taxpayers' money. He once bestowed an award on some psychologists who had received a federal grant to study how people fall in love. According to Proxmire the research was pointless because people do not want to understand love. They prefer, he said, to let such matters remain a mystery.

This module presents the information Senator Proxmire thought you did not want to know.

Establishing Lasting Relationships

Of all the people you meet, how do you choose those few who become your friends? (Or how do they choose you?) Here we consider factors relevant to both friendships and romantic relationships; later, we specifically discuss dating and marriage.

Proximity and Familiarity

Proximity means *closeness*. (It comes from the same root as *approximate*.) Not surprisingly, *we are most likely to become friends with people who live or work in close proximity and become familiar to us.* At the start of a school year, Robert Hays (1985) asked college students to name two other students with whom they thought they might become friends. After 3 months he found that more of the potential friends who lived close together had become friends than had those who lived farther apart.

One reason proximity is important is that people who live nearby have frequent opportunities to discover what they have in common. Another reason is the **mere exposure effect**, the principle that *the more often we come in contact with someone or something, the more we tend to like that person or object* (Saegert, Swap, & Zajonc, 1973; Zajonc, 1968). You can think of exceptions, of course; for example, frequent contact with a disease will not make you like it. However, mere exposure can elevate something from "neutral" to "liked." (Exactly why is not obvious.)

Similarity

Here's another finding that will hardly surprise you: Most close friends resemble one another in age, physical attractiveness, political and religious beliefs, intelligence, academic interests, religion, and attitudes (Laumann, 1969).

Choice of friends can be difficult for members of minorities. If your ethnic or religious group is greatly outnumbered where you live, your potential friends or romantic partners may be limited to individuals within your group who do not share your interests or members of other groups who do (Hamm, 2000).

Do you like people better when you learn that their beliefs and attitudes resemble yours? This question turns out to be more complex than it sounds. You probably like most of the people you meet until you have a reason to alter your judgment. If you think at all about a new acquaintance's beliefs and attitudes, you probably assume that he or she shares your own beliefs and attitudes . . . because most people do, don't they? After all, you believe your opinions and actions

▌ Behavior is guided by external forces, such as waves, and by forces within the individual. According to the determinist view, even those internal forces follow physical laws.

are normal and correct (Alicke & Largo, 1995). Therefore, finding a disagreement with someone *lowers* your regard for them more than finding an agreement *increases* your regard (Rosenbaum, 1986).

Confirmation of Self-Concept

You might well be saying, "Big deal. People make friends with others who live nearby and resemble them. Psychologists needed research to demonstrate *that?*" It is worthwhile to test the obvious because occasionally what seems obvious might be wrong. For example, suppose you are in a research study. First you are asked to describe yourself. Then two other people tell you their reactions. The first says, "You seem a pleasant, honest person. You're intelligent and you have some interesting ideas and a nice sense of humor." The second says, "I hate to be rude, but frankly you seem superficial. You're trying to make a good impression, but for me, you're failing. You drift aimlessly; you can't even organize your thoughts." Which one would you choose as a possible partner or friend?

The obvious answer is "the first one." However, many people with unusually low self-esteem choose the person who gave them a low evaluation (Swann, 1997). Evidently, people who think little of themselves find it satisfying to be with others who share that low opinion. You can see the potential harm. Someone with a low self-evaluation chooses friends and perhaps even a spouse who constantly criticizes. The result is even lower self-esteem.

The Equity Principle

According to **exchange** or **equity theories**, *social relationships are transactions in which partners exchange goods and services*. In some cases the businesslike nature of a romantic relationship is fairly blatant. In the Singles' Ads of many newspapers, those seeking a relationship describe what they have to offer and what they expect in return. Generally, women who describe themselves as attractive and men who describe themselves as wealthy set high demands on what they are seeking in a mate. People who have less to offer make fewer demands (Waynforth & Dunbar, 1995).

As in business, a relationship is most stable if both partners believe the deal is fair. It is easiest to establish a fair deal if the partners are about equally attractive and intelligent, contribute about equally to the finances and the chores, and so forth. With many couples one partner contributes more in one way and the other contributes more in another way. Those arrangements can also seem fair, although it is more difficult to be sure.

The equity principle readily applies while people are forming friendships or romances, but it is less applicable later. For example, you might nurse your spouse or lifelong friend through a long illness without worrying about whether you are still getting a fair deal.

CONCEPT CHECK   ☑

18. Someone your own age from another country moves next door. Neither of you speaks the other's language. What factors will tend to strengthen the likelihood of your becoming friends? What factors will tend to weaken it? (Check your answers on page 560.)

Special Concerns in Selecting a Mate

Choosing a partner for marriage or long-term partnership has special features because of the extra dimension of raising children. Yes, I know, not everyone wants to get married, not all married couples want children, and many unmarried people rear children. The following discussion does not apply to everyone—almost nothing in psychology does!—but it applies to those who hope to marry and have children.

Physical Attractiveness

What characteristics do you look for in someone you might date and eventually marry? You probably reply that you want "someone who is intelligent, honest, easy to talk to, with a good sense of humor." Now imagine a friend says, "Hey, you're not doing anything this weekend, right? How about going on a blind date with my cousin who is visiting for the weekend?" "Well, I don't know. Tell me about your cousin." "My cousin is intelligent, honest, easy to talk to, and has a good sense of humor." That description matches what you said you wanted, but you are skeptical. Your friend did not mention the cousin's appearance, so you assume the worst. Were you being dishonest when you said you wanted someone intelligent, honest, and easy to talk to? Not really. You did not mention appearance because you assumed anyone would take that for granted. (You also didn't say that you hope your date speaks English. You don't mention the obvious.)

In one study social psychologists arranged blind dates for 332 freshman couples for a dance before the start of classes. They asked participants to fill out questionnaires, but then the experimenters ignored the questionnaires and paired students at random. Midway through the dance, the experimenters separated the men and women and asked them to rate how much they liked their dates. The only factor that influenced the ratings was physical attractiveness (Walster, Aronson, Abrahams, & Rottman, 1966). Similarities of attitudes, personality, and intelligence counted for almost nothing. Surprising? Hardly. During the brief time they had spent together at the dance, the couples had little opportunity to learn about each other. Intelligence, honesty, and other character values do become important in a lasting relationship, but not on the first date or two, and certainly not in the first hour (Keller, Thiessen, & Young, 1996).

On the average, attractive people are judged more favorably than other people. They have more friends and they are treated better. The usual result is a self-fulfilling prophecy: Because people expect to like attractive people, they treat them better, and the attractive people therefore become more friendly and outgoing (Langlois et al., 2000).

The Possible Biological Value of Attractiveness

Why do we care about physical appearance? We take its importance so much for granted that we don't even understand why there is a question, so for a moment let's consider other species.

In many bird species, early in the mating season, females shop around and choose a brilliantly colored male that sings vigorously from the treetops. In several species, females also prefer males with especially long tails (Figure 14.8). From an evolutionary standpoint, aren't these choices foolish? The most "popular" males risk their lives by singing loudly from the treetops, where they call the attention of hawks and eagles. They also seemingly waste enormous energy on bright feathers. (It takes more energy to produce bright colors than dull ones.) A long tail may look pretty, but it interferes with flying. Why does the female prefer a mate who wastes energy and endangers his life?

FIGURE 14.8 In some bird species, males with long tails attract more mates. However, they pay a price: The long tail impairs their flying abilities. Only healthy males can afford this handicap.

Biologists eventually decided that wasting energy and risking life were precisely the point (Zahavi & Zahavi, 1997). Only a healthy, vigorous male has enough energy to make bright, colorful feathers (Blount, Metcalfe, Birkhead, & Surai, 2003; Faivre, Grégoire, Préault, Cézilly, & Sorci, 2003). Only a strong male can fly despite a long tail, and only a strong male would risk predation by singing from an exposed perch. In effect a col-

orful, singing male is showing off: "Look at me! I am so healthy and vigorous that I can afford to take crazy risks and waste energy frivolously!" The female, we presume, does not understand why she is attracted to colorful, loud, active males. She just is because, throughout her evolutionary history, most females who chose such partners reproduced more successfully than those who chose dull-colored, inactive males.

So it would seem, theoretically. The problem is that although a male's bright colors and vigorous singing do indicate health, his health depends more on his luck in finding a good feeding place than on his genes. The same is true for fish as well as birds (Brooks, 2000; Cunningham & Russell, 2000).

Now back to humans: Are attractive people more likely than others to be healthy and fertile? Theoretically, they should be. Certainly, many illnesses decrease people's attractiveness. Also, *good-looking* is in many regards similar to *normal,* which probably indicates *good genetics.* Suppose a computer takes photographs of many people and averages their faces. The resulting composite face has about an average nose, average distance between the eyes, and so forth, and most people rate this face "highly attractive" (Langlois & Roggman, 1990; Langlois, Roggman, & Musselman, 1994; Rhodes, Sumich, & Byatt, 1999) (see Figure 14.9). This is not to say that the average person is highly attractive, but a highly attractive person does have approximately average features. If we note anything "unusual" about an attractive face, it is the absence of irregularities—no crooked teeth, skin blemishes, or asymmetries, and no facial hair on women (Fink & Penton-Voak, 2002).

Why is normal attractive? One hypothesis is that normal means healthy. Presumably, the genes for an average face have spread in the population because they are linked to success. Any face far different from the average might indicate a genetic mutation. Researchers have found that even infants prefer to look at the same faces that adults consider attractive and that judgments of facial attractiveness are fairly consistent from one culture to another (Berry, 2000). A competing hypothesis, however, is that we like the normal, average face only because it is familiar, and we like anything that is familiar. Research has found that people tend to think that "average-looking" dogs, birds, and wristwatches are attractive (Halberstadt & Rhodes, 2000). Also, if you have recently seen many faces that are thinner than usual, fatter than usual, or in some other way distorted, your judgment of "attractive" is shifted slightly in the direction of the faces you have just seen (Rhodes, Jeffery, Watson, Clifford, & Nakayama, 2003). So our preference for normal faces might be unrelated to advantageous genes.

The best way to settle this issue is to see whether attractive people tend to be healthier or more fertile than others. In one study researchers

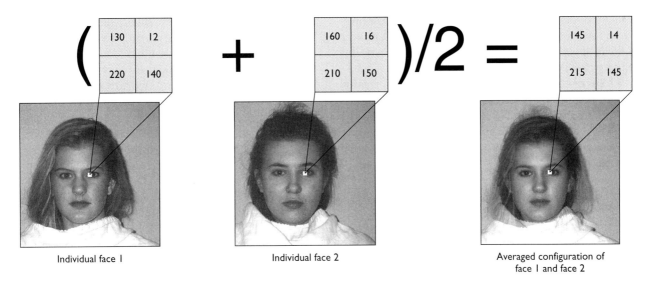

FIGURE 14.9 A computer measured the gray value of each point on each picture. It then produced a new picture with the average of the grays at each point. This set of photos illustrates the procedure for two original faces. The numbers are for illustrative purposes only. Most people rate the resulting face as highly attractive. (© *Langlois, Roggman, & Musselman, "Average Faces,"* Psychological Science, *Vol. 5, no.4.*)

obtained photos of hundreds of teenagers from long ago. They asked other people to rate the faces for attractiveness; they also obtained extensive medical records for the people in the photos. The ratings of attractiveness did not correlate reliably with health. People who were rated attractive were more likely to marry, and especially to marry early, but unattractive people who did marry were just as likely to have children as the more attractive people (Kalick, Zebrowitz, Langlois, & Johnson, 1998). Evidently, at least for this sample, attractiveness had nothing to do with health or fertility.

If facial attractiveness is a poor cue to health, what about the rest of the body? According to one theory, men should prefer women with a narrow waist and wide hips—a waist-to-hip ratio of about 0.7—because medical researchers believe women with that ratio are most likely to be healthy and fertile. Examine the drawings of women's figures in Figure 14.10. Which one do you consider most attractive? In the United States, both men and women rated thinner women as the most attractive (Tassinary & Hansen, 1998). In non-Westernized cultures of Tanzania and southeastern Peru, most men regarded heavier women as the most attractive (Marlowe

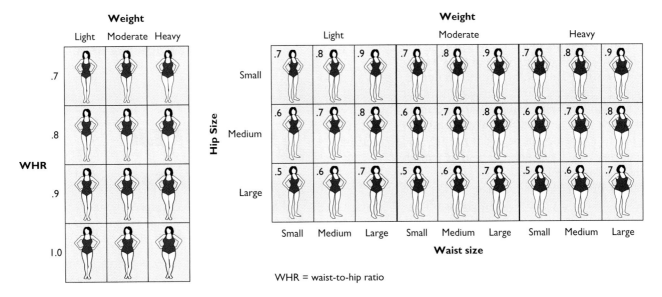

FIGURE 14.10 Which of these female figures do you find most attractive? Most fertile? Average ratings vary across cultures. (*From "A Critical Test of the Waist-to-Hip-Ratio Hypothesis of Female Physical Attractiveness" by L. G. Tassinary and K. A. Hansen,* Psychological Science, *1998, 9, 150-155. Copyright © 1998 Blackwell Publishers. Reprinted by permission.*)

& Wetsman, 2001; Yu & Shepard, 1998). In short, preferences for female shape vary somewhat across cultures and do not necessarily match what researchers consider healthy or fertile.

Where do all these studies leave us? Theoretically, it would make sense for good appearance to represent "truthful advertising" of healthful genes. However, so far researchers have not found a strong link between good appearance and healthful genes. Until we have more extensive research, we cannot be sure.

CONCEPT CHECK ☑

19. According to the evolutionary theory, attractiveness is a sign of good health. Why would it be difficult for an unhealthy individual to produce "counterfeit" attractiveness? (Check your answer on page 560.)

Men's and Women's Preferences

Imagine that two people have expressed a desire to date you, and you have reason to believe the date could lead to a long-term relationship and eventual marriage. You have to choose between the two; you cannot date both. Here are the descriptions. The choice for women: Man A is extraordinarily good-looking. He works as a waiter at a small restaurant and has no ambition to do anything more. Man B is about average looking. He patented an invention and sold it for a fortune. He was recently accepted to a prestigious medical school, and he is said to have an outstanding career ahead as a medical researcher.

The choice for men: Woman A is extraordinarily good-looking. She works as a waitress at a small restaurant and has no ambition to do anything more. Woman B is about average looking. She patented an invention and sold it for a fortune. She was recently accepted to a prestigious medical school, and she is said to have an outstanding career ahead as a medical researcher.

I have offered these choices to my own classes, and you probably can guess the results: Nearly all of the women chose man B. The men were divided, but most chose woman A. (Curiously, secret ballots gave different results from a show of hands, but the trend was in the same direction.)

The same trends occur in all cultures for which we have data (Buss, 2000). Both men and women prefer a physically attractive partner, if possible, but women have the additional concern of preferring a partner who can be a good provider. Most men are less concerned about a woman's potential job success.

Another trend found worldwide is that many men will accept almost any partner for a short-term sexual relationship, whereas most women either refuse a short-term sexual relationship or accept only a very appealing partner (Buss, 2000). Another is that men are more interested in sexual variety. As shown in Figure 14.11, in all of the 52 nations that were surveyed, men were more likely than women to want more than one sexual partner in the near future and in the long term (Schmitt et al., 2003). Still another trend pertains to jealousy: In most cultures men insist that women be sexually faithful more than women require fidelity from men. In some cultures, such as China, men and women are equally

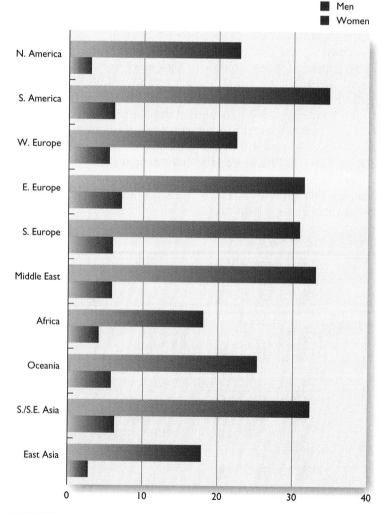

FIGURE 14.11 More than 16,000 people in 52 nations throughout the world were asked how many sexual partners they hoped to have in the next month. In all countries a higher percentage of men than women wanted more than one. *(Based on data of Schmitt et al., 2003)*

insistent on the other's sexual fidelity, and in Sweden both seem equally unconcerned, but in no culture do women demand more fidelity from men than men demand from women (Buss, Larsen, Westen, & Semmelroth, 1992; Buunk, Angleitner, Oubaid, & Buss, 1996).

All of those trends are well confirmed, but the explanation is not. One hypothesis is that we have evolved to act this way (Bjorklund & Shackelford, 1999; Buss, 2000; Gangestad, 2000; Geary, 2000). The argument goes as follows. First, consider short-term sexual relationships: A man who has a quick sexual relationship has some chance of spreading his genes if the woman becomes pregnant and manages to rear the child successfully. Therefore, a hypothetical gene that caused men to act this way would spread in the population. For a woman, having sex with many partners cannot give her more babies than sex with one partner. So a gene causing her to have sex with many partners would provide no advantage.

A man's other way of spreading his genes is to devote his energies to supporting one woman and her children (presumably his, too). However, this strategy succeeds only if the woman he marries is fertile. A young woman will be fertile for a long time, and an attractive woman is (perhaps) more likely to be fertile. So men increase their probable contribution to the gene pool if they marry young, attractive women. In contrast a woman can be less concerned about the age of her partner because men remain fertile into old age. However, she should prefer a man who can provide food and other resources while she is pregnant and caring for young children.

Theoretically, the reported difference in sexual jealousy might relate to the nature of human reproduction. If a man is going to pair with just one woman for life and help rear her children, he should make sure that she is sexually faithful; otherwise, he could be spreading another man's genes and not his own. A woman does not need to be equally jealous if her husband has a brief sexual affair because she doesn't have to worry about whether she is the mother of her child. She would, however, suffer a disadvantage if her husband stopped supporting her and shifted his attentions to another woman.

However, even if we accept these descriptions of male and female behavior, it is not necessary to agree that they are products of genetics and natural selection. The alternative view is that people throughout the world learn these preferences (Eagly & Wood, 1999). Yes, of course, the brain is subject to natural selection just as much as any other organ, but we need not assume that evolution has "micromanaged" our behavior with specific mechanisms for each decision.

Furthermore, many psychologists question the generalized descriptions of male and female behavior just discussed. For example, the strength of women's preference for financially secure men varies from culture to culture, largely dependent on women's ability to earn money and control resources of their own (Kasser & Sharma, 1999). Much of the evidence that men have stronger sexual jealousy than women rests on two kinds of studies—surveys of college students and crime records showing more jealousy-related violence by men. Surveys of older, more experienced people show less difference between men and women (Harris, 2002), and the crime records are indecisive because men commit more of almost *all* kinds of crime (Harris, 2003).

Finally, is it really true that women gain nothing from having sex with multiple partners? Sarah Hrdy (2000) has pointed out a number of potential benefits, including the following:

- Her husband might be infertile.
- Another man might have better genes than her husband and give her better children.
- The other man may provide her with additional resources and protection.
- If she has sex with many men, all of them may provide a modest amount of care and protection for her children.
- She might be able to "trade up," leaving her husband and joining the new partner.

A general point is that we cannot reconstruct the social life of our ancestors with great confidence. Mating customs vary from one human culture to another and even from one chimpanzee troop to another (Parish & deWaal, 2000). So reconstructing the evolution of human social behavior is uncertain. The case for evolutionary influence on mate choices would be stronger if someone found a gene that produces variations in preferences. (For example, imagine genes that caused men to prefer older women or women to prefer impoverished men.) Without evidence of genetic variation in mate choice, discussions of the evolution of social behavior will remain speculative.

CONCEPT CHECK ☑

20. Suppose astronauts discover humanlike beings on another planet, whose biology and culture resemble ours except that all men have exactly the same wealth and women remain fertile all their lives instead of losing their fertility at menopause. What would an evolutionary theorist predict about the mate preferences of men and women on this planet? (Check your answer on page 560.)

Marriage

A couple that decides to marry pledges that they will stay together as long as they both shall live, and yet a distressing percentage of marriages end in divorce. What went wrong?

Many couples date each other for a long time before exploring some of the issues that would become critical during a life together. Questionnaire studies have found that, as couples continue to date, their estimates of each other's sexual histories, activity preferences, and so forth become more *confident* without becoming more *accurate* (Swann & Gill, 1997). Answer the following questions, first for yourself and second *as you think your dating partner would answer them.* (Several questions assume a heterosexual relationship; disregard any items that do not apply to you.)

1. After you marry or establish another long-term relationship, how often would you want to visit your parents? Your in-laws?
2. How many children do you want to have? How soon?
3. If you have children, should one partner stay home with the children while they are young? Should both partners share the responsibility for child care? Should the children be placed in a day-care center as soon as possible?
4. Suppose the two of you are offered good jobs in cities far apart. Neither of you can find a satisfactory job in the other's city. How would you decide where to live?
5. Suppose a sudden financial crisis strikes. Where would you cut expenses to balance the budget? Clothes? Food? Housing? Entertainment?
6. How often do you plan to attend religious services?
7. How and where do you like to spend your vacations?
8. How often would you expect to spend an evening with friends, apart from your partner?

Were you uncertain about how your dating partner would answer any of these questions? If so, you are in the majority. Disagreements about such questions are common reasons for relationship conflicts. I do not suggest that you ask every person you date to fill out this questionnaire. However, before you get far into a relationship, you should discuss anything that is important to you.

Sometimes couples change in ways they could not have foreseen, but many breakups are predictable. Psychologists have studied recently married couples and related the observations to how the marriages developed later. Most of the problems and hostilities that eventually led to divorce were present early in the marriage. If a marriage ended in divorce within 7 years, in

most cases the couple showed mixed feelings toward each other even before marriage and made frequent negative comments about each other. Apparently, they married in hopes they could work out their problems, but matters just grew worse. Couples that divorced after more than 7 years started on stronger terms but became disillusioned and less affectionate within the first 2 years or so. Although they did not express overt hostility early in their marriage, they also did not show as much love and affection as most other couples whose marriages were going to last (Gottman & Levenson, 2000; Huston, Niehuis, & Smith, 2001).

There are probably some additional subtle cues, hard to quantify, that distinguish successful marriages from less successful ones. In one fascinating study, various kinds of people watched 3-minute videotaped conversations between 10 married couples and estimated how satisfied each couple was. Their estimates were then compared to reports by the couples themselves. People who reported that their own marriages were either highly satisfying or highly unsatisfying were the best at judging the quality of other couples' marriages. Marriage counselors and marriage researchers lagged behind, as did unmarried people (Ebling & Levenson, 2003).

Marriages That Last

When you hear about how many marriages end in divorce, it is easy to despair, but many marriages remain strong for a lifetime. Most characteristics of successful marriages are what you would probably expect (Howard & Dawes, 1976; Karney & Bradbury, 1995; Thornton, 1977). The following list is based on studies mainly in the United States in the late 20th century, so we do not know how they might differ for other times and places:

- The husband and wife have similar attitudes and personalities.
- They have sexual relations frequently and arguments infrequently.
- They have an adequate income.
- The husband has a good enough job to maintain self-respect.
- The wife was not pregnant before they married.
- The couple's parents also had successful marriages.

A successful marriage changes over the years, just as individual lives do. At first the couple has the intense excitement of learning about each other and doing new things together. Years later, although they do not arouse each other's emotions as intensely as before (Berscheid, 1983), they still love each other, perhaps even more deeply. If one of them becomes ill or dies, the emotion inherent in the mature relationship becomes vividly apparent.

■ In a mature, lasting relationship, a couple can count on each other for care and affection through both good and bad times.

Trying to Save a Marriage

Many couples with troubled marriages seek help from a marriage counselor. The results of marriage counseling are, unfortunately, not very encouraging. Of the couples receiving help, only about one third report improving their relationship during counseling, and even of those, half deteriorate later, leaving only about 15 to 20% that show any lasting improvement (Gottman, 1999). Even that 15 to 20% may overstate the success of marriage counseling, as some of those couples might have solved their own problems without counseling.

One reason for the disappointing results is, of course, that it takes two to save a marriage, and sometimes one partner has already given up before meeting the marriage counselor. Another reason, however, is that many marriage counselors have offered well-meaning but unhelpful advice. In particular, many counselors emphasize extremely open communication, including full expression of emotions. "Open communication" sounds like a good thing—after all, who is opposed to communication?—but venting hostile emotions toward your spouse is almost always harmful. The other person feels hurt and retaliates with equally insulting remarks (Fincham, 2003). The result is further deterioration of the relationship.

The distinction is this: If you have a complaint against your partner—an annoying habit, for example—yes, of course you should state it. However, state it politely, not angrily. And if the other person expresses hostile emotions, you are better off if you restrain your reaction.

In several studies dating or married couples recorded their emotional reactions toward each other

during a single conversation or on a daily basis; then each person reported what emotions they thought their partner had expressed. Happy couples expressed negative emotions only occasionally, and even then, the other usually did not report perceiving the negativity (Gable, Reis, & Downey, 2003; Simpson, Oriña, & Ickes, 2003). In other words successful couples limit both their expression and perception of negative emotions.

CONCEPT CHECK ☑

21. Why does the advice to "fully express your emotions" sometimes backfire in marriage counseling? (Check your answer on page 560.)

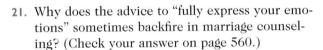

IN CLOSING

Choosing Your Partners Carefully

Few people enjoy living as a hermit, isolated from others. In prisons one of the harshest forms of punishment is solitary confinement. Almost any social contact is better than none at all. However, many people may choose their friends and their spouses poorly. In the first module of this chapter, we considered social perception—how we form impressions of other people. Finding friends and romantic partners is a special case, where more is at stake, but the processes are the same. In some regards forming impressions of romantic partners is especially difficult. A person you date is probably trying to make a good impression, and you *hope* to like the person. As the relationship progresses, another factor kicks in: Remember from the section on persuasion that anyone you like tends to be highly persuasive.

Life is like a roller-coaster ride in the dark: It has lots of ups and downs, and you never know what is going to happen next. Be sure you are riding with someone you like and trust.

Summary

* *Friendship choices.* People generally choose friends and romantic partners who live near them, resemble them, and confirm their self-esteem. Relationships are most likely to survive and grow if each person believes that he or she is getting about as good a deal as the other person is. (page 552)
* *Marriage and similar attachments.* People have special considerations when choosing a potential marriage partner because marriage usually implies a commitment to rearing children together. (page 553)

- *Physical attractiveness.* In many nonhuman species, physical attractiveness is a reliable cue to the individual's health, vigor, and therefore desirability as a mate. However, the relationship to genetics is unclear. In humans attractiveness is a powerful determinant of mate choice but has not been demonstrably linked to health. (page 553)
- *Men's and women's preferences in marriage partners.* In every human culture, men prefer young, attractive women and women prefer men who are good providers. Men tend to be more upset about possible sexual infidelity by their wives. Evolutionary theorists believe humans evolved to have these preferences to improve chances of reproducing. However, it is also plausible that people in different societies have learned these preferences. (page 556)
- *Marriage.* Marriage and similar relationships often break up because of problems that were present from the start. Marriages are successful when the partners have much in common and find ways to satisfy each other's needs. They are unsuccessful if the partners express too much hostility. (page 558)

Answers to Concept Checks

18. Proximity and familiarity will strengthen the likelihood of your becoming friends. The similarity principle will weaken it. Because of the difference in languages, you will have little chance, at least at first, to discover any similarities in interests or attitudes. In fact proximity will probably not be as a potent force as usual, because it serves largely as a means of enabling people to discover what they have in common. (page 553)
19. Attractive features such as bright feathers in a bird or large muscles in a man require much energy. It would be difficult for an unhealthy individual to devote enough energy to produce such features. (page 556)
20. If all men are equally wealthy, women would select men on some other basis, such as appearance. If women's fertility lasts as late in life as men's does, then the men on this planet should not have a strong preference for younger women. (page 557)
21. If the spouses exchange hostile comments, their relationship deteriorates. Better advice would be to discuss complaints or difficulties calmly. (page 559)

Interpersonal Influence

How are we influenced by other people's actions or inactions?

People tend to imitate one another, even when they have no apparent motive for doing so (Dijksterhuis & Bargh, 2001). If you see someone smile or frown, you briefly start to smile or frown also. Your expression may be just a quick, involuntary twitch, and an observer may have to watch carefully to see it, but it does occur. Similarly, people tend to copy the hand gestures they see. (You can demonstrate this tendency by telling someone, "Please wave your hands" while you in fact clap your hands. Many people copy your actions instead of following your verbal directions.)

Try It Yourself

Here is an even more surprising kind of imitation: Young adults performed a task in which different groups read different lists of words. After the study appeared to be over, the experimenters timed how fast the participants walked out of the room. Those who had just been reading a list of words like *gray, forgetful,* and *retired* that presumably reminded them of old people walked out of the room more slowly than the other participants (Bargh, Chen, & Burrows, 1996). In a similar study, students who had just been thinking about old people before filling out an attitude questionnaire expressed attitudes more consistent with their stereotypes of old people, such as supporting more government support for health care and opposing nudity on television (Kawakami, Dovidio, & Dijksterhuis, 2003). In effect the students conformed to the stereotype of the old people they had been thinking about!

In short, other people influence us constantly, even in ways we do not recognize. They influence us in two major ways: First, they provide us with *information* (or misinformation). For example, if almost everyone else is moving in the same direction, they might know something we don't. Second, people set *norms* that define the expectations of a situation. In much of our social behavior, we follow rules of politeness, such as "do not interrupt," "raise your hand if you want to speak," and "wait in line." In this module we encounter many examples of both informational and normative influences.

Conformity

Conformity means *maintaining or changing one's behavior to match the behavior or expectations of others.* The pressure to conform often exerts an over-whelming normative influence. For example, Koversada is a small, totally nudist city on the coast of the Adriatic (although people there sometimes dress for dinner at an elegant restaurant). If a first-time visitor walks around the city wearing clothes, other people stop and stare, shaking their heads with disapproval. The visitor feels as awkward and self-conscious as a naked person would be in a city of clothed people. Most visitors quickly undress (Newman, 1988).

If you exclaim, "I wouldn't conform," compare your own clothing right now to what others around you are wearing. Professors have sometimes reported the irony of watching a class full of students in blue jeans insisting that they do not conform to other people's style of dress (Snyder, 2003).

Conformity also serves informational functions, especially when we are not quite sure what we are seeing or hearing. One example is an illusion known as the **autokinetic effect:** *If you sit in a darkened room and stare at a small, stationary point of light, the point will eventually seem to move,* partly because of small involuntary eye movements that occur almost constantly. If some-

❚ People conform to one another in their clothing and other customs.

© Steve Thornton/CORBIS

561

one says, "I see it moving in a zigzag manner" or "I see it moving slowly in a counterclockwise direction," you are likely to perceive it the same way.

Conformity to an Obviously Wrong Majority

Early research suggested that people are most likely to conform their opinions in ambiguous situations that make it difficult to be sure of our own judgment (Sherif, 1935). For example, there are no absolutely right or wrong styles of clothing. In matters such as politics, religion, or the movement of a single point of light in a darkened room, the information we have is ambiguous, and we rely on other people's opinions to help form our own.

Would we also conform to opinions that were obviously wrong? To answer that question, Solomon Asch (1951, 1956) carried out a now-famous series of experiments. Asch assembled groups of students and asked them to look at a vertical bar, as shown in Figure 14.12, which was defined as the model. He also showed them three other vertical bars (right half of Figure 14.12) and asked them which bar was the same length as the model. As you can see, the task is simple. Asch asked the students to give their answers aloud. He repeated the procedure with 18 sets of bars.

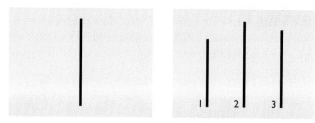

FIGURE 1.2 More than one third of psychologists work in academic institutions; the remainder find positions in a variety of settings. *(Based on data of Chamberlin, 2000)*

Only one student in each group was a real participant. All the others were confederates who had been instructed to give incorrect answers on 12 of the 18 trials. Asch arranged for the real participant to be the next-to-last person in the group to announce his answer so that he would hear most of the confederates' incorrect responses before giving his own (Figure 14.13). Would he go along with the crowd?

To Asch's surprise, 37 of the 50 participants conformed to the majority at least once, and 14 conformed on most of the trials. When faced with a unanimous wrong answer by the other group members, the mean participant conformed on 4 of the 12 trials. Asch (1955) was disturbed by these results: "That we have found the tendency to conformity in our society so strong . . . is a matter of concern. It raises questions about our ways of education and about the values that guide our conduct" (p. 34).

FIGURE 14.13 Three of the eight participants in one of Asch's experiments on conformity. The one in the middle looking uncomfortable is the real participant; the others are the experimenter's confederates. *(From Asch, 1951)*

Why did people conform so readily? When they were interviewed after the experiment, some said they thought the rest of the group was correct or they guessed that an optical illusion was influencing the appearance of the bars. Others said they knew their "conforming" answers were wrong but went along with the group for fear of ridicule. That is, they were subject to a normative influence even without any informational influence. The nonconformists were interesting too. Some were nervous but felt duty bound to say how the bars looked to them. A few seemed socially withdrawn. Still others were supremely self-confident, as if to say, "I'm right and everyone else is wrong. It happens all the time." Asch (1951, 1955) found that the amount of conforming influence depended on the size of the opposing majority. In a series of studies, he varied the number of confederates who gave incorrect answers from 1 to 15. He found that people conformed to a group of 3 or 4 just as readily as to a larger group (Figure 14.14). However, a participant conformed much less if he or she had an

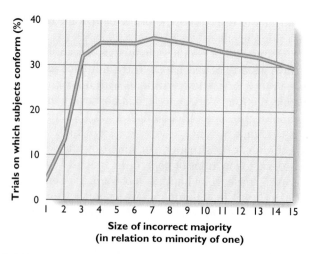

FIGURE 14.14 Asch (1955) found that conformity became more frequent as group size increased to about three, and then it leveled off. *(Adapted from "Opinion and Social Pressure" by Soloman Asch,* Scientific American, *November 1955. Copyright © 1955 by* Scientific American, *Inc. Reprinted with permission of the Asch estate.)*

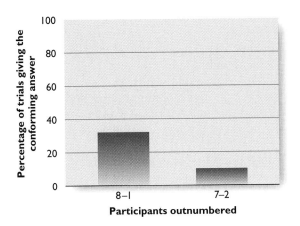

FIGURE 14.15 In Asch's experiments participants who were faced with a unanimous incorrect majority conformed on 32% of trials. Participants who had one "ally" giving the correct answer were less likely to conform.

Table 14.2 **Examples of Questions to Measure Collectivist Versus Individualist Attitudes**

T	F	I take pride in accomplishing what no one else can accomplish.
T	F	It is important to me that I perform better than others on a task.
T	F	I am unique—different from others in many respects.
T	F	I like my privacy.
T	F	To understand who I am, you must see me with members of my group.
T	F	I would help, within my means, if a relative were in financial difficulty.
T	F	Before making a decision, I always consult with others.
T	F	I have respect for the authority figures with whom I interact.

Note: The first four items measure individualism; the second four measure collectivist attitudes.
Source: From Oyserman, Coon, & Kemmelmeier, 2002.

"ally." Being a minority of one is painful, but being in a minority of two is not as bad (Figure 14.15).

CONCEPT CHECK ☑

22. Are you more likely to conform to a group when you are outnumbered 5 to 1, 10 to 1, or 10 to 2? (Check your answer on page 567.)

Cultural Differences in Conformity

Over the years since Asch's experiments, similar studies have been conducted in many countries. In the United States, most studies show a slight decrease in the amount of conformity since the 1950s. In most Asian cultures, the percentage of conforming answers tends to be relatively high, partly because people are trying to be polite and not embarrass the others by pointing out their error (Bond & Smith, 1996). That is, when researchers use the same procedure in different cultures, they may not be testing the same psychological processes.

Are people in certain cultures, particularly in southern Asia, in fact more prone to conformity as a general rule? The cultures of southern Asia, including China and Japan, are often described as more "collectivist" in contrast to the "individualist" cultures of the United States, Canada, Australia, and most of Europe. According to this view, Western culture encourages originality, competition, and individual freedom, whereas Eastern culture favors subordination of the individual to the welfare of the family or society. Originally, this contrast was based on observations of the Japanese during and shortly after World War II. However, Japan is a far different place today from what it was then. Acting collectively is a common response of any country when under attack or recovering from at-

tack (Takano & Osaka, 1999). After all, shortly after terrorists crashed four passenger planes on September 11, 2001, U.S. citizens showed a strong collectivist "we're all in this together" attitude.

Many studies have contrasted Japanese and U.S. attitudes, mostly using college students and relying on questions like those in Table 14.2. A few investigators have directly observed conformist, cooperative, and competitive behaviors in various countries. Most studies have found no significant difference between Japanese and American attitudes, and some have even found Japanese students to be slightly *more* individualistic than Americans (Bond, 2002; Oyserman, Coon, & Kemmelmeier, 2002; Takano & Osaka, 1999).

Some researchers therefore suggest that the "collectivist" notion is wrong, at least with regard to modern-day Japan (Takano & Osaka, 1999). Others point out that each country has multiple subcultures, and no generalization holds for an entire country (A. P. Fiske, 2002). Also, we need to measure collectivism or individualism more carefully and distinguish different aspects of each (Bond, 2002). For example, you can probably find fault with some of the items in Table 14.2. It is difficult to write questionnaire items that adequately measure cultural attitudes. In any case we should discard the simple, unqualified generalization that some cultures are more collectivist or conformist than others.

CONCEPT CHECK ☑

23. What is one possible explanation for why collectivism may have been a more prominent aspect of Japanese thinking in the past than it is today? (Check your answer on page 567.)

Accepting or Denying Responsibility Toward Others

Other people can encourage us to do something we would not have done on our own, as in Asch's studies. Other people can also inhibit us from doing something that we would have done on our own. We look around to see what others are doing—or *not* doing—and we say, "Okay, I'll do that too." Why do people sometimes work together to help one another and sometimes ignore the needs of others?

Bystander Helpfulness and Apathy

Suppose while you are waiting at a bus stop, you see me trip and fall down, just 10 meters away. I am not screaming in agony, but I don't get up right away either, so you are not sure whether I need help. Would you come over and offer to help? Or would you stand there and ignore me? Before you answer, try imagining the situation in two ways: First, you and I are the only people in sight. Second, there are many other people nearby, none of them rushing to my aid. Does the presence of those other people make any difference to you? (It doesn't to me. I am in the same pain, regardless of how many people ignore me.)

Late one night in March 1964, Kitty Genovese was stabbed to death near her apartment in Queens, New York. For 30 minutes, at least 38 of her neighbors listened to her screams. A few stood at their windows watching, but none called the police or helped in any other way. When interviewed later, several said they thought at first that it might be a lovers' quarrel. By the time they were sure it was a real attack, they assumed someone else must have called the police already. For detailed information, see:

**www.crimelibrary.com/serial_killers/
predators/kitty_genovese/**

Are we less likely to act just because we know that another person could act on the same information? Bibb Latané and John Darley (1969) proposed that being in a crowd decreases our probability of action because of **diffusion of responsibility:** *We tend to feel less responsibility to act when other people nearby are equally able to act.* Latané and Darley suggested that people ignored Kitty Genovese's distress because everyone knew that many other people *could* help her.

In an experiment designed to test this hypothesis, a young woman ushered one or two students into a room and asked them to wait for the start of a market research study (Latané & Darley, 1968, 1969). She went into the next room, closing the door behind her. There she played a tape recording that sounded as though she had climbed onto a chair and fallen off. For about 2 minutes, she could be heard crying and moaning, "Oh . . . my foot . . . I can't move it. Oh . . .

my ankle . . ." Of the participants who were waiting alone, 70% went next door and offered to help. Of the participants who were waiting with someone else, only 13% offered to help.

In a more recent study, investigators entered 400 Internet chat groups of different sizes and in each one asked, "Can anyone tell me how to look at someone's profile?" (That is, how can I check the biographical sketch that each chat room user posts?) The researchers found that the more people in a chat room at the time, the longer the wait before anyone answered the question. In large groups the researchers sometimes had to post the same question repeatedly (Markey, 2000).

▌ People watch other people's responses to help decide how they should respond. When a group of sidewalk Santas—who had gathered in Manhattan to promote a back-rub business—came to the aid of an injured cyclist, a few Santas made the first move and the others followed.

Diffusion of responsibility is one possible explanation. Each person thinks, "It's not my responsibility to help any more than someone else's." A second possible explanation is that the presence of other people who are also doing nothing provides information (or misinformation). At first the situation is ambiguous: "Do I need to act or not?" Other people's inaction implies that the situation requires no action. In fact the others are just as uncertain as you are, and they draw conclusions from *your* inaction. Social psychologists use the term **pluralistic ignorance** to describe *a situation in which people say nothing and each person falsely assumes that everyone else has a different, perhaps better informed, opinion.* Notice that the presence of other people exerts both normative and informational influences: Their inactivity implies that doing nothing is acceptable (a norm) and that the situation is not an emergency (information).

Social Loafing

When you take a test, you are required to work alone, and your success depends entirely on your own effort. In many other cases, however, you work as part of a team. For example, if you work for a company that gives workers a share of the profits, your rewards depend on other workers' productivity as well as your own. Do you work as hard when the rewards depend on the group's productivity as when they depend on your own efforts alone?

In many cases the answer is "no." In one experiment students were told to scream, clap, and make as much noise as possible, like cheerleaders at a sports event. Sometimes each student screamed and clapped alone; sometimes students acted in groups; and sometimes they acted alone but *thought* that other people were screaming and clapping too. (They wore headphones so they could not hear anyone else.) Most of the students who screamed and clapped alone made more noise than those who were or thought they were part of a group (Latané, Williams, & Harkins, 1979). Social psychologists call this phenomenon **social loafing**—*the tendency to "loaf" (or work less hard) when sharing work with other people.*

Social loafing has been demonstrated in many situations. For example, suppose you were asked to "name all the uses you can think of for a brick" (e.g., crack nuts, anchor a boat, or use as a doorstop) and write each one on a card. You would probably fill many cards by yourself but fewer if you were tossing cards into a pile along with other people's suggestions to be evaluated as a group (Harkins & Jackson, 1985). You probably wouldn't bother submitting ideas that you assume other people had already suggested.

At this point you may be thinking, "Wait a minute. When I'm playing basketball or soccer, I try as hard as

▌ During a catastrophe people abandon their usual tendencies toward bystander apathy and social loafing.

I can. I don't think I loaf." You are right; social loafing is rare in team sports. The reason is that observers, including teammates, watch your performance. People work hard in groups if they expect other people to notice their effort or if they think they can contribute something that other group members cannot (Shepperd, 1993; K. D. Williams & Karau, 1991). People also give full effort if it appears that the benefit to the group will be large compared to the cost to themselves (Goren, Kurzban, & Rapoport, 2003).

CONCEPT CHECK ☑

24. Given what we have learned about social loafing, why are most people unlikely to work hard to clean the environment?
25. In a typical family, one or two members have jobs, but their wages benefit all. Why do those wage earners *not* engage in social loafing? (Check your answers on page 567.)

Group Decision Making

An organization that needs to reach a decision will frequently set up a committee to look into the issues and make recommendations. A committee has more time, more total information, and fewer peculiarities and biases than any individual has. Research finds that a group generally makes better decisions than the average individual. However, the advantage of a group over an individual is often not as great as we might expect (Sorkin, Hays, & West, 2001). Groups sometimes rush to a decision, and many groups show social loafing. Some individuals conform to the majority opinion and discard their own, possibly better, opinions.

Group Polarization

If nearly all the people who compose a group lean in the same direction on a particular issue, then a group discussion will move the group as a whole even further in that direction. This phenomenon is known as **group polarization**. Note that it requires a fairly homogeneous group to begin with. If the group has several factions that disagree at the start, the effects are less predictable and harder to interpret (Rodrigo & Ato, 2002).

The term *polarization* does not mean that the group breaks up into fragments favoring different positions. Rather, it means that the members of a group move *together* toward one pole (extreme position) or the other. For example, a group of people who are opposed to abortion or in favor of animal rights or opposed to gun regulations will, after discussing the issue among themselves, generally become more extreme in their views than they had been at the start (Lamm & Myers, 1978).

Group polarization demonstrates both informational and normative influences (Isenberg, 1986). During the discussion, if most of the members were already leaning in the same direction, they hear new arguments favoring that side of the issue and few or none for the opposition (Kuhn & Lao, 1996). Also, as the members of the group become aware of the consensus during the discussion, the pressure to conform is especially powerful for those who do not feel fully accepted by the group (Noel, Wann, & Branscombe, 1995).

CONCEPT CHECK ☑

26. Is a jury more likely to reach a biased or extreme decision than a single individual would be? (Check your answer on page 567.)

Groupthink

One extreme form of group polarization is known as **groupthink,** when *the members of a group suppress their doubts about a group's poorly thought-out decision for fear of making a bad impression or disrupting group harmony* (Janis, 1972, 1985). The main elements leading to groupthink are overconfidence by the leadership, underestimation of the competitors or problems, and pressure to conform. Sometimes dissenters conform on their own; sometimes the leadership actively urges them to conform.

One dramatic example of groupthink led to the Bay of Pigs fiasco of 1962. President John F. Kennedy and his advisers were considering a plan to support a small-scale invasion of Cuba at the Bay of Pigs. They assumed that a small group of Cuban exiles could overwhelm the Cuban army and trigger a spontaneous rebellion of the Cuban people against their government. Most of the advisers who doubted this assumption kept quiet. The one who did express his doubts was told that he should loyally support the president. Within a few hours after the invasion began, all the invaders were killed or captured. The decision makers then wondered how they could have made such a stupid decision.

Groupthink often occurs in business decisions, especially in highly prosperous and successful companies. The leaders become overconfident and their critics become hesitant to speak up. For example, British Airways at one point discovered that 60% of its passengers were non-British. Its leaders therefore decided that it made sense to remove the British flag from the tailfins of the planes. This decision not only irritated the British public far more than the company expected but also outraged the employees who resented what seemed a pointless expense of £60 million to change

© Ali Meyer/CORBIS

❚ Many organizations try to resist the tendency toward groupthink, which stifles dissenting views. During the Renaissance, European kings sometimes called on a "fool" (or court jester) to describe some proposal in a fresh and possibly amusing light. In a court composed largely of yes-men, the fool sometimes was the only one who could openly point out the folly of a proposed action without fear of reprisals.

the company's logo at the same time the company was firing workers to save costs. By itself this decision was a small mistake, but it was part of a series of mistakes by British Airways executives at the time, who seemed to dismiss all criticism (Easton, 2001).

Groupthink is not easy to avoid. We generally admire government or business leaders who are bold, decisive, and confident. Groupthink occurs when they become *too* bold, decisive, and confident, failing to consider everything that could go wrong or failing to take the risks seriously. One strategy is for a leader to consult the advisers individually so they are not influenced by what they hear other advisers saying. A message for all of us is to be concerned when anyone in a position of power starts becoming too confident of success.

IN CLOSING

To Conform or Not?

Conforming to what others do is a good idea more often than not. For example, when we are on the road, it is safe to be surrounded by conformists who are willing to drive at the same speed as everyone else and on the same side of the road. Conformity is dangerous only when the group is doing something risky. However, even when we recognize a danger, for example, when people urge us to try drugs, it is seldom easy to resist the pressure to conform.

Summary

- *Types of social influence.* People influence our behavior by offering information (right or wrong) and by setting norms of expected conduct. (page 561)
- *Conformity.* Many people conform to the majority view even when they are confident that the majority is wrong. An individual is as likely to conform to a group of three as to a larger group, but an individual with an ally is less likely to conform. (page 561)
- *Diffusion of responsibility.* People in groups are less likely than an isolated individual to come to someone's aid because they experience a diffusion of responsibility. (page 564)
- *Social loafing.* People working together on a task tend to exert less effort than people working independently. However, people will work just as hard on the group task if they are evaluated on their individual performances or if they believe their contributions will make a big difference. (page 565)
- *Group polarization.* Groups of people who lean mostly in the same direction on a given issue often make more extreme decisions than most people would have made on their own. (page 565)
- *Groupthink.* Groupthink occurs when members of a cohesive group fail to express their opposition to a decision for fear of making a bad impression or harming the cohesive spirit of the group. (page 566)

Answers to Concept Checks

22. You would be about equally likely to conform when outnumbered 5 to 1 or 10 to 1. Any group of 3 or more produces about the same urge to conform. However, having even one ally decreases the pressure, so you would be less likely to conform when outnumbered 10 to 2. (page 563)

23. During and shortly after World War II, the people of Japan were under attack or recovering from attack. In that situation people of any country are motivated to work collectively. (page 563)

24. Social loafing is likely because many one-person contributions, such as picking up litter, would not earn individual credit or recognition. Also, each person thinks, "What good could one person do with such a gigantic problem?" (page 565)

25. The main reason is that the wage earners see they can make a special contribution that the others (children, injured, or retired) cannot. Also, their contributions are easily observed by the others. (page 565)

26. It depends. Group polarization would probably move a nearly unanimous jury toward a unanimous verdict. However, a jury that starts out divided would not experience group polarization. Most research has found that juries and similar groups are no more extreme than the average individual (Kerr, MacCoun, & Kramer, 1996). (page 566)

Why do people sometimes engage in self-defeating behavior?

In the 1960s world problems seemed to threaten the very future of civilization. The Vietnam War seemed to go on forever, the nations of the world were preparing for global nuclear war, racial injustice and other forms of discrimination were widespread, and we were beginning to recognize how terribly people were damaging the environment. As a high school and college student at the time, I had grandiose dreams of saving the world. I wasn't sure how, but I thought psychological research was a possibility. I hoped to somehow change human nature so that people would stop being so cruel and selfish.

Decades later, I reflect on the people who really did make the world a better place. Some made their impact through moral leadership, such as Martin Luther King Jr., Mother Teresa, Alexander Solzhenitsyn, and Nelson Mandela. However, many advanced the causes of peace and justice through technology—a route that I never even contemplated during my youthful "save the world" fantasies. For example, the engineers who devised spy satellites made possible the international treaties banning tests of nuclear weapons. (Without the capacity to watch one another, competing countries would never have agreed to the treaties.) The engineers who developed computers, printers, and modems spread freedom of the press, even in countries whose leaders did not want it. DNA testing has increased the accuracy of our criminal prosecutions and freed many people who were falsely accused. These technological advances changed human *behavior* without changing human *nature*.

The general point is that much of our behavior is controlled by the situation—sometimes the technological situation, sometimes the social situation. A situation can almost compel us to behave either in constructive ways or in uncooperative and self-defeating ways. We need to recognize the power of these situations so that we can avoid or change the most harmful ones.

What would you think of someone who knowingly paid a great deal more for something than it

was worth? Or someone who confessed to a crime even though the police admitted they did not have enough evidence for a conviction? Or someone who used all the available resources instead of saving some for later? You would probably question that person's intelligence or sanity. And yet, under certain circumstances, you would probably do the same. We can easily fall into a **behavior trap**—*a situation that coerces us into self-defeating behaviors.* We call such situations "traps" because people wander into them without realizing the danger. A simple example is being in a crowded theater when someone shouts "fire!" We all know we should file out calmly because a panic would jam the exits and no one could escape. In a real situation, though, we might decide that it is better to be among the first to panic than among the last! Therefore, a panic is

▮ A crowd of rock music fans can trample one another while trying to get close to the stage. Sometimes a situation becomes dangerous before people recognize the risk.

likely, no matter how many times we have been warned against it (Helbing, Farkes, & Vicsek, 2000). If you want to prevent panics in crowded theaters, don't tell people not to panic; build more exits. We shall consider four situations: escalation of conflict, the prisoner's dilemma, the commons dilemma, and obedience to authority.

Escalation of Conflict

Imagine that you, I, and a few other people are at an auction. The auctioneer explains that the next item up for bids is a dollar bill, to be sold to the highest bidder, even if the highest bid is only a few cents. There is one catch, however; at the end, when someone finally buys the dollar bill, the second highest bidder must pay his or her bid to the auctioneer also, receiving nothing in return. So, for example, if I bid 5 cents, you bid 10 cents, and the bidding stops there, you would buy the dollar bill for 10 cents and I would simply lose my 5 cents.

Suppose we plunge right in. I bid 5 cents, you bid 10, I bid 15, and so forth. Eventually, you bid 90 cents and I bid 95. Now what do you do? If you let me have the dollar bill for 95 cents, you lose 90 cents. So you bid $1, hoping to break even. What do I do? If I stop bidding, I lose 95 cents, but if I buy the dollar for $1.05, I sustain a net loss of only 5 cents. So I bid $1.05. Then you bid $1.10 because you would rather lose 10 cents than lose a whole dollar. The bidding continues. After a while, we start to become angry with each other. After all, as soon as one of us quits bidding, the other one will "win." Psychologists conducting such auctions usually manage to sell their dollar bills in the range of $3 to $5 and sometimes much more (Brockner & Rubin, 1985). As soon as the bidding goes over $1, bidders become increasingly distressed—sweating, trembling, sometimes even crying. (At the end of the experiment, the psychologists always return the money, although they had not promised to do so.)

The point of this study is *not,* "Here's a good scam you can use to make some quick money." The point is that if you get into a situation like this, it is hard to escape. Similar situations do arise in real life. For example, from the end of World War II until the Soviet Union collapsed in 1991, the United States and the Soviet Union devoted enormous sums of money to a weapons race. Critics often wondered whether the expenditures made sense. The reply was, "Having spent as much as we have already, we can't quit now and let the other side have more weapons than we do." Similarly, a manager who has already spent a fortune developing and advertising a product feels a need to continue developing the product because quitting would mean that the whole investment was wasted (Lant & Hurley, 1999). Perhaps you can think of additional examples. Note also the similarity of these examples to the sunk cost effect, mentioned in Chapter 8.

The Prisoner's Dilemma

Sometimes you have a choice between the action that seems best for you and one that seems best for your group. The most widely studied example is the prisoner's dilemma, *a situation where people must choose between a cooperative act and a competitive act that could benefit themselves but hurt others.* Let's start with the original version of this dilemma: You and a partner are arrested and charged with armed robbery. The police take each of you into separate rooms and ask you to confess. If neither of you confesses, the police do not have enough evidence to convict you of armed robbery, but they can convict you of a lesser offense with a sentence of 1 year in prison. If either of you confesses and testifies against the other, the confessor goes free and the other gets 20 years in prison. If you both confess, you each get 5 years in prison. Each of you knows that the other person has the same options. Figure 14.16 illustrates your choices.

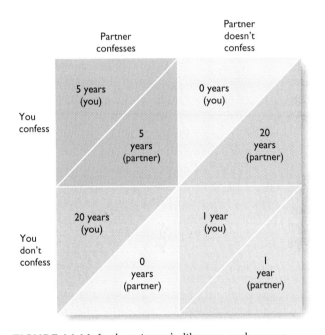

FIGURE 14.16 In the prisoner's dilemma, each person considering the choice alone finds it beneficial to confess. But when both people confess, they suffer worse consequences than if both had refused to confess.

If your partner does not confess, you gain by confessing because you will go free. (Your partner will get 20 years in prison, but let's assume you care mostly about yourself.) If your partner does confess, it is still to your advantage to confess because you will get only 5 years in prison instead of 20. So, you confess. Your partner, reasoning the same way, also confesses, and you both get 5 years in prison. If you had both kept quiet, you would each have served only 1 year in prison. The situation led you both to uncooperative, self-defeating behavior.

If you and your partner could have discussed your strategy, you would have agreed not to confess. Then, when the police took you to separate rooms, you would each hope that the other would keep the bargain. But can you be sure? Maybe your partner will double-cross you and confess. If so, you should too. And if your partner does keep the bargain, what should you do? Confess, of course! We're back where we started.

The two of you are most likely to cooperate if you can stay in constant communication with each other (Nemeth, 1972). If each hears what the other one says, you know that, if one confesses, the other will retaliate immediately.

The prisoner's dilemma can also be stated in terms of gains. Suppose you and another person have a choice between two moves, which we call *cooperate* and *compete*. Depending on your choices, here are the payoffs:

Here are the payoffs:

	Other person cooperates	Other person competes
You cooperate	Both win $1	Other person gains $2; you lose $2
You compete	You gain $2; other person loses $2	Both lose $1

Suppose you will play this game only once. The other person will answer by telephone, and the two of you will never meet. Which move do you choose? If the other person cooperates, your winning choice is *compete* because you will get $2 instead of $1. If the other person competes, again you gain by competing because you will lose just $1 instead of $2. Logically, you should choose to compete, and so should the other person, so you both lose $1. Here we encounter a classic behavior trap in which the situation logically leads people into self-defeating behaviors (Axelrod & Dion, 1988).

The strategy changes drastically if the two of you are going to play repeatedly. Unless you know what the other person will do, the recommended strategy is reciprocity, also called "tit-for-tat": Start with the *cooperate* move. If the other person cooperates too, then you continue to cooperate on later moves. If the other person makes a *compete* move, you retaliate with a *compete* move on your next turn. (Your retaliation should teach the other person not to try to take advantage of you.) You should refuse to play with anyone who is known to make mostly *compete* moves (D. S. Wilson, Near, & Miller, 1996). You can try this strategy and others at this Web site, where you compete against a computer opponent:

http://serendip.brynmawr.edu/bb/pd.html

This game is much more than a laboratory curiosity. First, it is a pretty good model of what happens in business deals, in which each person has to cooperate or the other person will retaliate. Second, it has implica-

tions for how human social behavior developed. From a biological standpoint, why should you ever cooperate with a nonrelative? A reasonable answer is **reciprocal altruism**: *You cooperate with someone who cooperates with you, or you help someone who may repay the favor later.* However, reciprocal altruism works only if you can keep track of who "cheats" by not helping in return. Therefore, reciprocal altruism and cooperative behavior in general require individual recognition. Otherwise, we could not distinguish between cooperators and cheaters. Reciprocal altruism—that is, cooperation—occurs mainly when people deal repeatedly with the same individuals and establish a reputation for cooperating or cheating. However, it also varies from one culture to another in ways that require further research to understand (Fehr & Fischbacher, 2003).

In species in which individuals cannot recognize other individuals, theoretically, reciprocal altruism should not develop. In fact altruism is rare in nonhuman animals.

CONCEPT CHECK ☑

27. Suppose you have been playing the prisoner's dilemma game as described, using the tit-for-tat strategy, and the other person has been cooperating on every move. When you get to the last move (so there will be no further chance to retaliate), what move would be best? Why? (Check your answers on page 574.)

The Commons Dilemma

Here is another case where people hurt themselves and others by considering only their own short-term interests (Hardin, 1968): In the **commons dilemma**, *people who share a common resource tend to overuse it and therefore make it unavailable in the long run.* The commons dilemma takes its name from this parable: You are a shepherd in a small village. Everyone shares one piece of land, called the commons. Ordinarily, your sheep graze on your own land, but when a few of them need a little extra grass, you can take them to the commons.

The village has 50 shepherds, and the commons can support about 50 sheep a day. So if each shepherd takes an average of one sheep per day to the commons, everything works out. Suppose a few shepherds decide to take several sheep per day to the commons to save the grass on their own land. Not to be outdone, other shepherds do the same. Soon the commons is barren and useless.

Social psychologists have simulated the commons dilemma in laboratory games. In one study college students were asked to sit around a bowl that contained 10 nuts (Edney, 1979). They were told that they could take as many nuts as they wanted whenever they chose. Every 10 seconds the number of nuts remaining in the bowl would double. The object of the game was to collect as many nuts as possible. The rational strategy is to let the nuts double every 10 seconds for a while and then let each participant occasionally harvest some. But most of the groups never made it past the first 10 seconds. The students simply plunged in and grabbed as many nuts as they could, immediately exhausting the resources.

Obedience to Authority

Another example of a self-defeating situation arises when people obey an authority who gives bad orders. Ordinarily, if a stranger ordered you to hurt another person, you probably would refuse. However, some situations can induce you to do something voluntarily that later leaves you feeling ashamed.

Decades ago psychologist Philip Zimbardo and his colleagues paid college students to play the roles of guards and prisoners for 2 weeks during a vacation period. The researchers set up the basement of a university building as a prison but gave the students only minimal instructions on how to conduct themselves. In this case the researchers gave no orders at all, although assigning people roles of prisoner or guard does have clear implications about how they were expected to behave. Within 6 days the researchers had to cancel the study because many of "guards" had become severely abusive toward the "prisoners," bullying them physically and emotionally (Haney, Banks, & Zimbardo, 1973). Why? None of these students were habitually cruel to others in everyday life. However, in this situation they could get away with cruelty, without any penalties or retaliation. Also, the students presumably inferred that cruelty was expected. After all, what would be the point of "playing prison" for 2 weeks while behaving politely? Although this is an interesting demonstration, beware of drawing strong conclusions, as no one has ever replicated the prison study. The results might be different with slight changes in instructions or procedure.

CRITICAL THINKING:
WHAT'S THE EVIDENCE?
The Milgram Experiment

A more extensive series of studies examined how people would react if an experimenter asked them to deliver shocks to another person, starting with weak shocks and progressing to stronger ones. At what point, if any,

would they refuse? This research by Stanley Milgram (1974) was inspired by reports of atrocities in the Nazi concentration camps during World War II. People who had committed the atrocities defended themselves by saying that they were only obeying orders. International courts rejected that defense, and outraged people throughout the world told themselves, "If I had been there, I would have refused to follow such orders" and "It couldn't happen here." What do you think? Could it happen here?

Hypothesis When an authority figure gives normal people instructions to do something that might hurt another person, at least some of them will obey.

Method Two adult male participants arrived at the experimental room—the real participant and a confederate of the experimenter pretending to be a participant. (They were not college students. The experimenters wanted results that would generalize to a broad population. They also wanted to minimize the risk that the participants would guess the true purpose of the experiment.) The experimenter told the participants that in this study on learning, one participant would be the "teacher" and the other the "learner." The teacher would read lists of words through a microphone to the learner, who would sit in a nearby room. The teacher would then test the learner's memory for the words. Whenever the learner made a mistake, the teacher was to deliver an electric shock as punishment.

The experiment was rigged so that the real participant was always the teacher and the confederate was always the learner. The teacher watched as the learner was strapped into the escape-proof shock device (Figure 14.17). The learner never received any shocks, but the teacher was led to believe that he did. In fact, be-

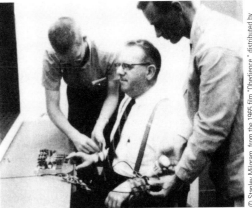

FIGURE 14.17 In Milgram's experiment a rigged drawing selected a confederate of the experimenter to be the "learner." Here the learner is strapped to a device that supposedly delivers shocks.

fore the start of the study, the experimenter had the teacher feel a "sample shock" from the machine.

At the start of the experiment, the teacher read the words and the learner made many mistakes. The teacher sat at a shock generator that had levers to deliver shocks ranging from 15 volts to 450 volts in 15-volt increments (Figure 14.18). The experimenter instructed the teacher to deliver a shock every time the learner made a mistake, beginning with the 15-volt switch and increasing by 15 volts for each successive mistake.

FIGURE 14.18 The "teacher" in Milgram's experiment flipped switches on this box, apparently delivering stronger and stronger shocks for each successive error that the "learner" made. The situation was designed to appear realistic, although the device did not shock the learner.

As the voltage went up, the learner in the next room cried out in pain and even kicked the wall. In one version of the experiment, the learner complained that he had a heart condition. If a teacher asked who would take responsibility for any harm done to the learner, the experimenter replied that he, the experimenter, would take responsibility but insisted, "while the shocks may be painful, they are not dangerous." When the shocks reached 150 volts, the learner called out in pain and begged to be let out of the experiment, complaining that his heart was bothering him. Beginning at 270 volts, he responded to shocks with agonized screams. At 300 volts, he shouted that he would no longer answer any questions. After 330 volts, he made no response at all. Still, the experimenter ordered the teacher to continue asking questions and delivering shocks. (Remember, the learner was not really being shocked. The screams of pain came from a tape recording.)

Results Of 40 participants, 25 continued to deliver shocks all the way to 450 volts. The people who did so were not sadists but normal adults recruited from the community through newspaper ads. They were paid a few dollars for their services, and those who asked were told that they could keep the money even if they quit. (Not many asked.) People from all walks of life obeyed the experimenter's orders, including blue-col-

lar workers, white-collar workers, and professionals. Most of them grew quite upset and agitated while they were supposedly delivering shocks to the screaming learner, but they kept right on.

Interpretation The level of obedience Milgram observed depended on certain factors that he injected into the situation. One was that the experimenter agreed to take responsibility. (Remember the diffusion of responsibility principle.) Another influence was that the experimenter started with a small request, asking the participant to press the lever for a 15-volt shock, and then gradually progressed to stronger shocks.

Figures 14.19 and 14.20 illustrate the results of a few variations in procedure that Milgram tried. For example, participants were more obedient to an experimenter who remained in the same room than to one who left. They were less obedient if they needed to force the learner's hand back onto the shock plate. If additional "teachers" divided the task—the other "teachers" also being confederates of the experimenter—a participant was very likely to obey if the others obeyed, but unlikely if the others did not.

FIGURE 14.19 In one variation of Milgram's standard procedure, he asked the teacher to hold the learner's hand on the shock electrode. This close contact with the learner decreased obedience to less than half its usual level; still, some teachers continued following orders to deliver shocks.

Still, the remarkable conclusion remains that, under a variety of conditions, many normal people followed orders from an experimenter they had just met, even though they thought they might hurt or even kill someone. Imagine how much stronger the pressure to obey orders from a government or military leader would be.

Ethical Issues Milgram's experiment told us something about ourselves that we did not want to hear. No longer could we say, "What happened in Nazi Germany could never happen here." We found that most of us do follow orders, even quite offensive orders. We

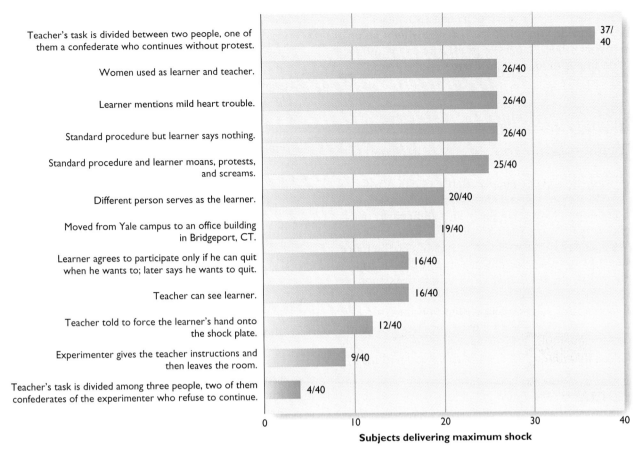

FIGURE 14.20 Milgram varied his procedure in many ways to find out what elements promoted or inhibited obedience. Division of responsibility increased obedience; an implication of personal responsibility decreased obedience.

are indebted to Milgram's study for this important, if unwelcome, information.

However, although I am glad to know about Milgram's results, I doubt that I would have enjoyed participating in his experiment. Most people were emotionally drained, and some were visibly upset to discover how readily they had obeyed orders to deliver dangerous shocks to another person.

Milgram's study prompted psychology researchers to establish much clearer and stricter rules about what an experimenter can ethically ask someone to do. Today, before the start of any psychological experiment—even the simplest and most innocuous—the experimenter is required to submit a plan to an institutional committee that can either approve or reject the ethics of the experiment.

If anyone today submitted a proposal to conduct research similar to Milgram's study, the local institutional committee would presumably refuse permission or require some changes in procedure. However, if the same rules had been in place *at the time* of Milgram's study, a committee might not have objected. Before the research, almost no one expected his results to

turn out as they did. Milgram asked various psychologists and psychiatrists to predict the results, and nearly all replied that only a rare psychopathic weirdo would press levers to deliver severe shocks. The distress experienced by so many participants underscores just how surprising Milgram's results were.

CONCEPT CHECK ✓

28. In what way did the obedience in Milgram's experiment resemble the foot-in-the-door procedure? How did it resemble Skinner's shaping procedure? (Check your answers on page 574.)

CRITICAL THINKING:
A STEP FURTHER
Modifying Obedience

Here is one version of the experiment that Milgram never tried: At the start of the experiment, we announce that the teacher and the learner will trade places halfway through the experiment so that the previous learner will start delivering shocks to the teacher. How do you think the teachers would behave then? What other changes in procedure can you imagine that might influence the degree of obedience?

Fix the Situation, Not Human Nature

If we want to prevent people from panicking when a fire breaks out in a crowded theater, the best solution is to build more exits. Similarly, it is difficult to teach people to behave productively in any of the behavior traps presented in this chapter. For example, the more shocks you have already given someone in Milgram's obedience study, the harder it is to quit. (As soon as you quit, you are taking responsibility for your actions, and you can no longer excuse what you have already done by saying, "I was just following orders.") In short, instead of just finding the right action to take in each situation, it is important to choose one's situations.

Summary

- *Behavior traps.* Certain situations pressure even intelligent people into self-defeating behaviors. (page 568)
- *Escalation of conflict.* In the dollar auction, the second highest bidder must pay the amount bid and receives nothing in return. If two people start bidding, it is difficult to stop. (page 569)

- *The prisoner's dilemma.* In the prisoner's dilemma, two people can choose to cooperate or compete. The compete move seems best from the individual's point of view, but it is harmful to the group. (page 569)
- *The commons dilemma.* If people can withdraw resources from a common pool while saving their individual resources, it is tempting to take as much as possible and therefore ruin the common pool. (page 570)
- *Obedience.* Many people obey the orders of a person in authority even if they believe their actions will injure someone else. They are less likely to obey if they can see the person who would be injured. They are more likely to obey if other people are following orders without protest. (page 571)

Answers to Concept Checks

27. If your identity is completely anonymous, you have something to gain and nothing to lose by choosing to *compete* on the final move—leaving aside issues of morality. However, if anyone will know your identity, it may be better to cooperate to protect your reputation as a cooperator. That reputation could help you the next time you play. (page 570)
28. In all three cases—Milgram's experiment, the foot-in-the-door procedure, and Skinner's shaping procedure—someone starts with a small, hard-to-refuse request and gradually builds up to bigger requests. (page 573)

Key Terms and Activities

Key Terms

actor-observer effect: the tendency to attribute internal causes more often for other people's behavior and external attributions more often for one's own behavior (page 540)

ambivalent sexism: an overt belief in equal treatment of the sexes joined with a lingering, often unstated belief that women should be treated differently (page 535)

attitude: a like or dislike that influences our behavior toward a person or thing (page 543)

attribution: the set of thought processes we use to assign causes to our own behavior and to the behavior of others (page 538)

autokinetic effect: the illusory perception that a point of light in a darkened room is in motion (page 561)

aversive racism: consciously expressing the idea that all people are equal, but nevertheless unintentionally discriminating against some groups (page 535)

bait-and-switch technique: the procedure of first offering an extremely favorable deal and then making additional demands after the other person has committed to the deal (page 548)

behavior trap: a situation that almost forces people into self-defeating behaviors (page 568)

bona fide pipeline: a task on which people alternate between looking at different kinds of faces, such as Black and White, and reading words that they need to classify as pleasant or unpleasant; investigators measure whether they respond "pleasant" faster after one kind of face or the other (page 537)

central route to persuasion: a method of persuasion based on careful evaluation of evidence and logic (page 544)

cognitive dissonance: a state of unpleasant tension that people experience when they hold contradictory attitudes or when their behavior is inconsistent with their attitudes, especially if they are displeased with this inconsistency (page 548)

commons dilemma: a situation where people who share a common resource tend to overuse it and therefore make it unavailable in the long run (page 570)

conformity: maintaining or changing one's behavior to match the behavior or expectations of others (page 561)

consensus information: comparisons of one person's behavior with that of others (page 538)

consistency information: observations of how a person's behavior varies from one time to another (page 538)

diffusion of responsibility: the tendency to feel less responsibility for helping when other people are around than when we know that no one else can help (page 564)

discrimination: in social behavior unequal treatment of different groups of people (page 534)

distinctiveness: observations of how a person's behavior varies from one object or social partner to another (page 538)

door-in-the-face technique: a method of eliciting compliance by first making an outrageous request and then replying to the refusal with a more reasonable request (page 547)

exchange (or equity) theories: theories maintaining that social relationships are transactions in which partners exchange goods and services (page 553)

external attribution: an explanation for someone's behavior based on the current situation, including events that presumably would influence almost anyone (page 538)

foot-in-the-door technique: a method of eliciting compliance by first making a modest request and then following it with a larger request (page 547)

forewarning effect: the tendency of a brief preview of a message to decrease its persuasiveness (page 547)

fundamental attribution error: the tendency to make internal attributions for people's behavior, even

when an observer sees evidence for an external influence (page 539)

group polarization: the tendency of a group whose members lean in the same direction on a particular issue to become more extreme in its views after discussing the issue as a group (page 565)

groupthink: a process by which the members of a group suppress their doubts about a group's poorly thought-out decision for fear of making a bad impression or disrupting the harmony of the group (page 566)

inoculation effect: the tendency of a persuasive message to be weakened if people first hear a weak argument supporting the same conclusion (page 547)

internal attribution: an explanation based on someone's individual characteristics, such as attitudes, personality traits, or abilities (page 538)

mere exposure effect: the tendency to increase our liking for everything and everyone that has become familiar (page 552)

peripheral route to persuasion: a method of persuasion based on such superficial factors as the speaker's appearance and reputation or the sheer number of arguments presented, regardless of their quality (page 544)

pluralistic ignorance: a situation where people say nothing and each person falsely assumes that everyone else has a different, perhaps better informed opinion. (page 564)

prejudice: an unfavorable stereotype; a negative attitude toward a group of people (page 534)

primacy effect: the tendency to be more influenced by the first information learned about someone than by later information about the same person (page 533)

prisoner's dilemma: a situation where people must choose between an act that is beneficial to themselves but harmful to others and an act that is moderately beneficial to all (page 569)

proximity: in social psychology the tendency to choose as friends people with whom we come in frequent contact (page 552)

reciprocal altruism: helping someone in the expectation that the other person will repay the favor, either now or later (page 570)

self-fulfilling prophecy: an expectation that alters one's behavior in such a way as to increase the probability of the predicted event (page 533)

self-handicapping strategies: techniques for intentionally putting oneself at a disadvantage to provide an excuse for an expected failure (page 541)

self-serving biases: attributions that people adopt to maximize their credit for their successes and to minimize their blame for their failures (page 541)

sleeper effect: delayed persuasion by an initially rejected message (page 544)

social loafing: the tendency to "loaf" (or work less hard) when sharing work with other people (page 565)

social perception and cognition: the process of gathering and remembering information about others and making inferences based on that information (page 533)

social psychologists: the psychologists who study social behavior and how individuals influence other people and are influenced by other people (page 532)

stereotypes: the overgeneralization of either positive or negative attitudes toward a group of people (page 534)

that's-not-all technique: a method of eliciting compliance whereby someone makes an offer and then improves the offer before anyone has a chance to reply (page 548)

Suggestions for Further Reading

Cialdini, R. B. (1993). *Influence: Science and practice* (Rev. ed.). New York: William Morrow. One of the most enjoyable and entertaining books in psychology. Take a copy with you for vacation reading.

Milgram, S. (1975). *Obedience to authority.* New York: Harper & Row. Describes Milgram's classic experiments on obedience.

Book Companion Web Site

Need help studying? Go to

http://psychology.wadsworth.com/kalat_intro7e/

for a virtual study center. You'll find a personalized Self-Study Assessment that will provide you with a study plan based on your answers to a pretest. Also study using flash cards, quizzes, interactive art, and an online glossary.

Check out interactive exercises on the companion site! These exercises will help you put what you've learned into action.

Your companion site also has direct links to the following Web sites. These links are checked often for changes, dead links, and new additions.

Implicit Association Test

https://implicit.harvard.edu/implicit/demo/

Test your own responses on the Implicit Association Test.

Groupthink: Theoretical Framework

choo.fis.utoronto.ca/FIS/Courses/LIS2149/Groupthink.html

This three-page series by Chun Wei Choo of the University of Toronto begins with an elaborate diagram showing the antecedent conditions and observable consequences of groupthink; pages 2 and 3 provide steps to minimize its development.

Social Psychology Network

www.socialpsychology.org/

This huge database includes more than 5,000 links to resources about social behavior.

Cross-Cultural Psychology

www.vanguard.edu/faculty/ddegelman/amoebaweb/index.cfm?doc_id=857

This page contains links to worldwide studies of cultural influences and culture differences.

Interpersonal Perception

nw3.nai.net/dakenny/interp.htm

David A. Kenny of the University of Connecticut, author of *Interpersonal Perception: A Social Relations Analysis,* offers an outstanding tutorial on the judgments that one person makes about another.

Prisoner's Dilemma

serendip.brynmawr.edu/bb/pd.html

Play the prisoner's dilemma game with a computer opponent. Try different strategies to see which works best.

 **Try It Yourself CD-ROM**
with Critical Thinking Video Exercises

Use your CD to access **videos** related to activities designed to help you think critically about the important topics discussed. For example, the video about implicit association relates to what you've learned in this chapter. You'll also find an easy portal link to the book companion site where you can access your personalized **Self-Study Assessments** and interactive **Try It Yourself** exercises.

PsychNow! 2.0

PsychNow! is a fun interactive CD designed to help you with the difficult concepts in psychology. Check out the Social Psychology section for the following topics that relate to this chapter:

Helping Others: the Kitty Genovese scenario, process of deciding whether or not to help, and scenarios of person getting/not getting help.

Attribution: choose reactions to situations, the attribution theory explained, and rate woman's and man's attributions.t know; didn't write this.>

Social Influence: moon/star exercise, watch a video of Milgram's experiment on obedience to authority, explore conformity in terms of the Asch experiment, and apply personal action decisions.

Attitudes and Prejudice: test your own beliefs, imagine people's responses, define attitudes, cognitive dissonance, prejudice, and stereotypes, and identify statements as representing belief, emotion, or action.

Aggression: take a contextual behavior quiz, explore an interactive analysis of "aggressive" behavior, and apply three perspectives on aggression to the Gulf War.

Environmental Psychology: casino environment and gambling behavior, six environments that determine behavior, and desk arrangements for different situations.

Abnormality, Therapy, and Social Issues

Over the past 4 months, George has injured several dozen people, most of whom he hardly knew. Two of them had to be sent to the hospital. George expresses no guilt, no regrets. He says he would hit every one of them again if he got the chance. What should society do with George?

1. Send him to jail.

2. Commit him to a mental hospital.

3. Give him an award for being the best defensive player in the league.

You cannot answer the question unless you know the context of George's behavior. Behavior that seems normal at a party might seem bizarre in a business meeting. Behavior that earns millions for a rock singer might earn a trip to the mental hospital for a college professor. Behavior that is routine in one culture might be criminal in another.

A protestor who spends years of his life picketing the White House in search of peace is statistically abnormal and puts himself at risk of harm. Still, most of us would not call him psychologically abnormal. Abnormality is hard to define.

Even knowing the context of someone's behavior may not tell us whether it is normal. Suppose your rich Aunt Tillie starts passing out money to strangers on the street corner and plans to continue until she has exhausted her fortune. Should the court commit her to a mental hospital and make you the trustee of her estate?

A man claims to be Jesus Christ and asks permission to appear before the United Nations to announce God's message to the world. A psychiatrist is sure that he can relieve this man of his disordered thinking by giving him antipsychotic drugs, but the man insists that he is perfectly sane. Should we force him to take the drugs, ignore him, or place his address on the agenda of the United Nations?

Abnormal Behavior: An Overview

What do we mean by "abnormal" behavior and how can we distinguish it from normal?

Students in medical school often contract what is known as "medical students' disease." Imagine that you are just beginning your training in medicine. One of your textbooks describes "Cryptic Ruminating Umbilicus Disorder": "The symptoms are hardly noticeable until the condition becomes hopeless. The first symptom is a pale tongue." (You go to the mirror. You can't remember what your tongue is supposed to look like, but it *does* look a little pale.) "Later, a hard spot forms in the neck." (You feel your neck. "Wait! I never felt *this* before! I think it's something hard!") "Just before the arms and legs fall off, there is shortness of breath, increased heart rate, and sweating." (Already distressed, you *do* have shortness of breath, your heart *is* racing, and you *are* sweating profusely.)

Sooner or later, most medical students misunderstand the description of some disease and confuse it with their own normal condition. When my brother was in medical school, he diagnosed himself as having a rare, fatal illness, checked himself into a hospital, and wrote out his will. (He finished medical school and is still doing fine today, decades later.)

"Medical students' disease" is even more common among students of psychological disorders. As you read this chapter and the next one, you may decide that you are suffering from one of the disorders you read about. Perhaps you are, but recognizing a little of yourself in the description of a psychological disorder does not mean that you have the disorder. All of us feel sad, nervous, or angry occasionally, and many of us have mood swings, bad habits, or beliefs that strike other people as odd. *A diagnosis of a psychological disorder should be reserved for people whose problems seriously interfere with their lives.*

Defining Abnormal Behavior

How should we define abnormal behavior? To try to be completely objective, we might define *abnormal behavior* as any behavior significantly different from the average. However, by that definition, unusually happy or successful people are abnormal, and severe depression would be normal if it became common enough. When we say "abnormal," we don't mean just "different"; we mean different in an undesirable way.

Another way to define abnormal would be to let people decide for themselves whether they are troubled. For example, someone who complains of feeling miserable has a problem, even if it is not apparent to anyone else. Fair enough, but what about certain people who insist that they do *not* have a problem? Imagine a woman who babbles incoherently, urinates and defecates in the street, insults strangers, begs for $1 bills and then sets them on fire, while claiming to be obeying messages from another planet. She reports feeling fine and does not

a

b

▮ What we consider normal or abnormal depends on the context. (a) People dressed as witches ski down a mountain as part of an annual festival in Belalp, Switzerland, in which dressing as witches is supposed to chase away evil spirits. (b) A woman walks through a public park carrying a large snake. We don't know why but "unusual" behavior is not necessarily a sign of psychological disorder.

■ Edvard Munch (1864–1944), *Self Portrait, The Night Wanderer*, 1923–24, Munch Museum, Oslo, Norway. The uncurtained windows and the bare room emphasize the feeling of loneliness and isolation.

regard herself as troubled, although most people would think she needs help.

The American Psychiatric Association (1994) defined abnormal behavior as any behavior that leads to distress (including distress to others), disability (impaired functioning), or an increased risk of death, pain, or loss of freedom. This definition presumably includes the woman just described. Its weakness is that it may be too inclusive. For example, when Dr. Martin Luther King Jr. fought for the rights of African Americans, he risked death, pain, and loss of freedom, but we regard his acts as heroic, not abnormal. Again, presumably, we want to limit our concept of "abnormal behavior" to conditions that are clearly undesirable.

CRITICAL THINKING:
A STEP FURTHER
What Is Abnormal?

How would *you* define abnormal behavior?

Cultural Influences on Abnormality

Each time and place has interpreted abnormal behavior according to its own worldview. People in the Middle Ages, for example, regarded peculiar behavior as a sign of demon possession that needed treatment with religious rituals.

In one culture in Sudan some years ago, women had low status and very limited rights; if a woman's husband mistreated her, she had no defense. However, people in this society believed that a woman could be possessed by a demon who caused her to lose control and scream all sorts of "crazy" things that she "could not possibly believe," including insults against her own husband (!). Her husband could not scold or punish her because, after all, it was not really she, but only the demon who was speaking. The standard way to remove the demon was to provide the woman with luxurious food, new clothing, an opportunity to spend much time with other women, and almost anything else she demanded until the demon departed. You can imagine how common demon possession became (Constantinides, 1977).

More examples: *Brain fag syndrome* is a psychiatric condition marked by headache, dizziness, eye fatigue, and inability to concentrate—a common complaint among high school and college students in sub-Saharan Africa (Morakinyo & Peltzer, 2002). You might ask your own professor to excuse you from a test tomorrow because of brain fag syndrome, but unless you live in sub-Saharan Africa, I doubt that your explanation will do you much good.

You have probably heard the expression "to run amok." *Running amok* is a type of abnormal behavior recognized in parts of Southeast Asia, where someone (usually a young man) runs around engaging in indiscriminate violent behavior (Berry, Poortinga, Segal, & Dasen, 1992). Such behavior is considered an understandable reaction to psychological stress, not a criminal offense. Does running amok remind you of anything common in North America or Europe? How about the celebrations that occur after a sports team wins a major championship? Like running amok, people often regard such wild displays as temporary responses to overwhelming emotion.

I do not mean to imply that brain fag, running amok, and demon possession are pretended. Presumably, those people are reacting to genuine stresses and problems. The point is that their way of reacting was

▌ Fans sometimes celebrate a major sports victory with a destructive rampage. In some ways this behavior is like "running amok"—it is an abnormal behavior copied from other people's example.

modeled on suggestions from others. For a Western-culture example, one Australian psychiatrist found three mental patients in one hospital who had cut off one of their ears. Assuming that this behavior must be a common symptom of mental illness, he contacted other psychiatrists to ask how often they had seen the same thing. They reported it was almost unheard-of. Apparently, when one patient in this hospital cut off his ear, the other two copied (Alroe & Gunda, 1995). (Why they copied is, of course, an interesting question.)

Suggestion is probably also a major influence in **dissociative identity disorder (DID)**, previously known as **multiple personality disorder**, in which *a person alternates among two or more distinct personalities, each with its own behavioral patterns, memories, and even name, almost as if each personality were really a different person.* Note that alternating among different personalities is *not* schizophrenia, although the media often mislabel it as such. We consider schizophrenia in Chapter 16, which treats in some detail four major categories of psychological disorders and the specific ways in which therapists treat them. Dissociative identity disorder was extremely rare before the 1950s, when a few cases received much publicity. Chris Costner White Sizemore was featured in the book and movie *The Three Faces of Eve*, written by her psychiatrists (Thigpen & Cleckley, 1957). Sizemore ("Eve") eventually told her own story, which was very different from her psychiatrists' version (Sizemore & Huber, 1988; Sizemore & Pittillo, 1977). A few other cases of dissociative identity disorder also received extensive publicity, such as the celebrated case *Sybil*, although one of the psychiatrists associated with that case later said he thought the author of the book about Sybil had greatly distorted the fact to improve sales of the book (Borch-Jacobsen, 1997). By the early 1990s, some ther-

apists were reporting many such cases. Why was this condition becoming so common?

A likely hypothesis is that overeager therapists notice minor symptoms and then through well-meaning questions, sometimes using hypnosis, suggest that the person might have an additional personality. At first, the person may have had only a small tendency toward different personalities at different times, but after a few therapy sessions, the dissociation becomes more severe (Lilienfeld et al., 1999). As mentioned in the last chapter, people often conform to the expectations of others, and an expectation of abnormal behavior can produce that abnormality in vulnerable people.

▌ Chris Sizemore, whose story was told in *The Three Faces of Eve*, exhibited a total of 22 personalities, including her final, permanent identity.

CONCEPT CHECK ✓

1. In what way might dissociative identity disorder resemble brain fag syndrome and running amok? (Check your answer on page 589.)

The Biopsychosocial Model

In Western cultures today, the predominant view is the **biopsychosocial model**, which emphasizes that *abnormal behavior has three major aspects: biological, psychological, and sociological.* Many researchers and therapists focus more on one aspect than another, but few deny that all three are important.

The *biological* roots of abnormal behavior include genetic factors, which can lead to abnormal brain development, excesses or deficiencies in the activity of various neurotransmitters or hormones, and so forth. Behavior can also be affected by brain damage, infectious diseases, brain tumors, poor nutrition, inadequate sleep, and the overuse of drugs, including nonprescription medications.

The *psychological* component of abnormality includes a person's vulnerability to stressful events. For example, people who are known to have been physically or sexually abused in childhood are more likely than others to develop psychological problems in adulthood (Johnson, Cohen, Brown, Smailes, & Bernstein, 1999).

Finally, the behavior must be understood in a *social* and cultural context. People are greatly influenced by how other people act toward them and what other people expect of them. Many people with strange behavior have disordered families or social networks.

Unfortunately, the agreement that abnormality depends on biological, psychological, and social influences doesn't tell us much about an individual case. For example, suppose you are a therapist and you meet someone who cries almost constantly. Before you begin treatment for depression, you need to rule out other possibilities, ranging from the recent death of a loved one to the presence of a brain tumor. Different people with apparently the same symptoms can have different underlying problems.

CONCEPT CHECK ☑

2. Of the three aspects of the biopsychosocial model, which one would be most prominent in explanations of brain fag syndrome and running amok? (Check your answer on page 589.)

Classifying Psychological Disorders

Any scientific study requires agreed standards for classifying information. If different psychologists conducting research on depression defined depression differently, chaos would result. That kind of chaos *has* sometimes occurred in psychology, and as a result psychologists have worked hard to establish uniform definitions and standards for diagnosis. One result is *a reference book called the **Diagnostic and Statistical Manual of Mental Disorders (DSM)***—now in its fourth edition and therefore known as *DSM-IV[1]*—which *lists the acceptable labels for all psychological disorders* (alcohol intoxication, exhibitionism, pathological gambling, anorexia nervosa, sleepwalking disorder, stuttering, and hundreds of others), including a description of each disorder and an explanation of how to distinguish it from similar disorders.

---

[1]A revised version is the *Diagnostic and Statistical Manual,* Fourth Edition, Text Revision, or DSM-IV-TR. The general principles are the same.

DSM-IV Classifications

The clinicians and researchers who use *DSM-IV* classify each client along five separate *axes* (lists). A person may have one disorder, several, or none at all. The axis that gets the most attention is *Axis I, clinical disorders.* Table 15.1 lists the major categories of disorder on Axis I.

Axis II, personality disorders and mental retardation, lists disorders that generally persist throughout life. *Axis III, general medical conditions,* lists physical disorders, such as diabetes, head trauma, or alcoholic cirrhosis of the liver. A psychotherapist does not provide treatment for Axis III disorders but needs to know about them because they influence behavior. *Axis IV, psychosocial and environmental problems,* indicates how much stress the person has had to endure. Stress can intensify a psychological disorder and thus affect the course of treatment. *Axis V, global assessment of functioning,* evaluates a person's overall level of functioning on a scale from 1 (serious attempt at suicide or complete inability to take care of oneself) to 100 (happy, productive, with many interests). Some people with a psychological disorder are able to proceed with their normal work and social activities; others are not.

Axis I Disorders

Most psychological disorders that are listed on Axis I have their onset after infancy and represent in some way a deterioration of functioning. Eating disorders and sleep disorders, which are listed on Axis I, have been mentioned in previous chapters. In Chapter 16 we shall concentrate on the most common Axis I disorders—anxiety disorders, substance-abuse disorders, and depression—as well as schizophrenia, a less common but often disabling condition.

As an example of an Axis I disorder, let's briefly discuss one that we haven't already considered and that we won't have occasion to discuss in Chapter 16: **attention-deficit disorder (ADD)**, which is characterized by *easy distraction from important tasks, impulsiveness, moodiness, and failure to follow through on plans* (Wender, Wolf, & Wasserstein, 2001). **Attention-deficit hyperactivity disorder (ADHD)** is *the same except with excessive activity and "fidgetiness."* Both are obviously a matter of degree, and it is often difficult to distinguish ADD or ADHD from normal high energy (Panksepp, 1998). (After all, how normal is it for a 6-year-old to sit still in school for hours at a time?) On the average, people diagnosed with ADD or ADHD have some minor abnormalities on brain scans, but no therapist relies on those to make the diagnosis (Giedd, Blumenthal, Molloy, & Castellanos, 2001; Ravizza & Ivry, 2001; Stefanatos & Wasserstein, 2001). For example, a well-behaved child with those brain abnormalities would not be labeled ADD.

TABLE I5.I Some Major Categories of Psychological Disorders According to Axis I of *DSM-IV*

Category	Examples and Descriptions
Disorder usually first evident in childhood	*Attention deficit hyperactivity disorder:* impulsivity, impaired attention *Tourette's disorder:* repetitive movements such as blinking, twitching, chanting sounds or words *Elimination disorders:* bedwetting, urinating or defecating in one's clothes *Stuttering:* frequent repetition or prolongation of sounds while trying to speak
Substance-related disorders	*Abuse of alcohol, cocaine, opiates, or other drugs*
Schizophrenia	Deterioration of daily functioning along with a combination of hallucinations, delusions, or other symptoms
Delusional (paranoid) disorder	Unjustifiable beliefs, such as "everyone is talking about me behind my back"
Mood disorders	*Major depressive disorder:* Repeated episodes of depressed mood and lack of energy *Bipolar disorder:* Alternation between periods of depression and mania
Anxiety disorders	*Panic disorder:* Repeated attacks of intense terror *Phobia:* Severe anxiety and avoidance of a particular object or situation
Somatoform disorders	*Conversion disorder:* Physical ailments caused partly by psychological factors but not faked *Hypochondriasis:* Exaggerated complaints of illness *Somatization disorder:* Complaints of pain or other ailments without any physical disorder
Dissociative disorders	Loss of personal identity or memory without brain damage
Sexual disorders	*Pedophilia:* Sexual attraction to children *Voyeurism:* Sexual arousal primarily from watching others undress or have sexual relations *Exhibitionism:* Sexual arousal from exposing one's genitals in public
Eating disorders	*Anorexia nervosa:* Refusal to eat, fear of fatness *Bulimia nervosa:* Binge eating alternating with severe dieting
Sleep disorders	*Sleep terror disorder:* Repeated sudden awakenings in a state of panic *Insomnia:* Frequently not getting enough sleep to feel well rested the next day
Impulse control disorders	Frequently acting on impulses that others would inhibit, such as stealing, gambling foolishly, or hitting people

In the United States, the ADD or ADHD diagnosis is applied to an estimated 3 to 10% of children, about 70% of them boys. Some of them "outgrow" the problem, but many have problems that persist into adulthood, impairing social behavior and job performance (Mannuzza, Klein, Bessler, Malloy, & LaPadula, 1998).

The causes are not known. Researchers have tentatively linked several genes to this disorder, but no one gene appears to have a strong relationship (Bakker et al., 2003; Faraone, Doyle, Mick, & Biederman, 2001; Ogdie et al., 2003). The environmental causes include fetal alcohol exposure, lead poisoning, epilepsy, sleep deprivation, emotional stress, and several kinds of mild brain damage (Pearl, Weiss, & Stein, 2001). In most cases the causes are unknown.

The most common treatment is stimulant drugs such as methylphenidate (Ritalin) (Elia, Ambrosini, & Rapoport, 1999). Stimulant drugs improve school performance and everyday behaviors (de Wit, Crean, & Richards, 2000; Jerome & Segal, 2001). However, the fact that stimulant drugs appear to help a given child should not be taken as evidence to confirm a diagnosis of ADD/ADHD. One study found that stimulant drugs increase the attention span even of normal children (Zahn, Rapoport, & Thompson, 1980).

Is it a good idea to prescribe drugs for so many young people? Psychologists disagree on this point. The idea of giving strong drugs to so many children is worrisome. In addition to or instead of drugs, psychologists recommend behavioral approaches to controlling ADD, such as controlling stress and distraction (Sohlberg & Mateer, 2001).

Researchers are trying to clarify exactly what they mean by "attention deficit." The problem is *not* simply a short attention span. Many ADD/ADHD children or teens can pay attention to a video game for hours. The problem lies more with controlling attention. Everyone, of course, has trouble paying attention to something that seems uninteresting, but people with ADD/ADHD have more trouble than others. They also have trouble restraining impulses, and following an impulse can interfere with controlling attention. Here are two tasks that measure impulsivity:

- **The Choice-Delay Task** Which would you prefer, a small reward now or a bigger reward later? Obviously, your answer depends on *how much* bigger and *how much* later. Most people with ADD or ADHD need a larger than usual incentive to choose the delayed reward (Solanto et al., 2001).
- **The Stop Signal Task** Suppose your task is to press a button whenever you see a circle on the screen, as fast as possible, but if you hear a "beep" shortly after you see the circle, then you should not press. If the circle and beep occur simultaneously, you can inhibit your urge to press the button. If the beep occurs after you have already started to press, it's too late. The interesting results are with short delays: After how long a delay could you still manage to stop your finger from pressing the button? Most people with ADD or ADHD have trouble inhibiting their response, even after short delays (Rubia, Oosterlaan, Sergeant, Brandeis, & v. Leeuwen, 1998; Solanto et al., 2001). To see for yourself go to http://psychology. wadsworth.com/kalat_intro7e, go to the student Web site, then to On-line Try It Yourself, and click on Stop Signal Task.

For links to many kinds of information about ADHD, visit this Web site:

www.add-adhd.org/

CONCEPT CHECK ☑

3. What are some possible causes of attention-deficit disorder?
4. Describe one of the behavioral tests used to measure deficits of attention or impulse control. (Check your answers on page 589.)

Axis II Disorders

Axis II of *DSM-IV* includes mental retardation and personality disorders, as listed in Table 15.2. If there is a distinction between Axis I and Axis II disorders, it is that Axis II disorders tend to be lifelong, whereas most Axis I disorders represent a deterioration of functioning. However, that rule has many exceptions. The main reason for distinguishing Axis II from Axis I is that Axis II disorders are generally less spectacular and less likely to be the main reason someone came to a therapist. By listing Axis II disorders separately, *DSM-IV* encourages the therapist to notice them. That is, a therapist fills out a diagnosis on Axis I and then comes to the question of what, if anything, to list on Axis II. It is possible to list "no diagnosis," but at least the therapist has to pause to consider the possibilities.

A **personality disorder** is *a maladaptive, inflexible way of dealing with the environment and other people*, such as being unusually self-centered. Some personality disorders are widespread; for example, one survey found that 5% of people had avoidant personality disorder, and about 2% each had paranoid and histrionic personality disorders (Torgerson, Kringlen, & Cramer, 2001). Most people with personality disorders do not complain about them or seek treatment, except when other people insist on it. Treatment is usually slow and difficult, as it implies changing someone's personality.

The Importance of Differential Diagnosis

In abnormal psychology, as in medicine, any diagnosis (identification) of a disorder requires ruling out other possibilities. For example, suppose someone says, "I feel unenergetic and pessimistic; I awaken often during the night; I don't have much appetite; and nothing brings me pleasure anymore." That description sounds very much like depression, but the same symptoms could be the result of a malfunctioning thyroid gland, a stroke, the side effects from certain medications, drug withdrawal, a grief reaction following the death of a loved one, nutritional deficiencies, or fatigue. Psychiatrists and clinical psychologists must learn to make a **differential diagnosis**—that is, *a determination of what problem a person has in contrast to all the other possible problems that might produce similar symptoms*. Only a therapist who understands the problem well can choose the best treatment.

Criticisms of DSM-IV

DSM-IV has helped standardize psychiatric diagnoses, but even its most loyal defenders admit it has flaws. Problems include the difficulty of distinguishing normal from abnormal and the question of whether *DSM-IV* is treating reactions to difficult situations as if they were mental illnesses.

Distinguishing Normal from Abnormal

Consider the sexual disorders such as *pedophilia* (sexual interest in children), *voyeurism* (sexual excitement from secretly watching others undress or have sexual relations), and *sexual masochism* (sexual pleasure from receiving pain). *DSM-IV* classifies each of these as a mental illness if it continues for at least 6 months. Obviously, it is arbitrary to say that 5 months of pedophilia is not a disorder but 6 months is. A more difficult question is whether an unacceptable sexual desire implies mental illness (Widiger & Clark, 2000). We can disapprove of something without calling it a mental illness. For example, we do not assume that all murderers are mentally ill.

TABLE 15.2 Some Major Categories of Psychological Disorders According to Axis II of *DSM-IV*

Category and Examples	Descriptions
Mental Retardation	Intellectual functioning significantly below average; inability to function effectively and independently
Personality Disorders	
Paranoid personality disorder	Suspiciousness, habitual interpretation of others' acts as threatening
Schizoid personality disorder	Impaired social relations and emotional responses
Schizotypal personality disorder	Poor relationships with other people; odd thinking; neglect of normal grooming. (Similar to schizophrenia but less severe.)
Antisocial personality disorder	Lack of affection for others; high probability of harming others without feeling guilty; apparent weakness of most emotions
Borderline personality disorder	Lack of stable self-image; trouble establishing lasting relationships or maintaining lasting decisions; repeated self-endangering behaviors
Histrionic personality disorder	Excessive emotionality and attention seeking
Narcissistic personality disorder	Exaggerated opinion of one's own importance and disregard for others. (Narcissus was a figure in Greek mythology who fell in love with his own image.)
Avoidant personality disorder	Avoidance of social contact; lack of friends
Dependent personality disorder	Preference for letting other people make decisions; lack of initiative and self-confidence
Obsessive-compulsive personality disorder	Preoccupation with orderliness and perfectionism. (Similar to obsessive-compulsive disorder, but less severe.)

Furthermore, every disorder varies in degree from mild to severe. Psychologists and psychiatrists do their best to make consistent diagnoses, but marginal cases call for difficult judgments. Therefore, any statistics about the prevalence of psychological disorders are somewhat uncertain. In one survey of a random sample of about 20,000 people in three U.S. cities, trained interviewers reported that about one fifth of all adults were suffering from a psychological disorder of some sort (as defined by *DSM*) and that close to one third had suffered from such a disorder at some point (Myers et al., 1984; Robins et al., 1984). A similar study 10 years later yielded somewhat higher numbers (Kessler et al., 1994), and a still later study found somewhat lower numbers (Narrow, Rae, Robins, & Regier, 2002). The discrepancies depend mostly on where the researchers draw the line between disordered and not disordered—that is, how many marginal cases are labeled as problems. All the surveys agree that the most common disorders are anxiety disorders, alcohol or drug abuse, and mood disorders (e.g., depression), as shown in Figure 15.1.

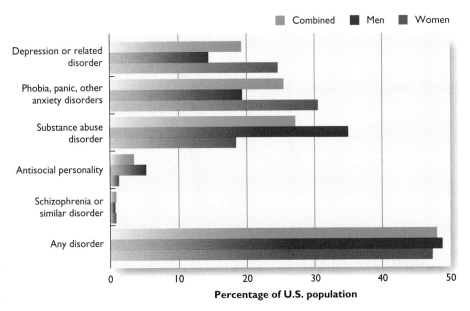

FIGURE 15.1 According to one extensive survey, about half the people in the United States will suffer at least one psychological disorder at some time. (The figures for the individual conditions do not add up to the total percentage for "any disorder" because some people have more than one disorder.) However, the exact percentages depend on where one draws the dividing line between "normal" and "abnormal." *(Based on data of Kessler et al., 1994)*

© Bob Daemmrich/The Image Works

❚ Almost everyone has an unpleasant mood or behaves strangely once in a while. Many people who qualify for a *DSM-IV* diagnosis are not very different from other people.

Is Abnormal Behavior in the Person or the Situation?

Another major criticism is that *DSM-IV* classifies understandable responses to difficult situations as if they were mental illnesses (Kutchins & Kirk, 1997). Suppose a child who is frequently bullied starts protesting vehemently against going to school, sometimes even vomiting on school mornings. Imagine a woman who has left an abusive relationship and is trying to restore her damaged self-esteem. It would seem pointless or harmful to give either of them the stigma of a psychiatric diagnosis. However, if a therapist diagnoses them as having anxiety disorders, the insurance company will pay for the treatment. Therefore, the authors of *DSM-IV* broadened the definitions of many disorders and described new disorders so that if you go to a therapist for almost any problem, you can receive a psychiatric diagnosis and your insurance company will pay for at least a few sessions of treatment.

CONCEPT CHECK ☑

5. Why should we be somewhat skeptical of all statistics about the prevalence of psychological disorders? (Check your answer on page 589.)

IN CLOSING

Is Anyone Normal?

DSM-IV gives both psychotherapists and researchers a way to use terms like *depression* or *phobia* in as consistent a way as possible. On the negative side, it encourages therapists to apply a psychiatric diagnosis, with its potential stigma, to almost anyone who seeks

help. Even someone who does not qualify for depression, anxiety disorders, schizophrenia, or substance abuse may qualify for a diagnosis of a personality disorder under Axis II.

According to the studies described in this module, about one third to one half of all people in the United States will have a *DSM-IV* disorder at some point in life. If those statistics are even close to accurate, the implication is obvious: Most of the people who qualify for a psychological diagnosis are not much different from everyone else. At some point in your life, you may have a bout of some kind of psychological distress. If so, remember that you have plenty of company.

Summary

- *Normal and abnormal behavior.* The American Psychiatric Association defines abnormal behavior as behavior that leads to distress, disability, or increased risk of harm. However, any definition of abnormal behavior has difficulties. (page 581)

- *Cultural influences on abnormality.* Every culture provides examples not only of how to behave normally but also of how to behave abnormally. (page 582)

- *Multiple causes of abnormal behavior.* Abnormal behavior is the result of various combinations of biological factors, early experiences, and learned responses to a stressful or unsupportive environment. (page 583)

- *The Diagnostic and Statistical Manual.* Psychological disorders are classified in the *Diagnostic and Statistical Manual of Mental Disorders, Fourth Edition (DSM-IV)*. This manual classifies disorders along five axes. Axes I and II contain psychological disorders; Axis III lists physical ailments that can affect behavior; Axes IV and V provide the means of evaluating a person's stress level and overall functioning. (page 584)

- *Axis I disorders.* Axis I of *DSM-IV* lists a wide variety of disorders, including anxiety disorders, substance abuse, and depression. (page 584)

- *Attention-deficit disorder (ADD) and attention-deficit hyperactivity disorder (ADHD).* ADD and ADHD are common diagnoses of a condition with a variety of causes, although usually the cause is unknown. Researchers have been trying to measure the attention and impulse-control problems to better specify the nature of the problem. (page 584)

- *Axis II disorders.* Axis II of *DSM-IV* lists mental retardation and various personality disorders. (page 586)

- *Personality disorders.* Personality disorders are stable characteristics that impair a person's effectiveness or ability to get along with others. Examples of personality disorders are excessive dependence on others and excessive self-centeredness. (page 586)

- *Differential diagnosis.* Psychiatrists and clinical psychologists need to learn to consider all the possible diagnoses of a given set of symptoms and to identify the correct one by eliminating all the other possibilities. (page 586)
- *Criticisms of DSM-IV.* In spite of the efforts of *DSM-IV* to provide clear guidelines, it remains difficult to distinguish between normal and abnormal. Also, *DSM-IV* has been criticized for labeling many people as psychologically disordered, when in fact they are reacting normally to an abnormal situation. (page 586)

Answers to Concept Checks

1. In each case people are reacting to real problems, but the way they react follows suggestions or expectations from other people. (page 583)

2. The social aspect would certainly be prominent because these disorders occur only in cultures that have made them seem like options. However, the people showing these symptoms may have biological and psychological problems as well. (page 584)
3. Possible causes include genetics, fetal alcohol exposure, lead poisoning, epilepsy, sleep deprivation, emotional stress, and mild brain damage. (page 586)
4. In the Choice Delay Task, the question is under what conditions someone will sacrifice a reward now for a larger one later. In the Stop Signal Task, one signal calls for a response and a second signal cancels the first signal; the question is under what circumstances a person can inhibit the response. (page 586)
5. Each disorder occurs in varying degrees, and the apparent prevalence of a disorder depends on how many marginal cases we include. (page 588)

15.2 Psychotherapy: An Overview

What methods are used to combat psychological disorders, and how effective are they?

Observation
If I don't drive around the park, I'm pretty sure to make my mark.
If I'm in bed each night by ten, I may get back my looks again.
If I abstain from fun and such, I'll probably amount to much.
But I shall stay the way I am, Because I do not give a damn.
—Dorothy Parker (1944)[1]

Psychotherapy is *a treatment of psychological disorders by methods that include a personal relationship between a trained therapist and a client.* But psychotherapy does little good unless the client gives the proverbial damn.

Psychotherapy is used for many well-defined disorders that are listed in *DSM-IV* and also for adjustment and coping problems. Some psychotherapy clients are virtually incapacitated by their problems, but others are reasonably happy, successful people who would like to function even more successfully.

Historical Trends in Psychotherapy

Psychotherapy has changed greatly since the mid-1900s for both scientific and economic reasons (Sanchez & Turner, 2003). Before World War II, almost all psychotherapists were psychiatrists. In the 1940s and 1950s, most therapists used Freudian methods and expected to see each patient frequently, perhaps even daily, for months or years. People who wanted therapy had to pay for it themselves, as almost no one had health insurance that covered psychiatric visits. (Most didn't have health insurance at all.) Therefore, few other than the wealthy received psychotherapy. At this time almost no research had been done concerning the effectiveness of psychotherapy, so clients had little choice but to trust whatever their therapists claimed. Some clients received a diagnosis such as depressed or schizophrenic, but many

were given either no diagnosis at all or a vague, almost undefined diagnosis like "neurotic."

Today all of that has changed, largely because health maintenance organizations (HMOs) and other health insurance programs will pay for mental health care, but only under certain conditions. HMOs try to restrain costs and make sure that money is spent effectively. If the man down the street pays for his own treatment, no one will object if he sees his therapist every day for the rest of his life. However, if his health insurance pays for the treatment, and you and I are under the same insurance program that he is, then we are helping to pay his fees. Suddenly, we and our insurance company want to know whether he needs that much treatment and whether the treatment is effective. Generally, insurance companies will pay for more treatment if someone has a diagnosed mental disorder. They limit the treatment to a moderate number of sessions and support only therapies that appear to be effective according to the best available evidence. The consequences have been, as you might guess:

- Therapists have listed more and more diagnoses of mental disorder so that more clients can qualify for insurance help. The previous module mentioned the huge number of diagnoses listed in *DSM-IV*, and now you understand why.
- Therapists have found ways to provide briefer and cheaper treatments, as we shall consider later in this module.
- Psychologists have conducted extensive research on the effectiveness of psychotherapy. Again, you will read about that research later in this module.
- Psychologists have made their treatment more systematic. Many follow published manuals that specify exactly how to treat various disorders.

Psychotherapists today employ a great variety of methods. Different therapists treating the same problem approach it in strikingly different ways. We shall review some of the most common types of therapy, exploring what they have in common as well as how they differ.

CONCEPT CHECK ☑

6. What is one major reason psychotherapists have added so many diagnoses to *DSM-IV*? (Check your answer on page 603.)

Psychoanalysis

Psychodynamic therapies *attempt to relate personality to the interplay of conflicting impulses within the individual, including some that the individual may not consciously recognize.* For example, both Sigmund Freud's procedure (looking for sexual motives) and Alfred Adler's procedure (looking for power and superiority motives) are considered psychodynamic despite the differences between them. Here we focus on the procedure developed by Freud, although its practitioners have modified and developed it further since Freud's time.

Psychoanalysis, the first of the "talk" therapies, is *a method based on identifying unconscious thoughts and emotions and bringing them to consciousness to help people understand their thoughts and actions.* Psychoanalysis is therefore described as an "insight-oriented therapy" in contrast to therapies that focus on changing thoughts and behaviors (Figure 15.2). Psychoanalysis was the dominant form of psychotherapy in the United States in the mid-1900s. Over the years it has declined in popularity and influence in the United States, although it remains more widespread in several European countries.

Freud believed that psychological problems result from unconscious thought processes and that the way to control self-defeating behavior is to make those processes conscious. Bringing them to consciousness, he thought, would produce **catharsis,** *a release of pent-up emotions associated with unconscious thoughts and memories.* Among Freud's methods of

A psychotherapist, like this military psychologist in a Haitian refugee camp, tries to help people overcome problems.

bringing unconscious material to consciousness were free association and transference. He also used dream analysis, as discussed in Chapter 5.

Free Association

In **free association** *the client starts thinking about a particular symptom or problem and then reports everything that comes to mind—a word, a phrase, a visual image.* The client is instructed not to omit or censor anything or even try to speak in complete sentences. The psychoanalyst listens for links and themes that might tie the patient's fragmentary remarks together. The assumption is that nothing happens without a cause, and every jump from one thought to another reveals a relationship between them.

Here is a paraphrased excerpt from a session of free-association:

> A man begins by describing a conference he had with his boss the previous day. He did not like the boss's policy, but he was in no position to contradict the boss. He dreamed something about an ironing board, but that was all he remembered of the dream. He comments that his wife has been complaining about the way their maid irons. He thinks his wife is being unfair; he hopes she does not fire the maid. He complains that his boss did not give him credit for some work he did recently. He recalls a childhood episode: He jumped off a cupboard and bounced off his mother's behind while she was leaning over to do some ironing. She told his father, who gave him a spanking. His father never let him explain; he was always too strict. (Munroe, 1955, p. 39)

To a psychoanalyst, the links in this story suggest that the man is associating his wife with his mother. His wife was unfair to the maid about the ironing, just as his mother had been unfair to him. Moreover, his

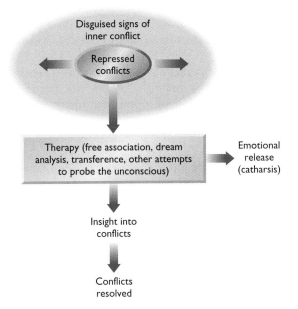

FIGURE 15.2 The goal of psychoanalysis is to resolve psychological problems by bringing to awareness the unconscious thought processes that created the difficulty. *Analysis* literally means "to loosen or break up, to look at the parts."

boss is like his father, never giving him a chance to explain his errors and never giving him credit for what he did well.

Transference

Some clients express love or hatred for their therapist because he or she reminds them of someone else. Psychoanalysts call this inappropriate reaction **transference**; they mean that clients are *transferring onto the therapist the behaviors and feelings they originally established toward their father, mother, or other important person in their lives.* Transference often provides clues to the client's feelings about that person.

Psychoanalysts offer **interpretations** of what the client says—that is, they *explain the underlying meaning*—and may even argue with the client about interpretations. They may regard the client's disagreement as resistance. For example, a client who has begun to touch on an extremely anxiety-provoking topic may turn the conversation to something trivial or may simply "forget" to come to the next session.

Psychoanalysts today modify Freud's approach in many ways. The goal is still to bring about a major reorganization of the personality, changing a person from the inside out, by helping people understand the hidden reasons behind their actions.

CONCEPT CHECK ☑

7. Name at least two methods psychoanalysts use to try to gain access to the unconscious mind. (Check your answer on page 603.)

Behavior Therapy

Behavior therapists assume that human behavior is learned and that someone can extinguish the learned response or learn a competing response. They identify the behavior that needs to be changed, such as a phobia or an addiction, and then set about changing it through reinforcement and other principles of learning. They may try to understand the causes of the behavior as a first step toward changing it, but unlike psychoanalysts, they are more interested in changing behaviors than in understanding their hidden meanings.

Behavior therapy *begins with clear, well-defined behavioral goals, such as eliminating test anxiety or breaking a bad habit, and then attempts to achieve those goals through learning.* Setting clear goals enables the therapist to judge whether the therapy is succeeding. If the client shows no improvement after a few sessions, the therapist tries a different procedure.

One example of behavior therapy is for children who wet the bed long after the usual age of toilet training. Most of them outgrow the problem, but it occasionally lingers to age 5, 10, or even into the teens. Many bedwetters have small bladders and thus have difficulty getting through the night without urinating. Also, many are unusually deep sleepers who do not wake up when they need to urinate (Stegat, 1975).

The most effective procedure uses classical conditioning to train the child to wake up at night when the bladder is full (Houts, Berman, & Abramson, 1994). A small battery-powered device is attached to the child's underwear at night (Figure 15.3). When the child urinates, the device detects the moisture and produces a pulsing vibration that awakens the child. (Alternative

FIGURE 15.3 A small device called a Potty Pager fits into a child's underwear and produces a vibration when it becomes moist. This awakens the child, who then learns to awaken when the bladder is full.

Courtesy of Ideas for Living, Inc.

devices work on the same principle but produce loud noises.) The vibration acts as an unconditioned stimulus (UCS) that evokes the unconditioned response (UCR) of waking up. In this instance the body itself generates the conditioned stimulus (CS): the sensation produced by a full bladder (Figure 15.4). Whenever that sensation is present, it serves as a signal that the vibration is imminent. After a few pairings (or more), the sensation of a full bladder is enough to wake the child.

Actually, the situation is a little more complicated because the child is positively reinforced with praise for waking up to use the toilet. Thus, the process includes both classical and operant conditioning. Training with an alarm or vibration eliminates bedwetting in most children, sometimes after as little as one night.

CONCEPT CHECK ☑

8. Contrast the goals and methods of behavior therapy with those of psychoanalysis. (Check your answer on page 603.)

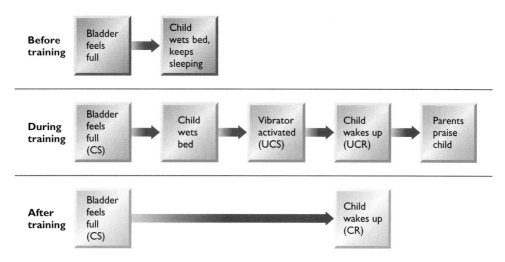

FIGURE 15.4 A child can be trained not to wet the bed by using classical conditioning techniques. At first, the sensation of a full bladder (the CS) produces no response, and the child wets the bed. This causes a vibration or other alarm (the UCS), and the child wakes up (the UCR). By associating the sensation of a full bladder with a vibration, the child soon begins waking up to the sensation of a full bladder alone and will not wet the bed.

Therapies That Focus on Thoughts and Beliefs

Suppose someone asks for your opinion on something and then asks someone else also. How do you react? You might think, "It's perfectly reasonable to get several opinions." Or you might feel hurt by the implication that your opinion wasn't trusted, wasn't good enough. Suppose someone invites several of your friends to a party but not you. Do you shrug your shoulders or do you take it as an insult? Your emotions depend not just on the events of life but on how you interpret them. Some therapists focus on the thoughts and beliefs that underlie emotional reactions. Unlike psychoanalysts, these therapists are more concerned about what their clients are thinking right now than about the early experiences that led to those thoughts.

Cognitive Therapies

Cognitive therapy *seeks to improve people's psychological well-being by changing their thoughts and beliefs—their cognitions* (Beck, 1976; Hollon & Beck, 1979). A cognitive therapist works to identify distressing thoughts and encourages the client to explore the evidence behind them. Usually, the client discovers that the beliefs are unjustified. Cognitive therapy also encourages people to monitor their daily activities and determine which ones provide opportunities for pleasure or a sense of accomplishment. The therapist helps the client overcome specific problems, such as poor social skills, and take a more active role in life.

(We shall discuss cognitive therapy for depression in Chapter 16.)

A related approach, **rational-emotive behavior therapy,** *assumes that thoughts (rationality) lead to emotions. The problem therefore is not the unpleasant emotions themselves, but the irrational thoughts that lead to them.* Rational-emotive therapists believe that abnormal behavior often results from irrational "internal sentences" such as these (Ellis, 1987):

- I must perform certain tasks successfully.
- I must perform well at all times.
- I must have the approval of certain people at all times.
- Others must treat me fairly and with consideration.
- I must live under easy, gratifying conditions.

The word *must* makes these beliefs irrational. Rational-emotive therapists try to identify irrational beliefs (which people may never have verbalized) and then contradict them. They urge clients to substitute other more realistic internal sentences. Here is an excerpt from a rational-emotive therapy session with a 25-year-old physicist:

Client: The whole trouble is that I am really a phony. I am living under false pretenses. And the longer it goes on, the more people praise me and make a fuss over my accomplishments, the worse I feel.

Therapist: What do you mean you are a phony? I thought that you told me, during our last session, that your work has been examined at another laboratory and that some of the people there think your ideas are of revolutionary importance.

Client: But I have wasted so much time. I could be doing very much better. . . . Remember that book I told you I was writing . . . it's been three weeks now since I've spent any time on it. And this is simple stuff that I should be able to do with my left hand while I am writing a technical paper with my right. I have heard Bob Oppenheimer reel off stuff extemporaneously to a bunch of newspaper reporters that is twice as good as what I am mightily laboring on in this damned book!

Therapist: Perhaps so. And perhaps you're not quite as good—yet—as Oppenheimer or a few other outstanding people in your field. But the real point, it seems to me, is that . . . here you are, at just twenty-five, with a Ph.D. in a most difficult field, with an excellent job, much good work in process, and what well may be a fine professional paper and a good popular book also in progress. And just because you're not another Oppenheimer or Einstein quite yet, you're savagely berating yourself.

Client: Well, shouldn't I be doing much better than I am?

Therapist: No, why the devil should you? As far as I can see, you are not doing badly at all. But your major difficulty—the main cause of your present unhappiness—is your utterly perfectionistic criteria for judging your performance. (Ellis & Harper, 1961, pp. 99–100)

CONCEPT CHECK ☑

9. How does the concept behind rational-emotive therapy compare to the James-Lange theory of emotions discussed in Chapter 12? (Check your answer on page 603.)

Cognitive-Behavior Therapy

Many therapists combine important features of both behavior therapy and cognitive therapy to form **cognitive-behavior therapy.** Cognitive-behavior therapists *set explicit goals for changing people's behavior, but they place more emphasis than most behavior therapists do on changing people's interpretation of their situation.* For example, most of us become very upset if we see a video news report showing a fatal automobile accident; we would be much less upset if someone told us that the film was a special-effects simulation (Meichenbaum, 1995). Similarly, cognitive-behavior therapists try to help clients distinguish between serious problems and imagined or exaggerated problems. They help clients change their interpretations of past events, current concerns, and future possibilities. Cognitive-behavior therapy has become one of

▌ Fictional tragedies in films, like the one in *Con Air,* are far less disturbing than real ones. The impact of any event depends not just on the event itself but also on its context and how we interpret it.

the most widespread forms of therapy in the United States.

Humanistic Therapy

As we saw in Chapter 13, humanistic psychologists believe that people can decide deliberately what kind of person to be and that we naturally strive to achieve our full potential. However, people sometimes learn to dislike themselves because others criticize and reject them. They become distressed by the **incongruence** *(mismatch) between their perceptions of their real self and their ideal self.* According to humanistic therapists, once people are freed from the inhibiting influences of a rejecting society, they can solve their own problems.

The best-known version of humanistic therapy is **person-centered therapy,** pioneered by Carl Rogers, which is also known as *nondirective* or *client-centered* therapy. *The therapist listens to the client with total acceptance and unconditional positive regard.* Most of the time, the therapist paraphrases what the client has said to clarify it, thus conveying the message, "I'm trying to understand your experience from your point of view." The therapist strives to be genuine, empathic, and caring, rarely offering any interpretation or advice. Here is an example (shortened from Rogers, 1951, pp. 46–47):

Client: I've never said this before to anyone. This is a terrible thing to say, but if I could just find some glorious cause that I could give my life for I would be happy. I guess maybe I haven't the guts—or the strength—to kill myself—and I just don't want to live.

Counselor: At the present time things look so black to you that you can't see much point in living.

Client: Yes. I wish people hated me, because then I could turn away from them and could blame them. But no, it is all in my hands. I either fight whatever it is that holds me in this terrible conflict, or retreat clear back to the security of my dream world where I could do things, have clever friends, be a pretty wonderful sort of person.

Counselor: It's really a tough struggle, digging into this like you are, and at times the shelter of your dream world looks more attractive and comfortable.

Client: My dream world or suicide.

Counselor: Your dream world or something more permanent than dreams.

Client: Yes. (A long pause. Complete change of voice.) So I don't see why I should waste your time. I'm not worth it. What do you think?

Counselor: It's up to you, Gil. It isn't wasting my time. I'd be glad to see you, whenever you come, but it's how you feel about it. If you want to come twice a week, once a week, it's up to you.

Client: You're not going to suggest that I come in oftener? You're not alarmed and think I ought to come in every day until I get out of this?

Counselor: I believe you are able to make your own decision. I'll see you whenever you want to come.

Client: I don't believe you are alarmed about . . . I see. I may be afraid of myself, but you aren't afraid for me.

The therapist provides an atmosphere in which the client can freely explore feelings of guilt, anxiety, and hostility. By accepting the client's feelings, the therapist conveys the message, "You can make your own decisions. Now that you are more aware of certain problems, you can deal with them constructively yourself." Few therapists today rely purely on person-centered therapy, but most users of other therapy methods have adopted its emphasis on the close, caring, honest relationship between therapist and client (Hill & Nakayama, 2000).

CONCEPT CHECK ☑

10. Answer the following questions with reference to psychoanalysis, cognitive therapy, humanistic therapy, and behavior therapy.
   a. With which type of therapy is the therapist least likely to offer advice and interpretations of behavior?
   b. Which type focuses more on changing what people do than on exploring what they think?
   c. Which two types of therapy try to change what people think? (Check your answers on page 603.)

Family Systems Therapy

In **family systems therapy,** *the guiding assumptions are that most people's problems develop in a family setting and that the best way to deal with them is to improve family relationships and communication.* Family systems therapy is not an alternative to other forms of therapy; a family therapist can use behavior therapy, cognitive therapy, or other techniques. What distinguishes family therapists is that they prefer to talk with two or more members of a family together. Even when they do talk with just one person, they focus on how that individual fits into the family and how other family members react to him or her. Solving the problem requires changing the family dynamics as well as any individual's behavior (Clarkin & Carpenter, 1995; Rohrbaugh, Shoham, Spungen, & Steinglass, 1995).

For example, a young woman with anorexia nervosa (as described in Chapter 10) may have excessively demanding parents or other family difficulties. Treating only the woman with anorexia would be pointless. A therapist needs to enlist her parents' help to monitor her eating without blame, criticism, or dominance (Eisler et al., 2000).

▌ Family therapists treat anorexia nervosa by trying to get the parents to supervise the patient's feeding, but without criticism or blame.

For another example, a young man who had been caught stealing a car was taken to a family therapist who asked to talk with the parents as well. As it turned out, the father had been a heavy drinker until his boss pressured him to quit drinking and join Alcoholics Anonymous. Until then the mother had made most of the family decisions in close consultation with her son, who had become almost a substitute husband. When the father quit drinking, he began to resume his authority within the family, and his son came to resent him. The mother felt less needed and grew depressed. Each member of the family had problems that they could not resolve separately. The therapist worked to help the father improve his relationship with both his son and his wife and to help all three find satisfying roles within the family (Foley, 1984).

Other Trends in Psychotherapy

Hundreds of types of therapy are available, including some that are quite different from the five discussed thus far (see Table 15.3). About half of all U.S. psychotherapists profess no strong allegiance to any single form of therapy. Instead, they practice **eclectic therapy,** meaning that they *use a combination of methods and approaches.* An eclectic therapist might use behavior therapy with one client and rational-emotive therapy with another or else start with one therapy and then shift to another if the first is ineffective. The therapist would probably borrow insights from several approaches, including person-centered therapy's emphasis on a caring relationship between therapist and client. Today, most therapists regard themselves as eclectic (Wachtel, 2000).

Because health insurance companies insist on limiting costs, psychotherapists have sought methods for quick and inexpensive help, such as brief therapy and group therapy. Self-help groups provide a no-cost alternative.

Brief Therapy

Some types of psychotherapy require a major commitment of time and money. You might see a therapist for a 50-minute session once a week, perhaps three to five times a week with psychoanalysis. The cost of each session varies, but it is seldom cheap. A physician who sees many patients per hour—a dermatologist, for example—might charge a moderate amount per visit, but a therapist who sees just one person per hour charges more. If the therapy will continue "as long as necessary," it might drag on for years.

However, most clients do not need such prolonged treatment. About half of all people who enter psychotherapy show significant improvement within 8 sessions, and three fourths improve within 26 sessions (Howard, Kopta, Krause, & Orlinsky, 1986). Insurance companies will pay for only a limited number of sessions.

TABLE 15.3 Comparison of Five Types of Psychotherapy

Type of Psychotherapy	Theory of What Causes Psychological Disorders	Goal of Treatment	Therapeutic Methods	Role of Therapist
Psychoanalysis	Unconscious thoughts and motivations	To bring unconscious thoughts to consciousness to achieve insight	Free association, dream analysis, and other methods of probing the unconscious mind	To interpret associations
Cognitive therapies	Irrational beliefs and unrealistic goals	To establish realistic goals, expectations, and interpretations of a situation	Dialog with the therapist	To help the client reexamine assumptions
Humanistic (person-centered) therapy	Reactions to a rejecting society; incongruence between self-concept and ideal self	To enable client to make personal decisions; to promote self-acceptance	Client-centered interviews	To focus the client's attention; to provide unconditional positive regard
Behavior therapy	Learned inappropriate maladaptive behaviors	To change behaviors	Positive reinforcement and other learning techniques	To develop, direct, and evaluate the behavior therapy program
Family system therapy	Distorted communication and confused roles within a family	To improve the life of each individual by improving functioning of the family	Counseling sessions with the whole family or with the individual talking about life in the family	To promote better family communication and understanding

As a result many therapists place limits on the duration of therapy. At the start of **brief therapy**, or *time-limited therapy, the therapist and client reach an agreement about what they can expect from each other and how long the treatment will last*—such as once per week for 2 months (Koss & Butcher, 1986). The therapy focuses on using the client's existing strengths to overcome difficulties. As the deadline approaches, both therapist and client are strongly motivated to reach a successful conclusion. (The same issue arose in the motivation chapter. Without deadlines, few people apply themselves diligently.)

Moreover, with a deadline that's agreed on in advance, clients do not feel deserted or rejected when the therapy ends. They may return for an occasional extra session months later, but for a time they must get along without help. Any client who fails to make progress by the deadline should consider going to a different therapist. Most clients with mild problems respond well to brief therapy.

Unfortunately, however, many HMOs have insisted on extremely brief therapy, in some cases as few as three sessions. Even a few sessions can be better than none, so the HMOs do make help available for many distressed people (Hoyt & Austad, 1992). However, many need more help than their insurance provides. Economically speaking, it is of course impossible to maximize the quality of care and minimize the cost at the same time. Working out a cost-effective solution is a serious challenge.

Group Therapy

The pioneers of psychotherapy saw their clients individually. Individual psychotherapy has advantages, such as privacy. However, therapists today frequently treat clients in groups. **Group therapy** *is administered to a group of people all at once*. It first became popular as a method of providing help to people who could not afford individual sessions. (Spreading the costs among five to ten people reduces the cost for each.) Eventually, therapists found that group therapy has other advantages as well. Just meeting other people with similar problems can be reassuring. People learn, "I am not so odd after all." Also, many clients seek help because of failed relationships or because they have trouble dealing with other people. A group therapy session enables them to examine how they relate to others, to practice better social skills, and to receive feedback from a variety of people (Ballinger & Yalom, 1995).

(Consider an analogy to education. Would you prefer your professor to teach you privately instead of in a large class? Perhaps so, but the cost of your tuition would sky-rocket. Besides, discussions with your fellow students are a valuable part of your education.)

Self-Help Groups

A **self-help group**, such as Alcoholics Anonymous, *operates much like group therapy, except without a therapist*. Each participant both gives and receives help. People who have experienced a problem themselves can offer special insights to others with the same problem. They are especially well prepared when someone says, "You just don't understand." They reply, "Oh, yes, we do!" Self-help groups have another advantage: The members are available whenever someone needs help, without an appointment and without charge.

Some self-help groups are composed of current or former mental patients. The members feel a need to talk to others who have gone through a similar experience, either in addition to or instead of seeing a therapist. For example, the Mental Patients' Association in Canada consists of former patients who were frustrated about their treatment (or lack of treatment) in mental hospitals (Chamberlin, 1978). Members share

a   © Richard T. Nowitz/CORBIS

b   © Getty Images

▌ (a) Individual therapy offers complete privacy and the opportunity to pursue individual problems in depth. (b) In group therapy participants can explore their ways of relating to other people.

experiences, provide support, and work together to defend the rights and welfare of mental patients.

The ultimate in self-help is to deal with your own problems without any therapist or group. In a series of studies, James Pennebaker and his colleagues have found that people with mild problems can do themselves an amazing amount of good just by organizing their thoughts about their emotional difficulties. Research participants have been randomly assigned to two groups. One group writes about their intense and difficult emotional experiences for 15 minutes on 3 or more days; the other group spends the same time writing about unemotional events. The people writing about their emotions consistently show improved mental and physical health over the next few months, especially those with much variation and flexibility in what they write (Campbell & Pennebaker, 2003; Pennebaker & Seagal, 1999). Apparently, writing about a difficult experience helps people to make sense of it and eventually put it behind them. In many cases writing about emotions prompts people to make decisions and change their way of life. In short, for mild problems you might be a good therapist for yourself.

CONCEPT CHECK ✓

11. Brief therapy is a goal or policy for many therapists. Why would it be less important in self-help groups? (Check your answer on page 603.)

CRITICAL THINKING:
WHAT'S THE EVIDENCE?
How Effective Is Psychotherapy?

The rise of HMOs and other insurance programs heightened interest in measuring the effectiveness of psychotherapy. Hans Eysenck (1952) pointed out that most of the people who receive no therapy neverthe-

less improve in a year or two. (Most psychological crises are temporary.) *Improvement without therapy* is called **spontaneous remission**. Psychotherapy is effective only if it does better than what we could expect by spontaneous remission.

In other chapters each What's the Evidence? section has highlighted a particular study. Here the section highlights a general research approach. Hundreds of research studies similar to this have been conducted, although they vary in their details (Kazdin, 1995).

Hypothesis Psychologically troubled people who receive psychotherapy will show greater improvements in their condition than similar people who do not receive therapy.

Method For the results to be meaningful, participants must be randomly assigned to the therapy and nontherapy groups. Comparing people who sought therapy to those who did not seek it would be unfair because the two groups might differ in the severity of their problems or their motivation for overcoming them. In the best studies, people who contact a clinic about receiving therapy are all given a preliminary examination and then randomly assigned to receive therapy at once or to be placed on a waiting list for therapy later. A few months later, the investigators compare the amount of improvement shown by the therapy group and the waiting-list group.

How should the investigators measure the amount of improvement? Researchers cannot rely on the judgments of the therapists; after all, they want to demonstrate the effectiveness of their procedures. For similar reasons researchers cannot ask the clients for an unbiased opinion; most clients exaggerate how much they improved (Safer & Keuler, 2002). Therefore, the researchers may ask a "blind" observer (see Chapter 2) to evaluate each client without knowing who has received therapy and who has been on the waiting list. Or they may ask each person to take a

▌ Because everyone's moods and effectiveness fluctuate over time, an apparent improvement between (a) the start of therapy and (b) the end is hard to interpret. How much of the improvement is due to the therapy and how much would have occurred even without it?

a
b

© Zigy Kalyuzny/Tony Stone Images/Getty Images

© Ken Fisher/Tony Stone Images/Getty Images

standardized personality test, such as the MMPI. None of these measures are perfect, of course, and they probably overlook some kinds of improvement.

Many experiments compare a group that received therapy to a control group that was on the waiting list. Other experiments, however, have compared groups receiving different kinds of therapy or different frequencies of therapy.

Results Here we do not focus on the results of any one study. Most experiments have included only a modest number of people, such as 10 or 20 receiving therapy and a similar number on the waiting list. To draw a conclusion, we need to pool the results from a great many similar experiments. Psychologists use a method called **meta-analysis,** *taking the results of many experiments, weighting each one in proportion to the number of participants, and determining the overall average effect.* According to one meta-analysis that pooled the results of 475 experiments, the average person in therapy shows greater improvement than 80% of similarly troubled people who do not receive therapy (M. L. Smith, Glass, & Miller, 1980). Figure 15.5 illustrates this effect.

Interpretation Every study has limitations, and even a collection of 475 studies has limitations. In particular, most research has dealt with relatively mild disorders, mainly because it seems unethical to assign anyone suffering from severe problems to a waiting list. Most research deals with fairly brief treatments, again largely because it is hard to keep anyone in a waiting-list control group for more than a few months. Also, most of the research has examined behavior therapy or cognitive therapy because these methods use consistent methods and set specific goals. It is more difficult to evaluate psychoanalysis or person-centered therapy.

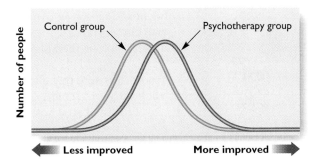

FIGURE 15.5 According to one review of 475 studies, the average person receiving psychotherapy shows more improvement than do 80% of similar, randomly assigned people who are not in therapy. This comparison lumps together all kinds of therapy and all kinds of disorders. *(From* The Benefits of Psychotherapy, *by M. L. Smith, G. V. Glass, and T. I. Miller. Copyright © 1980. The Johns Hopkins University Press. Reprinted by permission.)*

One could easily complain that investigators have invested a great deal of effort for rather little payoff. After 475 experiments, we can confidently say that therapy is usually better than no therapy for relatively mild psychological disorders. This conclusion is like saying that, if you are ill, medicine is usually better than no medicine. However, even if this conclusion seems unimpressive, it does pave the way for further, more detailed studies about how therapy produces its benefits and so forth. It also tells us something about the magnitude of psychotherapy's effects: The effects are real but usually not huge. Most clients benefit but perhaps not as much as they had hoped.

CONCEPT CHECK ☑

12. Although well-designed experiments on psychotherapy use a blind observer to rate clients' mental health, double-blind studies are difficult or impossible. Why? (Check your answer on page 603.)

Comparing Therapies and Therapists

Next we would like to know which kinds of therapy are most effective for which disorders. The practical problem for researchers is that therapists use hundreds of types of therapy for hundreds of psychological disorders. To test each form of therapy on each possible disorder would require tens of thousands of experiments, not counting replications. Furthermore, many clients have several problems, not just one, and most therapists use an eclectic trial-and-error approach instead of a single well-defined therapy (Goldfried & Wolfe, 1996).

Many studies have proceeded despite these difficulties, and they lead to a stunningly simple conclusion: For the disorders studied, researchers find only small differences in effectiveness between one type of therapy and another (Leichsenring & Leibing, 2003; Lipsey & Wilson, 1993; Stiles, Shapiro, & Elliott, 1986; Wampold et al., 1997). Even those differences are sometimes hard to interpret. For example, in some studies one kind of treatment produced better immediate benefits and another produced greater long-term benefits, so the apparent advantage depended on the time of measurement (Sandell et al., 1999). We should view this research with some caution, as it has dealt mainly with mild to moderate disorders suitable for brief therapy and mostly with behavioral and cognitive therapies. The effectiveness of psychoanalysis, for example, remains more controversial.

Furthermore, in Chapter 16 we shall encounter examples in which one type of therapy appears to have the advantage, such as behavior therapy for phobias and cognitive therapy for depression. However, even in these cases, the differences between one form of therapy and another are small, and the interesting point remains that therapies differing widely in their assumptions and methods produce results far more similar than most psychologists had expected.

Researchers also have compared the effectiveness of therapists with different kinds of training. The U.S. magazine *Consumer Reports* (1995) surveyed its readers about their mental health and their contact with psychotherapy. Of the thousands who said they had sought help for a mental-health problem within the previous 3 years, most said they were satisfied with the treatment and thought it had helped them. For measuring the effectiveness of psychotherapy, this study has some obvious problems: the lack of a random sample, the lack of a control group, and reliance on clients to evaluate their own improvement (Jacobson & Christensen, 1996). Nevertheless, the results indicated that people reported about equal satisfaction and benefits from talking with a psychiatrist, a psychologist, or a social worker (Seligman, 1995). They reported somewhat less satisfaction from consulting a marriage counselor or a general-practice physician (see Figure 15.6). A later survey of psychotherapy clients in Germany yielded similar results (Hartmann & Zepf, 2003).

The same general pattern emerged in a variety of other studies with different research methods: The type of therapist is not critical to the amount of improvement. Even the amount of therapist experience makes little difference in most studies (Christensen & Jacobson, 1994; Dawes, 1994).

❚ Just talking to a sympathetic listener, even someone without training, is helpful for many people with mild to moderate problems.

Is the conclusion, then, that if you are psychologically troubled, you may as well talk to your next-door neighbor as to a psychotherapist? No, for several reasons:

- The research comparing inexperienced to experienced therapists has examined clients with mild problems. We cannot assume that the same results would hold for more disabling conditions.

  - Few of us know someone with enough patience to listen to hours of our personal ramblings.
  - Conversation with a professional psychotherapist is confidential (except under special circumstances, such as if you tell your therapist you are planning to kill someone). You are less sure that a friend will keep your secrets.
  - A well-trained psychotherapist can recognize symptoms of a brain tumor or other medical disorder and can refer you to an appropriate medical specialist.
  - Clinical psychologists know enough about therapy research to avoid untested "fad" treatments (Maki & Syman, 1997).

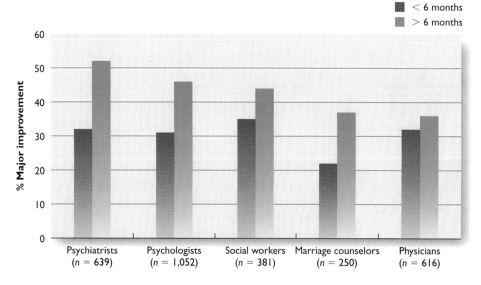

FIGURE 15.6 The percentage of *Consumer Reports* respondents who said they experienced great improvement in the problem that led them to treatment. (*From "The Effectiveness of Psychotherapy: The Consumer Reports Study," by M. E. P. Seligman,* American Psychologist, *1995, 50, 965–974. Copyright © 1995 by the American Psychological Association. Reprinted by permission.*)

In short, although you would probably benefit by talking to almost any sympathetic listener, there are important advantages to seeing a professional psychotherapist (Strupp, 1996).

Is More Treatment Better?

If seeing a therapist once per week for 3 months is helpful, would meeting twice per week for a year help even more? How much is the right amount?

Respondents in the *Consumer Reports* (1995) study were asked how much treatment they received and how much it helped them. Generally, those who received longer treatment reported that it helped them more. However, perhaps those who stayed in treatment the longest were those with the greatest problems at the start and therefore had the greatest room for improvement.

A somewhat better research design examines a single group of clients repeatedly as all of them progress through a given number of therapy sessions. Figure 15.7 shows the results of one such study. According to both the researchers and the clients themselves, most clients showed fairly rapid progress at first and then gradual additional progress (Howard et al., 1986). Evidently, prolonged treatment is at least somewhat more beneficial than brief treatment on the average.

An elaborate study of this issue was a 5-year study conducted at Fort Bragg, North Carolina. A government-supported program provided free clinical services for every teenager or child who needed psychological help and who had a parent in the military. Each client had a case manager who determined what treatment plan was best, made sure that the client received every necessary type of help, and coordinated all the service providers to make sure that each one knew what the others were doing. The goal was to demonstrate that a well-planned, integrated program would be highly effective and perhaps even inexpensive because it would avoid wasteful overlap of services. Results were compared to those in a similar community that offered the usual, less coordinated services. The result? The integrated program at Fort Bragg was no more beneficial, just more expensive (Bickman, 1996). We should not draw too strong a conclusion from this study or from any other single study. Still, most people had expected the integrated program to show clear advantages, and the results seem to imply that more therapy is not always better.

Similarities Among Psychotherapeutic Methods

What should we conclude from the observation that different forms of psychotherapy seem to be similar in their effectiveness? Consider an analogy to education: Suppose researchers found that, on the average, students learn about equally from lecture courses as from discussion classes, from experienced professors as from first-time instructors, and from one textbook as another. I, personally, would not be happy about that finding. As a professor and textbook author, I like to think that students learn *way* more from my lectures and textbook than from anyone else's! However, I should not be terribly surprised by those results. How much a student learns depends mainly on the student. A better lecture, a better class organization, or a better textbook presumably makes some difference, but it is surely a small difference compared to the difference between one student and another. Similarly, how much a client benefits from psychotherapy varies enormously depending on the client, and the difference between one therapist and another is relatively small and hard to measure (Bohart, 2000).

The similarity in outcomes among different forms of psychotherapy implies that they have much in common despite the differences in their assumptions, methods, and goals. One feature is that all rely on a "therapeutic alliance"—a relationship between therapist and client characterized by acceptance, caring, respect, and attention. This relationship provides social support that helps clients deal with their problems and acquire social skills that they can apply to other relationships (Krupnick et al., 1994).

Moreover, in nearly all forms of therapy, clients talk openly and honestly about their beliefs and emotions,

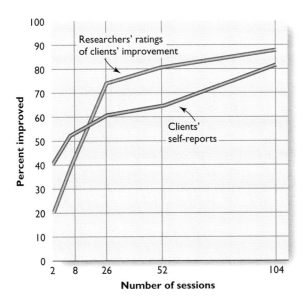

FIGURE 15.7 The relationship of the number of psychotherapy sessions to the percentage of clients who improved. *(From "The Dose-Effect Relationship in Psychotherapy," by K. I. Howard et al., American Psychologist, 1986, 41, 159–164. Copyright © 1986 by the American Psychological Association. Reprinted by permission of the author.)*

relationships with family members, and other issues that people ordinarily keep secret. They examine aspects of themselves that they usually take for granted; in so doing they gain self-understanding. Because of the expectation of self-disclosure, psychotherapy as practiced in North America and Europe does not transplant readily into other cultures. For example, most Chinese would consider it shameful to discuss personal or family matters with a stranger (Bond, 1991).

The mere fact of entering therapy, whatever the method, improves clients' morale. The therapist conveys the message "you are going to get better." Clients gain confidence in their ability to cope with and overcome their problems. The expectation of improvement can lead to improvement.

Finally, every form of therapy requires clients to commit themselves to changes in their lifestyle. Simply by coming to the therapy session, they reaffirm their commitment to feel less depressed, to overcome their fears, or to conquer some bad habit. They work on that change between sessions so that they can report at the next session, "I've been doing a little better lately." Improvement probably depends more on what clients do between sessions than on anything in the sessions themselves.

CONCEPT CHECK ☑

13. Name four ways in which nearly all forms of psychotherapy are similar. (Check your answer on page 603.)

Advice for Potential Clients

At some point you or someone close to you may be interested in seeing a psychotherapist. If so, here are some points to remember:

- Consulting a therapist does not mean that something is wrong with you. Many people merely want to talk with someone about difficulties they are facing.
- If you live in the United States, you can look in the white pages of your telephone directory for the Mental Health Association. Call and ask for a recommendation. You can specify how much you can pay, what kind of problem you have, and even what kind of therapist you prefer.
- Other things being equal, you may do best with a therapist from your own cultural background (Sue, 1998). Therapists are trained to be sensitive to people from different backgrounds, but a communication barrier often remains nevertheless. For example, certain responses to grief or fear that are considered abnormal by many Western psychotherapists are considered normal in many other cultures.

- You might prefer a therapist who shares your religious beliefs or lack of them (Worthington, Kurusu, McCullough & Sandage, 1996).
- Be skeptical of any therapist who seems overconfident. Clinical experience does not give anyone quick access to your private thoughts.
- Expect at least some improvement within 6 to 8 weeks. If you do not seem to be making progress, ask your therapist why. If you do not receive a convincing answer, consider seeing someone else.

IN CLOSING
Trying to Understand Therapy

As you have seen, therapists differ enormously in their assumptions and methods. A psychoanalyst hopes to uncover your unconscious thoughts, memories, and motives, on the assumption that knowing about them will help solve your problems. A cognitive or behavior therapist is more interested in changing your current thoughts and actions than in dwelling on the past and is skeptical about inferring any unconscious processes. A person-centered therapist provides a warm, supportive setting, in which you can set your own goals and decide for yourself how to achieve them. Despite these major differences, different forms of therapy are all effective and in many studies are almost equally effective. It is as if researchers found that when you are sick, one kind of medicine is as good as another.

Psychotherapy began with psychiatry, a branch of medicine, and we still treat it as analogous to medicine. That is, a client comes with a "disorder" that gets a medical diagnosis, the therapist provides a "treatment," and health insurance pays the bills. In some ways this analogy fails, and therapy is more like education. A client is like a student, and the therapist is like an instructor who tries to provide direction, but the amount of progress depends on the client's own efforts. This is not to say that the therapist is irrelevant; it is hard to doubt that some do a better job than others, just as some professors do. However, the variation between one client and another is greater than the typical difference between one treatment and another.

Summary

- *Psychoanalysis.* Psychoanalysts try to uncover the unconscious reasons behind self-defeating behaviors. To bring the unconscious to consciousness, they rely on free association, dream analysis, and transference. (page 591)
- *Behavior therapy.* Behavior therapists set specific goals for changing a client's behavior and use learn-

ing techniques to help a client achieve those goals. (page 592)

- *Cognitive therapies.* Cognitive therapists try to get clients to give up their irrational beliefs and unrealistic goals and to replace defeatist thinking with more favorable views of themselves and the world. Many therapists combine features of behavior therapy and cognitive therapy, attempting to change people's behaviors by altering how they interpret the situation. (page 593)
- *Humanistic therapy.* Humanistic therapists, including person-centered therapists, assume that, if people accept themselves as they are, they can solve their own problems. Person-centered therapists listen with unconditional positive regard but seldom offer interpretations or advice. (page 594)
- *Family systems therapy.* In many cases an individual's problem is part of an overall disorder of family communications and expectations. Family systems therapists try to work with a whole family. (page 595)
- *Eclectic therapy.* About half of all psychotherapists today call themselves "eclectic." That is, they use a combination of methods depending on the circumstances. (page 596)
- *Brief therapy.* Many therapists set a time limit for the treatment, usually ranging from 2–6 months. Brief therapy is typically about as successful as long-term therapy if the goals are limited. (page 596)
- *Group therapies and self-help groups.* Psychotherapy is sometimes provided to people in groups, often composed of individuals with similar problems. Self-help groups provide sessions similar to group therapy but without a therapist. (page 597)
- *Effectiveness of psychotherapy.* The average troubled person in therapy improves more than at least 80% of the troubled people not in therapy. In general, all therapies appear effective, and the differences among them are small. Psychiatrists, psychologists, and social workers provide approximately equal benefits on the average. (page 598)
- *Similarities among therapies.* A wide variety of therapies share certain features: All rely on a caring relationship between therapist and client. All promote self-understanding. All improve clients' morale. And all require a commitment by clients to try to make changes in their lives. (page 601)

Answers to Concept Checks

6. It is possible to get health insurance to pay for treatment if someone has a diagnosed disorder. (page 590)
7. Psychoanalysts use free association and transference to infer the contents of the unconscious. They also use dream analysis, as discussed in Chapter 5. (page 592)
8. Psychoanalysts try to infer unconscious thoughts and motives and try to trace current behavior to experiences of long ago. Behavior therapists pay little attention to thoughts, conscious or unconscious. They set specific goals and try to change current behavior regardless of whether they understand how the behavior originated. (page 592)
9. Rational-emotive therapy assumes that many thoughts lead to emotions. This assumption is the reverse of the James-Lange theory, which argues that emotion-related changes in the body give rise to thoughts. (page 594)
10. a. humanistic therapy;
    b. behavior therapy;
    c. psychoanalysis and cognitive therapy. (page 595)
11. One of the advantages of brief therapy is that it limits the expense. Expense is not an issue for self-help groups because they charge nothing (other than a voluntary contribution toward rental of the facilities). (page 598)
12. A double-blind design requires that neither the subjects nor the observers know which subjects received the experimental treatment and which ones were in the control group. It is not possible to prevent subjects from knowing whether they have received psychotherapy. (It is, of course, possible to use a treatment believed to be ineffective and call it psychotherapy.) (page 599)
13. Nearly all forms of psychotherapy include a "therapeutic alliance" (a close relationship between client and therapist), an effort to understand oneself and discuss personal difficulties openly, an expectation of improvement, and a commitment to make changes in one's life. (page 602)

| *How should society deal with psychological disorders?*

A group of nearsighted people lost in the woods were trying to find their way home. One of the few who wore glasses said, "I think I know the way. Follow me." The others burst into laughter. "That's ridiculous," said one. "How could anybody who needs glasses be our leader?"

In 1972 the Democratic party nominated Senator Thomas Eagleton for vice president of the United States. Shortly after his nomination, he revealed that he had once received psychiatric treatment for depression. He was ridiculed mercilessly: "How could anybody who needed a psychiatrist be our leader?"

As mentioned in the first module, about one third to one half of all people suffer from at least a mild psychological disorder at some point in life. However, many people prefer to struggle along on their own, like a nearsighted person who refuses to wear glasses, rather than seek help.

As a citizen and a voter, you should be aware of issues relating to psychological disorders and therapies: Who, if anyone, should receive psychiatric treatment involuntarily? Should mental patients have the right to refuse treatment? Under what circumstances, if any, should a criminal defendant be acquitted because of "insanity"? Can society as a whole take steps to prevent psychological disorders?

Deinstitutionalization

In the 1800s and early 1900s, growing numbers of people with severe psychological disturbances were confined in large mental hospitals supported by the government (Torrey & Miller, 2001). Most of these hospitals were understaffed and overcrowded. Residents included not only mental patients but also elderly people who could not care for themselves, probably suffering from Alzheimer's disease (Leff, 2002). Hospital attendants cooked the food, washed the laundry, and cared for the residents but did not try to teach them the skills they would need if they were ever to leave. After all, most would never leave. Some hospitals were better than others, but most were grim places.

Beginning in the 1950s and continuing since then, more and more hospitals moved toward **deinstitutionalization,** *the removal of patients from mental hospi-*

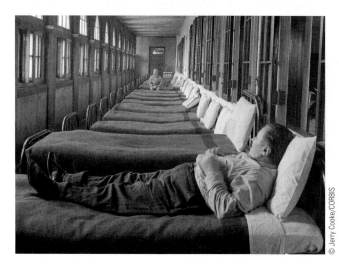

▐ Mental hospitals of the mid-1900s were unpleasant warehouses where people received minimal care.

tals, to give them the least restrictive care possible. Only people who were dangerous to themselves or others would stay for long. Others would live at home or in group houses and receive outpatient care as needed at community mental-health centers, which are usually cheaper and more effective than large mental hospitals (Fenton, Hoch, Herrell, Mosher, & Dixon, 2002; Fenton, Mosher, Herrell, & Blyler, 1998). The idea was that troubled people should receive appropriate supervision and care but should also have as much contact as possible with the outside world. As a result of deinstitutionalization policies, as well as the advent of antidepressant and antipsychotic medications, the number of long-term mental patients declined sharply. For example, England and Wales had 130 psychiatric hospitals in 1975 but only 12 in 2000 (Leff, 2002).

Unfortunately, most governments saw deinstitutionalization mainly as a way to save money; they discharged patients from the mental hospitals without planning adequate alternatives. Many people discharged from mental hospitals became homeless, especially those who had lost contact with their relatives and those with substance-abuse problems (Odell & Commander, 2000). Some ended in nursing homes or prisons. Deinstitutionalization was and is a good idea in principle, but only if implemented well, including much supervision and good opportunities for community health care.

■ Deinstitutionalization moved people out of mental hospitals, but many received little or no treatment after their release.

CONCEPT CHECK ☑

14. Why did deinstitutionalization seem to be a good idea? For what reason has it often not worked well? (Check your answers on page 609.)

Involuntary Commitment and Treatment

In a democratic society, we treasure both freedom and security. Sometimes these values are in conflict. For example, the right of a person with a psychological disorder to be free may conflict with the right of other people to feel safe and secure.

Imagine someone who mutters incoherently, cannot keep a job, does not pay bills or take care of personal hygiene, bothers the neighbors, and refuses treatment. Should it be possible to require treatment? We can argue this question either way. On the one hand, some of the most seriously disordered people fail to recognize that they have a problem. On the other hand, some families have been known to commit annoying relatives to mental hospitals just to get them out of the way, and some psychiatrists have given strong medications to people with minor problems, doing more harm than good.

Unfortunately, it is difficult to determine who really needs help and who doesn't. In the United States, laws vary from state to state, but typically, people can be involuntarily committed if they are dangerous to themselves or others or if they are incompetent to take care of their daily needs. In all cases a judge holds a hearing and makes the final decision (Weiner & Wettstein, 1993).

After people have been committed to a mental hospital, voluntarily or involuntarily, they still have the right to refuse treatment (Appelbaum, 1988). According to their psychiatrists, most of the people who refuse treatment are hostile, emotionally withdrawn, and prone to disorganized thinking (Marder et al., 1983). According to the patients themselves, they have good reason to be hostile and withdrawn; the hospital staff is trying to force dangerous treatments upon them. Either can be right in a given case. Studies find that the patients most likely to deny having a problem are those with the mildest problems and those with the most severe problems (Pyne, Bean, & Sullivan, 2001).

Figure 15.8 shows the results of one study that compared patients who refused drug treatment to those who accepted it. Understandably, it can be very difficult to make decisions about enforced treatment.

CRITICAL THINKING:
A STEP FURTHER
Involuntary Treatment

Thomas Szasz (1982) proposed that psychologically "normal" people write a "psychiatric will," specifying what treatments to give them, and what treatments to avoid, if they ever develop a severe psychological disorder. If you wrote such a will, what would you include? Or would you prefer to trust your judgment later, at the onset of the disorder?

The Duty to Protect

Suppose someone tells his psychotherapist that he is planning to kill his former girlfriend. The therapist doubts the threat and ignores it. However, a few days later, the client really does kill his ex-girlfriend . . . who happens to be your sister. Should your family be able to sue the therapist and collect damages?

Before you answer "yes," consider the following. First, psychotherapy is based on a trusting relationship in which the therapist promises to keep the client's comments secret. Second, therapists are seldom certain about which clients are dangerous (Monahan, 1993). Suppose you are a therapist. Over the course of a day, you see eight patients, and three of them say they are so angry they could kill somebody. How do you decide which ones, if any, to take seriously? (Have you yourself ever said you were so mad you could kill someone?)

FIGURE 15.8 (a) People with schizophrenia who refuse drug therapy impress their physicians as being seriously disturbed. High scores indicate greater ratings of disturbance. (b) Patients who refuse drugs rate themselves as dissatisfied with their physicians and their treatments. The higher scores indicate greater satisfaction with treatment. *(Based on data from Marder, et al., 1983.)*

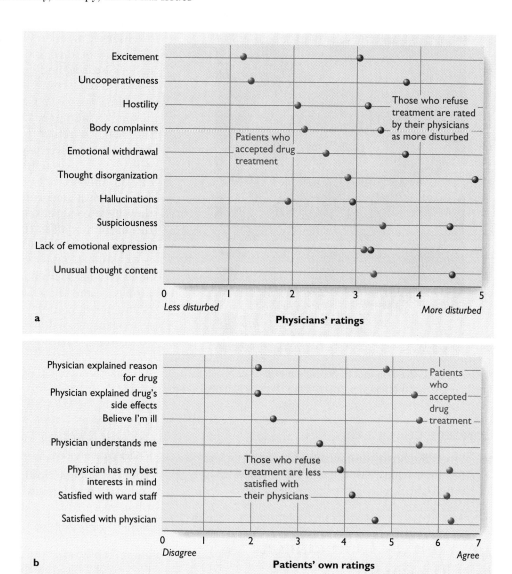

In 1976 a California court ruled in the *Tarasoff* case that *a therapist who has reason to believe that a client is dangerous must break the pledge of confidentiality and warn the endangered person* (Weiner & Wettstein, 1993). A Canadian court made a similar ruling in the case of *Wenden v. Trikha* (Truscott & Crook, 1993). However, applying such rules in practice is difficult because of the uncertainty about dangerousness. The courts have also ruled that the duty to inform applies only if the patient is a threat to a *specific* individual. For example, a therapist is *not* obligated to warn anyone about a drug-abusing client who is an airplane pilot. The client may be a danger to a huge number of people but not to any *specific,* identifiable person (Felthous, 1993). In fact the rules on confidentiality actually prohibit the therapist from informing the pilot's employer! We can sympathize with therapists who are puzzled and confused. So far, the courts have been reluctant to hold therapists legally accountable.

The Insanity Defense

Suppose that, in the midst of an epileptic seizure, you flail your arms about and accidentally knock someone down the stairs, who dies from the fall. Should you be convicted of murder? Of course not; you had no intention to do harm. Now suppose that, in the midst of severely disordered thinking and perception, you attack and kill what appears to be a giant insect but is in fact a human being. Again you intended no harm. You didn't even realize you were attacking a person. Should you be convicted of murder?

The tradition dating back to Roman times has been that you would be "not guilty by reason of insanity." Most people agree with that principle for extreme cases. The problem is where to draw the line. Under what conditions should someone be judged legally insane? *Insanity* is a legal term, not a psycho-

❚ Theodore Kaczynski (a), a brilliant mathematician who once had a promising career, became (b) a recluse who over the course of 17 years mailed bombs that killed 3 and injured 23 others. However, merely being "strange" or committing bizarre acts of violence does not qualify someone as legally insane.

a

b

logical or medical one, and its definition is based on politics more than science.

One point of broad agreement is that the crime itself, no matter how atrocious, does not demonstrate insanity. Jeffrey Dahmer, who was arrested in 1991 after murdering and cannibalizing several men, was ruled sane and sentenced to prison. Theodore Kaczynski, arrested for mailing bombs over decades, refused to plead insanity and probably would not have been ruled insane anyway. Bizarre crimes do not, in themselves, demonstrate insanity. In fact each of these murderers knew what he was doing and tried to avoid getting caught.

In many cases, however, a decision about sanity or insanity is difficult; lawyers, physicians, and psychologists have long struggled to establish a clear and acceptable definition of insanity. Probably the most famous definition, the **M'Naghten rule**, written in Great Britain in 1843, states:

> To establish a defense on the ground of insanity, it must be clearly proved that, at the time of the committing of the act, the party accused was laboring under such a defect of reason, from disease of the mind, as not to know the nature and quality of the act he was doing; or if he did know it, that he did not know he was doing what was wrong. (Shapiro, 1985)

In other words, *to be regarded as insane under the M'Naghten rule, people must be so disordered that they do not understand what they are doing.* Presumably, they would continue the act even if a police officer were standing nearby. Many observers consider that rule too narrow and would like to broaden the definition, but any definition requires a difficult judgment about the defendant's state of mind at the time of the act. To help make that judgment, psychologists and psychiatrists are called as "expert witnesses" to evaluate the defendant's state

of mind. If all the experts agree that the defendant is insane, the prosecution ordinarily accepts the insanity plea. If the experts agree the defendant is not insane, the defense abandons the plea. Therefore, the only insanity cases that come to a jury trial are the difficult cases in which the experts disagree. Those cases are rare. In the United States, fewer than 1% of accused felons plead insanity, and of those, only about 25% are found not guilty (Lymburner & Roesch, 1999). However, those few cases generally receive much media attention, and because people hear about them, they assume such cases are common. (Remember the availability heuristic from Chapter 8.) The insanity defense is just as rare in other countries.

Another common misconception is that defendants found not guilty by reason of insanity simply go free, where they are apt to commit further attacks. People found not guilty by reason of insanity are almost always committed to a mental hospital, and they usually stay at least as long in the hospital as they would have in prison (Silver, 1995).

Several states in the United States have experimented with allowing a verdict of "guilty but mentally ill," intended as a compromise between guilty and not guilty. However, the defendant actually receives the same sentence as if he or she had been simply found guilty and is no more likely to receive psychiatric care in prison than any other convicted person (Lymburner & Roesch, 1999). In short, the guilty but mentally ill verdict is the same as a guilty verdict. An appealing alternative proposal is to specify that anyone found not guilty by reason of insanity must be temporarily hospitalized and, when eventually released, must abide by many conditions and restrictions, similar to those of a released prisoner on parole (Linhorst & Dirks-Linhorst, 1999).

For more information about cases using the insanity defense, as well as other legal cases relevant to psychology, visit this Web site:

bama.ua.edu/~jhooper/tableofc.html

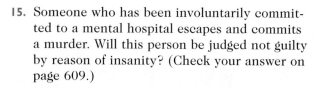

CONCEPT CHECK ✓

15. Someone who has been involuntarily committed to a mental hospital escapes and commits a murder. Will this person be judged not guilty by reason of insanity? (Check your answer on page 609.)

Preventing Mental Illness

Traditionally, psychotherapy has been a method to relieve psychological distress. More recently, community psychologists and others have made efforts at prevention. **Community psychologists** *focus on the needs of large groups rather than those of individuals.* **Prevention** is *avoiding a disorder from the start.* For example, in one study of "pessimistic" college students and another study with children of depressed parents, half of the participants were given cognitive therapy and half were not. In both studies fewer people in the therapy group became depressed over the next 2 or 3 years (Clarke et al., 2001; Seligman, Schulman, DeRubeis, & Hollon, 1999).

Prevention is distinguished from intervention and maintenance. **Intervention** is *identifying a disorder in its early stages and relieving it,* and **maintenance** is *taking steps to keep it from becoming more serious.* For example, therapists identify people showing early signs of schizophrenia and try to stop further deterioration (McGorry et al., 2002).

Just as our society puts fluoride into drinking water to prevent tooth decay and immunizes people against contagious diseases, it can take action to prevent certain types of psychological disorders (Albee, 1986; Wandersman & Florin, 2003). Here are some examples:

- **Ban toxins.** The sale of lead-based paint has been banned because children who eat flakes of it sustain brain damage. Other toxins in the air and water have yet to be controlled.
- **Educate pregnant women about prenatal care.** For example, women need to be informed that the use of alcohol or other drugs during pregnancy damages the brain of a fetus and that bacterial and viral infections during pregnancy can impair fetal brain development and increase the risk of psychological disorders in the child.
- **Outlaw smoking in public places and educate people about the risks of smoking.** Improvements in

physical health can improve psychological well-being too, and preventing smoking by pregnant women is good for the brain development of the fetus.

- **Help people get jobs.** People who lose their jobs lose self-esteem and increase their risk of depression and substance abuse.
- **Provide child care.** Improved, affordable day-care services would relieve stress for both parents and children.
- **Improve educational opportunities.** Programs that get young people interested in their schoolwork have made notable progress in decreasing juvenile delinquency.

These techniques are aimed at prevention for the entire community. Prevention or intervention techniques can be targeted at specific individuals who are beginning to show symptoms of a particular disorder. For example, psychologists identified fifth- and sixth-grade children prone to distress and then for 12 weeks taught them how to avoid negative beliefs about themselves. These children showed fewer signs of depression over the next 2 years compared to a similarly distressed group who did not receive this training (Gillham, Reivich, Jaycox, & Seligman, 1995).

Unfortunately, prevention is often more difficult than it might seem. For example, many programs designed to teach young people to avoid illegal drugs have produced no measurable benefits. In one study adolescents with a history of aggression met in groups to discuss their problems. Over the next year, they showed an *increase* in delinquent behaviors compared to a no-treatment control group (Poulin, Dishion, & Burraston, 2001). Evidently, associating with an all-delinquent group provided bad role models and did more harm than good. In another program patients recovering from anorexia nervosa or bulimia nervosa described their struggles to college women. The women who heard this presentation had an *increase* in eating problems over the next couple of months, whereas women who did not hear the presentation remained unchanged (Mann et al., 1997).

Attempts have been made to combat suicide, especially teenage suicide, by television programs about suicide and the pain it causes to friends and relatives. These programs have never decreased the suicide rate; in fact the research controversy is about how much the programs *increase* the suicide rate (Joiner, 1999). One study compared suicidal patients receiving brief crisis intervention to others receiving more prolonged therapy. Those receiving more help had a *higher* rate of suicide (Moller, 1992). The general point is that we cannot take it for granted that a procedure intended to help will succeed. Sometimes just talking about a behavior problem makes it more likely.

16. Why is it important to do careful research before initiating a new program to prevent a psychological disorder? (Check your answer on this page.)

IN CLOSING

The Science and Politics of Mental Illness

Suppose you are a storekeeper. Someone dressed as Batman stands outside your store every day shouting gibberish at anyone who comes by. Your once-thriving business draws fewer and fewer customers each day. The disturbing man outside does not seem to be breaking any laws. A psychologist consults *DSM-IV* and finds a couple of possible diagnoses. However, the man is not obviously dangerous or incompetent, just annoying, and he wants nothing to do with psychologists or psychiatrists. Should he nevertheless be forced to accept treatment for his odd behavior? If not, what happens to your rights as a storekeeper?

Similarly, the insanity defense and all the other issues in this module are complicated questions that require political decisions by society as a whole, not just the opinions of psychologists or psychiatrists. Regardless of what career you enter, you will be a voter and potential juror, and you will have a voice in deciding these issues. The decisions deserve serious, informed consideration.

Summary

- *Deinstitutionalization.* Today, few patients stay very long in mental hospitals. However, many states have released patients from mental hospitals without providing adequate community mental-health facilities. (page 604)
- *Involuntary commitment.* Laws on involuntary commitment to mental hospitals vary, but typically, people can be committed if they are judged to be dangerous or incompetent. It is difficult to frame laws that ensure treatment for those who need it while also protecting the rights of those who have good reasons for refusing it. (page 605)
- *Duty to warn.* The courts have ruled that a therapist who is convinced that a client is dangerous should warn the endangered person. Applying this rule in practice is difficult, however, because judging dangerousness is difficult. (page 605)
- *The insanity defense.* Some defendants accused of a crime are acquitted for reasons of insanity, which is a legal rather than a medical or psychological concept. The criteria for establishing insanity are controversial. (page 606)
- *Prevention of psychological disorders.* Psychologists and psychiatrists are increasingly concerned about preventing psychological disorders. Many preventive measures require the cooperation of society as a whole. Methods of prevention based on good intentions do not always succeed. (page 608)

Answers to Concept Checks

14. Deinstitutionalization appears to be a good idea because treatment in a community mental health center is more effective and less costly than treatment in a mental hospital. However, many states removed people from mental hospitals without providing adequate alternative care. (page 605)
15. Not necessarily. Having a psychological disorder, even a severe one, does not automatically qualify a person as insane in the legal sense. The judge or jury must also find that the psychological disorder prevented the person from knowing what he or she was doing or made law-abiding behavior impossible. (page 608)
16. In many cases a program intended for prevention has proved to be ineffective or counterproductive. It is important to test the effectiveness of a program before setting it up on a large scale. (page 609)

Key Terms and Activities

Key Terms

attention-deficit disorder (ADD): a condition marked by easy distraction from important tasks, impulsiveness, moodiness, and failure to follow through on plans (page 584)

attention-deficit hyperactivity disorder (ADHD): a condition marked by easy distraction from important tasks, impulsiveness, moodiness, and failure to follow through on plans, plus excessive activity and fidgetiness (page 584)

behavior therapy: treatment that begins with clear, well-defined behavioral goals, such as eliminating test anxiety, and then attempts to achieve those goals through learning (page 592)

biopsychosocial model: the concept that abnormal behavior has three major aspects—biological, psychological, and sociological (page 583)

brief therapy: treatment that begins with an agreement about what the therapist and the client can expect from each other and how long the treatment will last; also known as time-limited therapy (page 597)

catharsis: the release of pent-up emotions associated with unconscious thoughts and memories (page 591)

cognitive therapy: treatment that seeks to improve people's psychological well-being by changing their cognitions (page 593)

cognitive-behavior therapy: treatment that combines important features of both behavior therapy and cognitive therapy, attempting to change people's behavior by changing their interpretation of their situation (page 594)

community psychologist: a psychologist who focuses on the needs of large groups rather than those of individuals (page 608)

deinstitutionalization: the removal of patients from mental hospitals (page 604)

Diagnostic and Statistical Manual of Mental Disorders, Fourth Edition (DSM-IV): a book that lists the acceptable labels for all psychological disorders, with a description of each and guidelines on how to distinguish it from similar disorders (page 584)

differential diagnosis: a determination of what problem a person has, in contrast to all the other possible problems that might produce similar symptoms (page 586)

dissociative identity disorder: a rare condition in which the personality separates into several identities; also known as multiple personality disorder (page 583)

eclectic therapy: treatment that uses a combination of methods and approaches (page 596)

family systems therapy: treatment based on the assumptions that most people's problems develop in a family setting and that the best way to deal with them is to improve family relationships and communication (page 595)

free association: a procedure where a client lies on a couch, starts thinking about a particular symptom or problem, and then reports everything that comes to mind (page 591)

group therapy: treatment administered to a group of people all at once (page 597)

incongruence: a mismatch between the perceptions of one's real self and ideal self (page 594)

interpretation: a therapist's explanation of the underlying meaning of what a client says (page 592)

intervention: identifying a disorder in its early stages and relieving it (page 608)

maintenance: treating a disorder to keep it from becoming more serious (p. 608)

meta-analysis: a method of taking the results of many experiments, weighting each one in proportion to the number of participants, and determining the overall average effect (page 599)

M'Naghten rule: the rule that a defendant is not criminally responsible if, at the time of committing an unlawful act, the person was laboring under such a defect of reason, from disease of the mind, as not to know the nature and quality of the act he was doing; or if he did know it, that he did not know he was doing wrong (page 607)

person-centered therapy: a procedure in which a therapist listens to the client with unconditional positive regard and offers little interpretation or advice; also known as nondirective or client-centered therapy (page 594)

personality disorder: a maladaptive, inflexible way of dealing with the environment and other people (page 586)

prevention: avoiding a disorder from the start (page 608)

psychoanalysis: an approach to personality and psychotherapy developed by Sigmund Freud, based on identifying unconscious thoughts and emotions and bringing them to consciousness (page 591)

psychodynamic therapies: treatment that attempts to uncover people's underlying drives and motivations (page 591)

psychotherapy: the treatment of psychological disorders by methods that include a personal relationship between a trained therapist and a client (page 590)

rational-emotive behavior therapy: treatment based on the assumption that thoughts (rationality) lead to emotions and that problems arise not from the unpleasant emotions themselves but from the irrational thoughts that lead to them (page 593)

self-help group: an assembly of people with similar problems, who operate much like group therapy but without a therapist (page 597)

spontaneous remission: improvement of a psychological condition without therapy (page 598)

Tarasoff: the rule that a therapist who knew, or who should have known, that a client was dangerous is obligated to break the pledge of confidentiality and warn the endangered person (page 606)

transference: the extension of a client's feelings toward a parent or other important figure onto the therapist (page 592)

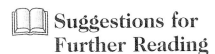

Suggestions for Further Reading

Dawes, R. M. (1994). *House of cards: Psychology and psychotherapy built on myth.* New York: Free Press. A harsh criticism of psychotherapists who rely on their intuition and experience instead of scientific evidence.

Seligman, M. E. P. (1993). *What you can change . . . and what you can't.* New York: Fawcett Columbine. Description of both the possibilities and the limitations of psychotherapy.

Sheehan, S. (1982). *Is there no place on earth for me?* Boston: Houghton Mifflin. The story of a young woman with schizophrenia and her life in and out of mental hospitals.

Book Companion Web Site

Need help studying? Go to

http://psychology.wadsworth.com/kalat_intro7e/

for a virtual study center. You'll find a personalized Self-Study Assessment that will provide you with a study plan based on your answers to a pretest. Also study using flash cards, quizzes, interactive art, and an online glossary.

Check out interactive **Try It Yourself** exercises on the companion site! For example, the Stop Signal Task exercise ties to what you've learned in this chapter.

Your companion site also has direct links to the following Web sites. These links are checked often for changes, dead links, and new additions.

Attention-Deficit Disorder

www.add-adhd.org/

This site offers a wealth of information and opinion about attention-deficit disorder, its causes, and treatment.

Landmark Cases in Forensic Psychiatry

bama.ua.edu/~jhooper/tableofc.html

In his excellent Forensic Psychiatry Resource Page, James Hooper offers brief summaries of criminal and civil cases in which mental disorders became an issue.

Try It Yourself CD-ROM
with Critical Thinking Video Exercises

Use your CD to access **videos** related to activities designed to help you think critically about the important topics discussed. You'll also find an easy portal link to the book companion site where you can access your personalized **Self-Study Assessments** and interactive **Try It Yourself** exercises.

PsychNow! 2.0

PsychNow! is a fun interactive CD designed to help you with the difficult concepts in psychology. Check out the Personality and Abnormal Psychology section for the following topics that relate to this chapter:

Abnormality and Psychopathology: six portraits—decide who looks normal, explore the biographies of the six people and the case histories of two men.

Nonpsychotic, Psychotic, and Affective Disorders: eight famous people with disorders, *DSM-IV* categories with examples, and case studies to review and diagnose.

Major Psychological Theories: five kinds of therapy with details and case studies and treatment.

Name Index

Subject Index/Glossary

External locus of control the belief that external forces are largely in control of the events of one's life, 507, *507*

Extinction (1) in classical conditioning the dying out of the conditioned response after repeated presentations of the conditioned stimulus without the unconditioned stimulus; (2) in operant conditioning the weakening of a response after a period without reinforcement, 198, 211
    classical conditioning and, 198, *198*
    operant conditioning and, 211, 216

Extrasensory perception (ESP) the alleged ability of certain people to acquire information without using any sense organ and without receiving any form of physical energy, 36
    experiments for testing, 38–39
    professional psychics and, 37–38

Extraterrestrials, 34–35

Extraversion the tendency to seek stimulation and to enjoy the company of other people, 509, 511, *511, 512*

Extrinsic motivation a motivation based on the rewards and punishments that an act may bring, 409–410, *409*

Eye-blink response, 198, *199*

Eyes
    brain hemispheres and, 88, *89*
    color vision and, 104–110
    dark adaptation of, 101–102, *102*
    disorders of, 99, *100*
    pathway of impulses from, 102–104, *103*
    structure and function of, 98–99, *98, 99*
    visual receptors of, 99–101, *100, 101*
    See also Vision

Eyewitness testimony, 260–261

F

Facial expressions
    cultural differences and, 457–458, *457*
    emotions and, 449, 452–453, *453*, 456–460, *456, 460*
    lie detection and, 471
    producing, 456, *457*
    understanding, 457–459, *457, 458, 460*

Facial features
    physical attractiveness and, 554–555, *555*
    recognition of, 129, *130*

Factor analysis, 509

False memory a report that someone believes to be a memory but that does not actually correspond to real events, 258–260, *260*

Falsifiable (with reference to a theory) making sufficiently precise predictions that we can at least imagine evidence that would contradict the theory (if anyone had obtained such evidence), 31

Families
    alcoholism in, 628–629
    birth order in, 392–393, *392*
    conflict and divorce in, 395–396
    day care and, 394–395, *394*
    nontraditional, 395, *395*
    parenting styles in, 393–394
    personality traits in, 511–512, *511, 512*
    schizophrenia in, 648–649, *649*, 652
    size of, 392–393, *392*

Family systems therapy treatment based on the assumptions that most people's problems develop in a family setting

and that the best way to deal with them is to improve family relationships and communication, 595–596, *595, 596*

Farsightedness, 99, *100*

Fear, 468
    anxiety and, 468–471
    facial expressions and, 458, *458*
    learning by observation, 619–620, *619*
    persuasive messages and, 545–546, *545*
    See also Phobias

Feature detector a neuron in the visual system of the brain that responds to the presence of a certain simple feature, such as a horizontal line, 129–132, *131, 132*
    evidence of, 130–132
    Gestalt psychology and, 136
    perception and, 132, *132*

Fetal alcohol syndrome a condition marked by stunted growth of the head and body; malformations of the face, heart, and ears; and nervous system damage, including seizures, hyperactivity, learning disabilities, and mental retardation, 359, *359*

Fetus an organism more developed than an embryo but not yet born (from about 8 weeks after conception until birth in humans), 358

Figure and ground an object and its background, 133, *133*

First impressions, 533–534, *533*

Fixation (a) in vision a period when the eyes are steady; (b) in Freud's theory a persisting preoccupation with an immature psychosexual interest as a result of frustration at that stage of psychosexual development, 314–315, *494*

Fixed-interval schedule a rule for delivering reinforcement for the first response that the subject makes after a specified period of time has passed, 215

Fixed-ratio schedule a rule for delivering reinforcement only after the subject has made a specific number of correct responses, 215

Flavor, 123

Flooding (or **implosion** or **intensive exposure therapy**) a treatment for phobia in which the person is suddenly exposed to the object of the phobia, 621

Fluid intelligence the basic power of reasoning and using information, including the ability to perceive relationships, solve unfamiliar problems, and gain new types of knowledge, 328

Flynn effect the tendency for people's performance on IQ tests to improve from one decade or generation to the next, 333–334

fMRI. *See* Functional magnetic resonance imaging

Folk psychology, 3

Food
    cultural cuisines and, 423–424, *424*
    dairy product consumption, 358, *358*
    dieting and, 419–420
    genetics and, 358, *358*
    learned associations with, 424, *424*
    selection motives relative to, 422–424, *423, 424*
    taste preferences and, 423
    See also Nutrition

Food and Drug Administration (FDA), 523

Footbridge Dilemma, 460, *460*

Foot-in-the-door technique a method of eliciting compliance by first making a modest request and then following it with a larger request, 547

Forebrain, 78–82, *79, 82*

Forensic psychiatry, 611

Forensic psychologist one who provides advice and consultation to police, lawyers, courts, or other parts of the criminal justice system, 12

Forewarning effect the tendency of a brief preview of a message to decrease its persuasiveness, 547

Forgetting
    brain damage and, 263–266
    infant amnesia and, 266–267
    interference and, 253
    See also Amnesia; Memory

Formal operations stage, 375

Fovea the central part of the retina that has a greater density of receptors, especially cones, than any other part of the retina, 98, *98*

Framing effect the tendency to answer a question differently when it is framed (phrased) differently, 298

Framing questions, 297–298, *298, 299*

Fraternal twins are twins who develop from two eggs fertilized by two different sperm; they are no more closely related than are any other children born to the same parents, 353–354, *353*
    See also Twin studies

Free association a procedure where a client lies on a couch, starts thinking about a particular symptom or problem, and then reports everything that comes to mind, 591–592

Freebase cocaine, 180

Free recall a method of testing memory by asking someone to produce a certain item (e.g., a word) without substantial hints, as on an essay or short-answer test, 234, *235*

Free will the doctrine that behavior is caused by a person's independent decisions, not by external determinants, 5–6

Frequency principle the identification of pitch by the frequency of action potentials in neurons along the basilar membrane of the cochlea, synchronized with the frequency of sound waves, 114

Freudian personality theories, 491–498

Friendships, 552–553

Frontal lobe a portion of each cerebral hemisphere at the anterior pole, with sections that control movement and certain aspects of memory, 81–82, *81*

Frustration-aggression hypothesis the theory that frustration leads to aggressive behavior, 472

Functional fixedness the tendency to adhere to a single approach to a problem or a single way of using an item, 297

Functionalism an attempt to understand how mental processes produce useful behaviors, 20

Functional magnetic resonance imaging (fMRI) a technique that uses magnetic detectors outside the head to measure the amounts of hemoglobin, with and without oxygen, in different parts of